Politics in the Marketplace

Politics in the Marketplace

*Work, Gender, and Citizenship
in Revolutionary France*

KATIE JARVIS

OXFORD
UNIVERSITY PRESS

OXFORD
UNIVERSITY PRESS

Oxford University Press is a department of the University of Oxford. It furthers
the University's objective of excellence in research, scholarship, and education
by publishing worldwide. Oxford is a registered trade mark of Oxford University
Press in the UK and certain other countries.

Published in the United States of America by Oxford University Press
198 Madison Avenue, New York, NY 10016, United States of America.

Some material in this book has been adapted from the following articles:
"Exacting Change: Money, Market Women, and the Crumbling Corporate World in
the French Revolution," *Journal of Social History* 51, 4 (2018): 837–868.
Reproduced by permission of Oxford University Press. © The Author 2018. All rights reserved.
"The Cost of Female Citizenship: How Price Controls Gendered Democracy in
Revolutionary France" was originally published in *French Historical Studies* 41, 4
(2018): 647–680. Copyright 2018, the Society of French Historical Studies. All rights reserved.
Republished by permission of the copyrightholder, and the present publisher,
Duke University Press. www.dukeupress.edu.
"'Patriotic Discipline': Cloistered Behinds, Public Judgment, and Female Violence in
Revolutionary Paris." In *Practiced Citizenship: Women, Gender, and the State in Modern France*,
edited by Nimisha Barton and Richard Hopkins, by permission of the University of Nebraska Press.
Copyright 2019 by the Board of Regents of the University of Nebraska.

Library of Congress Cataloging-in-Publication Data
Names: Jarvis, Katie (Katie L.), author.
Title: Politics in the marketplace : work, gender, and citizenship in revolutionary France / Katie Jarvis.
Description: New York : Oxford University Press, [2019] |
Includes bibliographical references and index.
Identifiers: LCCN 2018027020 (print) | LCCN 2018044300 (ebook) |
ISBN 9780190917128 (Updf) | ISBN 9780190917135 (Epub) |
ISBN 9780190917111 (hardcover : alk. paper)
Subjects: LCSH: Paris (France)—History—1789–1799—Economic aspects. |
Women merchants—France—Paris—Economic conditions—18th century. |
Women merchants—Political activity—France—Paris—18th century. |
Halles centrales (Paris, France) | Citizenship—France—History—18th century. |
Paris (France)—Commerce—History—18th century.
Classification: LCC DC194 (ebook) | LCC DC194 .J37 2019 (print) |
DDC 330.94/04—dc23
LC record available at https://lccn.loc.gov/2018027020

For my parents, Gay and David

CONTENTS

ACKNOWLEDGMENTS

Almost every day, it took the work of more than 1,000 market women to feed revolutionary Paris. A smaller but equally remarkable group of people supported this book, and it is my pleasure to thank them. Multiple institutions financed this project. Archival research in France and summer writing was funded by the Fulbright Program, the Council for European Studies, the Mellon Foundation, L'Institut Français d'Amérique, La Société des Professeurs Français et Francophones d'Amérique, the Society for French Historical Studies, the Western Association of Women Historians, Phi Alpha Theta, the University of Wisconsin–Madison Department of History, the Arts & Humanities Faculty Research Program and the Vice Provost for Research at Baylor University, and the Nanovic Institute for European Studies at the University of Notre Dame. The late Gerda Lerner left many legacies, including a Fellowship in Women's History that supported my first writing year. A Mellon/American Council of Learned Societies Dissertation Completion Fellowship allowed me to dedicate a second year to writing, at which point the University of Wisconsin–Madison Institute for Research in the Humanities granted me residency. Assistance from the University of Wisconsin–Madison, Baylor University, the University of Notre Dame, the University of Southern Denmark, and the Leverhulme Trust enabled me to travel to conferences where diverse audiences generated fruitful comments. The Institute for Scholarship in the Liberal Arts of the College of Arts and Letters at the University of Notre Dame granted a subvention for production and indexing costs, thereby permitting this book to appear in full form. Portions of the following chapters have appeared as articles, and I appreciate the permission of Oxford University Press, Duke University Press, and the University of Nebraska Press to use this material in modified form.

This project began at the University of Wisconsin–Madison, where I was extremely fortunate to work with Suzanne Desan. Suzanne has been an extraordinary mentor, engaged critic, generous colleague, and now friend. She has read countless versions of this material, attendant grant proposals, and multiple articles. All of it has benefited from her piercing insights, warm encouragement, and contagious enthusiasm. Our conversations continue to challenge me as a researcher and a writer. I thank her for these gifts. I am also indebted to Mary Louise Roberts and Laird Boswell for their mentorship and scholarly perspectives. Lou and Laird read numerous proposals, wrote funding letters, offered feedback on my dissertation, and led thought-provoking seminars. Anne Vila and Victoria Thompson also served on my dissertation committee, and this work has benefited from their insights. Paul Spagnoli and Virginia Reinburg sparked my love of French history at Boston College, where I first met the Dames. I thank Paul for his thoughtful comments on parts of this book and Ginny for productive conversations about framing.

Many people intellectually and personally enriched my research stays in France. During my preliminary research trip, Dominique Godineau, Lynn Hunt, and Jean-Clément Martin suggested archival paths of inquiry. For my Fulbright year, Pierre Serna granted me an affiliation with the Institut d'histoire de la Révolution française. In Paris, Steven Kaplan explained socioeconomic archival series, Allan Potofsky recommended municipal construction records, and Guillaume Mazeau offered his knowledge about revolutionary images. After a difficult first month in the archives, I was fortunate to meet Rachel Fuchs, who looked me in the eye and told me I would find the Dames' voices. Ever the champion of junior scholars, Rachel supported this project since that first café and suddenly passed away during its final phases. I hope that this book honors her personal dynamism and scholarly gumption. I am grateful for the intellectual solidarity of Anaïs Albert, Fanny Gallot, Anne Jusseaume, Eve Meuret-Campfort, Clyde Plumauzille, and Mathilde Rossigneux-Méheust. In our Groupe de travail autour du genre et des classes populaires, they introduced me to new theories, explained interdisciplinary methods, and graciously juggled time zones and technology for six years. Outside the archives, Clyde Plumauzille, fellow citoyenne, has been a spirited and generous friend. Martin Balc'h has animated visits with his stories. Clotilde Angleys has shared musical and historical interests along with her friendship. Romain Wenz, unofficial ambassador of Bretagne, knows endless medieval sites to explore and reacted to an early introduction. Time with Karena Kalmbach and Stefan Notthoff has been synonymous with relaxing meals and enjoyable adventures.

Many people shared their expertises to sharpen my understanding of the marketplace. This work was enhanced by discussions and exchanges with Rafe Blaufarb on property; Clare Crowston on guild regulations; Julie Hardwick on judicial practices; Jennifer Heuer on citizenship and public utility; Jacob Melish on women workers; Jack Santino on popular festivals; Anne Verjus and Nimisha Barton on citizenship and gender; Charles Walton on reciprocity and the social contract; Rene Marion on the Dames' origins; Michael Fitzsimmons on regional wages and tax requirements; David Garrioch on confraternities and street numbering; and Natalie Zemon Davis on precedents for the spanking images. I am indebted to multiple groups for hosting me and thank them for engaging with my work. I received productive feedback from the Boston College History Department Workshop; the Weidner History Workshop on Revolutionary Economic Practices organized by Rafe Blaufarb at Florida State University; the Premodern World Reading Group at the University of Illinois Urbana–Champaign, where Clare Crowston arranged a stimulating visit; and the Socioeconomic Rights in History Workshop convened by Charles Walton, Fabian Klose, and Claudia Stein at Das Leibniz-Institut für Europäische Geschichte in Mainz. Fellow conference panelists and audiences, especially those at the Society for French Historical Studies and the Western Society for French History, have provided timely food for thought along the way. For their suggestions in particular, I thank Micah Alpaugh, Claire Cage, Clare Crowston, Daryl Hafter, Carol Harrrison, Jennifer Heuer, Richard Hopkins, Nina Kushner, Kate Marsden, Katie McDonough, Meghan Roberts, and Laura Talamante. Meghan Roberts read key sections of my introduction. Nearly the entire Baylor Department of History rallied for my work-in-progress session, for which I remain grateful. William Doyle, Lynn Hunt, Sarah Knott, and Janet Polasky offered perceptive publishing advice in the penultimate stages.

I was fortunate to complete my revisions at the University of Notre Dame, where my colleagues in the Department of History advanced this manuscript in crucial ways. I offer them my sincere thanks. Elisabeth Köll and Brad Gregory have been unstinting mentors. Patrick Griffin's critiques improved my book proposal. Daniel Graff supplied leads on work and citizenship beyond France. Catherine Cangany, John Deak, Karen Graubart, Thomas Kselman, Paul Ocobock, and Emily Remus shared insights from their publishing experiences. Thomas Tweed explained contracts and production processes. The Notre Dame Department of History and the Institute for Scholarship in the Liberal Arts funded a transformative manuscript workshop. Paul Hanson, Laura Mason, Timothy Tackett, Thomas Kselman, and Jon Coleman generously read the full manuscript and offered suggestions in a full-day workshop moderated by Karen Graubart. Their pivotal feedback energized my final revisions. I thank Patrick Griffin and Ken Garcia for supporting this initiative and Lisa Gingerich for managing the logistical details.

My colleagues beyond the Department of History have also enriched this work. A semester fellowship at the Notre Dame Institute for Advanced Study propelled substantial revisions. I thank Brad Gregory, Don Stelluto, Carolyn Sherman, and Grant Osborn for creating this lively space for interdisciplinary dialogue. Alexander Martin, John Deak, Julia Douthwaite, Thomas Kselman, Tobias

Boes, Sabrina Ferri, and Vittorio Montemaggi of the Cultural Transformations in Modern Europe Reading Group at the Nanovic Institute for European Studies worked through an early draft of Chapter 6. Research assistants Tianyi Tan and Sara Abdel-Rahim assisted with secondary literature and footnotes. Matthew Sisk of the Hesburgh Libraries Center for Digital Scholarship expertly crafted the map of les Halles.

My gratitude goes to the press readers, Jennifer Heuer and Laura Mason, for their engaged reviews. I thank Susan Ferber, my editor at Oxford University Press, for soliciting excellent readers, sharpening nearly every page, and shepherding this book through press.

It is a pleasure to acknowledge the vibrant communities of people who have bolstered this project. I thank Alice Astarita, Sarah Britigan, Charlie Cahill, Hannah Callaway, James Coons, Erin Corber, April Dagonese, Skye Doney, Geneviève Dorais, Katherine Guenoun, Eric O'Connor, Terrence Peterson, and Britt Tevis for their camaraderie and collegiality as we worked on our projects together in Wisconsin and France. Grace Allen, John Boonstra, Abigail Lewis, and Jillian Slaight offered early reactions to material in Chapter 2. Kimberly Kellison, Thomas Kidd, Lauren Miller Poor, Joseph Stubenrauch, and Andrea Turpin volunteered strategies for writing while creating new classes. Jacqueline Mougoué continues to share her passion for gender history, scholarly tenacity, and kind heart. I sincerely appreciate the friendship of Lauren Capuano, Janna Doney, Connor Fitzpatrick, Jessica Moran, Abigail Ocobock, Katelyn Phelps, and Eileen Zeiger whose openness, honesty, and understanding have bolstered me throughout this process.

Finally, I thank my family. My grandmothers, Bernice Cook and Florence Jarvis, sustained this book with letters, phone calls, and memorable meals. My grandfather, Clyde Cook, passed away during my revisions but anticipated this book's completion with great faith. My brother, Kevin Jarvis; my sister-in-law, Alexandra Bisol; and my new family of Lechners shared meaningful conversations over the phone and quality time in person. I dedicate this book with love to my parents, Gay and David Jarvis, who encouraged my academic pursuits even when they sent me across states and continents. My mother's keen insights on teaching have influenced my historical writing. My father has always given me perspective and reminds me to find balance. They keep me in stitches when we are together. My profound love and gratitude go to Andrew Lechner, who has been my partner and teammate in every sense of the word. For the past four years, he has discussed the market women with me, has rooted for me, has moved across the country, and has shared his own aspirations. This is a book about people's everyday lives. I thank Andrew for bringing light and joy to my own.

Politics in the Marketplace

Introduction

Inventing Citizenship in the Revolutionary Marketplace

Four years into the French Revolution, on January 2, 1794, a group of women in aprons and wooden clogs commanded the attention of the National Convention. These Parisian market women, called the Dames des Halles, had addressed the deputies several times before. Three months after the revolutionaries stormed the Bastille, the Dames des Halles had led thousands of women to the royal chateau in Versailles. After demanding bread from the king, petitioning the National Assembly, and rallying National Guards, the Dames had triumphantly returned to Paris with bread and the monarch himself. Now, during the war-enflamed Terror of 1794, the Dames unleashed their patriotic reputation as "citizenesses of the Halles" to appeal to the deputies seated before them. The retailers were defending Jean-Jacques-Claude Vizon, their marketplace fish inspector, who had been convicted of counterrevolutionary remarks and faced deportation. Vizon had a lawyer, but it was the Dames' powerful speech on a national stage that convinced the deputies to reconsider his case.[1]

The Dames des Halles wove together their occupational services, patriotic activism, and gendered work to legitimize their demand and to prove Vizon's innocence. They began by praising the army's victory over Spanish and English invaders at Toulon. They honored the fallen soldiers by donating money to their widows and children. Alluding to the meager profits from their food trade, the Dames noted their "modest offering" was "a portion of the fruit of their painful savings" or "work."[2] Then, the Dames augmented their authority as patriotic activists, mothers, and wives. They proclaimed: "The women of the October Days [the march to Versailles], the mothers, the wives of so many volunteers armed in favor of liberty, would not raise their voice in favor of Vizon, if [he] were not liberty's friend." Among his "virtues," the Dames testified he was a "good citizen, good son" who provided for his elderly father and his brother's two sons "through his work." The Dames further asserted that he was "a Benefactor, a father" even to them. They explained that one of Vizon's market colleagues had

1

denounced him after they had fought. His remarks on "the rarity of bread," they protested, "were more indiscreet than criminal." Freeing Vizon would let him inspect fish again and, in the Dames' words, give "society a citizen who is not unworthy to serve it."[3]

At the climax of their passionate speech, the Dames des Halles couched their request as a right earned in return for their civic labors. They reminded the deputies: "Representatives of the People, they [the Dames] who have chased the tyrant from his hideout at Versailles have perhaps acquired some rights in relation to you: they dare claim this right today [that their] wish will not have been heard in vain."[4] Persuaded by the market women, the deputies moved to reconsider Vizon's fate.[5] For the Dames, their occupational labor, popular activism, and gendered duties worked hand in hand to validate their civic inclusion and claims on the state. Their idea of citizenship resonated powerfully with other revolutionaries, including the deputies who endorsed these "citizenesses of the Halles."[6]

On this and many other occasions, the market women and the marketplace influenced politics and economics in the capital. Les Halles, the main markets, were a lynchpin for public order and public opinion. They supplied 650,000 inhabitants with food everyday.[7] "Les Halles" most often referred to the central Parisian markets and assorted shelters that protected a staggering amount of trade. In 1789 alone, Parisians consumed 78,000,000 eggs, most of which passed through the central markets. There, the Dames des Halles (literally "women of the Halles") sold vegetables, fish, butter, eggs, and fruit from market stands. As retailers, the Dames subdivided carts of food that arrived from the countryside and sold small lots to consumers. The Dames' predecessors had traded in les Halles since the thirteenth century, when the king Saint Louis had granted poor women retail permissions as charity. Linked by shared privileges, the Dames maintained a quasi-corporate identity.[8] By the time of the Revolution, Parisians had supplemented their diet of bread with the Dames' foodstuffs for over 500 years. Within 6,000 crowded square meters, around 1,000 Dames des Halles hawked vegetables from stalls, approached customers with trays of fish, and bartered over vegetables under parasols.[9] Milling through the open square, winding among the pavilions, and darting in and out of shops, diverse customers searched for the best price or a familiar Dame willing to accept their IOUs. Never isolated from the provinces' rhythms, the Dames tied Parisians to the countryside through food supply chains and lending networks. Without their retail services, the capital's markets in fish, eggs, vegetables, butter, and cheese would collapse.

The "Dames de la Halle" most frequently referred to the central market retailers, but the term encompassed women selling in minor public markets as well.[10] Paris boasted several satellite markets around the city, such as the

Place Maubert and the Marché des Quinze-Vingts.[11] Due to their common occupations, Dames from across these markets shared the title by the mid-eighteenth century.[12] Thus, "Dames *de la Halle*" became a misnomer, since it implied a compact market in a single halle. To more accurately evoke the retailers from various Parisian markets, this book refers to them as the "Dames *des Halles*." According to revolutionary legislation, only impoverished individuals could secure a spot in the public marketplace and thus most Dames were poor. However, heritage, commercial networks, and a cultural milieu defined the group's identity more than legal apparatuses. The Dames relied on the same suppliers, credit, and money. Across barrels of fish and packages of butter, they traded resources, gossip, and insults. They took pride in their heritage and stamped their collective identity with a trademark dialect. Pairing singular nouns with first-person plural verbs (as in "I are all equals"), the Dames blurred the discursive boundaries between individual merchants and the wider group.[13] The collectivity subsumed individual Dames, and a single Dame channeled the speech of the entire collectivity. At once individuals and members of a corps, the Dames mirrored the subdivisions among citizens and the body politic.

The French celebrated the Dames as the leading emblem of the people, which granted the market women exceptional political influence. During the Old Regime, the Dames represented the Third Estate during royal rituals surrounding births, baptisms, and feast days. They performed the role of grateful subjects and showered the king with compliments. The king, in turn, acknowledged the Dames' crucial role in feeding his capital. For centuries, Parisians easily recognized them in literary, theatrical, and visual depictions. The Dames' repertoire of distinctive gestures and slang was unmistakable. Citizens continued to embrace the Dames as traditional representatives of the popular classes throughout the eighteenth century. The sans-culottes, often portrayed as embodying the people, did not monopolize this role until 1792. The Dames des Halles—more than any other group—represented "the people" at the outset of the Revolution. They frequently petitioned the National Assembly over crucial issues like money and food prices, they animated revolutionary festivals with songs and bouquets, and they took to the street to smoke out counterrevolutionaries. Their bold interventions and commerce in foodstuffs thrust them into the heart of revolutionary politics from 1789 to 1799.

In les Halles, Parisians fashioned a body politic far from the austere, polished allegories of revolutionary artists. Even in its most formal form, the body politic was mutable, dynamic, and spattered with fish guts. This book probes how the Dames conceptualized citizenship. They grappled with the political role of the popular classes alongside neighbors in marketplaces, legislators in assembly halls, judges in courtrooms, and playwrights in theaters. They and their fellow revolutionaries sought to imagine a new citizen, created unforeseen problems while correcting old ones, pursued countless solutions, and recast the fundamental relationships of society, economics, and politics in the process.[14]

Amid their modest market stalls, the Dames negotiated the dual rise of democratic aspirations and capitalism. This work argues that, at the crux of this volatile transformation, the Dames merged the budding social contract with the economic contracts of everyday trade. It analyzes the merchants' multifaceted concerns—ranging from practical cash to price controls, from occupational licenses to taxes, and from credit systems to the use of public space—to ask how the revolutionaries refracted economic concerns through the new prism of political reciprocity.[15] Across revolutionary regimes, the Dames espoused a triangular contract of mutual duties among the individual, society, and the state as the basis for citizenship. The market women pointed to their commercial service as merchants, to their political work as activists, and to their gendered labor as republican mothers to justify their marketplace demands. In short, they legitimized their civic membership and made claims on the state through their social utility. This approach, in part, corresponded with the autonomy requirements for suffrage, which always excluded women by gender and, at several points, excluded some men by age and income. In contrast to a model of citizenship rooted in voting, the market women thus articulated citizenship through the socioeconomic relationships of quotidian life. Ultimately, the Dames defined citizenship in terms of useful work, rather than predicating citizenship on gender from the outset. In these ways, the market women alter understandings of nascent citizenship at the cusp of modern democracy.

Capitalism, Economic History, and Social Identity

When the revolutionary deputies abolished Old Regime privileges and regulations, they threw centuries of commercial and social relationships into disarray. Recent studies have considered how global commerce, state policies, and officials' economic concerns shaped ensuing free market theories. But how did debates over economic liberty permeate street relationships? And how did street relationships complicate these new ideas? This study asks how the popular classes reformulated the free market ideas that historians often consign to economic theorists. Through their daily trade, the Dames negotiated the tenuous juncture of political and economic liberty with striking dexterity. On the one hand, the Dames broke up monopolies over market shelters by insisting that the nation, to which they belonged, owned the public space. On the other hand, they attacked price controls that resulted from sans-culotte demands for social equality but endangered their livelihoods. While struggling with the fallout of marketplace reform, the Dames advanced their own vision of just economic policy.

Analyzing the marketplace as a site of politics comes with abundant opportunities but it is also rife with historiographical tensions. Given the collapse of the Marxist narrative[16] and the rise of political culture approaches, historians of the Revolution have hesitated to reconsider economic issues at the core of the revolutionary narrative. Early revisionists so discredited the Marxist explanation of class struggle on the road from feudalism to capitalism that socioeconomic history became uncertain terrain.[17] Historians of the linguistic turn pivoted their analytical lens to discourse, further wresting significant causal power from the socioeconomic antagonisms of the Marxist tradition.[18] Rather than asking how an industrial class system possibly arose, social historians began to scrutinize how the corporate world collapsed. These scholars studied how abolishing and re-establishing the guilds affected socioeconomic footings, master–journeyman relations, and the world of craft labor.[19]

Most recently, economic historians of France and elsewhere have shifted their focus from workplace relations to institutions, broad networks, and theoretical imaginings.[20] Since the turn of the twenty-first century, historians reviving economic perspectives have debated the Revolution's financial origins, have considered the deputies' economic philosophies, and have examined the Revolution within global commercial networks.[21] In a related enterprise, historians have sought to redefine the "bourgeoisie" or ascertain if any such coherent group existed.[22] Urban historians, for their part, have trained an economic lens on the revolutionary state to ask how it ordered occupations, regulated commercial activity, and influenced labor markets.[23] Overall, most recent work has skirted the socioeconomic relations of the streets.[24]

This study reasserts the centrality of economics in everyday relationships among the revolutionaries and proposes new imaginings of citizenship from 1789 to 1799. Rather than clearly delineating socioeconomic identities, the Dames' case illustrates how economic issues inconsistently divided society and gave rise to various notions of citizenship. The Dames and the popular classes bucked the corporate model to forge innovative alliances in the marketplace, yet such coalitions were not necessarily class-based, nor were they permanent.[25] Merchants and consumers, for example, joined forces to demand special provisioning for Paris in 1789, but fell on opposing sides of price controls four years later.

Just as one's identity and political sentiments cannot be reduced to one's sex, the Dames' identity or political allegiances cannot be reduced to economic issues alone. It would be erroneous to homogenize 1,000 retailers' opinions or flatten their diverse experiences. The Dames sold a variety of goods in different markets dotting the capital. In order to collectively examine them, this work does insist on their shared marketplace concerns, their decision to appropriate the title "Dames des Halles" while acting en masse, their robust cultural heritage, and the revolutionaries' tendency to perceive them as a collectivity on the streets, stage, and printed page.

Because the market women were an occupational group, economic theories influenced popular and legislative attitudes toward their civic membership. During the Enlightenment, the physiocrats had reasoned that land generated all virtuous riches and accordingly placed their economic faith in property and agriculture. However, by the late eighteenth century, elite merchants repackaged trade as a societally oriented public service rather than an avarice-ridden enterprise.[26] They challenged the physiocrats' veneration of agriculture as more beneficial than commerce.[27] This shift primed the revolutionary environment in which the Dames could valorize their trade as productive work.[28]

Since their commerce served society, the Dames argued that their economic activity and political activity were one and the same during the Revolution. The Dames concretely demonstrate one of the ways in which Abbé Sieyès expanded the category of useful work in 1789. To bolster the Third Estate, Sieyès classified any occupation that benefited the body politic as legitimate labor.[29] He included commercial services like those of merchants, professional services like those of doctors, and even religious services like those of parish clergy. In a similar fashion, the Dames portrayed their small-scale trade as productive work that qualified them as citizens meriting the state's attention.[30] Their political imaginings were in no way insincere because profit partially motivated them. On the contrary, the Dames' ability to successfully integrate self-interest and collective interests under the umbrella of useful work made their vision of citizenship remarkably powerful.

Factional shifts and market crises continually refashioned the guiding principles of state economic policy and changed the context in which the Dames asserted their citizenship. In the eyes of the early revolutionaries, Old Regime monopolies, privileges, and controls had poisoned commerce and society. A free market, in contrast, would generate a just moral economy because it would be regulated by individuals' voluntary participation rather than state coercion.[31] During the radical and war-torn phase of 1793 to 1794, the deputies returned guardianship of the moral economy to the state and increased commercial regulations. Despite coercively enforcing their market policies, the Jacobins did not interpret their economic controls as antagonistic. Rather, they presumed that symbiotic regulations like price and wage controls mirrored fraternal relations among citizens. After the Terror, the Thermidorians and the Directory swung back toward a liberal market economy through "commercial republicanism." According to historian James Livesey, post-Terror republicans believed "intensive modern commerce promised to provide the basis for independent citizens ... the citizen's work, rather than their voice, would be their central contribution to the common good." Since individuals relied on one another's various occupational services, Directory officials presumed that citizens would seek just and cooperative commercial relationships.[32]

With striking dexterity, the Dames navigated the transition from a protectionist, Old Regime marketplace, to a liberated, protocapitalist one that supported free commerce, investment opportunities, and individually centered fiscal responsibilities. An attendant bourgeois culture celebrated autonomy, defended property, and rejected privileged corporations.[33] During the birth pangs of free market experiments, the Dames oscillated between a local moral economy dependent on paternalist protections and a liberated market ensconced in the body politic and standardized laws. As indigent retailers, they toed the precipice of economic failure with neighborhood credit and market privileges as their only safety nets. Consequently, the Dames clung to charitable benefits like license exemptions, yet they also cited free market reform to demand equal access to wholesalers.[34] Corporate privilege gave them marketplace advantages, but egalitarian discourses gave them legitimacy to make demands on the state. The Dames reveal how the revolutionaries negotiated democratic aspirations and burgeoning capitalist attitudes on the ground. They complicate the image of revolutionary merchants as bourgeois motors who readily propelled capitalist initiatives.

Although the Dames' modest stalls were far from the polished salons of economic debate, they demonstrate just how far theorists' ideas reached into the popular classes or were perhaps informed by them. It is highly unlikely that any literate Dame read economic treatises. They do not cite Rousseau, Sieyès, or Locke. Yet, their remarkable agility in maneuvering among logics of economists and social contract theorists suggests that, even at the start of the Revolution, these theoretical discourses were deeply entangled with everyday practice. In les Halles, through the most meager exchanges in the capital, market women drew on strands of welfare state logic, proposed their own vision for a liberated market, and molded the social compact to their commercial advantage. From 1789 to 1799, the Dames regularly engaged in acrobatics of free market principles and social egalitarianism. Seizing these discordant revolutionary ideals, they intervened in debates over political economy and influenced national legislation.

Les Halles, as the largest space of public exchange among citizens, became a microcosm of the body politic in 1789.[35] The revolutionaries insisted that the principles orienting political and social relations also apply in les Halles. Just as the deputies debated under the public galleries of the assembly halls, merchants and consumers bartered in the transparent environment of the public market square. As Dames sold to clients, brokers secured food from countryside suppliers, and consumers haggled over what constituted just prices, the revolutionaries negotiated how to create fraternal relations in one of the most basic, repetitive, yet foundational forms of workaday life: daily trade.

In this environment, the Dames developed a complex notion of economic citizenship or the ways in which an individual's economic activities (such as buying goods, selling food, or paying taxes) position him/her within the collective social body and enable him/her to make claims on the state. Diverse issues such as public space, wage limits, price controls, occupational licenses, and legal tender forced the revolutionaries to evaluate citizens' duties in an economic vein. In doing so, the revolutionaries asked how individuals' economic roles figured into the body politic. For example, price controls reflected the reach of the political imagination into the laws and attitudes that governed quotidian trade relationships. By determining the profits that merchants merited, officials delineated the worth of their occupational services to the nation. This differed from the Old Regime in which crown-granted permissions, not an individual's contributions, delineated their corporation's civic membership and privileges.

Revolutionary economic citizenship depicted work as an intangible personal property that tethered individuals to fiscal duties and public regulations. Thus, work both atomized and autonomized citizen-workers.[36] This ideal neatly dovetailed with the collapsing corporate world and rising republic from 1789 to 1794. However, beyond the scope of propertied men, the Directory struggled to reconcile this model with its shift toward the male-led familial political unit from 1795 to 1799. By probing the Dames' trajectory, this study reveals the revolutionaries' far-reaching attempts to merge political and economic citizenship in the rudimentary exchanges of everyday trade.

Citizenship and Gender

Les Halles offered a promising canvas for revolutionary reform, but it also bristled with social friction and commercial uncertainty. Here, citizens confronted the fundamental tensions of revolutionary politics: How could the indivisible general will and individual wills coexist? How could citizens reconcile private interests with public interests while buying fish, bartering with promissory notes, and displaying goods on public property? And where was this sovereign, Rousseauian Will if the mass of bodies crammed into les Halles outnumbered those tidily seated in the National Assembly? The question of where to locate revolutionary sovereignty was tightly linked to the question of how to define revolutionary citizenship.

Historians, political scientists, and philosophers rightly emphasize how the French Revolution created a foundation for democracy in modern Europe.[37]

Exploring socioeconomic relations unearths the multiple and potentially contradictory ways the revolutionaries invented citizenship from this outset. Historians have neglected the Dames since their activism did not take commonly recognized forms of democratic citizenship such as voting, bearing arms, participating in political clubs, or advocating through the press. If we project our modern institutional definitions of citizenship back upon the revolutionary model, we miss the opportunity to probe the myriad ways the revolutionaries conceptualized citizenship in its embryonic stages. Many of these revolutionary notions of citizenship challenged legal gendered divisions between men and women. In the case of the market women, the Dames considered useful occupational work to cut across gendered boundaries and form a crucial element of citizenship. Free market reform, state regulation, and socioeconomic changes deeply influenced how the Dames and others articulated their political rights and civic duties. Their experience challenges narrow definitions that reduce citizenship to voting rights and illuminates complex negotiations of political legitimacy across multiple sites and practices.

Revolutionary citizenship took many forms, and one could hold several simultaneously. In its most basic legal form, citizenship could denote inclusion in a system of rights and privileges, as it had during the Old Regime. Citizenship could mean membership in the body politic.[38] Yet, this approach makes it difficult to classify individuals who are included in some ways (such as having the right to a fair trial) but excluded in others (such as lacking the right to vote). Historian Harriet Applewhite reconciles this inconsistency by dividing citizenship into a receptive-creative dichotomy mirroring the revolutionaries' own distinction between passive and active citizens. Drawing from Sieyès, she explains, "Civil rights . . . guaranteed the protection of one's person, property, and liberty [and] were enjoyed by all the inhabitants of a country, while political rights allowed one to contribute to the formation of public authority, a direct application of the political power."[39] However, the deputies' legal binary failed to capture the cultural components of citizenship that they took so seriously. Historian Suzanne Desan thus further proposes three dimensions of citizenship: "civil rights" and juridical rights based on standardized laws that apply to members; cultural roles that integrate individuals into a "moral" community; and institutional access that allows individuals to express their sovereignty via the "formal" forums of "public politics."[40] Since definitions of citizenship are implicitly definitions of membership, most analytical models focus on the rights that states give included individuals. However, as Desan's cultural component suggests, the other side of the social contract required fulfilling duties as a member of the body politic.

For the revolutionaries, the relationship between duties and rights was up for debate. The two concepts unnervingly coalesced through linguistic ambiguity.

"Droits" cut both ways as rights and claims: the "droits" of citizens denoted civil rights (what the state owes the individual) but "droits" also referred to taxes (what the individual owes the state). The *Déclaration des droits de l'homme et du citoyen* could have been a list of fiscal obligations. "Droit" could also carry moral connotations as "jurisprudence." And the word could assume social virtues when describing a person.[41] Individual rights, participatory duties, and moral intent all fell under the same discursive umbrella.[42]

This fluidity helps explain why the banning of women's political clubs in 1793 merely registered as a blip in the Dames' civic trajectory. When the National Convention shuttered the clubs, it limited women's institutional citizenship and denied them the right to politically assemble. The deputies distinguished male citizenship from female citizenship and male rights from female rights. Yet, the market women continued to intervene in politics in diverse ways. What one assumes would have been a blow to the Dames' capacity to politically participate as women did not shake their sense of legitimacy.

The Dames des Halles remained unfazed by the new male definition of citizenship because they did not base their sovereignty on primarily gendered or institutional scaffolding. For the Dames, citizenship was not a static concept expressed through formal institutions. They constantly justified why their demands merited attention, sometimes as sovereign citizens, but never as a priori citizens by default. The Dames rarely appealed to universal, inalienable, or innate individual rights typically associated with modern citizenship. Instead, they portrayed revolutionary citizenship as contingent and temporal.[43] It was earned and continually renewed. When the Dames declared in 1791 that they did "not know any other virtues than those of being useful and serving their fatherland," they articulated their vision of participatory citizenship: Individuals joined the body politic through work that served society.[44] In other words, the Dames viewed citizenship as a set of societally useful practices that validated one's inclusion in the body politic. And this membership legitimated one's right to make demands on the state in return.

Although the Dames did not receive full institutional rights, they insisted that the state fulfill its reciprocal duties in other ways. The Dames demanded the government fairly regulate the market, defend patriotic families, and assist the poor. As citizens, they insisted that they could make these demands not *through* their representatives as sovereign conduits, but directly *on* their representatives (as hands of the state) through petitions, addresses, and protests. The Dames legitimized their demands through their contributions to the public good. They imagined their civic membership through their occupational work as traders, their patriotic work as activists, and their gendered work as mothers. Useful work, rather than gender, primarily validated the Dames' citizenship and allowed them to make claims on the government.

Consequently, this study challenges the argument that all revolutionaries conceived of citizenship as masculine in 1789. Proponents of this standard interpretation have highlighted how the deputies used gendered notions of autonomy to deny women suffrage in 1789 and then legally cast citizenship as male in 1793.[45] Although the state periodically classified some men as dependents through wealth or age requirements and thus ineligible to vote, it always classified women as dependents of their husbands or fathers and thus ineligible to vote. Some scholars point to these parameters to argue that when the deputies outlawed female political clubs in 1793, they legalized an implicit gendered divide between the masculine public sphere of politics and the feminine private sphere.[46] These scholars maintain that Rousseauian discourses of the Enlightenment, the threat of sexual dedifferentiation, and the contradictions of democratic universalism drove a firm wedge between masculine and feminine domains.[47] Discursive analyses along these lines define citizenship in its most formal sense as the right to vote, to keep arms, and to participate politically through clubs and assemblies. Such interpretations insist that the Revolution launched an inherently masculine trajectory for full citizenship that excluded women in its very definition.

Three groups of historians have contested these interpretations: the women's history vanguard, proponents of the crisis narrative, and scholars of political culture. Excavating moments of agency and activism, scholars of women's history have demonstrated how women intervened in the public sphere despite limitations on their citizenship.[48] Women, for example, reconceptualized their traditional roles in subsistence, religious, and familial arenas in the context of the Revolution.[49] Here, women's explicitly political actions influenced the very institutional politics that legally excluded them. They asserted their place in the nation by demonstrating, organizing, and engaging in public debate.[50]

Other scholars have highlighted women's political engagement but contend that, as "a period of crisis," the Revolution "open[ed] the political terrain to [women]."[51] They concluded that unusual circumstances granted women an exceptional ability to politically participate in societies, take up arms to defend their communities, and vote in some assemblies before such venues became exclusive male rights in 1793. However, this crisis framework assumes that all women politically identified by their gender over any other category like class, religion, or faction. It also assumes that revolutionary chaos created an anomalous opening for women, which limits historians to asking how women tapped into a preexisting form of citizenship rather than how the revolutionaries invented multiple interpretations of citizenship. The approach applies a homogeneous definition of citizenship and gender to a situation in which the historical actors themselves had yet to reach a consensus.

From a third perspective, gender scholars of political culture reject a firm divide between political public and domestic private domains.[52] The family proved fertile ground for these historians to question the politics of gendered relations by examining marriage and inheritance among other topics.[53] Other scholars have emphasized that revolutionary citizenship was not inherently sexist since lower income men, male servants, and male minors, as well as women, were considered "dependents" of a household. Thus, rather than resting on sex, the revolutionaries predicated full citizenship on independence assured by personal property and head of family status.[54]

All this vibrant work on gender has greatly advanced understandings of how women and men experienced the Revolution, how social relations evolved, and how the revolutionaries reconstructed political culture. Women's history and political culture approaches convincingly unhinged the private/public dichotomy. Nonetheless, their ambitious studies portray either vast thematic trends among women or amalgamations of scattered examples. To gain more nuance, gender historians have recently turned to group-anchored subjects and have examined broad social categories through case studies.[55] Petitions from potential soldiers, for example, demonstrate how male citizens interpreted paternal and military duties as complementary patriotic roles.[56] Priests and nuns released from their vows offer insights into the sexual politics of the Revolution.[57] And the treatment of prostitutes reveals how citizens, legislators, and the police confronted contradictory systems of "morals" and "droit de cité" during the Directory.[58] These targeted inquiries reveal the shifting role of gender according to context.

This book aims to advance scholarship by decentering gender in the formula of citizenship. As long as gender is used as the question of sociocultural differentiation, it becomes the answer for political delineation. The political scientist Anne Verjus similarly insists that analyses must extend beyond a history of women to avoid "going in circles by making the exclusion of women the explanation of their exclusion."[59] Gleaning perspectives on citizenship in which gender is not primary demands stepping away from gender as the principal vantage point. In order to understand how historical actors invented citizenship from other angles besides gender, they cannot immediately be cast as "male" or "female" citizens. Other approaches must be prioritized before considering how gender fits into this matrix of political identity. In analyzing the Dames des Halles, this book asks: How did the market women socially and economically integrate themselves into the body politic? How did malleable ideas of gender play into their notion of citizenship? And how did they continually adjust the balance between the socioeconomic and gendered attributes of their citizenship?

Sources and Structure

Accessing the experience of the popular classes often necessitates methodological creativity, and the Dames are no exception. The market women are eminent in revolutionary narratives, yet elusive in surviving sources. True to the tumultuous spirit of the marketplace, the Dames have scattered across the archives like runaway onions careening off a cart. They do not cohesively emerge from a single series, holding, or archival collection. They appear in dispersed reports written in pens that are rarely their own. The Dames' collective voice surfaces in the petitions they brought to the National Assembly or municipal government. But with the destruction of their confraternity records and those of Parlement's Chambre de la Marée, which judged all cases concerning fish en route from the sea to les Halles, there are few other places to tap into the Dames' collective thoughts.[60]

Nonetheless, judicial, police, legislative, visual, and print sources offer mediated points of contact with the Dames. For their part, police reported on the marketplace and apprehended retailers engaging in illegal activities. Subsistence committees monitored food supplies, prices, and trade between the capital and the provinces. The National Assembly studied market shelters to debate public domain and considered market cash while reforming currency. Individual Dames appear in the justice of the peace records where they settled disputes with their neighbors, pled for a lower tax bracket, or negotiated a license fee. From a visual perspective, revolutionary engravings depict the Dames' famous activism like the October Days, and architectural renderings hint at the built environment of the Dames' neighborhood. Hawked from street corners, newspapers and pamphlets describe the Dames' roles in festivals, street politics, and deputations to the government. And printers captured songs and plays that seized the Dames' likenesses for political and entertainment purposes. In short, this work reconstructs the Dames and their world, while also spotlighting the Dames' fellow revolutionaries. Chapters 1 and 2 establish the Dames' sociocultural environment and trace how the market women intervened in politics in and beyond the capital. Chapters 3 to 7 then move into the marketplace to explore how the Dames forged their citizenship through their occupations.

Chapter 1 establishes the influence the Dames derived from their commercial centrality as traders and their political centrality as traditional representatives of the Third Estate. It places the Dames in the marketplace and elucidates their relationships with clients, brokers, inspectors, and wholesalers. Evidence from 151 market women provide the contours of their everyday lives. It also demonstrates how the Dames' ritual relationship with the king and Old Regime literary precursors colored the Dames as mouthpieces of the people.

The pre-Revolutionary literary "genre poissard" created stock characters of the market women from which Revolutionary pamphleteers drew.[61] From 1789 to 1792, propagandists from rival parties appropriated the poissard style and deployed fictive market women to embody popular sovereignty.[62] These cultural constructions overlapped with the living Dames to inform their political influence.

Chapter 2 charts how, from the constitutional monarchy through the Terror, the Dames reinvented their place in the nation through their activism, which they framed as civic work, and through their maternal initiatives, which they framed as gendered labor. The Dames reasserted their role as communal guardians by collectively reacting to issues as they arose, whether seeking aid in subsistence crises or shunning the king after he fled France. Drawing on their legitimacy as republican mothers, they also compelled the government to pay special attention to soldiers' wives and spanked counterrevolutionary nuns who miseducated their children. However, the power of the Dames' sporadic interventions was challenged by the monarchy's decline and by the proliferating clubs and assemblies that became institutional venues for politics. Nevertheless, the Dames continued to promote an embodied and experiential social contract through notions of economic citizenship.

Chapter 3 examines the economically crucial and conceptually volatile debates over public space in the marketplace. From 1789 to 1792, the market women embraced new practices of citizenship to defend their trading spots and shelters. They seized revolutionary discourses to mark the earth as national property, to lambast monopoly-holders as privileged leeches, to appeal to the state's paternal duties, and to secure exceptions based on their work's public utility. The Dames began to shape their place in the body politic as they justified their personal profits on public space.

After the deputies overhauled national currency during the winter of 1789–1790, the Dames, their suppliers, their clients, and other merchants relied on new promissory notes for everyday trade. Chapter 4 reveals how small change shortages spurred market actors to ally across occupational boundaries and form their own innovative socioeconomic associations before the Assembly legally dismantled the corporate world. Money thus became a concrete conduit for effecting the core social transformations at the heart of the Revolution. Vegetable merchants aligned with carpenters to demand new denominations, retailers joined forces with brokers to protect promissory bills, and clients and merchants rallied to support overlapping credit networks. The Dames and their allies spurred the state to protect the monetary networks of productive citizens and together changed the trajectory of national currency reform.

Chapter 5 analyzes how contests over commercial regulations ultimately prompted the deputies to abolish women's political clubs. In 1793, the National

Convention passed a series of price controls called the Maximum. While debating the Maximum in the Convention, regulation-promoting Montagnards sparred with free market–defending Girondins over the political duties of buyers and sellers. Simultaneously, marketplace fights broke out between the Dames des Halles and the leading women's club called the Société des Citoyennes républicaines révolutionnaires. The Dames, whose retail profits the Maximum outlawed, repeatedly brawled with the Citoyennes républicaines, who supported stringent limits to protect consumers and criticized Montagnard attempts to accommodate merchant interests. To silence the club, the deputies argued that violent, irrational women had no place in politics and banned all female political assemblies. This chapter argues that the ban, long seen as a verdict on gendered citizenship, primarily emerged from disagreements over defining citizenship via commercial roles and subsistence regulation.

Days after banning women's clubs in November 1793, the Convention ordered Maximum reforms to include both wholesale and retail price ceilings. Chapter 6 dissects the treacherous late fall and winter during which Parisians waited for the new guidelines to be finalized and the Dames lacked a legal way to sell at a profit. As the Convention reformed the Maximum, the Dames, their commercial allies, and local police compelled the deputies to economically affirm and politically legitimize merchants as useful citizens. They highlighted marketplace practices to illustrate why retailers deserved to profit from their services. They also insisted that symbiotic trading relationships echoed the fraternal bonds among citizens and that workers' wages should be limited to ensure a balanced, reciprocal relationship for both sides of commerce. Ultimately, crippling inflation blurred the political interests of poor retailers and consumers when the Thermidorians abolished the Maximum in December 1794.

From 1791 to 1793 and again from 1795 to 1798, the deputies taxed work through occupational licenses called the patente. Chapter 7 unearths how the revolutionaries refracted the relationship among work, property, and autonomous citizenship through this tax. By exchanging fees for permissions, the patente created a fiscal contract between citizens and the state that mirrored the social contract.[63] Legislators assessed the patente according to criteria for full citizenship including independence and immobile property. From 1796 to 1798, the patente fashioned a type of economic citizenship not predicated on gender and enabled the Dames to form a fiscal contract with the nation, unlike all male wage laborers. In patente hearings before justices of the peace, the Dames articulated their trade as autonomous work.[64] When the deputies reorganized taxes by familial unit and exempted food retailers in 1798, the Dames lost their licenses and fiscal autonomy. At the same time, the Directory reconsolidated political authority into male heads of households.

By probing everyday experience, this book demonstrates how revolutionary market women envisioned citizenship as economic and social engagement. In les Halles, the Dames, brokers, clients, officials, police, and fellow citizens asked how fraternal relations assumed commercial forms. Citizens crafted civic membership and their right to make demands on the state by merging their understanding of the social contract with economic relations. The market women demonstrated in the streets to protect their communities. And they approached their representatives when they believed it would advance their interests. But the Dames des Halles did not look to parliamentary procedure to define the body politic. Rather, they negotiated economics, gender, and politics as complementary dimensions of their civic membership. Without predicating citizenship on gender, the Dames invented a work-based citizenship that included occupational, activist, and gendered components.

In casting away the teleological division of citizenship by sex and analyzing dimensions beyond its institutional expression, this study challenges the direct line between natural rights and the social contract so often cited by the revolutionaries. Instead, it exposes a triangular contract calibrated on reciprocal relationships among the individual, society, and the state. As citizens forged new relationships and remade old ones, they invented an experiential citizenship of social, economic, and political exchanges that permeated quotidian life. The market women point to the fundamentally messy but extraordinarily creative nature of developing democracies. By rejecting sex and institutions as the footings for civic membership but embracing the legitimizing power of useful work, the Dames reconfigure dominant understandings of nascent citizenship and its continued reverberations.

The Dames des Halles

Economic Lynchpins and the People Personified

On the evening of October 5, 1789, the king and his ministers conversed anxiously at his château in Versailles. Nearly three months had passed since the fall of the Bastille, but supply shortages and rumors of counterrevolutionary plots now threatened the capital. Outside the king's apartments, a deputation of five Dames des Halles trudged up the marble stairs. Their rain-soaked clothes weighed heavily on them as they followed the National Assembly's president into the king's rooms. Before them stretched a decadent green table surrounded by noble advisors in delicately carved chairs. The château's opulent frescoes discordantly soared above the ragged visitors. To onlookers, the poor petitioners seemed out of place. One of the women, Louison Chabry, approached Louis XVI. Echoing the language of the Third Estate, she told the king that she brought the "grievances [doléances] of the women & of the people." The seventeen-year-old fell on her knees before the monarch, lamented that the capital had no bread, and fainted at his feet.

Just as Louison Chabry had depleted her resources, so too had Paris exhausted its reserves. Earlier that morning, hundreds of Dames des Halles had abandoned their market stalls, gathered at the city hall, and demanded that officials solve the dire bread shortage. When municipal representatives could not alleviate the crisis, several hundred Dames and nearly 6,000 Parisians marched 12 miles to Versailles to appeal to the king. Several hours later, the monarch ordered brandy to revive Louison. The king embraced her and promised to send bread to the capital. Then, he dispatched her with declarations to reassure the crowds outside.

Since the capital also nervously awaited his word, the king arranged to send his reply. Instead of relying primarily on a court messenger, a minister, or a representative from the National Assembly, the king sent forty Dames des Halles in royal carriages to deliver his message. At 3:00 am, the Dames presented his letter to the frazzled Parisian mayor, thereby relaying Louis's promise to his faithful subjects.[1]

Why did the Dames des Halles audaciously assume the king would listen to them at Versailles? And why did the king not just receive the Dames in his private rooms, but deputize them to deliver his promise to Paris? The Dames' dual importance—as economic and political actors—clarifies these extraordinary moments from the October Days. In an economic vein, the Dames performed a vital commercial role as food retailers in the central markets. Since the thirteenth century, the monarchy had relied on the Dames to feed the capital. In a society that judged the government by its ability to guarantee bread, food equaled politics. In a political vein, the Dames were influential as traditional representatives of the Third Estate. During royal rituals stretching from holy days to military celebrations, the market women performed the part of grateful subjects. The Dames used their exceptional position to present the king with bouquets and to petition him at court. During the October Days, the Dames predicted the king would receive them and the king, in turn, channeled his message through the Dames with good reason. In 1789, the Dames held the keys to subsistence and sovereignty.

This chapter briefly outlines the Dames' origins from the thirteenth century and analyzes judicial evidence from 151 revolutionary Dames to sketch a collective biography and to explain how they conducted their commerce. Pairing the Dames' lives with the built environment of les Halles, it walks through the specialized markets to demonstrate the daily rhythms of trade. As they worked, the Dames formed the densest networks of women in the capital. Their occupational, familial, and neighborhood relationships dominated the marketplace. While police regulated fish sales and Parisians secured vegetables, they faced the Dames' centrality in provisioning 650,000 people.

Parisians had long recognized the Dames in commerce and royal rituals, but a literary style from the seventeenth and eighteenth centuries also primed them to accept the retailers. This style, named the genre poissard (after "fishwife"), sought to capture the daily lives of the Parisian popular classes, particularly the Dames, in a boisterous and hyperbolic form.[2] Parisians instantly identified the Dames in these texts and images. This chapter examines how propagandists used fictive Dames as mouthpieces and co-opted their popular sovereignty. From the Estates General to the fall of the king, rival propagandists channeled contradictory positions through the market women.[3] Royalists, who longed to return to an absolute monarchy, deployed the Dames in pamphlets, as did Fayettistes, who sought to consolidate the constitutional monarchy. Similarly, Orléanists, who supported the king's cousin as a liberal option for the throne, entered the fray by borrowing the Dames' likeness. Opposing factions thus appropriated the Dames' image and gritty straight talk to personify popular legitimacy. From 1789 to 1792, the Dames were the most recognizable and powerful symbol of the people.

Just as the Dames inspired pamphleteers' fictive fishwives, the propaganda influenced how others understood the living Dames. Their printed image circulated farther than the market women themselves. Encounters with fabricated "Dames" conditioned citizens, police, and government officials as they interacted with the actual market women. The Dames themselves even leaned on poissard stereotypes to advance their political causes. However, the style proved a double-edged sword: it celebrated the retailers as powerful figureheads but derided them as poor folk or irrational women to generate comedy. From 1789 to 1792, the Dames' place at the commercial and cultural crossroads of the Old Regime and the new nation set the stage for their revolutionary activism.[4]

Royal Power and Commercial Lineage in the Marketplace

Under the Old Regime, the king depended on a well-maintained food supply to keep order.[5] Therefore, the monarchy was heavily invested in activity in les Halles. Any nongrain foodstuff entering the capital was directly routed to les Halles, where officials regulated its distribution. This was no small feat: wholesalers annually sold 350,000 sheep, 120,000 calves, 80,000 cattle, and 40,000 pigs at les Halles.[6] Diverse customers and retailers from satellite markets purchased food from the Dames and fellow merchants.[7] The king relied on their centralized trade to maintain political control of the capital.

The Dames' special relationship with the monarch and their market privileges dated back to the Middle Ages. Records first mention the Dames in 1361. According to legend, saint king Louis IX distributed spaces in the central Parisian market "in alms to poor women, widows, orphans, and marriageable daughters." The state also granted owners of these "places Saint Louis" the title of "regratières," which permitted them to sell their own goods in limited quantities and subjected them to the regulations of the wholesalers and guilds. These fortunate recipients became the first Dames des Halles. Gradually, the *places Saint Louis* lost their strict charitable overtones as women passed them on to relatives or friends. Through generations of trading and residing in les Halles, the Dames established themselves as an enduring force in their community.[8]

Most sources on early modern Paris use the title "Dames de la Halle" to refer to retailers in the central market. However, by the end of the eighteenth century, Parisians called poor women retailers from satellite markets "Dames de la Halle" as well. The revolutionary market women themselves expressed this expansive identity. Just before the New Year in December 1789, Dames from several markets offered homage to the king and praised the National Assembly. Representatives from multiple sites signed under the collective title "us, the

Dames de la Halle," including Dame Dupray of the Marché St. Paul, Reine d'Ongrie (Hongrie) of the Marché d'Aguesseau, Dame Genti of the Marché des Quinze-Vingts, and Dame Doré of the central Halles.[9]

The Dames des Halles often presented themselves as a cohesive group by the late eighteenth century, but it is difficult to discern their number and individual identities. Although they were occupationally linked, they did not have a guild and corresponding corporate records. The 1700 inventory of the king's territory contains the last partial list of *places Saint Louis* holders before the Revolution.[10] However, May 1799 plans to reorganize rent in les Halles indicate that there were approximately 200 retail stalls in the fish market, 700 spots in the fruit and vegetable market, and 200 retail places for butter, cheese, and eggs.[11] Since about 75 percent of retailers in the central markets were women, and officials neglected to count some open-air fish selling places, at least 900 Dames likely sold in the central markets. Dames selling in satellite markets added to this number. For example, approximately 70 Dames traded on the Place Maubert on the Left Bank.[12] Thus, by 1789, at least 1,000 Dames des Halles sold fruit, vegetables, fish, butter, cheese, eggs, and occasionally flowers across the capital's markets. Their formidable group outnumbered bakers 2 to 1.[13] While bakers are seen as key to food politics, the Dames' comparative numbers suggest the need to examine their trade.

The World of the Market Women

A day that would unfold in the busiest artery in Paris began in solitude for Marie Jeanne Hollande at her humble one-bedroom apartment at n°598 rue de la Cossonnerie. The fish merchant rose from her straw mattress alone in the room. She was fifty-nine years old at the start of the Revolution, a widow of Étienne Pérault and mother to one daughter who had moved to the colonies. Her neighbors and fellow Dames were not only her colleagues in commerce—they were her lifelines.[14]

A glance at her small paper register would remind Hollande of the credit she gave customers and the debts she owed others. Taking stock of her limited clothing, she might pull a ragged pair of woolen stockings over her undergarments, as well as a corset of linen and cotton. After securing a blue and red camisole over her bosom, she might fasten a violet wool skirt around her waist. She would complete her chosen ensemble with two white merchant purses slung across her torso, a piqué bonnet tied under her chin, and a worn knife stowed in her pocket. Her outfit was as rough and colorful as the language of les Halles. The fish merchant reached for her crutch to steady herself as she shuffled forward in her heavy clogs. Slowly unlocking her door so as not to spill the chamber pot behind it, she hobbled down one flight of interior stairs and exited to the street.[15]

As a native of Paris, Dame Hollande knew the central market area illustrated in Figure 1.1. Across the street from her apartment stood the buildings most densely populated with Dames des Halles. Younger, more nimble retailers spilled

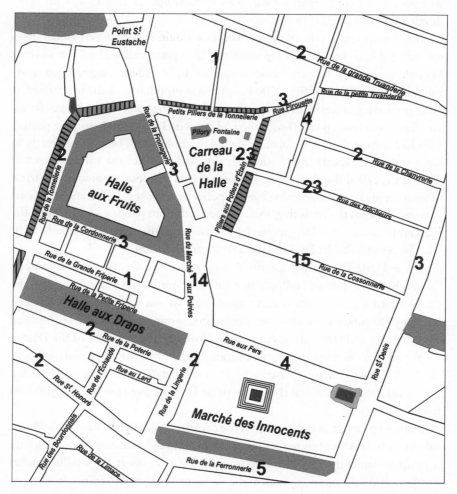

Figure 1.1 A Street Map of Les Halles in 1790. Dame Hollande lived on the Rue de la Cossonnerie, which intersected the southern point of the Carreau de la Halle. Note the open market spaces of Carreau de la Halle in the north, the Halle aux Fruits in the northwest, and the Marché des Innocents in the southeast. The numbers indicate the number of Dames' residences per street from the sample set of 151 market women. Drawn from BnF GR FOL LK7 6043 Edme Verniquet, "Atlas du plan général de la ville de Paris . . . Dessiné et gravé par les cens Bartholomé et Mathieu" (Paris: Rue de l'Oratoire, 1795).

out of the nearby doorways and passed Hollande as she walked one block west
toward the fish market square. On her way, she passed the old Halle aux Salines
to her left, where, tucked into a covered space off the public way, a few retailers
sold salted fish.[16] As Hollande approached the end of the rue de la Cossonnerie,
she may have veered toward a familiar woman who carried a tinplate container
on her back and took shelter under a Chinese parasol. In return for 2 sous, the
woman poured coffee with milk into an earthen pot for Hollande, who likely
drank it without pausing to sit.[17]

The sounds and smells of the marketplace would have attacked Hollande as
she handed back her cup. In the open market square, called the Carreau de la
Halle, there was, as one chronicler described it, "no silence, no rest, no inter-
mission." The earliest of the 6,000 countryside suppliers had already arrived at
1:00 am, having traveled 7 to 8 leagues while hauling carts of vegetables, fruits,
and flowers to the capital. Those who had unloaded their goods and the porters
who had helped them had fortified their early hours with brandy.[18] Directly in
front of Hollande, carts filled with fish still clattered into the southern part of
the square, called the Parquet de la marée. Here, wholesalers unloaded barrels
of seafood under the discerning eyes of police and brokers.[19] The shouts of cart
drivers peppered the air as they jockeyed for makeshift parking spots around the
marketplace. One Parisian gauging "the noise" and "the tumult" concluded that
"the Tower of Babel had not offered a stranger confusion."[20]

Dame Hollande headed for the storage space she rented with Antoinette
Douet, her neighbor and fellow fish retailer.[21] Among the more fortunate, she
could afford a place to stash two baskets and an oak table on which she laid
her scaly offerings. A few other retailers rented semipermanent stalls composed
of four posts and tattered canvas roofs.[22] However, the majority of the Dames
displayed their herring, mackerel, salmon, and cod in the open square. Some
of them rented collapsible parasols. Two dilapidated fish hangars bordered
the carreau to the west, but they were poised to collapse after four centuries of
trade.[23]

Setting up her chair on the edge of the carreau, Hollande surveyed the wholesale fish lots on which fellow retailers were about to bid. Entering from the south,
a group of Dames des Halles arrived from the Place Maubert, the satellite market
a mile away on the opposite bank of the Seine, to buy their fish from wholesalers.
The forts, or hired porters of les Halles, would soon be grunting under weight
of barrels of fish bought by these Dames.[24] With their cracked and calloused
hands, the forts expertly maneuvered carts of goods throughout the crowded
city center to retailers' spots in les Halles and the satellite markets.

Looking north, Dame Hollande could make out the silhouette of the royal
pillory, as seen in Figure 1.2, whose elevated stocks had punished criminals
during her youth. Although the state ceased using the pillory, a number of

Figure 1.2 The Carreau de la Halle. In the foreground, the Dames confront difficult customers in the open square. The fountain, pillory, and stocks occupy the middle ground. In the background, the dark recesses of the piliers are visible to the left while roofs of semipermanent market stalls appear on the right. Carnavalet G.13561, Jacques Aliamet (engraver) and Étienne Jeaurat (painter), "La Place des Halles," etching, 35 cm × 42 cm, (1757–1761). (c) Musée Carnavalet/ Roger-Viollet/The Image Works

permanent market stalls borrowed its base as a support wall, rendering its demolition a sore topic. To the right, under a cross that reached 10 meters into the sky, debtors had publicly surrendered their possessions. Perhaps the cross's presence explained why the neighboring old fountain, rebuilt in 1601, miraculously still worked at the start of the Revolution.[25] Leaning on the handle, oyster merchants summoned water from a pump that dipped into the Seine near Notre Dame.[26]

Hollande knew that, after buying a few fish from her stall, her customers might head for these northern reaches of the carreau to buy cheese, eggs, and butter from Isigny and Gournay.[27] They could also venture into the covered passageways or "piliers" that ran along the ground floors of houses and enclosed the market triangle to the north and east.[28] Within these recessed shops, bakers sold bread, the staple of Parisian diets.[29] Alongside them, frippery merchants displayed inexpensive used clothing.[30] The police worried that the woolen threads carried "contagious miasmas of different illnesses," but the poor could not resist the secondhand garments riddled with "hidden poisons." Still other clothes dealers sold from enclosed boutiques farther past the recesses of the piliers.[31] In the neighboring boutiques, Parisians browsed assorted furniture fit for bourgeois homes or Hollande's humble apartment.[32]

Above the eastern line of piliers, called the Piliers aux Potiers d'Étain, five other Dames des Halles began their day in the middle of the action. Dame Colin, Dame Boulanger, Dame Desmoulins, Dame Hartault, and Dame Mitaine resided in the five-floor building at n°19, with 2 one-room apartments on each landing.[33] Neighborhood gossip spread quickly through shared stairwells. In addition, the five Dames could only exit their building by weaving past merchants renting out the piliers below. None of them had a fixed place to sell. But they fanned out toward markets for their respective goods within les Halles.

Dame Boulanger, the vegetable retailer of n°19, headed south two blocks toward the Marché des Innocents. This market had previously been home to the Innocents Cemetery, a retail space where the living had bartered for vitals above the dead. Dame Boulanger recalled how, in 1780, the overstressed graveyard had exploded from the pressure of bodies below and commerce above. Underground remains had burst into the cellars of neighboring houses.[34] To remedy the problem, royal officials had relocated the corpses and dedicated the space to vegetable, herb, fruit, and flower markets.[35] Like the carreau with the fish market to the north, the Marché des Innocents was mostly an open square. Before 6:00 am, Dame Boulanger bought her baskets of potatoes or greens from vegetable wholesalers there. Then, the same space became the retail market, as depicted in Figure 1.3. The vegetable retailer could seek customers by strapping a portable tray to her back. Or she could rent a red parasol to shelter her goods. If Dame Boulanger displayed her pile near the center, she could hear water splashing from the fontaine des Innocents.[36] The fountain's sculpted facade was assessed at 10,800 francs and was a source of pride for the city. At its foot, Parisians approached the famous pea-shellers prepping their offerings and bartered with local gardeners selling their herbs.[37] Others continued one block south to the new flower market on the rue de la Ferronnerie.[38]

Plans were underway to move the wholesale fruit market into the Marché des Innocents alongside the vegetable and herb trade.[39] Parisians anticipated that this would give the area, as one guidebook wishfully put it, "a healthier air."[40] For now, Dame Boulanger could enjoy a little extra room as many fruit retailers clung to spaces elsewhere. In the rue du Marché aux Poirées, the street stretching to the northwest out of the Marché des Innocents, fruit merchants routinely clogged the throughway.[41]

Customers wishing to avoid being crushed by wagon wheels found it safer to frequent fruit merchants in the more spacious Halle aux Fruits, where customers could barter over peaches in the summer or oranges each winter.[42] Many fruit

Figure 1.3 The Marché des Innocents (detail). Note the circular parasols and covered makeshift stalls scattered around the large central fountain. Pierre Lafontaine, *Le marché des Innocents*, around 1791, oil on canvas, 49.5 cm × 60.5 cm, Musée Carnavalet, Paris. (c) Musée Carnavalet/ Roger-Viollet/The Image Works

merchants rented apartments in the slim buildings that surrounding this square. Of the six Dames des Halles who resided in n°22 rue du Marché aux Poirées, five of them retailed in fruit, while a lone retailer sold oysters.[43] Since apples were hardier and easier to transport than barrels of fish, the fruitières had more mobility than their neighbors hawking seafood. Dame Guérin and Dame Lapareillé, two of the fruit retailers of n°22, might sell directly next to one another in the Halle aux Fruits, or they could station themselves next to other Dames selling butter and cheese within the quadrilateral square. This flexibility did not necessarily translate to greater profits. Fruit seller Dame Gasseau, the neighbor of Guérin and Lapareillé, lived so far below the poverty line that officials dismissed all commercial fines she incurred.[44]

The mingling of goods in the Halle aux Fruits was convenient for the Dames' customers,[45] but it created headaches for market police, who wished to regulate the circulation of people, carts, and beasts. The police struggled to monitor food quality in this "chaos where all the food is piled up pell-mell." As the writer

Louis-Sébastien Mercier cheekily noted of marketplace life, "the fishwives make the law." The police were right to worry about the disorder—the exposed goods deteriorated in the sun or bathed in contaminated runoff from bordering roofs.[46] Customers squared off against merchants who escaped police regulation and attempted to sell them subpar merchandise. Citoyenne Le Fevre, a customer from another neighborhood, stood her ground against Citoyenne Chambourd, a vegetable and egg merchant. Customer Le Fevre deemed Dame Chambourd's eggs "too small" and refused to pay the price Chambourd demanded. The merchant responded by ripping her customer's apron, but Le Fevre won damages in court.[47]

To win customers and conduct their transactions, the Dames relied on a dense female network of occupational, neighborhood, and familial relationships. When she grew older, the fish merchant Dame Hollande hired Citoyenne Nicole as a marketplace assistant. Citoyenne Orevon, who lived two streets to the northwest, shuttled Hollande's linens to the laundress. And fellow fish merchant and neighbor Citoyenne Douet loaned Dame Hollande 20 francs when she became very ill.[48] Dames who were daughters, daughters-in-law, or sisters helped other Dames with their commerce. Fruit merchant Dame Pantureaux bought supplies on credit for the business of her widowed mother, Dame Largittere.[49] Citoyenne Limmonnet, a widowed fish merchant, entrusted her daughter to bring her commercial license to officials on her behalf.[50] Citoyenne Jeune Marie partnered with her mother-in-law, the former used her cart and a horse to haul fruit to the carreau where the latter sold the produce.[51] Sisters like Geneviève Travaut and Marie Anne Travaut, both fruit retailers, backed each other in marketplace conflicts. They smeared a rival fruit retailer's reputation by calling her a "slut," a "thief," and a "swindler."[52]

In addition to alliances among Dames, the marketplace was rife with rivalries. Exclamations in argot slang filled the air as merchants jockeyed for customers, haggled over prices, and disputed debts. As the Dames were potential competitors, economic and personal rivalries existed within their communities. In January 1792, three fruit merchants and one of their husbands teamed up against fellow fruit merchant Femme Metot. They accused her of failing to return a cloak that she borrowed and scathingly called her a "slut" and a "whore." The verbal assault so threatened Femme Metot's public honor that the judge condemned her rivals to pay damages.[53] Disagreements over deals between merchants sometimes turned violent. When Dame Droux insisted that Dame Le Clerc Jeune, a fellow retailer in the Marché des Innocents, pay her for having swept her place of sale, Le Clerc Jeune's sister leapt up from her own place to defend her. The sisters physically attacked Dame Droux. One threw a cabbage stalk into Droux's left eye, seriously drawing blood.[54] Surviving in the marketplace was not for the faint of heart.

Neighbors' brazen comments could destroy business reputations and trigger complaints of defamation.[55] In 1797, Citoyenne Lecureaux, a retailer, complained to the justice of the peace that Citoyenne Prieur, a fruit merchant, slandered her daughter by calling her a "maquerelle." The insult cleverly conflated occupational and gendered meanings. While the masculine "maquereau" was a mackerel, or fish, the feminine version, "maquerelle," meant brothel madame. The slur doubly condemned the daughter as a slippery merchant and a sexually corrupt woman.[56]

Although the Dames tenaciously competed for customers, a communal working and living environment tempered moments of daily discord.[57] Even without a formalized commercial organization, the shared identity of the Dames des Halles remained strong.[58] Neighborhood customs, ritual traditions, and at least two confraternities culturally glued the retailers together.[59] In addition, women retailers sold the majority of foodstuffs in les Halles.[60] All Dames ran their own businesses by definition, but many other women unofficially ran the stalls of husbands who belonged to foodstuffs guilds, including meat sellers. In a similar vein, widows frequently took over their husbands' food businesses.[61] The Dames des Halles, however, dominated the food retail scene through their numbers, occupational autonomy, and traditional importance.

As this glimpse into les Halles suggests, the marketplace drove its lively Parisian neighborhood. From 1791 to 1795, the Marché des Innocents section (which included les Halles) boasted the second-highest population density of all the revolutionary Parisian sections at 555 inhabitants per 1,000 square meters.[62] The Dames' apartments mixed in with those of prostitutes and other merchant families.[63] The magnitude of the Dames' continuous presence is especially striking, since other actors, such as the countryside wholesalers, left the market after sales. Parisians could find the Dames, like other working women, in habitually male-dominated local spaces like wine shops.[64] In short, the Dames' personal and occupational lives gave the market neighborhood its shape and character.

Who Were the Revolutionary Dames?

Although the Dames dominated les Halles as a group, they remain more elusive as individuals in archives of the late eighteenth-century. The last surviving records of the Dames' special market spaces, the *places Saint Louis*, trace back to 1700. These royal domain lists reveal some retailers who held places under the piliers outlining the marketplace, but they offer few clues about Dames selling in the open square or in semipermanent stalls.[65] As for the revolutionary archives, no lists of the Dames exist. It appears that the Dames' privileges became less tied

to permissions for physical places throughout the eighteenth century. The notion of "places Saint Louis" came to evoke the Dames' crown-endorsed access to
retail space, the preference they received from royally contracted parasol renters,
and the charitably few or nonexistent commercial fees they paid. The king's
hodgepodge efforts to reform and rebuild les Halles in the 1780s also hinder
tracking the Dames. Intermittent demolitions leveled semipermanent stalls and
displaced merchants from their habitual spaces. Since all ambulant retailers had
to swear before officials that they sold in a "place" and not in a boutique to pay
their 1798 taxes, it is evident that the government still had no list of assigned
market places at the end of the Revolution. Also, the revolutionaries' debates
over defining public property and regulating commerce frequently left market
administration in limbo. Finally, only one case survives from the Chambre de la
Marée, a government commission that regulated the sale, transport, and supply
of fish and tried offenders until 1791.[66] Although many of the Chamber's registered decrees appear elsewhere, its interactions with individuals like the Dames
are lost.

Consequently, this section calls on archival traces of 151 revolutionary
Dames from the court cases of the justices of the peace in the Marchés section
between 1791 and 1798.[67] Like all citizens, the Dames intermittently appeared
before these neighborhood judges in guardianship cases, arbitrations, commercial disputes, defamation suits, assault proceedings, and contests over debt
collection. The police and market inspectors also summoned Dames for commercial infractions. Tax officials likewise relied on neighborhood judges to track
down delinquent citizens. Records of these courtroom interactions offer fleeting
insights into the Dames' personal lives.

Revolutionary officials used the title "Dames des Halles" to refer to a group
of the market women in police reports and legislative matters but did not use it
to denote singular retailers in judicial records. Because the revolutionaries revised market ownership and indigence definitions, they rarely described one's
commerce with the Old Regime markers of "places Saint Louis" or "regratière."
In short, the revolutionaries and the market women themselves still considered
certain female retailers to be Dames des Halles, but the revolutionaries' reform
wiped away former legal categories that classified the market women as such.
Without these markers, this analysis defines a Dame des Halles through four
major traits: First, a Dame was ambulant in the open marketplace or sold from
under the piliers, a makeshift shelter, or a semipermanent stall.[68] As a recipient
of charitable exemptions, an indigent citizen, or a poor merchant, a Dame did
not sell from an enclosed boutique or permanent store. Second, a Dame was a
retailer. Revolutionary officials used inconsistent terminology to denote female
retailers including "revendeuse" (female reseller) and "détailleresse" (female
detailer). Moreover "fruitières" (female fruit merchants) or "marchandes de

poissons" (female fish merchants) could be retailers or large suppliers. Therefore, when a merchant's title was ambiguous, the categorization relies on contextual clues such as place of sale and supply quantities. Third, a Dame sold plant-based food, seafood, and occasionally flowers. In other words, a Dame retailed in eggs, butter, cheese, fish, herbs, vegetables, or fruit, but did not trade in poultry or cattle. Fourth, a Dame did not sell on behalf of her husband. She ran her own business under her own name.[69]

The Dames' residences were densely concentrated in the marketplace neighborhood. Out of the 151 sample Dames, 114 lived in or near les Halles, while 19 lived more than 2 blocks from les Halles. The residences for the remaining 18 Dames are unknown. The number of Dames' residences per street can be seen on the marketplace map (Figure 1.1). Approximately 22 percent of the Dames lived in the buildings between rue Saint-Denis, rue des Piliers-aux-Potiers-d'Étain, rue des Prêcheurs, and rue de la Cossonnerie, making it the block most populated with Dames. Half of all the Dames rented an apartment on rue des Piliers-aux-Potiers-d'Étain, rue des Prêcheurs, rue de la Cossonnerie, or rue du Marché aux Poirées. Fish merchants, fruit merchants, vegetable merchants, and butter merchants lived together in these four most heavily populated streets and they regularly crossed paths with other Dames who sold different goods in various spaces. For example, on the rue des Prêcheurs, one block east of the Carreau de la Halle, lived nine fruit retailers, two retailers of butter and eggs, three vegetable retailers, five unspecified retailers, two fish merchants (poisson), and two seafood merchants (marée).

Discerning the marital statuses of the 151 Dames poses several challenges. Prior to 1792, the justices of the peace and their clerks used dame/demoiselle and madame/mademoiselle as honor titles rather than as marital markers.[70] Beginning in 1792, the revolutionaries addressed all women as "Citoyenne" and men as "Citoyen," which intentionally flattened titles in legal records. The justices sometimes marked a woman as "wife of" or "without husband," but they inconsistently used this annotation. Justices noted a husband's presence if he was in the courtroom. But, in most instances, it was not legally necessary for a Dame's husband to accompany her. The only definitive way to discern whether a woman was single was if the clerk described her as "girl of majority age," which they rarely did.[71] Beyond this optional label, it is largely impossible to know whether a Dame was single. As for widowhood, judges consistently noted this status, since it could affect familial property ownership and legal liability. Given these hints and historical ellipses, the marital statuses of 47 percent of the sample Dames remain unknown. Many were likely single. However, of the other eighty-one Dames, forty-nine were married, twenty-nine were widowed, one was divorced, and two were single.

The married Dames' husbands appear more likely to be involved in commerce than in artisanal labor. Of the six husbands whose occupations are listed, one was a fort (porter) in les Halles, one was a merchant butcher, one was a seafood merchant like his wife, one was a shoemaker, and two served in army positions. The shoemaker also served as a firefighter.[72] This supports previous conclusions that the retailers' husbands were largely unskilled or skilled workers.[73]

The Dames' ages are their most elusive demographic trait. The exact ages of three of them are known: Dame Deswartitts was thirty-six, Dame Busson was thirty-four, and Dame Carpentier was forty-nine.[74] The average woman was married between the ages of twenty-three and twenty-six during the Revolution, and the average length of a first marriage was twenty years in the eighteenth century.[75] Therefore, the average age at which a woman became a widow can be estimated between forty-three and forty-six years old. Using these benchmarks for the eighty-one Dames for whom the marital status is known, the lowest possible average age within this group is 31.68 years.

As for their occupational distribution, the vast majority of the 151 Dames sold seafood or fruit. This lends truth to the stereotypical portrayal of the Dames as fish merchants. Overall, fifty-one of the market women sold fruit, thirty-nine sold seafood, thirteen sold vegetables, eight sold butter and/or eggs, three sold both fruit and vegetables, three sold herbs, and thirty-seven sold unspecified types of food. Given this collective picture, an "average" Dame in the Revolution, was much like Citoyenne Maillot: a fruit retailer who was married and lived on the rue des Prêcheurs.[76]

"The Universal Entrepôt"

For the capital, the 1,000 Dames' commerce was not a matter of convenience, but of logistical necessity. The market women acted as the lynchpin between countryside suppliers and local consumers.[77] Take the example of the fish market on the eve of the Revolution: while the capital slept, country wholesalers arrived with carts creaking under the weight of cod, salmon, mackerel, herring, and other fish. The suppliers traveled through cramped streets to the geographical heart of Paris—les Halles. In order to regulate trade, municipal law confined all wholesale transactions to the central markets. The suppliers could not legally bypass les Halles to trade elsewhere. Thus, the central markets acted as the fulcrum for food distribution.[78]

Since urban space was at a premium, the fish wholesalers could not park their carts in the market all day and sell their goods themselves. And even if the countryside suppliers could stay for the consumer market, they would not have enough time for their homeward journey. Rather, the wholesalers needed to unload their fish and leave the city center before other vehicles and people clogged streets. Consequently, six (usually) female fish brokers called "factrices" bought the suppliers' catch in one lump sum. Then, under the watchful eye of police inspectors, the factrices subdivided the fish into smaller lots. Next, retailers bid for the fish based on quality and quantity to set the daily price. The factrices then sold their baskets to over 1,000 Dames. The factrices kept accounts with the Dames and provided each with purchasing credit at various interest rates. Then, in the same market space vacated by the wholesalers, the Dames moved into their retail places and displayed their fish to consumers.

Finally, at the peal of a bell, the consumer market started. Parisians found a familiar Dame with whom they had credit or jostled to find the lowest price among the market women's shouts. The small marketplace accommodated trade on an astonishing scale. From 1781 to 1786, the Dames and their colleagues sold an average of 3,409,158 livres of fish per year. By 1790, the sum total of fresh- and salt-water fish sales rose to 4,960,000 livres.[79] Thus, at 1790 prices, the Dames channeled the equivalent of 4,464,000 small cod, 2,678,400 large cod, or 70,857,000 smoked herrings to consumers.[80] Of course, in reality, the Dames and other retailers sold various fish at different prices, but these figures convey to the sheer scale of the fish market. The other food markets of les Halles, such as the fruit and vegetables Marché des Innocents, followed similar sales systems by 1789. Each Dames' meager business enabled Parisians to buy small quantities of fish, fruit, vegetables, butter, and eggs to feed their families. The Dames who sold to other clients at some of the sixteen satellite markets across Paris also came to the central Halles for provisions.[81] Without the Dames' and brokers' services, the police could not entice wholesalers to undertake their journey to the capital. Without the retail system, Parisian police could not monitor food quality, prices, or distribution. In short, without the market women, the state could not ensure Parisians' daily necessities.

In addition to its role as "the stomach of Paris," les Halles was the most prominent public urban space,[82] one that fused key social, economic, political, communal, and religious aspects of life. St. Eustache, the neighborhood church, bordered the market so closely that carts arriving from the north could spray it with debris. It housed at least two of the Dames' religious confraternities and was a local rallying point. Just beyond the church's Gothic shadows, the monarchy had publicly executed criminals.[83] Government criers publicized royal decrees in the marketplace, and their revolutionary predecessors proclaimed the Constitution there.

Parisians recognized that the "public and political order" of the capital depended on the events that unfolded each day in les Halles.[84] If the retailers were upset by inadequate food regulations or neighborhood disturbances, the capital's tranquility could be in danger. Therefore, Parisians remained acutely attuned to the Dames' reactions and initiatives. Royal and revolutionary police understood that food and public space drove urban politics. Les Halles and the market women stood at the nexus of both.

Old Regime Subjects and the Leading
Symbol of the People

Although the Dames solidified their local influence through the marketplace, they became the most widely recognized symbol of the people through their privileged relationship with the king. Recalling Saint Louis's initial charity toward them, the Dames played the role of appreciative subjects in royal ceremonies. Several times a year, the king dispatched high officials to Les Halles and the Dames traveled to see the king. The royal administration openly favored the Dames des Halles to keep them content, to stabilize the markets, and to ensure their loyalty to the crown.[85]

Their relationship offered the crown a model of the paternal, benevolent king and his thankful subjects. On feast days and royal celebrations, the Dames des Halles showered the king with compliments and bouquets to show their approval.[86] Take, for example, a 1781 Versailles banquet celebrating the birth of the dauphin. Incarnating his subjects, a Dame addressed Louis XVI: "Sire, if heaven should give a son to a king who regards his people as his family, our prayers and our wishes have been asking for it."[87] The Dames then feted Louis by merging sacred and royal protection in song: "Do not fear dear papa / To see your family grow / The Good God will provide for it / . . . Where there are a hundred Bourbons, / There is bread, laurels for all."[88] In addition to these favored positions during court festivities, the Dames could access the king and queen's boxes at public events including performances at the Comédie-Française.[89] Thus, the Dames publicly built their political reputation through ritual and privilege.

The market women's status was so strong by the seventeenth century that they could temporarily transgress their ritual role without damaging their influence.[90] Moreover, they had strength in numbers. In a 1645 conflict over a priest vacancy at St. Eustache, the Dames des Halles blocked the archbishop's appointee from entering the church and insisted on an alternative candidate. They roused such a popular following that the king's archbishop had no choice but to concede to their wishes.[91] In national conflicts, the market women often sided with the Parlement of Paris. During the Fronde (1648 to 1653) and the fiscal reform attempts in the eighteenth century, the Dames defended Parlement out of fierce local pride.[92] The Dames invoked the king's duty to paternally protect them but forced him to uphold this obligation. During riots over mysteriously disappearing children in 1750,[93] the market women threatened to take their ritual route to Versailles to "tear the King's hair out" if he did not stop police suspected of orchestrating the kidnappings.[94]

The Dames' sporadic disagreements with the monarch before the Revolution were all minor spats compared to their political audacity in August 1787. Reacting

against the king's dismissal of his uncooperative Parlement, the Dames refused
to bring their habitual bouquet to the queen on the Feast of the Assumption
and boycotted their usual trip to Versailles. Moreover, they tried to avoid the
king a week later on the Feast of Saint-Louis. Such an impudent decision to snub
the monarch on his feast day could have been disastrous. However, the police
coerced the Dames into fulfilling their obligation to honor of Louis XVI and his
predecessors.[95] On the eve of the Revolution, the Dames' numbers and influence surpassed the king's control. However, writers and artists challenged the
market women's control over their own image.

Political Poissardes: Popular Representatives in Propaganda

For more than four centuries, the French bolstered or challenged the market
women's authority by calling them either "Dames" or "poissardes."[96] "Poissarde"
in the feminine form literally meant "fishwife" or "fish merchant." But, in the
broadest sense, "poissard" and "poissarde" respectively referred to any male or
female member of the popular classes.[97] Contemporaries employed "Dame" or
"femme" (woman) as a respectful title, whereas "poissarde" and "harengère"
denigrated the market women's dialect, culture, and social position.[98]
"Harengère" recalled the Dames' profession: it could refer to a woman who sold
fish like herring by shouting. No masculine counterpart existed for this occupational word—a rare French linguistic occurrence. Figuratively, "harengère"
could also mean "a woman who pleases herself by quarrelling and verbally
abusing others."[99]

As the Dames' two titles suggest, the contemporaries wavered between respect and ambivalence toward the popular retailers. While describing the
Dames' royal compliment for the dauphin's birth in 1781, Madame Campan,
the queen's lady in waiting, recounted how "Wanting to distinguish these female merchants from the poissardes who always made a disagreeable impression on him, the king gave a great meal to all these [female merchants]."[100] By
differentiating the merchants from "poissardes," Madame Campan and Louis
XVI consciously distanced the Dames from the overly gritty rabble. In Madame
Campan's eyes, the market women acted with decorum on this occasion and
thus merited the title "Dames."

Before the flood of revolutionary propaganda, the French most frequently
encountered written portrayals of "poissardes" in the literary genre of the same
name that was read by all levels of society. Rising out of the seventeenth-century
burlesque genre, parades, Italian Theater, and Theater of the Fair, the genre
poissard focused on "the low nature" of the Parisian streets. The style reveled

in volatile relations among popular-class characters including fishwives, porters, seamstresses, rag pickers, and ferrymen. Unlike writers such as Louis-Sébastien Mercier and Rétif de la Bretonne, whose "realist" style spotlighted societal relations and living conditions, most authors mimicked and parodied the popular classes in poissard works for entertainment value. In particular, writers exploited farce, parroted the rough dialect of les Halles, and focused on "the sly-naïve reactions of the popular mind" to create comic scenes and plots. Jean-Joseph Vadé mastered both elements—realism and parody—to launch the genre to its Old Regime zenith in the 1750s. Contemporaries hailed Vadé as the "Corneille des Halles" for his ability to imitate unrestrained quarrels, foul language, and the market women's butchered expressions.[101]

The genre poissard also incorporated marketplace elements to link fictional characters to their living foils in les Halles.[102] Even in other settings, poissard characters gestured to les Halles to mark their identity. In *Les Citrons de Javotte* (1756), merchant Javotte, a poissarde, ventures north of the marketplace to sell her fruit. As a customer inspects her "lemons" (a double entendre), Javotte comically attests to their quality by insisting they "are the most beautiful of les Halles."[103]

Old Regime propagandists assumed that the poissarde on the page could speak to her contemporaries in the street. During the Fronde, pamphleteers used poissard characters to critique Cardinal Mazarin's maneuverings. These "Mazarinades" highlighted the Dames' privileged position with the king and cast them as legitimate protectors of the people to condemn the chief minister's repression of rebels.[104] When famine struck Paris during the civil war, the pamphlet *Les Menaces des Harengères faites aux Boulangers de Paris, à faute de Pain* deployed an imaginary market woman's warning: "If you want, I will go with you to seek vengeance / On all the bakers that cause the famine, / Selling wheat and flour at too high a price."[105] Despite this bubble of Mazarinades, the genre poissard remained mostly literary before the Revolution.

At the call of the Estates General in 1789, an unprecedented wave of propaganda washed over France. Pamphlets, newspapers, and cheap images proliferated in the hands of hawkers. Clubs and wealthy individuals subscribed to periodicals. Peddlers trucked materials across provinces. Although those individuals with disposable capital printed the most, writers directed their political work at multiple audiences, including the poor.[106] A record number of propagandists turned to poissard characters to win readers.[107]

Revolutionary poissard pamphlets were part of an emerging subset of propaganda that harnessed popular characters and street slang. Père Duchesne, the pipe-smoking, eternally swearing sans-culotte, became the most famous character of this sort. Poissard pamphlets relied on the no-nonsense reputation of street characters, who appeared most qualified to access and freely communicate truths. However, to create humor, pamphleteers paradoxically portrayed their poissard characters as uneducated and lacking in social graces. Consequently, pamphleteers who relied on rough stereotypes of the Dames deployed them carefully: their brash traits could expose them to criticism as unrefined citizens.[108] The Dames' dialect in particular challenged the deputies' attempts to standardize and polish an official language for all citizens. Frank evaluations could slip into crude commentary, authentic sentiments into uncultured reactions, humorous expressions into grammatical errors, bold attacks into buffoon-like actions, and unapologetic opinions into physical violence.

From the grievance cahiers of 1789 to the monarchy's collapse in 1792, Parisian audiences eagerly devoured poissard pamphlets. The pamphlet *Cahier des plaintes & doléances des Dames de la halle & des marchés de Paris, rédigé au grand salon des Porcherons, pour être présenté à MM. les États-Généraux* was first printed at the call of the Estates General and had reached its eleventh edition by September 1789. The latter editions even added events since the fall of the Bastille.[109] The pamphlet's "Dames" complained, among other things, that the elite clergy squandered the Church's money and did not serve the poor. Citing the high price of sacraments and the threat posed to local girls by promiscuous priests, the author deployed the Dames' voice to intertwine economic grievances and collective moral rebuke.[110] The newspaper *La Chronique de Paris* attributed the pamphlet's enormous success to its brilliant poissard style: It had "that [quality] of gaiety, & did not lack salt. [The pamphlet is] a joke by a spirited man who perfectly succeeded in assuming the tone and bawdy turns, & who, while joking, lets escape some hard truths."[111]

Over fifty revolutionary pamphlets deploying a counterfeit Dame survive in the archives. These political works bolstered the living Dames' legitimacy by seizing their identity, but they also limited the market women's control over their own representation. The majority of the pamphlets were written in 1789. Although all of the 1789 pamphlets were prorevolutionary, different factions molded them to their agenda. While the Duc d'Orléans commissioned poissard pamphlets to critique the monarchy, the moderate Fayettistes used the same techniques to reduce anxiety and promote order in the capital.[112] By 1790, however, right-wing propagandists began to appropriate the Dames' image. By the time poissard pamphlets petered out in 1792 near the monarchy's end, a broad swath of writers had profited from poissard techniques.[113]

Pamphleteers assumed the Dames could appeal to all levels of society. The fictive Père Duchesne observed in 1791, "[The Dames] are good devils . . . & the great majority of people allow themselves to be directed by their influence."[114] Banking on this effect, the editor of the *Journal des Halles* explained his mission in poissard dialect. Posing as the Dames, he paired all his first-person singular pronouns with first-person plural verbs: "I imagined [J'avons imaginé] to print [a newspaper] from our manner of seeing [so that] that people of our station can understand without needing to know or have studied Latin. The *journal des halles* appeared to us our way; it's for this purpose that I tried [j'en hasardons] an issue in order to see if anyone will be able to latch onto it. I forewarn [J'avertissons d'avance] that I will say [je dirons] all that I have [j'aurons] on our heart."[115] Since part of the *Journal*'s audience was illiterate, this style would not necessarily increase readership. However, the announcement conceptually co-opted the popular classes and touted les Halles as the community most aligned with its message.

Pamphleteers harnessed the Dames' gregarious nature and spontaneity to present their position as agreeable.[116] In *Avis important d'une dame des Halles pour la diminution des vivres*, the author frames his pamphlet as a record of the "impromptu [discourse] of Madelon Friquet," a "charming poissarde." As Madelon speaks to the neighbors gathered around her, the narrator observed, "They judge her to be a good patriot capable of inspiring generous sentiments in others." The author-witness attests that "our beautiful Oratress possesses to the highest degree the art of making herself heard."[117] Tackling food issues, the exaggerated poissarde demanded affordable prices for bread, wine, meat, and rôgomme (cheap brandy). She demands that her listeners pay for her opinions with drinks and profits.

Other pamphleteers wrote fictive Dames into dialogues in which the market women, and the reader, learned the "correct" political opinion. These dialogues opened with a question, conundrum, or misconstrued notion to be debunked over the course of the conversation. In a 1791 conservative dialogue set in a cabaret, a "Dame de la Halle" drinks with a city gatekeeper, a ferryman, a roofer, and a carpenter.[118] As they discuss political topics, the characters learn of the revolutionaries' treachery. Within the ensemble of "pupils," the Dame shows increasing "comprehension" along this conservative slant. After she learns that revolutionary journalists are plotting to "assassinate" aristocrats with "regiments of bandits," her troubled reaction stands in for the popular audience and she speaks on behalf of the other previously uninformed neighbors beside her. The narrator leaves the scene convinced that "the people, that one thought to have tricked," now understood the truth.[119]

Other pamphleteers created flagrantly uneducated poissardes who, even in their naïveté, could arrive at "obvious" political conclusions. Market women could wonder: "all these things there, do they not see them every day? One does not have to be a great diviner."[120] Situational satire heightened the effect of self-evident truths. In the *Réclamation de toutes les poissardes avec un petit mot à la gloire de notre bonne Duchesse d'Orléans*, a fictive retailer denounces the Salic Law, which she humorously thought concerned salt instead of the rule that passed the throne through the male line. She reflects, "Ah! Dame I'm only a Poissarde, but . . . us, we see very clearly all the following consequences." After a scribe corrects her error and explains that the law, the poissarde reaims her critique. She asserts that the poor can reason as well as the rich and anyone can see that there are great French women such as the Duchesse d'Orléans and Saint Geneviève. In an unsubtle attack on Marie Antoinette, the market woman argues that French kings should not look "abroad" for wives.[121] The lowliest poissarde could easily, albeit humorously, discern political truth. Surely, the amused reader would agree.

Because humor operated outside the rules of correct political discourse, comedic pamphlets could point to others' transgressive behavior while freeing the author from those standards.[122] The author of *Harangue des Dames de la Halle aux citoyens du faubourg Saint-Antoine prononcée par Ma. Engueule, le 26 juillet 1789* crafted an amusing fake address by the Dames des Halles to celebrate the fall of the Bastille, rally support for Necker, and unmask counterrevolutionary plotters. The fictive Dames explain that they spoke to a government commission "to make you an emotion (or revolt) in order to this end speak reason wieth yous [sic]."[123] The mangled speech substitutes an "émotion" in place of a "motion" and then quickly puns on "raison" as "cold-headed and rational" but also alluding to "right and correct." Through their mispronunciation, the counterfeit Dames inadvertently gesture to their emotional authenticity and warn politicians they should be mindful of public opinion.

Pamphleteers frequently drew on the Dames' royal compliments and their role as traditional representatives of the Third Estate. In the 1789 dialogue *Les Poissardes à la Reine*, a pamphleteer fashioned his message as an address to the queen. Pledging her allegiance, his poissarde mouthpiece attests that others feel the same: "I'see ev'n [j'voyons mêm] twenty million o'hearts all ready to fly b'fore yer own."[124] In the 1789 pamphlet *Motion des harengères de la Halle*, counterfeit Dames send a petition to the Estates General. The "harengères" claim they intervene because their representatives had not accomplished anything. They acknowledge that they are of the "rabble," but insist that the term is better used for "the dogs of Parlement in this nobility" who dip into royal coffers and do not serve the king.[125] The author imitated the Dames' customary songs by composing his *Motion* in rhyming couplets.

Beyond their capital as ritual representatives, pamphleteers drew on the Dames' useful occupations to legitimize their demands as contributing citizens. In 1789, a pamphlet Dame justified her request by declaring, "I present us, as having as much right as any person, by our work, to be heard, by the sweat that we shed to support the life of the Nobility & the Clergy."[126] In a serial pamphlet from 1790 or 1791, the fictive Père Duchêne (also Duchesne) professed that he admired the Dames because of their market services. Addressing the "intrepid female merchants of the Halles," he explained that it's "you that [sic] I esteem and that I love, because you [sic] are excellent patriots, and because you sell what is the most essential to life and not useless trinkets." Père Duchêne warned the Dames that aristocrats would soon attack Paris with a counterrevolutionary army. He proposed that a "regiment of dames de la halle" follow him "in order to go guard the royal family." By evoking the living market women, Père Duchêne conflated the Dames' commercial work feeding Parisians with the Dames' duty to protect the royal family.[127]

From their elevated moral ground as productive traders, writers' poissardes could critique those who leeched off society. In one pre-1792 dialogue, four "dames de la halle" educate one another on current events. Manon l'écailleuse (Manon the Fish-scaler) asks Mère Saumon (Mother Salmon, a merchant), "Explain to us this word [aristocrat]." Mère Saumon instructs her comrades that "it's like what one would call those who want all the profit, without the hardship, [they are] no more nor less like these hornets who steal honey that the bees have gone to great pains to make; they pretend to have everything, the properties, the privileges, the special places, the honors, the distinguished titles . . . they want us, on the other hand, to pay for it all, and [they] spit on us down below."[128] Parasitic aristocrats were deficient citizens in contrast to workers of bee and merchant varieties.

Factional Pamphlet Wars

Neither the left nor right held a monopoly on effectively appropriating the Dames' popular legitimacy. Since the Dames traditionally represented the Third Estate, it would seem that left-leaning pamphleteers could most easily assume their voice. However, royalists and conservative pamphleteers also used the Dames to win supporters.[129] For example, the author of the counterrevolutionary *Grande motion des Halles* contends that his list of grievances originated in the marketplace. His refrain of "We don't want any more of your [insert revolutionary reform]" and "We want our [insert Old Regime counterpart]" drives a litany of demands. Ironically, the writer arms his counterrevolutionary critiques with popular legitimacy since his characters assert, "We demand it with all the power which belongs to the sovereign people."[130]

Juxtaposing right and left pamphlets on divorce illustrates how pamphleteers bent the Dames' political capital across diverging opinions. In the 1790 *Le Divorce, Dialogue entre Madame Engueule et Madame Saumon harengères, et M. Mannequin, fort de la halle*, the poissard characters praise the benefits of divorce. Madame Saumon argues, "For virtu' it's necessary't'be free, / Th' choice that'one makes by one's self is th' only good one." Madame Engueule seconds her friend and laments that an unwilling betrothed daughter is a "poor child that'one [*sic*] tyrannizes." A male character agrees that the threat of divorce would constructively force spouses to attend to each other.[131]

In contrast, the 1792 conservative pamphlet *V'là c'qui s'est dit passé à la halle* appropriates the Dames' influence in dialogue form to critique the Jacobins and support the king. The scene opens on a marketplace argument between "Brissotin" (Brissot was a Jacobin in 1792) and Madame Patureau, a fruit retailer in les Halles, who receives support from fellow fish merchants Commère (a gossip) Luce and Commère Marie. Brissotin attempts to hoodwink the poissardes by lowballing the price for peaches. His deceptive haggling quickly expands into a national metaphor in which the Jacobins abuse the popular classes. Commère Marie contrasts the parasitic Jacobins with "our' good king." She asks, "Is it not [the king] who ord'red some grain to be bought from almost two thousand places besides here'in order that we didn't lack?" Brissotin insults the royalists in response, but Madame Patureau turns on him: "Speak like that, eh! Morning [false oath], don't say bad things about the Royalists, otherwise you will have to pay us arrears. Learn here that we are Royalists and are prouwd [*sic*]."[132] Like the liberal pamphlet on divorce, the conservative pamphlet relies on the transparent and unapologetic outlook of poissardes to deliver its message.

Writers from opposing factions relied on the fictive Mère Saumon (Mother Salmon) to discern the truth and educate fellow Dames. Her name echoed the Dames' commerce, and the royal fish gestured to their relationship with the king.[133] In the left-leaning 1791 pamphlet *Le Goûter de la Courtille ou Dialogues sur les affaires présentes, entre quatre dames de la halle*, Mère Saumon explains to her colleagues that, since inheriting enough money to retire from commerce, she has attended the National Assembly to educate herself on political affairs. "It is necessary to be a good citoyenne," she insists, "& put one's instruction before one's pleasure." Mère Saumon instructs the other Dames to "listen to me" so that she can explain the Assembly's work. She reveals how the "good angels" of the Assembly have defended "the poor people" and corrects Mère Gogo's misperception that the Dames' lives have not improved since the Revolution. Before sharing one last drink, the Dames implore Mère Saumon, "Promise us to return another day to teach us again all the beautiful things that the National Assembly does for us." Mère Saumon swears by the "faith of a poissarde" to continue the instruction.[134]

With opposite goals but similar methods, the narrator of the 1792 royalist dialogue series *Les Entretiens de la Mère Saumon* listens to Mère Saumon give lessons to her fellow "female merchants of les Halles." The pamphleteer gives flesh to the Dames he "observed" by referring to their occupations, noting their participation in events like the October Days, and scattering a healthy dose of songs, alcohol, obscenities, and grammatical errors in their dialogue. The narrator protests that he is not a writer, and he is only going "to repeat what I heard" "in the middle of the Halle" in order to offer it "to the Public." Huddling her fellow Dames around her, "old sage" Mère Saumon gives nine days of political lessons. Each lesson begins with a Dame posing a question to Mère Saumon. For example, a lemon merchant asks "Learn-me therefore, Mère Saumon, what's that this-here Constitution? I don't understand too well wh't this-here word signifies." Mère Saumon invites the Dame: "You will be able to judge it for yourself, listen."[135] Following this question and answer formula, Mère Saumon's insights run the gamut of critical political topics: the Constitution, the nation, the law, tribunals, liberty, the National Assembly, the National Guard, priests, and the revolutionary paper money. Mère Saumon explains these concepts from the pamphleteer's royalist perspective to educate her listeners and the pamphlet's readers alike.

Picturing the Dames in Action

French citizens recognized the Dames in visual images as well, making them doubly potent as discursive mouthpieces and graphic markers. The Dames offered propagandists an especially powerful way to reach illiterate citizens. Illustrators drew on a common reservoir of gestures, subjects, titles, and captions to signal the Dames' presence and sketch them as the people incarnate. Since all citizens could easily assess visual material, artists significantly influenced the Dames' multidimensional reputation.

Citizens encountered images of the market women in prints for sale or posted around the city. Propagandists gave faces to their text by pairing images of Dames with their pamphlets. Hawkers at the Pont-Neuf and Palais Royal peddled caricatures of the Dames spanking counterrevolutionary nuns in 1791 to supplement a pamphlet recounting the true story.[136] Artists sold their prints at libraries, editors compiled them into series, and journalists attached them to newspapers. *Révolutions de Paris* commissioned event-based woodcuts to supplement their newspaper reports including several of the Dames during the October Days.[137]

Images of the Dames came in a variety of styles and prices. They could be black and white or bursting with color. One print nested a popular October Days scene of "Les Dames de Paris allant à Versailles" within a tricolor rosette to heighten its commemorative value.[138] Enterprising printers shrunk large prints into cheaper, more portable formats. The scene "Proclamation de la Constitution" came in at least three distinct forms. The first large print depicts the Dames listening to the proclamation among the marketplace masses. The second is the same image, but in sketch form. The third rescaled the image to medallion size.[139] These small tokens were often so blurry and rudimentary that one would need to have seen the larger versions to understand the smaller counterparts. Such necessity suggests that Parisians were well-acquainted with a core group of revolutionary illustrations featuring the Dames.

In addition to depicting the Dames in historical events, artists sketched the Dames into fictional scenes to evoke the Third Estate. One medallion featured a woman with her hand on her hip, clinking glasses with a fellow man of the popular classes. The caption reads: "I'are from the Third [Estate]." The image effectively identifies her as a market woman through her verb conjugation and stance associated with the Dames.[140] A 1789 image depicted a stereotypical poissarde to tout the Third Estates' victory after the Dames' march to Versailles. The poissarde rides on the back of a crawling royal Body Guard who had allegedly trampled the revolutionary tricolor. She yells at the defeated Guard, "And well, J . . . F . . . , [implied expletive] will you say long live the nobility again?"[141] The poissarde triumphantly reversed the iconic depictions of the First and the Second Estate riding on the back of the Third.

To signpost Dames and poissardes, artists drew on an iconography of dress and comportment specific to the market women. The living Dames and their graphic counterparts sported aprons, clogs, and floppy white bonnets. Viewers identified the Dames from their posts in les Halles, their retail sale of foodstuffs, and their occupational tools like trays or baskets.[142] Parisians also detected the Dames through their ritual behaviors. In the print "La Journée à jamais Mémorable aux François," Louis XVI formally arrives at the Parisian Hôtel de Ville after the Bastille's fall. Since the point of view is distant and elevated, the figures receiving the royal carriage are barely discernable. In a central space separated from the crowds by guards, a group of people with raised bouquets awaits the king. The written key confirms the viewer's immediate suspicion: the flower-carrying group is a contingent of Dames des Halles offering their ritual compliment.[143]

Whereas pamphleteers could fashion a lone "market woman" (marchande) or poissarde character to convey popular sentiment, artists only labeled their subject as a "Dame" if she was in the company of other Dames des Halles. Like their living counterparts, the visual market women embodied the collective sovereign people through their group presence. In these group images, artists spatially consolidated the Dames to convey their united voice. One artist who depicted the Dames congratulating the king on the Constitution huddled the merchants together despite much empty room space. The women eagerly lean forward, holding on to the person in front of them. This hodgepodge conga line continues all the way to the lead Dame, who presents a bouquet to the king, queen, and dauphin.[144] A colored image, depicted in Figure 1.4, similarly portrays three Dames holding laurel branches and decked out in the revolutionary tricolors en route to praise the queen. The woman in the rear holds the back of her foremost

Les Dames de la Halle de Paris .
Vont complimenter la Reine aux Tuilerie .

Figure 1.4 "The Dames des Halles Go to Compliment the Queen at the Tuileries"
BnF Estampes Réserve QB-370 (29)-FT 4 [De Vinck, 4857], "Les Dames de la Halle de
Paris vont complimenter la Reine aux Tuileries." watercolor; 20.5 cm × 15 cm (1792).

comrade's arm, clustering the three into a tight bunch. They would deliver one
collective message.

The Dames and those who depicted them drew from a repertoire of body
language to convey identity and meaning. One gesture in particular marked the
Dames des Halles: a hand on the hip or "arms akimbo." Parisians likely associated the stance with the Dames' aggressive trading posture or with their bracing
position to support the baskets and trays strapped to their backs. Since the seventeenth century, illustrations in poissard literary works had depicted market
women with hands propped on hips. *Riche-en-Gueule ou Le Nouveau Vadé,*

includes a foldout picture of Carnival carousers riding roughshod through les Halles while a retailer disapprovingly glares at them. Her fruit and vegetables threatened, the Dame bends toward the revelers, hands on hip, fist cocked in a ball, ready to spring at them.[145] With her arms akimbo, the Dame makes herself bigger, claims more territory, and looks ready for battle.[146] Such corporal tenacity fed into the Dames' tenacious reputation.

Some revolutionary illustrations creatively formed the arms akimbo pose by painting the market women gathering aprons on their hips. In the watercolor "Vive le Roi! Vive la Nation!" ("Long live the King! Long live the Nation!"), four boisterous Dames hold up their aprons in order to kick up their feet. They jubilantly thrust colorful orange tree branches into the air, they laugh and sing with mouths agape, and they wear colorful floral sashes and laurels around their torsos.[147] As seen in Figure 1.5, another drawing depicts dozens of people marching to Versailles, but in the foreground, three women walking with gathered aprons and arms akimbo are clearly Dames des Halles.

Revolutionary artists carefully tweaked small details of the hands-on-hip pose to tag a Dame while increasing their range of expression. Illustrators swung the hand around the back, side, and front of the hip, outlined open fingers or closed fists, and carefully considered the hand placement height to change the threatening severity of the pointed elbow. For example, a rosy allegorical image in

Figure 1.5 "The Dames de la Halle Leaving in Order to Go Find the King at Versailles on October 5, 1789" (detail). BnF Estampes Réserve QB-370 (18)-FT 4, Pierre-Gabriel Berthault, Jean Duplessi-Bertaux, and Jean-Louis Prieur, "Les Dames de la Halle partant pour aller chercher le roi à Versailles le 5 octobre 1789," etching, chisel; 24 cm × 29 cm (Paris: 1802).

which only soldiers hold weapons depicts the king's royal Body Guards and the National Guards reconciling after the October Days.[148] A woman watches with one hand on her hip and the other shepherding a child forward to look. Although the inferred Dame curls back the fingers of her resting hand, she appears more re-solved and self-confident than aggressive. As she leans forward to guide the child, she unbalances herself and vulnerably leads with her chest, suggesting no danger. Her hand-on-hip gesture marks her as a Dame without disrupting the peaceful scene. In the 1789 image "Le Roi reçoit les Femmes de la Halle," one of the many Dames before the king holds her hand on her hip. However, the market woman's head is tilted down, and her frame assumes a slightly concave, expectant posture. The king holds her colleague's hands as she delivers the deputation's message. In this instance, the Dame's stance did not suggest hostility toward the king but served as a graphic marker of identity for the delegation.[149]

Visual representations of the Dames occupied the midpoint between the dynamic world of the embodied Dames and the textual world that described them or their likeness. The Dames were both a tool for illustrators' revolutionary messages and a product of them.

The Dames' Hybrid Image and Singular Reputation

Some printed works did more than appropriate poissarde figures; they com-pletely conflated the Dames in the street with those on the page. Revolutionary pieces that mixed fictive and living Dames supported, undermined, and transformed the market women's reputation. They informed the market women's political authority.

In one blending method, propagandists recounted the Dames' true political activity as a base for their material. The 1789 pamphlet *Compliment des Poissardes de Paris, à MM. les électeurs, qui ont été à Versailles, pour solliciter l'amnistie des Gardes-Françaises, sortis de l'Abbaye Saint-Germain*, deploys this technique. The author begins by describing the Dames' actual trip to Versailles to thank the king and the National Assembly for allowing defected French Guards (royal infantry sympathetic to the revolutionaries) to join the National Guard. Having lauded the Dames' patriotic actions, the pamphleteer presents a fictive dialogue among multiple poissardes and a soldier. One fishwife asserts, "I are Poissardes, it's true. There is well difference between his occupation and our own; but I want [je voulons], like him, peace in our family."[150] The pamphleteer's fake dialogue fur-ther rationalized the French Guards' good intentions. To the modern reader, the abrupt juxtaposition of two stylistically different sections seems disconnected. But from the revolutionaries' perspective, each half derived its authority from the Dames—real or constructed.

In another twinning approach, the most-celebrated male poissard character, "Père Duchesne," rushes to rescue the Dames from aristocratic "slanderers." The pamphlet *Grande colère du Père Duchesne contre les jean-foutres de calomniateurs des Dames de la halle, & des Bouquetières du palais-royal, au sujet du beau discours qu'elles ont fait au roi* describes the Dames' actual February 1791 visit to the king during which they asked he prevent his aunts from fleeing Paris. Père Duchesne attests the Dames implored him, as "a good patriot," to publish their request to the king.[151] Indeed, his transcription is nearly an exact replica of the Dames' address printed in the reputable journal *La Chronique de Paris*.[152] Following the address, Père Duschesne defends the Dames as "the most patriotic women [who] continually make an effort to do service to the revolution." He crudely praises the Dames' linguistic style and sentiment: "There it is, fuck, that which calls itself beautiful and good eloquence, which comes from the bottom of the heart, that [language] that one makes in the crucible of the [French] Academy has no value compared to that."[153] Through a poissard character who narrated the Dames' real words, the pamphlet merged fact and fiction to defend the retailers.

Propagandists best intermingled fiction and reality in the person of a Dame named Reine d'Hongrie. The original Reine d'Hongrie may have been Julie Bêcheur, a retailer who lived in the market neighborhood. Popular legend maintains that she received the nickname "Queen of Hongrie" because Marie Antoinette said she resembled her mother.[154] Reine d'Hongrie also seemed to build on the aura of a famous literary precursor named Margot, Reine de la Halle.[155] By petitioning the National Assembly with other retailers, issuing invitations to the Dames' *Te Deum* masses, and leading a deputation to fetch the Comte d'Artois from Italy, Reine d'Hongrie became the most famous Dame des Halles during the Revolution. Government officials even leaned on d'Hongrie's political influence. After the fall of the Bastille, the District of St. Joseph sent a deputation and militia commander to ask d'Hongrie and her colleagues to sustain the food trade and encourage tranquility. Reflecting Reine d'Hongrie's communal clout, the officials entrusted her with 300 livres "to the benefit of unfortunate members of the District who have a pressing need for aid."[156]

As the "première Dame des Halles," Reine d'Hongrie channeled the Dames' nebulous authority into the flesh and blood of a recognizable figure. In the 1789 poissard pamphlet *Le Roi d'Yvetot à la Reine d'Hongrie tenant sa cour plénière aux Halles de Paris*, Reine's fictive lover praises her revolutionary virtues: "Your heart transmits its emotions to us. If you are angry, one sees clearly that you are angry: a strongly sonorous voice, a superb head, very sparkly eyes, bright blushing cheeks, cut by the most marked veins, the most rippling muscles; a magnificent throat, queen, to thus say, of all the charms of your person, and two querulous arms, pushed strongly upon two firm haunches." Roi repeatedly refers to Reine's popular influence, noting, "you speak & your orders are fulfilled." He recalls the "confidence that the distinguished citizens [revolutionary officials] had to invest in you."[157] He asks Reine to calm Parisians' fears and promote public order. Because of her living model, a stylized Reine d'Hongrie could serve as a commanding rallying point.

Writers so effectively co-opted Reine d'Hongrie that it is sometimes nearly impossible to separate what she actually did from what writers invented. A January 1790 pamphlet titled *Demande de la Reine d'Hongrie à M. le Directeur de la Comédie-Française* presents itself as an unfabricated letter to the Comédie. Reine d'Hongrie has "signed" the pamphlet, and explanatory notes testify that it was "Deliberated at our Palace of the Halles at 4 o'clock in the morning December 31, 1789." In the letter, Reine asks the director to play *Henri IV* so that everyone can fete the king for the New Year. The letter marries the Dames' customary rituals to the revolutionary spirit:

> I will assemble [Je ressamblerons]our ladies of honor, a'round, & all our Dames of the Palace, the nobles of our Court, there will not be a single aristocratic sympathizer. And at the instant when they [the actors] sing long live Henri IV, we will repeat it until we lose our breath & we will cry with all our force and beat our hands without even fearing that we will skin them, because I don't have [je n'avons pas] any vanity since we are Democratesses.[158]

Reine closes by asking for the actors to respond to her request in the *Journal de Paris*. The printed pamphlet included Director Molé's supposed response on January 3, 1790, that it was his troupe's pleasure to perform the piece.

Although no mention of Reine's request or the performance in the *Journal de Paris* can be found, the *Moniteur* reported that at the Théâtre de la Nation, "The king's ordinary French comedians, will perform today the 1st of January, *la Partie de chasse d'Henri IV*, requested."[159] If Reine's request been a fake written in hindsight, it would have more closely followed what the *Journal de Paris* did and did not publish. And, according to the *Courrier de Paris*, the Dames had already mounted the stage and drunk with the king character in a November play about Henri IV.[160] Thus Reine's request seems plausible. Whether or not Reine d'Hongrie and the Dames were actually the ones who demanded the January play, whether they wrote the pamphlet or it was written by an imposter to loosely fit events—these were unanswerable questions for most Parisians. Reine d'Hongrie's demand hung in limbo between reality and fiction for her contemporaries.

Even the police encountered the living Dames through the blurred lens of poissarde stereotypes. They used stock character names to describe market women in their notes.[161] Confronted with "rude, audacious, insolent, and formidable" retailers, the police recorded an anonymous Dame under the popular literary name "Margot."[162] Police Commissioner Dutrand even reported that one merchant called herself "Mère Duchêne" because "she resembles the Père Duchêne in his opinions and in the manner that she pronounces them."[163] Dutrand used the poissard name "Madame Saumon" to portray the stubborn opinions and loud objections of another nameless fish merchant. He depicted her as a "fat margot, one of a number of them who bring shame to la Halle."[164] The police turned stereotypes into reference points to convey their findings to superiors.

The boundary between fictive poissardes and their living models proved porous for civilians as well. Fournier l'Americain's memoirs illustrate how strongly the genre poissard influenced his interactions with the Dames. During the march to Versailles, he recounted how he "addressed five or six of these women who, with the name and outward appearance of poissardes, conceal moral qualities, and above all judgment, which always makes it possible for them to value sound advice." To speak to them, Fournier "stooped to their level of intelligence and borrowed the Père Duchesne's style."[165] Foreign diplomat Giuseppe de Lama flip-flopped between poissardes and the Dames without batting an eye. Lama described how, during the October Days, "the poissardes wanted to speak to [the king]" but then described how "His Majesty received the delegates of the Dames de la Halle."[166]

Even newspapers that normally reported the news, governmental debates, and economic developments occasionally incorporated fictive poissarde asides into "true" reports. The journal *L'Ami du Peuple ou le Défenseur des Patriotes persécutés* used a brief dialogue between "a Dame des Halles" and "her neighbor" to criticize deputies that it deemed too conservative.[167] The poissard scene was an uncharacteristic but striking tactic for a newspaper that habitually used formal rhetoric.

Without a standing organization, the Dames' political power was indelibly hitched to their reputation. No one understood the stakes of this relationship better than the market women themselves. The tarnish or brilliance of their image determined their legitimacy. Therefore, the Dames proactively defended and recast their name through print venues. After the fall of the Bastille, the Dames from the Marché St. Paul sent six retailers to the Parisian Assembly of General Electors. The six market women offered the Assembly bouquets and sang an air feting the deputies, the king, and the French Guards. After they finished, the Dames asked the Assembly to print their compliment and song "as soon as possible" in the *Journal de Paris*, which complied and copied the transcript verbatim.[168] For a profit-driven newspaper, the space dedicated to the Dames' address represented a substantial down payment on readers' interest in the market women's words.

The Dames occasionally hired writers to transcribe, if not embellish and partly write, their public compliments. Parisian bookseller Siméon-Prosper Hardy maintained that the Dames hired a poet named Sylvain Maréchal to convey their admiration for the Third Estate in 1789.[169] This is likely, as Maréchal was born on the rue des Prêcheurs, one of the streets most populated by the Dames des Halles.[170] In his diary, Hardy recorded that "eight of the best-mouthed" sang the song Maréchal helped compose. The Dames' compliment was printed as a standalone pamphlet.[171] As thanks, the Third Estate extended a 300-livre gift to the Dames.[172] Perhaps the gift underwrote the Dames' expenses or signaled the deputies' responsibility for poor, patriotic citizens. In either case, the printed copy extended the Dames' audience beyond those in the room of the Third Estate electors.

La Gazette des Halles (1789), a collection of poissard pamphlets, presents the most striking evidence that the Dames were acutely aware that their printed representations, popular interpretations, and malleable reputation depended on one another. After the October Days, the Dames commissioned this short series to channel their own opinions through fictive poissardes. They dramatically turned their fictionalized selves to their own advantage to shape and redeploy their political influence. And they entrusted hawkers to spread the pieces beyond their markets. The gazette's subtitle enticed readers with "dialogues mixed with songs, for those who love them." It clarified, "The mouth [within] speaks badly, but the heart [within] speaks well."

The second *Gazette* pamphlet contained a special wink for the reader. It narrates "fishwife" Catherine praising the king in her choppy dialect. She sings: "Oh from'that, he'z the fath'r of all (*repeat*) / It's in order to not make'jealous; (*repeat*) / Every single one he loves, / With a love that everyone returns back t' him all-the-same." When a "poet" walks by, Catherine and her friend implore him, "hey say Monsieu th'poetic-one, nightingale us [fashion us] thus a little air' in the mannar of verses."[173] In an ironic twist, the fictive scene mirrored how *La Gazette* was truly produced. The Dames had hired a writer to compose a scene in their stereotypical image.[174]

La Gazette des Halles mimicked the style other pamphleteers: fictive dialogues anchored each issue, humorous encounters advanced topsy-turvy plotlines, characters often broke out into song, and stylized dialect marked poissard characters. In the first eleven-page issue, fish merchant Margoton dresses up "in a nationau [*sic*] uniform." When Jérôme, another poissard character, greets her, she replies defiantly, "Margoton! ah weal yes, it weal that you speak to her. It's when she sells her fish that she takes that-there name; bwut in this'moment from here forward, it's Valor; Tranche-Montagne [Immovable-Mountain]; Heart-of-King that I'call'meself."[175] Margoton explains she has taken the National Guard uniform to pretend to be Lafayette, who is ill. She humorously tells Jérôme that she will drill the National Guard so that Lafayette's enemies will not notice his absence. Despite Jérôme's pressure to hand over the uniform so that he can join instead, Margoton insists that women can fight and that she can "serve her fatherland."[176] The pamphlet confirms the Dames' patriotism and ends in song praising Lafayette.

Another issue of *La Gazette des Halles* relied, like other pamphlets, on the poissardes' assumed frankness to correct false accusations. In this issue, the Dames sought to defend the king. Before sharing some brandy, poissardes Catherine and Javotte depict the king as a "good citizen." The poissardes angrily protest that printed libels smear the king's reputation. Catherine expresses her disdain for the slanderous words: "Oh go go; let it be! these duplicitous Aristocrats will soon have a foot in the nose as well as all the agents & these writings whose poisoned sheets are good for torching the ass of Monsieur Satan."[177]

If *La Gazette des Halles* so closely follows other poissard models, how can it be discerned that the Dames commissioned the work instead of another group? Several pieces of evidence point to the Dames as the sponsors of *La Gazette*. The two surviving issues are marked "printed at the expense of the Dames de la place Maubert." In contrast, fake pamphlets directly attribute authorship to the Dames. Printed at the expense of the Dames" is rather exact for a fake line and even decenters the Dames by removing them from the byline.

The *Gazette*'s publisher information further supports its authenticity. Unlike other poissard pamphlets that do not note a publisher or list a stock character such as Monsieur Josse or the Père Duchesne, the *Gazette*'s publisher line reads "from the printing house of N.H. Nyon, rue Mignon." Many poissard pamphlets chose a fictive press location that fits within the poissard ethos such as "pillars of les Halles" or somewhere in the marketplace neighborhood.[178] However, rue Mignon held no such cultural attachment and was located on the opposite bank of the Seine from the central Halles. But the address is a mere .4 miles from the satellite market at the Place Maubert whose Dames supposedly paid for the pieces. This proximity conforms to the logic that the merchants would use nearby printers, just as Parisians used neighborhood notaries.[179] In addition, a catalog of printers from 1789 confirms that Nicolas-Henri Nyon did run a printing shop on the rue Mignon. Moreover, Nyon was an official "Printer of Parlement, Bailiwick of the Palace, of the constabulary, of the Admiralty, and of the Water and Forests of France."[180] In addition to governmental notices printed by Nyon, some prints for private individuals have survived in the archives.[181] If all of these elements are taken into consideration, it is highly reasonable that the Dames did indeed commission *La Gazette des Halles* and redeployed stylized poissardes to their own advantage.

* * *

The Dames' crucial role as food merchants and as the most widely recognized mouthpiece of the people positioned them at the heart of revolutionary politics. Parisians relied on 1,000 Dames des Halles to buy supplies of fish, fruit, vegetables, cheese, eggs, and butter from the countryside. Without the Dame's retail services, the markets and public order across the capital would collapse. Due to their ritual relationship with the king, the Dames had represented the popular classes since the thirteenth century. After the opening salvo of the Revolution, most Parisians readily accepted the Dames' authority as the sovereign people incarnate. Fellow revolutionaries attempted to appropriate the Dames' substantial power in word and image. Especially from 1789 to 1792, pamphleteers and artists built from the genre poissard to snare, endear, or disgust readers.[182]

Citizens could recognize a fictive pamphlet dialogue, listen to a living Dame read a petition, or watch several of them trade in les Halles. Nonetheless, Parisians unconsciously absorbed the stereotypes that tied the fictive poissardes to the actual market women. Citizens' evaluations of fictive fishwives defined the true Dames des Halles and affected how they interacted with other citizens, groups, and institutions. Therefore, in the early Revolution, the Dames' political reputation rested in part on printed counterparts that they had little role in producing.

The market women, however, did not completely reject these cultural constructions. Rather, the Dames accepted their tremendous valence, which in part, stemmed from their own political power. The Dames built from poissard tactics and redirected them for their own ends. The market women even embarked on a campaign to cast their image in text and in action. Thus, the Dames' reputation resulted from both self-presentation and external appropriation, with each example repeatedly informing the other. In their revolutionary activism, the Dames would attempt to capture the clout and dodge the dangers of their malleable image.

Embodying Sovereignty

The October Days, Political Activism, and Maternal Work

On October 8, 1789, nine Dames des Halles unexpectedly appeared during the municipal government's session. Madame Lardin and her eight colleagues asked for the floor to prove their loyalty to the Revolution. During the October Days earlier that week, a much larger deputation of Dames des Halles had descended on the Hôtel de Ville to demand bread from the Commune officials before marching through the rain to petition the king at Versailles. The mud from the march could have barely dried on Madame Lardin's wooden clogs as she approached the podium. Before the municipal representatives, she voiced the Dames' fear that the public might conflate them with women moved "to the most violent excesses" in the morning confusion outside Versailles a few days earlier. Crowds infiltrating the chateau had, after all, left two royal guards headless.[1] Two-hundred-forty of Lardin's colleagues filed a similar complaint at the police bureau.[2] Madame Lardin elaborated that the Dames wished to keep order with the National Guard, especially regarding the suspect women.[3] They had already enforced "public tranquility" by seizing women who extorted money from citizens and bringing them to the police.[4] The municipal representatives were moved by the Dames' "patriotism." They posted 1,000 copies of Lardin's address around the city "so that the name of these *bonnes citoyennes* [good female citizens] be forever consecrated in public consciousness."[5]

Amid lively applause, the representatives showered the Dames with "marks of esteem."[6] Unpinning his tricolor from his hat, Mayor Bailly gave it to the head of deputation, who cut it into pieces to divide among her colleagues. When the assembly offered the Dames an "honorary [monetary] recompense," they protested, "One does not need a reward for doing one's duty." The representatives voted to inscribe the Dames' names on a bronze plaque and strike them four silver medals, each worth 28.4 days of bread.[7] Mayor Bailly explained, "This medal is the recompense for your good conduct at moments when so many people made their conduct reprehensible. The title *bonne citoyenne*, of which it bears the imprint, will recall to you without cease the duties that this title imposes on you."[8]

But what did it mean to be a "bonne citoyenne" in the early Revolution? What did the Dames and the Commune respectively mean by "doing one's duty" and "the duties this title imposes on you"? The medals they received, which bore the title "bonnes citoyennes" on one side and the city's coat of arms on the other, portrayed citizenship as built on reciprocal duties between citizens and the state.[9] The Dames' patriotic initiatives benefited the body politic, and the state repaid them by clearing their name. From 1789 to 1793, the Dames developed this model of a participatory social contract.

The market women framed their political and gendered interventions as civic responsibilities that served public interests. They petitioned the king as "faithful subjects" and called on the National Assembly as "representatives of the French nation of which we have the honor of being part."[10] As defenders of the Revolution, they pressured the royal family to support new legislation and exposed counterrevolutionary plotters who sought their assistance. In a similar vein, the Dames framed their gendered labor as a patriotic obligation. Once the daughters of Old Regime charity, the Dames became republican mothers in the regenerated nation. They cited their maternal duties to encourage support for soldiers' wives, protect defaulters on wet-nurse payments, and shield children from counterrevolutionary nuns. To describe the relationship between citizens and the state, they transferred paternal power from the king to revolutionary officials. All the while, they presented themselves as female guardians of their community. Thus, the market women embraced gendered work as a component of their citizenship without restricting citizenship to gendered roles.

Since the Dames did not have a standing organization, they reacted to issues in a piecemeal fashion and relied heavily on public display. Under Parisians' gaze, the Dames could become the organic face for the sovereign people. Their interventions offered them flexibility when tolerated. In the sectional assembly of les Halles, for example, the Dames responded as if they were part of the assembly vote by "applaud[ing] loudly" from the galleries to convey their opinions.[11] They acted as revolutionary heroines in national festivals and took oaths with National Guardsmen. The Dames so frequently feted military personnel on behalf of the nation that one lieutenant changed his troops' route to dodge their "laurel crowns and carafes of wine."[12] Without the restraints of institutional decorum or procedure, the Dames drew from a diverse pool of public demonstrations and changed tactics according to circumstance.

This chapter details the breadth of the Dames' activism, while closely analyzing three events. It scrutinizes the Dames' leadership in the October Days in 1789, their attempt to fetch the king's brother from Italy in 1790, and their spanking of counterrevolutionary nuns in 1791. In examining these moments, it excavates multiple layers of political practice and probes how other revolutionaries responded to the Dames' interventions.

The Dames' revolutionary activism corresponded to major political shifts. From 1789 to June 1791, the Dames des Halles imbued their Old Regime gestures and rituals with new political meaning. They presented bouquets to deputies who acted in their favor and invited politicians to patriotic *Te Deums*. In addition, the Dames experimented with revolutionary practices like petitioning the Commune and intermittently collaborating with neighborhood clubs. They continued to foster their special relationship with the king but also carved out space as autonomous popular representatives. As the market women wrestled for control of their public image, they built new alliances with the National Assembly, forged ties with the municipal government, and recast old relationships with the court.

After the king's flight to Varennes in June 1791, the market women dramatically cast off their connection with the monarch and turned to other signs of legitimacy. They completely replaced the king's broken paternal mandate with the authority of revolutionary representatives, but they held the deputies accountable for fulfilling duties toward them. During the period from June 1791 to spring 1793, local politics settled into novel institutional forms like elections, neighborhood assemblies, and the militia. Political clubs in particular began to compete with the Dames as the voice of the people. Groups with official-sounding charters and sustained structures gradually diluted the Dames' exceptional authority in the early months of the republic.

From 1789 to 1793, the Dames could only speak in the assembly halls if the deputies admitted them, could only effectively demonstrate in the street if the public noticed them, and could only change marketplace conditions if the police paid attention to them. Some revolutionaries lauded the Dames as exemplary figureheads, others ambivalently observed their activism, and still others feared that plotters manipulated them. All of their perspectives acknowledged the Dames' weight in national politics. The dual nature of the Dames' activism—public and embodied—was crucial to their influence and practices of citizenship. From the calling of the Estates General to the Jacobin Republic, the Dames framed their patriotic and gendered interventions as civic work integral to political reciprocity.[13]

Translating Ritual Practices to Revolutionary Relationships

During the Old Regime, the Dames had thrived by sanctioning the crown on behalf of "the people." From royal sacraments to military victories, the Dames sang the king's praises and showered him with bouquets. Since the Dames traced their origins to Saint Louis, they celebrated him and the king on his feast day every August 25.[14] Every New Year, the Dames also traveled to Versailles to offer the king "the homage of our hearts."[15] Since the last 1614 meeting of the Estates General, the Dames and their ancestors had formally addressed the king at least 350 times.[16] When the Estates General convened in 1789, the Dames reached into their long-established repertoire to develop new political relationships and endorse officials acting in their favor.

In March 1789, the Dames deployed their customary compliments to develop a relationship with the Third Estate representatives. The market women reminded their "brothers" that the first French king "was a soldier" who came "from the Third Estate." They professed their loyalty to the king, but also asserted a political role for themselves and the Third Estate representatives. They sang: "We defend, we love with zeal / We serve the State, / Let it always be faithful to Louis, / The Third Estate." The Dames told their electors, "we come to glorify ourselves in your eyes of the choice that was recently made in our favor, [which] nam[ed] you, by public voice, to support the interests of a People of which you are members."[17] Through their compliment, the market women took ownership of their electors and bolstered their own clout as organs of the popular classes.

After the National Assembly's creation in June, the Dames reacted to sudden ambiguities in political power by modifying their public interventions. In early July, they sent a deputation to compliment the electors-turned-deputies for the grace they extended to French Guards who had given up their royal posts.[18] They offered the deputies an address and a traditional song. However, the Dames explicitly distinguished their relationship with the deputies from their relationship with the king: "We will not be able to laud you, neither with gold, nor with incense, nor with laurels: these belong only to an esteemed monarch: but we laud you with flowers." A pamphleteer recounting the scene concluded that the Dames' embodied sanction was more potent than circulating political tracts. He noted, "One must not forget that [the Dames'] verses are the fruit of a sentiment, [they are] not an ordered work, not an exact production composed by a hired pen."[19]

The Dames drew more freely from their sanctioning toolbox throughout July 1789. When the capital welcomed the king at the Hôtel de Ville after the fall of the Bastille, the municipal government chose the Dames to represent Parisians. Channeling the good will between the king and his subjects, the market women presented him with "the Laurel, Symbol of peace."[20] Two days later, the Dames greeted the recently dismissed minister Necker with "cries of joy" when he returned to Paris. They offered Necker flowers to demonstrate how he had won their "hearts." To top it off, they enthusiastically showered his wife's hand with kisses.[21]

Over the summer, as the Dames attempted to validate their traditional influence in a revolutionary context, they forged relationships with emergent representative bodies. On July 20, 1789, the Dames of the Marché St. Paul brought
a bouquet to the new municipal committee. They congratulated the committee
on "the divine zeal which animates you, [through which] you bring hope for
the end of our miseries." They spoke to fellow listeners as "my dear comrades,"
called the officials "our great Deputies," and channeled a sovereign people that
surpassed the Third Estate. The Dames drove home their and the government's
broadening representative reach with a song celebrating "the three Orders
reunited."[22]

Similarly, on July 22, the National Assembly received a deputation of Dames
from multiple markets who claimed to speak "aloud from sincere devotion" on behalf of the wider public. Calling the deputies "braves defenders of French liberty,"
Dame Dupray of the Marché St. Paul, Reine d'Ongrie (Hongrie) of the Marché
d'Aguesseau, Dame Genti of the Marché des Quinze-Vingts, and Dame Doré of
the central Halles declared that they hoped "the end of your works will be [the
end] of our misery and the dawn of our Happiness."[23] Merchant Dupray composed a patriotic song whose lyrics literally took possession of the officials. The
singing Dames praised "King, Citizens, & Soldiers / O'r fath'r, our close friends,
our brothers." They invited fellow citizens to follow their lead: "Swear, all lik' we
will swear / To be faithful to the Nation."[24] The pamphlet version of Merchant
Dupray's song bore the mark, "Approved by Monsieur the Mayor of Paris," which
officially endorsed the Dames' logic. By the end of July, the market women had
reinvented their role as customary spokeswomen, had forged connections with
revolutionary bodies, and had asserted their vision of a politically reborn France.[25]

The market women used their privileged access to the king to comment on
revolutionary developments and to slowly reshape their connection with him. In
early August, forty Dames dressed themselves in white and gathered bouquets
to praise Louis XVI. Spokeswoman Mademoiselle Bourbau asserted that the
"People" had benefited from revolutionary events, and that God "ennobles all
of his [the king's] faculties" to benefit France. The Dames reassured the monarch, "we will not cease soliciting for you, & your venerable descendants."[26] The
market women implied that they would pray for the king while reiterating the
timeless nature of their own legitimizing abilities. They also recalled the king's
vow that "every time my people address me with confidence, they must expect
all of my generosity." By repeating the line word for word, the Dames reinforced
that their support could be contingent on the king keeping his promises. Later
that month, the Dames secured another audience to congratulate the king on the
start of the Constitution.[27] Pleased with the political developments, the Dames
called him "our dear man, our good close friend" and affirmed his continued position as "our father."[28]

The Dames also refashioned the traditional father–child political model that they had shared exclusively with the king. They extended the title of father, and its corresponding paternal obligation, to revolutionary figures. In August 1789, the Dames took up a collection throughout the city to free prisoners who defaulted on their wet-nursing fees.[29] Unlike their compatriots in the provinces, Parisian working women often sent their children to wet-nurses. The state monitored the payment of wet-nursing fees and could imprison parents for their debts.[30] To defend the defaulters, the Dames called on Lafayette as the "common Father of such a large family." They implored him to bring peace to Parisians, who were the "victims" of treacherous circumstances. Recalling the parent–child relationships in limbo, the market women insisted, "We feel that your presence already resurrects happiness and joy in the heart of this multitude of Children [Parisians] by whom you are so tenderly cherished and so religiously adored."[31] By asking the state to protect its citizen-children, forgive wet-nursing debts, and release debtors to return home to fulfill their parental duties, the Dames extended paternal authority to Lafayette and linked their nuclear families to the metaphorical national family.

Throughout the summer of 1789, the market women also wrapped revolutionary issues in religious displays that they were well versed in organizing. Dames from multiple markets staged Catholic processions and masses across the city. Four days after the fall of the Bastille, the Dames venerated Saint Geneviève and presented a bouquet to her relics in a Mass of Thanksgiving.[32] This patron saint of Paris had saved the capital from starvation and the Huns in the fifth century.[33] The revolutionary capital's bread shortages and rumors of hostile troops nearby echoed Saint Geneviève's own challenges.

When the Dames of the Marché Saint Martin hosted an elaborate Te Deum a few weeks later, they incorporated revolutionary officials into their celebration. Following musicians and a young girl crowned with flowers, five Dames transported an offertory bouquet with trailing ribbons through the streets. A National Guard detachment carried weapons decorated with flowers and escorted the procession.[34] At the church, the Dames' spokeswoman Mademoiselle Bourbau thanked Saint Geneviève for "preserving us from imminent danger." After the mass, the market women brought a bouquet to the head of the city militia, General Lafayette, whom they asked for lower bread prices.[35] They invited Lafayette to pray to Saint Geneviève and assured him that "all our parents & our friends join themselves to you." Together, their military protector and spiritual patron would safeguard the city.[36] The Dames of the Marché d'Aguesseau similarly incorporated members of the local community in another Te Deum. In the name of their colleagues, the daughter of Reine d'Hongrie and nine other market women sent out invitations asking participants to process 2.8 miles to the Church Saint Geneviève.[37]

Even as the revolutionaries invented new models of political practice like legislative proceedings, officials acknowledged the Dames' continued political valence and imitated their ritual gestures. On August 25, 1789, the Feast Day of Saint Louis, Parisian municipal officials and National Guardsmen mounted the road to Versailles to compliment the king. The revolutionary representatives and militia brought a metaphorical "bouquet for the king" composed of a "considerable sum" from "patriotic subscriptions."[38] They replicated the Dames' annual visit to express the nascent nation's unity much in the way the market women had expressed the collective gratitude of royal subjects for centuries. In the early months of the Revolution, it seemed as if the Dames' ritual repertoire could shape and be shaped by revolutionary politics.

The October Days and Their Aftermath:
Defining *Bonnes Citoyennes*

Not all revolutionaries embraced the Dames' direct interventions. Since officials could not control what the Dames did, the market women always represented some kind of wild card. As early as August 1789, the king himself was anxious over the Dames' upcoming visit for the feast of St. Louis. The king's Ministre de Maison wrote to Mayor Bailly and implored him to limit the number of Dames traveling to Versailles. Fearful of the unpredictable nature of a massive visit, the minister asked Bailly to stop the Dames from the Marché Saint Martin. He wrote that the king wished to receive only the "Femmes de la halle" (in this strict sense, Dames of the *central* Halles) to prevent a "storm."[39]

The real storm that should have worried the king grew over the six weeks that followed. In the fall of 1789, the dearth of bread and anxiety over counterrevolutionary conspiracies threatened to unhinge the capital. Rumors swirled that troops were approaching Paris to squash the Revolution, fear of hoarders heightened the bread crisis, and the press speculated about royalist plots to distance the king from the capital. The situation grew particularly tense in September, when, in protest over the National Assembly's refusal to give him an absolute veto, the king refused to formally accept the Constitution and the *Declaration of the Rights of Man and Citizen*. Then, in early October, the king's royal Body Guards held a banquet at Versailles that scandalized the capital. Parisians believed that, during the gathering, the Body Guards trampled the patriotic tricolor underfoot. Pamphlets maintained that the queen and her court handed out white and black cockades for the Bourbon and Hapsburg dynasties.[40] Rumors even spread that the banquet degenerated into a royalist orgy. The thought of counterrevolutionaries corrupting their benevolent king infuriated Parisians.[41]

On October 5, 1789, the Dames took action, drawing their authority from their traditional roles as local guardians, their ritual relationship with the king, and their developing relations with local officials. Leaving the marketplace, they went to the Hôtel de Ville to ask municipal officials for bread, which they considered the government's duty.[42] When the Commune failed to supply it, the Dames led over 6,000 other women and militiamen to Versailles to petition the king and the National Assembly.[43] The determined women dragged two cannons and assorted arms for 12 miles through heavy rain. At the château, the king promised the Dames he would send bread to Paris and dispatched some Dames to deliver his promise by carriage. That evening, the remaining women presented their grievances to the National Assembly next door. General Lafayette arrived with his Parisian National Guard and offered to protect the king. The Dames, other marchers, and the Parisian militia spread out to take shelter for the night.

The next morning, curious and exhausted marchers found their way into the château's courtyards. Chaos broke out among the confused guards and people. Some twelve people died in the ensuing clashes. Two Royal Body Guards lost their heads, and Marie Antoinette, fleeing the crowd outside her bedchamber, collapsed into her husband's arms.[44] In order to appease the Parisians flooding his courtyard, Louis addressed "my children" from his bedroom balcony. He agreed to relocate to Paris to prove his devotion.[45]

The October Days crystalized the social compact in practice. The Dames had set out for Versailles under the assumption that a patriotic king must protect his citizens. They seemed validated when they returned with thousands of people and the royal family in tow.[46] The National Assembly promised to move with the king as well. The Dames had forced the Commune, the National Assembly, and the King to uphold their duties to feed citizens, protect the capital, and demonstrate their revolutionary loyalty.

Through the dramatic and very public October Days, the Dames cemented their position linking the state and the people. Illustrations of the momentous event depicted the market women as the purveyors of political power. One etching features the Dames not only addressing the deputies of in National Assembly on October 5 but also integrating themselves alongside the deputies on the benches. A few market women brazenly approach the president's desk, others supplicate representatives on their knees, and many others gesture and speak freely.[47] Another engraver portrayed the pivotal moment when the king spoke to the crowd. The artist places the Dames closest to the balcony, in an area counterfactually set apart from the crowd and National Guards. The image depicts a visual hierarchy of political influence in which the Dames mediate the space, physical and political, between their fellow citizens and the monarch above.[48] Artists used the Dames to textually signal the sovereign people as well. The titles "Les Dames de la Halle partant pour aller chercher le Roi à Versailles le 5 octobre 1789,"[49] and "Départ des Femmes de la Halle pour Versailles"[50] employ the market women's name as a catch-all to describe scenes with hordes of other people.

Parisians found "the people" at the heart of the march to Versailles, and the Dames, in turn, at the heart of "the people." Reflecting on the October Days, *Révolutions de Paris* waxed poetically, "It was the people, of all ages, of all sexes, of all states, of all customs, but animated with one singular and same sentiment, very profound, very determined, very general, who went solemnly to Versailles."[51] As previously seen in Figure 1.5, one of the most widely reproduced and surviving images of the October Days, "Les Dames de la Halle partant pour aller chercher le roi à Versailles le 5 octobre 1789," spotlights the Dames among the sweeping panoply of marching people. They act as leaders encouraging fellow Parisians and as the visual figureheads for all the citizens depicted. Two women easily identifiable as Dames stand in the center foreground: one characteristically poses with her hand on her hip and another carries her basket on her back. Three Dames have mounted a carriage to rally bystanders. One on the roof raises a pike in determination. Another points forward with a child at her side. In the background, one man waves his hat and another applauds their actions. Most of the women have pikes and have arranged themselves like a ragtag army. They are also dragging a cannon. Meanwhile the National Guard, at the rear of the scene, stands at attention without intervening.[52] The National Guard's response mirrored the secondary role they played "in order to support the women," as one journalist described it.[53]

In accounts of the march, the Dames seemed to encapsulate the popular classes' gritty virtues. One pamphleteer asserted that the loud women vendors revealed the poor's merits beneath unpolished façades. He attested, "The women of the people hide great character which shows itself when needed," although it is often concealed by their "neglected and rough education."[54] *La Chronique de Paris* harnessed the Dames to evoke the patriotism of popular women in contrast to rich aristocratic ones. The editor asserted, "the *Dames de la Halle* have thwarted the plans of the *Dames du Palais*," who had participated in the scandalous royal banquet while Parisians hungered in the capital.[55] Other post–October Days images depicted the Dames as the allegorical people whose transparency reflected political virtue. These unrestrained Dames radiated joy with round rosy cheeks, singing mouths agape, arms tossed in the air, and skipping heels kicking up skirts. Of course, they decorated their outfits with revolutionary blue, white, and red.[56]

Some newspapers embraced the Dames as shrewd political actors who restored a broken compact. In his *Revolutions de Paris* following the October Days, even journalist Prudhomme, a known misogynist, praised how "the women of the people, principally the market women of les Halles[,] and the workers of the faubourg St. Antoine charge themselves with the safety of the fatherland." Because of officials' "ineptitude in provisioning projects, and their indifference toward public dangers," Prudhomme validated the Dames' grievances as "just." He even reported that royal Body Guards had tried to persuade the Dames that the capital would be provisioned if the Constitution guaranteed the king an absolute veto. Yet the market women, cognizant of the Assembly's efforts to pass the suspensive veto, refused to trade bread for the "price of liberty."[57]

In the context of the October Days, the revolutionaries painted the Dames in military terms not just to describe violence but also to metaphorically cast them as defenders of the nation. One medallion showed the Dames with an impressive artillery stash including two cannons, guns, pikes, scythes, halberds, and tridents.[58] Another artist called the Dames' journey their "Versailles expedition."[59] Others championed the Dames as "an army of Amazons," with all of their classical qualities, as "the French heroines," or as "the heroines of Paris."[60] In a newspaper advertisement, an engraver announced his commemorative stamp depicting their "bravery" and he "dedicated [it] to the women."[61] *Révolutions de Paris* vividly described how the "courageous women" assembled "instruments of death" for the march. The Dames had even co-opted military leaders by rallying the Volunteers of the Bastille who had attacked the prison three months earlier.[62] Another pamphleteer implored the Parisian women who had won "the entire liberty of France" to remain on alert and urged them "to charge themselves with policing respectably."[63]

However, not all French citizens were pleased with the Dames' October Days initiatives, especially those in favor of a strong monarchy. When the Dames sat among the National Assembly deputies on October 5, the Marquis de Maleissye recounted with disgust that the Assembly "did not believe that its dignity was soiled by letting the poissardes of Paris sit on its benches."[64] The violence and disorder of the October Days also exposed the Dames to critique.[65] A telling image titled "La terrible nuit du 5 au 6 octobre 1789" illustrates "poissardes armed with sabers" who, along with brigands, break into the queen's bedroom.[66]

Others resented that the market women had forced the king's hand and framed the Dames as plotters' tools. Pamphleteer Peltier scathingly concluded that false patriots conspired against the king, that the march was "conjured to destroy us," and that the people were pawns. He robbed the Dames of agency by viewing the event as a staged attack.[67] When the Parisian Comité des recherches, which was charged with monitoring treason, ordered the Châtelet (an Old Regime judicial body) to investigate the October Days, some witnesses hypothesized that schemers concocted a "project to rouse the Femmes de la Halle" and pay them off.[68] Over the course of seven months, the Châtelet compiled testimony from 395 individuals to denounce the massive breach of the château and name "the authors, troublemakers and accomplices" behind the event.[69] Some suspected the Duc d'Orléans of conspiring to steal his cousin's throne. Others thought Mirabeau aided d'Orléans to gain a less conservative monarch and a post as d'Orléans's minister. But the Châtelet investigation's failure to find significant evidence against either Mirabeau or the Duc d'Orléans greatly exonerates the two men.[70] The Dames and their fellow Parisians led the October Days, not factional plotters. When the National Assembly's Comité des rapports dismissed the increasingly unpopular investigation a year later, it concluded that the perhaps "the Châtelet was putting the Revolution on trial."[71]

The Dames, however, did not wait for anyone to clear their name. In fact, they used another public gesture to protect their image from being sullied. During their visit to request *bonnes citoyennes* medals at the Commune, 240 Dames expressed "the liveliest horror for the infamous libelers who use their pens to soil so many cherished names" such as Parisian heroes Lafayette and Bailly. The deputation asserted that they sought "to declaim against the indecency of these disgusting scenes [the October 6 violence], in which they protest that they did not have any part."[72]

Although the Dames' political legitimacy soared after the October Days, their influence remained dependent on their public image. This became clear when multiple newspapers incorrectly reported that Dames asked the queen to return all the effects of the Mont-de-Piété, a royal pawn-broking agency that acted as a charitable lending system for the poor. [73] The Dames, who protested the tarnish of the implied payoff, asserted that they must "clamor [in print] against this false complaint."[74]

The Dames aggressively recruited law enforcement to police their reputation. Dames Lefevre, Doyen, Franc, Petitpas, and Bijou, all fish and flower retailers, went to the bureau de police two weeks after the October Days. They told police officials that they had seen posters in which "some Dames des Halles make public their sentiments of respect and veneration for the king and his august family." Not to be left out of this "public" recognition, Dame Lefevre and her four colleagues testified they shared the "same sentiments." The retailers also complained that "slanderers, printers, & booksellers" who "only search to make money" caused "scandal" through their "indiscreet printed motions."[75] The police endorsed the Dames' testimony and copied their words, which would be "rendered public by printing notices and posting them." The Dames then requested "legal punishment" against authors of "injurious libels" and their distributors who "make them public."[76]

The New Year offered the Dames the opportunity to strengthen their relationship with the National Assembly. On December 29, 1789, the Dames des Halles congratulated the representatives on a successful year, as they routinely did for the king. Spokeswoman Dame Dupré (Dupray) praised the deputies' diligent acts as "enlightened labors." Highlighting the Dames' maternal patriotism, she concluded, "What glory, in effect, what a triumph for those who compose this honorable list [of deputies], since our children will say . . . behold our fathers!"[77] By embracing the children–parent relationship between citizens and the revolutionary state, the women diluted the king's paternal power.

The Dames emerged as revolutionary guardians again in February 1790, when they foiled a counterrevolutionary plot to disrupt the National Guard's oaths. As Dame Veuve Shubert of the Marché Saint Martin explained to the police, a few days earlier, a man had entered into Reine d'Hongrie's boutique and approached her colleagues. Dame Merillon testified that the man had tried to bribe the Dames "to buy a saber of wood or of white iron, and to go together to the lodging of M. Brillant [the National Guard captain], at the moment when the District and the Battalion would set out to march for the oath ceremony . . . [they] would present him their wooden sabers mocking them." When the man's servant returned to confirm the scheme, Dame le Coq (the daughter of Reine d'Hongrie) played along in order to uncover the plotters. The Dames even took up watch in the cabaret across from Monsieur Brillant's house to warn him. Having disrupted the plot, sixteen Dames from the Marché Saint Martin submitted into police evidence two sabers and a written note with Monsieur Brillant's address.[78] On the day of the oath ceremony, the Dames triumphantly carried flowers and tricolor ribbons past lines of spectators. Far from ruining the ceremony, the market women led the battalions' procession from the National Assembly to Notre Dame.[79]

Throughout the first half of 1790, other revolutionaries flaunted the Dames' praises as popular approval and publicized them to augment their effect. While celebrating the anniversary of the Tennis Court Oath in June 1790, the Club of '89 welcomed the Dames who asked admittance. Inside the banquet hall, the Dames implored the members, "On this day which recalls to us one of the most beautiful eras of the French nation, permit some *bonnes citoyennes* to make known to you their homage and respect." The Dames praised the club and National Assembly for writing "a constitution that we will bless all the days of our lives." The members excitedly threw open the windows and relayed the Dames' message and "patriotic song" to the crowd outside.[80]

Yet, factional opponents accused one another of co-opting the Dames as a political tool to manipulate popular legitimacy. *Révolutions de Paris* acknowledged the Dames' ritual leverage and reprimanded the Club of '89 for extending this "strategy" at the first anniversary of the fall of the Bastille. The editor wrote, when "Old ministers, old police wanted to make it appear that the public opinion favored one thing, they had women ready to play the role of dames de la halle. . . . The Club of 1789 enjoyed the same honors, one used the same ruse."[81] In the place of elite societies like the Club of '89, the newspaper called for open and frugal clubs where all revolutionairies could meet in public. The October Days cemented the Dames' political power, but the "appropriate" venue for their influence remained contested.

Defenders of the Revolution: From les Halles to Italy

As the first anniversary of the Bastille approached, the deputies planned a national festival to celebrate the Revolution's progress. At its climax, the king and the National Assembly would swear an oath to the Constitution on the altar of the fatherland. However, the absence of the king's brother, Monsieur d'Artois, cast a dark cloud over preparations. The prince had fled to Turin just two days after the Bastille fell. Making their 12-mile march to Versailles look like a short jaunt, the Dames des Halles decided to dispatch three merchants to travel 360 miles and to convince Monsieur d'Artois, his pregnant wife, and his court to leave Turin, come to Paris, and fete the new nation.[82]

Mindful of their image, the Dames sent their most widely recognized member, Reine d'Hongrie, to lead the group. A pamphleteer explained that Reine was "nearly always chosen by the Dames des Halles, to represent them, & to serve as an interpreter for their famed corps" because of her "spirit, sallies, and eloquence."[83] In her honor, Parisians had taken to calling the new street north of St. Eustache the "Passage of Reine d'Hongrie" by the late 1780s.[84] Reine also held distinctive revolutionary capital since she was associated with the fall of the Bastille and the October Days. During the Turin trip, the market women leaned on her credentials and clout with the hope of persuading the Comte d'Artois.

The traveling Dames drew from their ritual repertoire to impress communities en route and generate support for their trek. When Reine and her comrades passed through Dijon and arrived at Lyon, *Le Courrier de Lyon* marveled, "This heroine & her company honored some of our municipal officials with their kisses, they sang verses, & imbued their compliments and discourses, with this gaiety, this assortment of grandiose words which makes their reputation in Paris."[85] *La Chronique de Paris* likewise reported, "they sang, embraced, and swore [oaths] according to their custom."[86]

The Lyonnais government was struck by the blend of official and popular symbolism that enveloped the Dames' visit. General Lafayette, Mayor Bailly, and the king's minister of foreign affairs Montmorin had all signed the women's passports, which deputized them to conduct semiofficial business on the nation's behalf.[87] Their permission confirmed the Dames' role as a mouthpiece of the sovereign people even in light of new representative bodies that claimed the same legitimacy. A Lyonnais newspaper reporting the visit aptly painted the Dames as the "[female] sovereigns of the Halle."[88] Printed accounts labeled the women a "deputation." The Lyonnais municipal government acknowledged the Dames' diplomatic authority by providing accommodations for them.[89]

The extensive welcome the Lyonnais provided the Dames reflected their embrace of the Dames as not just guardians of Paris but also defenders of the nation. On the first day, the Lyonnais lavishly gave the Dames "places of honor" at a play performed just for them. The spectacle had a popular slant, complete with conversations between the parterre and the actors, and obscene songs against the clergy as a bonus.[90] Such festivities incorporated the Lyonnais into the Dames' journey to defend the Revolution. Of the visit, one pamphlet concluded: "They passed through the feasts, the balls, the spectacles, during their stay in this city; also they will never forget the Lyonnais, & they will not cease to sing their praises."[91]

Reports of the Dames' actions doubled back along their path between Paris and the provinces. Whether satirical and begrudging or serious and celebratory, written accounts used parliamentary vocabulary to shade the Dames' actions with legality. Multiple reporters described the trip as an "extraordinary diplomatic mission" undertaken by "our two ambassadors" or "the envoys of the Dames de la Halle."[92] The royalist newspaper *L'Ami du Roi* printed a letter supposedly from Lyon reporting that stomach problems had hospitalized one of the Dames. The dispatch irreverently noted the market women would not be stopped for lack of official passports but for indigestion.[93] From his base in Paris, diplomat Earl Gower even sent news to Britain of these "deputies of a different sort." He wrote that the Dames' quest generated "much astonishment."[94]

Once the Dames arrived in Turin, they established themselves as popular representatives through their trademark embellishments. One pamphlet described, "Our two ambassadors dressed in white, covered with ribbons of the nation, carried in their hands huge bouquets, traversing the streets of Turin surrounded by an innumerable crowd." When the two Dames entered Monsieur d'Artois's palace, they announced in their poissard dialect, "I comes in the name of the good people o' Paris, to engage you to return to the middler o' the family." They encouraged him "imitate rather your brother, err dear king." They paused to explain that, if "he [the king] wun't be err prince by heritage, I would has chosen him for his vartue." The idea that a people could choose their king dramatically reconfigured the monarchical mandate, but Reine d'Hongrie reminded d'Artois, "I are all equal." According to pamphlets, the Dames assured the prince of "Parisians' satisfactory sentiments in his regard" and their visit "at least had to make known to him the dispositions of the people." The Dames' public sanction could renew the civic bonds between the prince and his fellow citizens, but the market women demanded action. Monsieur d'Artois applauded their speech, embraced Reine d'Hongrie, held a magnificent meal in their honor, and dispatched them back to Paris. The Dames carried d'Artois's letter to the king, which promised his return.[95] He did not keep his word.

An Independent Collectivity: Navigating the Advantages and Liabilities of Extrainstitutional Activism

To maintain their political valence alongside revolutionary institutions, the Dames des Halles increasingly relied on state or popular approval for their sporadic interventions and sanctioning tactics. The municipality strengthened its connection with the market women in October 1790 by writing them into history. In their official narrative, the Commune deemed the Dames a "class of *citoyennes* who across time, exercised on the people great influence, [which] also put itself at the head of the revolution."[96] The anniversary of the October Days was the perfect moment to recall the Dames' patriotic model and reinforce the advantageous alliance. Moreover, on October 2, the National Assembly had rejected the Châtelet's investigation into suspected plots behind the march. Chabroud, the head of the Assembly's Comité des rapports, had applauded the October Days as "these pure days where the good citizens only have one soul."[97]

Unfortunately for the Dames des Halles, their patriotic reputation spurred fraud that sought to turn their political capital into financial capital. The market women had already distanced themselves from imposter alms-seekers in spring 1789, but in October 1790 women claiming to be Dames flattered wealthy individuals with bouquets and then asked for alms. The fake, money-grubbing Dames appeared unproductive, draining, and self-interested—the exact opposite of useful, virtuous, and community-minded citizens. *La Chronique de Paris* reported that the true Dames "demanded that a formal disavowal of this shameful collection be published and posted. No, they have no hand in taking up this collection; but one makes use of their name in order to undertake it." The editor observed that the Dames had needed "to denounce" the con-artists' reprise to restore their "honor."

Yet, the journal complained that Old Regime attitudes had inspired the solicitations and hinted that the Dames might still be tied to that world. The journal contended that, to maintain popularity, the Old Regime had treated "the female merchants of fish and the coal merchants, as representatives of the people."[98] But revolutionary society had recalibrated poor citizens' value according to the work they contributed to society. The journal concluded, "Today the Dames des Halles & the Dames du palais [probably Palais Royal], the male caterers and the female caterers, the courtesan & the courtesans, &c. &c.

are equal & all citizens. Each one must live from his/her work, & the municipality must treat like beggars all those who do not at all merit a salary."[99] The newspaper's assessment risked undermining the Dames' claims to legitimacy as productive citizen-workers.

The Dames' ritual exchanges also chanced appearing incompatible with the emerging regime of political etiquette. Three days after demanding that the market women take action against begging con-artists, La Chronique de Paris warned "the newly elected" deputies of the Legislative Assembly to ignore the Dames. The editor suggested their compliments were tinged by financial motives since they might expect a gift, like the king would have offered, in return.[100] Nonetheless, the Dames presented Representative Barnave with a bouquet for his new office as president of the National Assembly.[101]

By October 1790, the king had taken up a more or less ongoing residence in St. Cloud with his family and cabinet. Although he returned to Paris for the weekly Conseil d'État and state festivals and continued to correspond with the Assembly from his private retreat, some revolutionaries reasonably began to fear that counterrevolutionaries guided the king in St. Cloud. One pamphleteer conjectured that the Dames could solve the problem. He summoned them, "you who were armed with pikes, guns, and even cannons; you who led yourselves to Versailles; you who braved all dangers, to save your King and your fatherland from the peril which menaced it!"[102] "Virtuous Parisian [women]!," he implored them, "Would you have already forgotten this heroism which made you so famous and so commendable in the eyes of all other powers . . . which history will pass from age to age." He urged them, "For a second time make shine the courage, the honor and the independent virtue of the Parisian Amazons! Depart, go, find your King!" However, one senses that the market women's symbolic display of force appealed more to the pamphleteer than true bloodshed. He cautioned them to avoid "absolutely any violence."[103] Ultimately, the king consented to return to Paris without a visit from the Dames. Could the possibility have been on his mind? He reestablished his court at the Tuileries palace in early November.[104]

The market women welcomed public praise affirming their legitimacy throughout the winter of 1790–1791. When they showered New Year's compliments on the National Assembly at the close of 1790, Madame Dupray of the Marché St. Paul characterized their praise as the "most sacred of our duties toward the august assembly of representatives of the French nation of which we have the honor of being part."[105] The representatives bestowed honors of the session on them in return.[106] German playwright August Friedrich Ferdinand von Kotzebue, who was in Paris, was struck by how the revolutionaries lionized the "fish-women" and their grand reputation. Kotzebue was so impressed that he copied a description from the Journal de Paris in his diary:

The [National] Assembly received their [the Dames'] wishes with satisfaction as the voice of the people. It is known, that the *Dames de la
Halle* have often stepped forward in this revolution, and always full of
patriotism. Their character, at all times prone to independence, their
freedom of speech, which was even pardoned at a time when little was
pardoned, must naturally give them a distinguished zeal for liberty.

According to Kotzebue, the *Journal de Paris* commented that the elite could no
longer patronize or belittle the Dames. In his reading, the Revolution endowed
the market women with substantial authority as "the voice of the people."[107]
   Yet in the eyes of critics, fish guts and rough jargon did not befit the august assembly halls of a regenerated nation. The Jacobins' rivals accused them of using
the Dames' visit as a theatrical prop for artificially staging politics: "What deliberation had been truly free? Did not one know who should speak, who would be
applauded, who would be booed, who would be presented to the poissardes in
order to receive bouquets, or delivered to the va-nu-pieds [peasant rebels from
the seventeenth century] and barkers of conspiracy in order to be menaced with
the lantern?"[108] In *L'Ami du Roi*, far-right royalist Abbé Royou reported their
appearance in false glowing terms. After misinterpreting the article, the "extremely flattered" Dames decided to bring the Abbé his own bouquet. When
they arrived, they were informed that he had left to take his patriotic oath. This
excuse was likely a cruel joke, but the Dames, eager for signs of public approval,
lauded him in absentia.[109]
   In February 1791, the Dames and fellow Parisians became increasingly concerned about the strain that the gradual emigration of the royal family was putting on the Revolution and the king. Newspapers accused the king's aunts of
frequenting counterrevolutionary priests and planning escapes despite the great
alarm it would cause.[110] Not only would their flight condemn the Revolution,
but they, like other rich émigrés, would take money and jewels with them,
thereby draining the metallic money supply. For these reasons, the Dames went
to the aunts' country house in Bellevue and implored them to remain in Paris.
However, the aunts were frightened by the imposing group of market women
assembled at their home and rushed to take shelter with their nephew the king.[111]
   To make their case, the Dames petitioned the king through familial
metaphors, as they traditionally had, but this time they incorporated other civic
relationships. By February 1791 some Dames had become members of the
Société fraternelle, one of the Parisian political clubs that welcomed both men
and women, and they addressed the king on its behalf.[112] Showering Louis with
love like a "good father," they attested to citizens' "chagrin that from all sides your
[royal] family abandons you." They offered to grant the aunts political absolu-
tion within the national family. They told the king, "We will fete them, sire, as

soon as they appear beside your cherished person, & our love for you will wash over them." If his aunts "abandoned" him, the Dames assured Louis, "We, sire, your people, we will take the place of your family." Yet, the market women eerily warned Louis that he would be responsible if his aunts escaped, especially since some of the princes had already left.[113] In a nod to the increasing weight of the Parisian municipal government, the Dames went to the Commune to officially report their club's address to the king. The municipal deputies resoundingly applauded the Dames and ordered their patriotic speech printed for all citizens to see.[114]

When rumors swirled that the aunts would leave at midnight, the Dames transformed their ritual supplications into civic demands. *Le Creuset* reported that "a detachment of citoyennes de la halle ... went to the home of the hero of two worlds" (General Lafayette) to insist that the Commune and the National Guard intervene. But Lafayette and other officials did not arrive quickly enough.[115] The fed-up Dames hurried to the aunts' house in the outskirts of Paris. Although the aunts had already fled, the market women halted their baggage.[116] Next, the Dames set their sights on Monsieur, the king's brother, at the Luxembourg palace across the city. Monsieur was forced to admit the market women due to their ritual privilege. He swore to the Dames that he would not leave France as well.[117] The Dames and other Parisians next accompanied Monsieur to see the king and queen at the Tuileries. Trouble began when the palace guards opened the gate for Monsieur and some of the crowd leaked into the courtyard with him.[118] In response to this intrusion, the guards bolstered their watch, a cannon was summoned, and Lafayette arrived with militia. But it was to no avail. The Dames and the crowd refused to disperse for three hours while lamenting the aunts' flight.[119]

The incident added to aristocrats' growing distaste for the Dames' public displays that now forced, rather than bolstered, royal hands. The radical "Père Duchesne" rushed to rescue the Dames from "slanderers" who disparaged them. He informed readers that "aristocrats" shunned the Dames' actions, saying, "these women get themselves mixed up in things that don't concern them, that they would do much better to sell their fish, rather than rummaging through the king's palace because of their preference [their privileged connection with the king]." He scolded the hypocritical aristocrats and recalled how "their [the Dames'] frank & hardy repartees had [once] put joy in your hearts."[120]

After the aunts' flight, left-leaning factions exploited the line the Dames straddled between royal supplicants and revolutionary representatives. As the Jacobins planned festivities for Carnival in March 1791, they dispatched groups to invite "all the patriots, [and] to use all of the most engaging means to make at least the entire royal family [participate and] dance." The Jacobins enlisted "My Dames de la Halle" as messengers, no doubt because of their ritual association and continued access to the king as popular representatives. The Jacobins acknowledged the Dames as a political group by listing them alongside deputations of Parisian sections and clubs.[121] As an extrainstitutional group from the Old Regime in a field increasingly crowded by revolutionary representative bodies, the Dames needed such alliances to legitimize their periodic interventions.

Political Salvation: Republican Mothers and Spiritual Guardians

As the end of Lent approached, the Dames conflated their spiritual and political worlds and won acclaim as female protectors of both. In March and April 1791, rumors flew that counterrevolutionary nuns attended masses with nonjuring priests and aristocratic sympathizers. These nuns spanked their pupils, the Dames' children, for confessing to prorevolutionary priests. In response, the enraged Dames subjected the religious women to their own "correction." The market women dragged the nuns out of their convents, pulled aside their skirts, and spanked them in full view of the public. As patriotic mothers, the Dames asserted they protected their nuclear and national families from sterile, plotting nuns. Journalists and artists deployed gendered ideals to praise the Dames and to condemn the religious women. Few revolutionaries criticized the violence. Instead, as complicit spectators to the Dames' strikes, fellow citizens passed collective judgment, purged the nuns, and safeguarded national salvation.

In 1789, the National Assembly had begun to legally subordinate the Church to the state by nationalizing Church lands. By the winter of 1790–1791, the deputies were implementing the next steps of the Civil Constitution of the Clergy, which the Dames vocally backed. These laws forced Catholic parish priests and bishops to take an oath of allegiance to the new Constitution. Revolutionaries supporting the legislation interpreted those refusing to take the oath as counterrevolutionaries whose loyalties lay with the foreign pope. Worse still, the revolutionaries believed that nonjuring priests sympathized with the aristocratic forces that had controlled the Church under the Old Regime. Catholic celibacy also seemed to rob the nation of fathers, while priestly debauchery corrupted public morals.[122] In this pressure cooker, Parisians could barely stifle their anger at nonjuring priests who desecrated the body politic.[123] In January 1791, Bishop and former deputy Jean-Sifrein Maury received an anonymous threat to take the oath or else "the poissardes will hang him from the lantern."[124] Then, during the Holy Week in April, a journal speculated that "aristocrat-nuns" were secretly attending "good" Masses with priests who had refused the oath.[125] Gorsas, editor of *Le Courrier de Paris dans les 83 Départements*, reported that nuns were summoning refractory priests who, in private sermons, compared the counterrevolution to Christ, the governmental assemblies to tyrants, and the Revolution to hell.[126] However insulting this was to the nation, tensions exploded when the disgruntled nuns spanked their pupils for confessing to an oath-taking priest. Unluckily for the nuns, their pupils happened to be the Dames' children.[127]

The backlash would be remembered in "posterity," as one giddy witness put it.[128] Fed up, the Dames des Halles literally took matters into their own hands and submitted the nuns to their own "correction." On April 6, they dragged the counterrevolutionary nuns out of their cloistered convents into the public street.[129] As the nuns prayed to endure the trial, the Dames chased them down with bundles of sticks raised in the air. They unveiled the nuns' naked bottoms, submitting them to the public gaze and communal judgment. Spectators cheered on the spankings from the sidelines. The Dames boldly continued their rounds to several offending convents. The public took delight in what one artist described as the "good lessons" that the "citoyennes" gave to nuns who had aided "fanatic priests." Most newspapers, pamphlets, and images depicting the event assumed satirical or at least carnivalesque forms with sexual overtones. Citing an oft-repeated statistic, one watercolor proudly documented the Dames' accomplishment of "621 buttocks spanked; Total 310 and a half asses" since, as another pamphlet thankfully explains, "the Treasurer of the Miramionnes order only had one buttock."[130]

The Dames des Halles attacked the "enemies of God's servants" as a dual spiritual and civic duty.[131] The counterrevolutionary clergy's "fanaticism," according to one journal, had especially no place in the "holy week."[132] Another account reported that the head "Dame-Citizen" lambasted the nuns who had "dared" to choose the "house of God" for their mischief.[133] Many articles and illustrations depicting attacks refer to the spanking as "Corrected Fanaticism," implying that the violence carried broader ideological implications.[134] One pamphleteer argued, "This vengeance [of the people] is very useful, in as much as it acts when the law has no force."[135] The Dames had spiritually defended the nation when the government could not.

Several accounts of the convent visits legitimized the Dames' activism through ironic parliamentary overtones. *Révolutions de France* reported, "the Dames des Halles . . . held a National session at the Miramionnes, the Daughters of Sainte-Marie, and among the multitude of the Moustiers. Everything happened with great order. Each one was whipped in her own turn."[136] The popular engraving title "Patriotic Discipline" gives the sense of a state-mandated punishment.[137] By likening the Dames' judgment to a legislative session, presenting the chaos as ordered proceedings, and labeling their punishments as formally corrective, the descriptions paradoxically color the Dames' violence with a sense of civic order and legality.

The Dames' trusty tactical standby, public display, served two ends in the spanking spree. By chasing the nuns from their closed houses into the "open streets," the Dames unmasked counterrevolutionary forces while exposing the nuns' behinds. When one pamphleteer wrote that some bottoms saw air for the first time in 26 years, he also implied that the Dames brought the Counterrevolution (and the nuns' sexuality) out of a long-standing bastion of secrecy. According to the same witty pamphleteer, the Dames also permitted "surprised spectators" to partake in the judgment by "making them see" the nuns.[138] The exhibition underwrote a collective, and therefore sovereign, judgment. Although the Dames dealt the slaps, the spectators' gaze dealt communal authority. The *Liste de toutes les sœurs & dévotes qui ont été fouettées par les Dames des Marchés* described this dynamic between the Dames and the onlookers:

> It was truly a very-pleasing spectacle, to see each one of these good lively market women seize one of these sweet things, pull aside their skirts, and expose to the air their delicate posteriors on which, with their robust hands, our ladies applied redoubled strikes, the air resounded with the correction that these bigots had deserved.[139]

A journalist seconded the collective sentiment, asserting, "No part of the people is duped by their hypocrisy."[140] Another reported that the Dame swatted the nuns "under the eyes of the police," who in standing by conveyed their endorsement.[141]

As shown in Figure 2.1, the image "The miraculous thing which happened in Paris April 6, the Year of Grace 1791" parodies the nuns' fate while underscoring the spectators' role.[142] Several Dames armed with switches punish a bare-bottomed nun as other citizens gather around. The print pokes fun at the sisters' delusions of martyrdom by enshrining one nun's naked rear in a blinding halo of light. St. Benoît Labre descends from heaven carrying the monarchical fleur-de-lis and the papal proclamation forbidding the clergy from taking the oath to the Revolution.[143] Emerging from the clouds, he places a floral crown on the nun's beaming "saint behind," as the accompanying poem describes it. One of the Dames des Halles is taken aback by the descending saint, another falls on her knees praying, the one wielding the switch appears unmoved, but most importantly for communal judgment, one spectator wields a spy glass for a better look at it all. Though intentionally humorous, the detail drives home an important point: the Dames continued to publicly enact their citizenship by embedding their activism within a wider collectivity.

Splashed about in newspapers, pamphlets, and at least five published drawings, the Dames' spree left more than bodily marks and reached beyond firsthand witnesses. Printers rushed to cash in on the material. Some newspapers offered tongue-in-cheek accounts alongside serious reports. Journalist Gorsas

Figure 2.1 "The Miraculous Thing which Happened in Paris April 6, the Year of Grace 1791." BnF De Vinck 3497, "Fait miraculeux arrivé à Paris l'an de salut de 1791, le six avril," 1791, etching, 25.5 cm × 30 cm.

printed an erratum in his paper explaining that the Miramionnes' treasurer contacted him and offered to prove that she did, in fact, have two buttocks. He asserted that he would amend the count without requiring demonstrative evidence.[144] Even Baudouin, the National Assembly's prolific printer, published his own *Grand détail concernant les dévots et les dévotes qui ont été fouettés par les dames de la Halle à Paris*.[145]

Pamphleteers delighted in the Dames' paradoxical activism: it unveiled the surprisingly porous boundary between formal political discourse and rough-hewn popular tactics. The infamous *Liste des Culs Aristocrates et Anti-Constitutionnels, qui ont été fouettés hier* was an instant hit. Far from the sterile reports on government activity, the *Liste des Culs Aristocrates et Anti-Constitutionnels* rejoiced in the topsy-turvy. It proclaimed that thinking heads had been at the center the revolution but "who would have ever thought that ASSES would dare put themselves at the fore of the fatherland, & would want their turn to figure into history." The *Liste* played with the inverted order and chaos that allowed the "heroines of the Revolution" to pass "the judgment and punishment" they saw fit. The author describes at great lengths the physical appearance of each order's exposed behinds. He categorically describes the "truly beautiful perspective" of the Miramionnes' behinds, the Récolettes' "pumpkins of Moses," the ugly, blackened, and fouled rears of the Sisters of Saint-Sulpice, Saint-Laurent, Sainte-Marguéritte, la Magdeleine, Saint-Germain-l'Auxerrois, and warns that the deceptively tanned and fleshy bottoms of the Filles du Calvaire could be mistaken as patriot rears but, alas, they are also soiled. He closes the inventory by confirming that "an exact study" found 621 buttocks whipped.[146]

When the Dames des Halles "corrected" the nuns, they implicitly waged a war over patriotic womanhood and emerged victorious as "citizen mommies."[147] Parodies of the incident portray "true mothers" among the Dames forcing "saint women," who are not very holy after all, into compliance with the national community.[148] In the image "Le Fanatisme corrigée ou La Discipline patriotique," illustrated in Figure 2.2, a Dame spanks a nun who is praying in the shadow of a cross marked "obedience to the Law."[149] Trampled underfoot are three papers: "Bref de Pie VI," "Maniement de Msgr l'Archevêque de Paris," and "Actes d...Apo..." (presumably the royalist newspaper *Actes des Apôtres*). These papers serve as the only masculine presence. The domineering Dame has forced the nun into a submissive position. The sister is bent over, her tucked praying hands and elbows protect her flanks while she implores God. The market woman's breasts hang out of her dress in close proximity to the nun's naked rear. Like symbolic, if erotically charged, revolutionary allegories, the Dame's bare breasts hint at her "natural" rage as a mother against those who have poisoned her children. The Dame's fertile, reproductive parts sharply contrast with the nun's barren lower half.[150] The Dame-mother feeds familial and political life; the nun only produces fecal matter.[151]

Of course, the Dames' carnivalesque tactics sexually stigmatized the nuns and augmented the stinging gendered critiques. Since the nuns' virginity was supposed to reflect their spiritual purity, the revolutionaries could overturn their clout by attacking their sexuality. During the eighteenth century, the French believed that feminine moral authority was encoded in a woman's face.[152] Thus, the pamphlets undermined the nuns' feminine virtue by analyzing their character and counterrevolutionary intentions from their chaste naked rears. One sympathetic man protested that the Dames "exposed half-nude the poor recluses to the vilest and the most enthusiastic libertines of the capital."[153]

On the whole, the accounts stress that the majority of the direct contact occurred between the Dames des Halles and the nuns.[154] This physical separation of sexed bodies was crucial. Without male intervention, the Dames could invert the nuns' claims to bodily and religious purity, while protecting their violence from lewd critiques. Nonetheless, the Dames' "small correction on women by

Figure 2.2 "Corrected Fanaticism or Patriotic Discipline." BnF Estampes Réserve Fol QB-201 (124), "Le Fanatisme corrigée ou la Dicipline [*sic*] patriotique" (Paris: Chez Villeneuve, 1791), etching, 14.5 cm × 11cm.

women," as one paper defined it, relied heavily on approving spectators of both sexes.[155] In addition, two accounts carefully described how the Dames wielded "verges" against the nuns' naked rears. The word meant "switch" but could also imply "penis."[156] The first newspaper used the word to mock a lone man's complaint that libertines plotted the spankings. The newspaper satirizes his objection that there were "women armed with *verges*" who "stripped" the nuns.[157] The second journal defended the Dames' actions by characterizing them as "some strikes of *verges* given aptly and very decently to the nuns who let the sacred fire of patriotism extinguish within them."[158] Thus, the journalists portrayed the

Dames as an extension of male authority to further taint the nuns' past chastity and current nakedness.[159] Undersexed or oversexed, the nuns maternally and politically failed in contrast to the merchant mothers. Far from blaming the violence on women's emotional gendered deficiencies, most Parisians praised the Dames' strokes and the patriotic maternal ideal they protected.

The Dames' bold initiative raised a recurring question: how should citizens defend the fatherland outside formal institutions like government bodies, sectional assemblies, clubs, and the militia? *La Chronique de Paris* feared the "disorder" that the Dames' initiative caused: "If [these scenes] make young people laugh & amuse the unoccupied, they disagreeably affect the sensible man, the honest citizen."[160] The Commune itself was not amused, but hesitated to condemn the Dames' patriotic intentions. Peuchet, the chief of police, issued a statement declaring: "The latest disorders against the religious houses, against the individuals who live there, have a crude character and show a mindlessness unworthy of enlightened people." He insisted, "There exists a well-distinguished line of demarcation, in relation to social order, between individual acts of liberty and those of the public authorities."[161] On April 8, the municipal representatives decreed that no one could congregate in the religious houses and forbade anyone "to commit any excess against whoever this may be."[162] One month later, the Jacobin Society in conjunction with Mayor Bailly posted signs that if anyone rallied the "poissardes" to whip the cloistered nuns, or insulted citizens wearing religious symbols, they would swiftly receive "the penalty of an exemplary punishment!"[163]

Despite the Commune's objections, the Dames' actions decisively bolstered the Civil Constitution of the Clergy. Mere days after the spanking spree, 700 teachers of poor children lined up at the Commune to swear the patriotic oath.[164] Around the same time, posters spread rumors that the king received communion alongside aristocrats from nonjuring priests. When the king attempted to travel to Saint Cloud for Easter Mass on April 18, the Dames des Halles led crowds at the Tuileries shouting that the king "had at his home refractory bishops, he gives asylum at Versailles to refractory priests, the King himself is not complying to the law that he sanctioned; he escapes us [to Saint Cloud]."[165] The Parisian National Guard refused to cut a path through the crowds for the king to depart.[166] The Dames and the Parisians they rallied successfully blocked the king from leaving Paris.[167]

As the Dames backed the Assembly's religious reforms, their relationship with the reluctant monarch became increasingly tenuous. Rather than accepting royal sovereignty, the Dames acted frustrated with a king who would not respond to citizens' demands. To combat the nonjuring clergy, the Dames continued to employ public demonstrations, but they did not cast them as Old Regime rituals. Instead, they legitimized their activism as civic work that politically, maternally, and spiritually defended the nation. While this position empowered the market women, their extrainstitutional organization left them in limbo. Increasingly unhitched from the monarch, the Dames' political place became unclear alongside state representative bodies.

The King's Flight and the Flight from the King

On June 21, 1791, the king and his family fled the capital under the cover of night and headed for the German borderlands. Liberated from Parisian pressure, Louis planned to reverse the Revolution with military support. However, the townspeople of Varennes shattered the king's plans when they halted his carriage and returned him to the National Assembly.[168] After this flight to Varennes, the Dames boldly signaled their discontent with the king and politically abandoned him. The day after his return, the Dames marched through the National Assembly with the National Guard, the Forts de Halle, and some inhabitants of the Faubourg Saint-Antoine in order "to swear an inviolable patriotism." Before the deputies, they publicly professed their loyalty to the Constitution while omitting the king.[169]

Two months later, the Dames refused to give the king his ritual song and bouquet on Saint Louis's feast day. A British observer noted the Dames' cost them their "annual gift of a hundred louis" that the king usually offered them.[170] When five retailers went to perform the tradition without their colleagues' approval, the other Dames castigated the rogue merchants. They feared that the public would inadvertently associate the entire group with the appearance, which would tarnish their patriotic image.[171] Instead of complimenting the king, the Dames visited the National Assembly in the following months.[172]

The king's flight in June and the suppression of religious confraternities in August gave the Dames an opening to reconfigure their place within the spiritual triumvirate of religion, nation, and king.[173] On August 27, two days after refusing to pay the king homage on his feast day, the Dames des Halles appeared before the National Assembly. There, they dissolved their Old Regime confraternities dedicated to the Virgin Mary and Saint Louis, the king's ancestor.[174] The Dames' public gesture distanced them from the disgraced king and strengthened their ties to the indivisible body politic that rejected corporate divisions.[175]

On October 1, 1791, the newly elected Legislative Assembly assumed its post and by October 19, the Dames were requesting the floor. Their address made clear their loyalty to their deputies and transferred paternal authority from the king to the legislators. As revolutionary mothers and as representatives of the sovereign people, the Dames sanctioned the deputies' labor. Their spokesperson attested, "What gentle satisfaction, . . . what pleasure for a mother to say to her young children: Behold, our benefactors; behold, those who saved us." The Dames professed that they taught their children to admire their patriotic father-deputies.[176] At the rostrum, the President replied,

> When the nation was in irons, you were able to conserve a happy independence and one saw you often in their palaces [assembly halls] making the deputies hear the praise of Liberty. During the Revolution, you encapsulated the greatest energy accompanying your devotion to accelerating progress, accompanying your struggle against enemies [, which] will continue to merit the eternal goodwill of your fellow citizens for your unique virtues.

The President's speech acknowledged the Dames' exceptional initiatives, confirmed their patriotism, and indebted their "concitoyens" (fellow citizens) to their "example."[177]

Yet, not all the Dames' "concitoyens" eagerly accepted them as a serious political group in fall 1791. Shortly after the Dames' visit, a caricature satirized their motivations. In "Les Parques Nationales Parisiennes," three fishwives crowd around Pétion, Paris's new mayor, at the edge of the marketplace. Pétion is trapped in a barrel that perhaps held the merchants' cod or herring. Each of the three poissarde "Fates" holds a spool of thread and their fish. They have looped their threads over a lantern post and attached a sword dangling over Pétion's head. Punning on the mayor's name, the caption reads "Fart ["Pet"] . . . Asshole Go . . . since you [informal] do not want to give us anything to drink, we are going to cut your Cord. By the well intentioned [three poissardes], for his reception as Mayor October 18, 1791."[178] The caption suggests that the poissarde Fates sentenced Pétion to death for neglecting to offer them drinks at his inauguration. The artist critiques market women who measure justice by libations and who operate at the fringe of the revolutionary political system.[179] Nonetheless, by depicting them as "fates," the artist uneasily acknowledges the Dames' cheeky power. The humorous image bursts with condescension but concedes the market women's continued sway over political figures.

As citizenship became increasingly expressed through political institutions and societies,[180] the sea of proliferating revolutionary bodies diluted the Dames' influence. After the Legislative Assembly took its seat in the fall of 1791, the Dames focused their interventions more and more on commercial and subsistence concerns like access to public market space and practical currency. Officials, the police, and pamphleteers remained especially keen on co-opting the market women during food shortages. During the sugar crisis of January 1792, journalist Condorcet appealed to Parisians to give up sugar. He reasoned, "Let the Dames swear it with enthusiasm, & let all of France imitate them." According to

Condorcet, such a move would foil aristocrats causing chaos through soaring prices.[181]

While the Dames gradually reframed their occupational work as their primary contributions to the nation, they channeled their nonmarketplace performances into donations or revolutionary festivities. Through gift-giving, the Dames sustained a feedback loop of public display and governmental affirmation. In May of 1792, the Dames donated to the Legislative Assembly in light of war against the Austrians. Assuring the deputies of "our inalterable patriotism," the market women promised to make the same offering twice a year for the war's duration. In doing so, the Dames created space for officials to publicly confirm their patriotism twice a year.[182] On June 11, the Dames again donated to the Legislative Assembly and alluded to their reputation. They reiterated that their "vows are sincere; because we are known to love Liberty."[183]

From June to August 1792, French forces repeatedly lost against the advancing Austro-Prussian coalition, the king suspiciously vetoed the Legislative Assembly's decrees, and citizens multiplied their calls for a republic across France. Tensions burst on August 10, 1792, when the Parisian sections and fédérés from the provinces led an insurrection against the king. As they stormed the Tuileries, the king fled to the Assembly, where the deputies suspended him from his executive function. Some of the more moderate and conservative deputies fled in fear for their own lives and the remaining deputies soon called for a new assembly to discern France's undoubtedly republican future.[184]

By this apex of the republican surge, the king's supporters considered the Dames hostile to the monarchy. During the fallout from August 1792, police found the royal Intendant de la Liste Civile's private letters. Intendant Delaporte painted the market women as a threat to the king. He wrote to his allies that, when God judged the revolutionaries, "all the women will be shaved [guillotined] . . . finishing with the Dames de la Halle. These are women in love with independence and novelty, [they] who have led men astray; they deserve the whip; let us shave them, & let us obey God."[185] The Dames confirmed their monarchical indifference days before the king mounted the scaffold in January 1793 after De Salignac, a royalist pamphleteer, hatched a plot to rescue the king. He called on the Dames to lead the last-ditch effort:

> Citoyennes of Paris, women de la Halle, who every year brought bouquets to the queen, to the royal family, & from them received a welcome as gracious as generous, repair your past faults; bring Louis XVI back to his palace, this illustrious offspring of Saint-Louis, Charlemagne & Henry the Great. . . . Let Louis be delivered next Monday.[186]

The Dames ignored De Salignac's pleas. In reality, the Dames had already severed ties with the unfaithful monarch after his flight to Varennes. They were willing to allow the National Convention to sever his head too.

In October 1789, municipal officials had maintained that Dames' *bonnes citoyennes* medals were not motivated by "interest nor vanity" but were born "pure & in good conscience."[187] In contrast, during 1793, some Parisians complained that club members were wearing medals and "distinguishing themselves from other citizens." These Parisians protested that the markers "intended to resurrect distinctions," which were "contrary to equality."[188] Under the republic, the revolutionaries hesitated to embrace political exceptionality. These homogenizing impulses challenged the Dames' traditional gestures, issue-driven interventions, and special influence as popular representatives. The Dames' *bonnes citoyennes* medals no longer granted them unique status in 1793; in fact, the Dames risked estranging themselves from the general will if they touted their singularity.

Beginning with the Jacobin-dominated republic, the Dames principally became defenders of their local community who appealed to the national government. They lost the role they had played from 1789 to 1793 as titular defenders of the Revolution joined to the national government. With the formation of more political structures like clubs, neighborhood assemblies, and local militias, the Dames became superfluous as a link between citizens and the state. In addition, the king's fall had made the association between the Dames and the monarch less enticing in prorevolutionary propaganda.

Across these regime changes, the Dames consistently crafted their revolutionary citizenship via civic work. Through their situational activism, the Dames publicly incorporated themselves into the revolutionary body politic. They transformed their image as Third Estate representatives into a reputation as defenders of the Revolution. The Dames gradually divorced the source of their legitimacy from royal sanctioning rituals and inscribed it within the sovereign people. Because the Dames portrayed citizenship as societal engagement, they never created a formal political organization. Instead, the Dames rallied their numbers to respond to issues as they arose. This embodied activism proved flexible and advantageous early in the Revolution but became a liability by 1793 as representative politics became highly institutionalized.

From the outset of the Revolution, the Dames consistently advanced the idea of the familial state in which citizens had gendered duties. As poor mothers, the Dames financially and emotionally sustained their families, which they argued would serve the nation. And as citizens, they obliged first the king and then revolutionary officials to fulfill what they considered paternal duties. While confronting counterrevolutionary nuns, the market women performed female citizenship as republican mothers and spiritual guardians. Although the Dames considered gendered work a critical part of their citizenship, they did not artic-ulate gender as the initial filter for delineating citizenship or as its immutable starting point. Instead, they crafted their civic identity by together fusing their service as wives and mothers, their utility as citizen-workers, and their patri-otism as defenders of the nation.

As the Revolution progressed, the Dames developed notions of economic citizenship that complemented their civic interventions and gendered labors of 1789 to 1793. The Dames' occupational work became a particularly rich node through which they continually recast their rights and duties from 1789 to 1799. Through issues such as public commercial space, practical cash, price controls, occupational licenses, and taxes, the market women negotiated a new type of economic citizenship that, like their civic activism and gendered labor, turned to public utility as its legitimizing refrain.

3

Occupying the Marketplace

The Battle over Public Space, Particular Interests, and the Body Politic

On September 18, 1791, there was more commotion than usual at les Halles. National Guardsmen marched by retailers hawking fruits and vegetables, mounted officials weaved among parasols and makeshift stalls, and patrols squeezed through rare patches of space among Parisians buying food. Perched on the roof of storage facilities and leaning out of neighboring windows, workers and residents surveyed the scene below. Their gaze rested anxiously on the decorated liberty tree, where a crier proclaimed that Louis XVI had accepted the constitution. The elated crowd cheered around the liberty tree, whose branches towered over the bustling commerce below.[1]

The tree was an apt rallying point. It marked the commercial space with the optimism of regeneration. However, planting the liberty tree in the earth of les Halles proved far easier than implementing revolutionary ideology in les Halles. Like the tree's maze of roots, the revolutionaries' attempts to implement equality in the marketplace were fraught with twists. Officials revised Old Regime and revolutionary laws again and again as marketplace contestations arose. Legislators constantly reconsidered the best way to align revolutionary aspirations and socioeconomic practice in les Halles.

Merchants and consumers keenly understood that regenerating les Halles put their commercial positions and economic livelihoods at stake. Under their parasols near the liberty tree, the Dames des Halles celebrated the constitution. Across the square, the retailers traded from mobile stalls, shops, parasols, counters, and baskets.[2] Piled before them were fish, butter, eggs, vegetables, and fruit for sale. Although the revolutionaries considered les Halles a public space destined to benefit all citizens, the businesses of the Dames and other merchants dotted the landscape with private commercial interests.

When the revolutionaries attempted to dismantle Old Regime socioeconomic privilege in the marketplace, officials were forced to confront the paradox of particular interests on public domain.[3] During the Old Regime, the
king had owned all public domain, since he alone constituted the public body.
Consequently, the king had accorded permissions to individuals to use his domain, including the Parisian marketplace, for their personal benefit. In 1790,
the revolutionaries drastically reconceptualized public domain by insisting it
belonged indiscriminately to the nation's citizens. By reinterpreting the "public"
in "public domain" as the nation rather than the king, officials distinguished the
revolutionary body politic from its Old Regime predecessor.

Yet, the revolutionaries struggled to define the "public" as more than a vague
antithesis of its royal precursor. The 1792 collapse of the monarchy would further magnify the problem. Even if the revolutionary "public" negated past
definitions, the question remained: what was it? With no firm definition, the
concept shook the foundations of the state and the body politic. Citizens seized
the term for personal profit and administrators harnessed it to expand their
purview. Police official Lacorée cynically noted that entrepreneurs donned the
"cloak of public good" to advance commercial projects.[4] "Public utility" blurred
the interests of merchants and consumers and the divide between production
and consumption.[5] Diverse factions fashioned public utility as their legislative cornerstone. Constitutional monarchists, liberals, radicals, and Directorial
republicans alike justified their economic and political goals by their "utility."[6]
However, they pursued vastly different policies in les Halles.

To embed liberty and equality in the public marketplace, the revolutionaries
first resolved to banish exclusive privileges like royal permissions and monopolies.
But, when deputies and merchants offered diverging reforms for the space, their
disagreements revealed serious vulnerabilities in the revolutionary project. If the
regenerated marketplace were truly a public domain freed from feudal bonds,
how could officials regulate les Halles without shackling liberty? And if all citizens held equal claim to the marketplace, how could legislators allow merchants
to use public space for particular interests without resurrecting privilege? As the
staging center for the entire capital's food supply, les Halles became an especially
charged arena for such debates.

This chapter examines the economically and conceptually volatile debates
over market space from 1789 through 1793. It asks how les Halles became a site
for working out principles of liberty and equality while wrestling with the relationship among particular interests, public utility, and public space. On one side,
officials struggled to reform the market without creating special regulations.
On the other, marketplace actors demanded exceptional rules within supposedly national and universally just laws. Against this backdrop, governmental
institutions like the Commune, the Department, and the Assembly battled for

control of marketplace domain to assert their jurisdiction among overlapping "publics." The interpretive space surrounding the marketplace nearly dwarfed the rambling 6,000 square meters of trade in les Halles.[7]

The chapter begins by examining how legislators redefined the public marketplace through piecemeal reform. Property ownership and administrative privilege set the terms of debate over the market's uncertain future. Merchants and consumers simultaneously sparred, literally and figuratively, over marketplace earth. While struggling to justify their places of sale, the Dames navigated between particular and public interests.[8] In 1792, they collided with parasol renters and one another in a legal suit over royal contracts, revolutionary administration, and public ownership. The Dames who emerged victorious appealed to nascent institutions to defend their "useful" commerce. From 1789 to 1793, the Dames des Halles carved out physical space and their place in the body politic on the ground of les Halles.

Conceptualizing Public Domain and Regulating Les Halles under the Monarchy

During the Old Regime, the king contained the "whole public reality of the political sphere" in his person, so public domain could not exist apart from royal domain.[9] While "public space" could refer to a location where the populace gathered, the label of royal domain stressed that the king owned the physical property.[10] Thus, les Halles qualified as both public domain and a public space.

The marketplace belonged to the part of the king's domain known as the *voie publique* or literally the "public way." The *voie publique* encompassed all the roads, highways, rivers, ports, squares, parks, places, and markets included in the king's domain. In order to collect revenue and oversee his vast *voie publique*, the king granted privileges of "little voierie" to nobles and officials. With these royally sanctioned monopolies, nobles and officials could charge individuals to set up or rent commercial structures (like stalls and stands) on the *voie publique* and regulate their use.[11]

As part of the royal domain, les Halles fell under the king's personal discretion. In the thirteenth century, Saint Louis began the charitable tradition of giving permissions to poor widowed women and orphan girls to set up stalls and shops on his *voie publique*. These women retailers became the earliest Dames des Halles.[12]

By 1607, Henri IV allowed his agents to grant permissions more broadly to retailers in les Halles. Yet, in contrast to Saint Louis's original charitable goals, Henri IV developed his permission system to regulate merchants' chaotic and illegal usage of his *voie publique*. The proliferation of street-clogging stalls had sent his roads and markets sprawling out of control. Henri denounced this "kind of violation [as] all the more reprehensible as it became general by the liberty with which everyone allowed themselves to commit it." In exchange for permission to sell on the *voie publique*, Henri stipulated that the merchants' shops must not block throughways. For Henri and his successors, "liberty" on the *voie publique* was incompatible with the nature of the *voie publique* not only because it produced chaos, but also because individuals needed the king's permission to sell on his public territory.[13]

Despite Henri IV's crackdown, les Halles lapsed back into a congested and dangerous state. In 1784, Louis XVI conceived of his own project to tame les Halles once and for all.[14] Citing the overcrowded and dilapidated marketplace, he drafted plans to raze most of the terrain and reconstruct many of the permanent shelters. He hoped to separate wholesale and retail space, improve the circulation of provisioning traffic, and rebuild the overstressed, 200-year-old halles (market coverings) that bent over Parisians and their goods.[15] He would also streamline the web of marketplace permissions and structures that had multiplied exponentially since Saint Louis. In May 1784, the king ordered "the absolute demolition of sedentary & semi-sedentary Shops" in the Parisian region and stipulated that their owners absorb the costs. He denounced the makeshift sedentary stalls that "resemble[d] houses more than shops" and clogged his streets. Louis XVI lamented that merchants caused disorder when they did not secure permission to build such structures on the *voie publique*. Unlike Henri IV, who only sought to take stock of and redistribute permissions, Louis XVI planned to completely reconstruct the physical marketplace. Louis stipulated that any new personal structures must be "purely mobile." Merchants had to erect and remove their shelters from the *voie publique* each day.[16]

Despite these sweeping physical changes, Louis XVI continued some administrative mainstays in les Halles. For over a century, Louis's predecessors had farmed out privileges of spatial regulation, structural maintenance, rent collection, and parasol placement to special companies. Entrepreneurs paid annually for these privileges in the form of long-term leases called *baux emphytéotiques*.[17] In the marketplace, holders of the *baux emphytéotiques* gained exclusive rights to construct permanent shelters or place parasols on the king's domain. They made a profit by renting out these small sheltered spaces to merchants.[18] Retailers, including the Dames des Halles, depended on these parasols and structures to protect their goods and to conduct their daily trade. However, by the 1780s, the king had fractured his marketplace public domain into so many contracts, rights, and privileges that he could not reconstruct les Halles and reconcile them all.[19] So the king ordered all individuals to surrender their titles and receive an indemnity.[20]

Louis XVI then streamlined the unruly mass of parasol and stall renting permissions into two new monopolies. He consolidated control over the destruction, reconstruction, upkeep, and rent of the physical structures under one *bail emphytéotique* granted to Jean-Baptiste Doré. In exchange for annual rent of 6,000 livres and a large deposit to maintain the pavement, Doré's company gained the exclusive 99-year right to construct the new halles, shops, and boutiques on the king's domain and to rent out these spaces in les Halles.[21] Under this system, the king could still collect revenue on public property but would not have to administer or maintain the physical space. To continue Saint Louis's altruistic precedent, the king ordered Doré to rent parasols benevolently "in favor of the retail merchants, the [male] Détailleurs and [female] Detailleuresses, at all times."[22]

Thus, in 1789, the revolutionaries inherited a crucial public space powerfully centralized under one leaseholder who, quite literally, razed others' interests in the marketplace. For legislators, the *bail emphytéotique* fell squarely on the divide between royal privilege and entrepreneurial contracts. Its concerns extended to property law, everyday commerce, and notions of the "public." The Dames knew that any revisions in the lease or Louis's regulations would directly affect their ability to sell in the marketplace. In the revolutionary context of 1789, the deputies and merchants scrambled to rearticulate their support or rejection of the king's original modernizing plans for les Halles.

Reforming the Revolutionary Marketplace: Redefining Public Space and Legislating the *Voie Publique*

Revolutionary officials and journalists claimed that regenerating the marketplace could rectify the damage inflicted by Old Regime privilege on an inherently beneficial system. In a speech to the Legislative Assembly, Deputy Dufriche-Valazé argued that marketplaces first appeared because farmers lacked manufactured goods from the city and city-dwellers needed foodstuffs from the countryside. He enshrined the marketplace as the social cornerstone of primitive communities and concluded that "this institution was a natural order of human communications."[23] For Dufriche-Valazé, markets advantageously centralized commerce while fostering economic, social, and political bonds.

To purify market relations, the revolutionaries sought to end excessive dues. In their eyes, the burden of overwrought permissions had harmed the merchants and underpinned the Old Regime's abusive power. Journalist Prudhomme insisted that merchants had established the first periodic markets to escape the "oppressive" tariffs demanded by the nobles and clergy. In biting prose, he wrote that the merchants had been "pillaged and extorted by the henchmen of feudalism."[24] Prudhomme argued that marketplace reform should be a pillar of the revolutionary project. If privilege was correctly purged from "our public markets," then, Prudhomme reasoned, "nearly anyone who wanted to [re]establish the Old Regime would not succeed."[25] For Prudhomme, a free and just marketplace would provide a bulwark against counterrevolutionary agendas.

The deputies shared Prudhomme's reforming sentiment but waited seven months after abolishing feudalism to address marketplace privilege. In March 1790, the National Assembly officially suppressed, without compensation, all dues and privileges concerning the entrance and storing of goods in all fairs, markets, or halles.[26] To completely overhaul the marketplace, however, the deputies would have to do more than annul royally endowed permissions. The deputies would need to reconcile the entire balance of liberty, particular interests, and regulation within the marketplace.

Yet, the revolutionaries struggled to agree on the meaning of "liberty" and "freedom" in the marketplace. Some, like Prudhomme, advocated a radical laissez-faire policy in which the marketplace would not "follow any other law than the combined interest of sellers and buyers" since regulatory "mania is the plague of commerce." For like-minded revolutionaries, upholding the individual's political freedom meant honoring the individual's free economic will as well.[27] State regulation of the marketplace might slide into new privilege. Drawing on models of natural man, Prudhomme insisted that commerce "flourishes where it finds itself free: it is born completely and naturally there."[28] Consequently, he interpreted revolutionary "liberty" in the marketplace as the freedom of two or more individuals to exchange goods.

The Third Estate electors for the Parisian neighborhood of Saint-Gervais sought to segregate the commercial and social elements of "liberty" in the marketplace. They advocated a commercial liberty that would allow individuals to freely choose their own roles in market transactions while maintaining social privilege. Paradoxically, these electors argued that nobles should be able to participate in commerce, including retail, without forfeiting their titles.[29] Whereas Prudhomme viewed marketplace privilege as the lynchpin in the entire system of socioeconomic hierarchy, the Saint-Gervais electors sought to suppress economic prescriptions while upholding social distinctions. In a shackled marketplace, the social privilege of nobles as well as the social disadvantages of merchants could block "free" economic activity.

When the National Assembly purged the market of Old Regime permissions and institutions in pursuit of "liberty," it also destroyed the only regulatory system in place. Since many people shared the same space and used market structures, officials needed to implement new regulation in accord with revolutionary ideals or recast old approaches. To advocate for advantageous rules, citizens across France conceptually divorced utility from privilege. In December 1789, representatives from Bretagne presented the case that customs and marketplace dues collected in the king's name (rather than for the nobles' benefit) must qualify as "extractions," not "privileges." They argued that such dues were "more like taxes than feudal rights," were "useful to the public," and were payment for using the king's domain. As for the region's nobles, several had built the halles and market structures that played a pivotal role in sheltering and storing foodstuffs. Their Assembly deputies argued that nobles should continue to lease their structures on the king's land and that the revenue generated from the rent would offset construction and upkeep costs.[30] The nobles adopted the discourse of public utility to dodge the stain of privilege and defend their private enterprises.

Three months later, in March 1790, the National Assembly began to legally split useful proprietorship from privilege. The deputies separated the ownership of physical market structures from the dues on domain and commercial activity. The National Assembly decreed that buildings and halles would "remain the property of those to whom they belonged." Therefore, nobles and entrepreneurs could continue to rent out their market structures, but they could not charge rent for the earth. The ground itself remained public domain.[31] The deputies decreed that the rules would be standard for market structures across France. After all, if the "public" remained constant across the nation, must not the state uniformly regulate equivalent domains?

Since revolutionary notions of liberty in the marketplace favored democratizing space that was originally noble or royal domain, market reform extensively reconceptualized public domain and public space. As the revolutionaries abolished feudal privilege, different groups and individuals forfeited their property to the nation. Most of this property, like Church lands, became *biens nationaux* or national lands, which the deputies marked to sell off and disappear into private hands. The state would only "continue to hold things unsuitable for individual ownership, such as waterways and roads" and some markets.[32] Utility, or the state's reason for holding such property, thus assumed a legal civic quality. Although these spaces retained their "public" title, their classification now dovetailed with a new political public. This public no longer implied ownership by the king, but ownership by the sovereign nation, which would use it for public good.

Officials further distinguished between "national domain," which belonged to the national government, and "public domain," which could belong to the nation, departments, or municipalities. In November 1790, the National Assembly decreed that "the national domain . . . encompasses all the land property and all the real or mixed rights, which belong to the nation" whereas "all the portions of a national territory which are not susceptible to the title of private property, are considered to be dependents of public domain." Therefore, public domain became a gray area: it could include national domain (which belonged to the nation) as well as communal property like the marketplaces (which belonged to local municipalities). The deputies thus legally dismantled the king's property, but the ambiguity over how citizens would own the refashioned domain led to institutional contests to claim it. While the National Assembly gave police jurisdiction over order in what they called "public places," the balance of power between municipal and national governments in these spaces remained uncertain.[33]

Through their 1790 decrees, the National Assembly delineated the marketplace and the *voie publique* alike as "public domain." In Paris, the vast *voie publique* included not only the marketplace but also the roads, squares, and bridges. In their emerging logic, the deputies redefined public domain primarily through utility rather than ownership. They increasingly defined "public domain" primarily as a communal space that proved useful to multiple segments of the society and that any governmental branch could regulate. This major shift in property law transformed how individuals articulated their membership in the public and defended their quotidian access to the *voie publique*.

With the right to use the *voie publique* no longer emanating from the king's graces, officials struggled to balance citizens' competing interests. While trying to prevent religious groups' processions through the streets in February 1792, the Legislative Assembly asserted that the *voie publique* "belong[s] to the public, that is to say, equally and at all times, to all citizens . . . , [It] must therefore always be free to all and for all; but it ceases to be free, if an individual or a particular society ha[s] the right to divert it, even momentarily, to the destination of the particular usages which it would make it [exclusively] their own."[34] Because all people equally composed the "public," every individual streaming across the *voie publique* held equal ownership there. The Parisian municipal government seconded the Assembly's sentiment in August of 1792 when it reiterated that "the voie publique belong[s] to all, no one can dispose of it for their particular advantage." It thus needed to remain "free" and accessible.[35] Simply put, individuals shared ownership of the public domain with their fellow citizens. How the state should administer the domain and ensure just access was more difficult to discern.

Avoiding New Privilege in les Halles: Regulating and Negotiating Public Space

From 1790 to 1792, the deputies and merchants alike tackled a major ideological problem: How could a society abolish privilege in the name of freedom but then establish a new regulatory system in the name of this same liberty? Working out the administrative and regulatory details governing everyday market interactions brought multiple groups into the debate. Merchants, consumers, and entrepreneurs jockeyed to defend their commercial interests, while municipal, departmental, and national governments wrestled to seize the reins from one another.

In the Parisian markets, the Dames des Halles and other merchants contested the deputies' reform of commercial space and shelters. On the one hand, the Dames and other retailers protested that owners of permanent shelters exploited public space. Retailers tore down halles owned by private companies that charged high rental rates. On the other hand, retailers protected their own makeshift shelters from destruction. The king and Assembly had planned to raze these mobile structures in order to clear and reconstruct les Halles. To make their voices heard, some Dames and other sellers embraced new forms of political practice like petitions and justice of the peace suits as well as old standards of collective activism such as disregarding police orders. Despite their alliances, the Dames' claims to personal commercial space often conflicted with one another. While officials attempted to rebuild and regulate the marketplace, the Dames reinterpreted public space to defend their livelihoods.

Since the reconceptualization of the *voie publique* legitimized individuals' use of public domain, Parisian merchants found new ways to frame their commercial interests and to defend their right to sell on the *voie publique*. In June 1792, other merchants had complained that retailer Marie Leroy's stall structure impeded the Passage des Variétés. So police commissioners visited to investigate. The fruit seller told police that her commercial activity did not "disturb the voie publique" and that others would attest that she did not block her neighbors. Leroy did not defend her selling on the *voie publique* in terms of her personal rights. Rather, she spoke of how her commercial use of communal space did not impede her neighbors' own equal access. Leroy focused on collective ownership and positioned herself within that community to protect her business.[36]

Retailers straddled the tensions among particular use, communal ownership, and circulation in public space. Paradoxically, the *voie publique* explicitly facilitated commerce as a "public utility," but the revolutionaries feared that particular interests, including those merchants using stalls, might undermine traffic flow and the "terrain belonging to all the citizens."[37] Before the justice of the peace, Citoyenne Beau, a fruitière, challenged how fellow fruitière Aimée Capet sold on public domain. Beau complained that Capet had set up her stall on the Pont au Change "blocking the *voie publique* there." Capet's stall on the bridge caused traffic to bottleneck and a carriage wheel nearly crushed Beau as a result. The competing uses of the *voie publique*—namely commerce and circulation— inevitably conflicted with each other.[38] Moreover, mobile retail merchants like Marie Leroy and Aimée Capet did not pay taxes based on private commercial property, and the police found it difficult to regulate untethered commercial actors on the *voie publique* and in the public markets.[39]

In public markets, trade logistics required several merchants to employ the same space at different times of the day. The police constantly juggled these overlapping commercial permissions. While monitoring the Carreau de la Halle where butter and eggs were sold, Inspector Baude tried to enforce wholesalers' priority access in the morning and retailers' prerogatives for the rest of the day. Obstinate retailers like Citoyenne Duval encumbered his task by squatting in the wholesalers' morning spaces. The sharp-tongued retailer and her daughter refused to vacate the spot until "the others [retailers] pull out [also]." Duval only imagined the equal division of the *voie publique* within the context of rival retailers. She disregarded wholesalers' claims and focused on the unfair potential advantage of other retailers.[40] Inspector Baude's definition of fair use, in contrast, changed with the time of day.

As in the cases of Citoyennes Leroy, Capet, and Duval, retailers' commercial interests often conflicted with the interests of other merchants who sold on public domain and with consumers who used the *voie publique* for transport. As members of the regenerated public, all groups held theoretically equal claim to public property. Paradoxically, the "liberated" marketplace increased the need for state regulation. Thus, marketplace legislation became an inevitable laboratory for confronting revolutionary contradictions on the ground.

As officials struggled to reimagine ownership, rental systems, and legitimate use of the "public place," they waffled over jurisdiction. The Commune, the department, and the nation all shared legal prerogatives in the Parisian markets. At the local level, merchants and consumers held a distinct stake in les Halles through their municipal affiliation. In December 1789, the National Assembly approved legislation clarifying that "the [structures of the] Halles belong to the communities of their place and location."[41] In 1791, the Commune asserted its control by decreeing that any vehicles arriving to Paris must drive directly to les Halles for sale if they lacked an advance contract with a consumer.[42] But in 1793, the National Convention (previously the Legislative Assembly) went one step further by forbidding all wholesale exchange outside of the marketplace and ruled that provisioning could only take place "in the republic's markets and halles."[43] Les Halles belonged to a regenerated public, but it remained unclear if that public meant the city, the department, or the nation.

The Commune took the lead in applying new ideas of "public" to les Halles by delineating three types of property in the marketplace: permissions, structures, and earth. Since 1784, Doré, holder of the royal *bail emphytéotique* for les Halles, had the privilege of renting spaces and shelters to merchants at his personal discretion.[44] However, in November 1789, the municipal government recalibrated the rent for selling on market space by calculating charges based on the "place." In other words, the Commune directly correlated the merchants' rent to the actual earth on which they sold in les Halles. Under such a calibration, the representatives bypassed sweeping claims to privilege over marketplace property by materially apportioning communal space. The deputies hoped that such standards would appear rational, impartial, and thus just. Under this reorganization, the Dames would pay a flat rate of 6 sous per day to sell on plots of public space.[45]

In spring 1790, the Paris police took another step toward reorganizing open market space. They ordered that the leased hangars built for fruit and vegetable commerce in the old Grain Halls (now the Halle aux Fruits) be destroyed. The police anticipated the demolition would free the *voie publique* for commerce. Merchants would no longer have to rent sheltered spaces to use the marketplace. However, the king had granted Doré the privilege to build fruit halles and collect fees there. Doré's company refused to quickly demolish its structures. *La Chronique de Paris* lamented "the cupidity of a privileged company, sustained by the old police." After one of the fruit hangars had collapsed on four children playing, the paper demanded their immediate removal.[46]

After waiting three weeks for Doré to take responsibility, a group of fruit merchants took action. They accused Doré's company of grossly overcharging merchants to rent the shelters. His structures, they protested, were "a monument of usury on public property." Instead of paying to use the hangars, the merchants clamored that they "must have full liberty to install themselves." Determined to rectify the problem, they marched to the fruit halles to smash the structures. Once there, the merchants and supporters restated their goals in ways that, to one pamphleteer, echoed the order of a political assembly. With hammers in hand, the merchants listened as an "orator" addressed the crowd. He asked if they intended to destroy the shops that promoted usury, crippled "liberty," and were owned "by the old agents of despotism." The crowd responded "yes," the "public deliberation" closed, and the razing commenced. The group even enlisted the National Guard to impose order and limit crowds by closing roads. The merchants quickly reduced the hangars to rubble.[47]

The same pamphleteer juxtaposed corrupt privilege and revolutionary justice to describe how "the people" demolished the structures. The author asserted that the fruit hangars "had been built by the greedy intentions of people favored by the agents of despotism" but that "the vigilance of patriotism" would not permit privilege to continue. Portraying the merchants' actions as responsible, the pamphlet specified that blocking the roads "distanced the ill-intentioned and the brigands who run after groups to excite turmoil and to strike up discord." It closed by insisting that "the citizens of the capital always respect the laws, individual liberty, and legitimate properties." In the eyes of the pamphleteer, the merchants skillfully employed revolutionary liberty, sovereignty, and antiprivilege attitudes to legitimize their initiative.[48]

Pressured by the unrest and confusion over market property, the National Assembly and Louis XVI jointly resumed the king's crusade to clear, enlarge, and reorganize les Halles. The king issued a decree ordering those who had surrendered immobile structures (including houses) in marketplaces to redeem their compensation within three months or lose all indemnities.[49] The Assembly confirmed the Commune's 1789 intentions in July/August 1790. The Assembly reiterated that since "the feudal regime and seigneurial justice had been abolished" no individual (such as Doré) could claim to be the singular owner of or collect dues on the *voie publique*.[50] Therefore, it appears that the Dames des Halles and other retail merchants ceased to pay rent for their places on public earth in 1790. However, approved individuals like Doré could still rent structures on the *voie publique*. The earth of the public domain, the structures built on it, and the permission to rent the earth and structures remained distinct types of property.

Although the king's plan aimed to increase circulation, decrease accidents, and regulate use of the *voie publique*, it temporarily stifled the shelter options available to the Dames and other retailers. The shortage prompted departmental administrators to immediately request that the National Assembly pressure private owners of permanent halles to rent their structures. At the very least, the department suggested, the municipality could buy the private halles so that no shelter lay empty. The Commune could then collect rent on the structures from merchants to repay former owners.[51]

Over the next months, retailers in markets across Paris grew frustrated with their shelter options, which consumed valuable market space as well as their money. In May 1791, a National Guardsman burst through the police commissioner's door to report that the Dames of the Marché de la Place Maubert had taken matters into their own calloused hands. The enraged "fishwives" had torn down the stalls there and were threatening to march to the nearby Marché Saint-Germain to continue their destruction. The gatekeeper rushed to secure the entrance and protect the Saint-Germain shops from similar demise.[52]

Despite its visions for reform, the municipality soon found itself backpedaling to renew "the old rules & ordinances" on the timeless subject of congesting and endangering the *voie publique*. It clarified that "the public liberty does not give any citizen the right to do what harms others." These problems included obstructing the streets, parking carts in undesignated areas in the marketplace, creating opportunities for accidents, and, in the case of putrid makeshift stalls, endangering Parisians' health.[53]

Yet, merchants' habits and thinning patience proved resistant to revolutionary articulations of long-standing concerns. Police in the Arsenal section reported that they could not persuade retail merchants to relocate their stalls from the streets to the marketplace. A dense line of Dames selling fish, fruits, and vegetables refused to budge from their customary street locations. "Complaints, insults, and menaces" met the police's repeated efforts to disperse them. Retailer Marguerite Tripière obstinately occupied the entire corner of the rue St. Paul and the rue St. Antoine and would not change her position, while another fish merchant and her commercial tools clogged up the entrance of the rue St. Paul. The Dames cried so loudly in protest that the police gave up for fear of triggering "a general uprising in Paris." The commissioners reported that neighboring sections experienced similar problems.[54]

In light of the conflicts over stalls and the shops, the Commune negotiated how to regulate and legitimize merchants' use of the marketplace. Ultimately, officials were stymied by the same challenges that Henri IV had encountered two centuries earlier: an excess of liberty on the *voie publique*. Henri IV had interpreted these transgressions as attacks on his own authority and property, whereas the revolutionary officials believed that troublesome merchants misinterpreted the meaning of liberty in the marketplace. In October 1791, the Commune declared that "the right to occupy the *voie publique* [including the markets] whose use belongs to all, but whose exclusive use does not belong to anyone" must not be "abus[ed]" by "false ideas of liberty." Municipal representatives now reasoned that individuals could not erect permanent market structures on "the common terrain."

However, the Commune simultaneously recognized that retailers like the Dames relied on public space and shelters to earn a meager living. The majority of retailers who sold on public domain, rather than from permanent boutiques, were poor. As long as the merchants did not act "contrary to . . . public interest" or disrupt the *voie publique*, the Commune decreed that indigent citizens could sell fruits, vegetables, and herbs from mobile structures. The municipal government articulated that, to qualify for this special charitable permission, an individual had to live in Paris, be a parent, be infirm or over 50, and be impoverished. These stipulations created a quasi-contract between the city and individuals who gained exceptional permissions to occupy public space. The Commune's tolerant policy echoed one National Assembly member's acknowledgment that it was "important to leave to the poor" retail merchants "the means of living" by selling on public domain.[55]

The Commune's concessions reconfigured the paternalistic responsibilities of the state within the revolutionary framework.[56] Although the municipal and national representatives did not use faith-based justifications as had Louis XVI and the kings before him, they still assumed that the state had special responsibilities toward the poor. However, the fine line between Old Regime privilege and revolutionary benevolent permissions on the *voie publique* created major obstacles for marketplace legislation. The new charity requirements also overturned the Dames' advantageous claims to market space as a privileged group. Now, the Dames would have to seek access to space as indigent individuals.

Nonetheless, before the Dames and indigent retailers could secure the special permissions, the old semisedentary shelters still needed to be destroyed according to the king's 1784 plan. Only then could the reconstruction of les Halles continue. However, conflicts quickly arose over the immobile shelters slated for demolition. On October 21, 1791, twenty-eight retailers selling outside the Tuileries petitioned the municipal assembly to save their makeshift stalls. The merchants explained that they previously had shops outside the château at Versailles but had moved with the king and his court to Paris. Unlike the fruit merchants of les Halles who had been forced to rent hangars from Doré if they wanted shelters, the Tuileries retailers appear to have built their own immobile shelters to avoid rent. Appealing to the Commune's paternal responsibilities toward the working poor, the retailers asserted they had been "reduced to the most awful indigence" when they relocated to Paris. They testified that "a great number of poor working mothers" bought their daily scraps of meat from their stalls at low prices. Recalling the deputies' "justice" and "kindness," the merchants extended their request as "founded on humanity." And, reflecting their knowledge of the Commune's concerns, they testified that their shops did not disrupt the *voie publique* and that they locked them at night to ensure public safety.[57]

The male and female retailers on the quais de l'Infante et de l'École likewise feared that officials would force them to tear down their personal stalls. They took to the floor of the Legislative Assembly to reassure the deputies that "Obedience to the law is indisputably the duty of all good citizens." But when the merchants attempted to broach their concerns, the deputies shouted down the orator and ordered that the department directors deal with what they described as a municipal issue.[58] Undeterred, the retailers submitted a petition to the municipal assembly as well as the department directors. To dodge the exceptional appearance of their request, the merchants linked their demand to the plight of "more than 60,000 citizens" who would also suffer from the shops' suppression. They painted themselves as "citizens also inseparable from [the goals of] good order and public tranquility" who would secure their shops at night so as to guarantee public safety. Like the Tuileries merchants, they highlighted their "sad situation," but with a twist of revolutionary guilt. The merchants boldly declared that, since the Old Regime officials had benevolently tolerated their stalls, "they flattered themselves to find the current magistrates to have at least as much humanity and justice as the magistrates of the old government." In essence, the merchants challenged the deputies to have as much generosity as their Old Regime counterparts. Moreover, the merchants boldly hinted that benevolence was intrinsic to the revolutionary spirit.[59]

Retailers who attempted to protect their endangered structures through remnants of privilege fared worse than those who drew on revolutionary discourses of public space. In October 1791, the Dames des Halles who sold fish at the Saint-Germain market also petitioned the Legislative Assembly and the department to protect their stalls. The king's reconstruction project stipulated that three guardhouses would replace their selling posts. However, the female retailers pleaded in terms of the past. They argued that alternative spaces existed for the guardhouses and that it would be an "injustice to deprive them of places that they [the Dames] have occupied since time immemorial." The national and departmental officials did not take great interest in their predicament. By rooting their request in traditional exceptions rather than in antiprivilege frameworks, the Saint-Germain Dames partitioned themselves from the legitimate public. After three months in limbo, their petition disappeared, unresolved, from the administrative record.[60]

In response to the retailers' clamor and in dialogue with advice from the department, the Commune granted the semisedentary, makeshift shops a stay until April 1792. The department recognized that immediately destroying the structures before winter "would reduce to misery a considerable number of indigent families who did not have any other resources to survive." It would also increase the number of citizens who relied on the state for aid, thereby overwhelming the system. The department justified its suggestion as "prudent and humane," and therefore compatible with the revolutionary government's aspirations.[61] Commune officials agreed and expressed their desire "to favor, as much as public interest can allow it, the least fortunate class of merchants of the capital."[62] The municipality ruled that the stalls would not be demolished until the spring.[63] After the winter delay, the indigent merchants would have to surrender their makeshift structures and seek state-condoned shelters.

In their decision, the Commune officials recognized that free retail commerce in open places competed with rent-paying boutique businesses, which the street merchants often blocked.[64] To balance these rival groups, the representatives stipulated that any mobile structures which congested the streets, disturbed the *voie publique*, and measured over 28 inches would be immediately destroyed. In addition, the Commune stressed that the extension on the mobile shops until the following spring only applied to poor retail merchants who did not have "the means to conduct their Commerce in Boutiques."[65]

From 1790 to 1792, the Assembly and the Commune remained firm in their plan to reconstruct les Halles and marketplace permissions. To do so, however, officials had to negotiate new definitions of privilege, public space, and liberty in commerce. The Dames and other retailers immediately felt the weight of the modernizing campaign. The government outlined new parameters for indigent marketplace access, and police cracked down on their makeshift stalls that blocked the *voie publique*. The reform greatly increased pressure on the Dames' only alternative for affordable shelters—mobile parasols. With their stalls leveled and the stakes raised, the Dames navigated revolutionary ideology to vie for the invaluable parasols and secure the legitimacy to use the space beneath them.

The Battle of the Parasols: The Dames des Halles Stake Out Revolutionary Ideology in the Marketplace

The major conflict over parasols in les Halles illuminates how the Dames, shelter-renters, and officials negotiated public space and particular interests on the ground. Rented parasols were the lynchpin for many retailers' livelihoods. The Dames and other retailers relied heavily on them as the only low-cost shelter in parts of the market. The parasols granted the Dames more or less habitual spots in the marketplace and protected their goods so that their meager businesses could remain economically viable.[66]

The revolutionary state initially regulated how retailers occupied open space by tying their permissions to the parasol-renting companies contracted by Louis XVI. In his 1780s construction project, the king had made two sweeping reforms in les Halles: First, he granted the *bail emphytéotique* to Doré to rebuild the old halles in the fruit market. Second, he emptied the adjacent cemetery of Saint-Innocents. From this cleared cemetery, the king created an official open-air market in what had already become a bustling place of trade. In order to regulate mobile shelters in this new market and coordinate wholesale and retail waves, the king granted Hyacinthe Ignace Joseph Courvoisier a *bail emphytéotique* for the square in 1787. Although the king allowed Courvoisier to construct two rows of sedentary market shelters "to add to public utility," the lease largely set up Courvoisier to profit from renting parasols to retailers.[67]

Under the terms of his 99-year lease, Courvoisier gained the exclusive right to rent and place parasols for Dames des Halles who qualified for charitable privileges as outlined by the king's 1776 royal edict. This Old Regime edict had given permission to "poor women widows and orphaned girls" to sell on the king's *voie publique*.[68] However, by the eve of the Revolution, the vast majority of retailers, regardless of whether they met these 1776 charity requirements, relied on market parasols to protect their foodstuffs.

After 1789, Courvoisier's exclusive right to rent parasols created commercial and institutional conflict. As revolutionary officials attempted to sort out the complexities of a *bail emphytéotique* connected to a multilevel government rather than a king, institutional battles began over marketplace territory. Should the Commune, the department, or the Assembly protect the public and its domain in les Halles? Within the marketplace, several merchants questioned the legitimacy of Courvoisier's parasol company, which derived its monopoly from an Old Regime *rente*. The Dames and other retailers appealed to the municipal, departmental, and national governments and brought suits in court to jockey for shelters and space. Courvoisier's parasol-renting endeavor and the merchants' competing needs for space set into motion conflicting discourses of privilege, particular interests, and public good.

As the revolutionaries unpacked these concepts, the Dames des Halles felt the tangible consequences in the form of economic survival. The revolutionary government's efforts to standardize the marketplace by streamlining rent and charity requirements challenged the Dames' Old Regime advantages over other retailers. For centuries, and most recently in the 1776 edict, French kings had granted the Dames commercial exceptions and particular economic resources as a privileged group. In contrast, revolutionary legislation stressed that each merchant, as a member of the public, held equal claims to personal ownership of public domain. Revolutionary reforms required individuals to seek personal permissions to use stalls and limited their ability to commercially improvise on the *voie publique*. Thus, the Dames encountered obstacles to harnessing local resources, personal relations, and their former quasi-corporate identity for their benefit in the marketplace.

As Courvoisier marshaled his parasols into rank in les Halles, some retailers decided to wage a battle against his privileged company. Courvoisier's contract with the king explicitly favored renting parasols to "edict Dames" who met the 1776 charity requirements as "poor widows and orphaned girls" over other retailers. Consequently, his lease limited nonqualifying Dames' claims on market spaces. Thus, a division emerged within the Dames' own ranks and they interpreted revolutionary ideology differently according to their own interests. On one side, the edict Dames defended Courvoisier's lease and their premium access to marketplace parasols. They stressed the legality of revolutionary contracts that confirmed royal permissions. On the other side, nonedict Dames argued that competition between multiple parasol-providers would benefit all indigent merchants and help destroy the monopolistic privileges of the Old Regime. The nonedict Dames and their supporters maintained that the unrestricted use of parasols in the marketplace dovetailed with new notions of public space and liberty. To gain the upper hand, the Dames des Halles, other retailers, and their corresponding allies drew on the intricate nuances of revolutionary ideology.

Even before the legislative debate on the *baux emphytéotiques*, lessee Courvoisier rushed to get his exclusive parasol-renting rights confirmed in April 1790.[69] Initially, the municipality thought that well-aligned parasol placement could help organize the old Innocents cemetery-turned-market. City officials hoped the parasol-renting system would encourage "the safety of the *voie publique*" and bring order, which "alone can contribute to the advantage of all."[70] Coordinated parasols could stabilize the open space in les Halles and prevent merchants' piles from slipping into disarray.

Merchants and officials soon disputed whether *baux emphytéotiques* like Courvoisier's could continue in a society purged of privilege in which royal domain became national domain. And, if so, they questioned how the *baux emphytéotiques* could be brought into alignment with revolutionary ideology. The National Assembly needed to erase any lingering threats of privilege, ensure that legitimacy for using public domain originated in the nation, and give municipalities the legal tools to administer public space. In August 1790, the National Assembly proclaimed that, since feudalism had been abolished, no individual could claim ownership of or collect permission dues on the *voie publique*.[71] Consequently, all holders of royal *baux emphytéotiques* would have to submit their contracts to the government for revaluation. The leases would only remain valid if revolutionary officials confirmed the royal contract was just.[72] In addition, the Assembly replaced the king with the nation as the source of sovereign authority in public space. The deputies stipulated that "since the *baux emphytéotiques* make a true alienation, they are not reputed to have been made legitimately, and by consequence the buyers will not be held to their terms, until they [the leases] have been analyzed and re-vested with all the solemnities required by law, by place, and location."[73] The king, not the nation, had alienated the public domain, so any private contract on public land required reappraisal by representatives of the revolutionary public.

Despite the Commune's initial confirmation of his lease in April 1790, Courvoisier had to resubmit his contract on public domain to the National Assembly in accordance with its August decree. In March 1791, the Assembly confirmed Courvoisier's exclusive right to place parasols in the marketplace, but it flattened the other privileges originally attached to the king's agreement. The deputies insisted that Courvoisier reduce the price of all of his shelters to 4 sous per day "without distinction of person." The edict Dames, who had enjoyed preferential treatment, lost their exclusive claims to special places and parasol priorities. The Assembly guaranteed the equality of all retail merchants at the edict Dames' expense. It backed Courvoisier's lease and viewed the edict Dames as the overly privileged party in the royal arrangement. The standardized parasol rates would democratize the space and erase privilege. Frustrated with what seemed to be a tiny issue, one deputy declared, "It is unbelievable that [any]one comes to busy the National Assembly with the parasols of the Halles of Paris." He demanded that the issue be passed on to the department, which in turn passed the issue back to the municipality. [74]

The Commune responded to the Assembly's intervention in October 1791. The municipality reasoned that les Halles had been consolidated into the *voie publique* and, as such, belonged to the public domain of the city rather than the nation. In contrast to the National Assembly, the municipal assembly criticized Courvoisier's privileged business and condemned his particular ownership in a space destined "to the public use of the inhabitants." Rather than blame the edict Dames' priority rentals as the source of inequality, the municipal representatives attacked Courvoisier's exclusive monopoly (now legally backed by the Assembly) over parasols as the source of corruption. The Commune emphasized their paternal responsibility to guard against "speculation which could disrupt commerce and could be a considerable drain on the most useful and poorest inhabitants of Paris."[75] Rearranging the matrix of privilege, public space, and charity, the municipality refused to reconfirm Courvoisier's lease and defended their administrative turf.

The new phase in the parasol controversy exposed the divisions in the Dames' ranks. Although some of the indigent Dames des Halles fit the 1776 edict requirements for the king's charitable privileges "in favor of poor women widows and orphaned girls," better-off or married retailers across the Parisian markets did not.[76] Other Dames only fit the Revolution's more expansive definition of "indigent" as outlined in the Commune's October 1791 legislation that stressed residency, parental status, health, age, and need. Still others met neither condition.[77]

When another parasol provider, Sieur Thibault, challenged Courvoisier's monopoly in les Halles and forced officials to debate the terms of Courvoisier's lease, the minute distinctions among the Dames exploded into conflicting interests.[78] Courvoisier's royal contract had stipulated that he rent his Innocents parasols in favor of the Dames who met the 1776 edict requirements. In contrast, the Assembly ordered Courvoisier to treat all retail merchants equally when it reconfirmed his lease in March 1791. Despite the Assembly's orders, it appears that Courvoisier still favored the edict Dames and those Dames in their close circles. Therefore, the nonedict Dames stood to profit from competing parasol providers like Sieur Thibault.

While both groups of Dames deployed discourses of poverty and government responsibility in the ensuing conflict, they conceptualized privilege very differently. On the one hand, the royal edict Dames stressed the legality of Courvoisier's lease in the courtroom. These Dames argued that Courvoisier's original contract upheld their justly sanctioned, not exploitative, privilege in the Innocents market. On the other hand, the nonedict Dames downplayed their exceptionality in the assembly halls. These nonedict Dames positioned themselves within the patriotic "peuple" on communal space and aligned themselves with public interest more than particular interest. They attacked Courvoisier's monopoly and the edict Dames' privilege as relics of the Old Regime. As the Dames fought over parasol placement, they laid out claims to legitimacy in the marketplace, both ideologically and physically.

Tensions came to a head on May 5, 1792 at the sectional assembly of the Marchés neighborhood. Thibault, the bootleg parasol provider, had been offering his alternative services since 1790 to some merchants' delight but much to Courvoisier's chagrin. By May 1792, the state's stay on destroying makeshift stalls had expired and retailers' shelter options dwindled. At the sectional assembly, the nonedict Dames and other retailers insisted that the government abolish the "privileges which give certain citizens the exclusive right to place parasols." The neighborhood assembly agreed with the nonedict Dames and concluded, "the halles, markets, as well as the other public terrains destined to the usage of all must be a communal Property exempt from particular prerogatives."[79] The assembly circulated their petition to the 47 other Parisian sections and submitted their complaint to the Commune.

On the same day, the nonedict Dames began a multivisit crusade to the Legislative Assembly to end Courvoisier's lease and enable others to rent parasols in the markets. The nonedict Dames sweetened their request through a series of patriotic donations. When the nonedict Dames first spoke to the deputies, they gave 320 livres "to the fatherland" and asked "that it please the Assembly to very soon put on the order of the day the report on their petition against the privilege which the particular individual [Courvoisier] enjoyed, renter of places and parasols in the Innocents market."[80] The Assembly passed the Dames' petition on to its Commerce Committee for further evaluation. Nonetheless, the deputies applauded the Dames' donation and gave the retailers "the honorable mention in the minutes." The nonedict Dames returned on May 21 for a follow-up visit. Citing their revolutionary fidelity, they again offered a "tribute" and pledged to repeat their offering twice a year to support the war. In addition, the retailers turned in nonofficial coinage that had circulated in the markets. Although they would suffer "losses" as a result, the Dames resolved, "let this money no longer be a privilege of our exclusion." The nonedict Dames bluntly stated that they did not claim privilege, but rather associated themselves with the wider public.[81] They hoped to bypass the stigma of greedy merchants pursuing their particular economic interests.

In order to bolster their cause and distinguish themselves from Courvoisier's allies, the nonedict Dames and their partners painted Courvoisier and the edict Dames as perpetuators of Old Regime favoritism. Between the nonedict Dames' May visits, Courvoisier's rival Thibault appeared at the Legislative Assembly with his employees and some supportive rag merchants. They, too, directly demanded "the abolition of privileges and the liberty to sell goods by mobile display in the markets of Paris."[82]

Meanwhile, in the neighborhood tribunal, Thibault and 220 supportive merchants of les Halles and their lawyers brought a legal suit against Courvoisier and 122 edict Dames and their lawyers. Therefore, two groups under the influential title "Dames des Halles" squared off on opposing sides of the legal dispute. The case became even more complicated when the Commune asked its

prosecutor to intervene. The prosecutor sought to protect the municipality's interest in the marketplace, which the city sparred with the national government
to control. His addition brought the number of people involved to 544 interested parties, 5 lawyers, and 1 very nervous sectional commissioner. Courvoisier
argued that the revolutionary government had confirmed his lease numerous
times, which legitimized his exclusive authority to rent parasols in the marketplace. The edict Dames claimed that since the National Assembly had initially
approved Courvoisier's lease based on his original contract with the king, they
too maintained privileges in the Innocents market via their relationship with
Courvoisier. After two months of debate and analysis, the Commune's prosecutor contended that Courvoisier and the edict Dames' defense conflicted with
revolutionary principles. He dramatically concluded, "The French constitution
established that there is no longer for any party of the nation [,] nor any individual [,] any privilege nor exception to the common right of all the French
people. . . . The new laws suppressed all tolls in the public markets, it is without
regard to the laws that Sir Courvoisier and Company and the intervening women
of les Halles want to maintain a privilege."[83] In effect, the prosecutor's decision
seconded the Commune's challenge to the Assembly. Despite this municipal
ruling, the Legislative Assembly alone possessed the ability to rescind its confirmation of Courvoisier's lease.

However, the fall of the monarchy weeks later on August 10, 1792, overhauled
the political landscape and power dynamics in Paris. After the sections joined
forces to overthrow the king, the new municipal government emerged stronger
than before. The insurrectional Commune claimed the sovereignty of the people
and dominated politics in the capital. Virtually powerless and with no constitutional monarch, the Legislative Assembly called for elections to a National
Convention to establish a republic. Parisians began to eagerly strip all signs of
royalty and privilege from the city. Although the Legislative Assembly found
its power much reduced in the face of the Commune's claim to legitimacy, the
free-market-inclined Girondin deputies steered the Assembly through the in-
terim until the Convention convened in late September.[84] Panic over the war,
counterrevolutionary plotters, and fallout over the August 10 uprising fueled
massacres of prisoners in early September. The Girondin deputies, while re-
luctantly supporting the August 10 uprising and never condemning the violent
purge of early September, became acutely aware of the precarious situation and
the fear-fueled potential of the Parisian sections.[85]

The shift created a favorable atmosphere for the nonedict Dames' requests. On
September 12, 1792, the nonedict Dames pled their case against Courvoisier's
lease for the third time before the Legislative Assembly. In their petition, they
mobilized their own discourses of privilege, poverty, equality, and the state's
paternal responsibility. The retailers declared, "the exclusive privilege of the

parasols" "cannot continue under the reign of liberty and of equality, [it] would always weigh on the most numerous and most indigent class of the capital, if you do not prevent it [the privilege] from crushing it [the indigent class]." In this interpretative twist, the nonedict Dames undermined the edict Dames' exclusive claims to charitable prerogatives articulated in the 1776 edict in two ways. First, the nonedict Dames stressed that a wider and needier class existed that Courvoisier's lease harmed. Second, the nonedict Dames denounced parasol advantages as contrary to revolutionary equality. "In the name of humanity," the Dames asked "the fathers and representatives of the people" to erase "the traces of privilege against which the female merchants of les Halles have protested all along."[86] By extending their concern to all of "humanity" and evoking the representatives' paternal responsibilities, the nonedict Dames dodged the appearance of particular interests. Instead, they prevailed as steadfast revolutionary protectors against Old Regime privilege. In their equation, the nation's public domain could not be reminiscent of the king's public domain.

Swayed by the nonedict Dames' arguments, spurred by the monarchy's collapse a month earlier, and bolstered by both municipal support and Girondin free-market sympathies, the Legislative Assembly terminated Courvoisier's lease. It concisely proclaimed that "under the reign of Liberty, one does not know how to suffer [such] an establishment."[87] The king's arrest had crystallized the stark divide between the Old Regime and the Revolution. Journalist Prudhomme keenly summarized the issues at stake when he reported that the Assembly had annulled "an abusive lease, which turns a public place into a particular property."[88] Such an arrangement could not exist in republican imaginings. The Legislative Assembly could no longer refute the Commune's logic that Courvoisier was the offending privileged party.

The nonedict Dames and their allies won because they successfully navigated state institutions, turned the radicalization of politics to their advantage, and skillfully deployed revolutionary discourses to claim legitimacy. They presented themselves as members of the regenerated public who had equal rights on public domain. They best negotiated the powerful subtleties of particular interest, public interest, and communal space in the marketplace.

What, at first glance, seemed to be a negligible dispute over parasols in les Halles actually struck at the heart of major revolutionary contests by 1792. The revolutionaries' attempt to define and reform les Halles exposed the challenges of particular interests on public space. On the one hand, to erase privilege and assure public order, state officials reformed the *voie publique*, regulated commercial shelters, and restructured marketplace access. On the other hand, to protect their livelihoods, retailers reinterpreted economic relationships, occupied communal property, and insisted on the merits of working indigent citizens. While the deputies debated the legal inconsistences of a liberated market, the Dames confronted its tangible contradictions on the ground to survive. From under their parasols, the Dames carved out their place in the public marketplace and the revolutionary body politic.

The contests over space in les Halles intensified national debates over administrative turf, state duties, and civic membership. The legal shuffling furthered the rivalry among the municipal, departmental, and national governments as each jockeyed to command the capital. To redefine exceptional access to public space, officials from each level asked what the state owed indigent citizens and who was "worthy" of such assistance. The nonedict Dames and their allies responded by distinguishing the arbitrary charity and privileged monopolies of the Old Regime from the earned exemptions and commercial liberty appropriate for a republic. To retain their advantages, retailers cast themselves as members of the "people" who now owned public space and branded their private commerce as a public service. The nonedict Dames' court victory affirmed that individuals could forge civic membership via occupational activities and that citizens could use their productivity to make claims on the state. While the Dames developed these legitimizing discourses to defend their market use, they also directed them against another threat: the growing dearth of cash and credit. To confront this currency crisis, the Dames created new political alliances within the "public" in which they had literally staked out their membership with parasols.

4

Exacting Change

*Money, Market Women, and the Crumbling
Corporate World*

On May 21, 1792, the Dames des Halles filtered into the Legislative Assembly
to deliver a curious address. The deputies seated there had audaciously declared
war against Austria one month earlier. Offering a "tribute" to defend the nation,
the Dames presented the deputies with a modest purse filled with promissory
coins. Yet, as the clinking money settled on the desk, the merchants suddenly
complained about the literal tokens of their donation. Since revolutionary currency came in denominations far too large to sell a few fish or vegetables, the
Dames were forced to rely on these smaller promissory coins. The retailers lamented that the tender caused them "countless losses." They brazenly accused
the issuing banks of corporate privilege—the sinister ghost of the Old Regime.
"Let this money no longer be a privilege [of the issuers] that excludes us," the
Dames implored their representatives. Would the deputies, they asked, remedy
the small change crisis?[1] While addressing an Assembly rocked by war, why did
the Dames focus more on the physical money they offered than the troops it
would support? How could a critique of currency reform overshadow a looming
invasion?

Much to the deputies' chagrin, implementing the new revolutionary currency, called the assignat, was a collaborative project. Although historians have
discerned how the deputies intended the assignat to function through state
and financial institutions, questions remain about how it affected everyday
trade and how everyday trade influenced assignat policy.[2] The Assembly could
order printers to strike assignat notes and could back them with national lands.
However, the Assembly could not guarantee that citizens used the assignats,
nor could it legislate local confidence in them. There was no other place where
this reality was more evident or perilous than in the food markets of les Halles.
The volatile subsistence trade greatly informed Parisian politics, yet it hinged on

vulnerable systems of credit and supplies. As instability limited credit in commerce, small change became more valuable to buyers and sellers alike.[3] Rapid inflation compounded the lack of usable cash to stymie merchants' transactions. When, from 1790 to 1793, the overwhelmed government deferred to assignat-backed promissory notes to provide merchants with small denominations, the Dames landed in a maelstrom of monetary controversies. As the Dames joined forces with others to combat the small change shortage, they changed the trajectory of national currency reform. Moreover, Parisians reinvented socioeconomic and political alliances in the process.

Despite the sterile veneer of pecuniary formulas, the revolutionaries negotiated monetary reform as an ongoing project. This chapter first analyzes how the Dames and fellow Parisians coped with the disarray of cash and credit. Then, it discerns how diverse citizens banded together to defend necessary tokens for trade. Money became a concrete conduit for effecting the core social transformations at the center of the Revolution. That is, it encouraged people to look across the guild boundaries of corporate society to other shared socioeconomic interests. Vegetable hawkers, joiners, haberdashers, fish brokers, printers, and market goers gradually recognized common currency challenges. Thus, monetary problems inadvertently spurred the popular classes to restructure social identities through everyday trade.

When the Dames insinuated that "privilege" corrupted promissory coins, they exposed how local cash carried serious social and ideological ramifications. Privilege formed the core of the crumbling corporate world. Trade associations, religious institutions, social groups, and even geographical regions had their own, sometimes clashing, permissions stemming from the crown.[4] Guilds, in particular, segregated masters and workers by trade and represented collective interests to state officials.[5] This Old Regime occupational organization screeched to a halt in 1791, when the National Assembly abolished guilds. Since these corporations had held substantial legal and economic power, many studies spotlight the guilds and state officials as the major players in the corporate world's final chapter.[6]

In contrast, this chapter demonstrates how individual citizens, the Dames among them, played a leading role in unraveling the corporatist fabric from 1790 to 1793. It focuses on local experience to consider how all citizens effected the pivotal transformation to a postcorporate society. Using the ubiquitous lens of money, it asks how the revolutionaries recreated socioeconomic groups from below. The Dames and their neighbors reinvented the corporate world in ways integral to daily life rather than through responses to guild restrictions. When the deputies began to overhaul the nation's currency in 1789, they unintentionally opened the gates for coalitions cutting across corporate boundaries of trade and rank. Citizens formed novel alliances that centered on political and economic issues but did not constitute a continuation of corporate identities or an explicit reaction against them. Instead, the assignat's shortcomings galvanized alternative associations based on pragmatic concerns of credit and cash. These new coalitions of citizens pointed to their occupational utility, rather than corporate privilege, to demand the state protect their tokens. In short, the revolutionaries recast economic and political citizenship in tandem to defend their money. Consequently, this chapter reveals how the cash needs of everyday trade compelled the Dames and their neighbors to organically restructure socioeconomic identities, reconfigure political alliances, and experiment with new practices of citizenship. In les Halles, pocket money spurred these changes both before and after the Assembly abolished the guilds.

Reforming Cash, Credit, and Currency Communities

When the National Assembly swore to solve the national debt in 1789, it squared off against one of the most debilitating problems of the Old Regime. To pursue this ambitious project, the representatives began another: they overhauled the monetary system. Most official currency under the previous system consisted of coins whose value corresponded to their metallic worth.[7] In December 1789, the deputies switched to paper notes called "assignats," which they backed by the titles of *biens nationaux* or newly requisitioned Church properties. While the state assessed land acquisitions, collected revenue, and printed official assignats, the Assembly converted some bills of a private Parisian bank, the Caisse d'Escompte, into temporary "promises to be exchanged for assignats." The deputies planned to use these interest-bearing "promises" to pay state debts until the Caisse d'Escompte could pull them from circulation and redeem them for official assignats in fall 1790. At this point, the deputies reasoned, citizens could exchange assignats for deeds to national lands and the assignats would gradually disappear from circulation.[8]

In September 1790, with over 30,000 supporters and protesters outside, the deputies changed course.[9] They voted to make the assignats into national money without any interest. Officials portrayed the assignats as "circulating land" in paper form.[10] Nevertheless, the currency's value was less secure than this simple formula suggested. The assignat had partially liquefied backing from national land immediately sold. Tangible assets in the form of land yet to be sold constituted the remaining backing. Therefore, the assignats provided the state with interest-free IOUs on unsold land whose price and purchase were not certain. Nonetheless, by tying assignats to the national lands and circulating them across the nation, the deputies hoped to stabilize interregional trade, quell inflation, and reduce the debt.

Over one thousand Dames des Halles stood on the fault line of this seismic monetary shift. The assignats rocked the world of small change and credit, both long-standing pillars of the Parisian food trade. Microcredit networks relied on communal knowledge of who had a good reputation, who honored their debts, and what resources were available.[11] To buy supplies in les Halles, the Dames often took out "small weekly loans" from moneylenders whose offices dotted nearby streets. Each retailer contracted her own loans, but some moneylenders assembled groups of Dames and made them swear to be "all guarantors here, one for the other."[12] Thus, individual retail loans contributed to the collective fabric of the marketplace.

The Dames, their small change, and their credit networks followed a routine trajectory. First, provincial suppliers carted their foodstuffs to les Halles where brokers (factrices) bought these goods in wholesale. Next the brokers sold subdivided lots to individual Dames on credit or for cash and commercial bills. Finally, the retailers sold fish, butter, and vegetables to consumers, whom they attracted by extending their own credit or offering low prices. After collecting small change or promissory bills, the Dames would repay their debts to their brokers or private lenders.[13] This precarious mix of credit and small change supported astonishing trade. By 1790, the sum total of fish sales in Les Halles amounted to the equivalent of 4,464,000 small cod, 2,678,400 large cod, or 70,857,000 smoked herrings.[14] To win popular support in the capital, any national monetary project would have to satisfy the enormous food trade in les Halles and the market's influential retailers.

On a quotidian level, the Dames and their neighbors engaged in the Assembly's monetary project by trading assignats, assignat-backed bills, private notes, coins, or credit. Each time a citizen sold or purchased food in les Halles, he or she chose which forms of payment to accept. Although merchants were technically required to accept assignats, passing up a sale or accepting smaller substitutes was often more attractive because of impractical assignat denominations.[15] Through daily market purchases, citizens personally assessed the assignat's value and signaled their economic confidence in the nation's properties. As the assignats passed from one hand to another, the currency enmeshed citizens in revolutionary politics. Individuals who accepted the money inherently affirmed the state's just ownership of requisitioned Church lands. Deputy Jean-Baptiste Pinteville de Cernon, a noble on the Committee of Finances, predicted that the new currency would indeed "give all citizens an equal interest in maintaining and defending [the Constitution]."[16]

Parisian retailers understood that cash functioned as a political passport. In January 1790, the flower sellers of rue Neuve-des-Bons-Enfants left their street stands to take the assembly floor. Speaking on behalf of all Dames des Halles, the market women asked the deputies' permission to "establish a patriotic treasury in their hands." After amassing their donations in their treasury, the retailers would deposit its contents into the national treasury.[17] The Dames' financially superfluous request reflected their localized logic of money. In their understanding, the tender's origins created its cultural value and nominal worth. Although all assignat-backed tokens were theoretically equivalent, the Dames reasoned that they added patriotic value to the money as it passed through their hands. The Dames physically and figuratively merged their funds and loyalty with the new state.

The practical requirements of hard cash prevented the Dames from embracing the assignat in trade. Beginning in 1790, the government printed assignat bills in extremely large denominations of 1,000, 300, and 200 livres.[18] The deputies hoped to swiftly disseminate the currency through large sums handled by financial societies and wealthy citizens. But the logistical strategy of emitting large denominations marginalized the Dames and their neighbors. The popular classes actually relied more heavily on cash for transactions because they were less "credible" than the wealthy.[19] Moreover, the market women's trade fell far below the lowest threshold. For example, a Dame selling Neufchâtel cheese at 4 sous (.2 livres) per brick would need to sell a client 1,000 bricks of cheese to accept a single 200-livre assignat.[20] Clearly, the deputies' plan could not address the exigencies of marketplace trade.

The Dames were not the only citizens stymied by the new currency. Retailers of all sorts required small change to sell their goods and pay suppliers. Huge assignats risked paralyzing their businesses and politically marginalizing them. As financial problems exacerbated small change shortages in April 1791, one pro-Revolution pamphleteer unleashed Mère Duchêne, a fictive popular class character, to launch an unbridled critique.[21] "[S]mall change," Mère Duchêne declares, "is absolutely necessary for commerce in retail." She testifies that without practical denominations, consumers cannot pay her retailer husband, and she cannot pay her debts in turn. The deputies' tactics risked crippling "the most numerous portion of citizens." Mère Duchêne demands that the recalcitrant deputies start guiding monetary policy "more from practice than from theory; more from experience than from reasoning."[22] The National Assembly could continuously crunch numbers, but any currency that disregarded marketplace needs would fail.

From the opposing end of the political spectrum, a royalist pamphleteer likewise attacked the assignat's inadequacies through a fictive dialogue. His Dames Martinet and Margoton find themselves trapped with a 25-livre assignat, which they are unable to subdivide. After they pay for their dinner at a guinguette with the 25-livre note, the owner informs them that he does not have smaller denominations. Consequently, he refuses to give Martinet and Margoton their change. In the rough dialect of les Halles, Martinet complains of the "misery"

caused by the paper money. She protests, "now, if I are hungry, it will be necessary to go two leagues [to the guinguette] in order to have dinner [on remaining
credit]."[23] The lack of small assignats would weigh most heavily on the popular
classes.

In order to provide small bills and facilitate trade, the National Assembly
allowed citizens to create local substitutes. Financial societies called "caisses" issued assignat-backed promissory notes or coins. Run by municipalities, societies,
and private companies, these institutions issued their own billets de confiance
(literally "bills of confidence" or promissory notes) in small denominations
backed by their assignat holdings. By directly subdividing assignats into
smaller billets de confiance, the caisses and their clients could circulate notes in
denominations below the 200-livre assignat. Thus, banks and exchange caisses
played a vital role in local trade.[24] The decentralized system of small notes and
coins mixed public trust in national assignats with confidence in local purveyors
of credit.[25] To use promissory notes, citizens had to have confidence in the eq-
uity of the national lands as well as in the security of local monetary networks.

Financial companies found the billet de confiance system appealing. During
the Old Regime, financial societies had routinely issued commercial bills backed
by debt contracts or IOUs redeemable against assets. The revolutionary billets de
confiance allowed companies to expand their services or found a new business.
Some caisses profited by charging fees to convert large assignat denominations
into smaller promissory notes.[26] Others coupled exchange with auxiliary services
to attract banking clients. In contrast to the assignats backed by national lands,
the billets de confiance from exchange caisses were required to have completely
liquefied backing in the form of assignat reserves or bank assets.[27] However,
since any "convertible tokens are interest-free IOUs," many caisses waded into
illegal territory. They outpaced their assignat reserves and speculated with their
own promissory notes.[28] The deputies' attempt to provide small change spawned
unstable networks of ever-changing denominations and issuers. From these eclectic sources, a web of promissory bills flooded the marketplace.

Critics were quick to pounce on the vulnerable assignats and promissory
notes. One biting pamphleteer printed his own fake 100-sous note from the
"shitty caisse" to illustrate his lack of faith in the promissory money. On the satirical note, the author swapped the 1791 assignat's stoic emblem of a winged
man labeled "reign of law" for an unmistakable flying turd. And, in place of the
promise "to exchange against Assignats," the recipient of this fictitious bill would
trust the note's worth on the word of its issuer "Lichette," or little drunk person.
The satirical markings reveal how heavily the promissory notes depended on
local networks and public confidence in the issuing bank's credit. In this case,
the billet's origin from the "shitty caisse" coupled with the specification that it is
"payable in the mouth of the bearer" (instead of "payable to the bearer") suggests

that the holder of the insecure note would eat shit. The crude parody insinuated that the "Good-times" of usable currency were dead under the weight of promissory notes dubiously backed by assignats and local confidence.[29]

Despite their shortcomings, the exchange caisses and their promissory notes provided essential services to retailers in les Halles. Due to their low-volume commerce, the Dames were among the first hit by the problems of large-denomination assignats. The retailers relied on banks and exchange caisses to provide promissory notes in smaller, practical denominations. In Paris, the state sponsored some of these caisses and private companies ran others. Three new banks opened in 1791 and furnished marketplace money: the Caisse Patriotique (Patriotic Bank), the Maison de Secours (House of Aid) and the Caisse de Commerce (Bank of Commerce). These banks exchanged large assignats or even business credit for tokens that circulated as usable cash in the capital. As financial societies, they offered different banking services. For example, merchants could ask the Maison de Secours to liquefy their household assets in exchange for promissory notes. The Caisse de Commerce, in contrast, bought commercial contracts and solvent debts and offered billets in return. The caisses often specialized in particular denominations of promissory notes. With these new banks, the number of promissory notes backed by company assets, commercial IOUs, and assignats skyrocketed. Promissory notes frequently changed hands in the capital.

By accepting or rejecting assignats, promissory notes, metal coins, and credit, the Dames and other merchants intervened in currency valuation within local monetary networks. For example, beginning in May 1791, the private Caisse Patriotique issued its own subdivided billets de confiance that it guaranteed with its assignat holdings.[30] Not all merchants eagerly accepted the substitute. Journalist Prudhomme, who had supported the switch to assignats, lamented that it was impossible to force merchants to take the Caisse Patriotique's notes.[31] The merchants' refusal damaged confidence in an already fragile system. Prudhomme suggested that willing merchants encourage trade with a sign declaring, "here one takes as payment bills of the Caisse Patriotique."[32] The multiple note options placed significant power in the hands of consumers and traders. The assignat system could cripple their trade, but they too could cripple the assignat system.

In les Halles, the monetary situation exposed shared interests that cut across corporate and occupational boundaries. Clients and merchants could juggle credit, but they would eventually need cash to settle their accounts. Practical concerns over currency permeated relationships along entire supply lines. Without sufficient small bills, a vegetable-peddling Dame could not sell household quantities of peas to consumers. The Dame's broker, in turn, could not sell the retailer small lots without giving her extensive credit. But the broker would eventually need hard cash to pay the provincial wholesalers who carted food to the capital. Consider, for example, the challenges of the cheese-selling Dame in 1791. If she sold 15 bricks of cheese for 4 sous to clients, she would need to wait until her clients' debts reached an amount equal to the 2.5-livre denomination (the smallest assignat note at the time) to collect payment. Only then could the Dame pay her broker for her supplies. And only then could the broker pay the wholesaler who committed to carting the cheese over 125 kilometers from Neufchâtel to Paris. In les Halles, consumers, retailers, brokers, and wholesalers held a vested interest in common promissory notes for daily trade.

While denomination issues plagued promissory notes inside les Halles, the makeshift tender faced collapse at the market's edge. Since retailers circulated billets de confiance emitted by neighborhood banks, the substitute cash maintained its worth based on local confidence. Countryside suppliers who hauled food into the capital knew that Parisian promissory notes would be considered suspect outside the city. Therefore, provincial wholesalers balked at accepting Parisian notes. The assignat and the billets de confiance consequently encumbered trade between provincial suppliers and capital merchants who straddled different promissory-note networks. The problem extended beyond Paris. From 1790 to 1792, 71 percent of French departments had ten or more issuers of billets de confiance.[33] Instead of standardizing national currency as the deputies had anticipated, the assignat actually hardened regional boundaries forged by the reach of local caisses.

The assignat swept out completely new currency communities within Paris and throughout France—or groups of individuals who required the same denominations of cash, relied on overlapping systems of credit, and shared confidence in local issuers of promissory notes.[34] Parisians implicitly belonged to similar monetary networks and used informal IOUs during the Old Regime, but the assignat crisis thrust these latent common interests to the forefront of daily anxieties. The assignat system introduced new backers, new substitutes, and new rationales for monetary reform. The all-encompassing nature of the revolutionaries' monetary overhaul spawned new currency communities that relied on common tokens defined by denomination, region, and type of credit.[35]

Moreover, commercial relationships within revolutionary currency communities were more interdependent than former microcredit relationships. In contrast to microcredit networks where confidence was largely rooted in individuals' personal reputations,[36] billet de confiance networks depended more on the collective confidence of the community in specific cash. Previously, the Dames could vouch for each other to small moneylenders, but now the billets de confiance tied the Dames to a wider network welded to the credibility of local financial institutions. Therefore, when questionable notes circulated through the marketplace, prices quickly fluctuated. The fallout from even minor currency problems—like isolated counterfeits—dangerously resonated throughout commercial networks like les Halles. The Dames and other retailers fiercely protected fragile money throughout the Revolution. As late as 1797, Citoyenne Roudelle, one of the Dames des Halles, accused another, Citoyenne Fasche, of being "made of lead [a deceiving person], a thief, a maker of false assignats." Seven other Dames testified during Fasche's summons. Most cases between citizens at the justice of the peace involved three or fewer witnesses, so this high number signals how deeply the forgery insults affected the community. Fasche's individual honor and credit were at stake, but so too was the stability of the currency community.[37] The assignat's growing pains heightened the interdependence of tenuous commercial exchanges.

Rethinking Alliances to Defend Small Change

In the revolutionary marketplace, currency communities provided a framework for forging socioeconomic relationships that transcended traditional identities of the corporate world. Retail merchants of all varieties had a vested interest in small change because they all traded at the point of sale. Even shopkeepers and master artisans who sold their own goods needed small change to pay workers and settle credit accounts.[38] Because they were in the same monetary network, the Dames protested conversion policies alongside brokers.[39] Wine merchants signed petitions together with carpenters to protect tender. Male and female grain brokers seconded bakers' complaints against troublesome notes.[40] In short, market actors, workers, and artisans reconfigured corporate alliances and reinvented foundational socioeconomic relationships as they struggled to defend pocket change.

The Dames and their neighbors first campaigned for practical currency from the Assembly in September 1790. The deputies began to issue assignats of 100 and 50 livres in early fall 1790, a substantial improvement over the original large denominations, but the notes still remained above most marketplace trade. Therefore, the section assembly of les Halles sent a petition to the Committee of Finances. The section demanded "the establishment of a patriotic caisse for the exchange of 25-livre bills" which, they testified, the food markets required. Their proposed caisse would exchange these 25-livre denominations without "discrimination" and without a conversion fee.[41] These denominations would ease wholesale transactions, although they would not solve the small change shortage between retailers and consumers. In 1790, a Dame would still have to sell 25 pounds of fresh butter from Chartres, 55 white herrings, or 146 cheese bricks from Neufchâtel to equal just one 25-livre note.[42] Despite the continued inconveniences, any assignat subdivisions would facilitate credit networks and alleviate bulky debts in les Halles.

Shortly after the neighborhood assembly's deliberation in September 1790, more citizens brought their monetary grievances to the state. Only nine months after the assignat's birth and five months before the deputies attacked the guilds, ninety-three retail merchants of various trades signed a petition to the National Assembly.[43] They presented themselves as "merchants in Paris, and the majority as traders in retail." As sellers of various goods, they traditionally belonged to separate occupational corps. However, as members of the same currency community, they relied on similar denominations, local billets de confiance, and a shared regional cash network.

The unusual coalition of ninety-three retailers demanded that the National Assembly permit the Caisse d'Escompte to emit 30 million more livres in the smallest assignat denominations.[44] The petitioners pointed to the "great inconveniences for commerce in general, and in particular for retail commerce, caused by the rarity of small bills." The Caisse d'Escompte had already emitted a limited number of 200- and 300-livre assignats, but these bills had disappeared into the countryside after the government permitted their free movement. The retailers explained that since "the largest portion of interior circulation of the provinces takes place in small sums, the small bills are those which return the least to the capital." The provinces' own need for small assignats drained the capital's supply. The petitioners predicted that recent legislation enabling National Guards to carry "some small bills out of preference" across France would make these assignats "still more rare" within Paris. The merchants reasoned that circulating more small notes would rectify the potentially "fatal" "stagnation" of commerce.[45]

The hodgepodge coalition specifically called for small assignats to expedite their customers' debt repayments. The merchants explained that, to sell their goods, they had to extend credit to clients who said they could not make purchases for lack of small notes. When their credit came due, customers dodged repaying the merchants by attesting they did not have appropriate denominations.[46] Such actions stressed credit systems for everyday purchases and left merchants in the lurch: Should they lose sales by denying credit or should they sell on credit and risk never being paid?

Essentially, the small change crisis created a loophole that benefited buyers in their credit accounts with merchants. Technically, the Commercial Code required merchants to collect repayment within a year of sale or to draw up formal contracts.[47] By avoiding debt repayment for lack of monetary instruments, consumers could lengthen their initial debt and profit from assignat inflation. Thus, the small change shortage created credit resources for consumers similar to "obligations" (short-term demand loans) but put the borrower in control of the repayment schedule instead of the creditor.[48] Biding just a few months of revolutionary inflation could pay big dividends for customers and devastate sellers. Any consumer delaying repayment in Paris from January 1791 to January 1792 would have benefited from a 20% depreciation of the assignat and their debt.[49]

After the National Assembly hesitated to respond to their petition, the front of mismatched merchants sent a letter to the Caisse d'Escompte to accelerate their request. Three of the four leading signatories differed from the original petition, which suggested their budding collaboration lacked a standing organization. The merchants provided the Caisse with a copy of their petition and asked it to join their defense of small change.

The framing differences between the original petition and the follow-up letter signaled a striking evolution among the merchants. They signed each document as individuals, which spotlighted their political autonomy as citizens and jettisoned traditional guild representation. But, by the time they drafted the second piece, they corralled their signatures under the collective title "the retail merchants of Paris." The merchants notably abandoned traditional corporate bodies to portray a novel socioeconomic alliance. They referred to their first petition as a request, which they had signed "in harmony with many of our confrères" and asserted that they responded to "the general difficulty, which makes itself felt in all branches of trade."[50] "Confrères" was usually reserved for members within a common corporation or confraternity.[51] But the letter-writers altered its parameters to include diverse merchants facing the same monetary predicament. The shared hardship compelled the letter-writers to imagine themselves as an innovative community. Even before the Le Chapelier law wiped away the vestiges of the corporate world and the deputies banned collective petitions in 1791,[52] the ninety-three merchants understood their mutual monetary interests transcended corporate trade divisions.

To convince the National Assembly to solve their money woes, the ninety-three merchants and their Caisse d'Escompte supporters eschewed corporate privilege. The retail merchants claimed that public good, not particular interests, motivated them. They asserted that, regardless of the monetary reform's treacherous impact on their businesses, "they had supported it with courage and patience" because it was "for the advantage of the Revolution."[53] The Caisse d'Escompte administrators seconded the eclectic petitioners' demands and asked for permission to print more 200- and 300-livre bills "favorable to public good." The decision, they attested, weighed on "the commerce of the capital," which was aggravated by a "near general mistrust [that] had dried up the ordinary sources of credit."[54]

Government officials sensed the petitioners' shifting tactics and socioeconomic configuration. While discussing the Committee of Finance's report, the deputies abstracted the petitioners as "the commerce of Paris." Ultimately, the

National Assembly conceded to the ninety-three merchants and the Caisse d'Escompte: it issued 30 million more assignats to back smaller billets de confiance on September 16, 1790.[55] The government simply published the decree since the petitioners lacked a corporation to which to reply. Allying by currency community rather than by trade literally paid off for Parisian merchants.

The corporate world's demise in 1791 opened a new chapter in associative identities and collective petitioning for the Dames and other merchants. As legal entities, corporate bodies like guilds and confraternities had continued to interact with the state during the early Revolution. In hierarchical trade disputes, guild masters squared off against journeymen in court. Guilds also sued one another and solicited the state to consolidate commercial privileges. The d'Allarde and Le Chapelier laws overturned this entire system of corporations. Within the context of tax reform in February 1791, the deputies passed the d'Allarde law, which abolished the guilds and proposed an open license system in its place. Each citizen, the deputies reasoned, could pursue any occupation he/she chose as long as he/she bought the appropriate license. In June 1791, the deputies then disavowed workers' associations through the Le Chapelier law, which outlawed confraternities and forbade workers from assembling as an occupational group. Workers would be unable to collectively organize against their now isolated masters.[56]

By dismantling the guilds and banning corporate bodies from submitting collective petitions, the deputies inadvertently encouraged merchants to cooperate across trade boundaries.[57] Since the Constitution of 1791 still guaranteed the "liberty to address [to the government] individually signed petitions,"[58] citizens still needed to reconfigure their political alliances to maintain numerical strength but obey postguild restrictions. Two challenges loomed large. How could citizens channel a collective voice without corporate bodies? And how could interest groups transcend the specter of corporate privilege? Citizens needed wide-ranging alliances to legally pitch their monetary interests as public interests.[59]

By April 1791, two months into the guilds' death rattle, the waves of monetary confusion that pulsed through les Halles and other markets threatened to collapse the caisses and interregional economic networks. Numerous substitutes for the assignat, including assorted billets de confiance and coins from different caisses, shattered the mirage of a uniform monetary system. Despite the state's pragmatic goals in permitting financial societies to strike tokens, the caisses amplified the confusion as they emitted more and more specialized notes for local groups. In the capital alone, merchants and consumers navigated a maze of billets de confiance issued by sixty-three distinct societies.[60] These promissory notes held value based on consumer confidence in the signatures of the issuer and the notes' successive holders. The proliferating caisses compounded suspicion of Parisian issuers in the provinces. Backing signatures became less familiar to users the farther a billet de confiance traveled through networks of trade from its origin.[61] Since wholesalers came from the provinces to supply the capital's markets, the countryside's gradual loss of trust in Parisian notes directly affected the ability of the Dames, their brokers, and other retailers to buy their supplies.

In May 1791, a private company established the Caisse Patriotique and appeared poised to alleviate the practical note shortage for the Parisian popular classes. Until April 1791, the smallest assignat denomination had been 50 livres. In contrast, the Caisse Patriotique issued assignat-backed notes in denominations of 5, 10, 20, and 25 livres. Although the government planned to begin printing 5-livre assignat denominations in May, it could not match pace with the soaring demand.[62] The Caisse Patriotique's subdividing service proved so popular that it initially limited exchanges to 50 livres per person. Even then, caisse administrators could barely keep up with the mass of people flocking to their door.[63] By mid-August 1791, *La Chronique de Paris* alerted readers that the Caisse Patriotique would introduce a still smaller denomination: it would "incessantly emit notes of 50 sous" (50 sous = 2.5 livres).[64] To boost this production, the government exempted the exchange caisses from stamp taxes.[65] This decree gave billets de confiance "a quasi-official air." From citizens' perspectives, the assignat notes and the billets de confiance became more interdependent and less recognizable as distinct entities.[66]

The Caisse Patriotique's owners asserted that it strove to "relieve the artisan's and worker's demands of primary necessity," that is, to provide them with cash for everyday trade. Its services quickly became indispensable for the Dames and other merchants. The caisse's mission statement stressed that the popular class performed patriotic services and equated their needs with public needs. Parisian newspapers echoed their sentiments. *La Chronique de Paris* asserted that the small note shortage was "becoming each day more troublesome for the laboring classes of citizens, it is pressing to bring a remedy to this public unhappiness; and an aid . . . becomes a duty for the good citizens."[67] Banks like the Caisse Patriotique increasingly cited how Parisians relied on their promissory notes to justify their ventures. Private interests had to benefit the public in postcorporate politics. In the wake of the d'Allarde and Le Chapelier laws, retailers would bet their money on the same logic.

The Maison de Secours: Contending with Counterfeits and Local Monetary Networks

Besides cash, another currency roamed les Halles—credit. Some revolutionary caisses dealt with credit shortages rather than small change shortages. The Maison de Secours, for example, served the Dames des Halles and other Parisian retail merchants by liquefying tangible assets. In March 1791, this newly established caisse began "to accept furniture and household items in order to facilitate their prompt sale."[68] The caisse provided merchants the much-needed opportunity to turn their possessions into capital, and it offered them "secours" (aid) through this proxy service. Despite the charitable overtones, the Maison de Secours conducted its business for profit. It became a major player in the Parisian monetary market when it, like the Caisse Patriotique, began to issue its own billets de confiance in November 1791. The Maison de Secours similarly justified its subdividing services as a public good. The business announced that it directly responded to "the public's solicitations, notably the heads of manufacturing and the Dames des Halles." Indeed, the Maison de Secours supplied the Dames, other retailers, and their customers with small notes for daily commerce.[69] Unfortunately, within a month, counterfeit bills of 40 sous (2 livres) circulated throughout the city bearing the Maison's name.[70]

Counterfeiters profited more and more readily from copied billets de confiance in late 1791. Counterfeit bills of the Caisse Patriotique varied from the originals in color and signature but circulated through the Parisian markets without much resistance.[71] However, counterfeit tints sometimes mismatched denominations, which left illiterate retailers in the lurch. Vegetable merchant Michelle Feuillerade and flower seller Barthélemy Bureau faced criminal charges for using a fake billet copied from the Caisse Patriotique. The counterfeit was marked as 20 livres, but its yellow tint belonged to a different denomination.[72] Other Parisians knowingly overlooked counterfeits because they were eager to have even fake small bills for trade. When Dame Robert, a vegetable merchant, attempted to repay her 25-livre debt to Dame Maillot, another vegetable merchant, she partly paid with bills of 50 sous marked from the Caisse Patriotique. Dame Maillot immediately realized the notes were counterfeit and delivered them to the justice of the peace. Dame Robert defended herself by testifying that other market women had already circulated the counterfeits as practical money.[73] Just as the government had lost control of the assignat in the sea of promissory notes, the caisses lost control of their promissory notes in a jungle of counterfeits.

In January 1792, more forgeries put Parisians on edge in les Halles. A counterfeit fiasco related to the Maison de Secours in name, if not always in action, began to cripple the trust in commercial networks between the marketplace and the provinces. A printer in les Halles named Libarre set his press to produce 150,000 counterfeit livres in the form of 2-livre notes bearing the Maison de Secours's mast.[74] Just around the corner from the fruit market, the police discovered his stockpile of false bills and learned that some Dames had knowingly employed the counterfeit currency. To avoid detection in open trade, these Dames used the counterfeits to buy fruit and vegetables from their countryside suppliers under the cover of night.[75] Two weeks later, *La Chronique de Paris* warned the provincial wholesalers that the Maison de Secours itself could be involved in currency duplicity. The journal decried that the Maison inconsistently paired colors and denominations. Parisian retailers could take advantage of provincial wholesalers who, illiterate or less familiar with the notes, relied on color to recognize the bills' values.[76]

Thus, the promissory notes and their backing became a pivotal and volatile component in the relationship between the Dames des Halles, who dealt in local notes, and their provincial suppliers, who loathed the Parisian system of confidence. Representatives from Chartres, 54 miles southwest of Paris, complained to the Legislative Assembly that merchants coming to town with only Parisian billets de confiance worried their inhabitants. By February 1792, the Maison de Secours had emitted most notes foreign to Chartres' currency community.[77] Counterfeit fears further alienated provincial wholesalers from Parisian confidence networks.

The anticipated failure of the Maison de Secours threatened the supply and sale vectors of the Dames' trade. Consequently, in March 1792, an ally of the Dames made the Assembly a desperate offer. Femme Gond reported that the Dames agreed to incur losses on the Maison's overextended billets, on which they heavily relied, to prevent their complete collapse. After the troubled Maison de Secours declared bankruptcy and its director fled the city, Femme Gond had begun to talk with some Dames about the impending disaster. While buying her supplies from the retailers, Gond outlined a system to save the Maison's notes that the merchants needed for trade. The plan revealed how Parisians understood tender to derive its value from local users. Gond hypothesized that the Dames could collaboratively mitigate the setbacks caused by the Maison's doomed notes. Gond proposed that the Dames continue to trade the Maison's notes with their customers and among each other, but that they reduce the face value of each note by two deniers (1/6 sou or 1/120 livre) with each successive exchange. Each Dame would gradually absorb the losses through successive transactions within her monetary network.[78]

Apart from the Maison's bills, few other notes in practical denomination existed, and the available alternatives would not fill the enormous void. Therefore, the Dames remained willing to use the Maison's notes while Parisian municipal sections frantically struck replacement 10 sous coins backed by assignats. The Dames agreed to mark each Maison bill with small bars to diminish gradually each note's value. In doing so, the Dames would physically reduce the billets' capital after each marketplace transaction. These Dames promised Femme Gond to continue devaluing the Maison's notes until they could be withdrawn and replaced by the 10-sous coins.[79]

At the bar of the Legislative Assembly, Femme Gond told the deputies that the collaborative system would keep trade viable. She observed that the Dames supported this strategy, since "they would be able to live still; that would be better than nothing at all."[80] Little mention was made of the actual assignats and assets that should have backed the overextended notes in the first place. The currency community of les Halles determined the money's value—in this case, quite literally.

Despite the promissory notes' shortcomings, the battered assignat did not seem much more secure in Parisians' eyes. A royalist author channeled Mère Saumon, the fictive fish merchant, to express the general contempt for the revolutionary assignat in 1792. The fabricated Dame informs her neighbor that "silver" and the assignat are "not as equal as you'd weal believe." She protests that metal "h'as a real value, instead o' from one moment to the other, it can happen that th'paper isn't worth anything anymor." Old Regime coins appear superior to fickle paper assignats because metal tokens carry material value. Mère Saumon further explains that the unstable assignat causes marketplace wholesalers to hoard their merchandise "sinc' no one' has confidence in it."[81] Due to failed monetary reform, the marketplace lacked stable tender and reliable food supplies.

Transforming Local Networks into National Communities: Reining in the Caisses and Small Change Assignats

The billets de confiance crisis that the Dames and the popular classes experienced in 1792 forced the Assembly to debate their long-term goals for monetary reform. Whereas the Dames and their allies had initially complained about impractical large assignats, the patchwork of small promissory notes introduced additional stressors. Marketplace actors now sought government protection against counterfeiting, overextended caisses, and the general chaos created by too many tokens. Faced with the possible breakdown of means for barter in the capital, the deputies increasingly considered the workaday implications of revolutionary currency. Deputy Cartier-Douineau, a trader from Tours, testified on behalf of the Extraordinary Committee on Finances that the Legislative Assembly had yet to produce "a money useful to the people" for transactions between retailers and consumers.[82] By negotiating the state's duty in issuing small assignats and in regulating the substitutes it had permitted, the deputies confronted the place of money in the contract between citizens and the state.

The deputies looked with increasing concern on the labyrinth of small change. Old Regime coins, leather sous, assignats, caisse-issued billets, and counterfeit notes threatened to overwhelm retail trade. A few months earlier, Deputy Cartier-Douineau had convinced the Assembly that it could only prevent the abuse of proliferating promissory notes by issuing small assignat notes of 10, 15, and 50 sous (.5, .75, and 2.5 livres respectively).[83] Practical assignats would decrease Parisians' reliance on the caisses. Moreover, if individuals could redeem assignats for their billets de confiance, it would discourage the caisses from overextending their holdings.

The merchants of les Halles bristled at the Assembly's idea to issue small assignats in 1792 as far too late. According to the journal *Annales monarchiques*, the merchants feared that their notes from the Caisse Patriotique and the Maison de Secours would "no longer enjoy any confidence, or any credit" if official assignats took their place. Furthermore, the merchants shrewdly worried that the government would be unable to replace the massive amount of small change circulated by the Caisse Patriotique and the Maison de Secours.[84] Unconvinced, the deputies stood by their small assignats initiative.[85]

The Parisian retailers were justified in their fears. As the Legislative Assembly emitted small change assignats, its disdain grew for the promissory notes. The deputies viewed the substitutes that had initially saved commerce in les Halles as troublesome competitors with official currency. Immediately following the Maison de Secours's counterfeit fiasco in March 1792, the Legislative Assembly decreed that the municipal governments must audit the accounts of the private caisses, that private caisses must stop printing billets de confiance, and that only municipally run caisses could emit new billets de confiance.[86]

Unfortunately for the Dames des Halles, the Maison de Secours was deemed the most overextended and ubiquitous rival to the assignats. But the Assembly would need the Dames' and fellow retailers' cooperation to rein in the Maison's billets and throw confidence behind small assignats for everyday trade. The marketplace faced a major challenge when, in April 1792, the worried Assembly ordered the Maison to stamp all its notes and certify their assignat backing. Since many Parisians relied on the Maison's credit system, the mayor implored residents to seek gradual reimbursement for unstamped notes. The simultaneous influx of counterfeit billets under the Maison's mast widened the devastating gap between the company's assignat holdings and billets circulating in their name.[87]

The future of the Maison de Secours, their billets de confiance, and their users looked bleak. The Maison floundered in counterfeit scandals and could not refute accusations that it overextended its backings. Despite launching official 10, 15, and 50 sous notes, the state could not yet offer a comprehensive assignat network without decimating popular systems of billets and credit. When the Legislative Assembly declared war on Austria in April 1792, it added military payments to monetary needs. The Dames hitched the military emergency to their own concerns first regarding market space and then regarding cash. When the

Dames first donated to the war on May 14, 1792, they pleaded with the National Assembly to revoke Courvoisier's parasol monopoly in les Halles.[88] When they returned a week later to donate 112 promissory coins, they reminded the deputies of the small change shortage. Their orator noted that there "exists nothing more proper to fulfill our vow than this cash, we regret that its scarcity has limited our intent [the donation]."[89] For merchants and consumers, the deputies' commercial ideals, currency theory, and now war money considerations failed to solve local cash shortages.

The Caisse de Commerce: Banking on Political Contracts

The Dames' other recourse to small notes and credit during the 1792 impasse, albeit in 25-livre denominations, came from the Caisse de Commerce. In December 1791, the Legislative Assembly had allowed a network of privately owned offices called the Caisse de Commerce to act as a discount bank "to favor the merchants and the artisans." Rather than make change for large assignats, the Caisse de Commerce advertised that it would encourage trade "by facilitating ways private individuals could liquefy their effects that they could not circulate."[90] Merchants frequently sold goods on credit, but this left them with little cash to pay their debts and buy supplies. Therefore, the Caisse de Commerce offered to buy all solvent belongings, including contracted debts owed by clients to merchants, for a fee of 6% per year. In return, the Caisse issued redeemable "billets de commerce" that merchants could immediately use as tender in trade.[91] Sidestepping usury and speculation, the Caisse de Commerce promised "to feed, animate, and fortify all the products of agriculture, industry, and commerce."[92]

The Caisse de Commerce targeted retail currency communities and presented its services as charity. It advertised that it would assist small-scale merchants, specifically "the Resellers, the Women of les Halles and others." The owners announced that because these modest merchants "often cannot do anything without immediate assistance, the Caisse lends itself to their needs, less by [commercial] interest than by charity." The Caisse de Commerce offered moderate loans to retailers and exchanged their clients' outstanding debt for billets de commerce. The Dames considered these options godsends because if their customers defaulted on their accounts or did not pay their debts on time, the Caisse de Commerce, rather than the Dames, absorbed the loss. The Caisse de Commerce's owner asserted that if his company "experiences some losses on their [the Dames des Halles and retail merchants'] behalf, it expects them, and this service is less calculated on profit."[93] The caisse's presentation aimed to win over customers and public opinion.

Yet, the Caisse de Commerce also proved susceptible to the monetary turmoil in les Halles. In the month following the counterfeit debacle that sullied the Maison de Secours, the public began to lose confidence in the Caisse de Commerce as well. Parisians became as wary of the local credit that backed billets de commerce as they were of the supposed assignat holdings that backed billets de confiance. The Dames felt more billets and another credit resource begin to slip away.

On February 19, 1792, the Dames resolved to defend the Caisse de Commerce before the deputies. The market women bypassed the prerequisite Committee of Commerce and "captur[ed] the attention of the Assembly" with their urgent requests. Reminding the deputies that they were "the Dames des Halles, the friends of liberty," the merchants patriotically endorsed the Caisse de Commerce and condemned the "thousands of enemies" who sought to discredit it. They demanded that the Assembly publicly supervise the Caisse de Commerce and support its vital billets de commerce.[94]

To make their case, the Dames did not appeal to privilege or their identity as a corporate body. Instead, they called on the mutual duties of citizens and the state to legitimize their request to bolster the caisse. The Dames justified their value to the nation by citing the utility of the working classes and their consequent worthiness of the Assembly's protection. The Dames asked the legislators to protect a caisse that seeks "to come to the help of the laborer, the artisan, the merchant, not demanding any other guarantee than probity and talent; is it not [the caisse's goal] to give a free boost to industry and to furnish everyone the facility to occupy the post in the State where his/her capacity calls him/her."[95] No doubt thinking of the credit they extended to clients and received from brokers, the Dames implored the deputies "to give [the debtor] the greatest facility to liquidate his/her debt" through the billets. In its report of the Dames' visit, La Chronique de Paris stressed that the Dames sought to protect the monetary interests of "the indigent but active part of the people."[96]

The Dames appealed on behalf of the impoverished population—small merchants and consumers alike. Their orator insisted that "humanity" had always needed such a caisse, but that it had taken a "beneficial revolution" to enable its creation. The Dames asked the Assembly to consider how, without the caisse, greedy financial societies hoped "to attach themselves to the footsteps of the unfortunate to milk their blood until the last drop."[97] Thus, the Dames demanded the state's paternal protection as they would have under the Old Regime, but retailers refashioned the relationship as a reciprocal political contract. They attested to their civic contributions as traders and demanded the state match their contributions. Moreover, they petitioned the nation as members of a socioeconomic group, bound by productive labor rather than by corporate taxonomy.

The Dames also drew on national familial metaphors to bolster their revolutionary legitimacy at the bar. They deftly connected their monetary demands to their highest feminine duty as mothers.[98] They argued that the Caisse de Commerce's advantageous services assisted their trade, which ensured "ease and peace reigning in our families." This environment enabled them to nurture "Our children, what am I saying? the children of the fatherland" who would later serve as "virtuous wives and laboring men." The Dames told the legislators that they raised productive children sensitive to revolutionary values, who "satisfied with the honest gain that they take from their labor, already envision vice with horror."[99] Similarly, *La Chronique de Paris* credited the Caisse de Commerce with monetarily emancipating the Dames so they could foster families useful to the nation: "Becoming free, they [the Dames] promise to raise their children as citizens, & to teach them to enrich with one hand the state by their work, & to hold with the other the sword which must defend it."[100] In the Dames' schema, the benefits the nation would reap from hard-working citizens constituted the return on the state's protection of their monetary interests.

One week after the Dames' Assembly visit, the journal *Courrier des 83 départements* accused the Caisse de Commerce's owner of arranging for "some women of les Halles to appear at the bar to commit the Assembly to protect this caisse." The duplicitous caisse, it asserted, was tricking clients by reimbursing two-thirds of their own billets with "billets of other caisses" that were also failing.[101] The Caisse de Commerce's deficiencies magnified the concurrent problem of the Maison de Secours's billets.

Within four weeks, the Legislative Assembly confronted "public concerns" simmering in Paris over the Maison's notes. First, the deputies passed a special 3-million-livre advance to the capital's treasury. Then, they placed responsibility for local currency communities on the shoulders of municipalities across France. The Assembly charged each municipality with verifying that local caisses' emitted notes matched their assets. Private caisses were to stop producing new billets de confiance. Only caisses run by municipalities could continue to strike billets. Moreover, the municipal caisses were confined to backing their notes with assignats or metal coins (which necessitated the 3-million-livre advance to Paris). Department authorities would check these accounts weekly.[102] The revolutionaries had initially embraced private billets as a cash lifeboat. As that ship sank, citizens from disparate corporations pooled their political capital to defend their money.

Collective Identities in a Postcorporate World: Parisian Merchants Unite across Trades

Following the Dames' early lead, other retailers allied across trade boundaries to bolster the Caisse de Commerce during the Assembly's investigation. In June

1792, forty-eight citizens from diverse occupations signed a petition attesting to the "utility" of the Caisse de Commerce, which enabled their livelihood. Among the myriad supporters of the Caisse's monetary network were two beverage sellers, a naval wholesale supplier, a building painter, a secondhand clothes merchant, a baker, a printer, a National Guard commander, and a former lawyer. Their patchwork alliance of merchants, artisans, service workers, a man of letters, and a militiaman built from their 1790 predecessors. But their heterogeneous configuration also responded to the anticorporate Le Chapelier law that had outlawed collective protest by trade.[103] The two master fan makers might have needed the Caisse de Commerce's notes to square accounts with journeymen, and the two cobblers might have needed the same notes to trade with clientele, but both needed each other to legally defend currency communities after 1791.[104]

The forty-eight petitioners fervently defended the Caisse de Commerce as the only company that "gives even the artisan, the merchant, the producer, and all classes of citizens a way to find help and some resources." Like the Dames, these citizens perceived their families' well-being as inextricably tied to the Caisse de Commerce's financial services. If the deputies took exceptional measures to protect the caisse, the petitioners promised, "We will not cease repeating to our children that it is one of the benefits of the constitution, made from your love for the Public happiness."[105]

As the Caisse de Commerce's problems continued to fester over the summer of 1792, so did politics in the capital. A Parisian crowd invaded the royal palace on June 20 and an insurrection overthrew the king on August 10. With the government crumbling and political uncertainty mounting, the monetary situation became so tenuous that the overwhelmed deputies paused to scrutinize the Caisse de Commerce the day after the monarchy's downfall. The Assembly noted that the Caisse had given "the public a motive for confidence" but insisted that its billets must be backed by the real "solidity and credit of the establishment." Because the Caisse's account books failed this test, the deputies withdrew its private operating license. The Caisse had not fulfilled its promise of serving "public utility." Having been recently reacquainted with the strength of popular activism, the Assembly decreed that "there is an emergency" and lifted the freeze on the Caisse de Commerce's accounts on two conditions.[106] First, the Assembly ordered the Caisse to show the municipality the securities that "it presents to the public for the reimbursement" of their billets.[107] Second, it decreed that officials must stamp the caisse's billets de commerce to account for them as they were admitted.[108] This final stipulation on August 18 created a rush on the Caisse and left its directors nearly bankrupt.

In the face of quickly dwindling monetary resources, the Parisian "merchants and entrepreneurs" convinced more colleagues to craft a follow-up petition on August 26 defending the discredited Caisse de Commerce. This coalition of fifty-seven citizens objected that Assembly's "unfair" decree had "ruined and dishonored" the owners because it required them to pay in full commercial bills not yet due. They protested that since the notes of the Caisse de Commerce were "bills, letters of exchange, and other titles drawn on term, and not on the assignats," the Caisse should not have to retract its critical billets from circulation.[109] The united front complained that the Assembly had hastily passed the fatal decree with many members missing. They asked their representatives to revisit the decree and "render to the capital an establishment made for the happiness of commerce and industry."[110]

The 57 merchants and entrepreneurs had augmented their cross-occupational collaboration and strengthened their numbers since their June petition. In addition to some of the original petitioners, the merchants recruited allies from more assorted trades to protect their common currency community. Although 19 merchants omitted their occupation, left only illegible traces, or signed as an unspecified merchant, the remaining 36 petitioners paint a vibrant picture. Retail merchants such as the two grocers and the two beverage sellers participated, but so did two wholesale merchants of nonfood goods. According to pre-1791 guild delineations, twenty of the signers who specified their occupation would have belonged to ten separate corporations.[111] A building entrepreneur passed the pen to four haberdashers, two jewelry merchants teamed up with a printer, and two wine merchants partnered with a merchant wigmaker. Artisans from across the former guild ranks bolstered the alliance and encompassed a broad range of earning power. A master mason, a carpenter, and a master locksmith signed the petition alongside a small hardware merchant, a cobbler, and two joiners or finish carpenters. The four haberdashers may well have had elite merchandise networks across France and a rich clientele, while the wine merchants likely catered to local buyers.[112] The labored handwriting and spelling of Citizen Fenet, a caterer, suggests that he could barely sign his name.[113] The 19 individuals who left no occupation were likely less economically powerful.

In contrast with former corporate bodies, their collective request looked like a rag-tag alliance. However, threats to a common currency community encouraged citizens to reimagine associative identities. The petitioners rallied to save the Caisse that, they argued, "has for it the merchants of the capital, the national militia, on horse and on foot, the Dames des Halles, the merchant butchers, and bakers, who have presented petitions to you in favor of this Caisse." [114]

In light of the August 10 uprising against the king and the August 25 abolition of feudal indemnities, the coalition's claims to defend a broad swath of citizens gained potency.[115] The dramatic political turn raised the stakes in claiming sovereignty as "the people." The 57 citizens maintained the popular classes' collective sovereignty unified them and justified their request. They reminded their representatives that the services the Caisse de Commerce provided were "the resource of the people" which "is one of the benefits of the constitution that your justice will maintain." Hinting that sovereignty came from below, they concluded, "we will bless your work."[116] Associating "the people" with commerce and industry, the petitioners implied working citizens collectively composed "the people." The deputies reacted in piecemeal fashion in September as they scrambled to hold new elections and establish a republic.

By the government's estimate in early September, there were 1,834,292,175 livres circulating across France "as much in assignats as in caisses' billets or promissory notes for assignats."[117] Since late December 1791, the state had emitted 42 million assignat notes of 15 sous and 31 million assignat notes of 10 sous. Despite these efforts, Parisian merchants, artisans, and workers continued to deal heavily in billets de confiance.[118] The mounting pressure from Parisian petitioners to shore up local billets clashed with calls from deploying soldiers who needed small assignats to spend across regions.[119] The Legislative Assembly reacted by establishing Parisian exchange bureaus to provide small change, but these bureaus would only change citizens' billets worth 50 sous or less into assignats of 10 and 15 sous.[120] To fund the redemption, the Assembly ordered any "companies, banks, caisses, or citizens" that had issued billets of 50 sous or less to surrender their corresponding securities to the city. After pulling the promissory notes, the city would cancel and return them to the issuing caisses. Officials anticipated that 2,400,000 livres would be converted in the first wave. The deputies resolved to repeat the process "until the total extinction of the billets de confiance."[121] In the battle between a national currency community armed with small assignats and regional currency communities built on local promissory notes, the future looked bleak for the latter.

Where Is Sovereignty? National Policy, Parisian Pressure, and Vertical Alliances

The exchange plans of the expired Assembly along with the Republic's birth on September 22 wildly altered the parameters of the small change debate. The Convention's commitment to an assignat-only future nullified citizens' claims that protecting local notes benefited national interests. Yet, the Republic closed one door while opening another: the nascent government had been founded on the sovereignty of the people. The Dames and their factrices (brokers) seized this position to safeguard their billets throughout fall 1792. Abandoning discourses of exceptionalism, the retailers and brokers experimented with social contract logic and drew political legitimacy from their useful work. Their tactics further blurred the vertical boundaries within former corporate strata. While resisting the Republic's drive toward a standardized currency, the Dames and their factrices ironically escalated regional tensions influencing their trade. The provinces, buttressed by a tradition of regional corporatism and justifiable suspicion of Parisian policies, did not trust unfamiliar billets from distant Parisian banks. The Republic needed workaday solutions for cash and citizens' cooperation for its assignat-only policy to work.

The Convention's struggle to recall the billets de confiance made it painfully evident that the Dames still relied on the Maison de Secours notes. In October 1792, the Dames from the fish market petitioned the Convention to protest that they conducted their commerce with "only" the billets from the Maison de Secours. The Dames complained that they seemed to be "nearly the only victims" of the Maison's financial debacle. The radical deputy Louis Legendre, a butcher familiar with the capital's subsistence trade, confirmed the Dames' predicament.[122] He noted that "the majority of rich individuals" paid for their food from les Halles with billets from the Maison de Secours and the Caisse Patriotique, while countryside suppliers hesitated to accept these condemned notes from the Dames as payment for supplies.[123]

The Dames compelled the Convention to wrestle with a thorny question: who should reconcile the enormous discrepancy between the outstanding Maison promissory notes and its feeble remaining holdings? Must the nation or the city bear the burden of a financial remedy? Deputy Legendre argued that such a dire situation merited the Convention's attention, but the deputies decided to forward the Dames' demands to the municipality since the Maison de Secours was primarily a Parisian establishment. The Dames started shouting in the wings at the unfavorable motion. Despite initially agreeing to have their petition read, they now called for the floor. Deputy Charles-Nicolas Osselin, who was named to the Commune on August 10, had backed the Dames' original petition.[124] But upon the Dames' outburst, he asked the President to eject them in order "that the citizens learn to yield to the law."[125]

When the Convention denied the Dames' petition, it implicitly asked also who deserved its attention and why. In this case, the Convention dismissed the Dames because it viewed their problem as a municipal financial issue. Moreover, the Convention was not convinced by the Dames' entreaty for special treatment due to their occupational hardships.[126] With regard to the Maison de Secours, the Dames demanded highly localized exceptions without extending the gain to the popular classes as a whole.[127] The retailers unpersuasively strove to protect a single currency community rather than couching their request in national interest. Thus, the Convention evoked the law's sovereignty before any group's sovereignty. In an abrupt about-face from the Assembly's August decision to float an advance to the capital to redeem its troubled billets, the Convention rejected the Dames' appeal.

The next day, the Théâtre Français and Luxembourg sections wrote to the Convention and shifted the ideological stakes of the Dames' request. Rather than spotlighting the Dames' particularly difficult position, the sections urged the Convention to think of "the indigent class of citizens." They reported that they had sent representatives into the markets to encourage "the people" to retain confidence in the Maison's billets. The sections emphasized that the poorest swath of the population relied on these notes to buy their food. Girondin Deputy Jean-Bonaventure-Blaise-Hilarion Birotteau from the southwestern Department of Pyrénées-Orientales weighed the problem from municipal, departmental, and national perspectives.[128] Birotteau concluded that the sections ultimately made the same invalid requests as the Dames: the national treasury could not bail out private caisses serving only the capital region. Montagnard Deputy Marc-Antoine Jullien, who was also named to the Convention from a distant department (la Drôme in the southeast), pivoted to frame the suppliants as mouthpieces of the popular classes, rather than as Parisians.[129] Jullien cried, "We are the representatives of the poor, we are the fathers of the people who have been victims of the cupidity of the rich for a long time, we owe them help."[130]

The Convention's unfolding debate exposed the fundamental quandary in Rousseauian ideology: where to locate the general will. When Deputy Jullien insisted that "you [the deputies] have made sovereign the interests of the people," he butted heads with Deputy Marguerite-Élie Guadet, a leading figure from Gironde who was the Convention's president. Guadet was a rival of the pro-Parisian Montagnards and had even attempted to disband the Commune in late August.[131] He retorted that regional interests were not national interests, no matter the citizens' socioeconomic status. Guadet insisted, "There are no longer any sovereigns in France; but one sole sovereign, the people." Nonetheless, Jullien persisted. He asserted that the Convention should place a "patriotic tax" on the rich to back the Maison's promissory notes, which were vital to "the unhappiest class." Deputy Ignace Brunel, a moderate from the southern department of Hérault, responded that while Jullien's commitment to "the poor" was admirable, his solution would unjustly tax "the people" who lived outside of Paris.[132] Brunel convinced the Convention that Jullien "was not foreseeing that by exhausting the State's resources in favor of the people of one commune, one was bringing the biggest prejudice against the people from other parts of the Republic."[133] Unless the Dames and their neighbors could legitimize their monetary needs in broader terms, the Convention would deny their pleas as privileging Parisian interests over provincial ones.

Concerning the Maison de Secours's notes, the Convention's dichotomy between Paris and the provinces elided a far more complex reality. No group understood this better than the Dames' factrices, who functioned as a monetary link between countryside suppliers and more than 1,000 retailers. Consequently, these brokers were highly sensitive to assignat reform and public confidence in local notes. [134] On the sale side, the Dames and other clients operated on modest scales within Parisian monetary networks. The factrices recognized that the assignat-only system could ruin the Dames' small change. On the supply side, the factrices' provincial wholesalers conducted business on a larger scale and operated within the countryside's currency communities. The factrices felt how severely their provincial suppliers distrusted Parisian tokens. A wholesaler might have difficulty recirculating Parisian billets in the countryside where local caisses underwrote other notes. Since the most powerful wholesalers dealt in great quantities of goods and money, they preferred assignats in denominations of 50 livres that were portable and secure. To balance their two-directional accounts, the factrices dealt in assignats, promissory notes, and social capital.

By the end of October 1792, the factrices could hear the death bell for the Maison de Secours's overextended billets and the other varieties of small change with which the Dames paid them. Wholesale fish suppliers complained to the Commune that they received death threats if they refused the Maison billets. Parisians, in turn, worried that they might not receive supplies from reluctant wholesalers. [135] Officials from Nangis traveled over 37 miles to the Convention to attest that "public tranquility had been extremely troubled by the rumors spread that these [Maison] billets," imported by returning wholesalers, "would no longer have any worth." The Nangissiens demanded "the most serious and most prompt attention." [136] The Convention, which had attempted to pull the Maison's billets from circulation, faced the disconcerting reality that 2,936,063 livres of the Maison's notes still powered trade. Even more devastating, the Maison's holdings deficit, combined with that of the remaining Parisian caisses, hovered around 5 million livres. [137]

The factrices knew that Dames' businesses would fail if the deputies refused to cover the discrepancy between the emitted Maison notes and their assignat backings. Thus, to guarantee their own commerce with the Dames, the factrices of the fish market intervened on the retailers' behalf but strategized their entreaties as a campaign to help all indigent citizens. On November 6, 1792, the factrices addressed the Convention to ask that "the poor no longer be victims of the Maison de Secours." [138] The deputies sent their request to the Committee of Finances for further consideration.

Much to the factrices' dismay, the Convention stood firm in its plan two days later to terminate all billets de confiance. It forbade public and private caisses from striking any more promissory tokens. The deputies ordered municipalities to pull all billets from circulation by January, including those of the Maison, and to publicly burn them.[139] When new forms arrived to print 40 million livres of assignats in 10 sous notes, the deputies confirmed they would obliterate local cash.[140]

Nonetheless, the Convention heeded the factrices' appeal to consider "the troubles that this could bring" to "daily transactions." It ordered the departments and communes to cover any deficits created by caisses that had issued small notes below 25 livres without means to reimburse them. The Convention explained the addendum was "a duty" of the nation's representatives "in order that the segment of people who are the least fortunate do not fall victim to the insolvency or to the guilty maneuvers of people who emitted [the billets]."[141] Swayed by the threat of market paralysis and the factrices' appeal, the Convention begrudgingly advanced 1 million more assignats to Paris to replace the recalled promissory notes of less than 25 livres. It vehemently insisted that municipal debts and private caisses' debts "cannot in any case form a debt charged to the Republic." The advance was not a bailout.[142]

But, after one week, the Convention had still not sent the emergency funds. The Commune remained unable provide the factrices assignats for the Maison billets they turned in. Enraged, five factrices wrote to the minister of the interior Jean-Marie Roland threatening to halt their broker services, as they had once already, if they continued to bear the burdens of the assignat shortage. In their letter, the factrices brazenly threatened to send retailers who wanted to buy supplies directly to the minister's house. "Thus you can foresee it," they warned, "that tonight, perhaps at 3:00 in the morning, his house will be assailed by 300 or 400 women [Dames des Halles] who need to work; because we [the factrices] are firmly resolved to not sell any merchandise and to refuse the billets."[143] If the Dames could redeem their bills for assignats, the factrices' problems would also be solved. To buy time, Minister Roland negotiated a stay on the provisioning impasse. He could sleep soundly for at least two weeks.

The Convention's inadequate follow-up galvanized alliances across vertical levels of trade in the marketplace. In early December 1792, the Dames defended their shared cash before the Convention. At the bar, the Dames attacked the decree limiting each person's exchange of billets de confiance into assignats to 25 livres per day. This ceiling created an insurmountable obstacle for the factrices, who dealt in large quantities of money but received payment from the Dames in small Maison notes.[144] The deputation of Dames demanded that authorities continue reimbursing the factrices for all the Maison notes that the Dames paid them. They observed that, because their factrices could not exchange more than 25 livres of notes per day, "their position becomes as deplorable as our own." The Dames paid each factrice 500 to 700 livres in Maison notes per day. The retailers pointed out that they could not convert the Maison notes that they received from their customers into assignats to pay the factrices because the daily exchange lines were four hours long.[145]

Given the deputies' unwillingness to accord special monetary privileges to Paris, the Dames framed their grievance as integral to the wider "interests of the people" and painted its resolution as the deputies' benevolent duty. The Dames asked the deputies "to turn their paternal regards toward them and to steal a moment in favor of the public thing." They invited their political fathers to consider how their commerce "procures for over 20,000 families the means to subsist." Thus, the Dames hitched their occupational interests to the survival of other families within the national family. In addition, the Dames paraphrased the deputies' own conclusion from one month earlier: They reminded the Convention that they were not the aggressors, but "victims of the villainy of a man [the director of the Maison de Secours], who in the eyes of the Constitutional Assembly, abused public confidence." Evoking the social compact, the Dames insisted, "Deign to throw a glance, legislators, on our awful situation; we are unfortunate people in need: this title alone gives us some rights to your sensitivity."[146]

The same day, the factrices submitted a parallel petition to the Department of Paris pleading to redeem more than 25 livres per day. Introducing themselves first as "citoyennes" then as "brokers," the factrices asserted, "the provisioning of the capital and public tranquility" depended on their monetary requisites. Echoing the Dames, the factrices testified that the Maison billets were the "only cash that they receive from the fish retailers [the Dames] who rid themselves of it and which the wholesalers refuse." Provincial suppliers understood that the government's transition to an assignat-only system meant promissory bills could only be redeemed in their issuing city. By December, it was a worthless gamble for countryside wholesalers to transport Maison notes or other Parisian billets outside the capital. Stuck in the middle, the factrices demanded "special protection" and protested that they were inadvertently "becoming the intermediaries for withdrawing the Maison billets" from circulation.[147]

Like the Dames, the factrices depicted their commerce as serving citizens' stomachs as well as the peace-keeping state. The factrices impressed on the Department that their "fish commerce contains the existence of *20 thousand souls* of the most indigent class." Without reform, food supply chains would break down and bring about "an insurrection and the largest disorder." The factrices highlighted their public utility as part of the reciprocal contract between working citizens and the state. Rather than demand direct assistance or charity for disadvantaged individuals, the factrices asked the department to support "commerce" and working citizens by granting them exceptional permission to exchange Maison notes.[148]

Unable to grant the factrices an "exception to the law," the Department hurriedly passed the factrices' petition to Interior Minister Roland. The Department noted that the factrices had already accumulated a backlog of "more than *forty-thousand livres*" in Maison notes.[149] Department officials relayed the factrices' warning that their situation had grown "so urgent that if citizen Roland does not have the generosity to take into consideration our unfortunate and needy position, we will be constrained and forced to refuse the notes tonight at 2 am when our service begins and we are not responsible for what will result." Minister Roland called on the Convention to read the factrices' petition and the Department's assessment aloud.[150]

Compelled by the petitioners' logic and facing 650,000 potentially hungry Parisians, the Convention decreed that the factrices could exchange their Maison notes for assignats directly with the Department, thereby circumventing the 25-livre limit.[151] The Dames and the factrices had successfully collaborated across the vertical trade hierarchies to guarantee practical money. They had scrambled to defend a particular currency community, but they triumphed because they drew expansively on public utility over special interests, the social contract over corporate privilege, and national interests over Parisian exemptions. Marketplace actors revealed that the deputies could not establish a national currency community without catering to the local ones they aimed to obliterate.

In March 1793, the National Convention discontinued promissory notes. The substitute tokens, which had seemed like godsends in 1790, could no longer circulate as legal tender starting April 1, 1793.[152] Since the monarchy's collapse, the Dames and other merchants had continued to enlarge their socioeconomic alliances and decisively influence monetary reform. Early in 1793, the Convention attempted to close the Parisian caisse saga by convicting the Maison de Secours's directors of fraud and publicly burning their notes.[153] The deputies instructed all citizens to redeem any remaining billets de confiance for assignats from their issuing caisses.[154] The Convention hoped that its firm assignat-only strategy would streamline the chaos of confidence, credit, and tender. Since 1789, currency had become an economic, logistical, and political choice in everyday trade. But by spring 1793, the price of admission to the nation was payable only in assignats.[155]

Even after the billets' failure, citizens formed currency communities to protect local needs. Citizens across France, like the journeymen, artisans, and "local elite" protesting assignat hardships in the town of La Neuve-Lyre, continued to join forces across corporate strata to defend shared currency.[156] When Mayence (briefly seeking annexation to France) was cut off by Prussian siege in May 1793, the war council raised the value of each paper bill by signing the back. The counterrevolutionary army likewise created monetary rules in Vendée strongholds. Republican assignats only became acceptable tender if they were "signed and admitted in the name of the king."[157]

The lingering trauma of the billets de confiance, regional currency communities, inflation, and war weakened successive attempts to implement national paper money. In 1796, the revolutionaries replaced the failed assignats with a new currency called the "mandats." The Dames des Halles distrusted these notes even more than the assignats. The Commissaire de Police complained that "at the Halles of Paris one will not sell anything if he/she hears [the customer] mention the Mandat, [the merchants especially] won't consider it for the purchase of food, all the male and female merchants simultaneously shout all of their foodstuffs' prices in two amounts, one in assignats and the other in silver." The retailers, the commissioner explained, would either collectively attack the "poor holder of republican Money" or drive the holder to the local justice under a barrage of insults.[158] The mandat notes ultimately lost their value before workers could even finish printing them.[159] In 1803, Napoleon cautiously tried his hand by permitting the three-year-old Bank of France to emit paper notes in the capital. When he attempted to circulate the notes to the provinces in 1809, citizens remembered the assignat nightmare and how the Parisian caisses had been bailed out at their expense. The countryside clung to metal coins until officials printed smaller notes than those in Paris to cater to regional commerce.[160]

During the three years without sufficient assignats from 1790 to 1793, the billets de confiance exposed common economic interests among formerly disparate corporate groups. Citizens cooperated innovatively across trade identities to address shared monetary challenges introduced by currency reform. They joined forces along the contours of currency communities, which sometimes hinted at proto-class interests. Collaborations that began as economic alliances quickly morphed into political alliances. In this way, the assignats created within the popular classes venues for dialogue, cooperation, and cohesion that surpassed the occupationally bound identities of corporate society. These emerging groups tested new visions of citizenship while framing their requests as public interest rather than particular privilege.

Among baskets of fish and piles of vegetables, practical currency sparked a tremendous revolution in postcorporate society and citizenship. In Paris, the corporate titan of the Old Regime arrived tattered on the eve of 1791 antiguild legislation not only because of the deputies' preemptive attacks, but also because citizens themselves had already begun to reformulate political legitimacy and economic communities. Since 1790, marketplace actors had forged innovative socioeconomic identities to secure usable money. To avoid accusations of corporatism, Parisians continued these tactics after the deputies abolished the guilds. Thus, the assignat catalyzed the transition to a postcorporate world by complicating the material experience of cash, throwing currency communities into the spotlight, and triggering innovative political alliances. After the Republic's birth, these collaborators regrouped around popular sovereignty and emphasized how their work served the nation. Citizens' claims that their useful labor legitimated political demands would be echoed by the sans-culotte movement, which gained ground in the capital when the Parisian billets collapsed. By 1793, the Dames and their neighbors had unraveled the corporate world from below, had reinvented political coalitions, and had changed the trajectory of national currency reform to protect small change in the marketplace. In the months that followed, Parisians' concerns over small change morphed into dramatic battles over the price of goods themselves.

The Cost of Female Citizenship

Price Controls and the Gendering of Democracy
in Revolutionary France

In fall 1793, the revolutionaries found themselves squeezed by war, economic crisis, and factional rivalries. The upstart republic had just issued a mass military conscription to beat back foreign troops on its eastern border. In the West, civil war raged in the counterrevolutionary Vendée. Across France, inflation and shortages shook the food markets. Factional rivalries divided the National Convention. During the previous spring, the Girondins and the Montagnards had attempted to best each other in tactical economic contests and win grassroots support. On the right, the Girondins had supported free market legislation and believed that the Revolution was radicalizing too quickly. They opposed price controls that favored consumers at the expense of merchants and countryside producers. However, the leading Girondins had been purged from the Convention in June and were awaiting trial in prison during the fall of 1793.[1] On the left, the Montagnards had advocated for emergency economic regulation to protect the popular classes and to win the sans-culottes' support. The Montagnards dominated the Convention and many partisans, like Maximilien Robespierre, were leading members of the Jacobin club.[2] Although they embraced social equality, the Montagnards boldly presented themselves as a parliamentary middle path between popular radicals and the more centrist Girondins.[3]

In this tightening vise of war, dearth, and political polarization, the Convention passed two hallmarks of Jacobin legislation that set decisive precedents for state market regulation and gendered citizenship. The Montagnards' first program, extensive price controls called the General Maximum, appeared to pivot sharply from the early Revolution's free market reforms. Reacting to provisioning problems, spiraling inflation, and popular pressure, the deputies capped wages and the price of staple goods in September 1793. To drive an initial Maximum on bread past reluctant Girondins four months earlier, the Montagnards had temporarily aligned with a radical popular group called the Enragés. From Parisian clubs and neighborhood assemblies, the Enragés militantly called for direct democracy and pressured the Montagnards to decisively favor consumers over merchants.[4] The Enragés and their sans-culotte supporters continued to push the Montagnards left on the eve of the General Maximum.

The Montagnards' second momentous decree, the closing of women's political clubs, marked women's exclusion from institutional citizenship by barring women's political assemblies. Shortly after the Montagnards passed the General Maximum in September 1793, physical fights repeatedly broke out between two major groups of women. On the one side of the clashes stood several hundred Dames des Halles. The Maximum threated to cripple their livelihood and ruin their retail trade in fish, vegetables, cheese, and butter.[5] On the other side of the flying fists was the leading women's political club, the Société des Citoyennes républicaines révolutionnaires. These club women aligned with the Enragés and agitated for proconsumer legislation like price controls. Montagnard deputies used the brawls between the Dames and the Citoyennes républicaines to argue that women were irrational, emotional, and had no place in formal politics. Employing this discourse of gendered deficiencies, the Convention shuttered women's clubs on October 30, 1793. Some historians have interpreted this ban as codifying Rousseauian notions of gender and ideologically stunting women's citizenship at the outset of French democracy.[6]

This chapter argues that the revolutionaries' closing of the women's clubs and the General Maximum were the products of much more than gendered anxieties or competing economic agendas. Both the brawls among women and the conflicts over price controls tapped into the fundamentally political nature of daily trade. They were, in fact, interlocking efforts to articulate economic citizenship, or the ways in which an individual's economic activities, such as buying goods, selling food, or paying taxes, position him or her within the collective social body. A society's regulatory laws implicitly assign political value and social duties to economic roles. For example, what should retailers owe the body politic in exchange for profiting on public market space? What economic activities distinguish a retailer as a responsible citizen instead of a profiteering leech? Economic endeavors effectively include or exclude an individual from the cooperative body politic. If an individual's economic roles integrate him or her into this lived social contract, they enable him or her to make claims on the state in return. For example, police would likely listen to a compliant merchant's request to stop black market goods. And if retailers provided a useful service by provisioning citizens, the state might consider their demands to modify price caps.

Analyzing the Maximum throws light on the revolutionaries' tenuous attempts to translate the abstract social contract into daily commercial relationships.[7] However, historians have not paid enough attention to how the mechanics of economic policy unfolded in the marketplace and how the inner workings of Maximum rules created a new map of economic citizenship. While retailers demanded legal profit margins for their trade, club women denounced merchants as conspiring hoarders, and the Convention attempted to balance prices and wages, all appraised citizens' societal worth through their occupation. The revolutionaries assessed how the economic duties of merchants and consumers doubled as political duties and how the state should regulate this relationship.

To explore how the revolutionaries debated economic citizenship through daily trade while obscuring factional rivalries under gendered discourses, this chapter focuses on the confluence of the Maximum in the assembly hall and the confrontations between the Dames and the club women in the marketplace. While battling over price controls, the Dames and the Citoyennes républicaines clamored at the Convention's door to smear one another as transgressive women. At the same time, Montagnard deputies harnessed the conflict among the women to blame the disturbances on the free-market supporting Girondins to their right and to silence the proconsumer women's club that supported the increasingly radical Enragés to the Montagnards' left. The gendered debates on women's political clubs in 1793 thus became a convenient screen for factional clashes over inscribing the social contract in everyday trade.

Subsistence Problems and the First Maximum

The French had combatted subsistence problems since time immemorial, but the Revolution introduced new challenges. From 1789 to 1791, it appeared that the National Assembly's policies of economic liberalism had lowered bread prices. But a sugar crisis, foreign war, civil war, and the devaluation of the assignat soon threatened to send prices skyrocketing.[8] When France declared war on Austria in April 1792, the nation lost access to some external supplies.[9] Moreover, the government faced the critical problem of funneling food to armies within the country and abroad while continuing to feed large urban centers like Paris. In this charged environment, banks exploited the billets de confiance to speculate on the assignat, which led to spiraling inflation and pushed food prices higher.[10] In September 1792, the Commune established some price controls on bread, but no national legislation regulated its price.[11] The price of eggs the Dames sold surged by more than 28 percent over the course of 1792.[12] By early 1793, price increases on food and essentials outpaced wage increases.[13]

Within the Convention, the challenges were compounded by two factions whose economic strategies conflicted and who imagined different roles for the popular classes. Of the twenty-four Parisian deputies, twenty-one were Montagnards. The sans-culottes' proximity lent them muscle in the Convention.[14] As fierce defenders of the new Republic, the Montagnards were attuned to the powerful economic undertones of political equality. Robespierre and his allies loomed large in their ranks. The Girondins agitated for war against Austria and also approved the overthrow of the king in August 1792. However, they became wary of popular violence in the wake of the September Massacres shortly thereafter. By late fall 1792, the Girondins had come to believe the Revolution was unfolding at an unruly pace.[15] Since many of the faction's leaders came from the Gironde and other provincial departments, the Girondins' objections to the sans-culottes' violence made them appear generally resentful of the capital.[16] There was truth to this, as the Girondins desired a representative government expressed in parliamentary, rather than street, forms. They also located sovereignty more in the manifold provinces than in the powerful capital.[17] In late January 1973, the Girondins and the Montagnards further split over the guilty king's fate. The Montagnards demanded the king's immediate execution, while many Girondins unsuccessfully advocated for a plebiscite that might be more forgiving.[18] Between the Girondins and the Montagnards sat the deputies of the "Plain," whose votes shifted by issue and moment.[19]

As the assignat declined to 50 percent of its face value and supply problems from civil war in the Vendée drove prices higher in late winter 1793, the radical Enragés increased pressure on the Convention from the streets. The Enragés lobbied relentlessly to secure affordable food for wage laborers.[20] They were supported in this endeavor by sans-culottes, or militant members of the Parisian popular classes who participated in neighborhood sectional assemblies and held common political interests in subsistence and consumption.[21] When it abolished the guilds in 1791, the Assembly had outlawed workers' traditional methods of organizing stoppages and associations to secure higher wages.[22] Thus, in 1793, the sans-culottes turned to street activism and sectional assemblies to influence the Convention's policies. The sans-culottes believed that the food trade should ultimately serve "the people," whom they firmly interpreted as consumers, not sellers or producers. For example, the Gardes-Françaises section insisted that farmers and retailers consider their foodstuffs "as being goods placed in their trust for which [they are] to render an account to the Republic."[23] Food might pass through merchants' hands, but it was ultimately the nation's property from the perspective of the sans-culottes and their allies.

The Enragés and sans- culottes demanded the Convention protect consumer, not merchant, interests.[24] On February 12, 1793, the Parisian sections dispatched representatives to decry the Convention's free market approach to the grain trade. They lamented, "Do they [the pro–free market deputies], these self-styled economic theorists, these friends of absolute freedom of commerce in grains, not therefore see that in ripping away the poor's bread, they only enrich greedy speculators?" Eerily hinting that "where there is no bread, there are no longer any laws, any liberty, any Republic," the deputation called on the Convention to standardize the measures and maximum price of grain.[25] On February 25 and 26, Parisian crowds, composed of more women than men, rioted in the streets against high sugar prices and against shopkeepers they presumed to be profiteering.[26] Pierre-Gaspard Chaumette, a representative of the Commune, warned, "There are malicious individuals, hoarders. . . . Public misery is the cornerstone of an infinite number of capitalists' interested [private] speculations." Chaumette complained the Parisian poor were unable to "live free" because of the gulf between their wages and the exorbitant price of basic necessities. Lowering the cost of living, Chaumette insisted, would rally poor citizens to revolutionary causes.[27] Foreshadowing the Maximum's premises, he asked the Convention to restore a "healthy ratio" between wages and prices.

As the war against nearly every major European power escalated throughout February 1793, French citizens petitioned the Convention for relief from soaring bread prices. Assuring affordable food, they insisted, was the state's duty to loyal citizens. On behalf of wives of military volunteers from Paris and Versailles, Citoyenne Wuaflard expressed this sentiment before the Convention. She attested that while the wives "are sorry to watch their husbands, [and] their relatives leave for the frontiers, they are [simultaneously] frightened by the maneuvers of the hoarders." The women argued that if they sacrificed to protect the nation, the state must stabilize the food trade to protect them in return.[28]

Parisians vented their frustration over prices and the vulnerable food supply by condemning the Convention in the street, even with royalist remarks. Among clamors against high prices in February 1793, one police reporter wrote to his superiors, "It is impossible that the unhappy [people] can wait much more time, in spite of their patriotism, they also judge the Convention very severely, reproaching it with bitterness for consuming precious time disputing and maligning one another, and [they] demand that the hoarders be repressed and that it [the Convention] lowers the price of essential foodstuffs."[29] Enragé leaders sought to capitalize on the discontent to start an uprising, force price limits on all goods, and institute capital punishment for hoarders. These March attempts failed, but the police and deputies took note.[30]

In April, the Parisian sections, the Department of Paris, and deputations from other communes speculated on who caused high grain prices and how to resolve the problem. The petitioners who came in waves to the Convention's floor and to the Committee of Agriculture and Commerce frequently blamed farmers, field hands, and commercial agents. The Commune of Frett held producers and laborers accountable for grain prices, whereas the Commune of Saint-Germain-en-Laye sought to ban middle merchants and punish farmers who abandoned their fields.[31] Like many others, the Commune of Bercy asked the deputies "to fix the *maximum* price of essential food, [and] force the cultivators and farmers to supply the markets."[32]

Since the requests largely focused on grain prices, the Convention debated who owned grain as a fruit of the earth. The Committee of Agriculture and Commerce presented vice-president of the Department of Paris Alexandre-Louis Lachevardière's opinion that "the fixation of a maximum price of grains is just." Lachevardière explained that, when men form a society, "the principle condition of the [social] contract is that all must assure the existence of everyone, and give everyone the means to maintain existence. Among the other advantages that society assures, one must include property, but the *Declaration of Rights* wisely said: Let property always be subordinate to public necessity, and subject to a prior indemnity."[33]

Nonetheless, the Girondin deputies especially worried about limiting the free market through price controls. Economic liberalism had greatly informed the National Assembly's projects since the revolutionaries began dismantling Old Regime corporatism in 1789. Girondin deputies protested that state regulation would undermine liberty in the marketplace. In the fall of 1792, Deputy Jacques Pierre Brissot, a leading Girondin and recently ousted Jacobin, had attacked the Jacobins as " 'disorganizers who wish to level everything: property, leisure, the price of provisions, the various services to be rendered to society.' "[34] From the Girondins' perspective, the sans-culottes' 1793 demands for market regulation recalled Old Regime privileges and restraints.

The Girondins objected that capping grain prices would not respect property or commerce, would not correct the causes of high prices, and would disadvantage grain producers. Girondin Charles Barbaroux, a deputy from Creuse, insisted that men formed society to protect property as the source of subsistence.[35] He blamed war and the assignat for high prices. First, war disrupted supply lines and increased transportation costs between regions. It also reduced the number of field hands available to farmers. Second, farmers had to pay all their laborers in assignats, whose value was declining.[36] Despite shouts from Montagnards, Barbaroux asserted, "above all, let us thank commerce, the repairer of the faults of men and the harm of war."[37] Barbaroux then invited the sans-culottes, "O you [tu] who cry at the expense of bread! Honest artisan, come into the countryside, come I want you to converse with the laborer who nourishes you; I want you to embrace one another."[38]

The Girondins argued that price caps would only be just and effective if they encompassed each step from production to sale. But this would be nearly impossible. Barbaroux projected that, to stay viable with limited profit, farmers would demand the Convention place maximums on their farm animals, equipment, and laborers all while somehow preventing disease and crop-smashing weather.[39] Without these systematic checks, price limits would assist consumers to the detriment of producers and merchants. Three days later, Barbaroux's Girondin colleague Jean-François Ducos insisted that "if the fixation of the price of grain was not in proportion with the costliness of other goods, with the progress of the crop, with the salary of field hands, the cultivator would consequently receive no product from the exploitation of his field, [he] would cease to cultivate it such that most fields would be abandoned next year, and thus the people would die of hunger." Boos descended on Ducos from the galleries above and "violent murmurs arose" among the Montagnards.[40]

Despite their willingness to ally with radical popular groups in the spring, the Montagnards' attitudes toward price controls were more complex than both the Girondins' accusations and the sans-culottes' unwavering proconsumer line. The Montagnards had drawn attention to prices and the food supply in the winter. Food riots in the provinces had prompted Robespierre to insist, "the most fundamental law of society is . . . that which guarantees the means of existence to every person; every other law is subordinate to this one."[41] But the Montagnards hesitated to advocate heavy regulation without the sans-culottes' persistent pressure. Even in late April, Danton, a Montagnard deputy, could not ignore the haunting affront that price controls posed to physiocrat (free market and proagriculture) sensibilities. Danton unsuccessfully proposed that farmers freely set prices and then the government exercise "a tax on the rich" to cover the gap between the prices and working wages. But the Montagnards balked at determining whose food would be subsidized and at controlling local wages to keep the ratio balanced.[42] The Montagnards found themselves frequently backpedaling to explain how emergency market controls could correspond with revolutionary principles of liberty.

As people, petitions, and letters continued to pour into the Convention in favor of a maximum, the Montagnards became open to creating price ceilings as a tactical maneuver. Jean-Paul Marat, a far-left deputy and popular journalist, chastised the Girondins and drew the sans-culottes close to the Montagnards. He fumed, "You [the Girondins] have left the people without arms and without bread. You are spending your time listening to Encyclopedists on subsistence [laughter], and we die of hunger in the midst of abundance."[43]

On May 4, 1793, the Montagnards passed the first national Maximum on grain to satisfy the Enragés and Parisian sections to their left, to stifle the Girondins to their right, and to combat supposed subsistence sabotage by foreign enemies.[44] The deputies decreed that the "maximum prices of grains will be fixed, in all the departments of the Republic according to the maximum day's labor [wages]." The deputies aimed for "each consumer" to spend half their day's wages on bread. Municipalities would be responsible for finding the local "average price of a day's work" so that department directors could adjust regional grain maximums every May and November.[45] Therefore, the grain Maximum's guiding principles aligned with the Enragés' goals: the controls sought to protect the consumer by making bread affordable relative to a laborer's income. And while the law capped prices in accordance with workers' wages, it did not create a cap on wages that could inflate faster than the semiannual adjustment. Nor did the law curb farmers' costs in producing the grain, wholesalers' costs for transporting it, and merchants' costs in storing it.

To hand off the grain trade to local officials as quickly as possible, the Convention instructed officials to set the initial maximums by averaging departmental grain prices from January to May 1793.[46] All owners, farmers, and storers of grain were to report their holdings to the municipal authorities who would surveil supplies. The deputies reiterated that "Subsistence stuffs, like all properties, are sacred and inviolable" and decreed that arbitrary price limits on grain, like artificial price gouging, constituted a criminal act.[47]

Since the first Maximum only applied to grain and flour, neither of which the Dames sold, the market women experienced the law solely as consumers. As retailers of other foodstuffs, the Dames confronted the high bread prices in solidarity with other city-dwellers.[48] Regarding bread, they held the same commercial interests as wage laborers who were their own customers. Therefore, the proconsumer grain Maximum backed by the Montagnards and Enragés benefited the Dames. Ultimately, however, the Enragés' escalating accusations that all food merchants could be counterrevolutionary plotters marred the Dames' image.

On May 10, 1793, one week after capping grain prices, the Société des Citoyennes républicaines révolutionnaires convened its first women's club meeting in the capital. Since the start of the Revolution, women had formed at least thirty clubs across France,[49] had become members in mixed-sex clubs in Paris and elsewhere,[50] and had influenced men's club meetings through the lively galleries overlooking proceedings. The Société des Citoyennes républicaines révolutionnaires, however, became the capital's only political club exclusively for women. It boasted around 170 official members and averaged 100 attendees at the meetings it convened in the Jacobin library.[51] Pauline Léon, a daughter of a chocolatier, and actress Claire Lacombe, both political activists since 1789 who also participated in overthrowing the king, led the club along with lower-middle-class women.[52] The Citoyennes républicaines informed the municipal government that they aimed "to deliberate on the ways to disrupt the projects of the Republic's enemies."[53] To guard the interior of the fatherland, the club even agitated for women's right to bear arms. This simple goal carried significant political overtones, as the revolutionaries associated the right to bear arms with voting rights and full citizenship.[54]

Although the Citoyennes républicaines initially aligned more with the Jacobins than the inflammatory Enragés, the club's defensive mission led them to lambast merchants as tools in counterrevolutionary schemes or parasites who preyed on the popular classes.[55] One week after the club's founding, Claire Lacombe condemned wealthy traders and the Girondins in a passionate speech to the Jacobin club. She exhorted them, "Strike down the agitators, the hoarders and the egoistic merchants." "There exists," she proclaimed, "an awful plot to make the people die of hunger by raising prices of essential foodstuffs to colossal levels." In les Halles, some Citoyennes républicaines surveyed transactions as citizen-watchdogs.[56]

The Citoyennes républicaines frequently rallied crowds outside the Convention against Girondin policies that seemed to favor sellers over buyers and demanded "the removal of twenty-two [Girondin] deputies."[57] They rallied other women to join their cause, shouting "Long live the Montagnards! To the guillotine with the Brissotins [Girondins]!"[58] Inside the Convention, the Citoyennes républicaines pressured the Girondins with comments from the galleries. They even set the tone for legislative debates in late May by controlling entrance to the galleries. Girondin sympathizers found the Citoyennes républicaines periodically blocking their access.[59]

By the end of May 1793, the Montagnards and the Enragés had solidified their alliance on the back of the grain Maximum. Their parliamentary/popular coalition was too strong for the Girondins. On May 31, the Parisian sections started organizing an insurrection backed by a militia of 20,000 sans-culottes and assisted by the National Guard.[60] That same day, Claire Lacombe spoke at a club to rally section leaders and encourage "the sacred insurrection that would deliver the Mountain [the Montagnards] from its shackles."[61] The initial revolt failed, but on June 2 the Parisian sections surrounded the Convention again. The sections and the Citoyennes républicaines successfully petitioned the encircled Montagnards to purge the first wave of Girondins.[62] The strongest opponents to economic controls left the hall under arrest. One Enragé leader praised the Citoyennes républicaines' contributions and bestowed the club "the glory of having saved the Republic in the journées of May 31 and June 2."[63] When the revolting Federalists in Caen, Bordeaux, Lyon, and Marseille condemned the Montagnards' purge of the Girondins as another overstep of Parisian power, militant sans-culottes felt certain of having struck a blow against the counterrevolutionaries' partners in the Convention.[64]

Despite the Montagnards' Maximum and their arrest of the uncooperative Girondin deputies, the sans-culottes were far from satisfied with a price cap on grain products alone. In June, Enragé leader and municipal official Jacques Roux called for a maximum on all basic necessities, including key foodstuffs. He flipped the basis of economic liberalism on its head by arguing that "the liberty of commerce is the right to use and to put to use and not the right to tyrannize and to prevent use."[65] Before the Convention, he asserted that trade must serve basic popular needs rather than enrich "the merchant aristocracy, more terrible than the noble and priestly aristocracy." Before the Convention, Roux argued, "it's only by putting consumables within the reach of the sans-culottes, that you attach them to the Revolution and that you rally them around constitutional laws."[66] His speech echoed suspicions that greedy merchants stockpiled goods to gouge prices.

With the shared Girondin menace eliminated from the Convention, the contrast sharpened between the Enragés' radical democratic goals and the Montagnards' more moderate and parliamentary-centered visions. In June, the revised Constitution affirmed the universal manhood suffrage that the revolutionaries had implemented for the September 1792 elections. The Constitution's guarantees and its accompanying referendum further invigorated the Enragés to pursue a program of direct democracy bolstered by perpetual popular interaction—a model that endangered the Montagnards' representative system.[67] Although the members of Société des Citoyennes républicaines révolutionnaires' stretched across the political left from the Enragés to the Jacobins, Claire Lacombe and Pauline Léon began to lead the club closer toward the Enragés in July.[68] When Girondin supporter Charlotte Corday assassinated the radical journalist Jean-Paul Marat, the Citoyennes républicaines set about memorializing the "Friend of the People" who had supported the Maximum and the June revolt.[69]

The Enragés' and sans-culottes' crescendoing calls for price controls on more foods upset the Dames des Halles. The retailers dreaded limits on their butter, eggs, vegetables, and fish. In July 1793, police observer Dutrand wrote to the minister of the interior that, apart from the ones married to Jacobin sympathizers, the Dames cursed and grumbled.[70] They knew further price ceilings would decimate their profits. The police prudently tracked the Dames' discontent, since the Convention could not ensure the capital's food supply without the 1,000 retailers' cooperation. The deputies had learned this lesson six months earlier, when the Dames and their brokers threatened to stop selling food if the state did not address their assignat complaints. Much to the Dames' dismay, even center-left journals like Révolutions de Paris echoed the need for a maximum on foodstuffs beyond cereals by August.[71]

A national festival on August 10, 1793, offered the Montagnards the opportunity to co-opt the influential retailers. The deputies decreed that, throughout
France, citizens would celebrate the Constitution's successful referendum on the
first anniversary of the monarchy's collapse. The Convention invited municipal
delegates to bring their votes to the capital and embody the nation in festivities
there.[72] Citizens from across France poured into the streets of Paris and marched
between festival stops narrating the Revolution.[73] The second station featured the "heroines of 5 and 6 October" 1789, or rather, the Dames who had
marched to Versailles to bring bread and the king to Paris.[74] According to *Le
Créole patriote*, the women projected the same "proud attitude they had when
they had given the earliest examples of the superiority of free souls over those
submitted to servitude."[75] The Montagnard planning committee unambiguously
posed the Dames as martial figures: perched atop the artillery they had pointed
at the king's château, the Dames held tree branches and other "trophies" serving
as "unequivocal signs of the illuminating victory that these courageous female
citizens had won over the reviled [royal] Body Guards."[76] The Dames' soldierly
prowess was not lost on festival participants. Even departmental administrators
duplicating the festival noted the "male courage" of "the women of Paris."[77]
As the capital's parade paused in front of the Dames, Marie-Jean Hérault de
Séchelles, the Jacobin president of the Convention, praised the Dames' bravery.
He embraced the market women and symbolically erased the king by bestowing
"civic crowns" on the retailers, the traditional representatives of the people.[78]
Then, as the Jacobin planner Jacques-Louis David had instructed, the Dames
joined the procession to "reunite themselves with the sovereign."[79]

The August 10 festival appeared to wed the market women to the Montagnard-
led Convention, while the Enragé-supported Citoyennes républicaines were no-
ticeably left out of the spotlight.[80] The omission is all the more striking since, after
the 1792 attack on the king's palace, the fédérés (soldiers from the provinces)
had given three women civic crowns, including Citoyenne républicaine Claire
Lacombe, in recognition of their bravery.[81] Yet, in a national festival seeking to
glorify that August 10 victory, the deputies offered civic crowns to the Dames
des Halles rather than the Citoyennes républicaines.

Despite passing a dramatic *levée en masse* on August 23, 1793 to remedy
troop shortages at the front, the deputies still lacked a plan to remedy food
shortages at home. In late August, acute price swells multiplied sans-culottes'
cries for supply controls. The Dames' customers confronted surging food costs
in les Halles. Whereas it had taken three years for the price of butter to increase
by 90 percent from June 1790 to June 1793, the price soared an additional
33 percent from June 1793 to September 1793 alone. The drastic jump in the
price of eggs was even more shocking: the price climbed 31 percent from June

1790 to June 1793, but then spiked an additional 84 percent between June and September 1793.[82]

Presenting demands from the sans-culotte-backed Commune on August 31, Deputy Raffron asked the Convention for "a price control on the things necessary to life." Regulation, he argued, "conforms to the social economy" and past consumer protections had been deemed "just since common utility is the measure of justice." Raffron proposed that merchants in this cooperative society "are or should be citizens who, protected by the national authority, earn their living by furnishing to their fellow citizens the things that they need." He pleaded for checks "to oppose merchants' greed, [as] a brake on their bad [social] faith."[83]

The Montagnard deputies balked at transforming the Maximum on grain into a Maximum on all essential goods and foodstuffs. But the Parisian sansculottes responded by planning to converge on the Convention for the second time in four months. On September 4, the Parisian sections rallied at the Hôtel de Ville and began organizing popular pressure.[84] As the nervous Convention received reports of unrest, Deputy Raymond Gaston called for a maximum that covered "all the other essential goods."[85] He insisted that the solitary grain Maximum risked becoming a counterrevolutionary law that "weigh[ed] only on agriculture."[86] The Convention charged the Commission on Subsistence with formulating a plan to enact additional maximums.[87]

The next day, Parisian sans-culottes marched on the Convention to drive through broad price controls and measures against counterrevolutionaries.[88] Before introducing the deputation, Mayor Jean-Nicolas Pache recounted how Parisians had lined up "at the door of bakers" for over six weeks. They feared daily deliveries from the provinces would soon prove inadequate. The problem, Pache asserted, was that the grain laws were not enforced and wealthy grain storers hoarded supplies to inflate prices. Representative Pierre Gaspard Chaumette then spoke on behalf of the Commune and the crowd of sans-culottes outside. Despite the efforts of "the State's domestic enemies" who tried to corrupt citizens, Chaumette insisted that the people would not trade "its sovereignty for a morsel of bread."[89] The Parisian crowds had "only formed one vow," which was "Foodstuffs [Subsistence], and, in order to have them, the force of the law."[90] Chaumette insisted that the Convention act in the people's favor by creating a Revolutionary Army to requisition food from the countryside. The deputies acknowledged the request and citizens flooded the assembly hall with signs proclaiming, "War on the tyrants, war on the aristocrats, war on the hoarders."[91]

The Montagnard deputies capitulated and promised that they would create "a maximum price on all foodstuffs of the most important necessity."[92] These extensive price caps would be called the General Maximum. At the same time, the Convention created policing mechanisms to enforce these market controls and exterminate internal enemies, including a Revolutionary Army to act as the arm of the Convention. Citizen soldiers would smoke out counterrevolutionary hoarders, enforce the Maximum in the recalcitrant countryside, and ensure supply lines for urban centers and French troops.[93] Collectively, these measures cemented Parisian subsistence politics as the cornerstone of national economic policy. The revolutionaries formed part of the Terror's police scaffolding in the process. The Terror's overarching goal—to eliminate all counterrevolutionaries—targeted not only commercial offenders but also individuals waging civil war in the Vendée and supporting Federalist revolts against the capital.[94]

While the Commission on Subsistence failed to propose comprehensive price controls within its allotted eight days, marketplace trade grew more volatile in the capital. On September 11, the Convention passed an intermediary Decree on Subsistence to shore up the grain and flour trade with national, rather than regional, prices. But the Committee still toiled away on creating maximums for other critical foodstuffs.[95] By September 12, the Committee of Public Safety warned the minister of the interior that merchants in les Halles no longer obeyed the grain Maximum.[96] In this strained environment, the Montagnard Convention hedged its bets that a General Maximum, unlike its single-item predecessor, would stabilize inflation and the food supply.

Two Sides of the Tricolor: Merchants and Consumers in the Marketplace

The anticipated price controls escalated the tensions between the Dames des Halles on the one hand, and the Citoyennes républicaines and their Enragé allies on the other. Bread was a staple of the popular classes and the Spring Maximum had benefited the Dames. However, the Fall General Maximum would put price limits on many foodstuffs that the Dames sold such as butter, peas, and fish. Whereas the Spring Maximum helped the Dames as consumers, the Fall General Maximum threatened to cripple them as retailers. The Citoyennes républicaines increased their presence in les Halles in August, when they began holding their meetings at St. Eustache, the Dames' beloved neighborhood parish, just adjacent to the marketplace.[97] In mid-September, the Société des Citoyennes républicaines révolutionnaires made advocating for subsistence and basic necessities permanent club objectives.[98] Thus, within a stone's throw of the Dames, the club women repeatedly championed consumers and workers as the sovereign people while excluding merchants and their interests.

Economic concerns mainly divided the Dames and the Citoyennes républicaines, but the two groups diverged in other respects as well.[99] In contrast to the illiterate street vendors of food among the Dames, the leaders of the club women were more literate and came from the lower middle-class. Of the nineteen club women whose occupations are known, only 16 percent were merchants of edible goods.[100] And their food products—chocolate and cakes—drew a wealthier clientele and were not be subject to the General Maximum. Thus, the club women primarily acted as consumers. They were far more concerned with essential food prices than the effect such price limits had on food retailers. The visual differences between the two groups were also striking. If Parisians peered into St. Eustache during club meetings, they would notice the club women's red bonnets and might recall rumors of their demands for pants. However, if Parisians entered during Mass, they would see floppy white bonnets covering Dames' heads and skirts splattered with vegetable rot. Given the shared space, the Convention's budding dechristianization campaign likely exacerbated economic contests between the club and market women.[101] Whereas the Citoyennes républicaines were likely to support the new revolutionary calendar with its ten-day weeks and secular festivals, the Dames lamented the abolished Sabbaths of the Gregorian model.[102]

As Parisians waited three weeks for the new General Maximum to be published, the Dames and the Citoyennes républicaines acted out their ideological differences in battles over the revolutionary tricolor. The Citoyennes républicaines advocated that all women, like men, be legally obliged to wear the blue, white, and red cockade as a sign of citizenship.[103] But the Dames refused to wear an emblem that they associated more with the antimerchant Enragés than the Republic. On September 13, the day after the grain Maximum failed, brawls broke out across the city between women who donned the tricolor and the Dames who rejected it.[104] In the central markets, women wearing tricolors, some of whom were Citoyennes républicaines, lashed out against other women who rejected the rosette. In response, the Dames "tore to pieces," as one police observer put it, the women with the tricolored bull's eye. The Dames threatened to thrash cockade proponents again if they repeated their maneuvers.[105]

Three days later, the Citoyennes républicaines dusted off their tricolors to petition the Convention. They presented themselves as the authority on patriotic women and asked the deputies to imprison prostitutes who were "dangerous" to society. They also insisted that if male émigrés were arrested as suspected counterrevolutionaries, the deputies consider the same penalty for their wives. They asserted, "Legislators, it was up to the Citoyennes républicaines to frankly present some truths to you about our sex; it's up to us to deploy the proper ways to prevent these female beings from harming the Republic while harming themselves."[106] Certainly the Citoyennes républicaines' self-presentation as the female guardians of patriotism miffed the Dames and insulted the market women's authority as popular mouthpieces. After all, the Dames had received the very first *bonnes citoyennes* (good citizenesses) medals from the revolutionary state four years earlier.

On the same day as the Société's visit to the Convention, the Jacobin club confronted the Citoyennes républicaines' leader. The Jacobins accused Claire Lacombe of being "in collusion" with two famously radical Enragé leaders, Roux and the younger Leclerc. The Montagnard Convention had firmly turned against the most outspoken Enragé leaders by imprisoning Roux in late August. The Montagnards would also arrest Varlet and order Leclerc to stop printing his incendiary journal by the end of the month.[107] Jacobin François Chabot demanded that Lacombe, stained by association, "be seriously surveilled." The Jacobins then pivoted to accuse the entire Société des Citoyennes républicaines révolutionnaires of propagating street disturbances over soap and sugar supplies months earlier in February and June.[108] The Committee of General Security placed the indignant Lacombe under arrest for one day but failed to find any evidence of counterrevolutionary scheming.

The September 17 Law of Suspects significantly raised the stakes in the confrontations over the tricolor between the Dames des Halles and the Citoyennes républicaines by expanding the definition of malicious counter-revolutionary activity.[109] Just one day after passing the law, radical deputy Jean-Marie Collot d'Herbois expounded to the Convention: "It is time for you to deliver a last blow against the aristocracy of merchants. It is this aristocracy that has checked the progress of the Revolution and has prevented us thus far from enjoying the fruit of our sacrifices." He demanded that price-gouging merchants be considered suspect.[110]

Meanwhile, the Dames held fast against the tricolor and its proconsumer connotations in the marketplace. Among their stalls, they shouted that "if someone insulted [even] one woman citizen who did not have a cockade, they would all seek revenge for her."[111] Police observer Prévost reported that the Dames suggested "citoyenne cards" (female citizen cards) to replace the ambiguous tricolor. The market women attested they would gladly carry such "citoyenne cards" issued by the state.[112] For the Dames, the tricolor did not represent the nation or mark their citizenship. On the contrary, the Dames assumed they were already citizens who negotiated their status directly with the state.

In response to the festering unrest, the sans-culotte-backed Commune ordered all women to wear the tricolor cockade on September 18.[113] The Dames responded by dispatching forty retailers to organize their opposition across all city markets.[114] Police in the streets reported that recalcitrant Dames turned the Citoyennes républicaines' own indictments back against them. The retailers protested that it was only prostitutes "and those [women] who go to the Jacobins [club] who wear it [the tricolor]."[115] By portraying their opponents as sexually deviant women, the Dames sought to sharpen their moral advantage on the gendered playing field.

In the days following the Commune's tricolor ruling, the Dames expressed their frustration by spanking some Citoyennes républicaines who sported the tricolor.[116] The market women's tactics echoed the symbolic violence they had inflicted on counterrevolutionary nuns in 1791. With each strike, the retailers portrayed themselves as disciplinary mothers and framed the club women as errant children and transgressive women. Police observer Béraud connected the scuffles among women to soaring prices in the marketplace. He warned his superiors, "The people, above all the women, [are] speaking a thousand horrors of the Convention, one cries against it, the [prices of] primary foodstuffs augment from day to day."[117]

What began as a municipal dispute over the tricolor and its factional overtones quickly escalated into a national issue. Thirty-five clubs and Parisian sections had recently signed a petition to the Convention that was read by the female members of the mixed-sex Société fraternelle de la section de l'unité. The coalition had asserted the tricolor was a "revolutionary sign and that the citizenesses who share our works should equally share this advantage."[118] Two days after the Commune's tricolor decree, the overtaxed Parisian police added their own request that the National Convention outlaw those who "will rip off or profane the national colors." Meanwhile, the Dames looked to the Convention as a competing source of authority to dodge the Commune's ruling. One police observer reported that the Dames "show generally the deepest respect for the national representation . . . [yet the Dames] refuse to wear the cockade because the [initial] law that the Convention pronounced does not order it, they [the Dames] say, and let it be [the Convention's] decree and [they] will execute it."[119]

The National Convention responded to the unrest on September 21 by seconding the municipal government's decision and decreeing that "all women be required to wear the national cockade." It is critical to note that the Convention described the rosette as the "national" cockade instead of the "tricolor." In this way, the Montagnard-led Convention placated the Enragés by seconding the Commune's tricolor decree. But it robbed the Enragés of an ideological victory by characterizing the tricolor as an explicitly national, rather than factional, symbol.[120]

The Montagnards enforced the Convention's tricolor decree by welding it to the Terror. The deputies categorized attacking someone over the cockade or refusing to wear one as counterrevolutionary. They ordered police to imprison women without the cockade for eight days. Upon a second offence, a woman would become a counterrevolutionary suspect, and a justice of the peace would judge her political crimes. Furthermore, any woman who ripped the cockade off another woman would face six years in prison.[121] The Convention's decree complicated the ways the Dames could attack their local political rivals, whose economic agendas jeopardized their livelihoods.

In the wake of the tricolor showdown, the triumphant Société des Citoyennes républicaines révolutionnaires, the Enragés, and the Parisian sections redoubled their calls for proconsumer price controls and merchant restraints. The day after the Convention's ruling, the Citoyennes républicaines officially made it a club goal to secure "price controls on all commodities used by the people."[122] When, on September 22, the club women boldly sent a deputation to the Croix-Rouge neighborhood assembly to demand a "fixed price on all the staples used by the people," their rhetoric implicitly rejected merchants from "the people."[123] The Parisian sections lamented the delay in enacting the General Maximum to the Convention the same day.[124]

In light of the Convention's tricolor decision, the Dames des Halles did not slip into quiet complacency; on the contrary, they boiled with resentment. The Dames of the Place Maubert defiantly ripped tricolored bonnets from women's heads on the law's first day. The retailers threw the symbols in the mud amid a barrage of insults.[125] The disgruntled Dames of the central markets physically attacked a fabric merchant who was making tricolor bonnets. The market guard intervened to save her from being killed. The police reported that the Dames declared "one had forced them to take the cockade, that one apparently wanted to force them to wear one of these sorts of bonnets in order to humiliate them, and that they were not duped by what one desired of them."[126] Defiant women found creative ways to technically obey the decree but hide the required cockade under ribbons, handkerchiefs, and other coverings.[127] Nonetheless, the Dames had suffered a substantial political and economic defeat. With the General Maximum incubating behind committee doors and extensive price controls looming, the marketplace remained a hotbed for disputes over the civic responsibilities of merchants and consumers.

General Maximum: Symbiotic Trade for the Cooperative Body Politic

On September 28, three weeks after it promised to broaden price controls, the Convention presented its program. Although the sans-culottes had vehemently demanded ceilings to benefit consumers, the Montagnards felt uneasy about blatantly contradicting laissez-faire ideology to solely advantage buyers.[128] From a pragmatic perspective, marketplace police urged the deputies to pass dual controls on merchants and consumers to avoid a "continual and dangerous brawl between the buyer and the seller."[129] Therefore, on September 28 and 29, the National Convention advanced a symbiotic plan for price limits on foodstuffs and wages.[130] Ideally, this comprehensive General Maximum would not pit merchants against consumers. Instead, the holistic program would balance the cooperative body politic in which economic relationships carried social duties and political responsibilities.

The General Maximum transformed the local moral economy of the Old Regime into a national moral economy that included wages. The popular classes had often established a "just price" for the sale of goods during Old Regime riots.[131] They vindicated their actions as a way to protect the local, normally collaborative community from outsiders seeking to cart away supplies or drive up prices when resources were scarce. The General Maximum nationalized the scale of this vision. The state forbade the export of primary necessities for the war's duration.[132] In addition, the Maximum Commission assumed that local transactions wove a national web of economic relationships, all of which were predicated on universal duties of economic citizenship. Consequently, the commission cast counterrevolutionaries as outsiders who disrupted naturally stable political and economic relationships.

Despite the proconsumer movements that prompted the reform, the Convention insisted that it did not implement the General Maximum to correct antagonistic economic relationships between merchants and consumers. On the contrary, the Montagnard deputies insisted that the Maximum was simply an extraordinary and transitory measure to restore the harmonious equilibrium that counterrevolutionaries intentionally upset. The Maximum Commission reported, "In normal times prices are formed naturally by the reciprocal interests of buyers and sellers. This balance is infallible."[133] Buyers and sellers "naturally" worked like alternating pistons whose seemingly opposite movements propelled the nation forward. If each citizen fulfilled his/her commercial role in the subsistence trade as a civic duty, then the nation would benefit as a whole.[134]

The Convention blamed France's commercial crises on external enemies, since the economic duties of buyers and sellers were as resolutely symbiotic as the general will was indivisible. The Convention's stance now aligned with the Commune's demands presented by Deputy Raffron in the heated days of late August. Calling for a broader Maximum, Raffron had told his Convention colleagues, "The equilibrium between the essential goods and their value establishes itself nearly on its own, by the concurrence and by the routine of good faith, the precious fruit of interior peace. But, in a revolution, all this is different. The cupidity of speculators and malicious people makes them enemies of the fatherland. It's therefore necessary to apply a revolutionary remedy to the anarchical evil that torments us."[135] Extensive price controls would be the balm for wounds inflicted by counterrevolutionaries inside and outside the fatherland.

The deputies decreed that the General Maximum would include all essential foodstuffs and resources across France, but that their prices would be based on departmental averages. The deputies instructed department administrators to set prices by calculating the good's 1790 price, subtracting the customs duties and taxes of 1790, dividing that number by three, and then adding the third to the original price from 1790. To take an example relevant to the Dames: fresh butter from Chartres cost 1 livre per pound in 1790, of which 3 sous 6 deniers were the duties and taxes from 1790. Minus the duties and taxes, the butter cost 16 sous 6 deniers. The third to add would then be 5 sous 6 deniers, making the 1793 Maximum on fresh butter from Chartres 1 livre 2 sous per pound. Likewise, for the Dames' fish, a barrel of 108 salted small cod cost 120 livres in 1790, but since there were no duties and taxes on fish, the 1793 Maximum was 160 livres per barrel.[136] The General Maximum also included cheese and, although the Dames' eggs and vegetables were not originally included, they were quickly added.[137]

The National Convention decreed that workers would uphold their fraternal responsibilities in this economic partnership by adhering to corresponding caps on salaries, wages, and day labor. The deputies ordered each municipality to set wage maximums at 150 percent of their local 1790 rates.[138] This gave workers a slight advantage since their wages rose by one-half of the 1790 rates whereas food prices only rose by one-third.[139] Since the deputies' most pressing objective was to control consumer prices, fixing wages was a literal footnote to Montagnard deputy Raffron's original call for a General Maximum.[140] Nonetheless, the deputies concerned themselves with labor costs insomuch as it affected the overall economic and ideological balance.

Under the General Maximum workers, like merchants, had to imagine their livelihoods within a national economic equation. Because war demands had increased the cost of labor over the summer, workers' salaries were generally rising again in relation to the cost of living.[141] Since the Maximum set wages at 150 percent the rate of 1790, workers' income increased or decreased according to recent wage trends. On one extreme, harness-makers' wages had increased 180 percent between June 1790 and June 1793, so their wages decreased under the General Maximum, whereas masons' wages had only risen 50 percent between June 1790 and June 1793, so their wages increased under the General Maximum.[142] In either case, the parallel ceiling on consumer goods aimed to accommodate the difference and check the cost of living.[143] If carefully calibrated, the Maximum on workers' wages and merchants' prices would combat the inflation and supply challenges plaguing both groups.[144]

The General Maximum framed merchants' and laborers' occupational work as political responsibilities to the nation. Consequently, the Convention legislated punishments that made trade and labor into legal obligations. From a commercial standpoint, anyone who sold or bought above the Maximum would be put on the list of suspects. From a labor standpoint, the Convention gave municipalities the power to imprison for three days "workers, the producers, and different kinds of laborers who refuse, without legitimate reasons, to do their work."[145] Individual economic behavior carried political duties and judicial consequences.

To monitor citizens' joint political and economic responsibilities, revolutionary officials insisted that every aspect of trade take place on public land, among members of the public, and under the public eye. Since the first Maximum of May 1793, merchants could only sell grain and flour inside public markets and could not cut private deals.[146] In July 1793, the Convention further stipulated that merchants must expose their wares "daily and publicly." In early September, the deputies made stockpiling a public crime that could result in capital punishment.[147] With the General Maximum decrees, the Convention forbade new Parisian markets. In the existing markets, food exchanged hands in the open where citizens and the police could watch.[148] To correct commercial violations, the police reconstituted confiscated goods to the public by selling them in the open market square. For example, police caught Citoyenne Michel (sic) Roger, a Dame des Halles, with a basket of 820 eggs that she was selling above the Maximum, along with 10 cheese bricks, 40 cheese wedges, and a small duck. After detaining Citoyenne Roger, the police sold her supplies in les Halles and deposited the proceeds into the Commune's public treasury.[149]

To increase the transparency of trade and lower the price of goods, the General Maximum also emphasized that goods should pass through as few hands as possible. Montagnard officials and the public reasoned that the fewer people involved in commercial chains of sale, the less room there was for price manipulation, hoarding, or counterrevolutionary plotting. However, in practice goods often passed among many hands from their point of origin to market stalls. For example, fishermen who caught cod, salmon, and herring from the sea might sell their fish to wholesalers who transported the fish to Paris. At the central markets, brokers bought their lots, subdivided them, and sold these shares to the Dames. Finally, the Dames sold the fish in retail to consumers seeking modest quantities. Commissaire Dufourny recognized that the Convention's ideal, single-step transaction between buyers and sellers was a mirage. Disgusted, he said that the sans-culottes unfairly believed that "the man who speculates in foodstuffs for profit is a useless middleman, dangerous and guilty, a genuine monopolist, an enemy of society."[150]

Although the Montagnard deputies accounted for both prices and wages in their economic equation, the General Maximum overlooked the material cost of transporting goods and the complex chain of sale from fields, rivers, and workshops to household tables.[151] Moreover, it completely ignored the intermediary agents who transported and subdivided goods. In les Halles, these shortcomings wreaked havoc on the Dames' meager businesses and galvanized the Citoyennes républicaines' economic agenda. Rather than stabilizing commerce, the deputies' gross miscalculations further polarized merchants and consumers. Their oversight exacerbated factional rivalries in the marketplace.

Discerning Economic Citizenship: The Politics of Food, Factions, and Gender

The General Maximum spelled disaster for the Dames' livelihoods. It covered nearly all the foodstuffs the Dames sold, including butter, cheese, and fish, and eventually eggs and vegetables. The legislation's failure to delineate separate price limits for wholesale and retail trade especially frustrated the market women. To take a specific example, the Dames and other retailers who bought brie cheese from wholesalers, at the Maximum price of 57 livres 13 sous 4 deniers per dozen, could only subdivide and resell the brie at the same total price. The Dames lost their profit margin. This commercial stranglehold sparked physical ones as another month of confrontations began between the Dames and the Citoyennes républicaines. The marketplace chaos compelled the deputies to address the Maximum's grave deficiencies.

The Citoyennes républicaines and the Dames mounted their attacks as the Convention blew the opening whistle on the General Maximum. Although the Convention issued the Maximum's guidelines in late September, it gave districts an eight-day grace period to gather the 1790 prices necessary to calculate the local maximums.[152] On October 9, the Société des Citoyennes républicaines révolutionnaires protested to Commune that local price limits had not yet been implemented. The Citoyennes républicaines lamented that "The insolent merchant knows to profit from your slowness to execute this beneficial law."[153] According to the *Moniteur*, the club women complained that the government treated citizens like a "blind person to whom one promises light and who goes to his tomb with the regret of having badly chosen his doctor."[154] The Dames and other merchants did, in fact, refuse to follow the price caps until local authorities "promulgated" and posted the lists. Police reported that, in sectional assemblies, "when it is a question of subsistence, they [the merchants] raise their heads and it is impossible to speak of an issue as [seemingly] important."[155] The food trade remained in disarray as consumers and merchants dug in at the marketplace.

The last loophole closed for the Dames when the Parisian police posted and enforced the General Maximum on October 13, 1793.[156] With no way out, the frustrated Dames took aim at the "Phrygian caps" or red liberty caps that the antimerchant Citoyennes républicaines promoted. During antiquity, the emblem marked a freed slave. In the Revolution, the red cap was a more militant symbol than the tricolor and endorsed radical popular politics.[157] *Révolutions de Paris* had first referred to the sans-culottes as "the woolen caps,"[158] and the

Section de la Croix-Rouge even changed its name to "Bonnet Rouge" (Red Cap) shortly after the price controls passed.[159]

The lingering tensions over the tricolor and the fresh wounds of the Maximum quickly evolved into a battle over the red cap and its associated Enragé positions. On the first day of the General Maximum, the Dames hurled invectives against a woman selling Phrygian caps in the marketplace. Fearful they would have to wear the red cap, the Dames protested that they "wore the [tricolor] cockade, and that was enough." The Dames also expressed exasperation that the deputies were wasting time planning a "new calendar" when "it was more urgent to busy themselves with the endless lack of grain and flour in the capital." Within a week, the flawed Maximum compounded with shrinking supplies to send the Dames into what one spy called "the greatest consternation."[160]

The Terror gave the government new latitude for compelling the Dames and other merchants to obey Maximum. Battered by the Parisian sections' unrelenting demands and seeking to eschew elections, the National Convention had cited the wars to declare a "revolutionary" (i.e., emergency) government three days before enacting the General Maximum. Within four days of posting the price limits, the Paris Commune declared that merchants who gave up their trade would be suspect.[161] On October 27, the Convention created a Commission on Subsistence to enforce the Maximum.[162] It then followed the Commune's initiative by decreeing, "The merchants and the wholesalers who, since the law of the Maximum, would have ceased or would cease their production and their commerce will be treated like suspect persons."[163]

The new penalties greatly angered the Dames and imbued the food trade with life and death consequences.[164] Since wholesalers already sold supplies to the Dames at Maximum levels, the retailers could not resell at a profit. Nor could the retailers legally abandon their failing businesses. Police spy Prévost wrote to his superiors that "[the Dames] say that the Maximum had been made by some evildoers to provoke civil war; others [say] that those whom one calls republicans are the dregs of the people."[165] The Citoyennes républicaines, who advocated for the detrimental price controls, were foremost among these troublesome "republicans."

The Dames quickly aired their economic and political irritations against their rivals who championed the Maximum. During the morning market of October 28, women whom the populace took to be Citoyennes républicaines attempted to force the red cap on other women, mainly the "female citizens of the Halle."[166] The capless women lashed back with violent insults and threats. Soon an estimated 6,000 women came to blows and hurled insults among market stalls. Anti–red cap women, including the Dames, again cried that they would only follow the state's orders and not arbitrary rules others forced on them.[167]

Economically choked by the Maximum and agitated by the red cap campaign, the Dames armed themselves with proofs of patriotism directly from the government. After the brawl, the Dames appeared before the Commune and demanded it update the *bonnes citoyennes* medals it had awarded them after the October Days.[168] They asked to exchange their 1789 medals for the more recent August 10 medals that had been struck to commemorate the festival.[169] The Commune representatives agreed to bestow updated tokens on the "citizenesses whose patriotic zeal made them fly to Versailles in the journées of 5 and 6 October 1789" and furnished them with dispositions as "mothers of families which made them distinguished."[170] The Dames left the municipal assembly with government endorsements of their patriotism.

The conflict, nonetheless, quickly resumed when the Citoyennes républicaines held their meeting in the marketplace church of St. Eustache. Following the Société's normal procedures, the club president donned the red cap to bring the assembly to order. According to the Société's rulebook, the tricolor and the red cap were regular parts of the club's regalia. But, given the morning clash in the marketplace, the nonmembers in the church interpreted the president's red cap as a defiant gesture.[171] A nonclub woman cried from the gallery, "Down with the red cap, down with the [female] Jacobins, down with the [female] Jacobins, down with the [female] Jacobins & the cockade." The room grew chaotic. The neighborhood justice of the peace entered and shouted to the angry women, "Citoyennes, in the name of the law, silence . . . Citoyennes, the red cap is not in question, you will not wear it at all, and you will be free to style your hair (and decorations) any way you deem fit." He asked the president of the Société to doff her red cap, adjourned the Société's meeting, and declared that anyone was free to enter St. Eustache.[172]

Crowds soon flooded the church. They insulted the Citoyennes républicaines and attacked their regalia. Some Citoyennes républicaines took a stand in front of their symbols and flags. Seeing that they were outnumbered, one club member exclaimed, "Massacre us if you want, but at least respect the rallying point of the French." The Dames and other citizens descended on the Citoyennes républicaines to beat and drag them. The more fortunate Citoyennes républicaines fled to seek sanctuary at the marketplace neighborhood's Section Committee.[173]

Aware of the gravitas that legal procedure carried, the Citoyennes républicaines insisted that the Section Committee immediately hear their testimony and document their plight. However, a police officer burst into the Committee's room and alerted the group that the market crowd was coming fast on their heels. "The heads are heated," he warned, "the crowd is immense, one cries right now: *long live the republic*, down with the revolutionaries [the radical Citoyennes républicaines]." The cries backed the Dames' sentiment that one could support the Republic without supporting radical policies. The club members escaped in pairs through a secure passage.[174]

Like the Citoyennes républicaines, the Dames sought to co-opt the legitimacy of official institutions by filing a complaint at the Commune. They protested to the representatives that the Citoyennes républicaines wanted to legally oblige women to wear the red cap just as they had done with the tricolor. Convention representative Léonard Bourdon, a Jacobin who was at the Commune, lamented that counterrevolutionary nobles were trying to trouble the populace "above all on issues of subsistence." Le Moniteur noted that Bourdon demanded that the club "not trouble public order" by "wear[ing] markers [caps] by which they seem to want to distinguish themselves." It is crucial to note that Bourdon classified the red cap as a distinctive emblem. Unlike the tricolor or patriotic medals, the red cap could not pass as a national symbol because it was deeply affiliated with the Enragés and sans-culottes. A delegation from the market section committee, the justice of the peace from the church, and the municipal police also arrived to suggest that the government take "some measures to prevent this Society from assembling for some time."[175]

The next day, on October 29, a deputation of capless women sought to convince the Convention to dissolve the Société des Citoyennes républicaines révolutionnaires. The petitioners broadly presented themselves as "several united sections of female citizens," which likely included the Dames des Halles.[176] First, they urged the Convention not to pass a law requiring the red cap for women, which would "destroy the ways of commerce altogether."[177] Then, the petitioning women took aim squarely at the Société des Citoyennes républicaines révolutionnaires. "Citizen legislators," they lamented, "You will not ignore that the unhappiness of France was only introduced by a woman's voice [that of Marie Antoinette], we therefore demand the abolition of their club."[178] It should be noted that although the petitioners attacked the Citoyennes républicaines ("their club"), they did not condemn all women's clubs at first. In fact, the Dames themselves had previously addressed the state on behalf of some mixed-sex clubs such as the Société fraternelle.[179]

After reading the formal petition, the women recounted the previous day's events at St. Eustache. Their narrative seemed to associate the Jacobins, a Montagnard stronghold, with the chaos of October 28. They blamed women who "called themselves Jacobines and wore the red bonnet" for trying to force the headgear on others and instigating the fight. In response, Montagnard deputy Maribon-Montant rose to tell his colleagues that the Jacobin club never discussed a red cap requirement because they had far more serious things to debate. He asserted, "It's therefore wrong that one calls these women Jacobines."[180] With this clean cut, the Montagnards severed ties with the Citoyennes républicaines who had helped them arrest the Girondins in the spring, but who had sharpened the Enragé thorn in their side since July.

To paper over the Maximum's shortcomings and factional rivalries at the root of the marketplace fights, the Convention reframed the disturbances as a question of gender and women in politics. Montagnard Deputy Philippe-François-Nazaire Fabre d'Églantine argued that the leaders of shady "coalitions under the name of clubs . . . were not at all women occupied with the care of their households, [or] mothers inseparable from their children. . . . Instead they are a kind of knights errant . . . who spread out everywhere and cause trouble in the city." He maintained that "our enemies" strove to arm women because, since they did not know how to fire the weapons, plotters could seize them for violent ends. After discussion, the Convention decreed that both men and women could wear whatever they wanted without intimidation from others. The Dames and opponents of the Citoyennes républicaines did not have to adopt the red cap, but the tricolor requirement remained in force.[181]

Not until after Fabre d'Églantine lambasted women club members and raised the possibility of investigating all "revolutionary clubs" did one of the women petitioners rise again to ask "for the abolition of all special women's clubs."[182] Her impromptu request has become a turning point in the narrative of women's citizenship. Taken out of the political and economic context, this demand to close women's clubs appears to align with the Rousseauian undertones of Fabre d'Églantine's attacks. However, the Société des Citoyennes républicaines révolutionnaires was the only women's club in the capital and the petitioner's language deflected potential attention from women in mixed-sex clubs. In this light, the request appears to be a targeted way to bolster the capless women's original call to strike down "their club," that is, the Société des Citoyennes républicaines révolutionnaires. The deputies vowed to revisit the issue after their Committee of General Security (a Montagnard policing stronghold) finished investigating the fights that had rocked the markets and church.[183]

That same day, the department's Committee of Revolutionary Surveillance, which was investigating the turmoil, arrived at conclusions that strayed far from its evidence. The Committee acknowledged, but then brushed aside, the Dames' visit to the Commune the day before in which the "women of the Halle" explained their motives for attacking the "revolutionary women." The Committee embellished the Dames' testimony and asserted that the retailers had attacked the club because the Citoyennes républicaines "wanted to ask the Convention to decree that women be required to wear a red cap, and pants with pistols on each side."[184] The added weapons reference alluded to the Citoyennes républicaines' ill-received goal to arm women the previous May.[185] Despite the Dames' pointed testimony about the fights, the department's Committee insisted that larger, more nefarious forces manipulated the female combatants. Officials plastered 1,000 posters around Paris to "enlighten the public on the motive of the brawl," which they described as "a maneuver of the partisans of Brissot and of his [Girondin] accomplices," whose trial had just begun.[186] The Girondins had been mounting an eloquent public defense at the Revolutionary Tribunal.[187] In this way, the department's Committee publicly blamed the Girondins for the brawls before the national Committee of General Security completed its inquiry and the Convention debated the results.

The day after the Convention's Committee began their investigation and the department's Committee posted their conclusions, local officials began expressing anxiety over the confrontations in similar gendered and conspiratorial language. Marketplace observer Prévost feared that women were more susceptible to counterrevolutionaries' schemes. Like the department's Committee, he concluded that troublemakers spurred the violence among impressionable women at the St. Eustache meeting. He added, "It was humiliating for the masculine sex to see women wear the cockade and sow horror everywhere."[188] The market neighborhood assembly voiced its concern that counterrevolutionaries manipulated some women's patriotism at the very moment of "judgment of the leaders of the Brissotin and federalist faction [the Girondins]."[189] The neighborhood assembly requested that the Convention forbid anyone from interfering in another's dress and that "popular societies of women be strictly forbidden, at least during the revolution [i.e. the temporary emergency period of the Terror]."[190]

When the Convention's Committee of General Security gave its report on October 30, it offered conclusions on the cause of the brawl, on women's clubs, and on the issue of women in politics. The Committee explained that, to frame its investigation, it had asked itself: "Can women exercise political rights and take an active part in the affairs of the government?" Committee member and Montagnard deputy Jean-Pierre-André Amar proposed that women could attend club sessions as observers to keep abreast of politics necessary to educate their children. But he asserted that women must not participate in clubs lest political tempers corrupt their morals. Amar argued that excessive club attendance required women to "abandon" higher female duties like familial care and encouraging husbands' morals. He contended that women had "greater concerns to which nature calls them" than "these useful and laborious duties" of political institutions. According to Amar, women's lack of education and their natural weakness allowed nefarious nobles and plotting priests to manipulate them. The aristocracy, he asserted, had thus supported women's clubs "in order to excite troubles."[191] Women in formal politics, Amar feared, could become the republic's vulnerable Achilles heel.

Amar's focus on club membership as the popular gateway to politics inadvertently highlighted another factional dispute at play in the fall of 1793: Did political power come from above or below? The Montagnard deputies cast popular organizations in supporting roles to the Convention and happily received clubs like the Société populaire de la Rochelle, which praised them as "[the people's] representatives, the protectors of its rights, its fathers [who] have shared the sentiment of its indignation" against those who profited on the "subsistence of the unfortunate."[192] In contrast, the Enragés' vision of direct democracy championed neighborhood and popular societies as the sovereign organs to which national deputies were accountable. Given this cleavage, it is not surprising that Montagnard Deputy Amar claimed that the capless women lashed out against the club women because the capless women sought to obey "the laws made by the legislators and the acts of the people's magistrates . . . they would not cede to the will and caprices of certain idle and suspect women."[193] Thus, Amar harnessed gendered arguments to covertly advance the Montagnard hierarchy between legislators (whose "laws" are to be obeyed) and popular clubs (in this case "suspect women" whose "caprices" are not to be obeyed).[194]

A few deputies objected to Amar's conclusions, but the most vocal members of the Convention countered their objections through the proclaimed state of emergency. Montagnard Deputy Louis-Joseph Charlier protested that women had the right to assemble and that the Convention could not outlaw all women's clubs to silence a disorderly few. In response, Montagnard Deputy Claude Basire insisted that the debate was not over "principles" but that it was "uniquely a question of knowing if women's societies are dangerous." With Basire's lead, the deputies then cited "public safety" and recent "dangers" to extend the state of emergency. Finally, the Convention passed the sweeping wording that "these associations [women's clubs] be forbidden, at least during the revolution [emergency government]."[195] Montagnard Deputy Gilbert Romme noted that troublemakers could still meet in other clubs, and the Convention decreed that all societies' meetings be public for surveillance.[196] The deputies thus couched their decision as a temporary maneuver meant to serve public order rather than permanently decide women's intrinsic political rights. Nonetheless, the Convention disregarded the women petitioners' original request to disband only the Société des Citoyennes républicaines révolutionnaires and instead closed all female political clubs across France.[197]

During their debates, the deputies chose a gendered lens to explain disturbances that were most rife with economic tension: those in the marketplace. In the National Convention's proceedings, the marketplace serves as the wrestling ring for female violence instead of a site of commerce. In its ultimate report to the Convention, the Committee of General Security attributed the conflict to "a plot by the enemies of public interest." It did not acknowledge the Société des Citoyennes républicaines révolutionnaires' strident proconsumer campaigns. Nor did the deputies refer to the Dames as merchants or commercial actors.[198] For a legislative body that was so accustomed to receiving reports on market provisions, there are curiously few specifics on the price disputes that helped fuel the 12,000 flying fists of October 28. Instead, the deputies transformed a marketplace clash into generic female disorder. They ignored how marketplace violence reflected commercial problems between struggling retailers and consumer champions under the Maximum.

Despite their gendered arguments, the Committee of General Security, the Committee of Public Safety, and the Montagnards used the red-cap incident to foster support for their leadership and scapegoat factional rivals for disturbances linked to the Maximum's shortcomings.[199] The Revolutionary Tribunal was finally trying Brissot and other Girondin leaders on charges of counterrevolutionary plotting. Their fates had been all but sealed since the June purge shortly after the original bread Maximum. After the September General Maximum, pro-Montagnard popular societies continued to back the Convention's investigation into the Girondins' "treasons, hoardings, and speculations."[200] The Montagnard Convention and the Committee of Public Safety manipulated the conflict between the club women and the Dames des Halles to blame the Girondins once more. In his final analysis of the clash between the Dames and the women's club, Deputy Amar concluded, "At this moment when we judge Brissot and his accomplices, someone is trying to incite unrest in Paris."[201] Of course, thanks to his Montagnard Committee of General Security, 1,000 posters announcing this conclusion had been pasted to the walls of Paris before the deputies even discussed the investigation. And it was Deputy Amar who had delivered the Committee's charges against the Girondins weeks earlier.[202] Primed with the ability to make bolder accusations and inquiries after the recent Law of Suspects,[203] the Montagnard Committee of General Security had set up a circumstantial framework for disposing of the Société des Citoyennes républicaines revolutionaries. At the same time, the Montagnards could emerge as heroes to the sans-culottes for deposing the imprisoned Girondins.[204] Brissot and twenty-three fellow Girondins mounted the scaffold the day after Amar's report.

With less need for embodied popular legitimacy or physical force against parliamentary rivals, the Montagnard deputies used the women's club ban to strategically pivot against Parisian militants. The Montagnard majority resented the increasing pressure that the radical sections had placed on the Convention on issues including the Maximum. Thus, when the deputies closed women's clubs, they simultaneously weakened militant Parisian sans-culottes by decreeing that all assemblies would be public.[205]

Excavated from within this situational setting, Amar's discourse on gender emerges as a reactive strategy to advance the Montagnards' factional interests. Amar's speech was not a foundational inquiry into women's political capacities.

The Convention's goal was not to discern fundamental distinctions between male and female citizenship. Rather, the Committee formulated its analytical framework in the context of factional rivalries, contentious economic legislation, and the Terror. Amar posed the crucial question "Can women exercise political rights and take an active part in the affairs of the government?" to legitimize abolishing the Société des Citoyennes républicaines revolutionaries, allies of the Enragés, in a seemingly apolitical fashion. The Montagnard deputies seized gendered discourses to cover more salient factional goals, to strike out against uncompromising consumer demands in the marketplace, and to blame the General Maximum's failures on the Girondins. Thus, the Montagnards' gendered discourses were more tactical than ideological. As the tide turned for women's political clubs, gendered discourses danced on the surface. But conflicting views of economic citizenship drove the deadly undertow deep below.

Outside the assembly halls, the Dames themselves had skillfully hurled Rousseauian gender tropes to disarm their political rivals. In the marketplace, they had lumped together prostitutes and women who wore the tricolor.[206] And the police had reported that the Dames attacked tricolor-wearers by arguing, "the cockade should be worn by men; that [the women] should only occupy themselves with their household, and not with current affairs."[207] Although the Dames had likely never read Rousseau's *Émile* or *Lettre à d'Alembert*, they knew enough about others' objections to women in politics to strategically appropriate them.[208] Of course, the Dames themselves ignored the latter two-thirds of their own "imperative" by trading in the marketplace and frequently intervening in politics. In fact, the Dames had led over 6,000 men and women to Versailles in the largest political demonstration of 1789. The Dames had also policed the travels of the royal family in 1791, and in 1792 they cut deals to change national monetary policy. And now, in 1793, the Dames intervened yet again by pressuring the Convention to both outlaw the Citoyennes républicaines and revise the General Maximum to include profits for retailers. However, the Dames understood how to maneuver within normative gender discourses to challenge their adversaries' proconsumer agenda. Thus, the Dames applauded when the Convention outlawed female clubs because the decree undercut their economic opponents, not because the decree excluded women from institutional citizenship.

With the Girondins' blood on the scaffold and the Enragés checked by the ban on women's clubs, the Montagnard deputies turned to revising the crumbling General Maximum on prices. The Convention quickly moved to create separate price limits for wholesale and retail trade. The short two days it took the deputies to initiate price reform suggests that, despite their gendered explanations, they well understood the economic root of the St. Eustache violence. Journalist Prudhomme noted that the deputies' Maximum had not been "general enough" and failed to specify whether the price caps applied to wholesalers, retail merchants, or both. The Parisian "small retailers," he testified, hovered on the verge of collapse.[209] In an attempt to survive, the Dames had traded illegally, complained to police, or deserted the markets as their businesses folded. The Dames' actions paralyzed the food markets and ultimately changed the trajectory of national Maximum legislation.

On November 1, 1793, Deputy Bertrand Barère, a member of the Committee of Public Safety who was allied with Robespierre, presented a report to the Convention in which he "denounced" the General Maximum's lack of separate wholesale and retail price limits.[210] The Montagnard deputy argued that cultivators and wholesalers benefited at retailers' expense.[211] Barère urged the deputies to more fully conceptualize the Maximum as a society-wide project. He argued that "the law of the Maximum should cover each useful chain of producers, of technicians, of manufacturers, of producers, of wholesalers, of merchants, and of retailers."[212] In response, the Convention proposed a reform allowing the wholesaler to add 5 percent to the price of his original purchasing and transport costs. Then, retailers would double the percentage to 10 and sell.[213] As retailers, the Dames des Halles would be able to legally profit again.

According to this tiered Maximum, workers, retailers, and wholesalers provided distinct services to society and merited reimbursement for their labor. To defend a distinct Maximum for intermediary commercial agents, Barère highlighted the utility and patriotism of retail merchants like the Dames. He depicted them as "this class of good republicans who buy and live from day to day."[214] The deputies agreed and maintained the corresponding cap on wages as the counterbalance to price limits in a cooperative economic system. Workers and merchants had complementary requirements for economic citizenship. In creating price points for each type of work and commerce, the deputies acknowledged the public utility of diverse occupations and further codified economic roles as political duties to the nation.[215]

Less than a week later, on November 5, the former Citoyennes républicaines appeared at the National Convention to protest the closure of their club. Armed with the same gendered discourses that had legitimized their club's dissolution, they maintained that nearly all of their members were "mothers of families, wives of defenders of the fatherland." Boos and hisses drowned them out.[216] When the red-capped Citoyennes républicaines tried their hand at the Commune on November 17, Representative Chaumette undercut their appeal based on the Rousseauian vision of the domestic, moral wife, which had proved effective in the Convention. "Eh!," he declared, "Since when is it decent to see women abandon the pious cares of their households, the cradle of their children in order to come to the public place in the tribunal, at the bar of the senate, in the lines of our armies, to fill the duties that nature gave men alone?"[217] With the Girondins purged and studies for the tiered Maximum underway to revive the marketplace, Montagnard officials erased the Citoyennes républicaines' ability to protest.

The fall 1793 battles between the Dames des Halles and Société des Citoyennes républicaines révolutionnaires were not merely clashes between rival parties, nor were they reductive showdowns between opposing groups of merchants and consumers. The conflicts expressed fundamental disagreements over how to define citizenship via economic responsibilities and how to enact these ideals via subsistence regulation. The 1793 ban on female institutional citizenship was not the simple fulfillment of Rousseauian gender norms. Rather, the starting block for women in French democracy was forged from factional contests over modern state economic regulation. Nonetheless, both the Dames and the deputies wittingly expressed political rivalries and more salient socioeconomic concerns through gendered accusations. The primary stakes in the fall 1793 disputes among women were economic, whereas the primary discourses defending these stakes were gendered.

Dissecting how the Maximum worked in daily trade while probing the ban on women's clubs clarifies the relationship among economics, gender, and politics. Economic roles and gender roles both delineate duties for individuals within the body politic. But, economics and gender delineate different kinds of responsibilities between citizens and the nation. The club women, the Dames des Halles, and the deputies exploited this disjuncture to articulate the fall 1793 problems in different veins. Examining the mechanics of the Maximum also helps us break out of the overly simplistic buyers versus sellers analytical model. In reality, commercial relations were much more layered and intersected with gendered imaginings. Likewise, dovetailing economics with gender disrupts the deputies' superficial 1793 divide between female disorder and male order. Thus, probing gendered and economic citizenship in dialogue complicates dichotomies of consumer versus merchant or female citizenship versus male citizenship.

In searing irony, the Dames des Halles, the vanguard of revolutionary activism, supported the closure of one women's club in 1793 but inadvertently abetted the termination of all women's clubs across France.[218] Nonetheless, the Dames did not view the monumental ban on female assemblies as detrimental to their citizenship. The 1793 clashes between the Dames and the club women reveal two conflicting interpretations of citizenship while the concept was still being forged. The Citoyennes républicaines tied citizenship to innate rights and embraced new democratic institutions such as voting, serving in the militia, and acting in political clubs. In contrast, the Dames portrayed citizenship as contingent and earned through public utility. The market women demanded that the state address their grievances, like the Maximum's lack of retail prices, in exchange for the services they provided society. The Dames legitimized their civic membership through their useful work including, though not predicated on, their gendered labor.

Lest we trace the 1793 ban to latent, long-held attitudes toward women's (in)capacities, we should remember that the revolutionaries' attitudes toward the relationship among gender, violence, and citizenship were inconsistent at best. Contrary to the deputies' 1793 assertion that women's political activism caused troublesome violence, the revolutionaries had largely condoned the Dames' violent patriotic interventions since 1789. Two and a half years before their marketplace fights with the Citoyennes républicaines, the Dames had spanked counterrevolutionary nuns, and only the municipality and a few citizens scolded the Dames for the disorder they caused. Most Parisians celebrated the market women's violence as a moral and spiritual defense.[219] Similarly, three months before the October 1793 ban, the Montagnard deputies had upheld the Dames as models of martial courage atop cannons in the national August 10 festival. Then, mere hours before the October showdown at St. Eustache, Commune officials honored the Dames' maternal qualities and physical courage in tandem while updating their *bonne citoyennes* medals. In contrast to these three moments extolling female violence, the deputies framed the brawls between the Citoyennes républicaines and the Dames des Halles as the result of immutable female deficiencies and gendered disorder. This jarring discrepancy points to how gender could be a dynamic, fluid, and contingent component of citizenship instead of its immobile Rousseauian cornerstone.

Consequently, what has often been depicted as the disastrous ideological turn for gender and female citizenship over the longue durée stemmed in large part from commercial contests in the Parisian markets. In a new national moral economy predicated on citizens' symbiotic relationships, the duties of laborers and merchants became a point of economic and political contention. Crisis in the subsistence trade and the Maximum's failures shaped the deputies' October 1793 shutdown of women's clubs. This infamous ban was far from a comprehensive gendered manifesto on citizenship. Rather, it hinged on diverging ideas of market controls, state regulatory duties, and the economic dimensions of citizenship itself. Although the Dames had silenced their political rivals in the marketplace, the flawed Maximum still endangered their livelihoods and claims to citizenship as winter enveloped the capital.

6

Selling Legitimacy

Merchants, Police, and the Politics of Popular Subsistence

On the afternoon of February 28, 1794, les Halles looked strangely empty. The parasols that normally cluttered the marketplace were nowhere in sight. Silence filled the square. The eerie calm contrasted with the chaos from hours earlier. The Dames des Halles had pillaged grocers' boutiques for sugar, coffee, oils, and soap whose prices, they protested, soared beyond reach. The police dispatched patrols to break up the looting and disperse the recalcitrant retailers. The Dames booed as the police folded up their parasols and removed the foodstuffs they sold beneath them. Parisians deserted les Halles.[1]

Around 5:00 pm, the obstinate Dames flooded back into the marketplace. They defiantly sang and danced until officers arrived on horseback. Then, the Dames taunted the flustered force by running from one end of the market to the other. As hooves clattered behind them, the market women shouted insults over their shoulders. Les Halles soon resembled a giant wave pool of merchants, horses, and police futilely crashing back and forth across the open space.[2]

At the moment of the Dames' demonstration, the National Convention was struggling to stabilize the subsistence trade. Explaining the Dames' protest, one police officer observed that "exorbitant prices" greatly taxed the popular classes. His incredulous colleague, in contrast, accused counterrevolutionaries of provoking the Dames with "perfidious suggestions." But a third commissioner astutely discerned how Parisians' political and economic concerns were intertwined. "The unhappy people," he reported, "cannot possibly wait any longer, in spite of their patriotism. . . . They judge the Convention severely and bitterly reproach [the deputies] for wasting precious time arguing and slandering one another, and they demand that hoarders be stopped and that the Convention lower the price of basic foodstuffs."[3]

The Convention had started to reform the Maximum three months before the market showdown, but it had not yet enacted the revised price controls. These reforms would provide separate price limits for retail and wholesale transactions involving over forty types of essential goods. The wage controls that the Convention had passed as part of the General Maximum were equally stagnant. Officials had not enforced these wage ceilings despite their passage in September 1793. It had been ten months since the first grain maximum, and, although the political landscape changed from week to week, the exigencies of climbing prices, dwindling supplies, and unbalanced wages remained constant problems.

During the fall and winter of 1793–1794, the Montagnards' emergency decrees reordered political and economic life while attempting to supply citizens and soldiers. The deputies had instituted the General Maximum as the economic arm of the Terror, but the Terror proved more effective in corralling individuals' behavior than systemically imposing the Maximum. Consequently, studies of the Terror largely focus on revolutionary tribunals, civil war, violence, emotions, and factional maneuvering.[4] Yet, it was through the Maximum that most citizens tasted the Terror in their food, smelled it in their firewood, and felt it in their shoes. The deputies poured much sweat into their ubiquitous economic regulations and seized unprecedented control over national commerce, production, and labor. On October 27, 1793, the Convention created the Commission on Subsistence, whose chief policing goal was to enforce the Maximum. The Commission mobilized over 500 agents to create tiered price limits while tightly monitoring the nation's economy. The Comités révolutionnaires, another administrative unit of the Terror, locally policed the Maximum with uneven results.[5] After December 4, 1793, these Comités révolutionnaires were composed entirely of officials selected by the representatives on mission, who were themselves dispatched by the Committee of Public Safety in Paris. Despite such centralized initiatives, the emergency government remained dependent on marketplace actors to achieve the primary economic goal of the Terror—to ensure subsistence supplies. Thus, the Montagnards' economic initiatives were often reactions to local market practices.

The Maximum reform of 1793–1794 reveals a significant transition in political and economic theory from above and below.[6] During the Old Regime, ministers and police attempted to balance the "market principle" with the "marketplace." The market principle held that uncontrolled supplies, demand, and self-interest should freely set prices and guide commerce. The physical marketplace, in contrast, was "a designated site" that the monarchy sought to closely order, police, and restrain. The market principle's orientation toward liberty clashed with the marketplace predicated on "regulation."[7] These diverging impulses had undergirded struggles between merchants and consumers, market actors and the police, local communities and the royal state. In fact, subsistence riots were the most common disturbances in France throughout the eighteenth century.[8] The start of the Revolution continued the trend with 3,000 subsistence riots between 1788 and 1793 alone.[9]

If, in the Old Regime, the grain market drove royal officials to vacillate between the market principle and market regulations, the General Maximum crystallized this struggle for the revolutionaries. Through the Maximum, the revolutionaries simultaneously transformed the local moral economy of the Old Regime into a national moral economy. The moral economy of both periods attempted to balance consumers and producers, offer some paternal protections to poor consumers, and uphold private property and market competition.[10] Thus, to reform the Maximum, the revolutionaries experimented with a new politics, psychology, and language of price limits. The deputies' theoretical debates had pervasive consequences in the marketplace. Reforming the Maximum meant not only reconceptualizing the political economy but also reordering the social and political relations of buyers and sellers, reshaping collective commercial attitudes, and setting the threshold of material existence. Could there be anything more personal for 28 million French citizens than consuming revolutionary imaginings in a bit of fish, a wedge of cheese, or a heel of bread?[11]

Drawing heavily from the Convention's decrees, police reports, and justice of the peace records, this chapter argues that the hard-pressed deputies rationalized the Maximum and its revisions as an extension of cooperative relationships within the body politic. The Maximum did not cast the state as a protector in fundamentally combative relationships between buyers and sellers or between regional supplies and national commerce. Instead, the Maximum assumed the national economy was a symbiotic system. The Maximum made cooperative relationships between merchants and workers the organizing principle for economic citizenship. As the Montagnard deputies modified price controls, they considered the political duties and mutually beneficial roles of buyers and sellers. Each time the deputies revised the Maximum in May 1793, September 1793, March 1794, and December 1794, they asserted that plotters ruined the nation's natural circulation of goods and sabotaged the just equilibrium between fraternal merchants and consumers.[12]

The police also preferred cooperative marketplace relationships over punitive ones. Merchants and consumers vastly outnumbered the police in les Halles and the police needed marketplace partners, including the Dames, to sustain the commerce they could not tame. Consequently, the police implored the deputies to draw on their marketplace experiences, rather than theoretical models, to reform the Maximum. Local police and the Dames revealed how the September 1793 Maximum program, conceived in the assembly halls, failed in the marketplace. Since this Maximum discounted retail businesses, the Dames reacted to its flawed single sale premise in illegal and legal ways. Ultimately, the market women and their police allies pressured the deputies to enact separate price limits for wholesale and retail trade.

This chapter also argues that the Dames, their advocates, and officials recreated retailers' role in the body politic by defending their occupational utility and destabilizing the binary between merchants and consumers. Without effective price controls, the market's potential collapse threatened both buyers and sellers. The Dames politically morphed between both categories as merchants of a few goods and buyers of many others. Since each of the Dames sold only one type of food, they shared many price concerns with consumers. By providing retail services to fellow citizens, the Dames repelled charges that merchants were greedy counterrevolutionaries. The police likewise articulated the Dames' occupational legitimacy according to the Montagnard cooperative body politic and influenced how the deputies recategorized merchants as essential citizens in the final Maximum of March 1794.

Finally, this chapter argues that the Montagnards' inability to enforce wage ceilings, the end of the Terror in July 1794, and the Thermidorians' commercial deregulations rendered occupational distinctions less politically consequential than socioeconomic position. The economic fallout triggered by the Maximum's abolition on December 24, 1794 made purchasing power the new yardstick for sociopolitical categories. The Maximum's repeal marked a major step in the shift from economic citizenship based on individuals' occupational groups to modern economic citizenship based on capital, property, fiscal responsibility, and economic autonomy.

One Size Does Not Fit All: The Failure of a Single Price per Good

Despite the General Maximum's holistic vision of the body politic, the law fell apart in the fall of 1793 because the deputies modified prices by region but did not distinguish between levels of sale. For example, consumers in Dijon and Paris paid different prices according to regional limits. Citizens of Dijon bought their pound of butter for 13 sous 9 deniers in October 1793,[13] while Parisians paid 18 sous 1 deniers per pound of melted butter.[14] However, the regionally-calculated Maximum did not set different prices for wholesalers, brokers, and retailers which, as the October brawls demonstrated, commercially incapacitated the Dames and other middle merchants. If cultivators or wholesalers already sold their goods at the Maximum, brokers and retailers could not raise the price to profit from subsequent sales. The price controls threatened to erase the Dames' occupation altogether. In addition, the General Maximum prices completely ignored transport costs. Therefore, wholesalers could not recover trucking costs to sell goods beyond their place of origin. Since no region produced all its foodstuffs or essential goods, unrecoverable transportation costs could crush trade networks. Due to the September Maximum's omissions, symbiotic transactions among cultivators, merchants, and consumers remained impossible.

On November 1, 1793, deputy Barère presented a report to the Convention on behalf of the Commission on Subsistence and Provisioning as well as the Committee of Public Safety. He explained that, in their haste to restore supplies, the deputies had produced a flawed General Maximum. The deputies listening knew, of course, that the sans-culottes' uprising of September 5 had forced the Convention to pass controls without planning. But Barère blamed the British and greedy individuals for upsetting the markets. He concluded that the fall crisis brought "the misery of a large contingent of citizens, of this contingent [that is] of interest to the nation [and] who live from their work, and who have more right to the monitoring and solicitude of the legislator." According to Barère, the initial Maximum did have two problems. One problem was administrative: some local officials sought to bend the Maximum to favor personal interests or those of friends and relatives. Officials involved in manufacture, commerce, or agriculture unevenly applied the deputies' plan in their localities. Barère suggested the state override these particular interests by calculating and "set[ting] the price rates from the center" of government.[15]

The General Maximum's second failure was that it did not map onto how commerce actually worked. Barère "denounced" the September Maximum since cultivators and wholesalers benefited at retailers' expense.[16] The Maximum, he insisted, could fully become a society-wide project if commercial roles were subdivided. He argued that it "should cover each useful chain of producers, of technicians, of manufacturers, of producers, of wholesalers, of merchants, and of retailers." Without proper subdivisions, Barère declared that "commerce, so useful, so beneficial, so necessary in this revolution of liberty thus became a kind of miserly tyrant that one had to enslave to render it useful."[17] More legislation would correct this problem.

Although Barère condemned "retailing merchants' avarice" in their response to the September Maximum, he defended them as pivotal actors in the Commission's proposed reform. He confirmed what the Dames des Halles had already attested to for six weeks: The controls only benefited wholesalers and manufacturers who sold their own products. Retailers, in contrast, were sentenced to "an enormous loss." By reforming the Maximum with retail sales in mind, Barère attested, "you do an act of justice, you repair a loss of the little capital useful to retail commerce."[18]

Finally, Barère argued that retailers and sans-culottes lost the most. He explained that if new regulations compensated retailers' losses, the deputies would create "a sort of everyday commerce, more within the reach of the poor citizen, of the laborer, & of this class of good republicans who buys & lives from day to day."[19] A tiered Maximum, he insisted, would guarantee "the legitimate gain from work and industry, which is the product of operations that are useful to society."[20] Thus, a price control program that delineated multiple layers of trade could revive retailers' businesses and consumers' stomachs.

In order to correct the Maximum's deficiencies, Barère convinced the Convention to conduct price studies for a tiered Maximum, complete with transport costs, "in order to obtain just prices in the ladder of commerce."[21] His proposed reform would allow the wholesaler to add 5 percent to the price of his original purchasing and transport costs. Then, retailers like the Dames could double the percent to 10 so that they, too, could profit by 5 percent.[22] To reset the price limits, district commissioners would need to amass all local prices from 1790. Prices routinely diverged across France as they depended on regions' natural resources, trade routes, and supply partners. The Commission on Subsistence solicited 1790 prices since it believed that supply and demand, rather than artificial regulation, had balanced these levels.[23] This was a labor-intensive step, requiring each of the more than 550 districts within the 83 French departments to research their local historical prices.[24] After receiving the data, the Commission would draw up extensive regional tables for most merchandise from clothing to wood, and from butter to fish. These tables would include: "1° the production price of the merchandise in 1790, 2° the Price of transport, 3° the profit of the Wholesaler and of the Retailer."[25] After analyzing all the data and drawing up new regional tables, the Commission on Subsistence would bring their results to the Convention which, as the central authority, would then de-cree, print, and disseminate price lists back to each district.[26] These reformed food prices would be calculated and applied within one month.[27] Until then, the problematic September Maximum and its lack of retail prices would remain in effect.

The Convention made clear that the reformed Maximum would still be the policing arm of a national economy. The Convention offered indemnities from "the Public Treasury" to the "citizen merchants or producers, who, by the ef-fect of the law of the maximum, will attest to having lost their entire fortune" or who had less than 10,000 livres of capital. But it also threatened to unleash the Committee of Public Safety on regional authorities who did not enforce the Maximum. "Wholesale merchants who since the law of the Maximum have ceased or will cease their commerce" would also be suspect.[28]

Despite Barère's plan to carve out space for retailers, the Parisian Commune quickly undermined the Dames' businesses by granting consumers access to wholesalers. In November, the Parisian section Mucius Scaevola convinced the Commune to decree that "citizens" could buy food in les Halles before

retailers could secure supplies.[29] The Commune agreed that removing intermediary exchange would circumvent hoarding and price gouging.[30] Savvy
Parisians hesitated to buy from a retailer who hiked prices when they could
buy from a wholesaler at the yet-reformed Maximum. The Commune's con-
cession undermined the Dames' supplies and occupation. Although the Dames
had banished the Citoyennes républicaines from the marketplace and although
Barère depicted workers and small retailers on the same side within the "class
of little fortune," the Dames still faced detrimental sans-culotte demands. They
expressed their frustration by bullying and shouting against colporteurs who
hawked *Père Duschesne* and other radical titles supportive of the Maximum.[31]

Thus, from September through the Commission's statistical studies in the
winter months, the Dames were stymied by the lack of retail price limits. The deputies' legislative blunder produced two diverging socioeconomic relationships
for the market women: First, the problematic Maximum highlighted how
retailers and consumers had common interests in lower wholesale prices. As
consumers themselves, the Dames shared their clients' grievances over food
shortages, hoarding, and high prices. Second, the September Maximum put the
Dames in an impossible position with their clients. The single merchant category forced the Dames to illegally or creatively muster profits. Their desperate
survival tactics further perpetuated the image of price-gouging retailers. On
the one hand, the Dames' illegal strategies unintentionally sharpened a moral
dichotomy between patriotic consumers and greedy merchants. On the other
hand, their calls to implement the projected reform revealed a nation utterly dependent on their retail services.

Unlikely Partners in Reform: The Police and
the Dames des Halles

The Convention grossly underestimated how long it would take to complete the
statistical inventory for the reformed Maximum. The committee did not even
submit their proposed regulations to the Convention until February 24, 1794.
Even then, the reformed Maximum did not take effect in the capital until the
police posted the new wholesale and retail prices on March 25.[32] Therefore,
the Dames' businesses fell into ruin or hovered on the verge of collapse for six
months from September 1793 through March 1794.

When the Convention stalled in implementing retail price limits in November
1793, the market women found themselves trapped. On the economic front, se-
vere shortages, escalating prices, and the broken Maximum created a commercial pressure cooker during the winter of 1793–1794. The Dames, consumers,
and Parisian police all worried about the shrinking supply of affordable food.

On the political front, war, internal revolts, and the Terror superheated the relationship between politics and food. Without implementing retail price limits, the deputies blocked the Dames from legally staying in the black and undercut their occupational utility.

To eke out a living, shore up their commercial legitimacy, and assert economic citizenship, the Dames turned to a surprising ally—the police charged with enforcing the regulation that crippled their trade. During the three months that the Commission on Subsistence compiled local prices, legislators and officials relied on police reports to examine marketplace problems.[33] Despite the Committee of Public Safety's aspirations of a centrally dispensed Maximum that bypassed local administrative interests, the Parisian police became key players by funneling information and advice to the deputies. While reporting how the Dames and others reacted to price controls, the police unveiled the September Maximum's serious deficiencies and urged them to hasten their reform. In their intelligence, the commissioners examined the politics of Parisian trade and offered pragmatic suggestions based on marketplace transactions. They urged the deputies to address local grievances and fractured relationships instead of clinging to national economic formulas. The commissioners recognized the complexities of supply, distribution, prices, and public opinion. Their observations ultimately linked the Dames and the state. They validated retailers' essential role in provisioning the populace, even while chastising the Dames' illegal activities like selling above the Maximum or outside the marketplace.

The Minister of the Interior employed at least eighteen police commissioners to report on "the particular events and circumstances of all kinds that can characterize the general sentiment, indicate abuses, or announce troubles" in the capital. Of these informers, Grivel, Siret, Roubaud, Bacon, Prévost, Le Breton, Dugas, Mercier, Pourvoyer, Harivel, Monic, Perrière, and Charmont surveyed their territory most days and reported on food supply and trade conditions. From neighborhood cafés and offices, they wrote reports to the Minister of the Interior and the Provisionary Executive Council, which channeled information to the deputies and the Commission on Subsistence.[34]

As the tiered Maximum gestated from October to February, observers' reports on marketplace practices presented material for reform. The Commission on Subsistence especially praised commissioners Grivel and Siret as prolific marketplace spies who gave "the most advantageous information on commerce, agriculture, the sale of animals, on the Maximum and on the manner of provisioning Paris."[35] Grivel, a Jacobin, fearlessly voiced his opinions to his superiors and condemned what he saw as unbalanced price controls. He urged Jacobin officials to be moderate and fair in designing the Maximum wages and prices for wholesalers, retailers, and consumers alike. Grivel condemned consumers who sought to deny merchants profit just as much as he denounced merchants who traded illicitly. While observing the Dames and their neighbors in les Halles, Grivel became convinced that the Maximum could only succeed if it advanced a holistic program of economic trade. Marketplace exchanges, he argued, must be based on fraternal relations among citizens.

While assessing the Dames' behavior, the police proposed pragmatic strategies and sometimes unsolicited options to rescue the flawed Maximum.[36] During December 1793, Grivel complained multiple times that the deputies should heed his advice since the entire trade system was endangered. The Convention, he insisted, should immediately enact maximum reform. Otherwise, he warned, the capital would run out of provisions before the Commission finished its regional tables, already a month overdue. Rejecting the deputies' theory-based venture, Grivel insisted, "Experience, finally, confirms the truth of my observations and my calculations. Let one therefore take experience as a guide."[37] Commissioner Grivel asserted that only a tiered Maximum with an "honest profit" for wholesalers and retailers would restore commercial relations.[38] His pleas failed to accelerate the process enough. By January, some Dames had completely lost their ability to trade as retailers.[39]

In les Halles, Grivel drew on months of scouting to propose solutions premised on a symbiotic economy rooted in a cooperative body politic. He argued that price caps set below goods' intrinsic values stifled production and circulation, thereby harming the consumer. Each component in the chain of supply and demand needed to work together.[40] Despite the September Maximum on salaries, for example, Grivel noticed that workers' wages had nearly tripled. This gave workers an unfair advantage over merchants in buying food. He emphasized that "the law, like justice, must be impartial." The reformed Maximum needed to recognize that "all citizens are children of the Republic, all compose part of the people; therefore, one must not suffer by allowing certain classes and certain individuals to give themselves advantages at the detriment of other classes and other individuals."[41] In addition, Grivel urged his superiors to destroy the "moral barriers" that separated French municipalities and prevented supplies from circulating. He encouraged the government "to recall them all to the spirit of fraternity which must animate them and unite them."[42] For Grivel, a price and wage system that evaluated all parts of trade would naturally complement society's moral fibers.

Public Relations in Limbo: Buyers and Sellers Awaiting Reform

The public, like the police, attributed a moral and political dimension to various commercial roles. During the Maximum stalemate, Parisians sometimes held retailers, like the Dames, in higher esteem than their wholesale counterparts. In January 1794, Commissioner Pourvoyeur reported that "the people" in his section primarily blamed food troubles on "the rich merchants, brokers, farmers, etc., who only desire the unhappiness of the people."[43] The Défenseurs de la République (a club with Enragé sympathies) similarly pegged wholesalers and financiers as "the aristocracy of fortune."[44] This was partially because the Dames shared Parisians' consumer concerns with respect to the goods they did not sell. In early January, female fish and apple merchants who could not procure sugar from a grocer in the Faubourg Saint-Marceau lambasted him before fellow consumers. When a National Guardsman arrived, he asked the Dames, in their capacity as "good republicans," not to stir up the crowd. The guard then embraced the angriest woman as a sign of fraternity. Satisfied that the guard had publicized the injustice to buyers and had validated their patriotism, the other market women kissed the guard and cried, "Long live the Republic."[45]

The Dames similarly jeered at the hoarders who filed before the Revolutionary Tribunal throughout January. The Dames occupied the galleries with wage earners who were their clients and shared their disdain for the suspects. Police observer Monic reported that, because the Dames could not secure many supplies to sell in les Halles, they often went to the Tribunal instead.[46] With limited means to make money in the marketplace, some Dames even used the proceedings as an alternative commercial space. They peddled fruit to fellow spectators to eke out a few sous.[47]

Yet, as the pressures of war and the Terror bled into the Maximum's shortcomings, frustrated police and squeezed buyers ambiguously conflated the Dames, wholesalers, and aristocrats. Parisians were quick to condemn the Dames and other merchants whom they felt sold at unjust prices. After one vegetable retailer in the Marché Saint-Germain was dangerously called an "aristocrat" for setting her prices too high, another client accused all Dames of the Marché Saint-Germain of being "aristocrats who sell [food] so expensively."[48] The retailers attacked her in response. Commissioner Baron noted, "People loudly complained against the rich female merchants [grosses marchandes] of les Halles" and their greed.[49] "Grosses marchandes" could mean "fat/rich female merchants," but "marchand en gros" literally meant "wholesaler." In the context of the Terror, economic labels acquired moral overtones.

In les Halles, the populace cast commercial transactions as fundamentally political exchanges. Police spy Pourvoyer reported that citizens collectively monitored sales in December 1793. After one consumer bought eggs from a woman above the Maximum, "patriot" listeners pressed him that "it was his duty to take this woman to the first revolutionary committee."[50] In their eyes, the egg seller's price was a crime against the nation. In contrast, when one woman insulted a female fruit merchant whose price for a crate of onions she found exorbitant, onlookers backed the merchant. As the retailer and client came to blows, the spectators pegged the buyer as the unreasonable party and the police arrested her. The gathering crowd concluded the commercial dispute and cheered the police with cries of "Long live the Convention and the Republic."[51] Politics and trade appeared increasingly entangled in the marketplace.

While waiting for the deputies to separate wholesale and retail prices, the Dames developed a vibrant repertoire of illegal strategies to survive.[52] In one way, this was nothing new. Merchants and consumers across France had regularly engaged in illicit trade that affected commercial relationships.[53] However, the Dames' illegal maneuvers in the winter of 1793–1794 explicitly responded to the crisis produced by the not yet-revised Maximum. Ever deteriorating supplies augmented the strain between buyers and sellers from December through January.[54]

Most simply, the Dames increasingly ignored mandated price limits. In December 1793, the maximum on butter was 22 sous per pound, but it was sold illegally for 36 to 44 sous. Paris retailers illicitly sold twenty-five eggs at 80 sous. This was a leap from the illicit 50-sous rate of September[55] and more than triple the legal limits of 25 sous for eggs from Mortagne and 20 sous 8 deniers for eggs from Picardie.[56] Commissioner Le Breton wrote that the women retailers no longer observed the Maximum by January 1794.[57] Police spy Dugas seconded his account. "The maximum," he observed, "is only a joke for all the female merchants."[58] Even Grivel painted the Dames as "obstinate, often insolent, resellers" who forced mothers and cooks to pay above the Maximum or return home with "empty hands."[59] His colleague Siret found the Dames' price hiking doubly disheartening for those receiving state assistance. He noted, "One has seen more than one female citizen from this indigent class who, seeing the welfare of the sections, makes much more expensive the charity intended to relieve the poor."[60] Other Dames hedged their bets on wealthy customers' willingness to pay above the Maximum. These retailers confronted countryside producers outside the marketplace and forced them to sell them their supplies. Then, the retailers sold directly to well-off clients.[61]

By January 1794, the police appear to have inconsistently enforced the order of sale decreed in November by the Commune. Contrary to the municipal government's orders, the police allowed some retailers to buy supplies from wholesalers before consumers. One observer reported that if "only the public were admitted to provision itself" before the retailers, "it would be very advantageous for the indigent class."[62] The popular classes grew frustrated with the Dames' illegal maneuvers that, according to one police agent, burdened "the people alone."[63] But during the same scarce week, the Dames bitterly protested that they would not be able to pay market space rent.[64] By late January, buyers could not afford to buy food, but sellers could also not afford to sell it.

Backed into a Market Corner: The Pragmatic Solutions and Cooperative Ideals of Parisian Police

In late January, the very police who arrested Dames for illegal sales and annulled retailers' priority access to wholesalers became the Dames' principal advocates. The commissioners clung to the September Maximum's initial premise: symbiotic economic relationships mirrored the cooperative body politic. They pressured national officials to hasten the tiered price controls and release the legal stranglehold on marketplace trade. Police commissioner Siret noted that public opinion wanted the deputies to adjust the Maximum, but citizens needed to collectively agree on reform for it to be effective. The public, Siret argued, had to "put aside all particular interests and only occupy itself with the general interest." He called on the deputies to benefit merchants and consumers by finding a just "ratio" between the prices of goods and their intrinsic values. Regarding merchants, Siret suggested the deputies gradually diminish maximum prices to shake out hoarders by forcing them to sell quickly. Regarding consumers, he advocated punishing workers who organized to force up maximum wages. Siret framed workers' productivity as an issue of "sobriety and morals."[65] Like Grivel, he advanced a holistic project for the Maximum, which accounted for the economic responsibilities of all buyers and sellers.

Under such a cooperative revolutionary scheme, the police portrayed the Dames and other retailers as providing crucial services to wholesalers and consumers. Grivel objected that the police arrested one Dame who bought 100 eggs at 20 livres and was trying to resell them at the reasonable price of 25 livres. He argued that the retailer must be able to make some meager profit because she was a valuable link on whom consumers and wholesalers depended. If the countryside supplier had to retail his/her own eggs in Paris, he/she would not be able to sell across multiple markets, he/she would not be able to leave Paris in the morning to return to his/her farm, and he/she would have to pay to park his/her cart and horse in the capital. To compensate for these added expenses and loss of time, the wholesaler would have to sell his/her eggs at a higher price which would in turn harm the consumer. Therefore, Grivel argued, retailers deserved a profit to justly compensate their services that benefited suppliers and consumers.[66]

Grivel and Siret flagged how the Commune's reluctance to enforce the wage maximums undermined the more stringently enforced price maximums. Grivel and Siret eagerly demonstrated that consumers needed wage caps to stop the upward spiral of black market prices and the decline of actual supplies. In the absence of Maximum tables for Parisian wage limits, Grivel and Siret frequently used their knowledge of historical wage levels to infer what wage caps should have been and to complain about the discrepancy during the winter.[67]

On January 17, they observed that workers' wives could afford the best poultry and game in the market while their husbands demanded employers triple their wages. The commissioners deemed it unjust that "One has forcefully cried out against farmers and retail traders." They argued that wages as well as prices must be fairly balanced. "The Republic is a vast workshop," they lamented to their superiors, "where there is no boss. We are all workers in it. We work for the salvation of the fatherland." Merchants and laborers had mutually dependent economic duties which the General Maximum reflected. However, its lopsided enforcement harmed merchants who became deprived of their means to serve the nation and live above the subsistence line.[68]

By early February 1794, the surviving Dames complained that they could not secure anything to sell regardless of price and those remaining had mastered black market strategies to stay afloat. Police reporter Prevost noted that the few female fruit merchants who did procure food had completely abandoned the marketplace. They peddled directly to well-off customers' houses.[69] Retailers who procured supplies earlier in the chain of sale could bypass their brokers' cut in les Halles. Some Dames halted food-toting peasants outside the city en route to Paris. The populace summoned the police to stop this unregulated trade and steer the supply carts to les Halles for public sale.[70] Other Dames extended their businesses temporally. One fruit retailer complemented her daytime business with secret trade at night.[71] Still others manipulated neighborhood-based quotas to secure more supplies than allotted.[72] The insufficiencies of the General Maximum's merchant categories, the Commune's refusal to enforce the wage Maximum for four months, the dearth of reliable supplies, and the reforms in the lurch drove the lingering Dames' businesses to near ruin.

By early February shortages gripped the capital and the police continued tracking the Dames to illustrate how marketplace trade created mutual interests for buyers and sellers. Informer Prévost explained the Dames' precarious position as sellers of foodstuffs like vegetables and butter, but consumers of other foodstuffs like bread and sugar. Dames who sold marlins above the Maximum at 40 sous a piece had protested that they had to make some profit. If not, they could not afford to buy meat for themselves from the butchers.[73] Commissioner Bacon "chatted with different women of the Halle that I know" to collect insider information and protect consumer supplies. The Dames alerted him to a week-long conspiracy to deprive Paris of meat.[74] Police observer Pourvoyeur observed that the meat and grain shortages increased the demand for other food like vegetables, which the Dames sold.[75] But he noted that, like consumers, the Dames did not profit from this imbalanced food supply. Retailers faced an egg shortage as a result of the grain shortage: peasant suppliers who could not procure enough grain to feed their chickens sold them as meat or ate them at their own tables.[76]

The police noted that even while selling goods at illicit prices in les Halles, the Dames depicted themselves as legitimate actors in a local economy menaced by outsiders. Some Dames decried stockpiling consumers as violators of the moral community. Extravagant consumers' greed deprived their Parisian neighbors of supplies. In February 1794, after a Dame sold fish to a wealthy man's cook at a high price, she joined the chorus of complaints against gluttonous consumers. Police spy Perrière expressed his astonishment that "the female merchant was herself enraged with the expensive and delicate provisioning of these happy mortals since she must have gained a lot from it; but it's apparent that she was thinking about Equality."[77] Perrière approached the Dames, addressed them as "bonnes citoyennes," and implored them to not speak ill of their well-intentioned deputies who were revising the Maximum.[78] In the vegetable market two days later, another Dame scoffed at one consumer struggling to carry her many purchases: "Put them in your petticoat. Are you afraid of spoiling them? Go, you [tu] will not use them, we will be dead of hunger before they are used up. Do you not see that we already lack everything in Paris; turn your eyes on the market and you will be convinced of what I am telling you."[79]

Such seemingly mismatched alliances surprised police in les Halles. As poor consumers themselves, some Dames politically and economically sympathized with poor laborers' plight, even as they hiked prices. Like other consumers, the Dames railed against wholesalers who, anticipating that the Convention would release a higher revised Maximum, hid their goods.[80] On February 24, the very day that the Commission on Subsistence asked the deputies to vote on its re-formed Maximum, Perrière overheard a Dame share her clients' lament that the price of meat, vegetables, butter, eggs, and carp fluctuated so rapidly. The re-tailer explained that the instability resulted from "sad effects of the maximum." "Deprivations for some, exactions for the others," she sighed, "voilà the effect of prohibitive laws."[81]

Proposals, Promises, and Political Rivalries

From February 21 to February 24, the Commission on Subsistence presented the Convention with its ten-week-overdue proposal to reform price limits. Deputy Barère began by asserting that the General Maximum had been "a trap for the Convention set by the enemies of the Republic" in September 1793. He said that London and its contingent of Parisian allies had encouraged the original Maximum as a destabilizing economic measure. By only including price caps on some goods and not acknowledging multiple levels of trade, the September version had thrown commerce into disarray. According to Barère, the deputies had sought to correct the enemies' machinations on November 11, 1793, by ordering regional research for a more nuanced General Maximum. The tenacious people, Barère noted, refused to bow to enemies' plots. "The economy is the virtue of free peoples," he asserted, "the daily sacrifices are the privilege of those who battle for their rights."[82] Thus, Barère blamed the unreformed Maximum and five months of subsistence unrest on counterrevolutionaries rather than framing it as a legislative disaster.

Barère argued that the proposed Maximum reform amounted to nothing less than a transition from "monarchical commerce" to a Republican political economy. He maintained, "It is necessary for us to have a republican commerce, that's to say, a commerce that loves its country more than those of others, a commerce with moderated profits and virtues; republics have no other solid foundations." Consequently, the reformed Maximum would root the subsistence trade in republican morals. Barère emphasized that no other nation had instituted such a just or cutting-edge economic program. The new commercial regulations would overturn the plotters' nefarious intentions from the September Maximum. Barère proudly insisted:

> The tables [price lists] formed in virtue of the decree on the *maximum* on essential foodstuffs, merchandise and primary materials, is the newest and most important work on political economy. Thus all turns to benefit liberty; our enemies having offered [the Maximum] to us like a murderous weapon, we have made it into a useful and beneficial work for the people.[83]

The Commission maintained that their reformed Maximum would overhaul how citizens understood their role in a collaborative national economy. Under the monarchy, it argued, incomplete commercial figures and unbalanced trade regulations prevented subjects from seeing beyond their individual interests to the big economic picture. In contrast, the transparent Maximum tables would publicly reveal the rules and profit destined for each aspect of trade. The tables of regional prices and transport costs would embed the local economy within the national economy: "Envisioned under political relations, the table of productions and of industry for each district can make known the men's morals who inhabit [the district] and who are in some way shaped by common needs or works of the same nature." Thus, the reformed Maximum would be a political and economic project in which "all citizens" would collaborate. Through the tiered Maximum, "fraternity will be established between assistance and need, between the producer and the consumer." In the national economy, buyers and sellers would mutually benefit as cooperative citizens and symbiotic actors.[84]

To excuse the reform's detrimental delay, Barère explained that compiling the revised Maximum's tables had been a "gigantic and frightening work." More than 600 distinct maximums had existed across France as regions attempted to set their own prices. The Commission had invited all administrative units and popular clubs to submit historical local prices for the Maximum table studies. Barère assured the deputies that the reformed Maximum, backed by enormous research, would encompass "all the interests balanced."[85]

Although the deputies could decree the reform, the Commission noted that reviving the economy would be a society-wide enterprise. Barère called the Maximum "a public educational course for producers and consumers." Citizens' willing adherence would bring commerce to its fullest fraternal and economic potential: "The people will see in it [the Maximum] the ways to modify, to measure profit, and to regulate the true ratio of commerce, which will finally become patriotic, and which will cease to be foreign to the interests of liberty which makes it prosper."[86]

After three days of presentations and debate, the Convention and the Committee of Public Safety decided they would implement the tiered Maximum prices and allowances for transport costs (based on the distance between place of production and point of sale). The Convention declared that each of the 548 districts would have to enforce unique price controls for each good at wholesale and retail levels. Wholesale prices for each good would be calculated by adding 5 percent to the producer's price plus local transport costs. An additional 5 percent would then be added to "form the price to sell to the consumer by the retailer."[87] Every commercial link in the chain of sale should profit. The next day, Barère congratulated the Convention on passing "a democratic institution, a truly republican law." The Maximum would make "a nation of free men, of citizens more attached to their fatherland than to fortune."[88] The Convention planned to mail the Maximum tables from Paris and enact them across the nation on March 23, 1794.[89]

When Deputy Barère presented the reformed tables with distinct wholesale and retail prices, he acknowledged that retailers held little sway over consumer prices. Barère argued that the excessive number of intermediary agents, whose trade the public did not see, actually posed the biggest threat to buyers. These "parasites" would have no role under the third Maximum. Rather, Barère insisted that in open trade among commercial parties, "the secret of commerce will be known, [and] the operations of industry will be divulged."[90] Transparent trade between consumers and retailers in the public marketplace would foil intermediary agents. Thus, the reformed Maximum finally legitimized the retailers' work as a crucial public service. The projected tiered prices would enable the Dames to profit legally once again. Unfortunately, the Convention's national mailing procedure meant the Dames would have to wait one more month before they could legally sell above the old limits.

Almost immediately, rumors swirled around the projected Maximum prices and speculation further inflamed trade in the capital. Peddlers began hawking copies of the "Tableau de maximum, etc." which contained eight pages of bogus prices masquerading as the legislative decree. The Commune posted warnings that "foreign plotters" authored the work.[91] The Commission on Subsistence reiterated that the real Maximum would be posted on March 23, and the Convention charged the revolutionary tribunal with exposing the seditious authors. "Is he not one of the most dangerous counterrevolutionaries," Barère asked, " . . . that one who divides the interests of the buyer and of the vendor by deceiving them both, . . . who provokes the murmurs of the people around commercial shops and who irritates merchants' interest?"[92]

The Convention's promise to implement a tiered Maximum on March 23 galvanized some Parisians, while the delay angered others. Bolstered by both patriotic and alcoholic spirits, women in a cabaret on rue Dominique refused to be deterred after the Convention decreed the reformed Maximum would be posted within a month. The women exclaimed, "The aristocrats are waiting for an uprising, but, as long as the Seine flows and as we will have bread, we will be republican [women], and we are f***ed for being it." They punctuated their resolve, which nearly guaranteed hunger, with cries of "Long live the Republic!"[93] In contrast, police observer Rolin recorded, the Dames des Halles already "permitted themselves some unpatriotic remarks" in their continued desperation the next day.[94]

By late February, the butter and egg shortage was so dire that the police feared the popular classes would erupt if the Convention did not immediately provide relief.[95] The Dames, of course, had contributed to this dearth by participating in black market maneuvers to stay afloat. After the Convention decreed its plan, Parisian police realized the captial would be unable to wait four weeks for the new Maximum to be printed and implemented. Therefore, the police gained the Convention's permission to block retailers once again from buying supplies until "the Citizens had been provisioned."[96] In doing so, the police backpedaled to paint Parisian consumers as citizens but exclude the Dames from the same category.

Still unable to profit legally on resale and now unable to buy supplies, the Dames rushed to the Convention the same day. They testified that they could only profit by selling above the Maximum. However, the Convention refused to permit them to sell at a higher price since the reformed Maximum had yet to be posted.[97] The Dames also objected that the Commune had forbidden them from buying any vegetables at all to resell. Deputy Ducos replied that the original spirit of the Commune's decree was to "prevent monopolies." But the petitioning Dames protested that "this measure will deprive two thousand families of the means to subsist." Echoing the balancing theory behind the Maximum, Deputy Cambon defended the Dames: "It is necessary that the Committee of Public Safety and that [commission] which is occupied with the law of the Maximum research how to reconcile the supply of the markets, with a guarantee of profit for the poor women who have no other means to live apart from commerce in vegetables." The Convention decided that the Dames' request concerned policing practices, not law, so it passed the Dames' petition to the police administration.[98] Practice and legislation, however, were not easily untangled.

Besides supply problems, another major challenge remained for the Dames and the revised Maximum. Over the winter, a pro-sans-culotte faction led by Deputy Jacques Hébert had broken away from the Montagnards in the Convention and firmly dominated the Parisian municipal government.[99] More radical than the Robespierre-led Montagnards who controlled the Committee of Public Safety, these Hébertists sought to quicken the pace of revolutionary change and expand the Terror against suspected enemies. The Hébertists were the strongest advocates of using the Revolutionary Army to forcefully requisition food from the countryside to send to urban markets. The Hébertists called for more stringent protection of workers' interests, similar to the proconsumer call of the Enragés in 1793.[100] In his popular newspaper *Père Duschesne*, Hébert even began to skewer small merchants like the Dames des Halles: "I will no longer save the female merchant of carrots more than the richest wholesaler, because f***, I see a front formed from all those who sell against those who buy and I find as much bad faith in the small shops as in the big stores."[101]

The Hébertists sprang into action against the projected Maximum revisions that would weaken consumers' advantage. After Barère's presentation, Hébert rang the alarm bell at the Cordeliers club. Heated discussions ensued. Hébert called for an insurrection against the Montagnard deputies who supported the reform.[102] On March 1, posters attributed to the Hébertists plastered the walls of the capital. They warned the sans-culotte that he must fight "for his fatherland" or "die in the famine." Citing the new Maximum prices, the posters charged the government of collusion with evil merchants. They warned Parisian citizens, "You are a toy of all the crooks who govern the self-called Republic. These are the conspirators along with all the merchants of Paris. I denounce them."[103] On March 2, Hébert and his allies demanded a trial of some still-imprisoned Girondins whom Robespierre had initially saved from the scaffold. Hébert called on the people to overthrow the colluding Montagnard "oppressors."[104]

Montagnards who allied with Robespierre and the Committee of Public Safety still supported the Maximum's cooperative ethos and remained confident that the revised controls would restore the natural equilibrium of fraternal commerce. However, the Montagnards deftly spotlighted the backlash against their own reform to eliminate rival factions from the Convention. In the wake of Hébert's attack, Montagnard Barère blamed the marketplace dearth on those who posted incendiary posters calling for revolt. He accused the Hébertists of being paid by Pitt. Then, Barère blamed the Indulgents, the Montagnards' more moderate adversaries, for aspiring to weaken the nation by calling to release enemies from prison.[105] Like the Hébertists, the Indulgents had also broken off from the Montagnards during the winter of 1793–1794, but for opposite reasons. Led by Georges Danton and Camille Desmoulins, the Indulgents had begun to denounce the Terror as too excessive and accused the Committee of Public Safety of hijacking the Convention's powers. Therefore, in the weeks following Barère's proposed Maximum, the price of the fish trading hands in the marketplace became wedded to the central issue of parliamentary politics—the future of the Terror.

The Dames' reactions to the promised revisions and the factional turmoil surrounding it reflected how they envisioned the relationship between commerce and citizenship. An exasperated Dame declared on March 2 that she could not procure any fruit to sell. She complained in the marketplace, "In spite of the police and the commissioners' surveillance, it is still necessary to fight with all one's strength, it's that which made me abandon the fatherland."[106] The Dame forfeited her loyalty to the nation because the state did not fulfill its duty in the new national moral economy. It had yet to guarantee subsistence and legitimize retailers as fraternal partners in trade. However, even after the Convention dismissed the Dames' pleas to allow them to buy supplies before consumers, many of the Dames continued to support the Revolution or at least Robespierre, the Montagnards, and the Committee of Public Safety who supported the revised Maximum. It appeared that future maximum retail prices might be the only way to save the Dames' business.[107] The Montagnards were also the Dames' only check against the sans-culotte-controlled Commune. Thus, some retailers distinguished economic discontent and factional frustrations from blatant counterrevolutionary sentiment. From his post in les Halles, Grivel remained optimistic that the tiered Maximum would work because of its joint economic and political duties. He applauded one citizen's observation that the new Maximum must, like the government, rest on "the unity, the right and the duty of each citizen to rally to public good."[108] On March 4, Grivel reported with pride and great interest that:

Yesterday the majority of the citizenesses of the Halle, while setting up in the places that they occupy in the market, found circulars and anonymous letters, in which the authors told them that one must not suffer the cruel oppression exercised by the Convention, that it was necessary to return to one unique head [of state] and to displace the 700 tyrants who reign arbitrarily in his [the king's] place, that, in order to bring an end to the unhappiness that consequently devastates all, we exhort the Dames de la Halle to rise up and go, with 1,200 [Dames], to the National Assembly in order to eradicate tyranny and the tyrants.

Dames in neighboring markets found similar letters "addressed to the citizeness merchants of the Halle" in their stalls.[109] However, police observer Grivel was happy to report that "far from producing the effect that one had desired from it, [the pamphlets] enraged the citizenesses who found them."[110] The Dames grew infuriated over the counterrevolutionary sedition and brought the inflammatory pamphlets directly to the police.[111] The Dames' economic attitudes certainly informed their political attitudes. However, the Dames' revolutionary allegiance could never be simply derived from their economic experience. Alarmed by the pamphlet, the Convention charged the revolutionary tribunal with finding the responsible parties.[112]

Ironically, the day after he praised "the citizenesses of the Halle" for rejecting counterrevolutionary sedition, police commissioner Grivel took safeguards against the Dames' "recalcitrant spirit" and disregard for the supply laws. He looked suspiciously on the Dames' visit to the Convention to protest the order of sale: "The women, who call themselves citizenesses of the Halle and who are not it, have tried, through the favor of this name, to fool the Convention." Grivel observed that the consumer-first policy was the only way to prevent the Dames from forcing wholesalers to sell at the Maximum, but then selling to consumers above the Maximum themselves. Parisians complained to the Commune that the market women blatantly ignored the recent supply rules. Grivel warned that the Dames committed "excesses" in the marketplace including "invectives, cries, and violence." [113]

Grivel castigated the Dames' defiant transactions as "uncivic conduct" and brought an armed force to les Halles to underscore his point. Unfazed, the Dames still broke the Maximum and the order of sale. Chaos erupted in the marketplace as the Dames unleashed "a great tumult and much trouble and disorder." The confrontation between the Dames and the commissioner only ended after the police managed to arrest 200 of the Dames and hold them in a revolutionary timeout in the church St. Eustache.[114] The Dames may have maintained revolutionary allegiance, but they would not let their businesses disintegrate nor let the Convention wipe away the political legitimacy of their retail occupations.

As the Maximum faltered in March 1794, allegations of counterrevolutionary sympathies flared up in les Halles. With supplies dwindling, tempers rising, and retailers abandoning their commerce, Police reporter Rolin accused the Dames of acting like "perfect aristocrats" whom counterrevolutionaries "paid to spy on citizens."[115] No show of wealth went unsuspected. One inebriated merchant from les Halles inadvisably displayed her husband's expensive possessions. Since she claimed to make only 15 livres per day selling fruit and fish, she drew accusations of aristocratic payoffs.[116] By mid-March, the Dames sold mostly to rich clients, and some merchants smuggled butter out of les Halles to their houses.[117] The sectional committee reported that butter in the marketplace had even been stamped with the royal fleur-de-lys.[118] In response, the Comité de sûreté générale confiscated foodstuffs illegally destined for private houses. They sold the contraband in the public market to signal victory over aristocratic forces, but these small corrections were ineffective.[119]

The Convention had attempted to bypass retailers in les Halles, but it mattered little, as fewer goods arrived or remained in the market for sale. Although the police attempted to directly distribute butter to consumers, the daily queues of female consumers grew agitated.[120] Women repeatedly pillaged carts of butter and eggs in the markets across the city, and fed-up wholesalers vowed not to return.[121] Food became even scarcer. On March 11, several women beat one woman so severely during a butter dispute that the police evacuated her from les Halles on a stretcher. She later died from her wounds.[122]

Dames who sold fish felt the tremors from the butter shortage and dealt with their own irregular supplies. Clients passed by the Dames' stalls asking, "What would we do with our fish, we don't have any butter to prepare them with."[123] Although the popular classes might find a "morsel of butter" to cook cheap salted herring and local vegetables, retailers had trouble selling their reliable supplies of salmon and pike that were more expensive to buy from wholesalers and thus unaffordable in retail quantities for most Parisians.[124] A few scrappy fish merchants abandoned their usual commerce to switch to other markets. Five of them conspired to collect the pork rations for the décade (the revolutionary week) multiple times from different sections. These Dames speculated they could resell their dubious rations.[125]

By mid-March 1794, many consumers were calling on each Parisian section to provision its own inhabitants instead of funneling foodstuffs through the central markets. This would prevent individuals from buying from multiple satellite markets and then hoarding goods. However, one commissioner noted that despite their good intentions, these citizens did not realize that such a measure "would reduce all the female merchants in boutiques of the Halle to begging."[126] It would be another blow to marketplace retailers and their commercial raison d'être. *Révolutions de Paris* noted that the Dames aired their irritation by shouting "My faith! it would be better to have a king."[127]

Although some Dames willingly disparaged the deputies' decrees and traded illicitly, Parisian police understood that the 1,000 retailers were the lynchpin to order in the capital. On March 13, the Commandant général of the armed forces encouraged the Dames to partner with local troops. He called on the group to protect the subsistence trade. He wrote to the city gatekeepers: "I like to believe that the virtuous republicans [the Dames] will be the first to establish tranquility. The female merchants of fish are beginning to do the policing themselves."[128] The police sought to convince the deputies they could defend consumers' interests by defending retailers' commercial interests. For example, the police noted that when the Dames bought butter in les Halles but then had to flee the markets and sell to rich customers to make their profits, they deprived poor families of foodstuffs.[129] Police observer R.J. reasoned: "It would be much better for the rich as well as for the poor, if the maximum price were augmented, because the former [rich] would pay less than they pay [now], and with this security in price the others [the poor] would obtain these foodstuffs which they [currently] cannot have at all, it is infinitely preferable to pay a little more for the objects of necessity than to be absolutely deprived of them."[130] The commissioners implicitly backed the Dames' own assertions that retailers provided a useful public service.

The Commune and the Convention had taken great pains to supply the capital, but neither the requisitioning Revolutionary Army nor exceptions to the chain of sale in the marketplace, nor the 16 million livres the Committee of Public Safety spent on the capital's shortages since November had permanently solved the problem. The Dames found it difficult to supply themselves, as fewer wholesalers found it profitable to come to les Halles. Suppliers complained that they lost incentives to come to Paris after officials forbade them from leaving the capital with any candles, soap, or sugar that they usually brought back to the countryside.[131] The lack of vegetables grew so dire that on March 11, that the Commune encouraged the sections to cultivate public park spaces and turn them into vegetable gardens.[132] The forthcoming revised Maximum, with its cooperative and comprehensive vision of trade, offered hope to some and anxiety to others.

The Third Maximum: Economic Responsibilities, Commercial Utility, and a Specialized Body Politic

Nine days before the police enacted the reformed Maximum, it appeared that merchants might still be able to prove their revolutionary worth through their occupational services. On March 15, the Bonne Nouvelle section complained to the Convention that the "mercantile aristocracy" was still plaguing the nation but the section seemed softer on retail merchants. It demanded the deputies "decree that merchants will be excluded from all public functions until the peace and that any citizen who is not a merchant can only buy from retailers." Since consumer access to wholesalers had not worked, the section appeared willing to try retail trade to democratize sales. At the tribune the next day, Robespierre protected merchants from blanket accusations by Hébert. He argued, "If the merchant is necessarily a bad citizen, it is evident that no one can sell anymore; therefore this natural exchange which enables members of society to live is ruined and by consequence society is dissolved." Robespierre maintained that the nation's enemies denigrated merchants' merits to weaken the country.[133] In essence, Robespierre was returning to themes from his famous February 4 "Report on the Principles of Political Morality," when he called for "a society in which 'commerce is the source of public wealth rather than solely the monstrous opulence of a few households.'"[134] Robespierre rightly feared that wage laborers (and their Hébertist supporters) did not comprehend how intricate levels of trade determined prices. According to police agent Mercier, the public did not witness how high retailers had to bid to secure goods from wholesalers before the consumer market began.[135]

By late March 1794, it was abundantly clear that the Convention needed to release the reformed Maximum as soon as possible. Neither merchants nor consumers could survive without a maximum that distinguished between wholesale and retail prices. Against the backdrop of an unpredictable marketplace, a police observer reported an "image of desolation" during a March 23 crush:

> What is certain, it's that les Halles resembled a battlefield; one heard the cries of young women and pregnant women who felt themselves pressed in the most sensitive places; children were on the verge of suffocating in their mothers' arms, unleashing lamentable screams; the [market] guards, covered in sweat, hurt with their arms those whom they intended to protect: one woman had her wrist cut in this manner; another woman thought her eye had been punctured by a halberd.[136]

Not far from the gruesome scene in les Halles, Robespierre and his Montagnard supporters launched an attack on the most vocal opponents of their political and economic projects: the radical Hébertists. The Convention, spurred by the Committee of Public Safety, accused Hébert and his faction of being "hoarders/speculators having sought in the public's misery a way to enrich themselves, having wanted to use famine to bring about civil war and the fall of Robespierre."[137] The Hébertists were executed on March 24. The Montagnards then turned their attention to the right and attacked Indulgents who remained critical of the Committee of Public Safety's growing power and the quickening Terror.[138] The leading Indulgents mounted the scaffold on April 5 under charges of plotting to dismantle the Republic and restore the monarchy.[139]

With the Hébertist resistance quelled and district transport costs calculated, the Convention finally enacted the reformed General Maximum. The revised price lists amounted to 1,200 pages of tables. The state had requisitioned 15 presses to print 4,000 copies for regional officials.[140] The police posted the tiered prices in Paris on March 25, 1794. In total, Parisians had weathered the General Maximum's deficiencies for six months as officials researched and disseminated the new Maximum. The police reports and the Dames' illegal maneuverings worked in tandem to compel the Convention to create prices for all levels of commerce. Moreover, the six-month crisis demonstrated that retailers were essential in facilitating trade. Paradoxically, the fiasco that destroyed many Dames' businesses also legitimized the Dames' work as a pivotal service to the nation.

The reform finally endorsed retailers' occupations and profits in a regenerated nation of interdependent citizens. The tiered prices provided retailers with a 5 percent profit on top of wholesale prices. For example, a wholesaler could sell 100 stock fish (like cod) to a Dame at a maximum of 54 livres 10 sous. The Dame could then profit by reselling the fish at a maximum retail price of 60 livres per 100 cod.[141] The Dames could finally pursue their livelihood once again through legal means.

In the difficult weeks that followed, public opinion split over the reforms' fairness and effectiveness. Some Parisians objected to the tiered Maximum because it raised prices for consumers. Others critiqued this third iteration of the Maximum as a violation of the law's own holistic goals: they argued that it privileged one group over another. On the one hand, some individuals complained that the Maximum was "very advantageous" to provincial suppliers and was "absolutely to the advantage" of merchants.[142] On the other hand, wholesalers complained that the tiered Maximum was "much less favorable [to them than to] retailers."[143] Marketplace suppliers moaned that transport costs were still too high for them to profit.[144] Parisian consumers, in turn, protested that the third Maximum unreasonably doubled the price of butter from Isigny. Others complained that only the rich would be able to buy meat since poor sans-culottes could not afford the new prices.[145] Many consumers objected that the reform catered "to the profit of merchants" by unnecessarily inflating retail prices.[146] Still others doubted that the system could entice suppliers to bring more goods to the capital and that the ineffective decrees were "meant to entertain us."[147] A mere three days after enacting the Maximum, police accused wholesalers of engaging in "liberticide traffic" for striking deals outside the market under the cover of night.[148] In short, most critics agreed that equilibrium was necessary to make subsistence trade a cooperative society-wide enterprise, but they disagreed on its enforceability and fair price ratios.

Optimistic Parisians hoped that the tiered prices would revive and stabilize the subsistence trade. Groups gathered around the decree posters sighed that the high prices would at least encourage the provincial suppliers to return to Parisian markets.[149] Other consumers noted that, although butter prices seemed a bit expensive, they would be satisfied if it attracted wholesalers and their provisions again.[150] Hopeful Parisians anticipated that, by balancing production, transport, commercial, and labor prices, the legislation would be "the despair of all of the Republic's enemies."[151]

Reform in the Balance: Mobilizing the Maximum in the Marketplace and the Workshop

Unfortunately for Parisians, the tiered Maximum did not fulfill their hopes. Six months of marketplace turmoil proved difficult to correct. The reformed Maximum failed because supplies still arrived irregularly, the police could not enforce the new prices, and government officials did not uphold the corresponding Maximum on wages. Although the battered Maximum would legally last eight more months until December 1794, the controls barely limped along in the capital by Robespierre's fall in July.[152]

By late March 1794, marketplace trade was so desynchronized that when countryside supplies did arrive in the capital, they sometimes converged in quantities too large to sell. Just two days after police posted the new prices, deliveries of seafood flooded the fish market. Since the fish arrived in large waves, the Dames could not sell them all and, to the police's chagrin, threw out rotting fish carcasses.[153]

The national committees tasked with inventing the Maximum on paper sought to stem the law's hemorrhaging in Paris. Supply to the capital might be insured if the government smoked out peripheral black-market activity and harnessed tools of the Terror. On April 12, the Commission on Subsistence suggested secret agents infiltrate regions surrounding Paris to expose fraud and Maximum infractions. On April 19, the Commission de Commerce assumed emergency responsibility for delivering food and essential goods to the capital as "a place of war." However, by the end of the reformed Maximum's first month, Parisian police struggled to enforce sales at the revised prices. It took 400 men to guard les Halles during volatile cheese sales on April 18.[154] Moreover, the rising legal and illegal food prices contributed to worker unrest in Paris after mid-April.[155] The Committee of Public Safety and the Commune attempted to settle stomachs and tempers by issuing ration cards for meat supplies. Each household member would only receive ½ pound of meat every five days.[156] The Commune promised to work with supply merchants. On May 18, the representatives appealed directly to retailers' obligations and patriotism: "Retail merchants, cease from resting, with guilty inertia, on the government's resources in that which you are capable; the law assures you the proper advantages to encourage you; it [the law] guarantees you the free circulation and peaceful arrival of your merchandise; it assures you a sufficient profit for commerce; but a more gentle recompense is offered to you, that of serving your fatherland."[157] After eight months of commercial turmoil and imbalance, legal threats and patriotic appeals did not deter buyers and sellers from violating the Maximum.

None of the painstakingly recalculated price controls on goods mattered if the corresponding wage ceilings on which they were predicated did not take effect. The balance among producers, buyers, and sellers remained skewed in the capital. In Parisian arms workshops, the Commune never implemented the wage Maximum. The workshops' output was crucial to the war effort and the Commune feared providing fodder for work stoppages. In addition, municipal governments administered the Maximum and, as a sans-culotte stronghold, Commune officials imposed price limits while generally ignoring wage limits. This clashed with employers who viewed work as an object for sale like all other goods and insisted the Commune mandate local ceilings on wages as the Convention had instructed. Without caps on wages, Parisian employers complained, production costs would surpass maximum sale prices on manufactured goods such as wool, linen, coal, candles, and soap.[158]

Having purged the sans-culottes' greatest allies, the Hébertists, from the Convention, Robespierre and the Montagnards began to pressure Parisian workers on wages in late Spring.[159] On June 3, the Convention requisitioned the labor of those who transported food supplies and threatened to punish anyone who resisted. Four days later, the Commune blamed "malicious persons" for encouraging workers to strike, especially those who worked with foodstuffs, to sabotage the nation. Like the Convention, the Commune promised an audience with the revolutionary tribunal and possible death to laborers who stopped work, collectively organized, or individually demanded higher wages.[160]

After months of punitive laws for merchants who abandoned their jobs, workers received parallel consequences. The Convention's decree made the unmistakable statement that the state regarded workers who did not fulfill their occupational duties, who ceased to serve the nation by abandoning their work, or who pursued profit outside the confines of the Maximum, as having committed crimes against the nation. Such workers' occupational deviance broke the social contract. As the September Maximum had intended, political and economic contracts now went hand in hand for producers, sellers, and wage laborers. On June 1, the Committee of Public Safety formally issued a warning "forbidding administrations, sections, entrepreneurs to give workers and laborers employed by them a salary above the maximum."[161] The Committee of Public Safety underscored its commitment to the equilibrium theory behind the Maximum on June 10 by ordering its agents to establish the Maximum on wages in areas where the municipal councils had not done so.[162] By mid-June, many different occupational groups who saw their purchasing power decline threatened to strike and demanded higher wages.[163]

On June 19, the municipal government reported that many parties had violated the Maximum. One observer concluded that it was impossible for the police to surveil everything, everywhere. The best system, he suggested, would be to have consumers report fraud and infractions. But he acknowledged consumers would not do so since they obtained supplies through these illegal transactions.[164]

On July 23, the Commune formally complied with the September Maximum by issuing local wage tables at 1.5 times the 1790 rates. The list ran 61 pages and carefully subdivided wages within industries. For example, nine occupations existed within the sword makers category ranging from the sword assemblers to the polisher's wheel turner. In les Halles, porters' rates varied by the type of butter, fish, or vegetables they carried and took into account the quantities moved and equipment used. Remunerations also considered nonmonetary compensation. Printers who received room and board were paid lower wages than those who did not. The marketplace pea shellers' custom of receiving possible partial payment in a cup of coffee or brandy was finessed into their wages. Articles II and IV of the Commune's decree reiterated that accepting wages above the published rates was a crime. It would be the legal responsibility of the worker and those who employ him/her to obey the Maximum.[165]

Although Commune officials carefully calculated the Maximum wages in proportion with the Maximum food prices, the result angered sans-culottes who saw their wages decline. A carpenter of the 1st class whose wages had peaked at 8 livres during Messidor an II (June/July 1794) saw his wages reduced to 3 livres 15 sous under the published rates (calculated on the 1790 rate of 2 livres 10 sous).[166] The Parisian wage Maximum made the sans-culottes and the Parisian sections less enthusiastic about rescuing Robespierre when the Convention arrested him four days later. Disgruntled workers were less likely to save the Montagnards who capped or even decreased their salaries.[167] A few Parisians cheered "f*** [the] Maximum!" as Robespierre's cart clattered by them to the guillotine. The Great Terror largely expired with Robespierre's final breath on July 28.[168]

Repealing the Maximum: Liberal Visions of Economic and Political Contracts

Although laborers resented that the Commune bowed to the Committee of Public Safety in setting the nine-month delinquent wage rates in the capital, most workers had seen an increase in their standard of living from June 1793 to July 1794. Even with rising food prices and limited meat rations under the Terror, Parisian workers' disregard for maximum salary caps meant that their income outstripped living costs.[169] These gains eroded precipitously as the Thermidorian Convention gradually loosened the Maximum's strictures. Within a week of Robespierre's fall, the Committee of Public Safety promised Parisian workers that they would revise the Maximum "so that the price for a day of work can be proportioned to those of subsistence."[170] The Commission du commerce et des approvisionnements drew up a study to base wage rates on "the current value of consumables, above all the vegetables and fruits which are one of the principal foods of the workers."[171] In other words, the maximum wages would no longer be based on the 1790 rates but on current food prices. Such a move would again legally advantage buyers over sellers, whose legal price limits did not change. However, the sans-culottes were no longer strong enough to push the Convention to follow through. Ultimately, after the fall of the Jacobins in July 1794, the Thermidorians criticized the Maximum as a radical project that limited economic freedom. From the perspective of Thermidorian officials, any wage increase would raise war production and supply costs. It would also jettison the Maximum's theoretical balance between merchants and consumers. Thus, the proposed revisions indefinitely languished in the Comité de commerce and never made it to a vote on the Convention floor.[172]

Throughout the late summer and fall, the General Maximum came under attack by the Convention as the deputies struggled to "exit the economic terror" and resume economic liberalism once again. Given the shifting tides of politics and war, many of the same deputies who had initially supported the Maximum questioned if continued regulation would bring prosperity.[173] Deputy Joseph Éschassériaux turned the very argument that justified the Maximum in September 1793 against it in August 1794. He argued that the deputies should loosen the grain maximum since the counterrevolutionaries, paid by foreign governments to cause chaos in the food trade, had been recently eradicated by the guillotine. The economy's problems, Éschassériaux insisted, had been sparked by malice, not by profit-oriented business. His colleagues Villiers, Petit, and Blutel likewise extolled commercial liberty in the Convention's September 1794 debates. They argued that relaxed trade controls would allow the natural equilibrium between merchants and consumers to emerge, which would bring supplies and domestic prosperity. Deputy Blutel argued that the nation needed to rehabilitate the image of useful business owners to revive the economy. He asked, "Does there exist a man who despises himself sufficiently to be willingly exposed to a state of commerce that would bring suspicion down upon his head?"[174]

Logistical problems throughout fall 1794 further eroded the Convention's incentive to maintain the Maximum. Some district committees discovered data errors in the original tables, which unintentionally skewed prices for several months. Deputy Jacques Isoré argued that manufacturers lacked motivation to produce goods since raw material costs were too high compared to the Maximum sales price of finished goods.[175] To keep pace with rising costs and inflation in October, the Convention bolstered merchants by raising prices from the original 1 ⅓ of the 1790 rates to 1 ½ of the 1790 rates. Workers were now proportionally disadvantaged, as they received no corresponding increase in wage ceilings.[176] Their purchasing power decreased with rising costs, and their standard of living plummeted. Nonetheless, by December 1794, Deputy Legendre complained to the Convention that no honest trader could stay in business under the restrictions. He observed that the individuals remaining in commerce were those willing to engage in illegal activity. Economic regulation had driven out law-abiding citizens.[177]

The death knell sounded for the Maximum in December, as the Convention pursued liberal economic policy rooted in free trade and the protection of private property. Proponents of deregulation asserted that the Maximum created fundamental antagonisms in commerce. Others again insisted that nefarious plotters had put the Maximum into motion. Jean-René Loyseau contended that centralizing subsistence trade made citizens dependent on the "despots" of government and "our internal and external enemies" like "Robespierre and his accomplices."[178] Giraud, presenting on behalf of the Committee of Commerce and Provisioning, noted that enemies who had implemented price controls "killed agriculture, suffocated commerce, they annihilated all types of industry and ruined the retail merchant."[179] Éschassériaux called for deregulation to create a just economy for all actors and commercial arenas: "A system of economy is good," he explained, "when work and the products of the earth are regarded as the nation's primary wealth ... when the farmer, the manufacturers, and the trader enjoy the full liberty of their property, their production, and their industry."[180] The Maximum's attack on private property not only abused individuals' natural rights but also undermined relations among citizens. Loyseau argued that the "law," including economic regulations, must match "our social relations."[181] This perfect fusion of economic and political relations, of course, had been the General Maximum's initial goal fifteen months earlier.

On December 24, 1794, the Convention abolished the Maximum.[182] In a proclamation explaining its decision, the Convention argued even "the least enlightened individuals" could see that the Maximum harmed food supplies. The emergency war conditions that "perhaps justified its birth" were no longer relevant. The government would maintain some regulations on grain and special provisions for the army, but, regarding other food and wages, the deputies concluded, "the more this law was strict, the more it became impractical." The deputies decisively embraced free trade as the "regenerated commerce" in which "the Republic's provisioning will be entrusted to liberty, the sole base of commerce and agriculture." The Convention guaranteed citizens that fraternity in commercial relations would now stem from the voluntary good will among citizens and market interests: "Fraternity will not be a vain word among you," the Convention reassured citizens, "it will equally repel the calculations from avarice and false alarms" that create artificial supply shortages.[183]

Thus, the optimistic leitmotif of fraternal commercial relations undergirded opposing economic systems supported by many of the same deputies during the radical Republic and the Thermidorian reaction.[184] The deputies pursued a symbiotic economy of citizens via centralized regulation under the Terror and via market liberalization under the Thermidorian Convention. In this concert of commerce, war and factional rivalries frequently modified the key of debate. Ultimately, the revolutionaries on both sides of 9 Thermidor believed that balanced players could harmonize a symphony of interests. Whether that equilibrium was achieved through economic controls or the free market remained a dissonant chord. However, the basic premise remained: citizens' economic duties were bound to their political duties in a new national moral economy. Thus, economic contracts became political ones.

In the Maximum's Shadow: The Rise of Class Concerns and the Collapse of Popular Activism

The Maximum's abolition caused the assignat to depreciate severely and catapulted food prices again. In Ventôse an III (February/March 1795), Parisian police called on the state to regulate bread once again to improve supplies for the poor. One commissioner cited the ideological value of working citizens in addition to practical concerns for public order: "it is of the greatest importance and the greatest justice to come to the help of the indigent class which cannot procure for itself the most indispensable goods . . . it is of the greatest importance, above all, to reassure this laboring and useful class."[185] In exchange for their "useful" work and fidelity, citizens expected the state to provide bread. These reciprocal services remained at the heart of their social contract. As Parisian workers later succinctly put it, "We want the Republic . . . but with it we want bread."[186]

Due to soaring food prices unleashed by deregulation, Parisian sans-culottes revolted against the Convention twice in Germinal and Prairial an III (April and May 1795). The uprisings reflected the utter failure of liberated commerce to foster fraternal equilibrium. Since the Thermidorians did not adjust wage ceilings during the summer and fall of 1794 and the free market caused food prices to spike, Parisian workers' standard of living was reduced to famine levels worse than 1789 for the first time.[187] The price of butter increased 1,415 percent between June 1790 and April 1795.[188] The price of a single egg went from 4 sous to 8 sous between December 1794 and April 1795 alone.[189] Thus, a carpenter spending his entire Maximum wage on the eve of the Maximum's abolition could only buy around 19 eggs.

In this dire context, the sans-culottes launched their last major uprisings on 12 Germinal and 1 Prairial (April 1 and May 20) demanding "Bread and the

Constitution of 1793."[190] The police called high prices a mere "pretext" for plotters "to encourage the most violent measures against the national representation [the Convention]."[191] But, in reality, popular activism starved to death at the hands of imbalanced regulation and unchecked deregulation. Terrified by the Parisians who invaded the assembly hall, the deputies swiftly shut down avenues for popular politics. The Convention purged its Jacobin deputies and soon ordered all Jacobin clubs to close across France. It also dismantled the Parisian municipal government, a seat of sans-culotte power. The Directory would continue to centralize political practice into restricted state institutions.[192] While the deputies were quick to stifle popular activism after Germinal and Prairial, they were less successful in checking the inflation and food shortages causing the discontent.

Without maximum wages divided by occupation or privileges oriented by trade identities, purchasing power more forcefully delineated society than before. By first instituting and then retracting the General Maximum, the revolutionaries had laid a stepping stone to class-based identities. The Maximum's categories of buyers and sellers initially streamlined, though oversimplified, the myriad parts of Old Regime trade. When the deputies endeavored to distinguish wholesalers from retailers, they bit off more than they could logistically chew. They could not successfully regulate remuneration for every occupational subdivision in the national economy. Ironically, the Commune's failure to enforce the elaborate wage limits rendered the commercial distinctions among laborers less relevant. Finally, the Thermidorians' deregulation and the drastic rise in the cost of living aligned most Parisians' political and economic concerns, and thus separated society by class. During the Directory, wealthy elites would expand such class divisions into cultural ones to justify their political leadership over the "uncivilized" poor.[193]

As the Thermidorians and then the Directory enacted free trade strategies, economists and the police worried about the pragmatic effects of deregulation in the marketplace. This led them to experiment anew with controls in les Halles. In July 1795, the Committee of Public Safety rationed out some foodstuffs, including the cod and herring that the Dames des Halles sold, to "the indigent class of citizens" and others without steady income. The Committee planned for each household to receive ration coupons to buy their goods "from the grocers and female fish retailers, of their choice, and known for their probity and their intelligence in retail commerce."[194] The Dames and other retailers, in turn, would submit their coupons for reimbursement by the "national treasury." But, in the late summer of 1795, the deputies waffled. They tried to slash food prices by cutting retailers like the Dames from the chain of sale, as they had in winter 1793–1794.

When officials once again decreed that consumers could purchase directly from wholesalers before retailers could, economist Camille Saint-Aubin rushed to the resellers' defense. The economist attested to retailers' utility for consumers. He argued that consumers who spent their mornings waiting in wholesale lines sacrificed valuable working time. Their lost wages actually made it more expensive to buy from wholesalers. Moreover, wholesalers set their prices in bulk and would dislike selling individual quantities to consumers. Nothing would stop rich consumers from buying more than their fair share and then reselling, as illegal retailers, in smaller quantities at higher prices. Citing the proverb "an onion merchant should know all about his scallions," Saint-Aubin maintained that retailers, who navigated everyday trade logistics, rather than governmental officials, best understood the economic intricacies of the food trade. The state should allow retailers to conduct their beneficial commerce.[195]

The Maximum was gone but not forgotten after the Directory was established in November 1795. Government supporters feared that unattainable food prices would rally the popular classes and incite violence akin to the uprisings of Germinal and Prairial.[196] Seven months after Saint-Aubin plead on behalf of retailers, the journal Le Miroir accused Jacobins of sparking radical sympathy by slipping secret messages into foodstuffs. The journal explained how a market woman had sold a bundle of radishes to another woman with egalitarian political tracts hidden inside. These radical pro-Babeuf titles included "The Legion of Police for Itself," "The Memories of a Democrat," and "Does One Owe Obedience to the Constitution of '95?"[197] Babeuf had been arrested 15 days prior for conspiring to overthrow the Directory and to reinstate the Constitution of 1793 but, as Le Miroir's report suggests, conservatives remained convinced that plotters were stirring hungry sans-culottes to attack the government.[198] In les Halles, food and the commercial relations surrounding it remained literally wrapped in politics, if no longer in regulation.

The Maximum, its failures, and its aspirations set the stage for nineteenth-century anxieties over subsistence policy and for the 1,300 food riots that ensued from 1800 to the 1850s.[199] Much like the regional maximums, local controls on bread continued to be applied in patchwork fashion into the nineteenth century despite efforts to nationalize the system. For decades following the Maximum, diverse political parties advocated for price controls for reasons ranging from public order to paternalistic state duties. Notwithstanding these different logics, all elites remained acutely aware of food riots' revolutionary potential and this social anxiety underscored most subsistence legislation in the years following the Maximum.[200]

Each time the deputies passed one of the three Maximum programs from May 1793 to March 1794, they reconfigured the web of economic relations among the Dames des Halles and their fellow citizens. During the arduous revision of the General Maximum and its ensuing enactment, the Dames culturally, if not commercially, survived great ideological challenges to their occupation's worth. The retailers attempted to dodge the political and literal mud flung at merchants whom citizens accused of hoarding, price gouging, and manipulating market chaos to fatten their purses. By condemning counterrevolutionary sedition, responding to patriotic appeals, and voicing consumer concerns over goods like bread and meat, the Dames carved out ideological space as useful merchants whose commercial and political interests overlapped with those of their clients. Commercial frustration did not automatically translate into counterrevolutionary sentiment, nor did it create irreversible antagonistic relations between buyers and sellers. To survive within the marketplace, the Dames bent the deputies' decrees to their economic advantage or disregarded them altogether.

While officials legislated economic policies, they implicitly judged the social utility and, consequently, the political legitimacy of various occupations. Price controls demanded the revolutionaries ask whether merchants could politically justify their profits. Did merchants assist fellow citizens? Or did gluttonous merchants pander to rich clients and cheat vulnerable worker-consumers? In short, how could egalitarian impulses assume economic forms in the marketplace? Disagreement over the answer revealed competing visions of societal relations within the regenerated body politic. The reformed Maximum solidified retailers' commercial responsibilities as patriotic duties. As the deputies put a price on food, they put a price on merchants' occupational worth to the nation. Consequently, the Dames and their supporters fought unfavorable aspects of the Maximum by asserting that retailers indispensably served society. By petitioning their representatives and complaining to the police, the Dames insisted the state reform the Maximum to support their crucial retail businesses.[201]

Police observers became the Dames' unexpected allies. They simultaneously chastised the Dames' black-market strategies, enacted emergency measures that bypassed retailers, and defended them as essential commercial actors in les Halles. Similar to the Montagnards on the Committee of Public Safety and in contrast to the Hébertists, the police recognized the market women's pivotal role in provisioning the city. As agents of the state, observers in les Halles revealed the General Maximum's shortcomings to the Convention and the Commission on Subsistence. They contrasted their on-the-ground experiences with the deputies' sterile calculations. Police observers expounded to the deputies that the tiered Maximum must correct local problems in les Halles and that equilibrium between the market principle and market regulation defied static, formulaic theories.

Ultimately, the Dames, the police, and the National Convention all engaged in the Maximum reform of March 1794, which legally coded retailers' work as indispensable to the nation. The Dames, the police, and the retailers' supporters interpreted and protected retail trade within the framework of a fraternal society. If the *Encyclopédie* had described retailers as "more convenient than necessary" in 1753, the revolutionaries' experience from 1793 to March 1794 convinced them otherwise.[202] In the tiered Maximum, the deputies confirmed that retailers like the Dames not only served public good but also played an essential role in trade and the body politic. By establishing retail limits, the revolutionaries validated resellers' work. Thus, the Maximum's various iterations profoundly affected how the Dames could affirm their occupational utility, legitimize their economic citizenship through their work, and make claims on the state.

Although the reformed General Maximum subdivided wholesale, retail, and transport costs to align multiple levels of sale, it also depended on the corresponding wage maximums to balance the economy. Until 5 Thermidor (July 23, 1794), Parisian officials catered to sans-culottes' interests and largely disregarded the controls on wages. Thus, although the deputies endorsed retailers' useful services to the nation and advanced a cooperative economic model of the body politic, local officials failed to enforce the wage limits required for the model. The one-legged regulation could not stand.

After the Thermidorians repealed the General Maximum in December 1794, legal distinctions softened between merchants and workers within the popular classes. The Thermidorian Convention's focus on property and purchasing capital as economic and political delineators rendered class, rather than occupation, a more salient social cohesive. Political grievances incubating in the unresolved problems of the subsistence trade reflected class concerns. Free trade jettisoned the occupational subdivisions of the Maximum and further loosened the trade-based compartmentalization of workers. Despite the common goals of an entire Parisian social strata struggling to eat, the deputies crushed the popular insurrections against the Convention in Germinal and Prairial an III (April and May 1795). Nonetheless, under the Directory's economic liberalism, the Dames could still posit useful work and reciprocal duties as the enduring basis of the social contract. After the fall of the Maximum, the Dames would recast their economic citizenship by insisting that fiscal contracts mirrored political ones.

Commercial Licenses as Political Contracts

Working Out Autonomy and Economic Citizenship

On August 27, 1791, the Dames des Halles appeared before a National Assembly vexed by the king's recent flight from the Revolution. At the bar, the market women announced that they had dissolved their confraternities dedicated to the Virgin Mary and Saint Louis, the king's ancestor. They swore, "Today, we have no other corporation than the French, no other confraternity than the patriots, no other cult than that of liberty."[1] The deputies applauded as the Dames donated their confraternities' 1,500 livres in money, precious metals, and ceremonial ornaments to the nation.[2] Referencing the patriotism of "the citizens of all classes," the Dames portrayed themselves as useful citizens implanted in the body politic, rather than privileged members of a corporation.[3] Their spokeswoman asserted, "The (female) inhabitants of les Halles, for whom all politics, all refinements are foreign, do not know any virtues other than those of being useful and serving their fatherland."[4] Yet, far from detaching the Dames from politics, the fish merchant had actually articulated the Dames' model of economic citizenship: Individuals joined the body politic through beneficial work that served society. For the Dames, civic labor, rather than gender, served as the organizing principle for citizenship. For them and others, the fiscal world associated with that labor consequently defined civic membership.

When the revolutionaries demolished the guilds in 1791, much of the fiscal system also disintegrated into the rubble. Without guilds to levy occupational taxes, the state's corporate revenue vanished. At the same time, the revolutionaries lost the internal policing measures the guilds had provided. To fill this double void, the revolutionaries invented a new personal occupational license system called the patente. Under this annual direct tax, each citizen would pay graduated fees in exchange for permission to conduct his/her trade. Officials announced that they would only grant licenses to holders "conforming themselves to the laws and police regulations."[5] This clause provided modest inroads to postguild surveillance. The patente's fiscal potential was much greater than its policing power. Therefore, the money-strapped legislators fashioned the patente first and foremost as a tax instrument.

As a fiscal tool informed by cultural assumptions, the patente sheds light on the revolutionaries' endeavors to define the relationship between autonomous work and civic membership. Their imaginings grew out of discussions from the second half of the eighteenth century, when many political economists began to portray farmers, producers, and traders "as acting out of civic regard for their fellow citizens." Some believed this "patriotic" economic engagement might compensate for an individual's lack of immobile property. Economic activity could incorporate him/her into society.[6] As the French prepared to convene the Estates General in 1789, Abbé Sieyès further developed this logic to define the nation through various types of labor in *What Is the Third Estate?* As historian William Sewell succinctly summarizes, Sieyès maintained that "the nation was constituted by useful work—either private or public—and by the citizens who performed that work." On the one hand, the collective mentality of Old Regime corporatism lingered in this idea of the body politic. After all, the revolutionaries similarly predicated civic membership on serving society writ large.[7] On the other hand, the revolutionary individual needed nothing but his/her work to enter autonomously into such social and political relationships. In such a work-based vision of the nation, the Dames des Halles earned membership by providing food to fellow citizens and by paying taxes on this labor.

By erasing corporate intermediary bodies, the patente created a new type of fiscal contract between the individual and the state. As historian Yannis Kotsonis has argued, national economic planning and yearly taxes compelled the modern European to "reconsider himself or herself as an integrated citizen whose economic activities had state significance and who should be viewed primarily in economic terms." Direct taxes like the patente washed away the guilds' delineations and substituted novel, equally politicized, national economic traits.[8]

From 1791 to 1798, revolutionary officials jettisoned guild delineations and erected new scaffolding for occupational taxes. To determine patente fees, legislators experimented with yardsticks of occupational profitability, immobile property, and work-based independence. The deputies' changing approaches to assessing the license tax paralleled shifting definitions of autonomy and citizenship.

In the eyes of the Physiocrats and most Enlightenment thinkers, sovereignty emanated from the land, and ownership of immobile property conferred full citizenship.[9] It comes as no surprise, then, that the National Assembly gauged its earliest direct taxes and the right to vote on property. Using the assessment standards for the patente from 1791 to 1798, this chapter reveals how occupational traits came to delineate fiscal responsibility and civic membership in ways analogous to this immobile property. In the legislation on occupational licenses, the deputies not only evaluated citizens' tangible properties to determine tax rates but also accounted for citizens' commercial independence and the social utility of their services. Consequently, this chapter argues the revolutionary patente transformed occupational labor into intangible personal property, i.e. a movable but nonphysical possession considered a legal asset. Unlike guild masterships or venal offices, this intangible personal property was limited to the working life of an economically independent citizen. As citizens individually contracted their occupational permissions with the state, they incorporated work into the social contract.

Second, this chapter argues that, as officials mapped fiscal duties onto wider ideals of contractual citizenship, they came to consider both material possessions and occupational labor as twin types of property that signaled individuals' civic autonomy. While officials appraised citizens and individuals vied for the most advantageous tax bracket, both groups sought to recreate the connection between work and property. The debates surrounding the patente's creation in 1791, its interruption in 1793, and its ensuing reform from 1795 to 1798 demonstrate how the revolutionaries dovetailed notions of work and individual autonomy.

Finally, this chapter asks how citizens without immobile property became personally categorized and fiscally attached to their state through their work in ways that disrupt gendered binaries of citizenship. In 1796, the deputies expanded the patente qualifications and integrated the Dames des Halles as independent commercial agents. While the Directory enlarged the patente to include more autonomous workers like the Dames, it simultaneously excluded all dependent wage-laborers, most of whom were men. Given this surprising contrast, how did the patente affect or reflect the Dames' position in the body politic? How did the market women rethink their economic identities, fiscal responsibilities, and political duties to maneuver into the lowest tax bracket? And how did they refashion their occupational identities before justices of the peace to secure a desirable license? The Dames' position as female merchants illuminates how the revolutionaries conceptualized, for the first time, material possessions as well as the act of immaterial work as personal property that constituted civic autonomy. Both property and self-directed labor signaled citizens' independence and rendered them members in fiscal contracts. And both placed the taxpayer within a body politic in which, as the Commune of Paris insisted, "Taxes are an obligation which derive essentially from the social contract."[10] The patente transformed work into a type of property, one that signified civic independence without gendered foundations.

Replacing the Guilds: Fiscal Contracts
and Legitimate Work

Officials and citizens alike believed that taxes, the Achilles' heel of the Old Regime, needed to be fundamentally overhauled to remake the relationship between citizens and the state. On June 17, 1789, the first day of its existence, the National Assembly declared that all former taxes were "'illegal, null, and void because they had not been consented to by the nation."[11] The deputies argued that taxes could only be just if citizens or their representatives negotiated them.[12] Fair taxes could only be "determined by the general will" and formed "an offering to public utility."[13] In place of the "impôts" (literally "imposed" taxes) of the absolutist system, the deputies planned for revolutionary "contributions," which evoked the "voluntary and civic dimension of the fiscal gesture."[14] In the August *Declaration of the Rights of Man and Citizen*, the platform for the future Constitution, the deputies confirmed that "a common contribution is indispensable" and that it would be "divided among all the citizens."[15]

After negating the Old Regime's ideological basis for collecting and assessing taxes, the deputies faced a self-inflicted hole in state income in addition to the national debt it had inherited. The French detested the indirect taxes of the Old Regime, in part because they were unevenly distributed across the population and much heavier than other taxes. Because the king only levied indirect taxes on a few consumer products and the regional movement of goods, he did so at high rates. But, in disavowing the Old Regime indirect taxes such as the gabelle (salt tax) and octrois (customs duties) the cash-strapped National Assembly lost 150 million livres in annual income.[16]

With the bitter taste of indirect taxes lingering, the deputies focused on creating new direct taxes with national standards. In general, the revolutionaries and their nineteenth-century descendants considered direct contributions that taxed personal material objects more just than those that taxed a person's income and social rank. Officials could visually, unobtrusively, and objectively assess material objects as "indicators" of wealth, whereas considering values attached to "the person" relied on the "inquisitorial" assessment that caused "horror,"[17] appeared invasive, seemed "subjective," and socially ranked people rather than things.[18] In December 1790, the National Assembly passed its first direct tax, called the "contribution foncière." Officials calculated this land tax based on "the net revenue of the earth" defined as the profit "which stays with its owner, after deducting the cost of cultivation, seed, harvesting and upkeep from the brut product."[19] The deputies hoped the *contribution foncière* would net 250 million livres a year.[20] They followed this land tax with a second direct tax called the "contribution mobilière," which drew mostly on the rental value of one's dwelling.

The deputies hoped the bulk of the tax would target "capitalists" whose business involvement and profit resulted from their role as investors and administrators rather than as "workers."[21] In the Assembly, La Rochefoucauld justified the gauge as an equitable, since "It is in general true that each person is lodged according to his faculties [wealth]."[22] In addition, individuals who earned more than the average daily wage would pay the regional equivalent of "three days' work." This was the same sum that conferred active citizenship and voting rights.[23] At the *contribution mobilière*'s passage in February 1791, the revolutionaries estimated the it would generate 39 million livres a year.[24]

The *contribution foncière* and the *contribution mobilière* left the Committee on Taxation still searching for some way to tax commerce comparable to the abolished customs duties of the Old Regime.[25] Taxing inanimate land and immobile property proved much easier than taxing the socially embedded world of work. After all, officials had charged themselves with finding a fiscal model that would mirror ideal social and political relationships among citizens themselves.[26] Commerce, production, and labor were rarely isolated personal activities. Consequently, they held promising potential as sinews of the revolutionary body politic. However, the legal organization of trade had also underpinned Old Regime social hierarchies. Before the National Assembly, Pierre d'Allarde contended that the revolutionaries could only throw off the guilds' "tyrannical privilege" if they completely replaced the fiscal system on which it depended.[27] Any revolutionary solution would need to tax citizens as individuals, not as members of corporations, and account for the disparate occupational clout of taxpayers. In February and March 1791, the Assembly began its quest by dismantling the corporate world and abolishing occupational privilege. Through the d'Allarde Laws of March 2 and 17, the deputies requisitioned the guilds' property, assumed their debts, reimbursed their titles, and incorporated their holdings into the *biens nationaux*.[28] In the same sweep, the Assembly eliminated all *droits d'aides* (indirect taxes on some transportation, food, drinks, and goods).

In this clearing, the National Assembly passed its third direct tax, called "the patente." The tax would generate revenue previously supplied by guild masters' license fees. The patente would also replace the dreaded *vingtième* or a periodic 5 percent income tax, which essentially taxed the fruits of labor.[29] The Assembly optimistically projected the patente would pump 34 million livres into state coffers each year.[30]

This third direct tax borrowed its name from its Old Regime cousin. Under the monarchy, "lettres patentes" (patente letters) were a form of "lettres royaux" (royal letters) or orders in the king's name.[31] According to its 1772 definition, *lettres patentes* were "letters emanating from the King, stamped with a grand seal, & countersigned by a Secretary of the State." *Lettres patentes* contained open, public knowledge. They included the "ordinances, edicts, and Declarations that form the general laws," but they also included permissions "given to a province, city or corporation, or to a private subject, with the effect of affording them some grace, privilege, or other right."[32] For guilds, their *lettres patentes* granted them monopolies over the production, regulation, policing, and trade of a specific good or service in a given region. Individuals who bought masterships from the guild accepted the guild as their link to the crown in occupational and political issues. Some masterships also carried voting rights in a representative assembly. As purchased privileges, guild masterships were defined as individual property that one could bequeath after death. Thus, like venal offices, a guild membership was a piece of property whose existence transcended and existed independently of any individual's life.[33]

The 1791 patente sought to transform this relationship among work, property, and sovereignty by taxing citizens and their work without intermediary bodies and by directly granting personal licenses to each citizen taxpayer. In fall 1790, the deputies had attempted to institute an *impôt personnel* (personal tax) without success.[34] Deputy d'Allarde, of the Comité des contributions publiques, presented the patente as a way of reorganizing the *impôt personnel* to suppress the guilds, destroy their monopoly over labor practices, and erase their "exclusive" advantages.[35] The patente would refashion occupational permissions to emanate "From the Law and the King" as the licenses proclaimed.[36] It would also shift responsibility for *occupational* taxes to individuals and citizens would have to annually renew their patente. Thus, the patente continued to treat occupational permissions like a type of private property, but reframed individuals' work as serving society rather than serving a corporate body.[37] Unlike a guild mastership, the occupational permission expired with the autonomous work life of the individual or when the individual ruptured their relationship with the state. The patente was thus truly a contract on both material and ideological levels. Citizens received personalized licenses from the state in return for paying the patente fees. No other revolutionary direct taxes involved a one-to-one exchange.

The patente also became the only truly personal direct tax of the revolutionary era. That is, the patente was the one direct tax whose rates varied according to changes in the taxpayer's individual situation, rather than according to regional collection quotas that officials subdivided among inhabitants.[38] This individual and independent assessment of the patente is unsurprising since, after eradicating corporatism, the deputies sought to atomize the autonomous worker's relationship with the state. In doing so, they dramatically redefined fiscal citizenship.

By destroying guild fee structures, annulling trade monopolies, and forbidding corporations from mediating permissions between individuals and the state, the patente created a work-based political contract between each citizen and the nation. In his 1791 patente report on behalf of the Comité des contributions publiques, Pierre-Louis Roederer insisted to the Assembly that "the ability to work" was a natural right and that "this right is his property."[39] At the climax of his own patente speech, d'Allarde likewise argued, "the faculty to work is one of the first rights of man." He asked his fellow representatives to agree with Anne Robert Jacques Turgot, the 1776 antiguild controller-general, that work was "the first property, the most sacred, the most imprescriptible."[40] The state, d'Allarde argued, should protect individuals' ability to pursue any occupation because this freedom would benefit society writ large. When choosing their occupations, citizens would naturally gravitate toward the work or commerce others needed.[41]

It is important to note that d'Allarde's definition of work as property referred to the immaterial and individual act of working rather than the material results of any such work. This was not a sans-culotte struggle over the means to production. Nor was it a Marxist view of alienated labor. Nor was it even Turgot's hierarchy of property ascending from urban equipment to landed property.[42] Rather, d'Allarde's vision fashioned work as the autonomous property of an independent citizen. This notion of work stressed the private, unmediated ownership of occupational acts. In other words, anything under an individual's direction, including material production, immaterial labor, and immobile property qualified as his or her taxable "propre" or "own" items.[43] Such a distinction was crucial for those like merchants, whose work provided services instead of tangible goods.

The patente, the deputies hoped, would erase the old maze of commercial privileges and defend the freedom to work on ideological and practical levels. It would open occupations. As long as each citizen secured a patente through governmental authorities, the deputies proclaimed, "it will be free for any citizen to conduct any commerce, or to exercise any profession, art, or trade that he will find good."[44] For citizens who chose to be merchants, the patente tax streamlined or even nullified other marketplace fees that could accumulate.[45] Since traveling merchants paid one patente fee to conduct their business anywhere, the system granted them newfound geographical freedom.[46] For all self-employed individuals, paying the variable patente would be less cumbersome and risky than saving and advancing large amounts for corporate privileges.[47] In short, the patent gave citizens more occupational choices, expanded commercial opportunities, increased mobility, decreased investment risk, and provided new guidelines for delineating labor-based identities.

In contrast to corporate classifications, the patente's broad tax brackets cut across previously disparate trades. To calculate graduated patente fees, the Assembly sought to gauge the economic prowess of each self-employed worker. The Assembly first analyzed the rental value of an individual's occupied property, which citizens would annually report to local administrators.[48] Officials then assigned a tiered rate based on "the rental value of the dwelling, of boutiques, of stores, and of workshops." The deputies reasoned physical property was the "only approximate measure of the importance of commerce" or work-based in-come.[49] For traveling merchants, the deputies even considered their transport vehicles as a way of evaluating their trade.[50] By focusing on immobile property or commercial possessions as "manifestations of wealth," the revolutionaries could ignore the particular person from which subjective privileges had for-merly radiated.[51] Like all four revolutionary direct taxes, known as the "quatre vieilles," the patente sought to combat this Old Regime heartburn by taking ma-terial objects as proxy gauges for economic strength.[52] Officials calculated citi-zens' patentes based on the categories shown in Table 7.1.

Despite these property markers for assessment, the deputies did not envision the patente as taxing material possessions or a distinct trade. Rather, the act of individual labor rather than the specific craft practiced was the ultimate object of assessment. Work became a novel type of personal property for which au-tonomous citizens were fiscally liable. Autonomous will, not skill, became the defining trait of occupational labor.

The deputies anticipated there would be 659,712 French citizens who would require a license based on the patente criteria.[53] To give their new system teeth, the deputies decreed that individuals who evaded the patente would be fined four times their license cost and any person who reported a nonpatented indi-vidual would profit from the sale of their confiscated goods.[54] The Assembly instructed municipal police to enforce the patentes and local judges to prosecute those who shirked their fiscal duties.

The deputies issued some patente exemptions that echoed supply concerns and notions of political dependency. Bakers only paid half rates so as not "to aug-ment the price of consumptions of the poor."[55] To avoid straining production, the deputies exempted rural farmers who raised beasts, cultivated foodstuffs, or produced essential goods on their lands (many of whom already paid the *contri-bution foncière*). Since state officials held public offices whose salaries came from the public treasury, the deputies excused them from licenses.[56] Wage and day laborers (whose employers held patentes) did not have to pay a patente much in the same way guilds had barred them from membership as occupational dependents.[57] Finally, just as one could not be an independent, active citizen without paying three days' work in taxes, the Assembly excused from the patente "people who are not included in the tax rolls of the *contribution mobilière* for the tax of three days' labor."

The National Assembly wanted to expand the labor market rather than re-strict it and acknowledged that even graduated taxes might surpass the means of some citizens. Deputy Martineau praised "the honest indigent man" who worked to survive. He cautioned that the patente would overwhelm the poorest workers and encourage "vagabondage" in place of useful labor.[58] With this in mind, the deputies proposed Article 8 to exempt "male and female sellers of

Table 7.1 **Patente Rates by Occupation and Rent in March 1791**[a]

Occupation	Criteria for Graduated Evaluation	Annual License Tax Rate
Standard Rate (most citizens participating in commerce, arts, trades, and professions)	For rents up to 400 livres	2 sous per livre of rent
	For rents from 400 to 800 livres	2 sous 6 deniers per livre of rent
	For rents over 800 livres	3 sous per livre of rent
Bakers	For rents up to 400 livres	1 sous per livre of rent
	For rents from 400 to 800 livres	1 sous 3 deniers per livre of rent
	For rents over 800 livres	1 sous 6 deniers per livre of rent
Peddlers and Wholesalers Who Travel to Sell Their Goods	For merchants carrying their goods on their backs	Whichever is greater: 10 livres or the Standard Rate
	For merchants using a cart of any kind	Whichever is greater: 25 livres or the Standard Rate
	For merchants using any animal to transport their goods	Whichever is greater: 50 livres or the Standard Rate
Merchants of Wine, Brewers, Lemonade Makers, Distillers, Vinegar Makers, Merchants of Beer and Cider, Innkeepers, Innkeepers Selling Food and Beverages, Caterers, Manufacturers and Dealers of Playing Cards, Manufacturers and Dealers of Tobacco[b]	For rents up to 200 livres	30 livres
	For rents from 200 to 400 livres	3 sous 6 deniers per livre of rent
	For rents from 400 to 600 livres	4 sous per livre of rent
	For rents from 600 to 800 livres	4 sous 6 deniers per livre of rent
	For rents 800 livres and above	5 sous per livre of rent

[a] Table compiled from "Décret portant suppression de tous les droits d'aides, de toutes les maîtrises et jurandes, et établissement des Patentes," March 2–17, 1791, in *Recueil Général des Lois, Décrets*, vol. 2, n°100, 36–37.

[b] These professions paid *droits d'aides* on their goods and services under the Old Regime, so the deputies ordered a higher patente rate to "replace [them] in the least imperfect manner." The *droits d'aides* most commonly taxed beverages but occasionally covered meat and fish. See "Rapport sur les Patentes," in Roederer, *Œuvres*, vol. 6, 527; "L'Assemblée Nationale aux Français," in Roederer, *Œuvres*, vol. 6, 546, 549.

flowers, fruits, vegetables, fish, butter and eggs" without immobile commercial property.[59] The exemption classified together all "the male and female retailers, selling in the streets, halles, and public markets" based on their ambulant use of public space. In this occupational category, the deputies strikingly ignored traditional trade boundaries that divided commerce by types of goods.[60] Despite their charitable intentions, the deputies hesitated to pass the exception for fear of creating new privileged groups. Deputy Aubry-Dubochet summed up the general sentiment: "At its core, this [exemption] article is an indirect privilege; but it is fair to favor the indigent class, which can only subsist on the product of their retail."[61] However, the deputies feared the license tax might also disrupt the small food trade, always a precarious subject. In order to avoid "augmenting the price of the poor's consumptions," the deputies passed the exemption article. They completely excused "those who sell vegetables, fish, or who display their goods in the markets and the streets."[62] Even though the poor Dames des Halles did not require a patente according to this ambulant retailer and food trade loophole of 1791, the Dames' very exemption reshaped their occupational identity. Their lack of physical commercial property and use of public space became legally more important than their type of trade.

On June 17, 1791, the deputies delivered the final blow against the corporate world in the Le Chapelier law. After the d'Allarde law, artisans working in former masters' workshops had benefited from their now-isolated employers' reduced power, so the Le Chapelier law leveled the playing field by barring workers' associations. The legislation prohibited individuals of "a same state or profession" from gathering into committees, keeping collective records, forming rules concerning their occupation, and submitting collective "addresses and petitions" to government bodies. In this way, neither groups of workers nor groups of employers could maintain the socioeconomic privileges they had held under the Old Regime.[63] In response to the Le Chapelier law, the Dames des Halles dissolved their confraternities, as we have seen, in August 1791 and severed the last institution circumscribed by their collective occupational identity. Although the Dames did not yet pay the patente, the Le Chapelier law began to atomize their legal occupational identities. As disbanded individuals, the Dames readily asserted that, like "all classes," their patriotic "virtues" stemmed from "being useful and serving the fatherland."[64]

While the Assembly continued to eliminate the vestiges of corporatism into the fall of 1791, it struggled to compel local communes to enforce its replacement—the patente.[65] To simplify the new patente tax brackets and improve lackluster collection after the first six months, the deputies delineated three broad patente types in September 1791. Significantly, these licenses would have no "designation of any profession" printed on them. The reform subtly, but critically, depicted a citizen's occupation as a choice resulting from the license level purchased rather than a preexisting trait informing the level to be purchased. Citizens could secure the *demi-patente* (the half patente), the *patente simple* (the simple patente), or the *patente supérieure* (the superior patente). Each level granted the holder a set range of commercial rights.[66] Reflecting national concern over bread supplies, only bakers paid the cheap *demi-patente*. Anyone who bought a *patente simple* could exercise any profession except for the commercial professions that offered lodging, entertainment, or refreshments for consumption in their place of business. Finally, a citizen who purchased the expensive *patente supérieure* could exercise any occupation "without exception."[67]

Patente posters in les Halles reminded artisans and merchants with boutiques to estimate the value of their residence, workshops, stores, and shops before municipal authorities in exchange for exercising nearly any "profession that will please him/her."[68] Through this process, citizens annually renewed their personal fiscal contracts with the state.[69] As factrices and local pub owners also began to pay for patentes, the Dames remained excused. Yet, the very logic of their exemption occupationally redefined the poor retailers. Until 1793, the Dames continued to trade in the marketplace without licenses or direct occupational taxes.

The Public Value of Particular Acts: Hope for Work and Disappointment for the Patente, 1793

While the sans-culottes are commonly portrayed as the champions of labor in the radical Revolution, the valorizing nature of work struck a common chord among multiple political factions in 1793. The joint economic and political importance of commercial labor, for example, resonated with Pierre-Louis Roederer, a moderate who had helped craft the 1791 patente as part of the Comité des contributions publiques.[70] The sans-culotte-backed Commune and the Jacobin-dominated Convention interpreted the relationship between work and property differently than Roederer and his Girondin supporters, but they too framed work as the cornerstone of citizenship. Ironically, the nation's occupational license system became untenable at the precise moment when work became a legal proof of patriotism in 1793.

Roederer began to deliver a series of lectures in January 1793, three months after the rivalry between the Girondins and Montagnards began to escalate. His orations amounted to "a defense of private property," but he expanded the definition of private property to include immaterial commercial work. Rendering the legal categories of property pliable took some conceptual acrobatics. According to historian Ruth Scurr, Roederer redefined contemporary "*propriété foncière* [real property] as land and *propriété mobilière* [mobile property] as the land's produce" and maintained that the capital holders benefited civilization more than the landholders.[71] Roederer recounted how early societies had become divided into individuals who owned immobile property, those who worked the land, and those who owned capital.[72] Originally, individuals who freely worked the land to fulfill their family's needs maintained ownership of most *propriété mobilière*.[73] But, Roederer argued, as society developed, farmers needed investment capital and auxiliary services to reap the fruits of their land. Producers could not harvest crops, transport their goods to clients, and sell to customers. The new services of investors and traders liberated some agricultural producers, who, similarly supported, became manufacturers. Manufactured goods then "augmented" those of the earth.[74] In sum, the useful services of commercial actors like traders and investors made possible the time and capital essential for modern agriculture and manufacture. Because merchants and investors catalyzed production processes originating in the fruits of the earth, Roederer reframed commercial activity as *propriété mobilière* owned by merchants.[75]

Roederer's ultimate goal in redefining property was to overturn the idea that political rights only originated in landed property. The physiocrats, Old Regime jurists of domainial rights, and some moderate and conservative revolutionaries had defined land ownership as the source of sovereignty. But Roederer insisted that those whose immaterial capital contributions facilitated the production and sale of goods from the earth likewise deserved full citizenship.[76] In short, their mobile property stemmed from immobile property. Consequently, Roederer's reconsideration of private property to include commercial and financial work strikingly realigned sovereignty and civic membership.

Roederer's expanded category of private property clashed with the most radical sans-culottes, who sought to jettison property entirely. Roederer fiercely denounced calls to abolish private property as detrimental to the moralizing effects of self-directed work, to the freedom to work, and to productivity. He denied that property disparity created social inequality. Instead, he argued in a liberal vein that work by both the rich and poor would improve social relations and politically glue citizens together:

> It is this complete and entire institution of work in a great nation that
> I call the great, the true principle of morals and of good mores; and
> I mean by good mores not only the habit of domestic virtues, but that
> of social virtues in all their reach. It is this complete and entire insti-
> tution that, developing in talents, multiplying riches, strengthening
> the common patrimony, multiplies still, tightens, ennobles all the re-
> lations of man with his fellow men, restores natural equality in social
> disproportions.... [Work] creates the fraternity of talents, and brings to
> the common good the diverse gifts that nature has given to individuals;
> [work] guarantees property . . . guarantees liberty, by doubling the

rich's need of the poor, while freeing [the poor individual] from all the degrading qualities of his dependence."[77]

To celebrate all types of work and engrain occupational virtues in popular culture, Roederer called for each department to honor a different job in a festival every Sunday. Citizens would display, at the altar of the fatherland, tools of the featured trade. They would celebrate the job's "utility" in song and dance. The rotating festivals would provide fraternal spaces among citizens and "attach them to the fatherland, to public interest."[78]

Tangentially, the sans-culottes and the Jacobins agreed with the strand of Roederer's argument that insisted a wide range of occupations undergirded society rather than just those attached to the land.[79] In the fiscal realm, paying taxes on immobile property and dwellings (the *contribution foncière* and the *contribution mobilière*) and on work (the patente) reflected a citizen's double contribution to the body politic. On January 31, 1793, the Commune declared, "the first proof of civic duty is the payment of contributions [taxes]."[80] For those without land, this largely referred to the *contribution mobilière* and the patente. Dovetailing the logic of the sans-culottes-backed municipality, the national government declared work one marker of citizenship in the law of March 21, 1793. The law stipulated that *certificats de civisme* (certificates of patriotism) should be given to many types of individuals, including "all indigenous adult males who had a job, duly acquitted their civic responsibilities and had four guarantors in the locality."[81] In the same round of legislation, the deputies established municipal committees to register foreigners and to issue *certificats de civisme*. These committees would become Comités de surveillance révolutionnaire.[82] Defining civic inclusion was on the agenda across the nation. Performing useful work and paying corresponding taxes became part of the equation.

However, the very same day the Convention updated the *certificats de civisme*, the deputies moved to revoke the patente. The annual licenses were supposed to have generated 23 million in revenue a year, but they only brought in 6 to 7 million with a collection price tag of 800,700 livres. Moreover, sixty of eighty departments requested the deputies extend their collection deadlines or reduce their regional assessments.[83] The patente had turned into a logistical nightmare.

Some officials feared that keeping the patente would fan the flames of counterrevolutionary resistance. Some rural citizens initially evaded the patente because it appeared to replace the hated *vingtième* (a periodic Old Regime income tax). To supervise license registering and tax collecting in municipalities, the central government had dispatched *visiteurs de rôles* (visitors of tax rolls) since September 1791. But, as Deputy Cambon noted, these circulating officials were "suspect, because they represent the collecting agents of the *vingtième*, the ferrets of the former chambres des aides, . . . in another form a resuscitated fiscality."[84]

The budding civil war in the Vendée further complicated the collection of countryside patente fees by early spring 1793.[85] In addition, the patente rates seemed out of balance across France, since city rents surpassed their rural counterparts and the three broad patente categories lumped together modest merchants with formidable brokers. The exasperated Convention admitted, "This law, too favorable to some, too rigorous for the others, gave rise to unfaithful declarations, oppressions, refusals, countless complaints."[86]

Rather than patch up a sinking ship, the Convention abandoned its project of occupational licenses on March 21, 1793, and voided all licenses required since the start of the year.[87] The deputies consolidated the patente fees that had taxed dwellings into the *contribution mobilière*.[88] But by April, moderate voices in the Convention like Deputy Balthazar Faure objected that eliminating the patente was a mistake that had drained the nation's production as much as its fiscal revenue. Faure lamented, "It is necessary that we have farmers, manufacturers, workers, physical laborers; and it's only in order to distract themselves from the most useful work that a mass of people abandon these professions to become merchants, resellers, second-hand clothes dealers, cabaret owners, and it is in order to easily win everything without hardship [i.e. taxes] and without difficult work."[89] Nonetheless, Faure remained a minority voice. The Convention held fast to its decision throughout the Jacobins' tenure and the Terror.

The notion that taxes constituted the threshold to basic citizenship did not disappear with the troubled patente. The nation leaned heavily on its remaining direct taxes as it dug in for internal and external war. The Commune even made paying taxes a requirement for obtaining municipal *certificats de civisme* on December 2, 1793.[90] The Convention may have abandoned the patente, but the revolutionaries did not discard the centrality of work or taxes in citizenship.

Defining Civic Autonomy: Work, Property, and Gender, 1795–1798

The debt, war, and uncertainty continued to weigh heavily on the state through the Thermidorian Convention. First the Thermidorians and then the Directory were anxious to contrast their republic with the radical republic that had threatened property and which popular politics rendered unstable. As the Council of Ancients (the Directorial upper house) later explained, their Thermidorian predecessors had wrung their hands over the lack of "equilibrium between public receipts and expenditures" and the direct taxes that only taxed buildings and land. Locked in a fiscal crucible and desperate for income, the deputies reconsidered an occupational tax that generated public revenue from the pursuit of commercial activities. Declaring, "it is just that commerce and industry contribute to the needs of the Republic," the Thermidorian Convention reinstated the patente as an "act of urgency" on July 22, 1795.[91] Once again, working citizens would have to pay patente fees calculated on their immobile property and occupation type. However, when the deputies reinstated the patente, they continued to excuse ambulant merchants who sold in public spaces without a fixed boutique. In other words, the deputies again exempted the Dames des Halles.[92]

However, given persistent debt problems, the Conseil des Cinq-cents (the Directorial lower house) reconfigured the patente in August 1796 to include all independent workers, even those without immobile property.[93] The Conseil decreed: "Each citizen must push himself to come to the aid of the public thing, according to his/her faculties; let not agriculture alone bear nearly all the state's burdens [large farmers incurred heavy patente fees], and let commerce and industry contribute as well because of the protection that is granted to them and the advantages that they receive from the system." In effect, the Conseil reformed the patente according to the Constitution of 1795. Passed one year earlier, it proclaimed, "All contributions [taxes] are established for the general utility; they must be divided among the tax-payers, according to their faculties."[94] Since the 1796 revision did not exclude poor working citizens without immobile property, the Dames des Halles no longer escaped the patente's fiscal demands.

By forcing the ambulant Dames and other propertyless merchants to pay for a patente, the state formed a direct contract with each retailer who contributed to the "public thing" and financed the "public treasury." The political resonance of paying this direct tax would not have been lost on the Dames. During the earliest patente debates, Deputy Vernier of the Committee of Finances had maintained, "our fiscal contributions [are] the first and the most sacred of all debts for true republicans."[95] And in 1792, the Commune had campaigned to show how "public contributions" defended the fatherland from enemies and included taxes in the oath of "fidelity to the Law."[96] The National Assembly had already found itself in an uneasy ideological position in 1791 when it clarified that, as part of the *contribution mobilière*, each male citizen had to pay the same tax "equivalent to three days' work" that conferred active citizenship and voting rights, but so too did "women enjoying their [personal economic] rights and taxable minors although they are not active citizens."[97]

Magnifying these tensions, the 1796 patente continued to emphasize that each individual was responsible for his/her own tax and his/ her own occupational permission. Article IX declared, "The patentes will be personal and will only serve those who have taken them."[98] Therefore, as the Dames contributed to the nation via their personal license tax, they fulfilled their fiscal duties as individual citizens. These fiscal parameters of citizenship notably surpassed gendered boundaries of electoral citizenship. Thus, the 1796 patente gave the

Dames autonomous claims to citizenship based on an economic, rather than gendered, contract with the nation.[99]

Since the revolutionaries considered taxes central to citizenship and the patente's criteria closely aligned with voting qualifications, many people conflated the occupational license with full citizenship in 1797. In response, the minister of the interior had to publicly clarify that paying the patente did not guarantee the right to vote.[100] The confusion was understandable. Autonomy, as variously measured by property, occupation, and taxes, constituted the prerequisite for citizenship since 1789. The earliest revolutionaries had maintained that full political independence was impossible under the Old Regime's tenurial model of real property, which included multiple layers of ownership on the same piece of land. They had concluded that practices offering "private ownership of public power," such as venal offices, further compounded the problem. Thus, as historian Rafe Blaufarb argues, "absolute, individual property . . . was the essential basis of political liberty [in revolutionary reform], for property-ownership alone provided the personal independence required for citizenship."[101] In the various qualifications for citizenship from 1789 to 1795, the deputies substituted tax contributions as a proxy measurement for property that provided political autonomy. Yet, tax quotas for voting requirements were not usually quantified as a cash sum, but as a number of days of labor. For example, in 1789, the deputies set the economic bar for voting at taxes amounting to at least three days of labor. In effect, the revolutionaries measured the autonomizing and sovereignty-endowing effects of real property (material personal property) in tax contributions generated by both real property and work. This elision effectively rendered occupational labor immaterial personal property that endowed the "owner" with political powers and civic rights.[102] Thus, the trinity of work, property, and autonomy as expressed by taxes was present since the very outset of the Revolution.

Citizens could draw a variable, but undeniable path from property to taxes to work to civic autonomy in definitions of citizenship from 1789 to 1795. Each constitution strove to block those who were dependent or under the potential influence of others from the voting. For example, the Constitution of 1791 deemed those who were servants or slaves too dependent to vote. Voting citizens also had to have the makings of financial independence by paying taxes equivalent to three days of work (3 livres), while bankrupt individuals could not be active citizens. Although the unimplemented Constitution of 1793 removed all property and tax requirements to vote, it required a minimum age of presumed independence (21 years old) and stipulated that foreigners could only vote if, among other conditions, they worked and had some sure source of personal income. As the Thermidorians reduced the number of people who could vote, they still left a door open via taxes. All voting citizens had to be men who had served in the military or paid direct taxes. Those men who did not pay direct taxes could purchase voting rights by paying the sum of three-days' work.[103] Such fiscal yardsticks reflected the emerging attitudes of "commercial republicanism" which was "committed to . . . the idea that the labor of every person qualified him or her for participation in political life."[104]

Herein lay the confusion under the Directory: the patente was a direct tax like those referenced in the voting qualifications and even the alternative option for purchasing enfranchisement was articulated through the lens of labor. Although Directorial officials sought to limit the number of citizens eligible to vote,[105] the criteria for political autonomy seemed to incorporate occupational autonomy in ways that could broadly legitimize artisans and modest merchants. By expanding the patente to tax more independent yet economically marginalized workers like the Dames des Halles, the deputies further agitated the paradox of citizenship from 1796 to 1798. Insofar as direct taxes equivalent to three days' labor signified the property and autonomy necessary for voting, the state solidified work as immaterial personal property.

This ambiguous connection between work and civic rights might seem like a moot point for the Dames, who could not vote as women. However, paying the patente shook the very premise of their gendered omission. As political scientist Anne Verjus has argued, the revolutionaries did not simply prohibit women from voting because they were women. Exclusion from the vote cannot be reduced to sexual difference alone, since the revolutionaries variously banned other groups like children, servants, and vagrants. Rather, the "common trait" among these disenfranchised members of society was their perceived dependence within or alienation from the nuclear family.[106] As they moved toward the nineteenth century, lawmakers increasingly adopted a "familialist" model of political representation that considered fathers to have a "socio-political nature as head of the family."[107] Women, in the words of Roederer, "have the same intellectual faculties as men, [but they] have many other occupations," such as reproductive and domestic duties. The "familialist" model assumed, like Roederer, that women needed men to undertake political duties on behalf of the family because feminine duties alone amounted to nearly overwhelming responsibilities.[108] In line with this "familialist" model, elite wives during the Directory politically participated not through activism, but through fashion. They wore Greco-Roman outfits inspired by ancient republican predecessors and advertised through new women's journals.[109] Some elite women hosted salons in their homes or threw balls, but their influence derived from their social capital, not their political autonomy.[110]

The Dames des Halles, their work, and their 1796 patentes flew in the face of this Directorial familialist model. The patente considered the Dames autonomous agents apart from the family, with fiscal responsibilities based on their personal work. When officials had reintroduced the Patente in 1795, the annual tax categorized and assessed citizens in two parts. First, each self-employed working citizen paid a *droit fixe* (fixed duty), which directly corresponded to one of eight brackets based on his or her occupation. All independent, working, citizens (including the Dames starting in 1796) had to pay the *droit fixe*. To take a few examples from among the Dames' retailing ranks: The patente guide stipulated that resellers of clothes or other goods pay 30 francs for a patente of the sixth class, merchants of fresh and salted fish pay 20 francs for a patente of the seventh class, and ambulant merchants pay 10 francs for a patente of the eighth class. The majority of the Dames and other modest retailers who sold from baskets or mobile stands qualified for the eighth and lowest patente class.[111] Thus, the patente continued to delineate commercial actors in ways similar to the Maximum: it separated professions and commercial occupations by perceived economic clout rather than by type of good or skill. Wealthy wholesalers occupied a higher tax bracket than their poor and propertyless retail counterparts. After his or her bracket was determined, each citizen's *droit fixe* was further adjusted based on the size of his/her municipality. For example, a chocolate or macaroni merchant (in the fifth class) would pay 40 francs for his *droit fixe* in Paris or Bordeaux (more than 100,000 inhabitants), 32 francs in Nantes (between 50,000 and 100,000 inhabitants), and 10 francs in Tours (5,000 to 25,000 inhabitants). An architect (in the second class) would pay 100 francs, 80 francs, and 40 francs in these respective cities.[112]

Second, all patente holders paid a variable *droit proportionnel*. This "proportional duty" was based on material property holdings. Each citizen's *droit proportionnel* was equivalent to 10 percent of the rental value of his/her dwelling and building spaces used for work. The deputies assumed that wealthier merchants would own or rent more immobile property, which would generate higher *droits proportionnels*.[113] Combined with the *droit fixe*, the *droit proportionnel* on property would further graduate the license taxes. Thus, from a fiscal perspective, the patente fees closely followed the 1795 Constitution's material and immaterial definitions of property as "the right to enjoy and dispose of one's lands/goods, one's revenues, and the fruits of one's labor or industry."[114]

Even the patente's exemptions sharpened how the revolutionaries imagined work as a type of personal property and civil autonomy that carried fiscal duties. In the 1796 patente, the deputies only excused wage earners who worked under someone else, public officers who worked for the state, and small farmers who worked their own land.[115] Male and female wage earners who worked on someone else's account could not claim autonomous ownership of their labor. As a result, the state interpreted them as lacking civic independence and exempt them from the corresponding fiscal responsibility of the patente. Civil servants could not be taxed on their work as a property because public offices could not be subjected to private ownership. This was a decisive reaction to Old Regime venal offices. And the deputies hesitated to double tax small farmers who already paid the *contribution foncière* on their landed property, which as the source of their production, would have also counted as commercial property under the patente.

In contrast to these exempt groups, the two-pronged 1796 patente required all merchants from the lowliest peddler to the most powerful wholesaler to pay at least an annual *droit fixe* and secure occupational licenses.[116] By individually assessing retailers like the Dames for patentes without intermediaries, officials made them legally independent commercial actors. Therefore, the patente allowed the Dames to enter, as autonomous agents, into a personal political contract with the state predicated on their own work.

The Parisian government tellingly referred to patentes as "voluntary declarations" when instructing police on procedures.[117] The burden to register for a patente, to provide the information for assessing the patente, and to pay the annual patente fell squarely on each citizen's shoulders. A Dame des Halles would have to report to her neighborhood bureau de l'enregistrement in order to request a patente, present her classification criteria, and pay for the anticipated license.[118] First, she would tell the clerk her name, occupation, and the rental value of her dwelling and any permanent occupational structures.[119] The Dame would prove these amounts by presenting a lease or document showing the real property value taxed in the *contribution foncière*.[120] To determine the fees and patente class, the clerk would note the local population size, in this case that of Paris. Municipal officials would later deliver, at the Dame's expense, a personal numbered patente certificate, which the administration duly tracked in the city's registers.[121] A citizen's license was only attached to the profession "under [his/her] personal name."[122] Each Dame would have to keep her license at the ready while hawking foodstuffs. Because the patente process relied on citizens' initiative, the Commune instructed police inspectors to monitor merchants' licenses to prevent illicit trade and tax evasion in les Halles.[123]

When the legislators passed the 1796 patente reform, they stipulated, "the patentes will be personal, and can only serve those who have taken them." However, the representatives made a special case for the marital unit. Husbands and wives who lived together and participated in the same commerce or occupation only needed one patente under the husband's name.[124] Thus, Citoyen Boullanger, a wholesale grocer, could send his wife to the police to defend his patente for their family business.[125] Since they worked together, the couple only needed one patente in the husband's name. When the deputies issued their model forms for the 1796 patente, they included only masculine forms of verbs and adjectives, exposing their assumption that the holder would be male.[126]

In contrast, most Dames des Halles conducted their commerce independently of their husbands' trade. The patente stipulated that both the wife and husband pay for separate patentes when each "exercis[ed] a particular profession, under his/her personal name." Although only one spouse would be responsible for paying the *droit proportionnel* on their residential property, each spouse would have to pay the *droit fixe* and receive a personal patente based on their independent occupations.[127] For example, when the police summoned Citoyenne Bouchard, a fish seller, to prove that she had paid her patente, her husband accompanied her to the courtroom. Although her husband was also a fish seller, each spouse conducted his/her business independently. Therefore, Citoyenne Bouchard directly addressed the judge to secure her own patente. The couple's similar occupations did not have any impact on Citoyenne Bouchard's personal commercial permission and fiscal duty. Commercially active widows held their own patentes following the same logic. For female retailers like the Dames, the occupational tax marked them legally independent in work relations with the state.[128] The patente framed the Dames as citizen-workers.

In addition, the 1796 patente gave most Dames des Halles more fiscal responsibility, and thus stronger claims to autonomy, than all male wage earners. The 1796 patente requirement did not apply to "workers working in the Workshops or Boutiques of others who employ them."[129] According to officials' logic, wage earners who worked under the direction of others could not be independent laboring agents. Therefore, wage earners could not acquire their own patente. A few Dames, like Citoyenne Thabaroie, did sell on behalf of another individual. As a result, this vegetable retailer did not have to secure her own patente when she appeared before the justice of the peace in September 1797.[130] However, the majority of the Dames did require a patente based on the self-governing nature of their work.

The patente functioned as a sign of economic agency and self-sufficiency. Directory officials assumed that only economic independence could underpin political autonomy, much in the same way domestic servants could not vote because of their "dependent" state. As Roederer wrote in 1795, "I say that in order to be a citizen, one must have the interest and means of serving the State. . . . I say a direct interest in order to distinguish [citizens from] the women, the children, the servants, all those who live under the domination and protection of the family, and have only a distant interest to public prosperity."[131] But in qualifying for a patente, the Dames proved both "direct interest" and a "means of serving the State." Their patentes indicated that they acted as independent commercial agents whose social utility transcended auxiliary roles in a workshop, family business, or domestic realm. Unlike the exempt groups, the Dames' autonomous work directly served fellow citizens and they paid public fees for conducting this work. Thus, in contrast to all male and female wage laborers, the Dames des Halles held more substantial claims to work-based contracts with the nation. The patente strikingly legitimized the Dames as autonomous citizen-workers and taxed their work in ways that mimicked intangible personal property.

Defining Fiscal Duties in the Courtroom and Marketplace

When the Directory required the Dames to buy occupational licenses from the state, the market women consciously navigated the sociopolitical ideals that underwrote their taxes. In the courtroom, they obtained or objected to their patentes. In light of police surveillance and judicial regulation, they negotiated their financial responsibilities to the nation and evoked the state's reciprocal obligations to the working poor. The Dames demanded fiscal leniency due to the fragility of their businesses. Yet, they affirmed their right to trade on public property. The license system required the Dames des Halles to consider their work as part of an individual contract with the state with economic and judicial ramifications.

The neighborhood justices of the peace and the police worked hand in hand to uphold the license laws and to summon noncompliant merchants. Negligent Dames found themselves explaining their commercial and fiscal transgressions before local justices of the peace.[132] In the market neighborhood, Judge Nicolas Alexandre Herbault held his court directly in the Bâtiment de la Halle aux Draps which bordered the food markets.[133] The police sent violators like Citoyenne Tenaille, a female fruit merchant in les Halles, to Judge Herbault's nearby bureau. Citoyenne Tenaille had been unable to produce her patente for police in the marketplace, but she brought her patente to the courtroom to prove she legally conducted commerce. Herbault dismissed the charges against her. In contrast, another fruit merchant named Citoyenne Fastielle failed to keep pace with the license requirements and let her patente expire before renewing it. Consequently, Judge Herbault ordered her to pay the standard court appearance fees of 3 livres for consuming the nation's resources. Considering that Citoyenne Fastielle had only paid 10 livres for her annual patente, the fees were a heavy penalty.[134] The Dames knew that officials would pursue them for evading the patente and that they could face a costly fine if caught.

Given the significant gamble in dodging the patente, the Dames attempted to pay as little as possible for the mandatory license. After the 1796 reform, the Dames staked out their commercial identities according to their lack of immobile property to avoid the *droit proportionnel* and to fit in the cheapest patente bracket of the *droit fixe*, which included ambulant merchants. In August 1797, Citoyenne Veuve Lalouette, a retailer, appeared before the justice of the peace to prove that she sold only in the streets. As a merchant without a permanent shelter, Lalouette insisted that she owed only the *droit fixe* of the eighth and lowest class. She reduced her annual taxes by 20 livres, or 66 percent, by successfully reclassifying herself.[135] A fruit merchant named Citoyenne Berdaut quite literally negotiated her commercial identity with the police. When they demanded she pay fees for a sixth-class patente, she retorted she had already offered to pay them the smaller 10-livre fee for an eighth-class patente. Berdaut swore she was "only a retailer in the Streets or under a mobile shelter, and not in a boutique." Consequently, she belonged in the lowest class.[136] Fellow fruitière Citoyenne Sainte-Beuve similarly presented herself as "only an ambulant reseller" and pleaded with the court to forgive the amend she had incurred by refusing to pay the higher patente class. She underscored her weak economic position by requesting a delay on her patente payment.[137] Deploying another approach, a fish merchant named Citoyenne Gagnery testified that she conducted her commerce on public space under a parasol rather than on private property. By focusing on property ownership, Gagnery strove to disqualify herself from the *droit proportionnel* and qualify for the cheapest *droit fixe* in one fell swoop. She asked the court to reevaluate and lower her occupational tax level.[138]

Whereas the Dames frequently identified themselves as "Dames des Halles" in addresses, petitions, and pamphlets, they do not appear to have identified themselves as such in court cases concerning occupational licenses. This is striking, as the Dames did not shy away from invoking their collective title and political prowess during the battles over public space from 1789 to 1792, in the struggles over cash from 1791 to 1792, in their confrontations with the rival Société des Citoyennes républicaines révolutionnaires in 1793, and during the Maximum reform of 1794. The absence of the title "Dame des Halles" suggests that the patentes spurred the market women to abandon recourse to their traditional rights or exemptions. Because the patente levied personal taxes on individuals, it rendered the Dames' occupational sisterhood fiscally irrelevant. To secure the cheapest personal patente, the Dames defined themselves before officials primarily through the patente's modes for individual categorization. In addition, the Dames helped to redefine one another by serving as witnesses in patente hearings. If a market woman disputed her patente assessment, her neighbors could testify as to the type of commerce she conducted. When Citoyenne Veuve Lalouette filed for a patente of the ambulant eighth class even though she had been classified as a revendeuse (sixth class), her neighbors verified in court that Lalouette did, in fact, only sell in the streets.[139] Before state officials, the Dames actively labeled one another through the patente's occupational categories instead of their traditional collective identity.

Thus, in the postcorporate world of the patente, individuals fiscally reclassified themselves based on material property-holdings and autonomous labor. As officials divided merchants by their use of immobile property, they grouped the Dames des Halles with other, formerly disparate, actors in the marketplace. Due to their different market spaces and types of goods, female butchers did not consider themselves Dames des Halles. However, like the fruit and fish retailers, Citoyenne Haucot, a butcher, claimed that she belonged to the lowest patente bracket since, she too, "only sells under eves, and not in a boutique."[140] Likewise, ambulant Dames found themselves in the same patente class as male fruit merchants who sold from stalls in the Marché aux Poirées.[141] The patente's occupational yardstick transcended gender and long-standing corporate categories. Through the patente, legislators and their constituents alike rethought the relationship among work, property, and citizenship.

Reforming the Patente in 1798

From 1796 to 1798, the departments, municipal police, and local judges struggled to collect payment for the *droit fixe* they attached to the licenses of self-employed workers without immobile property. After requiring all merchants to pay the patente, legislators juggled their wish to encourage the poor to work without unnecessary burdens with their conflicting desire to compel each citizen to finance the state. In the courtroom, the justices of the peace improvised to show leniency to the least fortunate. Some judges granted impoverished citizens grace periods for their patente payments. Judge Herbault in les Halles took pity on Citoyenne Maillot, a poor fruit merchant who defaulted on her patente. He dismissed her fine and gave her ten days to pay the license tax to police.[142] By October 1797, the Directory formally enabled struggling citizens to appeal for a lower patente class on the basis of "modest trade or particular burdens."[143] Although the post-1796 patente stipulated that individuals owed the state fiscal duties, officials also considered what duties the state owed indigent citizens.

By October 1797, the representatives concluded that the patente fees taxed the lower-class workers beyond their means. To streamline the patente and reduce tax hardships, officials abolished the *droit proportionnel* based on immobile property for all merchants below the fifth class. As a result, the merchants and workers of the sixth, seventh, and eight classes only paid the *droit fixe*, which could not surpass 30 francs.[144] The modest retailers, cobblers, and tripe sellers of the eighth class would no longer pay a tax on the rental value of their property just like the shearers of wool of the sixth class, or the assemblers of books or makers of clogs of the seventh class.[145]

However, in the next reform of November 1798, officials reorganized patente to take into account the type of goods merchants sold. This reform specifically protected the subsistence trade and exempted "ambulant sellers in the streets, in places of passages, and in the common markets, of fruits, vegetables, butter, eggs, cheese and other foodstuffs." Ambulant merchants who sold other goods (mostly nonfoodstuffs) still had to purchase a patente at half the boutique rate for sellers of the same object.[146] Therefore, as propertyless food retailers, the Dames des Halles no longer had to buy a patente to conduct their commerce.

At the same time, officials reestablished the family household, rather than the individual, as the fundamental fiscal unit. If husband and wife both qualified for a patente by their personal occupations but held their immobile property in common, they would only pay the patente fees of the higher class.[147] In the families of married and exempt Dames, only their husbands would hold a patente if eligible by trade. The state soon redefined leniency along family criteria as well. Officials instructed the police in les Halles to modify patente fees by taking note of "a state of misery or distress, apparent by a large family."[148] This "familialist" vein doubly disqualified many Dames from obtaining personal occupational licenses. Thus, in the November 1798 patente, legislators reclassified the Dames as financial dependents of the state, their households, and potentially their husbands once again.

Citizenship, Work, Taxes, and Property, 1796 to 1804

From 1796 through 1798, the patente had significantly recalibrated work in ways analogous to personal property to determine fiscal autonomy and responsibility. If one considers the trajectory of gender, citizenship, and property over the same time period, the results are striking. Just as material personal property (signified by taxes equivalent to three days' wages) defined political autonomy and the right to vote in the Constitution of 1795, work as a type of intangible personal property defined fiscal autonomy and civic membership in the patente legislation. Moreover, the revolutionaries articulated the minimum material property requirement for voting as taxes equivalent to three days' wages. Measurements rooted in occupational language, not gender, signified civic independence in both electoral rights and fiscal duties.

From 1796 through 1798, the Dames des Halles could point to their patentes as proof of their occupational pact with the nation. In December 1798, the national cap on the tax representing three days' wages was 4.5 francs.[149] Until the 1798 reform, the Dames had paid at least 10 francs annually for their personal patente. Therefore, the Dames surpassed the minimum direct tax requirement for electoral citizenship applied to men. And, unlike both dependent workers and women who shared an occupation with their husbands, the Dames had to obtain patentes for their autonomous trade. In contrast to all male and female wage laborers, the Dames held more substantial claims to work-based contracts

with the nation. Thus, three years after the deputies outlawed women's political clubs, the patente paradoxically included the Dames in a political and economic contract predicated on individual agency and work. In the patente, the
revolutionaries conceptualized the Dames' civic identity by drawing on socioeconomic categories, rather than drawing primarily on gendered categories. In
short, the tax combined political notions of autonomy with economic notions
of autonomy.

When officials restructured the patente in 1798, their new categories
exempted most Dames. On one hand, the state lifted the financial burden from
the backs of the poorest food merchants, which included most of the ambulant
retailers among the Dames. On the other hand, even for the few Dames selling
from permanent boutiques, the reform eliminated their independent contract
with the state if they were married. As a result, the 1798 patente effaced the
Dames' autonomy as citizen-workers who fiscally supported the nation.

Like other Directorial legislation, the 1798 patente recentered the household as the basic economic and political unit. Husbands mediated their wives'
labor, civic duties, and fiscal obligations as they would in the Napoleonic Era.
Even when the Constitution of Year VIII (which established the Consulate in
December 1799) lifted the tax requirements for the popular vote, it still excluded
minors, women, and individuals who labored in someone else's household.
Napoleon's Civil Code of 1804 dramatically changed married women's legal autonomy in commerce. Title V, Chapter VI stipulated, a "wife cannot plead in
her own name, without the authority of her husband, even though she should
be a public trader, or non-communicant, or separate in property." Even those
women who could maneuver more freely in the commercial realm as "public
traders" legally attached their husbands to all of their business agreements.[150] As
such, a married woman could no longer be the sole proprietor of her own work
under Napoleonic law. She held no absolute autonomy in her business nor derived civic autonomy from that business.

Equally noteworthy, the definition of property became consolidated in physical objects and capital during the Empire. The Dames lacked these bourgeois
staples. In the Civil Code, property constituted "The right to enjoy and to dispose of goods in the most absolute manner."[151] Thus, the *act* of work as a revolutionary marker of civic autonomy became less important than the economic or
material product of that work as measured by household units.[152]

With pressures accumulating from the failed paper currency, forced loans, and
the 1797 bankruptcy of two-thirds, the Directory and the Consulate abandoned the revolutionary revulsion toward indirect taxes to generate revenue.[153]
Yet, the patente and other direct taxes persisted as the load-bearing pillars of
fiscal policy. The deputies supplemented revenue with their fourth and final

revolutionary direct tax, an *impôt sur les portes et fenêtres* (a tax on doors and windows), in November 1798.[154] Even after reducing the number of eligible patente payers in 1798, officials collected 15,868,578 francs in Year VIII (1799–1800),[155] 16,000,000 francs in Year IX (1800–1801), and 17,000,000 francs in Year X (1801–1802). The Directorial model of assessing the patente through the *droit fixe* and the *droit proportionnel* continued for nearly two centuries.[156] Thus, the revolutionary drive to keep direct taxes "indiciaires" (measured by signs of wealth) and graduated in order to avoid income-based assessment persisted in French taxation.[157] The patente remained "personal" or individually contracted by citizens with the state based on their condition. Because there was no income tax until 1914, the French state continued to measure independent work as a form of intangible personal property delineated by occupation and related property rather than as an abstracted monetary figure.

In 1791, the deputies had invented the patente as a tool for reconfiguring the corporate world. The direct tax overhauled the nature of occupational permissions and work. As a truly reciprocal exchange of taxes for licenses, the patente created a fiscal contract between individual citizens and the state. These fiscal contracts mirrored the nascent social contract. Moreover, in its innovative assessment guidelines, the patente effectively reconceptualized work as an intangible personal property and limited the life of occupational permissions to the life of an economically independent individual. The personal, the temporal, and the continuous contractual nature of the patente sharply diverged from the venal offices and guild masterships of the Old Regime.

While crafting and revising the patente, officials traced fiscal categories onto political imaginings. Despite the patente's technical permutations, the revolutionaries consistently assumed that useful work was a political virtue with fiscal duties attached. In determining who should pay the patente from 1791 through 1798, the revolutionaries did not just consider how economic dependence affected individual free will and political autonomy. They also considered who directly benefited from each individual's work. As the heirs of Sieyès circa 1789, they deemed that individuals who served citizens beyond the household proved their social utility. The nature of this work, akin to intangible personal property, earned the worker an autonomous civic position by fiscal standards. In electoral and fiscal codes, taxes symbolized the independence of will, the property, and the social contribution necessary for citizenship. The patente drew on these exact categories of atomization, autonomization, and utility. Occupational taxes were fundamentally connected to the question of full citizenship.

From 1789 through 1798, the Dames, police, and state officials grappled with the Dames' political duties as retailers. Public space, hard cash, food supplies, and state finances created opportunities for the Dames to redefine themselves within shifting economic systems and, by extension, the body politic. The patente of

1791 initially released the Dames from paying taxes based on their commerce. Yet, rather than referencing the Dames' traditional economic privileges, the deputies legitimized their exception through new fiscal categories of public and private property. From 1796 to 1798, the patente enabled the Dames to form a fiscal contract with the nation, in contrast to all male wage laborers. The requirement compelled the Dames to rearticulate their occupations before the justices of the peace to secure the cheapest bracket possible. Within the patente criteria, all retail merchants without fixed commercial property became a legal occupational class in their own right for the first time. The patente thus further catalyzed the Dames' transition from a corporate, collective identity to atomized citizen-workers.

The patente was the last major revolutionary project to cast the Dames as economic citizens with autonomous rights from and duties towards the state. It marked them as citizens whose trade not only directly served the public good, but also fiscally supported the nation. The patente created an economic, rather than gendered, pact with the nation whose logic of utility and independence mirrored the revolutionaries' criteria for political citizenship. By the end of the Directory, the Dames, officials, and fellow citizens had confirmed the centrality of retailers' work and had firmly embedded it within revolutionary imaginings as a useful service to the nation. However, when the deputies reorganized taxes based on familial units and exempted food retailers, the Dames lost their fiscal autonomy. By extending the "familialist model" from the electoral to fiscal system in 1798, the Directory subsumed the Dames' work into that of their households led by men. The market women no longer secured occupational licenses.

As Anne Verjus has argued, "Revolutionary society socializ[ed] its definition of the political individual much more than we do today."[158] This is clear to see in Dames' criteria for a patente from 1796 through 1798. The type of work the Dames conducted (modest food commerce) and the recipients of their services (nonfamily members) determined whether and how much they paid for a license. In the Revolution, the atomization and autonomization of citizens could only be defined within the context of human relationships. The Dames' patentes suggest that, in the eyes of the revolutionaries, these requirements for entry into the social contract were not sexed traits written on human bodies at birth. The patente exposed the dangerous contradiction in sifting out citizens' civic duties from their civic rights.

In analyzing capitalist Europe after the Revolution, scholars often delineate gendered spheres according to where individuals worked—either inside or outside the home. The start of this metanarrative maintains that the revolutionaries defined legal citizenship as masculine, irreversibly conflated gender and citizenship in the process, and then bifurcated politics as well as gendered work into separate spheres. The Dames' experience suggests it would be productive to further consider how the revolutionaries divided members of the body politic by the nature of their work rather than the location of their work. Following Roederer, the revolutionaries distinguished those whose work "directly" served nonrelatives in society from those whose work was one step removed from society. For example, a republican mother could serve the nation by raising a moral son. But her son would be the one whose work immediately impacted society beyond the family; therefore, the mother's work was mediated in relation to the wider body politic. As the 1796 patente rules demonstrated, the same principle would hold true for a woman who labored in her husband's trade. By paying a single patente that included his spouse's work, the husband mediated his wife's labor in relation to the nation. If spheres of labor are conceptualized along these revolutionary parameters, individuals whose personal occupation directly served nonfamily members in society could legitimate their citizenship by their social utility.

Rather than fusing together sex and citizenship, this approach spotlights how the revolutionaries divided civic work into two types that informed political categories. This perspective privileges work as a marker for individuals' socially oriented roles in the body politic. Such an interpretation posits citizenship as earned through societal engagement rather than being an innate, a priori right. The Dames did not hesitate to appeal to the state through a gendered lens as mothers, through a political lens as patriotic defenders, or through an occupational lens as useful traders. At the advent of modern society, the Dames drew political legitimacy without contradiction from what would be considered domestic and public spheres by post-revolutionary standards.

The patente continued to politically resonate in the nineteenth century. When Deputy Tallendier suggested revising the patente in 1843, he had to clarify he was not proposing to decrease the commercial tax burden (the patente) as an underhanded way of reducing the number of poor people eligible to vote.[159] Legislative bodies rarely challenged the structure of the patente itself, but disputes arose from conflicting views over calculating the appropriate ratio of the two gauges. As building rents (on which the *droit proportionnel* was based) outpaced the growth of commercial profits (the revenue of self-employed individuals), citizens called for the state to lower the assessment rate on the *droit proportionnel*. Regional variations in rent further aggravated the disparities. In a similar fashion, the legislators of 1791 could not have foreseen how the rise of the Grands Magasins would disadvantage small shopkeepers in their tax code. Nineteenth-century shopkeepers loudly objected that each Grand Magasin only paid one patente for several departments and dozens of wage-laborers, while modest boutique owners paid a single patente for selling one type of good with a handful of employees.[160] Despite these challenges, the patente still brought in 23.6 percent of French direct tax revenue by 1913.[161]

The changing financial, commercial, and bureaucratic landscape collided with the threat of war to bring the first substantial shift in French tax policy since the Revolution.[162] In 1914, the French government threw off its abhorrence for assessing "the person" rather than tangible "signs" of wealth and instituted the first income tax since the Old Regime.[163] But far from replacing the patente, the state merely shifted all of its revenues from national to regional coffers in 1917. To match pace with the evolving occupational landscape, the patente code bulged with *droits fixes* for 1,400 professions and their occupational subdivisions by the mid-twentieth century. The state finally replaced the patente with a *taxe professionnelle* (professional tax) in 1975. This plan maintained the regional beneficiaries but focused on self-employed business owners by assessing the rental value of their property, the tangible assets of their business, and a percentage of wages paid to their employees.[164] It removed the *droit fixe* and a tax on the self-directed individual from its calculations. Consequently, the patente as a personal occupational license was replaced by a tax more concerned with targeting commercial profits still estimated by signs.[165] In this equation, the act of independent work was no longer an intangible personal property that citizens contracted with the nation.

The patente, quickly conceived in the heat of overhauling taxes and the corporate world, remained in effect for 184 years. The license system survived two empires, two monarchies, and five republics. It spanned the industrial revolution, remained in force even with the establishment of the income tax, weathered the financial turmoil of two world wars, and only succumbed to the professional tax in 1975. Its resiliency suggests that the patente tapped into slippery yet remarkably enduring notions of work, property, and autonomy as the baseline for fiscal and electoral citizenship. Born of revolutionary aspirations to join the independent worker and the state, the patente redefined work and the social contract for modern France.

Conclusion

Fruits of Labors: Citizenship as Social Experience

On August 15, 1852, the Dames skipped their commerce in the central markets. Instead of bursting with fruits, vegetables, eggs, butter, and fish, les Halles overflowed with 6,000 cookies, 20,000 pieces of fruitcake, 50,000 frozen desserts, and 60,000 servings of flavored water. Dragging the Dames' shelters to the side, municipal workers erected a temporary dance hall and rigged the Innocents fountain to illuminate the square. They were preparing for the "Feast of Saint Napoleon."[1] Prince-President Louis Napoleon had seized the presidency through a coup d'état eight months earlier, and he planned to shore up his power by reinstituting the feast day. But, rather than celebrating the Bonaparte Prince-President, the official program noted, the "ball will be offered [in honor of] the Dames des Halles on the spot of the Innocents Market."[2] Anticipating the occasion, the Théâtre de Vaudeville performed a new play featuring the iconic and perpetually entertaining market women. Its fictive orange merchant kicked up a fuss preparing for the ball. Asserting "Never does my head speak without my heart," the poissarde encapsulated the Dames' beloved reputation for straight-talk.[3] On the day of the celebration, the living Dames and 20,000 Parisians crammed into the marketplace to eat, drink, and dance. Songwriter Louis-Charles Durand contributed an "homage" to the retailers in verse: "Women of the people with frank smiles, From our markets joyous queens. Honor to the sovereign Dames of the Halles of Paris!"[4]

The Dames seemed to float timelessly above the political symbolism. Crimson drapes decorated with Napoleonic eagles and trimmed with flower garlands drew Parisians' gaze up ten grand arches. Their keystones bore the inscription "Vox populi, vox Dei" ("Voice of the people, voice of God").[5] August 15 was also the Feast of the Assumption, the day when the market women would bring bouquets to Old Regime queens, the day when they would give voice to the Third Estate at Versailles. The message could not be clearer. Louis Napoleon, like his emperor uncle, appropriated the date's religious and political overtones through the dubious Saint Napoleon and the Dames. After the tumultuous French sampler of empire, monarchy, and republic, Louis Napoleon insisted that the festival would "bring together all minds in a common sentiment of national glory."[6] The careful staging implied that the market women, the "voice of the people," did not earn their sovereignty because of any action, but because they were unchanging representatives of the popular classes. However, the festival planners of 1852 grossly oversimplified the complex ways the Dames and others had imagined citizenship since the Revolution.

Despite their Old Regime ritual roles and special connections with the state in 1789, the revolutionary Dames des Halles invented citizenship in ways that surpassed institutional scaffolding. For the market women, the neatly seated representatives of the National Assembly did not channel the General Will alone. Nor did the Dames interpret voting or participating in political clubs as the primary expression of the social contract. Nor did they find citizenship engraved on sexed bodies as an a priori right. Instead, to the Dames in the market, the social contract smelled like melting cheese, tasted like ripe fruit, and felt like soft butter. It took the form of merchants and consumers haggling over prices and cutting deals on credit. It surfaced while carrying the king to Paris, addressing his brother in Italy, and lobbying officials over public space. It crystallized in licenses and petitions to protect small change. And it took the shape of mothers raising children for the fatherland. According to the Dames, individuals earned citizenship in the body politic by serving society through useful work. They assumed that an individual's occupational, civic, and gendered work legitimized his or her demands on the state in return. Theirs was a truly social contract.

While the Dames carved out their influence from 1789 to 1799, other revolutionaries seized the Dames' image to navigate the profound anxieties produced by a rapidly evolving social order. Writers latched onto the Dames as shorthand for the popular classes. In doing so, they papered over socioeconomic diversity to create culturally legible categories. Pamphleteers channeled their opinions through the merchants' rough but influential tongues. These representations informed and were informed by the living Dames' political legitimacy. Such portrayals implicitly asked who spoke for the people, what constituted popular sovereignty, and how citizens should live out the Revolution in their everyday lives. Whether constructing or consuming fictive market women, pamphleteers, journalists, and Parisian audiences wrestled with the political and economic role of the popular classes in the nation. A glance at the wildly popular Madame Angot, a fictional Dame who headlined nineteen plays from 1796 to 1803, suggests that the late revolutionaries normalized work as the popular classes' contribution to society. In each play, Madame Angot attempts to climb into bourgeois society but comically slips off the social ladder. The fish merchant's repeated decision to renounce her ambitions and return to work in les Halles redeemed her in the eyes of sold-out audiences prior to the Empire.[7]

Beyond the page and stage, other revolutionaries seized the Dames' ideas, begrudgingly acknowledged their demands, arrived at similar conclusions, or flat out rejected the retailers' interventions. In the streets, the Dames used the politically charged, yet conceptually amorphous ideas of utility and public good to create wide-ranging associations. Joining political clubs and state bodies, the market women celebrated favorable advancements through festivals and processions. Rallying their ranks across markets and bringing other Parisians into the fold, the Dames marched to Versailles to fetch the king and chased counterrevolutionary nuns out of convents. Armed with a rhetorical toolbox bolstered by liberty, equality, fraternity, and paternalism, the Dames frequently set their sights on the assembly halls. They addressed officials to alternatively make demands or sanction government policies. Their petitions and threats changed the trajectory of national policy, including monetary reform and the foundations of political economy. Factions redeployed the Dames to advance their own goals. The Montagnards profited from the Dames' support to silence their Enragé rivals and ban women's clubs. Police in les Halles grew frustrated as the Dames violated market rules and licensing requirements. But they also threw up their hands and acknowledged the market women understood the nature of retail trade more than the unversed deputies holding the commercial reins. Finally, justices of the peace mediated disputes between Dames and their clients while considering the social dimensions of economic contracts and fielding appeals to the state's paternal duties.

The retailers' notion of earned citizenship appealed to diverse groups. The virtuous and political nature of work evolved but endured across the constitutional monarchy from 1789 to 1792, the radical republic of 1792 to 1794, the Thermidorian backlash of 1794 to 1795, and the Directory of 1795 to 1799. These discourses even stretched to the colonies where abolitionists seized personal work and service as bargaining chips in the pact of citizenship. On behalf of French officials in Saint-Domingue in 1793, Louis-Pierre Dufay argued that the Convention should ban slavery because "freedmen and women would indemnify France by producing workers for the *patrie*." A deputation of slaves similarly testified, "We will fight for France, but in recompense we demand our liberty."[8] Such visions assumed that the work of freed slaves, whether it be fighting in the military or laboring in fields, would benefit the nation and earn them citizenship in return. Like the market women, revolutionaries inside and outside of the metropole cast the reciprocal contract in a utilitarian mold.

The Dames des Halles negotiated the ambiguities of citizenship while it was conceptually developing. They intervened in exceptional ways that both harnessed the legitimacy and challenged the primacy of formal politics. Scholars who argue that the social contract was predicated on male citizenship justly assert that the Convention denied women institutional citizenship in 1793. However, the Dames illustrate how women were not conceptually written out of the initial contract, nor was it contingent on their exclusion. Contrary to the deputies' 1793 efforts to paint it as such, the social contract was not a sexual contract at its outset. At the core of their cooperative vision of the nation, the Dames insisted on reciprocal duties between the citizen and the state. The Dames could petition the Assembly to adjust price controls, could insist on support for indigent parents, and could demand that officials correct libel smearing their livelihoods, precisely because the Dames believed they had earned the state's support in exchange for their useful work. The Dames did not reject the social contract model that formed the cornerstone of modern democracy; they embraced it, reshaped it, and deployed it for their own ends.

In les Halles, the social contract dovetailed with economic contracts. Economic exchanges such as buying goods, selling food, or paying taxes created micro-relationships among citizens that mirrored the macro-relationships of the cooperative social body. These interactions formed the core of an economic citizenship that permeated quotidian life. Regulatory laws over currency, food prices, occupational licenses, and particular interests in public spaces governed marketplace roles through commercial and political lenses. The laws implicitly assigned political value to marketplace actors based on public utility and collective needs. Throughout the Revolution, the government recognized the necessity of jointly incorporating retailers and consumers into the body politic. However, the optimal balance for these relationships remained a constant debate. Especially in 1793 and 1794, officials struggled to reconcile subsistence needs and commercial profits as symbiotic interests. From 1791 to 1798, the patente provided an alternate vehicle to mediate economic relations among citizens by amassing national taxes for collective expenditures. Simultaneously, the licenses oversaw how marketplace actors could legally offer occupational services to fellow citizens. In short, the social contract of the Dames and their neighbors was incubated in the everyday trade of the marketplace.

Ultimately, the Dames' vision of citizenship based on useful work that included, but did not hinge on, gendered components did not prevail. The Napoleonic Civil Code consolidated legal and judicial power into male heads of households in 1804.[9] These laws codified the shift toward a public/private dichotomy in nineteenth-century politics and culture. Yet, we should be clear that the discourses of 1789 did not predetermine or inevitably distill citizenship into voting rights for property-holding men. Rather, the revolutionaries experimented with multiple pathways to citizenship for over a decade. Moreover, the logics of these myriad definitions were not resolutely incongruent. Rather, the potency of the Dames' influence suggests the market women hit on salient and lasting components of citizenship that resonated with their fellow revolutionaries and would reemerge as points of contestation in the nineteenth century.

The Dames' notion of citizenship powerfully aligned with three revolutionary tenets: it had the potential to be universally applicable, it took autonomous individuals as the starting point for citizenship, and it oriented individuals' actions toward the collectivity. First, the Dames' vision of citizenship seemed to have universalizing potential.[10] Diverse types of work created a uniform measuring stick for civic virtue without homogenizing citizens.[11] As the patente illustrated, the revolutionaries assumed that citizens could choose to devote their labor to a variety of essential activities from farming and building to printing and doctoring. Men and women of all classes could undertake civic work by defending communal interests, smoking out counterrevolutionaries, and agitating for favorable legislation. Citizens of both sexes could engage in gendered work as soldier-fathers or mother-wives. In sum, virtuous work could cut across the urban/rural dichotomy, transcend and incorporate gendered divides, and surpass factional particularities from 1789 to 1799.[12] Second, although the legal requirements for active citizenship such as property, age, and sex changed with different revolutionary regimes, these various markers always sought to establish autonomy. The Dames redeployed the revolutionaries' prerequisite of independence and self-direction when they framed personal and socially productive work as political agency. Finally, the Dames embedded citizenship into mutually advantageous relationships with other citizens. By arguing that society ultimately benefited from their services, the Dames integrated themselves into a cooperative body politic that needed merchants as much as consumers, men as much as women, and urban commerce as much as rural supplies. This final tenet mastered the critical, yet elusive, logic of the general will. It reconciled particular interests and individual actions with public good and the indivisible body politic.

Although revolutionary ideas of citizenship "centered on the individual and his or her rights and obligations" and a "compact among individuals," the Dames offer insights into how group identities could be translated into viable political identities.[13] The Dames are a reminder that the radical autonomization of citizens did not effect an immediate atomization of society. Nor did the corporate identities of the Old Regime directly morph into protoindustrial class identities. Rather, the Dames demonstrate how the revolutionaries forged new socioeconomic associations based on changing circumstances. The Dames maintained a cultural and occupational identity that allowed them to intervene collectively to defend market spaces, shelters, and supplies, even if they did not always agree with one another. At the same time, the Dames responded to economic challenges such as currency reform by forming new coalitions with powerful brokers, middling artisans, and their marketplace clients. By the time the

Le Chapelier Law and d'Allarde Decree dismantled guilds and confraternities in 1791, the Dames had already negotiated new alliances to protect their commercial interests. In effect, the anticorporate laws legally confirmed the process that the Dames and their neighbors had previously begun. The pressures of the Maximum further compelled the Dames to identify with other retailers and the patente codified their socioeconomic positions through property and commercial prowess. The Dames' old inclination toward collective identities informed complex civic constellations at the crossroads of corporate privilege, liberal autonomy, and capitalist hierarchies.

From their stalls in les Halles, the Dames offer an especially rich node for examining the history of work as the French dramatically pivoted toward free markets. On the one hand, much of the social history on work in the revolutionary era equates "work" with manual labor conducted by propertyless citizens. From this perspective, work becomes the world of wage labor.[14] On the other hand, the history of commerce spotlights entrepreneurs, wholesale merchants, and brokers. Histories concerning revolutionary merchants usually ask questions about the bourgeoisie, capitalism, entrepreneurial nobles, the rise of new notables, and what constitutes commercial activity.[15] As retailers with little capital, the Dames underscore that work did not necessarily mean wage labor and that not all commercial agents were capitalist entrepreneurs or savvy notables. The Dames depended on charity privileges for market permissions, but they are not easily lumped into the laboring masses. The retailers, after all, clashed with the Citoyennes républicaines révolutionnaires, who backed consumer interests and the sans-culottes. In short, the Dames defy and disrupt socioeconomic classification within the capitalist paradigm. By framing their shape-shifting labor as a pillar of their citizenship, the Dames allow us to read socioeconomic relationships from a fluctuating cultural and situational perspective, rather than through Marxist lenses.

As they negotiated economic citizenship, the Dames wrestled with the tension between the democratic ideals of social equality and the burgeoning ideals of the free market. The Dames harnessed free market discourses to rent cheap parasols and to demand access to public space. They appealed to democratic notions of fraternity and a cooperative body politic to attack price maximums as unjust. Yet the Dames also expected protectionist advantages in the liberated marketplace. They demanded exceptions to currency policy and profited from paternally motivated leniency in license fees. Over piles of fruits, vegetables, and eggs, they drew on egalitarian principles and free market tenets in fluid and contradictory ways.

Through their marketplace experiences, the Dames reinterpreted the volatile leitmotifs of liberty and equality, while actively producing the salient paradoxes of nineteenth-century politics. The recurring clashes over economic citizenship eventually gave shape to the barricades of 1848.[16] However, the Dames and other members of the popular classes did not cohesively set the agenda in 1789. Rather, the market women appropriated liberty and equality in highly contingent and inconsistent ways. The Dames maintained conceptual flexibility and consistency by navigating among useful work of occupational, activist, and gendered varieties.

The Dames compel a reconsideration of the modern starting line for gender, work, and citizenship. The revolutionaries certainly inscribed gendered duties on citizens' sexed bodies, but gendered divisions did not fundamentally order every element of citizenship. In contrast to this messy embryonic state of gender and republican citizenship, scholars of post-Rousseauian Europe often portray gendered and political binaries as inevitably begetting public and private spheres. Much nineteenth- and twentieth-century labor history leans heavily on the two spheres by analyzing work and gender according to where individuals work—either inside or outside of the home.[17] The spatial dimensions contained within the very metaphor of public and private "spheres" linguistically conflate gender and place. "Home" has become scholars' code word for "familial space." In this symphony of meaning, gender, work, and politics frequently take their pitch from the public or private character of space.

Yet, automatically linking the theoretical public and private of politics to physical locations of work creates two analytical shortcomings for the nineteenth century. First, if environments are assumed to have gendered and political significance independent of the actors who inhabit these spaces, the ways that historical actors assign gendered and political meaning to these spaces through experience are lost. Second, assuming political and spatial congruency between public and private risks making the mere location of an individual's work the gauge of its subversive or conforming nature. Thus, women working outside the home appear to transgress gendered and political norms, while their domestic counterparts appear to reinforce the status quo. This methodological compass is understandably enticing for social historians of women and the popular classes whose subjects leave few discursive sources to describe their experience. However, additional means exist to explore how historical actors attributed political, cultural, and spatial significance to their work.[18]

In light of the Dames' experience, it would be productive to consider how the revolutionaries divided members of the body politic by the type of work rather than the location of work. After the collapse of the corporate world, work enabled individuals to frame themselves as autonomous liberal subjects who could productively labor for the collectivity. Their service to other citizens legitimated the demands they could make on the state as repayment. This political contract between the individual and the state mirrored the social contract between the individual and society. These two pacts formed the twin pillars of liberal citizenship.[19] The state (the institutionalized body politic) fulfilled its duties toward the citizen because the citizen served other citizens (the incarnated body politic). Individuals like the Dames, whose work directly served society, could make a stronger case for citizenship than those whose families alone seemingly profited from their labor.[20] Women and men conducted both types of labor into the nineteenth century. Consequently, certain types of work, not places of work, posed the most serious ideological threat to the liberal model of institutional citizenship that excluded women. At the advent of modern society, the Dames drew political legitimacy without contradiction from what would be considered public and private spheres by bourgeois definitions of politics and work.[21]

Rather than fusing together sex, space, and citizenship, this analytical approach highlights how the revolutionaries built political categories on multidimensional work. Such an interpretation posits citizenship as contingent and earned rather than as an innate, independent right. While the notion of earned citizenship was potentially liberating to classes marginalized under the Old Regime, this definition proved equally dangerous. Factional shifts and cultural tides easily changed the bar that defined entry to and exclusion from earned citizenship.

The long-term implications of this revolutionary perspective on democratic society emerge when contrasted with debates over work, gender, and citizenship in the nineteenth century. Historians who study urban spaces agree that female factory workers disrupted bourgeois gender ideals by acting outside the home. These female laborers destabilized how the middle class imagined the masculine public sphere. Tracing debates over work, wages, and economic markets, historian Victoria Thompson argues that by the 1840s, women workers posed an additional danger: they undercut male workers' calls for higher wages as family breadwinners.[22] In this formula, French men and women equated work with remuneration. In other words, they asked whom workers' wages benefited rather than who benefited from the act of work. Opponents of female wage labor seized the logic of the Napoleonic Civil Code that a family's political and economic existence was mediated through a male head of household. But flipping the analytical viewpoint to ask whom one's labor serves reveals how women producing goods and services ideologically unhinged male institutional citizenship. Society at large consumed the goods that a female worker created, whether she spun at home or produced cloth in a factory. Focusing outward toward the collectivity as the direct beneficiary of their work rather than inward toward their families as the recipient of their wages provided a means for women to integrate themselves into the body politic.[23]

Mid-nineteenth-century writers who advocated for higher wages for women workers sensed the powerful connection between those whom one's labor benefited and political legitimacy. In 1848, activists preferred to construct images of marital sacrifice to describe how women contributed to the community rather than appeal for greater wages in order to support their families. Supportive journalists portrayed women workers as "'amazons of peace'" who promised to draw ranks "'in order to prove, by energetic demonstration, that they also know how to devote themselves to the good of humanity.'" Since the Civil Code granted some commercial independence to *femmes marchandes publiques*, some female traders bolstered their political claims through their work's public utility. In 1837, journalist Madame Poutret de Mauchamps agitated for women's legal and political equality by asserting, '"in Commerce, women are useful, necessary, almost indispensable."' Despite women's contributions in trade, police in les Halles increasingly sought to regulate the occupational exceptions, public visibility, and commercial influence of the Dames' descendants by the mid-nineteenth century.[24]

Briefly comparing the market women of the 1790s to the male workers of 1848 reveals major benchmarks on the trajectory of work and citizenship. Historian William Sewell demonstrates that socialist workers could trace the germ of "sovereignty of labor" to Abbé Sieyès and illustrates how the discourse had evolved over fifty years.[25] In contrast to the revolutionary Dames des Halles, male workers of 1848 focused on "the right to labor" more than rights that derived from labor. In socialist imaginings of citizenship, work became the thing citizens demanded from the state more than a way to legitimize diverse demands on the state. If 1848 was a triumph of the "working classes," it could only be because the notion of "worker" and "labor" had been distilled into one dominant type of worker (the wage laborer) and type of labor (production) from among the many types present in the imaginings of 1789. Work remained a salient component of citizenship in 1848, but its political meaning and social reality had shifted since the first revolution.

The birth of modern citizenship among the revolutionary market women was one of exploration, perpetual negotiation, and invention. The Dames derived their traditional authority from Old Regime state rituals, yet they deftly deployed revolutionary notions of popular sovereignty. They did not appeal to individuals' natural rights, yet they interpreted citizenship as an autonomous status. They did not esoterically discuss capitalist theory, yet they effectively spoke with a free market vocabulary. The Dames did not debate these ideas in salons, closed clubs, or coffee houses. Rather, they worked through an array of challenges, opportunities, and paradoxes as they encountered them in the streets and the marketplace. In their actions, the Dames pursued a triangulated compact among individuals, society, and the state, which assumed that individuals earned and continually renewed citizenship through action. For the Dames and many other revolutionaries, citizenship and rights were contingent, not innate. This paradigm provided them new opportunities in the postcorporate world of

1789 but became treacherous as governing factions settled into the familialist model by the Directory's end.

Politics in the Marketplace has attempted to holistically bring into dialogue the myriad components of the Dames' revolutionary experience as they lived it. Tracking the Dames' diverse sites of political negotiation necessitates probing poissard pamphlets hawked from street corners; reading petitions from the retailers' coalitions; peering into assembly halls where deputies debated fiscal policies; intercepting police reports detailing market price controls; and listening in the courtroom as citizens explained themselves before local judges. The Revolution cut across all aspects of the Dames' daily life and the Dames' daily life informed national policy in return.

The Dames des Halles offer a rich window into the revolutionaries' quest to remake society and politics from 1789 to 1799. Rather than presenting a neat, comprehensive vision of the regenerated body politic, the market women illustrate how the revolutionaries forged a path to citizenship around unforeseen obstacles. Their mutable goals changed according to the situation. However, the Dames' logic of citizenship remained constant: individuals earned membership, and thus the right to make demands on the state, through useful work. The Dames' vision diverged from institutional models of citizenship that assumed certain individuals had a priori rights inscribed on their sexed bodies. The market women included gendered duties as a pillar of citizenship in their useful work but did not posit gender as its cornerstone. In regard to European democracy, the story of the Dames challenges the dominant analytical binary in which gender acts as the primary instrument for political differentiation. From the heart of les Halles, the Dames force us to rethink our understanding of work, gender, and nascent citizenship.

NOTES

Abbreviations

AdP   Archives de Paris
AdPP   Archives de la Préfecture de police
AN   Archives nationales
AP   Madival, J., and E. Laurent, eds. *Archives parlementaires de 1787 à 1860: recueil complet des débats législatifs & politiques des chambres françaises.* Series I. 102 Volumes.
BHVP   Bibliothèque historique de la Ville de Paris
BnF   Bibliothèque nationale de France
Carnavalet   Musée Carnavalet

Introduction

1. AN C 287, n°866 (pièce 3), L-G Calner, défenseur officieux de Vizon et défenseur gratuit des prisonniers indigents, (incorrectly dated 7 nivôse an II).
2. AN C 287, n°866 (pièce 3); *Journal de la Montagne*, 14 nivôse an II, n°54, as reprinted in *AP*, 13 nivôse an II, 82:583. The *Journal de la Montagne* replaced "savings" with "work" in their report.
3. *AP*, 13 nivôse an II, 82:583; AN C 287, n°866 (pièce 3).
4. AN C 287, n°866 (pièce 3).
5. Although Vizon's fate disappears from the Convention's paper trail, he appears to have resumed his post as fish market inspector. Departmental records indicate that five of the six brokers' counters were under his control during a dispute in 1800. AdP D.Q^{10} 482 Marée à la Halle, Enquête sur la compagnie Vison [*sic*], an VII-an IX.
6. The Dames referred to themselves "Citoyennes des Halles" six times during their address.
7. Sigismond Lacroix, ed., *Actes de la Commune de Paris pendant la Révolution*, series 1, vol. 1 (New York: AMS Press, 1974), viii.
8. Rene Marion, "The Dames de la Halle: Community and Authority in Early Modern Paris" (PhD diss., Johns Hopkins University, 1994), 21, 162. Marion's important dissertation remains the most detailed study of the Dames before the Revolution. Jehanne d'Orliac's survey of the Dames from 1181 to 1939 is a brief sketch. Although Dominique Godineau's crucial book on Parisian women analyzes how the Dames confronted the women's clubs, *Politics in the Marketplace* is the first comprehensive study of the Dames during the Revolution. Orliac, *Dames de la Halle* (Paris: Eds. Frances, 1946); Godineau, *Citoyennes tricoteuses: Les femmes du peuple à Paris pendant la Révolution française* (Aix-en-Provence: Alinéa, 1988).
9. I have calculated the square meters based on figures from AdP D.Q^{10} 39, Département de la Seine, Bureau des 3e & 4e arrondissements, "Les Droits qui se perçevoient anciennement, qui se perçoivent actuellement ou se percevoir dans les différentes communes de la République à raison des foires, marchés, & a."

10. For example, the following cross-market petition was signed by representatives Dame Dupray of the Marché St. Paul, Reine d'Ongrie of the Marché d'Aguesseau, Dame Genti of the Marché Quinze-Vingts, and Dame Doré of the central Halles: AN C 128, n°435, "Adresse de reconnaissance et de dévouement à l'Assemblée nationale, par les dames des divers marchés de la capitale." The revolutionaries usually referred to the central markets when using the singular "la halle." However, the revolutionaries also used "les Halles" to emphasize the several markets (vegetables, fish, cloth, etc.) within the central markets. In addition, "les Halles" could broadly refer to the central and satellite markets scattered across the city.

11. Fellow Dames from the Place Maubert trekked across the Seine to supply themselves from the retailers of les Halles. Marion, "Community and Authority," 120.

12. The Dames were not an indivisible group, as no thousand people could be. The retailers did not usually present themselves under the title "Dame des Halles" individually but did so in the company of others. As a group, the Dames called their name to their advantage to evoke their numbers and shared identity.

13. BnF Lb39 9193, "Départ de M. d'Artois pour se rende à Paris et détail intéressant de la réception qu'il a faitte [sic] aux dames de la halle pour le ramener à Paris" (Imprimerie de Calais & Dubois), 5–6: "je sommes tous égaux."

14. Lynn Hunt has argued that the revolutionaries "consciously" endeavored to "reconstitute society and social relations" and that "members of society could invent culture and politics for themselves." By creating a new political culture, the revolutionaries also changed "the category that one calls 'politics.'" Hunt, Politics, Culture, and Class in the French Revolution (Berkeley: University of California Press, 2004), 12, 88; Hunt, "Relire l'histoire du politique," in La Révolution à l'œuvre: Perspectives actuelles dans l'histoire de la Révolution française, ed. Jean-Clément Martin (Rennes: Presses Universitaires de Rennes, 2005), 121, 123; William Doyle stresses the revolutionaries responded by situation. They had a clearer view of what they struggled against than what would replace it. Doyle, "The Outbreak of the Revolution, 1787–1789," in The French Revolution: Conflicting Interpretations, 5th ed., ed. Frank A. Kafker, James M. Laux, and Darline Gay Levy (Malabar, FL: Krieger Publishing Company, 2002), 1.

15. On the evolution of reciprocity in the eighteenth century, see Charles Walton, "Reciprocity and the French Revolution (abstract)," in e-France: New Perspectives on the French Revolution, 4 (2013), and Charles Walton, "Capitalism's Alter Ego: The Birth of Reciprocity in Eighteenth-Century France," Critical Historical Studies 5, no. 1 (2018): 1–43.

16. Albert Mathiez, La Révolution française, 3 vols. (Paris: Armand Colin, 1922–1924); Albert Soboul, "Classes and Class Struggles during the French Revolution," Science and Society 17 (Summer 1953): 238–257; Albert Soboul, The Parisian Sans-culottes and the French Revolution, 1793–1794, trans. Gwynne Lewis (Oxford: Clarendon Press, 1964); Georges Lefebvre, The Coming of the French Revolution, trans. Robert R. Palmer (Princeton: Princeton University Press, 1947); Soboul, "The French Revolution in the History of the Contemporary World," reprinted and abridged from Albert Soboul, Understanding the French Revolution, trans. April Ane Knutson (New York: International Publishers, 1988): 274–299, in The French Revolution: Recent Debates and Controversies, ed. Gary Kates (New York: Routledge, 2006), 24.

17. Alfred Cobban, The Social Interpretation of the French Revolution (Cambridge: Cambridge University Press, 1964); Colin Lucas, "Nobles, Bourgeoisie, and the Origins of the French Revolution," Past and Present 60 (August 1973): 84–126. For the trajectory of revisionist scholar scholarship, see William Doyle, Origins of the French Revolution, 3rd ed. (Oxford: Oxford University Press, 1999), 10–11; Kates, The French Revolution: Recent Debates and Controversies; Kafker et al., The French Revolution: Conflicting Interpretations.

18. François Furet, Penser la Révolution française (Paris: Éditions Gallimard, 1978); Keith Baker, Inventing the French Revolution (Cambridge: Cambridge University Press, 1990).

19. Recurring questions include: how the sans-culottes united or did not unite over socioeconomic interests; how wage laborers clashed with or shared their master's aspirations; how the Le Chapelier and d'Allarde anticorporation laws affected worker identity; and how opening trade to talent changed the occupational landscape. Liana Vardi, "The Abolition of the Guilds during the French Revolution," French Historical Studies 15 (1988): 704–717; Steven Kaplan, "Social Classification and Representation in the Corporate World of Eighteenth-Century

France: Turgot's 'Carnival,'" in *Work in France*, ed. Steven Kaplan and Cynthia Koepp (Ithaca: Cornell University Press, 1986); Michael Sonenscher, "Les sans-culottes de l'an II: Repenser le langage du travail dans la France révolutionnaire," *Annales: Économies, Sociétés, Civilisations*, 5 (1985): 1087–1108; Gail Bossenga, "Protecting Merchants: Guilds and Commercial Capitalism in Eighteenth-Century France," *French Historical Studies*, 15 (1988): 693–703; Michael Fitzsimmons, "The National Assembly and the Abolition of Guilds in France," *The Historical Journal*, 39 (1996): 133–154; Clare Haru Crowston, *Fabricating Women: The Seamstresses of Old Regime France, 1675–1791* (Durham: Duke University Press, 2001). Gary Kates observes, "recent scholars define class more in terms of specific professions and occupations with varied social interests than in terms of a solid group with political interests." Kates, "Introduction," in *The French Revolution: Recent Debates and Controversies*, 9.

20. For eighteenth-century Europe, histories of banks, money, credit, ports, smuggling, and international trade along with a return to political economy have offered new entries on intricate socioeconomic networks. For Britain, see: Steven Pincus, "Rethinking Mercantilism: Political Economy, the British Empire, and the Atlantic World in the Seventeenth and Eighteenth Centuries," *William and Mary Quarterly* 69, no. 1 (January 2012): 3–34; Christine Desan, *Making Money: Coin, Currency, and Capitalism* (Oxford: Oxford University Press, 2015); James Livesey, "Free Trade and Empire in the Anglo-Irish Commercial Propositions of 1785," *Journal of British Studies*, 52 (2013): 103–127; Christopher Dudley, "Party Politics, Political Economy, and Economic Development in Early Eighteenth-Century Britain," *Economic History Review*, 66 (2013): 1084–1100. For France, see: Julie Hardwick, *Family Business: Litigation and the Political Economies of Daily Life in Early Modern France* (Oxford: Oxford University Press, 2009); Rebecca Spang, *Stuff and Money in the Time of the French Revolution* (Cambridge: Harvard University Press, 2014); Rebecca Spang, "The Ghost of Law: Speculating on Money, Memory, and Mississippi in the French Constituent Assembly," *Historical Reflections/Réflexions historiques* 31, no. 1 (Winter 2005): 3–25; Rebecca Spang, "Money, Money, Money," *History Workshop Journal* 69, (Spring 2010): 225–233; Michael Sonenscher, *Before the Deluge: Public Debt, Inequality, and the Intellectual Origins of the French Revolution* (Princeton: Princeton University Press, 2007); Michael Kwass, *Contraband: Louis Mandrin and the Making of a Global Underground* (Cambridge: Harvard University Press, 2014). For Europe, see: Steven Kaplan and Sophus Reinert, eds., *The Economic Turn: Recasting Political Economy in Eighteenth-Century Europe*, 2 vols. (London: Anthem, forthcoming); Robert Fredona and Sophus Reinert, eds., *New Perspectives on the History of Political Economy*, 2 vols. (Springer Nature: Palgrave Macmillan, 2018). William Sewell has appealed to historians to reintegrate economic concerns into cultural analysis. He challenges historians to consider how capitalism developed as "a power-laden yet long-enduring structure" via wide-ranging sites of cultural practice. Sewell, *Logics of History: Social Theory and Social Transformation* (Chicago: University of Chicago Press, 2005), 52, 149, 159–165. Michael Kwass attributes the mounting interest in the history of capitalism, in part, to the economic downturn of 2007–2009 and growing socioeconomic disparities in borderless global markets. Kwass "Capitalism and Inequality in Eighteenth-Century France: Writing History after the Great Recession" (plenary lecture, Society for the Study of French History, Warwick, July 2018). For the postrevolutionary evolution of French capitalism and market regulations in a European context, see Alessandro Stanziani, *Rules of Exchange: French Capitalism in Comparative Perspective, Eighteenth to Early Twentieth Centuries* (New York: Cambridge University Press, 2012).

21. James Livesey, *Making Democracy in the French Revolution* (Cambridge: Harvard University Press, 2001); Charles Walton, "*Les Graines de la Discorde:* Print, Public Spirit, and Free Market Politics in the French Revolution," in *Into Print: Limits and Legacies of the Enlightenment, Essays in Honor of Robert Darnton*, ed. Charles Walton (University Park: Pennsylvania State University Press, 2011), 158–174; Paul Cheney, *Revolutionary Commerce: Globalization and the French Monarchy* (Cambridge: Harvard University Press, 2010); Michael Kwass, "The Global Underground: Smuggling, Rebellion, and the Origins of the French Revolution," in *The French Revolution in Global Perspective*, ed. Suzanne Desan, Lynn Hunt, and William Max Nelson (Ithaca: Cornell University Press, 2013), 15–31; Lynn Hunt, "The Global Financial

Origins of 1789," in *The French Revolution in Global Perspective*, ed. Desan et al., 32–43; Charles Walton, "The Fall from Eden: The Free-Trade Origins of the French Revolution," in *The French Revolution in Global Perspective*, ed. Desan et al., 44–56; Lynn Hunt, "The French Revolution in Global Context," in *The Age of Revolutions in Global Context, c. 1760–1840*, ed. David Armitage and Sanjay Subrahmanyam (New York: Palgrave Macmillan, 2009); Michael Kwass, *Privilege and the Politics of Taxation in Eighteenth-Century France: Liberté, Égalité, Fiscalité* (Cambridge: Cambridge University Press, 2000); Gail Bossenga, "Financial Origins of the French Revolution," in *From Deficit to Deluge*, ed. Thomas Kaiser and Dale Van Kley (Stanford: Stanford University Press, 2011), 50–79; Thomas Kaiser, "From Fiscal Crisis to Revolution: The Court and French Foreign Policy, 1787–1789," in Kaiser and Van Kley, *From Deficit to Deluge*; Steven Pincus, "Empires and Capitalisms: Competing Political Economies and Eighteenth-Century Imperial Crises" (paper presentation, Social Science History Association, Vancouver, November 2012); Nicolas Delalande, *Les batailles de l'impôt: Consentement et résistances de 1789 à nos jours* (Paris: Seuil, 2011).

22. Sarah Maza, *The Myth of the French Bourgeoisie: An Essay on the Social Imaginary, 1750–1850* (Cambridge: Harvard University Press, 2003). For the most recent collective work on the bourgeoisie debate, see Jean-Pierre Jessenne, ed., *Vers un ordre bourgeois? Révolution française et changement social* (Rennes: Presses Universitaires de Rennes, 2007); For peasants, see Jean-Pierre Jessenne, "Une Révolution sans ou contre les paysans?," in *La Révolution française: Une histoire toujours vivante*, ed. Michel Biard (Paris: Éditions Tallandier: 2010), 253–267.

23. Allan Potofsky, *Constructing Paris in the Age of Revolution* (London: Palgrave Macmillan, 2009); Jean-Louis Harouel, "La question financière et ses rapports avec l'aménagement urbain," in *À Paris sous la Révolution: Nouvelles approches de la ville*, ed. Raymonde Monnier (Paris: Publications de la Sorbonne, 2008), 29–38; Anne Cochon, "Paris et les transports sous la Révolution," in Monnier, *À Paris sous la Révolution*; Eric Szulman, "Les évolutions de la boucherie parisienne sous la Révolution," in Monnier, *À Paris sous la Révolution*.

24. In one of the rare recent studies, Clare Crowston has analyzed how networks of "moral credit" from the Old Regime continued to inform merchant–client relations during the Revolution. Crowston, *Credit, Fashion, Sex: Economies of Regard in Old Regime France* (Durham: Duke University Press, 2013). Historians of the Old Regime, less restrained by strident ideological conflicts, continue to produce innovative analyses of socioeconomic relations, life, and work. See, for example, Nina Kushner and Daryl Hafter, eds., *Women and Work in Eighteenth-Century France* (Baton Rouge: Louisiana State University Press, 2015); Merridee Bailey, Tania Colwell, and Julie Hotchin, eds., *Women and Work in Premodern Europe: Experiences, Relationships, and Cultural Representation, c. 1100-1800* (London: Routledge, 2018); Hardwick, *Family Business.*

25. Since I do not contend the Dames emerged from the Revolution as part of a well-defined class, I use the term "popular classes" to broadly describe their socioeconomic milieu. The term emphasizes the group's limited economic resources while avoiding a strictly Marxist sense of class-consciousness based on the categories of a preindustrial society. By using "popular classes," I also seek to avoid the pejorative cultural shades often attached to the term "lower classes."

26. Amalia Kessler argues that this reconceptualization paralleled the shift from mercantilist regulation to free market attitudes. The risks of negotiability became acceptable in the latter half of the eighteenth century as merchants argued their exchanges benefited society. Kessler, *A Revolution in Commerce: The Parisian Merchant Court and the Rise of Commercial Society in Eighteenth-Century France* (New Haven: Yale University Press, 2007), 3, 226.

27. John Shovlin, *The Political Economy of Virtue: Luxury, Patriotism, and the Origins of the French Revolution* (Ithaca: Cornell University Press, 2006), 184.

28. Much scholarship on women and work during the eighteenth century has focused on female work within the family economy. In contrast, the revolutionaries defined commercial work in ways that focused on individual initiative and ambition. This atomization dovetails with the notion of a revolutionary citizen as an autonomous individual. Scholars have recently begun to look beyond the family economy to study female work. See Kushner and Hafter, *Enterprising Women in Eighteenth-Century France*; Maria Ågren, ed., *Making a Living, Making a*

Difference: Gender and Work in Early Modern European Society (New York: Oxford University Press, 2016).

29. Jacques Guilhaumou paraphrases Sieyès's writings to explain, "L'étape décisive [of the formation of the Nation] est celle où 'l'association,' issue de 'l'acte libre de volonté' constitutif de la nature humaine, se situe sur le terrain de 'l'engagement réel,' là où 'tout individu s'engage et s'oblige lui-même envers les autres." Guilhaumou, *Sieyès et l'Ordre de la Langue: L'invention de la politique moderne* (Paris: Editions Kimé, 2002), 85.

30. While defending their utility as working citizens, the Dames reinforced Sieyès's efforts to unhinge productivity from agricultural labor, as the physiocrats defined it. Catherine Larrère notes that, to valorize work not connected to the land, Sieyès "efface la distinction entre valeur d'échange et valeur d'usage." Larrère, "Sieyès, lecteur des physiocrates: Droit naturel ou économie?" in *Figures de Sieyès*, ed. Pierre-Yves Quiviger, Vincent Denis, and Jean Salem (Paris: Publications de la Sorbonne, 2008), 203; William Sewell has illustrated how, during the Revolution, attitudes toward work reflected the transition from corporations to autonomous labor. This occupational shift mirrored how new autonomous citizens interacted with one another and how the state defined their fiscal obligations. Since work often provides a service or a good, it provides a means of integrating the individual worker among other members in society. Sewell, *A Rhetoric of Bourgeois Revolution: The Abbé Sieyes and "What is the Third Estate?"* (Durham: Duke University Press, 1994), 148–149.

31. Charles Walton has argued that in 1789, "From the perspective of free market republicans . . . if citizens were to be empowered and markets freed, the masses would have to be trained to think about their interests and duties in a new way. Securing both free markets and a more democratic government would require nothing less than moral regeneration." "*Les Graines de la Discorde,*" 161; Haim Burstin describes efforts to find the fair balance between work and wages as "une sort d'économie éthico-politique." Burstin argues that by providing wages for patriotic labor like military service, the revolutionaries no longer calculated compensation merely "de la justice et de l'équité morale, mais du patriotisme et de la citoyenneté." The new moral economy categorized political work as wage labor. Burstin, "Travail et citoyenneté en milieu urbain sous la Révolution," in *Citoyens et citoyenneté sous la Révolution française*, ed. Raymonde Monnier (Paris: Société des Études Robespierristes, 2006), 268. John Shovlin argues that the moral economy was an important component of the political economy of eighteenth-century theorists and ministers. Drawing on notions of "patriotism," they strove "to create a political community in which citizens subordinated private interests to the welfare of the public." Shovlin, *The Political Economy of Virtue*, 4–5.

32. James Livesey, "The Political Culture of the Directory," in *A Companion to the French Revolution*, ed. Peter McPhee (Oxford: Wiley-Blackwell, 2013), 337–338; Elsewhere, Livesey explains, "The force of the republican argument derived from its protection of the moral autonomy of the citizen. The democratic institutions of the republic stabilized the beneficent effect of commercial society." Livesey, *Making Democracy in the French Revolution*, 81.

33. I define capitalism similarly to Colin Jones and William Sewell as a set of attitudes favorable to diverse entrepreneurial endeavors and which dovetailed with liberal individualism. Jones and Sewell conceive of capitalism as more connected to cultural and economic attitudes than a predetermined economic path. The notion diverges from the Marxist definition that firmly links capitalism to the development of an industrial society. Jones, "Bourgeois Revolution Revivified: 1789 and Social Change," reprinted in an abridged format from *The French Revolution and Social Change*, ed. Colin Lucas (Oxford: Oxford University Press, 1990): 69–118, in Kates, *The French Revolution: Recent Debates and Controversies*; Sewell, *A Rhetoric of Bourgeois Revolution*. On the revolutionary bourgeoisie and state regulation, see Philippe Minard, "L'héritage historiographique," in Jessenne, *Vers un ordre bourgeois?*, 26.

34. Free market proponents feared that welfare made individual citizens economically dependent. This reliance robbed them of their free and autonomous will, which was ideologically sacred. To uphold their marketplace advantages, the Dames recast themselves as the deserving, productive poor rather than dependent recipients of charity. In the eighteenth century, the Dames referred less frequently to their market spots as "places Saint Louis," which recalled the king's charity. Marion, "Community and Authority," 24, 71.

35. Victoria Thompson has analyzed market women in the nineteenth century to examine debates over the morality of women in public, the cultural value of women's work, and women's role in society. See especially "Policing the Free Market" in Thompson, *The Virtuous Marketplace: Women and Men, Money and Politics in Paris, 1830–1870* (Baltimore: Johns Hopkins University Press, 2000), 86–129.

36. Pierre Rétat illustrates how the revolutionaries used "citizen" as a hyphenated adjective to denote patriotism or "social utility." Rétat, "The Evolution of the Citizen from the Ancien Régime to the Revolution," in *The French Revolution and the Meaning of Citizenship*, ed. Renée Waldinger, Philip Dawson, and Isser Woloch (Westport, CT: Greenwood Press, 1993), 13.

37. I acknowledge that democracy in Europe, as in other parts of the world, has taken various forms. Indeed, it is a central argument of this work that the revolutionaries themselves contested the meaning of democracy. Therefore, I assume Lynn Hunt's broad definition of democracy as "the continual struggle over the boundaries of citizenship." Hunt, "Afterword," in Waldinger et al., *The French Revolution and the Meaning of Citizenship*, 213. The year 1789 continues to be an international starting point in comparative studies of citizenship. See Anne Epstein and Rachel Fuchs, eds., *Gender and Citizenship in Historical and Transnational Perspective: Agency, Space, Borders*, (London: Palgrave, 2017).

38. Gail Bossenga, "Rights and Citizens in the Old Regime," *French Historical Studies* 20, no. 2 (Spring 1997): 217–218, 221–222. According to Bossenga, citizenship's "juridicial" nature enables individuals to make "legal claims on the state."

39. Harriet Applewhite, "Citizenship and Political Alignment in the National Assembly," in Waldinger et al., *The French Revolution and the Meaning of Citizenship*, 50.

40. Suzanne Desan, *The Family on Trial in Revolutionary France* (Berkeley: University of California Press, 2004), 48; See also Philip Dawson, "Introduction," in Waldinger et al., *The French Revolution and the Meaning of Citizenship*, xiii–xxi, and Pierre Rétat, "The Evolution of the Citizen from the Ancien Régime to the Revolution," in Waldinger et al., *The French Revolution and the Meaning of Citizenship*, 3–16.

41. "Droit," in *Dictionnaire de l'Académie française*, 5th Edition (1798), Project ARTFL, http://artfl-project.uchicago.edu/content/dictionnaires-dautrefois.

42. The deputies explicitly connected rights and duties in the 1795 *Declaration of Rights and Duties of Man and Citizen.*

43. The Dames' vision of citizenship, as I discern it, sharply contrasts with Darline Gay Levy and Harriet Applewhite's tableau of militant Parisian women who "grounded their action in universal claims" and whose campaign for "recognition as citizens . . . necessarily identified them as subjects of universal rights." Levy and Applewhite, "A Political Revolution for Women? The Case of Paris," reprinted from *Becoming Visible: Women in European History*, 3rd ed., ed. Renate Bridenthal, Susan Mosher Stuard, and Merry E. Weisner (Boston: Houghton Mifflin Company, 1998), 266–291, in Kafker et al., *The French Revolution: Conflicting Interpretations*, 5th ed., 345, 346.

44. *AP*, August 27, 1791, 29:754.

45. As proxy voters, a small number of women had elected deputies to the Estates General. Lynn Hunt, *Inventing Human Rights: A History* (New York: W.W. Norton & Company, 2007), 169.

46. Joan Landes, *Women and the Public Sphere in the Age of the French Revolution* (Ithaca: Cornell University Press, 1988); Joan Scott, *Only Paradoxes to Offer: French Feminists and the Rights of Man* (Cambridge: Harvard University Press, 1996); Geneviève Fraisse, *Muse de la Raison: La démocratie exclusive et la différence des sexes* (Aix-en-Provence: Alinéa, 1989); Carole Pateman, *The Sexual Contract* (Stanford: Stanford University Press, 1988). Karen Offen characterizes the revolutionary ban on women's clubs as "one aspect of a far deeper, centuries-old French male anxiety about women's wielding of political authority." Offen, *The Woman Question in France, 1400-1870* (New York: Cambridge University Press, 2017), 47.

47. Lynn Hunt initially argued that male revolutionaries feared sexual dedifferentiation and thus sought to exclude women from citizenship. Hunt, *The Family Romance of the French Revolution* (Berkeley: University of California Press, 1992).

48. Marc de Villiers, *Histoire des clubs des femmes et des légions d'amazones* (Paris: Plon-Nourrit, 1910); Marie Cerati, *Le Club des Citoyennes Républicaines Révolutionnaires* (Paris: Éditions Sociales, 1966).

49. Marie-France Brive, ed., *Les femmes et la révolution française: Actes du colloque international, 12-13-14 avril 1989*, 3 vols. (Toulouse: Presses universitaires du Mirail, 1989–1991).

50. Harriet Applewhite and Darline Levy, eds., *Women and Politics in the Age of Democratic Revolution* (Ann Arbor: University of Michigan Press, 1990); Darline Levy and Harriet Applewhite, "Women and Militant Citizenship in Revolutionary Paris," in *Rebel Daughters: Women and the French Revolution*, ed. Sara Melzer and Leslie Rabine (New York: Oxford University Press, 1992); Olwen Hufton, *Women and the Limits of Citizenship in the French Revolution* (Toronto: University of Toronto Press, 1992); Carla Hesse, *The Other Enlightenment: How French Women Became Modern* (Princeton: Princeton University Press, 2001); Dominique Godineau, *The Women of Paris and Their French Revolution*, trans. Katherine Streip (Berkeley: University of California Press, 1998); Christine Fauré, "Doléances, déclarations et pétitions, trois formes de la parole publique des femmes sous la Révolution," *Annales historiques de la Révolution française*, 344 (2006): 5–25; Laura Talamante, "Les Marseillaises: Women and Political Change during the French Revolution, 1789-1794," PhD diss., UCLA, 2003; Lisa DiCaprio, *The Origins of the Welfare State: Women, Work, and the French Revolution* (Urbana: University of Illinois Press, 2007).

51. This type of women's history approach has appeared more frequently in French than in Anglo-Saxon studies. For example, see Martine Lapied, "Histoire du genre en Révolution," in Martin, *La Révolution à l'œuvre*, 77; Martine Lapied, "Une absence de Révolution pour les femmes?" in Biard, *La Révolution Française: Une histoire toujours vivante*, 304.

52. For a summary of trends in the historiography of women and gender during the Revolution until 2000, see Suzanne Desan, "What's after Political Culture? Recent French Revolutionary Historiography," *French Historical Studies* 23, no. 1 (2000): 187–192; For pre-1990 work on women's rights and citizenship, see Karen Offen, "The New Sexual Politics of French Revolutionary Historiography," *French Historical Studies* 16, no. 4 (1990): 909–922. Dena Goodman, "Public Sphere and Private Life: Toward a Synthesis of Current Historiographical Approaches to the Old Regime." *History and Theory* 31, no. 1 (1992): 8–9, 15, 19. With an eye to political culture and sociability, Goodman has convincingly argued that the two spheres overlapped and did not "oppose" one another during the Old Regime and the Revolution. Annie Smart argues that the "home is the site of both domestic and civic virtues," but retains the sphere dichotomy. She maintains, "When we [scholars] declare that *citoyennes* do not exist or that women are excluded from civic identity, we make two assumptions: first, that political right is a necessary—and almost sufficient—condition for citizenship, and second, that only actions in the public sphere can be considered civic." Smart, *Citoyennes: Women and the Ideal of Citizenship in Eighteenth-Century France* (Newark: University of Delaware Press, 2011), 3, 6.

53. Suzanne Desan, "The French Revolution and the Family," 481; Desan, *The Family on Trial in Revolutionary France*; Jennifer Heuer, *The Family and the Nation: Gender and Citizenship in Revolutionary France, 1789-1830* (Ithaca: Cornell University Press, 2005).

54. Anne Verjus, *Le bon mari: Une histoire politique des hommes et des femmes à l'époque révolutionnaire* (Paris: Fayard, 2010), 26–28. See also her discussion of the "patriarchal paradigm" in Verjus, "Gender, Sexuality, and Political Culture," in McPhee, *A Companion to the French Revolution*, 203, and Verjus, *Le Cens de la famille: Les femmes et le vote, 1789-1848* (Paris: Editions Berlin, 2002). William Sewell also demonstrates how property separated "passive" male citizens from "active" male citizens who could vote. In his reading of Sieyès, Sewell gives the following three-part formula for citizenship in 1789: A citizen is "(1) a French national (2) who is the head of a household and (3) performs useful work." Sewell, *A Rhetoric of Bourgeois Revolution*, 149; William Sewell, "Le Citoyen/la Citoyenne: Activity, Passivity, and the Revolutionary Concept of Citizenship," in *The French Revolution and the Creation of Modern Political Culture: The Political Culture of the French Revolution*, vol. 2, ed. Colin Lucas (Oxford: Pergamon Press, 1988).

55. For an overview of recent scholarship on gender in the Revolution, see Guillaume Mazeau and Clyde Plumauzille, "Penser avec le genre: Trouble dans la citoyenneté révolutionnaire," *La Révolution française*, 9 (2015), http://lrf.revues.org/1458, 14 (accessed October 24, 2016) and Suzanne Desan, "Recent Historiography on the French Revolution and Gender," in Special Forum: "The French Revolution is Not Over: An Introduction" *Journal of Social*

History 52, no. 4 (Summer 2019). Microhistory approaches also illustrate how political tides affected relationships among spouses, parents, and children. See Anne Verjus and Denise Davidson, *Le Roman conjugal: Chroniques de la vie familiale à l'époque de la Révolution et de l'Empire* (Seyssel: Champ Vallon, 2011); Lindsay Parker, *Writing the Revolution: A French Woman's History in Letters* (Oxford: Oxford University Press, 2013).

56. Jennifer Heuer, "Citizenship, the French Revolution, and the Limits of Martial Masculinity," in Epstein and Fuchs, *Gender and Citizenship in Historical and Transnational Perspective*, 19–38.

57. Claire Cage, "'Celibacy Is a Social Crime': The Politics of Clerical Marriage, 1794–1799," *French Historical Studies* 36, no. 4 (2013), 601–628; Claire Cage, *Unnatural Frenchmen: The Politics of Priestly Celibacy and Marriage, 1720–1815* (Charlottesville: University of Virginia Press, 2015). Kathryn Marsden, "Married Nuns in the French Revolution: The Sexual Revolution of the 1790s" (PhD diss., University of California-Irvine, 2014).

58. Clyde Plumauzille, "La nouvelle publicité de la prostitution dans le Paris révolutionnaire: Information, marchandisation et banalisation d'une transgression sexuelle (1789–1799)," in *Le Genre entre transmission et transgression*, ed. Lydie Bodiou, Marlaine Cacouault-Bitaud, and Ludovic Gaussot (Rennes: Presses Universitaires de Rennes, 2014), 79–93; Clyde Plumauzille, *Prostitution et Révolution: Les femmes publiques dans la cité républicaine (1789–1804)* (Paris: Ceyzérieu, 2016).

59. Anne Verjus studies suffrage over several decades to ask what qualities excluded women *and some men* from the right to vote. The Dames des Halles were less interested in the theory of representation encapsulated in voting than in using their socioeconomic services to legitimize their demands on the state. However, these logics of suffrage and economic citizenship powerfully intersect in fiscal reform. Verjus, *Le Cens de la famille*, 19, 80.

60. Suzanne Clémencet, "Chambre de la Marée," in *Guide des recherches dans les fonds judiciaires de l'Ancien Régime*, ed. Michel Antoine (Paris: Imprimerie nationale, 1958).

61. A. P. Moore, *The Genre Poissard and the French Stage of the Eighteenth Century* (New York: Institute of French Studies, 1935).

62. For a partial list of pamphlets and analysis, see Ouzi Elyada, *Presse populaire & feuilles volantes de la Révolution à Paris 1789–1792* (Paris: Société des Études Robespierristes, 1991). The Fronde was the last time the genre poissard became deeply politicized before the Revolution. See Jeffrey Merrick, "The Cardinal and the Queen: Sexual and Political Disorders in the Mazarinades," *French Historical Studies* 18, no. 3 (Spring 1994): 667–699.

63. Nicolas Delalande and Alexis Spire argue that taxes construct political and social relations in tandem. Delalande and Spire, *Histoire sociale de l'impôt* (Paris: Editions Berlin, 2002), 5.

64. William Sewell asserts that the revolutionaries believed "the nation was constituted by useful work—either private or public—and by the citizens who performed that work." He adds, "all useful work, whether menial or distinguished, was a contribution to the well-being of the nation. Only *idleness* was to be despised." Sewell, *Work and Revolution in France: The Language of Labor from the Old Regime to 1848* (Cambridge: Cambridge University Press, 1980), 80, 81.

Chapter 1

1. This account draws from: Sigismond Lacroix, ed., *Actes de la Commune de Paris pendant la Révolution*, series 1, vol. 1 (New York: AMS Press, 1974), 173; Deposition CLXXXIII, Deposition CLXXXVII, and Deposition CCLXXXI of the subsequent investigation ordered by the National Assembly. *Procédure criminelle instruite au Châtelet de Paris, sur la dénonciation des faits arrivés à Versailles dans la journée du 6 Octobre 1789*, vol. 1 (Paris: Chez Baudouin, 1790); Henri Leclercq, *Les journées d'octobre et de la fin de l'année 1789* (Paris: Librairie Letouzey et Ane, 1924), 54.

2. On the literary genre, see A. P. Moore, *The Genre Poissard and the French Stage of the Eighteenth Century* (New York: Institute of French Studies, 1935).

3. Ouzi Elyada, *Presse populaire & feuilles volantes de la Révolution à Paris 1789–1792* (Paris: Société des Études Robespierristes, 1991).

4. On the later theatrical representations of the Dames, see "Playing the Poissarde: Madame Angot, the Dames des Halles, and Political Influence, 1795–1804" in Katie Jarvis, "Politics in

the Marketplace: The Popular Activism and Cultural Representation of the Dames des Halles during the French Revolution" (PhD diss., University of Wisconsin-Madison, 2014), 398–485.

5. Rene Marion, "The Dames de la Halle: Community and Authority in Early Modern Paris" (PhD diss., Johns Hopkins University, 1994), 151.

6. David Garrioch, *Neighbourhood and Community in Paris, 1740–1790* (Cambridge: Cambridge University Press, 1986), 101. Daniel Roche, *The People of Paris: An Essay in Popular Culture in the 18th Century*, trans. Marie Evans (Berkeley: University of California Press, 1987), 243.

7. Marion, "Community and Authority," 14–15.

8. Marion, "Community and Authority," 21, 23, 35, 68–69, 58–59. By the end of the seventeenth century, three-quarters of the *regratières* who held *places Saint Louis* were parishioners of St. Eustache (the church connected to les Halles) while one-third of the total market women lived in houses directly attached to the *piliers des halles* (bordering arcades and shops).

9. AN C 128, n⁰ 435, "Adresse de reconnaissance et de dévouement à l'Assemblée nationale, par les dames des divers marchés de la capitale."

10. Marion, "Community and Authority," 153–154, 26.

11. AN F⁷ 7611, dossier 69, "Tableau approximatif du Produit de la location des Places sur les halles, marchés, ports, et chantiers, 29 ventôse an 8"; AN F¹³ 1161, "Poyet architecte des Travaux publics au Ministre de l'Intérieur," n°1022, le 3 brumaire an 5.

12. AN F¹³ 1162, Préfecture de Police, "État des Marchés de Paris et du Nombre des places qu'ils contiennent," September 16, 1812.

13. Paris had 530 bakers. Marcel Reinhard, *Paris pendant la Révolution* (Paris: Centre de documentation universitaire, 1962), 71.

14. Much of the information on Hollande comes from judicial and police dossiers after her death in 1799. The police recorded their walkthrough of her apartment and vividly described the space. I have extracted rare details from her exceptionally rich death records, an inventory of her possessions, neighbors' testimony, and contemporary sources to approximate what her life, possessions, and occupation would have been like ten years earlier. AdP D.4 U¹ 30, "Extrait des Registres des Actes de Décès de Marie Jeanne Hollande, Veuve d'Étienne Perault," 26 germinal an 8, n°167.

15. AdP D.4 U¹ 30, "Extrait des Registres des Actes de Décès de Marie Jeanne Hollande."

16. Léon Biollay, *Les anciennes Halles de Paris*, in *Mémoires de la Société de l'Histoire de Paris et de l'Île-de-France*, vol. 3 (Paris: Société de l'Histoire de Paris, 1877), 65.

17. BnF 8-Z Le Senne 6366 (9) Louis-Sébastien Mercier, *Tableau de Paris*, vol. 9 (Amsterdam: 1788), 296; BnF 8-LI3-52 (1,4) Mercier, *Tableau de Paris*, vol. 4 (Amsterdam, 1782), 154.

18. Mercier, *Tableau de Paris*, vol. 4, 151–152.

19. Biollay, *Les anciennes Halles*, 2.

20. BnF 8-LI3-52 (J,1) Mercier, *Tableau de Paris*, vol. 1 (Amsterdam: 1793), 129.

21. AdP D.4 U¹ 30, "Extrait des Registres des Actes de Décès de Marie Jeanne Hollande."

22. "La maison des Pocquelins et la Maison de Regnard aux Piliers des Halles, 1633–1884," in *Mémoires de la Société de l'Histoire de Paris*, vol. 11, (Paris: Chez Champion, 1885), 271–272.

23. Biollay, *Les anciennes Halles*, 57.

24. Garrioch, *Neighbourhood*, 120.

25. "La maison des Pocquelins," 271–272.

26. J.-A. Dulaure, *Histoire Civile, Physique et Morale de Paris*, vol. 9 (Paris: Baudoin Frères, 1825), 227.

27. Garrioch, *Neighbourhood*, 116; Biollay, "Les anciennes Halles," 59.

28. These are the "Petits Piliears de la Tonnellerie" and the "Piliers des Potiers d'Étain" in Figure 1.1.

29. Garrioch, *Neighbourhood*, 244.

30. Biollay, *Les anciennes Halles*, 66.

31. Mercier, *Tableau de Paris*, vol. 9, 295.

32. BnF 8-LI3-52 (I,2) Louis-Sébastien Mercier, *Tableau de Paris*, vol. 2 (Amsterdam: 1782), 265–266. For a social, economic, and cultural perspective on the luxury and master merchant boutiques in Paris, the antipodes of the Dames' mobile food stands, see Natacha Coquery,

Tenir boutique à Paris au XVIIIe siècle: Luxe et demi-luxe (Paris: Comité des travaux historiques et scientifiques, 2011).

33. AdP D.4 U^1 29 n°293, Cne Colin; AdP D.4 U^1 29, n°294, Cne Boulanger; AdP D.4 U^1 29, n°295, Cne Desmoulins; AdP D.4 U^1 29, n°297, Cne Hartault; AdP D.4 U^1 29, n°305, Cne Mitaine. The number of floors has been taken from Turgot's elevated map. I have discerned the apartment and building structure from architectural drawings of the cadastre records. BnF Département Cartes et plans, GESH18PF37DIV3P56, "Paris au XVIIIe siècle. Plan de Paris: en 20 planches, . . . levé et dessiné par Louis Bretez" (Paris: 1739); AN F31 79^{01} Cadastre de Paris par îlot (1810-1836), 15e quartier, Marchés, Tableau d'Assemblage; AN F31 79^{20} Cadastre de Paris par îlot (1810–1836), 15e quartier, Marchés, îlot n°19.

34. David Garrioch, *Making of Revolutionary Paris* (Berkeley: University of California Press, 2002), 206.

35. Anne Lombard-Jourdan, *Les Halles de Paris et leur Quartier (1137–1969)* (Paris: École Nationale des Chartes, 2009) 96–97, 101; Mary Durham Johnson, "Old Wine in New Bottles: Institutional Changes for Women of the People during the French Revolution," in *Women, War, and Revolution*, ed. Carol Berkin and Clara Lovett (New York: Holmes & Meier Publishers, Inc., 1980), 11.

36. BnF Estampes Réserve Fol VE-53 (F), Jacques François Joseph Swebach, "Fontaine des innocents, Élevée sur la place de la halle. Les bas-reliefs des Cens Jean-Gougeon [*sic*], et de Pujet," Drawing with pen and brown ink, 26.7cm × 19.6cm (1793).

37. Mercier, *Tableau de Paris*, vol. 1, 126.

38. Biollay, *Les anciennes Halles*, 63.

39. The market officially moved in 1790. Biollay, *Les anciennes Halles*, 63.

40. Thiery, *Le Voyageur à Paris: Extrait du Guide des amateurs & des étrangers voyageurs à Paris*, vol. 2 (Paris: Chez Gattey, 1790), 15.

41. Biollay, *Les anciennes Halles*, 46.

42. Mercier, *Tableau de Paris*, vol. 1, 126; Mercier, *Tableau de Paris*, vol. 9, 119.

43. AdP D.4 U^1 29, n°311, Cne Ruiné; AdP D.4 U^1 29, n°313, Cne Gasseau; AdP D.4 U^1 29, n°314, Cne Guérin; AdP D.4 U^1 29, n°315, Cne Lapareillé; AdP D.4 U^1 29, n°317, Cne Lécureux.

44. AdP D.4 U^1 29, n°313, Cne Gasseau.

45. Mercier notes the "poissardes" made this point to insist that the markets stay clustered in the city center. BnFZ Le Senne 6366(11) Louis-Sébastien Mercier, *Tableau de Paris*, vol. 11, (1788: Amsterdam), 157–158.

46. Mercier, *Tableau de Paris*, vol. 1, 127, 126.

47. AdP D.4 U^1 25, n°927.

48. AdP D.4 U^1 30, "Extrait des Registres des Actes de Décès de Marie Jeanne Hollande."

49. AdP D.4 U^1 24, n°417.

50. AdP D.4 U^1 29, n°298, Cne Limmonnet.

51. AdP D.4 U^1 27, n°1579, 21 germinal an III.

52. AdP D.4 U^1 29, police municipale, 17 pluviôse an 7.

53. AdP D.4 U^1 24, n°452, Femme Metot vs. Pasquier, January 31, 1792.

54. AdP D.4 U^1 29, n°425, vendémiaire an VI.

55. Marion, "Community and Authority," 218.

56. AdP D.4 U^1 28, n°351, 7 thermidor an V.

57. Marion, "Community and Authority," 237.

58. As David Garrioch explains, "in terms of sociability and solidarity . . . the division here is between those who belonged to the local community and those who did not. It is a difference in the way of life, in the attitudes and in forms of behaviour." *Neighbourhood*, 254; Garrioch, *Making of Revolutionary Paris*, 16–19.

59. According to David Garrioch, the confraternity's records have not survived.

60. Mercier, *Tableau de Paris*, vol. 9, 174.

61. Marion, "Community and Authority," 114, 202, 112, 205. When Louis XVI reestablished the guilds in 1776, he opened all the corporations to both sexes. But he also undermined female economic authority for those occupations with women-only guilds by abolishing them. However, the Dames skirted these restraints since they did not have a corporation. Steven

Kaplan, "Social Classification and Representation in the Corporate World of Eighteenth-Century France: Turgot's 'Carnival,'" in *Work in France*, ed. Steven Kaplan and Cynthia Koepp (Ithaca: Cornell University Press, 1986), 211; Before Turgot closed the guilds, at least six corporations had been exclusively female at different points, including "the dressmakers, linen weavers, midwives, makers of floral bouquets, flax makers, women's hairdressers, and sellers of women's fashion clothes." Garrioch, *The Making of Revolutionary Paris*, 67.

62. George Rudé, *The Crowd in the French Revolution* (New York: Oxford University Press, 1967), 242–243.

63. Arlette Farge, *La Vie fragile: violence, pouvoirs, et solidarités à Paris au XVIIIe siècle* (Paris: Hachette, 1986), 188.

64. Garrioch, *Neighbourhood*, 117, 182.

65. Marion, "Community and Authority," 26.

66. AN Z^{11} 1, Chambre de la Marée; Suzanne Clémencet, "Chambre de la Marée," in *Guide des recherches dans les fonds judiciaires de l'Ancien Régime*, ed. Michel Antoine (Paris: Imprimerie nationale, 1958). "Chambre de la Marée," in *Encyclopédie, ou dictionnaire raisonné des sciences, des arts et des métiers*, ed. Diderot and d'Alembert, vol. 3, (1751–72), 54 on ARTFL, http://portail.atilf.fr/encyclopedie/.

67. The records of the "Justice de Paix du 4ème Arrondissement Ancien, Section du Marché des Innocents, puis des Marchés" are organized chronologically in departmental archives in the following cartons: AdP D.4 U^1 23; AdP D.4 U^1 24; AdP D.4 U^1 25; AdP D.4 U^1 26; AdP D.4 U^1 27; AdP D.4 U^1 28; AdP D.4 U^1 29. Most individuals brought civil disputes before the justice of the peace in their neighborhood, occupational tax agents summoned delinquent citizens in their section of residence, and the police brought market violators from les Halles before the Marchés judge. Therefore, the Dames appear much more frequently in these cartons than elsewhere. Court officials most often recorded litigants' names, spouses, occupations, and residences as identifying information. In a typical case, Citoyenne Marault appeared before the Marchés justice of the peace in his office on the rue de la Chauverrerie in July 1793. Marault and a fellow merchant sought arbitration over a debt. From the court record, we learn that Marault was a fish merchant, she lived on the rue Pirouette, and her husband's name was Marie. See AdP D.4 U^1 25, n° 939.

68. Any merchant with a patente (occupational license) of the eighth class was ambulant by definition. Thus, the patente records reveal this category even when no other commercial details are offered.

69. To make the database as statistically robust as possible, I only included the 151 Dames for whom we have at least three pieces of the following information: a name, where she traded, the type of good she sold, her marital status, her husband's name, her husband's occupation, her age, and/or her place of residence. Those Dames for whom we have less information appear elsewhere in this book, but they have been omitted from the database. To create a cohesive sample, the set focuses on those Dames who worked in the central markets. Dames from satellite markets like the Place Maubert fall beyond the purview of the following numerical analysis.

70. My thanks to Julie Hardwick for confirming that this legal trend continued from seventeenth-century practices.

71. The age of majority for women was 21. Suzanne Desan, *The Family on Trial in Revolutionary France* (Berkeley: University of California Press, 2004), 293.

72. AdP D.4 U^1 24, n°226, Dame Fou; AdP D.4 U^1 24, n°452, Dlle Marie Benaied; AdP D.4 U^1 26, n°970, Citoyenne Granger; AdP D.4 U^1 25, n°351, Citoyenne Bouchard; AdP D.4 U^1 29, n°475, Cne Vve Romain; AdP D.4 U^1 29, n°490, Cne Ravet.

73. Garrioch, *Neighbourhood*, 115, 119.

74. AdP D.4 U^1 24, April 4, 1793, see Dame Madeleine Deswartitts and Dame Marie Busson; AdP D.4 U^1 24, Dame Carpentier.

75. Suzanne Desan, "Making and Breaking Marriage: An Overview of Old Regime Marriage as Social Practice" in *Family, Gender, and Law in Early Modern France*, ed. Suzanne Desan and Jeffrey Merrick (University Park: Pennsylvania State University Press, 2009), 2; Janine Lanza, *From Wives to Widows in Early Modern Paris: Gender, Economy, and Law* (Aldershot: Ashgate, 2007), 165.

76. AdP D.4 U¹, n°237.
77. Mercier gave les Halles the title "the Universal Entrepôt" in his work on Parisian city life. Mercier, *Tableau de Paris*, vol. 4, 152.
78. I have constructed this three-paragraph narrative to describe how the fish market functioned on the eve of the Revolution. The details come from the following sources: AdP D.Q^{10} 482 Marée à la Halle, Enquête sur la compagnie Vison, an VII-an IX, n°3353, L'administration Centrale du Département de la Seine au Directeur du Domaine Nationale, signed Picard Paris, 28 Pluviôse an 7; AdP D.Q^{10} 742, Papiers Lenoir (Halles et marché) Dossier: Halles et marchés d'approvisionnements et du facturât dans les marchés, questions d'administration et réformes proposés (1807–1836); AdP D.Q^{10} 742, Papiers de Lenoir, Dossier: Personnel des Halles et Marchés (1828–1841); AdP V2F^4 9, Halles, poisson et divers, le 19ième siècle, Dossier: n°19 Vente en gros du poisson; AN F^7 7745^a, Dossier n°40, "Arrêté du préfet de police sur le commerce des beurres, fromages, et œufs à Paris" (an VIII); AdP D.Q^{10} 742, Papiers de Lenoir, Subdossier: Personnel, Service; AdP D.Q^{10} 743, Papiers de Lenoir, Dossier Octrois, Subdossier: Octrois, volaille; AdP D.Q^{10} 743, Papiers de Lenoir, Dossier: Dépouillement d'un travail fait l'an 6 par M. Gansouard; AdPP D^B 515, Préfet de Police, "Ordonnance concernant le Commerce des Fruits, Légumes, Herbages, Fleurs en bottes et Plantes usuelles" December 2, 1816; Marion, "Community and Authority," 19; Anne Lombard-Jourdan, *Les Halles de Paris*, 100–101.
79. 5,000,000 francs (des ventes de la marée) + 1,200,000 francs (ventes de Poisson d'eau douce) / 1.25 = 4,960,000 livres. Calculations based on AdP D.Q^{10} 742, Papiers Lenoir (Halles et marchés: Recherches particulières classées par établissement et par nature de marchandises), Dossier: Statistiques des Marchés de Paris.
80. I have used the 1790 base prices from the 1793 price control legislation to calculate these quantities. Cod cost 120 livres per barrel of 108 small fish or 200 livres per barrel of 108 large fish. Smoked herring cost 70 livres per barrel of 1,000 fish. AdPP D^B 387, "Tableau du maximum des Denrées et Marchandises, Stipulées dans l'article premier de la Loi du 29 septembre 1793."
81. Thiery, *Le Voyageur à Paris*, vol. 2, 91–92.
82. Émile Zola famously labeled les Halles "the stomach of Paris" in his novel set in the marketplace during the nineteenth century. Zola, *Le Ventre de Paris*, Paris: Charpentier et Cie, 1873.
83. Marion, "Community and Authority," 106, 15, 12. Many occupational bodies had confraternities during the eighteenth century. Confraternities, like those of the Dames, fused occupational association and collective religious practice.
84. Marion, "Community and Authority," 264.
85. Jehanne d'Orliac, *Dames de la Halle* (Paris: Éditions Francex, 1946), 34.
86. Marion, "Community and Authority," 8, 258, 256, 261.
87. As quoted in Orliac, *Dames de la Halle*, 121.
88. The spelling discrepancies in the song reflect the author's attempt to capture the characteristic *poissard* pronunciation of the Dames des Halles through phonetic transcription. As quoted in Orliac, *Dames de la Halle*, 121. "Ne craignez pas cher papa / D'voir augmenter vot'famille / Le Bon Dieu s'y pourvoira / Fait z'en tant que Versailles en fourmille. / Y eut-il cent Bourbons chez nous, / Y 'a du pain, du laurier pour tous."
89. Orliac, *Dames de la Halle*, 21. Marion, "Community and Authority," 293.
90. On ritual as "theatrical spectacle" and a tool for royal power, see Joan Landes, *Women and the Public Sphere* (Ithaca: Cornell University Press, 1988), 18.
91. Marion, "Community and Authority," 260–261.
92. For a discussion of the relationship between Parisians and Parlement, see Colin Lucas, "The Crowd and Politics between the Ancien Régime and Revolution in France," *Journal of Modern History* 60, (1988): 421–457, 440.
93. See Farge's explanation of the tensions between the police and the populace in *La Vie fragile*, 87.
94. Carla Hesse, *The Other Enlightenment: How French Women Became Modern* (Princeton: Princeton University Press, 2001), 87.
95. Marion, "Community and Authority," 310–316.
96. Marion, "Community and Authority," 220.

97. Orliac, *Dames de la Halle*, 19. BnF Lb39 7354, *Compliment des poissardes de Paris à MM. les électeurs, qui ont été à Versailles, pour solliciter l'amnistie des gardes-françaises*. Given the subject matter, the pamphlet is likely from 1789.

98. Marion, "Community and Authority," v, 2, 7.

99. "Harengère" was so closely associated with the Dames des Halles that the 1798 academy dictionary gives "Les harangères de la halle" as the example in context. In addition to the literal and figurative definitions, it offers phrases that blend the occupation and character traits associated with the word: "Crier comme une harengère. Dire des injures comme une harengère. Parler comme une harengère." "Harengère" in *Dictionnaire de l'Académie française*, 5th Edition (1798), Project ARTFL, http://artfl-project.uchicago.edu/content/dictionnaires-dautrefois.

100. As quoted in Orliac, *Dames de la Halle*, 121.

101. Moore, *The Genre Poissard*, 1, 3, 4, 45, 121, 126, 141.

102. Marion, "Community and Authority," 288; Carla Hesse, *The Other Enlightenment*, 22; Elyada, *Presse populaire*; Ouzi Elyada, ed., *Lettres bougrement patriotiques de la Mère Duchêne suivi de Journal des Femmes, 1791* (Paris: Les Éditions de Paris/EDHIS, 1989); Moore, *The Genre Poissard*, 5, 25, 178–179; See, for example, how the following author situates his male and female characters within the marketplace: BnF Arts du spectacle, Ra4 659, Augustin de Piis, *Le Bouquet du vaudeville, ou Dialogue d'un charbonnier et d'une poissarde sur la naissance de Mgr le Dauphin* (Imprimerie de Chardon, 1781).

103. BnF Z Le Senne 4329, Anne Claude Philippe de Pestels de Lévis de Tubières-Grimoard, *Les Citrons de Javotte. Histoire de Carnaval* (Amsterdam, 1756), 5.

104. Moore, *The Genre Poissard*, 43. See also Christian Jouhaud, *Mazarinades: la Fronde des mots* (Paris: Éditions Aubier Montaigne, 1985) and Jeffrey Merrick, "The Cardinal and the Queen: Sexual and Political Disorders in the Mazarinades," *French Historical Studies* 18, no. 3 (Spring 1994): 667–699. Even church leaders, ensconced in the world of universities, harnessed a carnivalesque form of poissard propaganda. They used the fishwives' association with Lenten dietary practice to resist Jansenist attacks against the Church. Hesse, *The Other Enlightenment*, 19.

105. Moore, *The Genre Poissard*, 52.

106. Lynn Hunt, "Engravings" in *The French Revolution: Conflicting Interpretations*, 5th ed., ed. Frank A. Kafker, James M. Laux, and Darline Gay Levy (Malabar, Florida: Krieger Publishing Company, 2002), 276.

107. Moore, *The Genre Poissard*, 340.

108. Marion, "Community and Authority," 288.

109. *La Chronique de Paris*, September 8, 1789, n°16.

110. *Cahier des plaintes et doléances des Dames de la Halle et Marchés de Paris, Rédigé au grand salon des Porcherons, le premier dimanche de Mai, pour être présenté aux Messieux les États-Généraux, Avec des augmentations sur la nouvelle du premier samedi du mois de Juin, au sujet du pain* (1789), reprinted in *Réclamations de Femmes, 1789* (Paris: Côté femmes éditions, 1989), 71–75.

111. *La Chronique de Paris*, September 8, 1789, n°16.

112. Elyada, *Presse populaire*, iii, iv, 3, 11–14. Ouzi Elyada has analyzed 41 of these poissard pamphlets. Most of them were independent, onetime publications. He does not include the following potential series in his tallies: *Dialogues entre une poissarde et un fort de la Halle, La Gazette des Halles, Finissez Donc Cher Père, Le Goûter de la Courteilles, Journal des Halles, Le Groupe Sire Jean ou Club du Savatier*, and *Le Club des Halles*.

113. Elyada, *Presse populaire*, 3. Of the poissard pamphlets Elyada has documented, the following reflects the total pamphlets by year: 1789, 19 pamphlets; 1790, 11 pamphlets; 1791, 6 pamphlets; 1792, 4 pamphlets.

114. BnF NUMM- 42495, Jacques-René Hébert, *Grande colère du Père Duchesne contre les jean-foutres de calomniateurs des Dames de la halle, & des Bouquetières du palais-royal, au sujet du beau discours qu'elles ont fait au roi* (Paris: Imprimerie de Tremblay, 1791), 7.

115. BnF Lc2 2382, "Petit mot d'avis en passant. Lettre du général La Pique aux dames de la Halle," in *Journal des Halles*, n° 1, June 1790, 1–2.

116. The Dames had a long-established reputation for their frank and free speech. A revolutionary reprint of Montaigne's works noted his desire to speak honestly, like the market

women. In the sixteenth century, Montaigne admired the direct transparency of the poissard dialect: "Eloquence injures things, which diverts us from the self. As with clothes, it's the pusillanimity of wanting to mark oneself in some particular and archaic way.... Why may I not make use of those [ways of speaking] that serve [those of] les Halles of Paris?" Michel de Montaigne, *Essais de Michel de Montaigne*, vol. 1 (Paris: Chez Jean Serviere et Chez Jean-François Bastion, 1793), 221.

117. BnF Lb39 9028, *Avis important d'une dame des Halles pour la diminution des vivres* (Paris: De la Cloye), 3, 7.

118. If the café was a site for the political education of the bourgeoisie, the cabaret was the alcohol-infused counterpart for the popular classes. The cabaret setting welded together components of oral speech, unfiltered frankness, and lively dialogue.

119. BnF Arsenal GD-9001, *Dialogue pas mal raisonnable, entre un ancien commis de barrière, un passeur, un couvreur, un charpentier et une Dame de la Halle*, 12, 13. (likely January 1791).

120. BnF Lb39 7577, *Premier dialogue entre une poissarde et un fort de la Halle*, 16.

121. BnF MFICHE Lb39- 2352, *Réclamation de toutes les poissardes*, 5–8.

122. Nevertheless, the genre's farcical elements revealed a lingering tension between the entertainment value of the poissardes' culture and the Dames' capabilities as intelligent political players. Marion, "Community and Authority," 288.

123. BnF Lb39 6294, *Harangue des Dames de la Halle aux citoyens du faubourg Saint Antoine prononcée par Ma. Engueule* (1789), 1.

124. BnF Lb39 2089, *Les Poissardes à la Reine* (Paris: Imprimerie P. de Lormel, 1789). There is no standardized way to translate argot slang or irregular poissard spellings into English. In addition to manipulating verb conjugations, French authors frequently clipped letters and mispelled words to evoke, in textual form, the dialect and mispronunciations of the popular classes. I have attempted to mimic the textual effects in the English translations throughout this chapter.

125. BnF RES- YE- 3065, *Motion des harengères de la Halle* (Paris: 1789), 1.

126. BnF MFICHE Lb39 1229, *Les trois poissardes, buvant à la santé du Tiers-État*, 9. *Premier dialogue entre une poissarde et un fort de la Halle*, 16.

127. BnF Lc2 513, Le Père Duchêne, *Je suis le véritable père Duchêne, foutre*, n°8 (Paris: Imprimerie du véritable père Duchêne), 1, 2.

128. BnF Lb39 8416, *Le Goûter de la Courtille ou Dialogues sur les affaires présentes, entre quatre dames de la halle: Mme Saumon, La Mère Gogo, La Mère Écorche-Anguille et Manon L'Écailleuse*, 3.

129. Public opinion carried legitimizing power for all political positions in the 1780s. Even the monarchy hired pamphleteers to stir up popular support at the end of the Old Regime. Robert Darnton, *The Literary Underground of the Old Regime* (Cambridge: Harvard University Press, 1982), 202. See also Keith Baker, "Public Opinion as Political Invention," in *Inventing the French Revolution* (Cambridge: Cambridge University Press, 1990).

130. BnF Lb39 10208, *Grande motion des Halles* (1791), 5, 6.

131. BnF Réserve YE 3069, *Le Divorce, Dialogue entre Madame Engueule et Madame Saumon harangères, et M. Mannquin, fort de la halle* (1790), 2–4. "Pour la vertu faut zêtre libre, / L'choix qu'on fait soy même est l'seul bon."

132. BnF Lb39 5296, *V'là c'que s'est dit et passé à la Halle. V'là la grande dispute entr'un Jacobin et des marchandes de fruits*, 7, 9–10. (likely early 1792).

133. Hesse, *The Other Enlightenment*, 22, 26.

134. BnF Lb39 8416, *Le Goûter de la Courtille*, 2–4, 8. (likely April 1791).

135. BnF Z Le Senne 5128, *Les Bienfaits de l'Assemblée Nationale ou entretiens de la Mère Saumon, doyenne de la Halle: suivis des vaudevilles* (Paris: Au Palais Royal, 1792) 6–7, 11, 15.

136. BnF Estampes P 22029, "La Discipline patriotique ou le fanatisme corrigée." According to the BnF catalog, "On distribuait sur le Pont-Neuf et au Palais-Royal des caricatures avec un libelle portant le titre qui suit: *Liste de toutes les sœurs et dévotes qui ont été fouettées par les Dames des Marchés de Paris, avec leurs noms.*"

137. When jewelry thieves invaded the marketplace in 1792, the journal's artist realistically scattered the Dames among the terrified market goers. BnF Estampes P23880bis, "Événement de 14 7bre 1792," from *Révolutions de Paris*.

138. BnF Estampes P 21390, "Les Dames de Paris allant à Versailles."

139. AdPP D^A 23, The two large prints are entitled "Proclamation de la Constitution," while the medallion is labeled "Proclamation de la première Constitution." Since the latter bears the number 72 and implies the second Constitution exists, it is likely part of a commemorative series.

140. BnF Estampes M 99968, "J'sommes du Tiers."

141. BnF Estampes P 21379, "Eh bien, J . . . F . . . , dira-tu encore vive la noblesse?" (London: 1789).

142. Carnavalet G 27952, "Les Dames de la Halle partant pour aller chercher le roi à Versailles le 5 octobre 1789."

143. Carnavalet G 29383, "La Journée à jamais Mémorable aux François où Louis XVI Restaurateur de la liberté Françoise se rendit à l'Hôtel de Ville le 17 du mois de Juillet 1789."

144. Carnavalet G 2796, "Les Dames de la Halle félicitant leurs Majestés sur le commencement de la Constitution."

145. BnF YE 32173, Riche-en-Gueule ou Le Nouveau Vadé publié par un enfant de la joie et dédié aux dames des halles et marchés (Paris: Quai des Augustins n° 9).

146. A rigid elbow cocked out to the side signals confidence and is a way to claim territorial dominance. Joe Navarro with Marvin Karlins, What Everybody Is Saying (New York: Harper Collins, 2008), 119, 125.

147. Carnavalet G 25375, "Vive le Roi! Vive la Nation!"

148. Carnavalet G 27982, "Journée Memorable du 6 octobre 1789."

149. Carnavalet G 2796, "Le Roi reçoit les Femmes de la Halle" (1789).

150. BnF Lb39 7354, Compliment des poissardes de Paris à MM. les électeurs, qui ont été à Versailles, 2, 4.

151. BnF NUMM- 42495, Hébert, Grande colère du Père Duchesne contre les jean-foutres de calomniateurs des Dames de la halle, 3.

152. La Chronique de Paris, February 19, 1791, n°50.

153. BnF NUMM- 42495, Hébert, Grande colère du Père Duchesne contre les jean-foutres de calomniateurs des Dames de la halle, 4–5, 1.

154. Félix Lazare and Louis Lazare, Dictionnaire administratif et historique des rues et monuments de Paris (Paris: Bureau de la revue municipale, 1855), 671.

155. See, for example, Reine de la Halle in BnF Arsenal BL 19584, Étrennes aux Messieurs les Ribauteurs les Supplémens aux Écosseuses, ou Margot La Mal-Peignée en Belle Humeur, et ses qualités (1759) in Recueil d'œuvres comiques et poissardes (1756-60).

156. Journal de Paris, July 30, 1789, n° 211.

157. BnF Lb39 11705, Le Roi d'Yvetot à la Reine d'Hongrie tenant sa cour plénière aux Halles de Paris (Paris: Chez Debray), 5–6, 4, 8.

158. BnF Lb39 8267, Demande de la Reine d'Hongrie à M. le Directeur de la Comédie-Française, 2.

159. Réimpression de l'ancien Moniteur: Depuis la réunion des États-Généraux jusqu'au Consulat, January 1, 1790 (Paris: Plon-frères, imprimeur-éditeur, 1854.)

160. Laura Mason, Singing the French Revolution: Popular Culture and Politics, 1787–1799 (Ithaca: Cornell University Press, 1996), 70–71.

161. Dominique Godineau, The Women of Paris and Their French Revolution. Trans. Katherine Streip (Berkeley: University of California Press, 1998).

162. Reinhard, Paris pendant la Révolution, 104.

163. AN F^1c III Seine 27, Citoyen Dutard, Commissaire Observateur local pour le Département de Paris, May 17, 1793.

164. AN F^1c III Seine 27, Citoyen Dutard, Commissaire Observateur local Pour le Département de Paris, June 24, 1793.

165. F.-A. Aulard, ed., Mémoires secrets de Fournier l'Américain (Paris, 1890), 27–35, reprinted in Darline Gay Levy, Harriet Branson Applewhite, and Mary Durham Johnson, Women in Revolutionary Paris, 1789–1795 (Urbana: University of Illinois Press, 1980), 46.

166. Jean Loup de Vireau-Beavoir and Giuseppe de Lama, "October 12, 1793," in La Révolution française racontée par un diplomate étranger. Correspondance du bailli de Virieu, ministre plénipotentiaire de Parme (1788–1793), ed. Emmanuel Henri Vicomte de Grouchy and Antoine Guillois (Paris: E. Flammarion, 1903), 143.

167. *L'Ami du Peuple ou le Défenseur des Patriotes persécutés*, le 3 brumaire an V, October 24, 1796, n°212.

168. *Journal de Paris*, July 22, 1789, n° 33, Reporting on July 20, 1789.

169. BnF Lb3⁹ 1635, *Compliment des dames poissardes à leurs frères du Tiers État* (1789).

170. Françoise Aubert, *Sylvain Maréchal: Passion et Faillite d'une Égalitaire* (Paris: Gliardica, 1975), 9; See also "La mémoire des Lieux," Paris Révolutionnaire, http://www.parisrevolutionnaire.com/.

171. BnF Lb3⁹ 1635, *Compliment des dames poissardes*.

172. Charles-Louis Chassin, ed. *Les élections et les cahiers de Paris en 1789*, Vol. 3 (Paris: D. Jouaust, Charles Noblet, and Maison Quantin, 1889).

173. BnF Arsenal GD 11044, *La Gazette des Halles*, n° 2 (Paris: Imprimerie de N.H. Nyon, 1789), 7, 9.

174. A. P. Moore concludes, because the constructed poissardes coexisted with their living inspirations, the literary genre lacked strong conventions. Moore, *The Genre Poissard*, 5.

175. BnF Lc2 2268, *La Gazette des Halles*, n°1 (Paris: Imprimerie de N.H. Nyon, 1789). 3.

176. BnF Lc2 2268, *La Gazette des Halles*, n°1, 8.

177. BnF Arsenal GD-11044, *La Gazette des Halles*, n°2 (1789), 7.

178. For example, the following pamphlet lists "the printing press of the Halles" as its place of publication: BnF Lb39 9542, *Le Club des Halles établi à l'instar de celui des Jacobins à la nouvelle Halle ci-devant le charnier des innocents* (Paris: Imprimerie des Halles, 1790).

179. BnF Arsenal GD-11044, *La Gazette des Halles*, n°2; BnF Lc2 2268 *La Gazette des Halles*, n°1.

180. Augustin Martin Lottin, *Catalogue chronologique des libraires et des libraires-imprimeurs de Paris, Depuis l'an 1470, époque de l'établissement de l'Imprimerie dans cette Capitale, jusqu'à présent* (Paris: Chez Jean-Roch Lottin de S. Germain, 1789).

181. For example, see BnF Lb39 7802 Louise-Félicité Guinement de Kéralio, *Observations sur quelques articles du projet de constitution de M. Mounier* (Paris: Imprimerie de N.H. Nyon, 1789). Carla Hesse judges considers this piece authentic. Hesse, *The Other Enlightenment*, 92.

182. The Dames des Halles gradually lost their centrality in revolutionary political pamphlets by 1793. Ouzi Elyada has found only four nonserialized poissard pamphlets published in 1792. Elyada, *Presse populaire*, iv, 3.

Chapter 2

1. Sigismond Lacroix, ed., *Actes de la Commune de Paris pendant la Révolution*, series 1, vol. 2 (New York: AMS Press, 1974), 214–215, 223. There are no surviving copies of this address.

2. *La Chronique de Paris*, October 10, 1789, n°47.

3. *Actes de la Commune* 1, 2:214–215, 223; *La Chronique de Paris*, October 13, 1789, n°51.

4. M. Godard, *Exposé des Travaux de l'Assemblée-Générale des Représentans de la Commune de Paris, Depuis le 25 Juillet 1789, jusqu'au moi d'Octobre 1790, époque de l'organisation définitive de la Municipalité* (Paris: Imprimerie de Lottin l'aîné, 1790), 84.

5. *Actes de la Commune*, 1, 2:214–215, 223.

6. Godard, *Exposé des Travaux de l'Assemblée-Générale*, 84.

7. *La Chronique de Paris*, October 10, 1789, n°47; *Actes de la Commune* 1, 2: 215; AdP D.24-26 (current call #VD* 3), n°222, p. 70. "13e fournitures et ouvrages divers concernant la Maison commune, les différentes administrations Municipales, excepté la Mairie, les fêtes Publiques et autres objets cy," The Commune paid 25 livres 8 sous for 4 medals. Thus, one medal cost 6 livres 7 sous. If we use the August 1789 Paris bread price of 3 sous per retail pound (Albert Mathiez, "Étude critique sur les journées des 5 & 6 octobre," *Revue Historique*, vol. 67 [1898]), then 6 livres 7 sous can buy 42.7 pounds of bread. In 1789, the average person consumed 1.5 pounds of bread per day (Georges Lefebvre, *The Coming of the French Revolution*, trans. R. R. Palmer (Princeton: Princeton University Press, 1947), 102). Therefore, one medal could purchase 28.4 days of bread rations for one individual.

8. *Actes de la Commune*, January 1790, 1, 3. Haim Burstin discusses this negotiation over patriotic medals as part of the struggle to define "the new hierarchy of revolutionary merit" and to delineate political distinctions. Burstin, *Révolutionnaires: Pour une anthropologie politique de la Révolution française* (Paris: Vendémiaire, 2013), 287.

9. BnF Estampes M 98953, "Médaille aux bonnes citoyennes le 8 octobre 1789, donne par la commune de Paris." BnF M 99487 depicts a larger version of the medal. In August, the Commune had given medals to sympathetic French Guards in a similar fashion. They labeled these medals "the price of patriotism." *Révolutions de Paris*, August 2–8, 1789, n° 4.

10. BnF Lb39 7744, Lebois, *Récit exact de ce qui s'est passé hier à Sainte Geneviève par les Dames du Marché Saint Martin; & de-là à l'Hôtel-de-Ville; avec Compliment prononcé au Roi par Mlle Bourbau, âgée de 17 ans au nom des dames du Marché Saint Martin; Et la réception agréable de la part de Sa Majesté*, (Imprimerie Ballard) 5, 6; AN C 48, n° 476; AP, December 30, 1790, 21:719.

11. AN W 76, "Déclarations des citoyens de la section des Marchés," 21 au 22 nivôse an II.

12. Marquis de Maleissye, *Mémoires d'un Officier aux Gardes Françaises (1789-1793)* (Paris: E. Plon, Nourrit, 1897), 26.

13. On reciprocity in a wider context, see Charles Walton, "Reciprocity and the French Revolution" (abstract) in *e-France: New Perspectives on the French Revolution*, vol. 4, ed. Alex Fairfax-Cholmeley and Colin Jones (2013).

14. *Révolutions de Paris*, August 20–27, 1791, n°111.

15. AN C 128, n°435, "Adresse de reconnaissance et de dévouement à l'Assemblée nationale, par les dames des divers marchés de la capitale" (likely 1789).

16. The Dames visited the king at least twice a year for the Feast of Saint Louis and the New Year. The minimum number of compliments is 350, since it does not include variable visits for other rituals such as royal baptisms, marriages, the queen's feast day on the Assumption, and military celebrations.

17. BnF Lb39 1635, *Compliment des Dames poissardes à leurs frères du Tiers-État avec des couplets* (likely 1789), 2, 4.

18. On the French Guards in the summer and fall of 1789, see Samuel Scott, *The Response of the Royal Army to the French Revolution: The Role and Development of the Line Army, 1787–93* (Oxford: Clarendon Press, 1978), 53–54, 59, 72–73.

19. BnF Lb39 7354. *Compliment des poissardes de Paris à MM. Les électeurs qui ont été à Versailles pour solliciter l'amnistie des Gardes Françaises*, 2.

20. Carnavalet Histoire G 29383, "La Journée à jamais Mémorable aux François où Louis XVI restaurateur de la Liberté Françoise se rendit à l'Hôtel de Ville le 17 du Mois de Juillet 1789."

21. BnF Lb39 2085, *Entrée triomphante de M. Necker à l'Hôtel-de-Ville, accompagnée du compliment de M. le marquis de la Fayette & de M. Bailly, maire, suivie de la réponse de M. Necker, & de la présentation du bouquet des poissardes* (Paris: Chez Cressonnier, 1789?); *Révolutions de Paris*, July 26–August 1, 1789, n° 3.

22. *Révolutions de Paris*, July 20, 1789.

23. AN C 128, n°435, "Adresse de reconnaissance et de dévouement à l'Assemblée nationale, par les dames des divers marchés de la capitale."

24. BnF Microfiche M-12884, Mme Dupray, *Chanson des Dames des Marchés Saint Paul; des Quinze-Vingts, la Halle & d'Aguesseau* (likely 1789).

25. *Le Journal de Paris*, July 22, 1789, n°33, *La Chanson nouvelle chantée par les dames députées du même marché.*

26. BnF Lb39 7744, Lebois, *Compliment prononcé au Roi par Mlle Bourbau, âgée de 17 ans au nom des dames du Marché Saint Martin*, 5, 6.

27. BnF Estampes QB-1 (1789-10-08)–FOL, "Les Dames de la halle félicitant leurs Majestés sur le commencement de la Constitution," etching, 1789 or 1790.

28. *Révolutions de Paris*, August 8, 1789, n°4, compliment pronounced on August 7.

29. BnF Lb39 7705, *Procession solennelle des dames fripiéres de la Halle et des marchandes du c imetière des innocents, suivie du Compliment à M. de la Fayette* (Paris: Imprimerie de la Jorry, 1789).

30. P. Galliano, "Nourrices" in *Dictionnaire des institutions de la France aux XVIIᵉ et XVIIIᵉ siècles*, ed. Marcel Marion (Paris: A Picard, 1923); J. Charpentier, "Enfants Trouvés" in *Dictionnaire de l'Ancien Régime: Royaume de France, XVIᵉ–XVIIIᵉ siècle*, ed. Lucien Bély (Paris: Presses universitaires de France, 1996). In 1769, Paris officials started regulating wet-nurse activity to prevent parents from abusing the Enfants Trouvés as free temporary care.

31. BnF Lb39 7705, *Procession solennelle des dames fripiéres de la Halle et des marchandes du cimetière des innocents, suivie du Compliment à M. de la Fayette*, 3.

32. *Journal de Paris*, July 22, 1789, n°33.

33. Moshe Sluhovsky, *Patroness of Paris: Rituals of Devotion in Early Modern France* (Leiden: Brill, 1998), 11–12, 162.

34. *Révolutions de Paris*, August 9–15, 1789, n°5.

35. Augustin Challamel and Wilhelm Ténint, *Les Français sous la Révolution* (Paris: Imprimerie Duccessois, 1843), 242.

36. BHVP 7530, *Récit exact de ce qui s'est passé hier à Sainte Geneviève par les Dames du Marché Saint Martin*, 5–6.

37. BnF Lb39 7758, Reine d'Hongrie, Mesdames Pluvinet, DeVille, Chevalier, Lefebvre, Lamy, Doute, Genet, Cochois, Baronet, *Lettre d'invitation des dames marchandes du marché d'Aguesseau, à un Te Deum* (1789). The other nine retailers included Mesdames Pluvinet, Deville, Chevalier, Lefebvre, Lamy, Doute, Genet, Cochois, and Baronet.

38. BnF Lb39 2239, *Bouquet du roi: Pour le 25 août 1789* (Versailles: Imprimerie Royale, 1789).

39. AN O¹ 5000, fol. 400, "Lettre du Ministre de la Maison du Roi à M. Bailly," August 20, 1790.

40. *Le Mercure de France* pointed out that the Body Guards' white cockades were part of their regular uniform. "Défense des Gardes-du-Corps, compte rendu par le Mercure de France, des journées des 5 & 6 octobre," in *Révolutions de Paris*, October 17–24, 1789, n°15.

41. Katie Jarvis, "Allez, Marchez Braves Citoyennes: A Study of the Popular Origins of and the Political Reactions to, the October Days of the French Revolution" (bachelor's thesis, Boston College, 2007). On the song and banquet, see Pierre Dominique, *Paris enlève le roi: octobre 1789* (Paris Librairie Académique Perrin, 1973), 83; Laura Mason, "Oh Richard, Oh, My King!" *Liberty, Equality, Fraternity: Exploring the French Revolution*, http://chnm.gmu.edu/revolution/.

42. October Days images frequently highlight bread as a rallying point. The drawing "Le Roi arrivant à Paris avec sa famille, escorté de plus de trente mille âmes" depicts women joyfully touting bread on pikes alongside the royal carriage. See also Carnavalet Histoire PC 010, Chemise D, G 26247, "La Journée Mémorable de Versailles, Le lundi 5 Octobre 1789"; Johann Anton Otto, *Der König kömt mit seiner Familie unter einer Bedeckung von mehr den dreißigtaud Menschen in Paris an den Oktober 1789*, (1815) reproduced in *La Révolution par la Gravure: Les Tableaux historiques de la Révolution française*, ed. Claudette Hould, Annie Jourdan, Rolf Reichardt, and Stéphane Roy (Vizille: Musée de la Révolution française, 2002), 131.

43. The crowd was largely Parisian, although some individuals from other towns joined en route. Dom Leclercq, *Les journées d'octobre et de la fin de l'année 1789* (Paris: Librairie Letouzey et Ane, 1924), 54.

44. The Comte de Montgaillard and Jules Michelet each estimated that twelve people died. Marc de Villiers, *Reine Audu: Les Légendes des journées d'octobre* (Paris: Émile-Paul Frères, 1917), 224.

45. *Révolutions de Paris*, October 3–10, 1789, n°13; Carnavalet, Histoire PC 007, Chemise C, G 27973 87CAR 037NB, "Le Roi paroisseant au Balcon donnant sur la Cour de marbre."

46. Louis Gottschalk and Margaret Maddox, *Lafayette in the French Revolution Through the October Days* (Chicago: University of Chicago Press, 1969), 379–381.

47. BnF Estampes M 99404, "4e événement du 5 8bre 1789: Les Femmes Parisiennes siégant à l'Assemblée Nationale parmi les deputés."

48. BNF Estampes M 99442, "Vue du Château de Versailles à l'époque du 5 8bre 1789: Le Roi la Reine et Msr le Dauphin présentant au Balcon donnant sur la Cour des Miracles, La Garde Nationale de Paris et de Versailles au nombre de plus de 20,000 sans y comprendre plus de 12,000 âmes Hommes et Femmes armés de différentes armes, qui adressoient au Roi des plaintes sur le manque de pain dans la capitale, et priant le Roi de venir faire son séjour à Paris."

49. BnF Estampes P21381 Berthault, "Les Dames de la Halle partant pour aller chercher le roi à Versailles le 5 octobre 1789."

50. Carnavalet Histoire PC 007, Chemise C, G 27958, "Départ des Femmes de la Halle pour Versailles"; Carnavalet Histoire PC 007, Chemise C, G 26246, "Pariser Poisarden sonst Fisch Weiber."

51. *Révolutions de Paris,* January 22–29, 1791, n° 81.

52. BnF Estampes Réserve QB-370 (18)-FT 4, Pierre-Gabriel Berthault, Jean Duplessi-Bertaux, and Jean-Louis Prieur, "Les Dames de la Halle partant pour aller chercher le roi à Versailles le 5 octobre 1789," etching, chisel; 24 cm × 29 cm (Paris: 1802); Other popular crowd images feating the Dames during the October Days include: BnF Estampes M 99431, Événement du 5 octobre 1789: Les Dames de la Halle et autres femmes partant de Paris pour Versailles; BnF Estampes M 99412 S, "S, 8bre Départ des Dames de la Halle pour aller chercher le Roi à Versailles."

53. Prudhomme, *Révolutions de Paris,* n° XIII, 3 au 10 octobre 1789.

54. BnF Lb39 2411, *Les héroïnes de Paris, ou l'entière liberté de la France par les femmes, police qu'elles doivent exercer de leur propre autorité* (Paris: Knapen).

55. *La Chronique de Paris,* October 9, 1789, n°47.

56. BnF Estampes P21409, "Vive le roi! Vive la Nation! Lang leeve de Koning! Lang leeve de natie!" "Vive le roi! Vive la Nation!" BnF Estampes P-23748, "Les dames de la Halle de Paris vont complimenter la Reine aux Tuileries," Gravure à l'eau forte, anonyme, colorée.

57. *Révolutions de Paris,* October 3–10 1789, n°13.

58. BnF Estampes P 21385, "À Versailles! À Versailles: ou la Journée du 5 Octobre 1789."

59. Carnavalet, Histoire PC 007, Chemise C G 27983, "Retour des Héroïnes Parisiennes après l'expédition de Versailles du 6 octobre 1789."

60. BnF Estampes M 99429 Guyot, "Arrivée des Femmes à Versailles le 5 Octobre 1789" (Paris: Chez Graveur et Md d'Estampes Rue S. Jacques n°10); Carnavalet Histoire PC 007, Chemise C, G 27978, "Époque du 6 octobre 1789, l'après dîné à Versailles"; BnF Lb39 2411, *Les héroïnes de Paris, ou l'entière liberté de la France par les femmes, police qu'elles doivent exercer de leur propre autorité.*

61. BnF Estampes M 99433, Ph. Caresme, *Dédiée aux Femmes: Bravoure des Femmes Parisiennes à la Journée du 5 octobre 1789, Paris* (Paris: rue de la Lune, n°38, 1789); advertised in *Révolutions de Paris,* December 19–26, 1789, n°24.

62. *Révolutions de Paris,* October 3–10, 1789 n°13.

63. BnF Lb39 2411, *Les héroïnes de Paris, ou l'entière liberté de la France par les femmes, police qu'elles doivent exercer de leur propre autorité.* As historians Darline Gay Levy and Harriet Applewhite have observed, the show of force propelled "the transformation of subjects into a militant citizenry." Darline Gay Levy and Harriet Applewhite, "Women and Militant Citizenship in Revolutionary Paris," in *Rebel Daughters: Women and the French Revolution,* ed. Sara Melzer and Leslie Rabine (New York: Oxford University Press, 1992), 85.

64. Maleissye, *Mémoires d'un Officier,* 108.

65. For a discussion of violent and nonviolent protests early in the Revolution, see Micah Alpaugh, "The Politics of Escalation in French Revolutionary Protest: Political Demonstrations, Nonviolence and Violence in the Grandes journées of 1789," *French History* 23, no. 3 (Fall 2009): 336–359; Micah Alpaugh, *Non-Violence and the French Revolution: Political Demonstrations in Paris, 1787–1795* (Cambridge: Cambridge University Press, 2015).

66. BnF Estampes P21428, "La terrible Nuit du 5 au 6 Octobre 1789."

67. BnF Lb39 2472, Peltier, *Domine salvum fac regem,* October 21, 1789.

68. *Révolutions de Paris,* November 21–28, 1789, n°20.

69. "Dénunciation Municipalité de Paris," as reprinted in *Procédure criminelle instruite au Châtelet de Paris, sur la dénunciation des faits arrivés à Versailles dans la journée du 6 Octobre 1789,* vol. 1 (Paris: Chez Baudouin, 1790), 6–7.

70. For the arguments for and against a conspiracy by the Duc d'Orléans, Mirabeau, or Lafayette as well as an analysis of the available evidence, see Jarvis, "Allez, Marchez Braves Citoyennes."

71. *AP,* 29:364. On the relationship among shifting political factions, judicial power, and public opinion, see Barry Shapiro, *Revolutionary Justice in Paris, 1789–1790* (New York: Cambridge University Press, 1993).

72. *La Chronique de Paris,* October 10, 1789, n° 47.

73. "Mont-de-Piété de Paris," in *Dictionnaire de la Révolution française: Institutions, Hommes & Faits,* ed. Elphège Boursin and Augustin Challamel (Paris: Librairie Furne, 1893). One such false report was in *La Chronique de Paris,* October 9, 1789, n°47.

74. BHVP 600056, Claude-François de Beaulieu, *Assemblée nationale. Séance et suite des Nouvelles de Versailles du 8 octobre 1789. Découverte d'un complot contre la liberté nationale. Réclamation des dames des halles et marchés contre des faussetés publiées contre elles* (Paris: Imprimerie de Seguin-Thiboust, 1789).

75. *Révolutions de Paris,* October 17–24, 1789, n°15.

76. *La Chronique de Paris,* October 17, 1789, n°55.

77. AN C 33, n°285, and *AP,* December 31, 1789, 11:56, "Adresse présentée à l'Assemblée par une députation des marchés de Paris pour la féliciter de ses travaux."

78. AdP D.51–52, #474, p.45 et 47 (current call # VD* 47), "Procès-verbal de la déclaration faite par 16 femmes du marché Saint-Martin qu'un individu les a sollicitées moyennant argent à se rendre avec des sabres de bois ou de fer blanc chez M. Briffaut, capitaine des gardes nationales, pour lui proposer par dérision de se battre avec elles, au moment où le district et le bataillon se mettront en marche pour la cérémonie du serment," February 18, 1790.

79. Gottschalk and Maddox, *From the October Days through the Federation,* 226.

80. *La Chronique de Paris,* June 21, 1790, n° 172.

81. *Les Révolutions de Paris,* July 10–17, 1790, n° 53.

82. *La Chronique de Paris,* July 1, 1790, n°182. Artois was the future King Charles X.

83. BnF Lb39 9193, *Départ de M. d'Artois pour se rendre à Paris et détail intéressant de la réception qu'il a faitte [sic] aux dames de la halle pour le ramener à Paris* (Imprimerie de Calais & Dubois).

84. Félix Lazare and Louis Lazare, *Dictionnaire administratif et historique des rues et monuments de Paris* (Paris: Au bureau de la revue municipale, 1855), 671. Anne Lombard-Jourdan, *Les Halles de Paris et leur Quartier (1137–1969),* (Paris: École Nationale des Chartes, 2009), 98.

85. *Courrier de Lyon,* June 24, 1790, n°47.

86. *La Chronique de Paris,* July 1, 1790, n° 182.

87. George Granville Levenson-Gower Sutherland, "July 2, 1790," in *The Despatches of Earl Gower, English ambassador at Paris from June 1790 to August 1792,* ed. Oscar Browning (London: C. J. Clay and Son, Cambridge University Press Warehouse, 1885), 8.

88. *Courrier de Lyon,* June 24, 1790 n°47.

89. "Nouvelles des Provinces: Extrait d'une Lettre de Lyon, du 25 juin," *L'Ami du Roi,* July 2, 1790, n°32.

90. *L'Ami du Roi,* July 2, 1790, n°32

91. BnF Lb39 9193, *Départ de M. d'Artois pour se rendre à Paris,* 3.

92. BnF Lb39 9193, *Départ de M. d'Artois pour se rendre à Paris,* 2, 8, 5.

93. "Nouvelles des Provinces," *L'Ami du Roi,* July 2, 1790, n°42.

94. Levenson-Gower Sutherland, "July 2, 1790," 8.

95. BnF Lb39 9193, *Départ de M. d'Artois pour se rendre à Paris,* 5–8, 14.

96. Godard, *Exposé des Travaux de l'Assemblée-Générale,* 82–83.

97. *AP,* 19:367.

98. *La Chronique de Paris,* October 18, 1790, n°291.

99. *La Chronique de Paris,* October 18, 1790, n°291.

100. *La Chronique de Paris,* October 21, 1790, n°294.

101. BnF Estampes M 100435.

102. BnF Lb39 9451, *Adresse aux dames parisiennes. Le voyage à St. Cloud. Paris ou Le Service du Bout de l'An, Pour faire suite au Voyage de Versailles* (Paris: Imprimerie de J. Legueum, 1790), 3.

103. BnF Lb39 9451, *Adresse aux dames parisiennes. Le voyage à St. Cloud,* 4, 7.

104. Ambrogio Caiani, *Louis XVI and the French Revolution, 1789–1792* (Cambridge: Cambridge University Press, 2012), 94.

105. AN C 48, n° 476; *AP,* December 30, 1790, 21:719.

106. *La Chronique de Paris,* January 1, 1791, n°1.

107. August Friedrich Ferdinand von Kotzebue, *Sketch of the Life and Literary Career of Augustus Von Kotzebue with the Journal of His Tour to Paris at the Close of the Year 1790,* trans. Anne Plumptre, December 31, 1790 (London: C. Whittingham, 1800), 303.

108. François-Alphonse Aulard, ed., *La Société des Jacobins: Recueil de documents,* vol. 2, January 1791 (Paris: Librairie Jouaust, 1899), 53–55.

109. *La Chronique de Paris*, January 2, 1791, n° 3.

110. *La Chronique de Paris*, February 25, 1791, n° 56.

111. Jean Loup de Vireau-Beavoir and Giuseppe de Lama, "February 14, 1791," in *La Révolution française racontée par un diplomate étranger. Correspondance du bailli de Virieu, ministre plénipotentiaire de Parme (1788–1793)*, ed. Emmanuel Henri Vicomte de Grouchy and Antoine Guillois (Paris: E. Flammarion, 1903), 235–236.

112. BnF Lb40 1245 *Discours adressé au roi par les dames de la Halle, membres de la Société Fraternelle, dont, le 14 février 1791, elles sont venues donner lecture au Conseil-Général de la Commune, qui en a ordonné l'impression à la distribution* (Paris: Imprimerie de Lottin l'aîné & J. R. Lottin, 1791), 3.

113. *La Chronique de Paris*, February 19, 1791, n° 50.

114. BnF Lb40 1245 *Discours adressé au roi par les dames de la Halle, membres de la Société Fraternelle, le 14 Février 1791*, 3.

115. James Rutledge, *Le Creuset, Ouvrage Politique et Critique*, March 3, 1791, n°18, vol. 1, (Paris, 1791), 345.

116. Levenson-Gower Sutherland, "February 25, 1791," in Browning, ed., *The Despatches of Earl Gower*, 63.

117. Vireau-Beavoir and Lama, "February 28, 1791," in Grouchy and Guillois, *La Révolution française racontée par un diplomate étranger*, 248–249.

118. Levenson-Gower Sutherland, "February 25, 1791," 64.

119. Vireau-Beavoir and Lama, "February 28, 1791." Meanwhile, the king's aunts encountered many obstacles in their flight. The citizens of Moret stopped them. It took 100 troops and the mayor's men to force open the city gate so they could continue. Then, the inhabitants of Arnay-le-Duc momentarily retained the aunts because they did not have passports from the National Assembly.

120. BnF NUMM- 42495, Hébert, *Grande colère du Père Duchesne contre les jean-foutres de calomniateurs des Dames de la halle*, 5, 6, 1–2.

121. Aulard, *La Société des Jacobins*, March 2, 1791, vol. 2, 157.

122. E. Claire Cage, *Unnatural Frenchmen: The Politics of Priestly Celibacy and Marriage, 1720–1815* (Charlottesville: University of Virginia Press, 2015), 5.

123. *La Chronique de Paris*, April 9, 1791, n° 99. Michael Fitzsimmons, "The National Assembly and the Invention of Citizenship," in *The French Revolution and the Meaning of Citizenship*, ed. Renée Waldinger, Philip Dawson, and Isser Woloch (Westport, CT: Greenwood Press, 1992), 33.

124. Vireau-Beavoir and Lama, "January 2, 1791," in Grouchy and Guillois, *La Révolution française racontée par un diplomate étranger*, 235.

125. Levenson-Gower Sutherland, "April 15, 1791," in Browning, ed., *The Despatches of Earl Gower*, 79.

126. *Le Courrier de Paris dans les 83 Départements*, April 6, 1791; *Le Courrier de Paris dans les 83 Départements*, April 3, 1791.

127. *Révolutions de Paris*, April 9–16, 1791, n °92.

128. BnF Lb39 5505, *Liste des Culs Aristocrates et Anti-Constitutionnels, qui ont été fouettés hier au soir à tour de bras, par les Dames de la Halle, et du Faubourg Saint-Antoine* (Paris: Imprimerie Patriotique, 1791), 3.

129. Only one pamphlet asserts the Dames spanked priests and monks whom they also found in the religious houses. BnF Ld⁴ 7148, *Liste de toutes les sœurs & dévotes qui ont été fouettées par les Dames de Marchés des différents Quartiers de Paris, avec leur nom, celui de leur Paroisse, & un détail très-véritable de toutes leurs aventures avec les Curés Vicaires à Habitués desdites Paroisses* (Paris: L'imprimerie de Tremblay, 1791), 2–4.

130. BnF Estampes, Collection de Vinck 3376, "La Discipline patriotique ou le fanatisme corrigée," watercolor, reproduced in Antoine De Baecque, *La caricature révolutionnaire* (Italy, Presses de CNRS et l'imprimerie Arti Grafiche Vincenzo Bona, 1988), 98–99. Journals reported the nun lost her buttock in an "indecent" and unrepeatable "accident." BnF Ld⁴ 7148, *Liste de toutes les sœurs & dévotes qui ont été fouettées par les Dames des Marchés*, 8.

131. Voltaire's quote appears on several images to condemn the nuns. See BnF De Vinck 3497, "Fait miraculeux arrivé à Paris l'an de salut de 1791, le six avril," 1791.

132. BnF MFILM-8-Lc2-161, *Le Courrier de Paris dans les 83 Départements*, April 3, 137.
133. BnF Lb39 5505, *Liste des Culs Aristocrates et Anti-Constitutionnels*, 6.
134. One sees a similar motif and title in BnF Estampes P23562, "La Correction Républicaine." The image shows two French generals whipping the bare bottoms of the Duke of York and Cobourg with switches. The drawing figuratively uses individuals to reify the military violence and political victory. The images of the Dames whipping the nuns likewise depict discrete violent "corrections" as well as a larger ideological one. The only other revolutionary image I have encountered in which a woman is being spanked is Carnavalet, Histoire 8 Chemise C couleurs G 23922, "Une femme de condition, fouettée pour avoir craché sur le portrait de Mr Necker." Three men spank the woman while men and women watch at the Palais Royal.
135. *Liste de toutes les sœurs & dévotes qui ont été fouettées par les Dames des Marchés*, 1.
136. *Révolutions de France*, n°73, reproduced in *Révolutions de France et de Brabant par Camille Desmoulins*, ed. Gary Kates (Frankfurt: Antiquariat und Verlag Keip GmbH, 1989), 355.
137. BnF Estampes, Collection de Vinck 3376, "La Discipline patriotique ou le fanatisme corrigée," watercolor, reproduced in De Baecque, *La caricature révolutionnaire*, 98–99.
138. BnF Lb39 5505, *Liste des Culs Aristocrates et Anti-Constitutionnels*, 5, 6.
139. BnF Ld4 7148, *Liste de toutes les sœurs & dévotes qui ont été fouettées par les Dames des Marchés*, 3.
140. *La Chronique de Paris*, April 9, 1791, n° 99.
141. *Le Courrier de Paris dans les 83 Départements*, April 10, 1791.
142. BnF Estampes P22034, "Fait miraculeux arrivé à Paris l'an de salut de 1791 le six avril."
143. Saint Benoît Labre embraced mortification and was recently canonized.
144. *Le Courrier de Paris dans les 83 Départements*, April 12, 1791, 186–187.
145. BHVP # 31 598 (n°2) in 8°, "Grand détail concernant les dévots et les dévotes qui ont été fouettés par les dames de la Halle à Paris" (Paris: Baudouin) (likely April 1791). Jean-François Baudouin printed most of the 20,000 revolutionary decrees for which there is a database. See Anne Simonin and Pierre Serna, *Décrets et Lois 1789–1795: Collection Baudouin* http://collection-baudouin.univ-paris1.fr/ (accessed August 1, 2017).
146. BnF Lb39 5505, *Liste des Culs Aristocrates et Anti-Constitutionnels*, 2, 4–5, 7–8. In contrast to these extraordinary pamphlets, popular female violence is largely absent in eighteenth-century police records. See Clara Chevalier, "Des émeutières passées sous silence? 'invisibilisation de la violence des femmes au prisme du genre (Paris, 1775),'" in *Penser la violence des femmes*, ed. Coline Cardi and Geneviève Pruvost (Paris: La Découverte, 2012), 85–94.
147. BnF Estampes 3494.
148. *Révolutions de Paris*, April 9–16, 1791, n° 92.
149. BnF Estampes Réserve Fol QB-201 (124), "Le Fanatisme corrigée ou la Dicipline [*sic*] patriotique," (Paris: Chez Villeneuve, 1791), etching, 14.5 × 11cm.
150. On nuns, celibacy, and motherhood, see Mita Choudhury, *Convents and Nuns in Eighteenth-Century French Politics and Culture* (Ithaca: Cornell University Press, 2004), 5.
151. On caricature and visual propaganda during the Revolution see De Baecque, *La caricature révolutionnaire*.
152. Physiognomy was so important to self-presentation that it shaped wig-styling in the eighteenth century. See Michael Kwass, "Big Hair: A Wig History of Consumption in Eighteenth-Century France," *American Historical Review* 111, no. 3 (June 2006): 631–659.
153. *Le Courrier de Paris dans les 83 Départements*, April 10, 1791, 154.
154. The *Liste* concedes that one male citizen, caught up in the excitement, slapped some of the Daughters of the Precious Blood. BnF Lb39 5505, *Liste des Culs Aristocrates et Anti-Constitutionnels*.
155. *Révolutions de Paris*, April 9–16, 1791, n °92.
156. The 1762 French Academy Dictionary defines "verge" primarily as a "Sorte de petite baguette longue & flexible." However, the fourth definition is "Le membre viril." *Dictionnaire de l'Académie française*, 4th Edition (1762), Project ARTFL, http://artfl-project.uchicago.edu/content/dictionnaires-dautrefois.
157. *Le Courrier de Paris dans les 83 Départements*, April 10, 1791.

158. *Révolutions de Paris*, April 9–16, 1791, n °92.
159. These images also evoke illustrations of domestic violence. See Katie Jarvis, "'Patriotic Discipline': Cloistered Behinds, Public Judgment, and Female Violence in Revolutionary Paris," in *Practiced Citizenship: Women, Gender, and the State in Modern France*, ed. Nimisha Barton and Richard Hopkins (Lincoln: University of Nebraska Press, 2019); For more on "unruly women" and gendered inversions, see Natalie Zemon Davis, "Women on Top" in *Society and Culture in Early Modern France* (Stanford: Stanford University Press, 1975), 131–151.
160. *La Chronique de Paris*, April 9, 1791, n° 99.
161. *Le Moniteur Universel*, April 14, 1791, n° 104.
162. *La Chronique de Paris*, April 11, 1791, n° 101.
163. "Extrait des registres de l'Assemblée du manège et de celle des Jacobins Saint-Honoré, fait le 25 mai 1791," reprinted in Aulard, *La Société des Jacobins*, May 25, 1791, vol. 2, 456.
164. *La Chronique de Paris*, April 16, 1791, n° 106. In Year II, the government ordered teachers to acquire a *certificat de civisme* to influence burgeoning citizens. Isser Woloch, "The Right to Primary Education in the French Revolution: From Theory to Practice," in Waldinger et al., *The French Revolution and the Meaning of Citizenship*, 140. The memory of the Dames' activism reverberated well into the fall. In November, the Filles du Croix refused the oath and the Commune ejected them from their convent. However, nonjuring priests convinced the counterrevolutionary nuns to return to their posts and teach young girls. The panicked curé of Saint-Paul and warned the department that it was urgent "to take rigorous measures for the sake of public tranquility. The poissardes' heads are <u>heating up</u> [emphasis in the original]; a longer delay can have upsetting consequences." AN S 4688, November 21, 1791, "Mémoire de M. Brugière, curé de Saint-Paul, au Directoire du Département."
165. Vireau-Beavoir and Lama, "April 24, 1791," in Grouchy and Guillois, *La Révolution française racontée par un diplomate étranger*, 263.
166. Micah Alpaugh, *Non-Violence and the French Revolution*, 87.
167. *Révolutions de Paris*, April 16–23, 1791, n° 93.
168. For more details, see Timothy Tackett, *When the King Took Flight* (Cambridge, MA: Harvard University Press, 2003).
169. *AP*, June 22, 1791, 2:iv.
170. Stephen Weston, Letter XXXIX, August 1791, in *Letters from Paris during the Summer of 1791* (London: J. Debrett, Piccadilly, and W. Clarke, 1792), 225.
171. *Révolutions de Paris*, August 20–27, 1791, n° 111.
172. *Révolutions de Paris*, October 15–22, 1791, Reporting on October 9, 1791 session, n° 119.
173. On August 18, all religious communities and confraternities were ordered to disband. Colin Jones, *The Longman Companion to the French Revolution* (Abington, UK: Routledge, 2014), 17.
174. BnF Le29 1729 *Adresse des Dames de la Halle, à l'Assemblée nationale, séance du 27 août 1791* (Paris: Imprimerie Nationale, 1791), 2; See also AN C 75, n°745, August 27, 1791.
175. BnF Le29 1729 *Adresse des Dames de la Halle, à l'Assemblée nationale, séance du 27 août 1791*, 2.
176. *La Chronique de Paris*, October 20, 1791, n°293.
177. AN C 139, n° 97; *Procès-verbal de l'Assemblée nationale*, vol. 1 (Paris: Imprimerie Nationale, 1791), 172, 173; *AP*, October 19, 1791, 34:289.
178. BnF Estampes P22731, "Les Parques Nationales Parisiennes."
179. BnF Estampes P22731, "Les Parques Nationales Parisiennes."
180. There were 434 Jacobin clubs across France in July 1791. Michael Kennedy, *The Jacobin Clubs in the French Revolution, 1793–1795* (New York: Berghahn Books, 2000), 5.
181. *La Chronique de Paris*, January 26, 1792, n° 26, "Aux Parisiens & Parisiennes."
182. AN C 149 n°252; *AP*, May 21, 1792, 43:621.
183. AN C 152, n°270; *AP*, June 11, 1792, 24:80.
184. C. J. Mitchell asserts that although only 284 of over 600 deputies appeared on the Legislative Assembly's roll call for August 10, attendance records for its committees and later group

votes indicate that deputy attrition rates were relatively low before the National Convention replaced the Assembly. Mitchell, *The French Legislative Assembly of 1791* (Leiden: Brill, 1988), 261–263.

185. As recorded in *Révolutions de Paris*, September 29–October 6, 1792, n° 169.

186. The pamphlet, *Bréviaire des dames parisiennes pour la défense de Louis XVI* by De Salignac was quoted in *Révolutions de Paris*, January 19–26, 1793, n°185.

187. *La Chronique de Paris*, October 10, 1789, n°47.

188. AN F⁷ 3688³, Charmont, reprinted in Pierre Caron, *Paris pendant la Terreur: Rapports des agents secrets*, vol. 1, 279.

Chapter 3

1. BnF Département des Estampes, M 100995, "18 septembre Proclamation de la première Constitution"; M 100996, "Proclamation de la Constitution Place du Marché des Innocens le 14 septembre 1791"; M 100997, Detail of "Proclamation de la Constitution Place du Marché des Innocens le 14 septembre 1791."

2. Alfred Franklin, *Dictionnaire Historique des Arts, Métiers et Professions depuis le Treizième siècle* (Paris: Chez H. Welter, 1906).

3. I borrow the phrase "particular interests" from the revolutionaries' vocabulary. For the revolutionaries, "particular" referred to a discreet individual within the general will. "Private," in contrast, disconnected the individual from the public body politic and suggested a government based on the majority interests of private interests.

4. AN F¹² 1266, "Rapport de Cen Bulliot Lacorée demeurait à Paris, fait passé au ministre avec sa lettre du 14 courant, des observations sur l'établissement d'un meilleur ordre dans les marchés de Paris." 14 floréal an 8.

5. I am indebted to Clare Crowston for this observation.

6. James Livesey argues, "'Utility' was an abstract concept through which differing conceptions of the common good could be articulated and compete." I argue that the adjective "public" was just as malleable and value-laden. Since revolutionary utility is directed toward the public, debates over utility shed just as much light on its moving target. When the revolutionaries spoke of public utility, they inherently imagined, defined, and located the public. Utility was a mutable concept precisely because the revolutionaries intertwined it with their fluctuating interpretations of the public. James Livesey, *Making Democracy in the French Revolution* (Cambridge: Harvard University Press, 2001), 72.

7. I have only included the dimensions for the retail markets of the central Halles in this calculation. Innocents: 4000m²; Tonnellerie and a portion of rue Montmartre: 190m²; Piliers: 18 m²; Pointe St. Eustache: 185m²; Carreau des Halles: 1800m²; Rue Fromagerie: 258m²; right angle in front of the halle aux draps: 348m²; AdP D.Q¹⁰ 39, Département de la Seine, Bureau des 3e & 4e arrondissements, "Les Droits qui se perçevoient anciennement, qui se perçoivent actuellement ou se percevoir dans les différentes communes de la République à raison des foires, marchés, &a."

8. In a similar vein, Suzanne Desan has examined how revolutionaries and aristocrats projected and worked out their various aspirations on land in Ohio. Desan, "Transatlantic Spaces of Revolution: The French Revolution, Sciotomanie, and American Lands," *Journal of Early Modern History* 12 (2008): 467–505.

9. Marcel Hénaff and Tracy Strong, "The Conditions of Public Space: Vision, Speech, Theatricality" in *Public Space and Democracy*, Marcel Hénaff and Tracy Strong, eds. (Minneapolis: University of Minnesota Press, 2001), 15.

10. The 1762 Dictionary of the French Academy defines "Lieux publics" as "Les lieux où tout le monde a droit d'aller." On the other hand, the dictionary links "l'autorité publique" to officials who act "sous l'autorité du Prince." "Public," in *Dictionnaire de l'Académie française*, 4th Edition (1762), Project ARTFL, http://artfl-project.uchicago.edu/content/dictionnaires-dautrefois.

11. BnFZ Le Senne 2974, Perrot, "Voierie," *Dictionnaire de voierie*, 438.

12. Rene Marion, "The Dames de la Halle: Community and Authority in Early Modern Paris" (PhD diss., Johns Hopkins University, 1994), 21.

13. AdPP D^B 258, Dossier: Voierie, Échoppes, Démolition des Échoppes & Maisons, "Ordonnance du Bureau des Finances de la Généralité de Paris Concernant les Échoppes" (Paris: Imprimerie Royale, 1776).

14. For histories concerning the construction of physical structures in les Halles and its neighborhood, see: Anne Lombard-Jourdan, *Les Halles de Paris et leur Quartier (1137–1969)* (Paris: École Nationale des Chartes, 2009); Jean Martineau, *Les Halles de Paris des Origines à 1789: Évolution matérielle, juridique, et économique* (Paris: Éditions Montchrestien, 1960); Françoise Boudon, André Chastel, Hélène Couzy, and Françoise Hamon, *Système de l'Architecture Urbaine: Le Quartier des Halles à Paris*, vol. 1 (Paris: Éditions du Centre National de la Recherche Scientifique, 1977); M. Baurit, *Les Halles de Paris des romains à nos jours* (Paris: Chez M. Baurit, 1956); David Garrioch, *The Making of Revolutionary Paris* (Berkeley: University of California Press, 2002).

15. AN Q^1 1183, "Lettres Patentes du Roi, qui ordonnent la construction d'une nouvelle Halle à la Marée à Paris, le 21 août 1784."

16. AdPP D^B 258, "Lettres Patentes du Roi, Portant suppression des Échoppes de la Ville de Paris, 27 mai 1784" (Chez Simon, 1784).

17. On the varieties of royal domain and its historical alienability or inalienability, see Rafe Blaufarb, *The Great Demarcation: The French Revolution and the Invention of Modern Property* (New York: Oxford University Press, 2016), 136–138.

18. AN Q^1 1186, Quartier des marchés, "La Copie informe d'un arrêt du Consigne portant Bail Emphytéotique au profit de Jean Baptiste Doré," September 30, 1784.

19. AN Q^1 1183, "Lettres Patentes du Roi, qui ordonnent la construction d'une nouvelle Halle à la Marée à Paris, le 21 août 1784."

20. AdP D.Q^10 1, Dossier n°572: Picard, "Réclamations pour la démolition d'échoppes dont il était propriétaire aux Halles," 1674-an III; BnF F-21216 (31), "Arrêt du Conseil d'État du Roi, qui fixe l'époque à laquelle seront démolies les échoppes du parquet à la Marée, du Carreau du Pilori & du Marché aux Poirées" (Paris: L'imprimerie Royale, 1786); AN Q^1 1187, Les Halles, Renseignements sur divers places et échoppes, Bureau de Liquidation de Maisons et Échoppes à Paris, 1786.

21. AN Q^1 1186, Quartier des marchés, "La Copie informe d'un arrêt du Consigne portant Bail Emphytéotique au profite de Jean Baptiste Doré," September 30, 1784.

22. AN Q^1 1183, "Lettres Patentes du Roi, qui ordonnent la construction d'une nouvelle Halle à la Marée à Paris, le 21 août 1784."

23. Dufriche-Valazé also maintained, "the establishment of the Halles dates from the first progress of society and from the foundations of cities." *AP*, November 29, 1792, 53:673.

24. *Révolutions de Paris*, April 9–16 1791, n°92.

25. *Révolutions de Paris*, June 23–30, 1792, n°166.

26. *Révolutions de Paris*, March 13–20, 1790, n°36.

27. *Révolutions de Paris*, April 9–16, 1791, n°92.

28. *Révolutions de Paris*, June 23–30, 1792, n°155.

29. "D'instructions pour MM. les électeurs nommés par l'assemblée du tiers-état, tenue en l'église de Saint-Gervais, commencée le 21 avril 1789," in *AP*, 5:312.

30. *AP*, December 9, 1789, 10:479. "Observations relatives au droit féodal de la province de Bretagne sur les droits féodaux supprimés sans indemnité."

31. *Révolutions de Paris*, March 13–20, 1790, n°36.

32. Blaufarb, *The Great Demarcation*, 121.

33. *AP*, November 8, 1790, 20:328; *Révolutions de Paris*, November 13–20, 1790, n°71. The Assembly also charged the police with surveilling foodstuffs "for public sale." *AP*, August 16, 1790, 18:112.

34. *AP*, February 10, 1792, 38:382.

35. *La Chronique de Paris*, September 1, 1792.

36. AdPP AA 88, Dossier: Butte des Moulins, Janvier 1792–Octobre 1792, "Le procès-verbal des commissaires de police, 4 juin 1792," n°376.

37. *AP*, February 10, 1792, 38:383.

38. AdP D.4 U^1 29, Dossier: Police: Vendémiaire, Pluviôse et Prairial, an VII, Citoyenne Beau contre Aimée Capet, 1 vendémiaire an VII.

39. In February 1791, the deputies also promoted commercial circulation by abolishing taxes on moving goods between two territories and entrance taxes into cities. *Révolutions de Paris,* February 19–26, 1791, n°85; *Révolutions de Paris,* November 13–20, 1790, n°84.

40. AdP D.4 U¹ 29, Justice de Paix du 4ème Arrondissement Ancien, Section Marché des Innocents, Dossier: Police: Vendémaire, Pluviôse et Prairial, an VII, Inspecteur Baude contre Citoyenne Duval et sa fille, 13 pluviôse an 7.

41. *AP,* December 22, 1789, 10:725.

42. AdPP D^B 387, "Municipalité de Paris par le Mairie et Les Officiers Municipaux. Extrait des Délibérations du Corps Municipal," May 26, 1791.

43. *AP,* April 30, 1793, 13:634.

44. Perrot, "Voierie," in *Dictionnaire de voierie,* 438.

45. Perrot, "Place," in *Dictionnaire de voierie,* 343; AdPP D^B 387, Assemblée des Représentans de la Commune de Paris, Comité de Police, "Affiche du samedi 14 novembre 1789."

46. *La Chronique de Paris,* May 23, 1790, n°143.

47. BHVP in 8° #959 739, "Démolition totale des harangues de la halle, faite hier au soir par le peuple" (Paris: LL Girard). From context, I date this pamphlet in late May or June 1790. Records of the event do not leave clues as to who was among the mixed group of merchants.

48. BHVP in 8°, #959 739, "Démolition totale des harangues de la halle, faite hier au soir par le peuple."

49. AdPP D^B 258, Dossier: Voirie, Échoppes, Démolition des Échoppes & maisons, "Arrêt du Conseil d'état du Roi, qui ordonne que les Propriétaires de maisons & échoppes supprimées à Paris, remettront leurs titres à M. le Contrôleur général, pour être procédé à la liquidation des indemnités qui peuvent leur être dues, 8 août 1790."

50. BnF F-23631 (891), "Lettres Patentes du Roi, sur un Décret de l'Assemblé Nationale, du 26 Juillet 1790, relatif aux droits de Propriété & de Voyerie sur les chemins publics, rues & places de villages, bourgs ou villes, & arbres dépendans," August 15, 1790 (Paris: Chez Nyon, 1790), 1.

51. *AP,* August 9, 1790, 17:692.

52. AdPP AA 166 Luxembourg, Procès-verbal des commissaires de police, May 10, 1791, "Déclaration concernant les troubles causés au marché de la place Maubert par les poissardes qui ont abattu les échoppes et paraissent disposées à en faire autant dans le marché Saint-Germain."

53. BHVP in 8°, #10 073 (T. II, n°57), "Municipalité de Paris par le maire et les officiers municipaux, Extrait du registre des délibérations du Corps municipal. Du samedi 24 septembre 1791 (Paris: imprimerie Lottin l'aîné et JR. Lottin, 1791), 2–4; BHVP in 8° 10 073 (t. II, n°59), Municipalité de Paris par le maire et les Officiers-Municipaux, "Arrêté sur les échoppes et étalages fixes et mobiles," Extrait du registre des délibérations du Corps municipal, October 3, 1791 (Paris: Lottin l'aîné & J.R.-Lottin, 1791), 2. Under the previous system, the king had similarly charged voyers (collectors of dues on the *voie*) with the responsibility of regulating dangers that structures might have posed on the *voie*. See BnF F-23675 (99), Parlement de Paris, Arrêts de Règlement du Parlement de Paris, "Concernant les Droits de Voierie, des 21 juillet & 27 août 1779" (Paris: Imprimerie de Ph. D. Pierres, 1779), 9–10.

54. AdPP AA 68, Commissaires de police (Arsenal), November 5, 1791, "Procès-verbal de transport du commissaire de police de la section de l'Arsenal, dans toutes les rues et places de la section, afin de mettre à exécution les arrêtés de la Municipalité des 3, 14, et 29 octobre."

55. *AP,* February 17, 1791, 23:230.

56. BHVP in 8° #10 073 (t. II n°59), "Municipalité de Paris . . . Du lundi 3 octobre 1791." For a discussion of charity in the marketplace during the Old Regime see Marion, "Community and Authority."

57. AdPP D^B 258, Dossier: Voirie, Échoppes, Démolition des Échoppes & Maisons, partial copy from *Actes de la Commune,* October 21, 1791, 295–296.

58. *AP,* October 18, 1791, 34:268.

59. AdPP D^B 258, Dossier: Voirie, Échoppes Démolition des Échoppes & Maisons dans différents lieux de Paris et démolition du Bâtiment du Pilori, a filed copy from *Actes de la Commune,* in éclaircissements of October 21, 1791.

60. AN F^{12} 1239, Dossier: Foires et Marchés, Paris 1705-an II, "Lettre du procureur Gen. Syndic du dept. de Paris relative à une demande présentée par les femmes du Marché aux poissons de l'abbaye St. Germain pour la considération de leurs places, malgré la construction proposée de 3 Corps de gardes, 16 octobre 1791"; "Lettre de M. Roederer, procureur général syndic du Département au président du Comité du commerce, accusant réception du mémoire présenté à l'Assemblée nationale par les Dames du marché aux poissons de la ci-devant Abbaye-de-Saint-Germain . . . ."

61. AdPP D^B 258, Dossier: Voirie, Échoppes Démolition des Échoppes & Maisons, copy from *Actes de la Commune*, éclaircissements of October 29, 1791, Letter from the Directory of the Department of Paris to the Municipal Assembly concerning the marchandes des quais de la Ferraille, de l'infante et de l'école, 445–446.

62. Sigismond Lacroix, ed., *Actes de la Commune de Paris pendant la Révolution*, October 29, 1791, series 2, vol. 12 (New York: AMS Press, 1974), 425.

63. *AP*, November 3, 1791, 34:622.

64. *Actes de la Commune*, October 29, 1791, 2, 12:425.

65. BHVP, in 8° #10073c (tome II, n°68), Municipalité de Paris par le maire et les officiers municipaux, "Extrait du registre des délibérations du Corps municipal Du vendredi 4 novembre 1791 . . . ." (Paris: Lottin l'aîné et J.R. Lottin, 1791).

66. BnF LK7 31662, "Adresse à M. le Maire de Paris, ou à son lieutenant, pour les marchands merciers-fripiers-tailleurs, et autres habituellement attachés au marché des SS Innocens" (Paris: Imprimerie de Hérault, 1790).

67. AN E 2653, fol. 33, 74.

68. AN E 2653, fol. 33, 74; AN X^{1b} 9084 See "Lettres patentes" 8 février 1789 for the reference indicating that the 1776 edict must serve as the parameters for the special permissions. The quote and explanation of 1776 qualification requirements appear here: AdPP, D^B 258, "Ordonnance du Bureau des Finances de la Généralité de Paris Concernant les Échoppes, 1 février 1776" (Paris: Imprimerie Royale, 1776).

69. AN E 2653, fol. 33, 74; X^{1b} 9084, "Lettres patentes" of February 8, 1789, March 14, 1789, April 21, 1790.

70. BHVP in 4° 131912, Municipalité de Paris, Département de police. "le M. le Maire, M. le lieutenant de Maire et MM. les Conseillers, Administration règlement provisoire, pour le Marché des SS Innocents," May 2, 1790 (Paris: Lottin l'aîné & Lottin, 1790).

71. BnF F-23631 (891), "Lettres Patentes du Roi, sur un Décret de l'Assemblé Nationale, du 26 juillet 1790, relatif aux droits de Propriété & de Voyerie sur les chemins publics, rues & places de villages, bourgs ou villes, & arbres dépendans," August 15, 1790 (Paris: Chez Nyon, 1790), 1.

72. *Révolutions de Paris*, July 10, 1790, n°52. Report on the session of June 27, 1790.

73. *AP*, August 9, 1790, 17:696.

74. *AP*, March 6, 1791, 23:710.

75. *Actes de la Commune*, October 29, 1791, 2, 7:427.

76. AN E 2653, fol. 33, 74; AN X^{1b} 9084 See "Lettres patentes" 8 février 1789; AdPP, D^B 258, "Ordonnance du Bureau des Finances de la Généralité de Paris Concernant les Échoppes, 1 février 1776" (Paris: Imprimerie Royale, 1776).

77. Regardless of these legal divisions, all the Dames des Halles had shared a collective identity driven by occupational and cultural cohesion. See chapters 1 and 2.

78. For other retail merchants also affected by the parasol issue, see: "Adresse à l'Assemblée nationale, pour les marchands forains et autres de la Halle de Paris, dont l'emplacement du cimetière des Innocents fait partie, renvoyée au Comité de commerce et d'agriculture le 14 novembre 1790," reprinted in *Actes de la Commune*, October 29, 1791, 2, 7:450–451, and BnF Lk7-31662, "Adresse à M. Le Maire de Paris pour les marchands-fripiers-tailleurs, et autres habituellement attachés au marché des SS. Innocents" (Paris: Impr. de Herault, 1790). Throughout the records, pamphlets, and petitions on the parasol issue, Thibault, Thibauld, and Thibaut all refer to the same parasol renter.

79. AdP VD* 8, #912 and BnF Manuscrits Nouv. Acq. Fr. 2651, fol 187.

80. *AP*, May 5, 1792, 43:8.

81. *AP*, May 21, 1792, 43:641.

82. *AP*, May 18, 1792, 43:534.
83. AdP D.Q^{10} 1392, Dossier 3048 Innocents (Marché des).
84. Frédéric Braesch, *La Commune du dix août 1792: Étude sur l'histoire de Paris du 20 juin au 2 décembre 1792* (Paris: Librairie Hachette et Cie, 1911), 428.
85. Braesch, *La Commune du dix août 1792*, 392. Slavin argues the Girondins "applauded the September massacres until they realized that indignation over them could be utilized as a weapon against their enemies." Slavin, *The Making of an Insurrection: Parisian Sections and the Gironde* (Harvard University Press, 1986), 4, 7. Patrice Higonnet argues that although the Girondins and the Montagnards were both of bourgeois stock, the Girondins became wary of popular violence first in the fall of 1792 because they came to power first. On the other hand, the Montagnards, as the minority group, were more willing to continue to draw from sans-culotte support. The Girondins were more likely to be sons of businessmen than Montagnards, who were more frequently the sons of lawyers. This divide may have made the Girondins more inclined to support free market policies. Patrice Higonnet, "The Social and Cultural Antecedents of Revolutionary Discontinuity: Montagnards and Girondins," *The English Historical Review* 396 (1985): 516, 526.
86. AN C 167, n°411; *AP*, September 12, 1792, 51:578.
87. AN C 163, n°377, September 12, 1792.
88. *Révolutions de Paris*, September 15–22, 1792, n°167.

Chapter 4

1. AN C 149, n°252, "Compliment adressé par les Dames de la Halle à l'Assemblée législative, en remettant leur don patriotique pour les frais de la guerre, consistant en une monnaie particulière frappée au nom des sieurs Lefèvre, Lesage et Cie"; *AP*, May 21, 1792, 43:621.
2. For a general overview of the revolutionary assignat, see S. E. Harris, *The Assignats* (London: Oxford University Press, 1930) and Jean Morini-Comby, *Les Assignats: Révolution et Inflation* (Paris: Nouvelle Librairie Nationale, 1925). On the long history and evolution of IOUs, see Thomas Sargent and François Velde, *The Big Problem of Small Change* (Princeton: Princeton University Press, 2002). On Parisian banks and financial companies, see Jean Bouchary, *Les Compagnies financières à Paris à la fin du XVIIIe siècle*, vols. 1 and 2 (Paris: Librairie des Sciences Politiques et Sociales Marcel Rivière et Cie, 1941). With the proliferation of numerous promissory notes, counterfeiting became a major problem. For details on the situation in Paris, see Jean Bouchary, *Les Faux-Monnayeurs sous la Révolution Française* (Paris: Librairie Marcel Rivière et Cie, 1946). Georges Depeyrot has assembled a collection of monetary laws and legislative decrees in *Monnaie et Papier-Monnaie Pendant la Révolution (1789–1803)* (Paris: Maison Florange, 1996). Rebecca Spang has closely analyzed the players who devised and produced the currency. Rebecca Spang, *Stuff and Money in the Time of the French Revolution* (Cambridge: Harvard University Press, 2015).
3. Spang, *Stuff and Money*, 74.
4. Jeff Horn, *Economic Development in Early Modern France: The Privilege of Liberty, 1650–1820* (Cambridge: Cambridge University Press, 2015), 21.
5. Clare Haru Crowston, *Fabricating Women: The Seamstresses of Old Regime France, 1675–1791* (Durham: Duke University Press, 2001), 257; Steven Kaplan, *La Fin des corporations*, trans. Béatrice Vierne (Paris: Fayard, 2001), 600.
6. Recent work has demonstrated that eighteenth-century guilds were dynamic organisms during Louis XVI's reign. Jeff Horn has shown how masters negotiated market demands and evolving economic policies. Jeff Horn, *The Path Not Taken: French Industrialization in the Age of Revolution, 1750–1830* (Cambridge, MA: The MIT Press, 2006). Scholars such as Steven Kaplan, Michael Sonenscher, Clare Crowston, and Michael Fitzsimmons have emphasized how guild relations were shaped by litigation, employment patterns, reactions to state rationalization, and tensions among masters and workers. Kaplan, *La Fin des corporations*; Michael Sonenscher, *Work and Wages: Natural Law, Politics and the Eighteenth-Century French Trades* (Cambridge: Cambridge University Press, 1989); Crowston, *Fabricating Women*; Michael Fitzsimmons, *From Artisan to Worker: Guilds, the French State, and the Organization of Labor, 1776–1821* (Cambridge: Cambridge University Press, 2010). Earlier research focused on the

degree to which guilds fed prerevolutionary social tensions or were viable representative units. George Rudé and Liana Vardi have argued that conflicts within outdated hierarchies of masters and journeymen drove the Revolution forward as a social engine. However, other scholars like Gail Bossenga, William Sewell, and Michael Sonescher make the case that the guilds were not anachronistic in 1789, since they still successfully protected their members' commercial interests. They argue that few revolutionaries sought to destroy immediately these socioeconomic alliances. George Rudé, *The Crowd in the French Revolution* (London: Oxford University Press, 1967); Liana Vardi, "The Abolition of the Guilds during the French Revolution," in *French Historical Studies* 15 (1988): 717; Gail Bossenga, "Protecting Merchants: Guilds and Commercial Capitalism in Eighteenth-Century France," *French Historical Studies*, 15 (1988), 695, 703; William Sewell, *Work and Revolution in France: The Language of Labor from the Old Regime to 1848* (Cambridge: Cambridge University Press, 1979); Michael Sonenscher, "Les sans-culottes de l'an II: repenser le langage du travail dans la France révolutionnaire," in *Annales. Économies, Sociétés, Civilisations*, 5 (1985): 1087-1108. Other research has spotlighted how Louis XVI changed corporate life by opening all guild memberships to women. This echoed the eighteenth-century trend of more women holding personal occupations. Crowston, *Fabricating Women*, 209. The number of women who listed a profession separate from that of their husband in tax rolls, judicial testimony, and police documents increased throughout the eighteenth century as women came to identify more with their occupation. See James Collins, "Women and the Birth of Consumer Capitalism," in *Women and Work in Eighteenth-Century France*, ed. Daryl Hafter and Nina Kushner (Baton Rouge: Louisiana State University Press, 2015), 163; Daryl Hafter, "French Industrial Growth in Women's Hands," in Hafter and Kushner, *Women and Work*, 195; Daryl Hafter and Nina Kushner, "Introduction," in Hafter and Kushner, *Women and Work*, 3; Dominique Godineau, *Les Femmes dans la France moderne, XVIe-XVIIIe siècle* (Paris: Armand Colin 2015), 81. Michael Fitzsimmons has argued that the National Assembly undermined the corporate world beginning with the dissolution of the three orders on the night of August 4, 1789, the reform of the judicial system that uncoupled privilege and justice, and with the restructuring of municipal administrations that jettisoned guilds as representative units of economic and political interest. Fitzsimmons, "The National Assembly and the Abolition of Guilds in France," *The Historical Journal*, 39 (1996): 137, 152, 153.

7. On early modern French coinage and minting, see Jotham Parsons, *Making Money in Sixteenth-Century France: Currency, Culture, and the State* (Ithaca: Cornell University Press, 2014), 3-11. After John Law's attempt to introduce state paper money in 1718 caused rapid speculation, inflation, and a market meltdown, the French deeply distrusted paper forms of currency. See Philip Hoffman, Gilles Postel-Vinay, and Jean-Laurent Rosenthal, *Priceless Markets: The Political Economy of Credit in Paris, 1660-1870* (Chicago: University of Chicago Press, 2000), 69-95.

8. Jean Lafurie, *Les Assignats et les Papiers-Monnaies émis par l'état au XVIIIe siècle* (Paris: Léopard d'Or, 1981), 118; Rebecca Spang, *Stuff and Money*, 68, 77, 83.

9. Micah Alpaugh, *Non-Violence and the French Revolution: Political Demonstrations in Paris, 1787-1795* (Cambridge: Cambridge University Press, 2015), 82.

10. Harris, *The Assignats*, 12; Rebecca Spang, *Stuff and Money*, 72.

11. Julie Hardwick, *Family Business: Litigation and the Political Economies of Daily Life in Early Modern France* (Oxford: Oxford University Press, 2009), 170; Clare Haru Crowston, *Credit, Fashion, Sex: Economies of Regard in Old Regime France* (Durham: Duke University Press, 2013), 10.

12. Laurence Fontaine, *L'économie morale: Pauvreté crédit et confiance dans l'Europe préindustrielle* (Paris: Gallimard, 2008), 156.

13. This sequence describes how the fish market functioned on the eve of the Revolution. I assembled the details from the following sources: AdP D.Q^{10} 482, Marée à la Halle (Commerce de la) Enquête sur la compagnie Vison, an VII-an IX, n°3353, L'administration Centrale du Département de la Seine au Directeur du Domaine Nationale, signed Picard, le 28 Pluviôse an 7; AdP D.Q^{10} 742, Papiers de Lenoir, Dossier: Halles et marchés d'approvisionnements et du facturât dans les marchés, questions d'administration et réformes proposés (1807-1836); AdP D.Q^{10} 742, Papiers de Lenoir, Dossier: Personnel des Halles et Marchés (1828-1841); AdP V2F^4 9, Halles, poisson et divers, le 19ième siècle, Dossier: n°19, Vente en gros du poisson; AN F^7 7745^a, Dossier n°40, "Arrêté du préfet de police sur le

commerce des beurres, fromages, et œufs à Paris" (an VIII); AdP D.Q^{10} 742, Papiers de Lenoir, Subdossier: Personnel, Service; AdP D.Q^{10} 743, Papiers de Lenoir, Dossier: Octrois, Mélanges et feuilles numérotées éparses, Subdossier: Octrois, volaille; AdP D.Q^{10} 743, Papiers de Lenoir, Dossier: Dépouillement d'un travail fait l'an 6 par M. Gansouard, Commissaire de la Comptabilité Nationale, sur les taxes et produits des droits d'entrée de Paris sous le régime de la Ferme Générale; AdPP D^B 515, Préfet de Police, "Ordonnance concernant le Commerce des Fruits, Légumes, Herbages, Fleurs en bottes et Plantes usuelles," December 2, 1816; Rene Marion, "The Dames de la Halle: Community and Authority in Early Modern Paris" (PhD diss., Johns Hopkins University, 1994), 19; Anne Lombard-Jourdan, *Les Halles de Paris et leur Quartier (1137–1969)* (Paris: École Nationale des Chartres, 2009), 100–101.

14. I have used the 1790 base prices from the 1793 price control legislation to calculate these quantities. Cod cost 120 livres per barrel of 108 small fish or 200 livres per barrel of 108 big fish. Smoked herring cost 70 livres per barrel of 1,000 fish. AdPP D^B 387, "Tableau du maximum des Denrées et Marchandises, Stipulées dans l'article premier de la Loi du 29 septembre 1793, l'an II de la République Française."

15. Spang, *Stuff and Money,* 7, 116.

16. Morini-Comby, *Les Assignats: Révolution et Inflation,* 17; "Jean-Baptiste Pinteville baron de Cernon," in *Dictionnaire des Constituants, 1789–1791,* vol. 2, ed. Edna Hindie Lemay (Paris: Universitas, 1991), 181–182.

17. *AP,* January 23, 1790, 11:295. Rebecca Spang also argues that revolutionaries continued to consider personal confidence in individuals who issued assignat-backed promissory notes despite the national monetary system. Spang, "Money and Liberty in the French Revolution" (paper presented at the annual meeting for the Western Society for French History, November 12, 2011).

18. Harris, *The Assignats,* 24.

19. Spang, *Stuff and Money,* 49.

20. AdPP, D^B 387, "Tableau du maximum Des Denrées et Marchandises, Stipulées dans l'article premier de la Loi du 29 septembre 1793, l'an II."

21. For the publishing background of this serial pamphlet, see Ouzi Elyada, "La Mère Duchesne. Masques populaires et guerre pamphlétaire, 1789–1791," *Annales historiques de la Révolution française,* 271 (1988): 10–11.

22. "Dixième lettre bougrement patriotique de la Mère Duchêne," April 2, 1791, reprinted in *Lettres bougrement patriotiques de la Mère Duchêne, suivi du Journal des Femmes: Février–Avril 1791,* ed. Ouzi Elyada (Paris: Éditions de Paris/EDHIS 1989), 89–96.

23. BnF Lb39 9938, "Grand événement arrivé à un patriote de la Halle, à cause de l'échange d'un assignat. Grande difficulté à ce sujet. Formation d'un club aux Halles," 4. This pamphlet is undated, but since it discusses the king's sanction of the constitution and other National Assembly projects, we can assume that the pamphlet dates to 1791.

24. Harris, *The Assignats,* 24.

25. In times of prior monetary instability, merchants had often explicitly, if illegally, stipulated the form of money attached to business contracts. In 1541, the king had outlawed, without much success, individualized valuations of currency during singular transactions, 206. Sargent and Velde, *The Big Problem of Small Change,* 206, 329.

26. F. Hincker, "Billets de Confiance," in *Dictionnaire historique de la Révolution française,* ed. Albert Soboul (Paris: Presses Universitaires de France, 2006), 123–124.

27. Spang, *Stuff and Money,* 117.

28. This definition of exchange tokens comes from Sargent and Velde. For more on shifting monetary doctrines in early modern Europe, especially those concerning banknotes, see Sargent and Velde, *The Big Problem of Small Change,* 330–331.

29. Bibliothèque nationale de France Réserve QB-370 (19)—FT 4, "Caisse merdeuse Billet de cent sous: pryable [*sic*] dans la bouche du porteur . . . ." Paris (1790–1792) in *Collection de Vinck: Un siècle d'histoire de France par l'estampe, 1770–1870.* n° 3123; Franz Gabriel Fiesinger, engraver, "Assignat de vingt-cinq livres" (Paris: Domaines nationaux, 1791), in *Images de la Révolution française: catalogue du vidéodisque* (1990) 35034–2506; Digital version Stanford University Libraries and the Bibliothèque nationale de France, *French Revolution Digital Archive,* http://frda.stanford.edu/ (accessed July 2014).

30. Bouchary, *Les Faux-Monnayeurs sous la Révolution Française*, 82.

31. Andrew Dickson White, *Fiat Money Inflation in France* (San Francisco: Cato Institute, 1980, original 1933), 16.

32. *La Chronique de Paris*, June 11, 1791, n°162.

33. Spang, *Stuff and Money*, 114.

34. Rebecca Spang notes, "Those who willingly use any particular currency form a community of believers: they have faith in particular objects and assume all their cocommunicants share their basic convictions." Spang, *Stuff and Money*, 174.

35. Sargent and Velde, *The Big Problem of Small Change*, 203. For example, merchants in Angers circumvented a 1577 shortage by conducting trade with their own parchment notes that each merchant marked with the symbol that identified their silverware. In the nineteenth century, debtors' and creditors' newspapers created a new way to delineate confidence networks among small traders. See Erika Vause, "'The Business of Reputations: Secrecy, Shame, and Social Standing in Nineteenth-Century French Debtors' and Creditors' Newspapers," *Journal of Social History*, 28 (2014): 47–71.

36. Julie Hardwick's study of civil court cases in the seventeenth century demonstrates that individuals participated in "litigation communities" to forge familial credit in local networks. Hardwick, *Family Business*. On the postrevolutionary relationship between debt and honor, see Erika Vause, *In the Red and in the Black: Debt, Dishonor, and the Law in France between Revolutions* (Charlottesville: University of Virginia Press, 2018).

37. AdP, D.4 U^1 28, n°357, Citoyenne Fasche contre Citoyenne Roudelle, le 12 thermidor an V.

38. Sonenscher, "Les sans-culottes de l'an II," 1089. In 1790 and 1791, scores of masters filed employee lists with sectional officials in order to request the smallest assignat denominations with which to pay workers.

39. "Mémoire présenté au département," in *AP*, December 9, 1792, 54:726.

40. *Les Facteurs et factrices à la Halle aux Farines, à leurs concitoyens* (France: 1792).

41. AN D VI 8, n° 70, "Délibération de la section du Marché-des-Innocents, réclamant une émission suffisante d'assignats pour le remboursement de la dette exigible, émission qui comprendrait un certain nombre de petits billets de 100, 50 et 25 livres, et l'établissement d'une caisse patriotique pour l'échange des billets de 25 livres," to the Committee of Finances, September 9, 1790.

42. I calculate these examples based on the survey of 1790 prices that the department assembled to prepare the 1793 Maximum. In 1790, fresh butter from Chartres was 1 livre per pound, a barrel of 120 white herrings was 55 livres, and cheese from Neufchâtel was 2 livres 5 sous per dozen. AdPP, D^B 387, "Tableau du maximum Des Denrées et Marchandises, Stipulées dans l'article premier de la Loi du 29 septembre 1793, l'an II."

43. Berthellemot, Degland, Briot, Brunet, Bigeon, et quatre-vingt-huit autres, "Pétition adressée à l'Assemblée nationale par plusieurs commerçants en détail, de Paris, et renvoyée par elle au comité des finances," in *AP*, September 16, 1790, 19:1–2.

44. Bouchary, *Les Faux-Monnayeurs sous la Révolution Française*, 11; Harris, *The Assignats*, 12.

45. "Pétition adressée à l'Assemblée nationale par plusieurs commerçants en détail," in *AP*, September 16, 1790, 19:1–2.

46. "Pétition adressée à l'Assemblée nationale par plusieurs commerçants en détail," in *AP*, September 16, 1790, 19: 2.

47. Crowston, *Credit, Fashion, Sex*, 180.

48. Hoffman et al., *Priceless Markets*, 15, 158, 181.

49. See "Chart on Depreciation of the Assignat in the Department of the Seine," in Harris, *The Assignats*, 127.

50. "Seconde lettre des marchands en détail, de Paris, à MM. les administrateurs de la caisse d'escompte. Paris, le 14 septembre 1790," in *AP*, September 16, 1790, 19:6.

51. "Confrère," in *Dictionnaire de l'Académie française*, 4th Edition (1762), Project ARTFL, http://artfl-project.uchicago.edu/content/dictionnaires-dautrefois.

52. For the National Assembly's related attempt to ban petitions from political clubs in September 1791 (which the Legislative Assembly did not enact), see Malcolm Crooks, "The New Regime: Political Institutions and Democratic Practices under the Constitutional Monarchy, 1789–1791," in *The Oxford Handbook of the French Revolution*, ed. David Andress

(Oxford: Oxford University Press, 2015), 231–232; Bronislaw Baczko, *Ending the Terror: The French Revolution after Robespierre* (Cambridge: Cambridge University Press, 1994), 107–112.

53. "Pétition adressée à l'Assemblée nationale par plusieurs commerçants en détail, de Paris, et renvoyée par elle au comité des finances," *AP*, September 16, 1790, 19:4.

54. "Seconde lettre écrite par MM. les administrateurs de la caisse d'escompte à M. le président du comité des finances." Reprinted in *AP*, September 16, 1790, 19:3–4.

55. "Projet de décret présenté par le comité des finances," reprinted in *AP*, September 16, 1790, 19:4.

56. Fitzsimmons, "The National Assembly and the Abolition of the Guilds," 149, 150, 152.

57. Not all merchants readily abandoned the corporate system to forge new cross-occupational alliances. Gail Bossenga has argued that, unlike those in Paris, the merchants of Lille sought to protect their commercial interests and integrate revolutionary principles into their guilds rather than jettison corporate bodies. Bossenga, *The Politics of Privilege: Old Regime and Revolution in Lille* (Cambridge: Cambridge University Press, 1991).

58. French National Assembly, "The Constitution of 1791," in *The Old Regime and the French Revolution*, ed. Keith Baker, vol. 7 of University of Chicago Readings in Western Civilization (Chicago: University of Chicago Press, 1987), 250. For overarching debates concerning free speech during the Old Regime and the Revolution, see Charles Walton, *Policing Public Opinion in the French Revolution: The Culture of Calumny and the Problem of Free Speech* (Oxford: Oxford University Press, 2009).

59. Vardi, "The Abolition of the Guilds," 715.

60. Hincker, "Billets de Confiance," 123–124.

61. *AP*, April 17, 1791, 25:172–174.

62. Harris, *The Assignats*, 26.

63. "Instruction sur la caisse patriotique," in *La Chronique de Paris*, May 26, 1791, Supplément au n°146.

64. *La Chronique de Paris*, August 19, 1791, Supplément au n° 231.

65. "Décret sur les billets de confiance," May 19, 1791, in Depeyrot, *Monnaie et Papier-Monnaie*, 95.

66. Morini-Comby, *Les Assignats: Révolution et Inflation*, 38.

67. *La Chronique de Paris*, "Instruction sur la caisse patriotique," May 26, 1791, Supplément au n°146. To complement the Caisse Patriotique, another caisse opened in July 1791 to exchange 5-livre assignats for small money. Its services were so popular that the caisse restricted each individual to exchanging one 5-livre assignat per day for smaller change. Morini-Comby, *Les Assignats: Révolution et Inflation*, 56.

68. Bouchary, *Les Compagnies financières*, vol. 2, 73–74.

69. Elphège Boursin and Augustin Challamel, "Maison de Secours," *Dictionnaire de la Révolution française: Institutions, hommes et faits* (Paris: Jouvet et Cie, 1893), 458. The small Caisse Lefèvre, Lesage et Cie, which opened to exchange assignats for small money coins on May 29, 1792, also justified its establishment as a response "public sollicitations, notably from heads of manufactures and the Dames des Halles." Bouchary, *Les Compagnies financières*, vol. 2, 158.

70. Bouchary, *Les Faux-Monnayeurs sous la Révolution Française*, 83.

71. Bouchary, *Les Faux-Monnayeurs sous la Révolution Française*, 82.

72. AN Z^3 85, December 28, 1791–April 30, 1792, "Procédure instruit au 5e Tribunal criminel contre Barthélemy Bureau et Michelle Feuillerade."

73. AdP D.4 U^1 23, Justice de Paix, Dame Robert contre Dame Millot, n°413, December 20, 1791.

74. Bouchary, *Les Faux-Monnayeurs sous la Révolution Française*, 83.

75. *La Chronique de Paris*, January 13, 1792, n° 13. According to Bouchary, the police arrested some implicated Dames des Halles along with the printer.

76. *La Chronique de Paris*, January 29, 1792, n°29. In November 1791, counterfeiters had similarly switched green and red paper for false bills of 5 and 20 livres marked with the Caisse Patriotique's mast. Bouchery, *Les Faux-Monnayeurs sous la Révolution Française*, 82.

77. The deputies from Chartres arrived at the Legislative Assembly in February 1792. Bouchary, *Les Compagnies financières*, vol. 2, 85.

78. AN C 147, n°218, "Lettre de la femme Gond, veuve Boulliaud, au président de l'Assemblée législative," March 31, 1792.

79. AN C 147, n°218, "Lettre de la femme Gond," March 31, 1792.

80. *AP*, March 31, 1792, 41:104

81. BnFZ Le Senne 5128, *Les Bienfaits de l'Assemblée Nationale ou entretiens de la Mère Saumon, doyenne de la Halle: Suivis des Vaudevilles* (Paris: Au Palais Royal, 1792), 138–140, 144.

82. *AP*, December 12, 1791, 36:37; "Cartier-Douineau," in *Dictionnaire des Législateurs, 1791–1792*, vol. 1, ed. Edna Hindie Lemay (Paris: Ferney-Voltaire, 2007), 124–125.

83. "Cartier-Douineau," in Lemay, *Dictionnaire des Législateurs, 1791–1792*, vol. 1, 124–125; 1 livre = 20 sous = 240 deniers.

84. Bouchary, *Les Compagnies financières*, vol. 2, 28–29.

85. Harris, *The Assignats*, 25–26. Many Parisian caisses issued far more billets de confiance than they could back. The Caisse Patriotique had 5 million assignats in reserves in April 1792, but it had issued 17.5 million livres in billets de confiance.

86. "Décret sur la vérification des caisses patriotiques ou de secours," March 30, 1792, in *Monnaie et Papier-Monnaie*, 174–175.

87. Bouchary, *Les Faux-Monnayeurs sous la Révolution Française*, 84.

88. "Lettre des Dames de la halle occupant le marché des Innocents," May 14, 1792, as reprinted in *Procès-Verbaux des Comités d'Agriculture et de Commerce de la Constituante de la Législative et de la Convention*, vol. 2, ed. Fernand Gerbaux and Charles Schmidt (Paris: Imprimerie Nationale 1906), 748.

89. *AP*, May 21, 1792, 43:621.

90. AN D VI 1, "Prospectus, Caisse de Commerce" (Paris: Imprimerie de la Veuve Hérissant), 1.

91. Bouchary, *Les Compagnies financières*, vol. 1, 105, 106–108.

92. AN D VI 1, "Prospectus, Caisse de Commerce."

93. Bouchary, *Les Compagnies financières*, vol. 1, 109.

94. AN C 143, n° 158, "Proces-Verbal de la séance [of the Legislative Assembly] du Dimanche 19 février l'an 4 de la liberté," February 19, 1792.

95. *AP*, February 19, 1792, 38:655.

96. *La Chronique de Paris*, February 20, 1792, n°51. On the session of February 19, 1792.

97. *AP*, February 19, 1792, 38:652. See also AN C 143, n°158.

98. Suzanne Desan, *The Family on Trial in Revolutionary France* (Berkeley: University of California Press, 2004), 72, 212.

99. *AP*, February 19, 1792, 38:655.

100. *La Chronique de Paris*, February 20, 1792, n°51. Reporting on the Session of February 19, 1792.

101. Bouchary, *Les Compagnies financières*, vol. 1, 112.

102. Depeyrot, *Monnaie et Papier-Monnaie*, 174–175.

103. The full list of 48 citizens who signed the collective petition included: 12 who were labeled "merchant" without a trade or were illegible; 1 wholesale supplier of the navy; 1 building contractor; 6 intermediary traders; 5 beverage sellers; 1 manager; 2 haberdashers; 2 grocers; 1 metal smith; 1 building painter; 1 seller of lathes; 1 secondhand clothes dealer; 1 oats merchant; 1 baker; 1 cobbler; 1 leaseholder of a furnished house; 1 coquilles; 1 money broker; 1 former lawyer; 1 commander from the National Guard; 1 National Gendarme stationed near the tribunals; 1 furrier; 2 master fan-makers; 1 master carpenter.

104. Master artisans paid most workers daily rates, which made it difficult to delay settling accounts. Although payment could take other forms like meals and lodging, Parisian employers would especially need cash for wages in this insecure monetary environment. Sonenscher, *Work and Wages*, 190–192.

105. AN D VI 1, "Pétition adressée par des marchands à l'Assemblée législative en faveur de la Caisse de commerce," June 19, 1792.

106. *Collection Générale des Décrets rendus par l'Assemblée Nationale Législative, avec la mention des sanctions et des mandats d'exécution donnés par le Roi*, vol. 3 (Paris: 1792), 144.

107. Bouchary, *Les Compagnies financières*, vol. 2, 175.

108. Depeyrot, *Monnaie et Papier-Monnaie*, 208; *AP*, August 18, 1792, 48:331.

109. To stop caisses from rampantly issuing billets de confiance (which surpassed the value of the *biens nationaux* and caused the assignat to inflate) the Assembly had begun to pull some "paper money" from circulation in March 1792. Consequently, the petitioners strove to disassociate the Caisse de Commerce's billets from the assignat. AN D VI 1, "Pétition

adressée par des marchands à l'Assemblée législative en faveur de la Caisse de commerce," June 19, 1792.

110. The complete list of petitioners included: 19 merchants, no title, or illegible; 4 haberdashers; 2 grocers; 1 clockmaker; 2 brokers; 1 varnisher; 2 cobblers; 2 wine merchants; 1 paper merchant; 2 jewelers; 3 tailors; 1 draper; 2 makers of small objects; 2 joiners; 1 innkeeper; 1 keeper of valet cars; 1 printer; 1 building entrepreneur; 2 beverage sellers; 1 entrepreneur; 1 wigmaker; 1 ironmonger; 1 master mason; 1 master locksmith; and 1 carpenter. AN D VI 1, "Pétition des marchands & Entrepreneurs de Paris" from the [Legislative Assembly] Morning Session of August 26, 1792.

111. I calculated this figure according to the 6 merchant guilds and 44 trade guilds that Louis XVI established in 1776. See BnF F-21193 (22) *Édit du Roi, Par lequel Sa Majesté en créant, de nouveau, six Corps de Marchands & quarante-quatre Communautés d'Arts & Métiers, conserve libres centaines genres de Métiers ou de Commerce: Réunit les Professions qui ont de l'analogie entr'elles; & établit à l'avenir des règles dans le régime desdits Corps & Communautés* (Paris, 1776).

112. Bossenga, "Protecting Merchants: Guilds and Commercial Capitalism," 702.

113. AN D VI 1, "Pétition des marchands & Entrepreneurs de Paris" from the Legislative Assembly session of August 26, 1792.

114. AN D VI 1, "Pétition des marchands & Entrepreneurs de Paris," Session of August 26, 1792.

115. John Markoff, *The Abolition of Feudalism: Peasants, Lords, and Legislators in the French Revolution* (University Park, PA: Pennsylvania State University Press, 1996), 465.

116. AN D VI 1, "Pétition des marchands & Entrepreneurs de Paris," Session of August 26, 1792.

117. *AP*, September 3, 1792, 49:198.

118. Harris, *The Assignats*, 26.

119. *AP*, September 3, 1792, 49:602. For conflicts in other regions between locals and deploying soldiers who attempted to use hometown billets de confiance, see Spang, *Stuff and Money*, 122.

120. Depeyrot, *Monnaie et Papier-Monnaie*, 225.

121. Plon-frères, ed., *Réimpression de l'ancien Moniteur*, September 16, 1792, n°260 (Paris, 1854), 701.

122. "Louis Legendre," in *Dictionnaire des Conventionnels* by A. Kuscinski (Paris: Société de l'histoire de la Révolution française, 1916), 392–394.

123. *AP*, October 18, 1792, 52:567.

124. "Charles-Nicolas Osselin," in Kuscinski, *Dictionnaire des Conventionnels*, 470–471.

125. *AP*, October 18, 1792, 52:567.

126. "Décret du 11 octobre 1792," in Depeyrot, *Monnaie et Papier-Monnaie*, 230.

127. William Scott has argued that the revolutionaries frequently upheld special interests, like those of the poor, as long as the members belonged to an oppressed group. However, if the demands of special interest would give the collectivity an advantage over another interest group, the special interest could no longer be legitimate. William Scott, The Pursuit of 'Interests' in the French Revolution: A Preliminary Survey," *French Historical Studies* 19, no. 3 (Spring 1996): 816. Scott quotes Sieyès's pamphlet *What Is the Third Estate* to show the basic contrast: "All classes of the Third are linked by a common interest against oppression by the privileged."

128. "Jean-Bonaventure-Blaise-Hilarion Birotteau," in Kuscinski, *Dictionnaire des Conventionnels*, 58.

129. "Marc-Antoine Jullien," in Kuscinski, *Dictionnaire des Conventionnels*, 354.

130. *AP*, October 19, 1792, 52:569–570.

131. "Marguerite-Élie Guadet," in Kuscinski, *Dictionnaire des Conventionnels*, 312–314.

132. "Ignace Brunel," in Kuscinski, *Dictionnaire des Conventionnels*, 95.

133. *AP*, October 19, 1792, 52:570.

134. During the Revolution, the government relied on the factrices (especially those in the Halle à la marée) to guarantee supplies from the countryside, distribute goods wholesale in the market, and give retailers presale credit. The factrices ordered commercial transactions, despite the fact that the state did not commission their regulatory responsibilities. AdPP D^A

24, Caisse de la vallée et de la Marée, in Dossier n°301: Poissons et huîtres, caisse de la marée, organisation du service de la caisse de la marée (1830s).

135. Bouchary, *Les Compagnies financières*, vol. 2, 113. Bouchary calls the merchants who complained to the Commune on October 24, 1792, "marayeuses." This appears to be a female form of "mareyeurs" or the usually male wholesalers of fish.

136. *AP*, November 6, 1792, 53:203.

137. Bouchary, *Les Compagnies financières*, vol. 2, 116.

138. *AP*, November 6, 1792, 53:202.

139. Louis Joseph Hullin de Boischevalier, *Répertoire, ou Almanach historique de la Révolution française*, vol. 2 (Paris: Lefort, 1793), 372–373. "Du 8. novembre 1792. Vérification de l'état de situation des caisses des corps administratifs et municipaux, compagnies et particuliers qui ont émis des médailles, billets de confiance, patriotiques, de secours et autres. Le jour de la publication du présent décret, toute émission desdits billets cessera, et les planches qui ont servi à leur fabrication seront brisées. Ce décret a été scellé le 9 dudit mois."

140. *AP*, November 6, 1792, 53:207.

141. *Journal des débats et des décrets*, Session of November 11, 1792, n°53.

142. "Décret concernant les billets au porteur, billets de confiance, patriotiques, de secours, etc.," November 8, 1792, in Depeyrot, *Monnaie et Papier-Monnaie*, 237–240.

143. Bouchary, *Les Compagnies financières*, vol. 2, 122. The quote is from factrice citoyenne Rigaud's November 15, 1792 letter to the Minister of the Interior. *Le Courrier des 83 départements* reprinted the inflammatory ultimatum.

144. "Mémoire présenté au département" by the five factrices, in *AP*, annexe December 9, 1792, 54:726.

145. *AP*, December 9, 1792, 54:724.

146. *AP*, December 9, 1792, 54:724. The Dames shared the same assumptions of women workers in state-sponsored spinning workshops who agitated to support their families. They insisted on what Lisa DiCaprio has called "the obligation of a secular republic towards its citizens." DiCaprio, *The Origins of the Welfare State* (Urbana: University of Illinois, 2007), xii.

147. "Mémoire présenté au département" by the five factrices, in *AP*, annexe December 9, 1792, 54:726.

148. "Mémoire présenté au département" in *AP*, annexe December 9, 1792, 54:726 (emphasis in original).

149. *AP*, "Au ministre de l'intérieur," annexe December 9, 1792, 54:726 (emphasis in original).

150. *AP*, "Le ministre de l'intérieur au président de la Convention Nationale," annexe le 9 décembre 1792, 54:726.

151. *AP*, December 10, 1792, 54:748.

152. Louis Joseph Hullin de Boischevalier, *Répertoire, ou Almanach historique de la Révolution française*, vol. 2 (Paris, 1793), 374. Although they banned billets de confiance in March 1793, the revolutionaries did not attempt to partially reestablish a metallic standard until fall 1796. Harris, *The Assignats*, 215.

153. Bouchary, *Les Compagnies financières*, vol. 2, 131, 143.

154. Spang, *Stuff and Money*, 188.

155. Of course, illicit currency still circulated among merchants without regulation. During the Terror in January 1794, police spies observed many merchants making change for assignats with "small écus" (Old Regime money) or with coins worth 6 and 13 sous. AN D XLII 11, 14 nivôse an II, reprinted in Pierre Caron, *Paris pendant la Terreur: Rapports des agents secrets du ministre de l'intérieur*, vol. 4 (Paris: A. Picard, 1964), 30.

156. Spang, *Stuff and Money*, 159.

157. Lafurie, *Les Assignats et les Papiers-Monnaies*, 132–133, 135.

158. AN F[11] 1185, Approvisionnement de Paris. Le Commissaire de Police de la Section de Brutus au Ministre de l'intérieur, n° 8254, le 9 floréal l'an 4; *La Chronique de Paris*, June 11, 1791, n°162.

159. Lafurie, *Les Assignats et les Papiers-Monnaies*, 9–10, 122.

160. Tristan Gaston-Breton, *Banque de France: Deux siècles d'histoire* (Paris: Cherche Midi, 1999), 23, 26.

Chapter 5

1. Frédéric Braesch, *La Commune du dix août 1792* (Paris: Hachette, 1911), 392; "Girondins," in *Historical Dictionary of the French Revolution*, by Paul Hanson (Lanham, MD: Scarecrow Press, 2004), 141–144; Patrice Higonnet, "The Social and Cultural Antecedents of Revolutionary Discontinuity: Montagnards and Girondins," *The English Historical Review* 396 (1985); Morris Slavin, *The Making of an Insurrection: Parisian Sections and the Gironde* (Cambridge: Harvard University Press, 1986), 4,7; See also Paul Hanson, *The Jacobin Republic under Fire: The Federalist Revolt in the French Revolution* (University Park: Pennsylvania State University Press, 2003), 8.

2. Before 1793, some of the Girondins had also been members of the Jacobin club.

3. Hanson, "Montagnards," in *Historical Dictionary of the French Revolution*, 221–222.

4. George Rudé, *The French Revolution* (London: Weidenfeld and Nicolson, 1988), 84, 91.

5. Sigismond Lacroix, ed., *Actes de la Commune de Paris pendant la Révolution*, series 1, vol. 1 (New York: AMS Press, 1974), viii.

6. Because the Dames vehemently rebuffed the Citoyennes républicaines' attempts to make all women wear the cockade, some historians have concluded that the Dames were too conservative to support radical republicanism and too traditional to support democratic female citizenship. For example, Shirley Roessler argues that although the Dames des Halles "recognized the need for change, they despised the Revolution." Roessler, *Out of the Shadows: Women and Politics in the Age of the French Revolution, 1789–1795* (New York: P. Lang, 1996), 133. Many historians have depicted the Citoyennes républicaines as the zenith of women's revolutionary citizenship by the modern standards of institutional politics. In this vein, Dominique Godineau primarily examines the contest between the Dames and the Citoyennes républicaines to ask questions about female inclusion or exclusion from formal politics. Therefore, Godineau characterizes the Société's intense focus on socioeconomic demands (such as a pro-consumer Maximum) after September 1793 as a "retreat" from "politics." Godineau, *The Women of Paris and Their French Revolution* (Berkeley: University of California Press, 1998), 163–172.

7. Dominique Godineau, Olwen Hufton, Scott Lytle, Patrice Higonnet, and Albert Soboul in particular have acknowledged that differences in economic theory drew factional lines at the closing of the women's clubs. Since the Société was linked with the Enragés who the Jacobins attempted to silence in the fall of 1793, Patrice Higonnet argues that the closure was a "straightforward political strategy" and that "the Jacobins also decided that the involvement of women in politics ran against nature's dictates." Higonnet, *Goodness beyond Virtue: Jacobins during the French Revolution* (Cambridge: Harvard University Press, 1998), 56. Scott Lytle acknowledges that the Société greatly concerned itself with socioeconomic issues since its founding in May 1793. However, Lytle fails to acknowledge the socioeconomic issues at play in the Société's brawls with the "fishwives." Scott Lytle, "The Second Sex (September, 1793)" *Journal of Modern History* 27, no. 1 (March 1955): 14–26. Olwen Hufton argues that, by closing the women's clubs, "antifeminism was there; but the timing of the closure within the context of a concerted attack upon the Enragés and the use of market women who had been the targets of Roux's [a head Enragé] inflammatory exhortations to pillage suggest that more practical considerations were at issue." Hufton, *Women and the Limits of Citizenship in the French Revolution* (Toronto: University of Toronto Press, 1992), 37–38. Albert Soboul notes the Société's political and socioeconomic surveillance of the Dames in "Un Épisode des luttes populaires en septembre 1793: la guerre des cocardes," *Annales historiques de la Révolution française*, 163 (1961): 52–55.

8. Albert Mathiez, *La vie chère et le mouvement social sous la Terreur* (Paris: Payot, 1927), 26.

9. Mathiez, *La vie chère*, 116.

10. Mathiez, *La vie chère*, 530.

11. A. Chéruel, "Maximum," in *Dictionnaire historique des institutions, mœurs et coutumes de la France* (Paris: Librairie de L. Hachette, 1855), 758.

12. According to George Rudé, the price of eggs increased from 42 livres per 1,000 to 54 livres per 1,000. Rudé, "Wages and Popular Movements in Paris during the French Revolution," *The Economic History Review* 6, no. 3 (1954): 253.

13. Mathiez, *La vie chère*, 582.

14. "Montagnards," in Hanson, *Historical Dictionary of the French Revolution*, 221–222.

15. Braesch, *La Commune du dix août 1792*, 392; Slavin, *The Making of an Insurrection*, 7; Higonnet, "The Social and Cultural Antecedents of Revolutionary Discontinuity," 516, 526.

16. "Girondins," in Hanson, *Historical Dictionary of the French Revolution*, 141–144.

17. Hanson, *The Jacobin Republic under Fire*, 8.

18. Higonnet, *Goodness Beyond Virtue*, 40–43.

19. Slavin, *The Making of an Insurrection*, 157.

20. Rudé, *The French Revolution*, 83.

21. Albert Soboul, *The Sans-Culottes: The Popular Movement and Revolutionary Government, 1793–1794*, trans. Remy Inglis Hall (Princeton: Princeton University Press, 1980), 43.

22. Mathiez, *La vie chère*, 582.

23. As quoted in Soboul, *The Sans-Culottes*, 53. Petition presented on February 17, 1793.

24. For more on the Enragés' concerns, see William Shepard, *Price Control and the Reign of Terror: France, 1793–1795* (Berkeley: University of California Press, 1953), 4.

25. *AP*, February 18, 1793, series 1, vol. 58: 475; for context see Godineau, *The Women of Paris*, 114.

26. Godineau, *The Women of Paris*, 116–117.

27. As quoted in Mathiez, *La vie chère*, 160.

28. Mathiez, *La vie chère*, 146.

29. AN AF^{IV} 1470, "Extrait des rapports et déclarations reçus au Bureau de surveillance de la Police," February 26 and 28, 1793.

30. Rudé, *The French Revolution*, 84.

31. *AP*, Une députation des citoyens de la Frett, April 21, 1793, 63:89; *AP*, Une députation des citoyens de la commune le Saint-Germain-en-Laye, April 25, 1793, 63:302.

32. *AP*, Une députation des citoyens de la commune de Bercy, April 21, 1793, 63:89.

33. "Opinion: Est-il juste, est-il utile de fixer le maximum du prix des grains?," in *AP*, April 25, 1793, 63:341.

34. As quoted from Brissot's *Appel à tous les républicains de France* in October 1792 by Peter McPhee, *The French Revolution, 1789–1799* (Oxford: Oxford University Press, 2002), 109. See also "Brissot, Jacques-Pierre (1754–1793)," in Hanson, *Historical Dictionary of the French Revolution*, 46–47.

35. On Barbaroux, see "Charles-Jean-Marie Barbaroux," *Dictionnaire des Conventionnels* by A. Kuscinski (Paris: Société de l'histoire de la Révolution française, 1916), 21–23.

36. *AP*, April 27, 1793, 63:428.

37. *AP*, April 27, 1793, 63:429.

38. *AP*, April 27, 1793, 63:427.

39. *AP*, April 27, 1793, 63:430.

40. *AP*, April 30, 1793, 63:644; "Jean-François Ducos," *Dictionnaire des Conventionnels*, 218–219.

41. As quoted in McPhee, *The French Revolution*, 110.

42. Mathiez, *La vie chère*, 174–175.

43. As quoted in Shepard, *Price Control and the Reign of Terror*, 9. The Girondins had unsuccessfully brought up conspiracy charges against the opinionated Marat in April. "Jean-Paul Marat," in *A New Dictionary of the French Revolution*, by Richard Ballard (London: I.B. Yauris, 2012), 222–224.

44. Mathiez calls the Montagnards' resort to economic regulation "an alliance in which the maximum was the price." Mathiez, *La vie chère*, 178–187.

45. *AP*, May 4, 1793, 64:114–115.

46. *Révolutions de Paris*, May 4–11, 1793, n°200.

47. *AP*, May 4, 1793, 64:114–115.

48. G. LeMarchand states that the Maximum proved difficult to enforce because many departments remained committed to economic liberalism and would not force agricultural laborers to comply with the new regulations. LeMarchand, "Maximum," in *Dictionnaire historique de la Révolution française*, ed. Albert Soboul (Paris: Presses Universitaires de France, 2005), 730.

49. The earliest women's societies focused on patriotic philanthropy, but by 1792, most like the Citoyennes républicaines acquired a radical political edge. Godineau, *The Women of Paris*,

102,103. In Paris, Etta Palm d'Aelders had unsuccessfully proposed one "Amies de la Vérité" women's club for each Parisian section. Théroigne de Méricourt also unsuccessfully sought Parisian club support for a "company of Amazons" in March 1792. Marie Cerati, *Le Club des citoyennes républicaines révolutionnaires* (Paris: Éditions sociales, 1966), 20–21. For clubs outside of Paris, see Suzanne Desan, "'Constitutional Amazons': Jacobin Women's Clubs in the French Revolution," in *Re-creating Authority in Revolutionary France*, ed. Bryant T. Ragan Jr. and Elizabeth A. Williams (New Brunswick: Rutgers University Press, 1992), 11–35.

50. Godineau, *The Women of Paris*, 105.
51. Godineau, *The Women of Paris*, 119, 121.
52. On Pauline Léon, see Claude Guillon, "Pauline Léon, révolutionnaire" *Annales historiques de la Révolution française*, 344 (2006): 147–159.
53. As quoted by Cerati, *Le Club des citoyennes républicaines révolutionnaires*, 23.
54. Godineau, *The Women of Paris*, 173.
55. Godineau, *The Women of Paris*, 121. Although little information has survived about the club's individual members, at least two haberdashers, two cake merchants, and one press owner contributed to the club's ranks. Cerati, *Le Club des citoyennes républicaines révolutionnaires*, 30–31.
56. As quoted in Mathiez, *La vie chère*, 202.
57. Godineau, *The Women of Paris*, 125.
58. Godineau, *The Women of Paris*, 127.
59. Godineau, *The Women of Paris*, 126.
60. Rudé, *The French Revolution*, 85.
61. As quoted in Slavin, *The Making of an Insurrection*, 138.
62. Godineau, *The Women of Paris*, 130.
63. Slavin, *The Making of an Insurrection*, 186.
64. Hanson, *The Jacobin Republic under Fire*, 9–11.
65. As quoted in Mathiez, *La vie chère*, 217.
66. Jacques Roux, "Le Manifeste des Enragés," in *Scripta et Acta*, ed. Walter Markoc (Berlin: Akademie-verlag, 1969), 141, 142.
67. Slavin, *The Making of an Insurrection*, 127. Rudé, *The French Revolution*, 86.
68. Godineau, *The Women of Paris*, 151. In addition to Lacombe and Léon, Jacques Roux, Jean Varlet, and Théophile Leclerc were the most vocal Enragés. Slavin, *The Making of an Insurrection*, 129.
69. "Jean-Paul Marat," in Ballard, *A New Dictionary of the French Revolution*, 222–224.
70. "Rapport de l'observateur Dutrand à Garat ministre de l'intérieur," July 23, 1793, in *Répertoire Général des sources Manuscrits de L'Histoire de Paris pendant la Révolution Française*, ed. Alexandre Tuetey, vol. 9, #712.
71. *Révolutions de Paris*, July 20–August 3, 1793, n°211.
72. The Convention had issued a referendum on the completed Constitution of 1793 in late June. Timothy Tackett, *The Coming of the Terror in the French Revolution* (Cambridge: Belknap Press of Harvard University, 2015), 296–298.
73. Marie-Louise Biver, *Fêtes révolutionnaires à Paris* (Paris: P.U.F., 1979), 185. See also Mona Ozouf, *Festivals and the French Revolution*, trans. Alan Sheridan (Cambridge: Harvard University Press, 1988), 155.
74. Historians have debated whether the women seated atop the cannons were actual Dames des Halles or performed the role. However, multiple sources indicate that the women were the actual women who participated in the October Days march. The official planning report, the subsequent follow-up report, a personal letter, and accounts from newspapers like the *Feuille de Correspondance et Nouvelles Patriotiques* and the *Créole patriote* suggest that the women at the station were Dames des Halles. In the Department du Chers, officials even instructed the local substitutes to "Receive, in the name of the heroines of Paris, this prize honoring their civic audaciousness during the journées of 5 and 6 October 1789, enjoy in their name the honor of seizing these canons and igniting them." For four years, the revolutionaries had given the market women the title of "heroines" in connection with their political activism, and the populace easily made such associations. Jean-Paul Marat called the Dames "the heroines of the Halles who delivered us from the conspirators of 5 and 6 October," the *Correspondance Littéraire Secrète* refers to the

market women as "our heroines of the Halle" during the departure of the king's aunts, and the popular pamphlet names the Dames "heroines of the Revolution" as they spanked counterrevolutionary nuns. See Darline Levy and Harriet Applewhite, "Women and Militant Citizenship in Revolutionary Paris," in *Rebel Daughters: Women and the French Revolution,* ed. Sara Melzer and Leslie Rabine (New York: Oxford University Press, 1992), 94; *Feuille de Correspondance et Nouvelles Patriotiques,* vol. 2, no. 4, July 15, 1793, 15; *Feuille de Correspondance et Nouvelles Patriotiques* vol. 2, no. 8, August 12, 1793, 31; AP, Report of Pierre-Anastase Torné on the August 10 festival in the Department du Chers, August 21, 1793, 72: 566, 570. For Pinet's description, see Tackett, *The Coming of the Terror,* 297; Marat, *L'Ami Du Peuple,* no. 269, February 11, 1790; *Correspondance Littéraire Secrète,* no. 8, February 20, 1791, 71. See also the language in BnF Lb39 5505, *Liste des Culs Aristocrates et Anti-Constitutionnels, qui ont été Fouettés Hier au Soir à Tour de Bras, par les Dames de la Halle* (Paris: Imprimerie Patriotique, 1791), 4–5. I am indebted to Suzanne Desan and Jillian Slaight for bringing some of these articles to my attention.

75. *Le Créole patriote: bulletin de Milscent-Créole: journal du soir,* n°18, August 11, 1793.
76. BnFZ Le Senne 9438 *Recueil complet de tout ce qui s'est passé à la fête de l'Unité et de l'Indivisibilité de la République Française, suivi des inscriptions tracées sur les pierres de la Bastille et sur les monumens destinés pour cette cérémonie* (Paris: Imprimerie de Chaudrillié), 3.
77. AP, August 21, 1793, Pierre-Anastase Torné's Report on the August 10 festival in the Department du Chers, 72:570.
78. Jean Loup de Vireau-Beavoir and Giuseppe de Lama, "August 12, 1793," in *La Révolution française racontée par un diplomate étranger,* ed. Emmanuel Henri Vicomte de Grouchy and Antoine Guillois (Paris: E. Flammarion, 1903), 466.
79. BnF 8 Le38 344, Jacques Louis David, Convention nationale, "Rapport et décret sur la fête de la Réunion républicaine du 10 août, présentés au nom du Comité d'Instruction publique," July 11, 1793 (Paris: Imprimerie Nationale, 1793).
80. See Levy and Applewhite, "Women and Militant Citizenship in Revolutionary Paris," 94.
81. Godineau, *Women of Paris,* 111.
82. See charts in Rudé, "Wages and Popular Movements," 254, 257.
83. AP, August 31, 1793, 73:258.
84. Pierre Caron, ed. *Le Maximum général: Instruction, recueil de textes et notes* (Paris: Imprimerie Nationale, 1930), 8.
85. AP, September 4, 1793, 73:391.
86. *Journal des Débats et des Décrets,* n°351, as reprinted in AP, September 4, 1793, 73:391.
87. AP, September 4, 1793, 73:391.
88. Caron, *Le Maximum général,* 8.
89. *Réimpression de l'ancien Moniteur: seule histoire authentique et inaltérée de la Révolution française depuis la réunion des États-Généraux jusqu'au Consulat,* September 7, 1793, vol. 73, n°520. The *Moniteur* incorrectly dates this session as September 4, 1793, but it was actually September 5, 1793; AP, September 5, 1793, 73:411; AP, September 4, 1793, 73:391.
90. AP, September 5, 1793, 73:410.
91. *Réimpression de l'ancien Moniteur,* September 7, 1793, 73, n°520, 411. Reporting on the session of September 5, 1793.
92. Mathiez, *La vie chère,* 369. AP, September 6, 1793, 73:461. Soboul, *The Sans-Culottes,* 60.
93. On the revolutionary armies, see Richard Cobb, *The People's Armies,* trans. Marianne Elliott (New Haven: Yale University Press, 1987); AP, September 5, 1793, 73:414.
94. For the Terror and the repression of the Federalist Revolts, see Hanson, *The Jacobin Republic under Fire,* 185–196, 221–232.
95. AP, September 11, 1793, 73:691–697.
96. AN BB³ 81ᴬ fol. 299, "Délibération du Comité de salut public du Département de Paris," September 12, 1793.
97. Olwen Hufton also notes the importance of the church's proximity to the marketplace. *Women and the Limits of Citizenship,* 36. Godineau, *The Women of Paris,* 120.
98. Godineau, *The Women of Paris,* 154.
99. Timothy Tackett characterizes most members of the Citoyennes républicaines as "middle class" women who butted heads with "working women." Tackett, *The Coming of the Terror,* 313–314.

100. Godineau, *The Women of Paris*, 121.
101. The Convention's fall dechristianization campaign, which included suppressing the Mass in Paris and instituting the Revolutionary Republican Calendar, likely contributed to the tension at St. Eustache. Tackett, *The Coming of the Terror*, 315–316.
102. In November 1793, the Dames protested that no one said Sunday Mass at St. Eustache. Prévost, le 27 brumaire an II, reprinted in Pierre Caron, *Paris pendant la Terreur: Rapports des agents secrets* (Paris: Libraire Ancienne Honoré, 1943), vol. 6, 288.
103. The club's demands were a reprise of their insistence in one of their earliest visits to the Jacobin club in May 1793 that women also wear the tricolor. Godineau, *The Women of Paris*, 158.
104. Prévost, September 13, 1793, reprinted in Caron, *Rapports des agents secrets*, vol. 6, 231–232.
105. AN F⁷ 3688³, Harivel, September 14, 1793, reprinted in Caron, *Rapports des agents secrets*, vol. 1, 94.
106. *AP*, September 16, 1793, 74:284. Controlling prostitution became a topic of debate throughout fall 1793. See Clyde Plumauzille, *Prostitution et Révolution: Les femmes publiques dans la cité républicaine (1789–1804)* (Paris: Ceyzérieu, 2016), 224–251.
107. "Jacques Roux, (1752–1794)," in Hanson, *Historical Dictionary of the French Revolution*, 286; "Jean-François Varlet (1764–1832), in Hanson, *Historical Dictionary of the French Revolution*, 323; "Jean-Théophile-Victoire Leclerc," in Hanson, *Historical Dictionary of the French Revolution*, 190.
108. Claude Guillon, *Deux Enragés de la Révolution: Leclerc de Lyon & Pauline Léon* (Quimperlé: Éditions La Digitale, 1993), 77–79.
109. *AP*, September 18, 1793, 74:368.
110. R. R. Palmer, *The Twelve Who Ruled* (Princeton: Princeton University Press, 2005), 68.
111. Prévost, September 18, 1793, reprinted in Caron, *Rapports des agents secrets*, vol. 4, 233.
112. Prévost, September 18, 1793, reprinted in Caron, *Rapports des agents secrets*, vol. 4, 233.
113. Jennifer Heuer has examined debates throughout the Revolution over who should or should not wear the tricolor cockade to mark their citizenship. The question centered on individuals who sometimes appeared as dependents of others and their claims to citizenship. Jennifer Heuer, "Hats on for the Nation! Women, Servants, Soldiers and the 'Sign of the French,'" *French History* 16 (2002), 28–52.
114. AN F⁷ 3688³, "Rapport du Cn (l'observateur) Bigeot," September 18, 1793.
115. Prévost, Septembre 18, 1793, reprinted in Caron, *Rapports des agents secrets*, vol. 4, 233.
116. AN F⁷ 3688³, "Rapport de l'observateur Rousseville," September 20, 1793; See also AN F⁷ 3688³, "Rapport de Dugar," September 20, 1793.
117. AN F⁷ 3688³, "Rapport de l'observateur Béraud," September 20, 1793.
118. *AP*, September 16, 1793, 74:284–285.
119. AN F⁷ 3688³, "Rapport de l'observateur La Tour La Montagne," September 21, 1793.
120. *AP*, September 21, 1793, 74:571–572.
121. *AP*, September 21, 1793, 74:571–572.
122. As quoted in Godineau, *Women of Paris*, 163.
123. AN F⁷ 3688³, Rossenville, September 22, 1793, reprinted in Caron, *Rapports des agents secrets*, vol. 1, 171; See also Mathiez, *La vie chère*, 356.
124. Caron, *Le Maximum général*, 9.
125. AN F⁷ 3688³, Observations du citoyen Rolin, September 21, 1793. Although, on the whole, fewer Parisians came to blows over the tricolor after the Convention's ruling, the Dames did not relent in the days that followed. AN F⁷ 3688³, Rapport de Leharivel, September 22, 1793; AN F⁷ 3688³, Rapport de l'observateur Rousseville, September 24, 1793.
126. Prévost, September 25, 1793, reprinted in Caron, *Rapports des agents secrets*, 240.
127. AN F⁷ 3688³, Beraud, September 29, 1792, reprinted in Caron, *Rapports des agents secrets*, vol. 1, 226.
128. Soboul, *The Sans-Culottes*, 253, and Palmer, *The Twelve Who Ruled*, 70.
129. AN F⁷ 3688³, Roubaud, September 28, 1793, reprinted in Caron, *Rapports des Agents secrets*, vol. 1, 233.
130. *AP*, September 29, 1793, 75:321–323. Caron, *Le Maximum général*, 9.

131. Cynthia Bouton, "Les Mouvements de Subsistance et le problème de l'économie morale sous l'Ancien Régime et la Révolution française," *Annales historiques de la Révolution francaise*, 319 (Janvier/mars 2000), 71-100; Cynthia Bouton, *The Flour War: Gender, Class, and Community in Late Ancien Régime France* (University Park: Pennsylvania State University Press, 1993). E. P. Thompson, "The Moral Economy of the English Crowd in the Eighteenth Century" *Past & Present*, no. 50 (February 1971): 76-136. For an analysis of how the moral economy could apply to revolutionary reform, see Dominique Margairaz and Philippe Minard, "Marché des subsistances et économie morale: Ce que 'taxer' veut dire," *Annales historiques de la Révolution française*, 352 (2008): 53-99.

132. Shepard, *Price Control and the Reign of Terror*, 14.

133. Speech by Committee on Subsistence in the National Convention on September 29, 1793, as quoted in Palmer, *The Twelve Who Ruled*, 70.

134. Soboul, *The Sans-Culottes*, 253; Palmer, *The Twelve Who Ruled*, 70.

135. "Second discours prononcé à la Convention nationale par le citoyen Raffron, député de Paris; Sur la taxe des choses nécessaires à la vie; ou de la Police du commerce intérieur ou des choses de consommation," *AP*, August 31, 1793, 73:258.

136. AdPP DB 387, "Tableau du Maximum des Denrées et Marchandises, Stipulées dans l'article premier de la Loi du 29 septembre 1793."

137. The original list of goods included: "fresh and salted meat, lard, butter, oil, cattle, salted fish, wine, eau de vie, vinegar, cider, beer, firewood, charcoal, coal, candles, fuel oil, salt, soda, soap potash, sugar, honey, white paper, hides, iron, brass, lead, steel, copper, hemp, flax, wool, cloth, linen, raw materials for manufacturing, boots, shoes, rope and tobacco." Shepard, *Price Control and the Reign of Terror*, 13-14. The National Convention added nearly all food goods in their modified October 2, 1793, decree. AdPP DB 387, "Décret de la Convention Nationale, du 2 Octobre 1793, qui comprend tous les Comestibles dans la Loi du maximum."

138. "Décret qui fixe le maximum du prix des denrées et marchandises de première nécessité. Du 29 septembre 1793," reprinted in Caron, *Le Maximum général*, 33.

139. Mathiez, *La vie chère*, 374.

140. *AP*, August 31, 1793, 73:258. After his verbose speech on price controls, Raffron added a terse "A tax on salaries is a necessary consequence of what I have proposed" as a footnote in the printed version.

141. Mathiez, *La vie chère*, 585.

142. See the statistics compiled by Rudé, "Wages and Popular Movements," 254.

143. Mathiez, *La vie chère*, 586.

144. AdP D.1 U³ 35, "Arrêté du 29 octobre 1793 qui fixe le maximum du prix des Denrées en marchandises de première nécessité, publié le 22 du 1 mois de l'an 2."

145. "Décret qui fixe le maximum du prix des denrées et marchandises de première nécessité. Du 29 septembre 1793," reprinted in Caron, *Le Maximum général*, 33.

146. *Révolutions de Paris*, May 4-11, 1793, n°200.

147. Mathiez, *La vie chère*, 252.

148. Decree of 18 vendémiaire an II, Jean Tulard, ed., *Almanach de Paris: De 1789 à nos jours*, vol. 2 (Paris: Encyclopaedia universalis, 1990).

149. AdP current code: VD* 40; old system: D.389, #6800.

150. As quoted on September 1, 1793, in Soboul, *The Sans-Culottes*, 60.

151. Mathiez, *La vie chère*, 377.

152. Mathiez, *La vie chère*, 377.

153. *Moniteur*, le 20 du 1er mois, l'an 2, n°20, 81, Reporting on the General Council session of October 9, 1793; Mathiez, *La vie chère*, 392.

154. *Moniteur*, le 20 du 1er mois, l'an 2, n°20.

155. AN D XLII 11 Prévost, October 12, 1793, reprinted in Caron, *Rapports des agents secrets*, vol. 6, 250.

156. Mathiez, *La vie chère*, 392.

157. Albert Soboul, *The Sans-culottes*, 223-226. Jennifer Harris, "The Red Cap of Liberty: A Study of Dress Worn by French Revolutionary Partisans 1789-94," *Eighteenth-Century Studies*, 14, no. 3 (Spring 1981), 283-285. See also Colin Jones, *Longman Companion to*

the French Revolution (New York: Longman, 1990), 404. Cissie Fairchilds, "Fashion and Freedom in the French Revolution," Continuity and Change 15, no. 3 (2000): 426.

158. Les Révolutions de Paris, 15–22 brumaire an I, n°214, in an article entitled "Origine, définition, moeurs, usages, & vertus des sans-culottes."

159. Jones, Longman Companion, 223.

160. Prévost, October 22, 1793, reprinted in Caron, Rapports des agents secrets, vol. 6, 262. In mid-October, the Dames complained that they could not secure any foodstuffs. Prévost, October 17, 1793, reprinted in Caron, Rapports des agents secrets, vol. 6, 256.

161. Mathiez, La vie chère, 394.

162. Jones, Longman Companion, 105.

163. "Décret relatif au compte à rendre de l'exécution de la loi du maximum pour les denrées de première nécessité. Du 7 brumaire an II," reprinted in Caron, Le Maximum général, 40.

164. Farmers surrounding Paris had already faced the ultimatum to produce grain for the requisitions or be arrested as "public enemies." Mathiez, La vie chère, 465.

165. AN W 174, Prévost, October 28, 1793, reprinted in Caron, Rapports des agents secrets, vol. 6 (Paris: Librairie Klinckscieck, 1964), 267.

166. Moniteur, October 30, 1793, n°39.

167. AP, 9 brumaire an II, 78:49.

168. La Chronique de Paris, October 10, 1789, n° 47; Lacroix, ed., Actes de la Commune, series 1, vol. 2, 214–215, 223.

169. On the bronze medals struck for the August 10, 1793, festival, see Marie-Louise Biver, Fêtes révolutionnaires à Paris, 74.

170. Annales Patriotiques et Littéraires de la France et Affaires Politiques de l'Europe, 9 brumaire an II, n°301. Reporting on Commune of Paris session of 7 brumaire.

171. Société des citoyennes républicaines révolutionnaires de Paris, Règlement de la Société des citoyennes républicaines révolutionnaires de Paris (Paris, 1793); See also Godineau, The Women of Paris, 167.

172. Although the club women were politically closer to the Enragés than the Jacobins, the nonclub women probably called the Citoyennes républicaines "jacobines" because they supported the Jacobin Convention's recent subsistence decrees. Révolutions de Paris, 23–30 brumaire an II, n°215.

173. Révolutions de Paris, 23–30 brumaire an II, n°215.

174. Révolutions de Paris, 23–30 brumaire an II, n°215.

175. Moniteur, October 30, 1793, n°39. Reporting on council of 7 brumaire an II; See also Mathiez, La vie chère, 357.

176. AP, 8 brumaire an II, 78: 20. The petition was signed by twelve women. Various records label these petitioners as "femmes" [women] or "citoyennes" [female citizens]. In conjunction with the market brawl, I agree with Dominique Godineau, Darline Gay Levy, and Harriet Applewhite that these women are likely Dames des Halles. See Levy and Applewhite, "Women and Militant Citizenship in Revolutionary Paris," 95.

177. AP, 8 brumaire an II, 78:20; See also Mathiez, La vie chère, 357.

178. AP, 8 brumaire an II, 78:20; The Archives Parlementaires' singular wording of "club" reflects the official procès-verbal recorded in AN C 280, dossier n°761. However, some newspapers misprinted the quote so that it appeared that the women asked the Convention to close all female political clubs. The confusion may have arisen from the plural description of Citoyennes républicaines révolutionnaires and the single entity in which they were members. Or, the newspapers may have conflated the disconnect between the women's targeted appeal regarding one female club and the Convention's debate of all female clubs in response. Robert Blackman has examined how conflicting reports of a speech by Mirabeau affected secondary audiences. Robert Blackman, "Did Cicero Swear the Tennis Court Oath?" French History 28, no. 4 (2014): 471–497.

179. BnF Lb40 1245 Discours adressé au roi par les dames de la Halle, membres de la Société Fraternelle, dont, le 14 Février 1791, elles sont venues donner lecture au Conseil-Général de la Commune, qui en a ordonné l'impression à la distribution (Paris: Imprimerie de Lottin l'aîné & J. R. Lottin, 1791). The Fraternal Society of les Halles even drew its membership from among the Dames. Godineau, The Women of Paris. Until 1793, other mixed sex

clubs in Paris included the Fraternal Society of Nomophiles and the Fraternal Society of Minimes.

180. *AP*, 8 brumaire an II, 78:21.
181. *AP*, 8 brumaire an II, 78:21, 20, 33.
182. *AP*, 8 brumaire an II, 78:20–21.
183. On the Committee of General Security as "a Montagnard fief," see Jones, *Longman Companion*, 93.
184. AN BB³ 81ᴬ fol 394, 8 brumaire an II, séance du matin, "Extrait du registre des procès-verbaux et délibérations du Comité de surveillance du Département de Paris, Délibération du Comité de salut public du Département de Paris."
185. On the club's initial arms goal, see Godineau, *The Women of Paris*, 122–123.
186. AN BB³ 81ᴬ fol 394, le 8 brumaire an II, "Extrait du registre des procès-verbaux et délibérations du Comité de surveillance du Département de Paris."
187. Tackett, *The Coming of the Terror*, 308–309.
188. AN F⁷ 3688³, Prévost, October 29, 1793, reprinted in Caron, *Rapports des agents secrets*, vol. 6, 270.
189. As paraphrased in the *Journal des Débats et des Décrets* and reprinted in *AP*, 9 brumaire an II, 78:50.
190. *AP*, 9 brumaire an II, 78:50.
191. *AP*, 9 brumaire an II, 78:49–51.
192. *AP*, Address by the Société de la Rochelle, 8 brumaire an II, 78: 12–13.
193. *AP*, 9 brumaire an II, 78:49.
194. The cockade resurfaced as a point of contention later in the Revolution. The ambiguity between the cockade as a factional or a national symbol continued to play a role in the confusion. In late November and early December 1794, some women refused to wear the cockade because the Montagnards had passed the law and they had been defeated. During the subsistence crises and popular uprisings of Prairial and Germinal an III, Parisian women once again ripped cockades off one another and cried that "they [female plural] would not wear the cockades anymore until they had enough bread," and insisted that "one must not be Republican when one does not have bread." Even in Spring 1795, the cockade continued to be a contested symbol in the performance of factional loyalty or citizenship. See Aulard, *Paris pendant la réaction thermidorienne et sous le directoire*, vol. 1, November 30, 1794, 288; Aulard, *Paris pendant la réaction thermidorienne et sous le directoire*, vol. 1, December 3, 1794, 293; See also a March 21, 1795 report that "troublemakers" were telling women, "Citoyennes, if you do not want to be taken for Jacobines and be insulted, remove your cockades." François-Alphonse Aulard, ed., *Paris pendant la réaction thermidorienne et sous le directoire*, vol. 1, March 21, 1795 (Paris: Librairie Léopold Cerf, 1899), 591; AN AFⁱᵛ 1472 Dossier Frimaire an II, 8 germinal an III; Archives de Paris D.1 U³ 35, Laws sent by the Ministre de la Justice to the Tribunal du Commerce, 16 prairial an III; AdP D.4Z Dossier: Germinal à Prairial an III, 26 germinal, 370, 372.
195. *AP*, 9 brumaire an II, 78:51.
196. Recorded in the *Journal des Débats et des Décrets* and reprinted in *AP*, 9 brumaire an II, 78:50. On Romme, see "Gilbert Romme," in Kuscinski, *Dictionnaire des Conventionnels*, 533–535.
197. *AP*, 9 brumaire an II, 78:51. Timothy Tackett also acknowledges the market women only asked for the abolition of the one, specific club. He concludes that the National Convention took advantage of the club's Enragé ties to abolish all women's societies through "misogynistic rhetoric." Tackett, *The Coming of the Terror*, 314.
198. *AP*, 9 brumaire an II, 78:49.
199. Darline Gay Levy and Harriet Applewhite sense this convergence as well. "Women and Militant Citizenship in Revolutionary Paris," 95.
200. Address by the Société populaire de Saint-Quentin, *AP*, 8 brumaire an II, 78:11.
201. *AP*, le 9 brumaire an II, 78:49. Amar also called the affair "a plot by the ennemies of the public thing" permitting that the clubwomen were possibly motivated by "even an excess of patriotism."
202. Tackett, *Coming of the Terror*, 307.
203. Jones, *Longman Companion*, 123.

204. On the Girondins' trial, see Hanson, *The Jacobin Republic under Fire*, 13–21, and Tackett, *Coming of the Revolution*, 306–311.
205. Although women were unable to form women-only clubs, they could still sit in the galleries of local and national political assemblies.
206. Prévost, September 18, 1793, reprinted in Caron, *Rapports des agents secrets*, vol. 4, 233.
207. Prévost, September 25, 1793, reprinted in Caron, *Rapports des agents secrets*, vol. 6, 241.
208. On the relationship among the monarchy's patriarchal form, marital roles, and family law, see Julie Hardwick, *Family Business: Litigation and the Political Economies of Daily Life in Early Modern France* (Oxford: Oxford University Press, 2009), 6–10, 224–225.
209. *Révolutions de Paris*, 7–14 brumaire an II, n°21.
210. For Barère's political trajectory, see "Barère, Bertrand (1755–1841)," in Hanson, *Historical Dictionary of the French Revolution*, 26.
211. Mathiez, *La vie chère*, 433.
212. *Révolutions de Paris*, 7–14 brumaire an II, n°213.
213. Mathiez, *La vie chère*, 433.
214. Mathiez, *La vie chère*, 433.
215. In reality, the balance between buyers and sellers remained skewed in the capital. Since municipal officials administered the Maximum and the Parisian government was a sans-culotte stronghold, Parisian officials tended to enforce price limits on consumer goods more than limits on wages until the Spring of 1794. Robert Palmer, "Popular Democracy in the French Revolution: Review Article," *French Historical Studies* 1, no. 4, (Autumn 1960): 460.
216. As quoted by *Journal des Débats et des Décrets* and reprinted in *AP*, 15 brumaire an II, 78:364. See also Mathiez, *La vie chère*, 360.
217. *Les Révolutions de Paris*, 1–9 frimaire an II, n°216.
218. For the growing ambivalence toward women's clubs in the provinces, where citizens felt the effects of the club ban but did not directly experience the confrontation between the Dames and the Société, see Suzanne Desan, "'Constitutional Amazons,'" 30–35.
219. See, for example, BnF Lb39 5505, *Liste des Culs Aristocrates et Anti-Constitutionnels, qui ont été fouettés hier au soir à tour de bras, par les Dames de la Halle, et du Faubourg Saint-Antoine* (Paris: Imprimerie Patriotique, 1791); BnF Ld4 7148, *Liste de toutes les sœurs & dévotes qui ont été fouettées par les Dames des Marchés des différents Quartiers de Paris* (Paris: L'imprimerie de Tremblay, 1791).

Chapter 6

1. AN AF[IV] 1470, "Extrait des rapports et déclarations reçus au Bureau de surveillance de la Police," February 26, 27, 28, 1794. The Dames had also pillaged grocers' boutiques the day before.
2. AN AF[IV] 1470, "Extrait des rapports," February 27, 1794.
3. AN AF[IV] 1470, "Extrait des rapports," February 26-28, 1794.
4. For recent work on the Terror, see: Timothy Tackett, *The Coming of the Terror in the French Revolution* (Cambridge: Harvard University Press, 2015); Marie-Hélène Huet, *Mourning Glory: The Will of the French Revolution* (Philadelphia: University of Pennsylvania Press, 2015); Marisa Linton, *Choosing Terror: Virtue, Friendship, and Authenticity in the French Revolution* (Oxford: Oxford University Press, 2013); Peter McPhee, *Robespierre: A Revolutionary Life* (New Haven: Yale University Press, 2012); Sophie Wahnich, *In Defence of Terror: Liberty or Death in the French Revolution* (London: Verso Books, 2012); Michel Biard, ed., *Les Politiques de la Terreur, 1793–1794: Actes du Colloque International de Rouen, 11–13 janvier 2007* (Paris: Société des Études Robespierristes, 2008); Dan Edelstein, *The Terror of Natural Right: Republicanism, the Cult of Nature, and the French Revolution* (Chicago: University of Chicago Press, 2009); Paul Hanson, *The Jacobin Republic under Fire: The Federalist Revolt in the French Revolution* (University Park: Pennsylvania State University Press, 2003); and Arno Mayer, *The Furies: Violence and Terror in the French and Russian Revolutions* (Princeton: Princeton University Press, 2002).
5. Colin Jones, *The Longman Companion to the French Revolution* (New York: Routledge, 2013), 105. See also John Black Sirich, *The Revolutionary Committees in the Departments of France, 1793–1794* (Cambridge: Harvard University Press, 1943).

6. Morris Slavin, *The Making of an Insurrection: Paris Sections and the Gironde* (Cambridge: Harvard University Press, 1986), 157.

7. Steven Kaplan, *Provisioning Paris: Merchants and Millers in the Grain and Flour Trade during the Eighteenth Century* (Ithaca: Cornell University Press, 1984), 25–27.

8. See Jean Nicolas, *La rébellion française: Mouvements populaires et conscience sociale (1661–1789)* (Paris: Éditions du Seuil, 2002), and John Markoff, *Abolition of Feudalism: Peasants, Lords, and Legislators in the French Revolution* (University Park: Pennsylvania State University Press, 1996).

9. Cynthia Bouton, "Les Mouvements de Subsistance et le problème de l'économie morale sous l'Ancien Régime et la Révolution française," *Annales historiques de la Révolution française*, 319 (2000): 72–73.

10. Dominique Margairaz and Philippe Minard, "Marché des subsistances et économie morale: Ce que 'taxer' veut dire," *Annales historiques de la Révolution française*, 352 (2008): 58.

11. Population according to Paul Spagnoli, "The Unique Decline of Mortality in Revolutionary France," *Journal of Family History* 22, no. 4 (1997): 433.

12. Margairaz and Minard note Barère's emphasis on circulation as essential to the national domestic economy, "Marché des subsistances et économie morale," 75.

13. Louis Hugueney, *Les Clubs Dijonnais sous la Révolution* (Dijon: J. Nourry Libraire-Éditeur, 1905), 176.

14. BnF YE 14068-71, Citoyen B***, *Almanach républicain chantant pour l'an 2e de la République française: commençant le 22 septembre 1793, et finissant le 21 septembre 1794* (Paris: chez Lallemand, 1793), 120.

15. *AP*, November 1, 1793, 78:143, 144.

16. Albert Mathiez, *La vie chère et le mouvement social sous la terreur* (Paris: Payot, 1927), 433.

17. *Révolutions de Paris*, 7–14 brumaire an II, vol. 17, n°213.

18. *AP*, November 1, 1793, 78:143–145.

19. *Révolutions de Paris*, 7–14 brumaire an II, vol. 17, n°213.

20. *AP*, November 1, 1793 78:145.

21. *AP*, November 1, 1793, 78:144–145.

22. Mathiez, *La vie chère*, 433.

23. Margairaz and Minard, "Marché des subsistances et économie morale," 75.

24. Melvin Edelstein counts 548 districts in 1790, but the number fluctuated through war and annexations. Edelstein, *The French Revolution and the Birth of Electoral Democracy* (London: Routledge, 2006), 159.

25. AN AF^{II} 42, (Subdossier: AFII 333), Comité de Salut Public, "Répertoires des arrêtés, Table Alphabétique des décrets de feuilleton," Germinal, an 2; Pierre Caron, *La Commission des Subsistances de l'an II: Procès-verbaux et Actes*, XIII (Paris: E Leroux, 1925); See also "Décret relatif au compte à rendre de l'exécution de la loi du maximum pour les denrées de première nécessité. Du 7 brumaire an II," reprinted in Pierre Caron, ed., *Le Maximum général: Instruction, recueil de textes et notes*, Bulletin Trimestriel (Paris: Imprimerie Nationale, 1930), 40.

26. *AP*, November 1, 1793, 78:142.

27. AdPP DB 387, "Décret de la Convention Nationale, du 7e jour du 2e mois de l'an second de la République," "Relatif au compte à rendre de l'exécution de la Loi du Maximum pour les Denrées de première nécessité."

28. *AP*, November 1, 1793, series 1, vol. 78:142–143.

29. *Révolutions de Paris*, 15–22 brumaire an II, n°214.

30. Grivel or Siret observed that, under the current system, three parties raised prices before the public could purchase food at les Halles. Grivel or Siret, 26 nivôse an II, Ernest Leroux, ed., *Commission de Recherche et de Publication des Documents Relatifs à la Vie Économique de la Révolution*, Bulletin Trimestriel (Paris: Imprimerie Nationale, 1907), 129–130.

31. Paul d'Estrée, *Le Père Duchesne: Hébert et la Commune de Paris (1792–1794)* (Paris: Librairie Ambert, 1908), 337.

32. Pierre Caron divides the General Maximum into two periods separated by 6 ventôse an II (February 24, 1794) reform. However, police reports reveal that the reformed General Maximum was not posted and enforced in Paris until 5 germinal an II (March 21, 1794). The month delay caused additional confusion, which inflamed marketplace tensions and

generated more debate over the reform within the capital. Therefore, I use the enactment of the reformed Maximum on March 21 as the turning point in my analysis of socioeconomic relations. Caron, *Le Maximum général*, 3.

33. For an overview of the police commissioners, their instructions, their attitudes, and their observatory practices, see: Richard Cobb, *The Police and the People: French Popular Protest, 1789-1820* (Oxford: Oxford University Press, 1970), 14-26.

34. As quoted in Pierre Caron, "Rapports de Grivel et Siret, Commissaires Observateurs Parisiens du Conseil Exécutif Provisoire sur les subsistances et le maximum," *Bulletin d'histoire économique de la Révolution* (Paris: Imprimerie Nationale, 1907), 67.

35. As quoted in Caron, "Rapports de Grivel et Siret," 69.

36. Caron, "Rapports de Grivel et Siret," 67, 69.

37. AN F^{11} 201, Grivel, 20 frimaire an II, reprinted in Pierre Caron, *Paris pendant la Terreur: Rapports des agents secrets du ministre de l'intérieur* (Paris: Librairie Alphonse Picard, 1914), vol. 1, 255.

38. AN F^{11} 201, Grivel, 20 frimaire an II, reprinted in Caron, *Rapports des agents secrets*, vol. 1, 255.

39. By January 1794, Commissioner Monic reported that the number of Dames who attended the revolutionary tribunal swelled because they had nothing to sell and therefore had much free time. Commissioner Prévost similarly observed some female fruit merchants complained that they simply had nothing to sell. AN F^7 3688^3, Monic, 21 nivôse an II, reprinted in Caron, *Rapports des agents secrets*, vol. 2, 291-292; AN W 191, Prévost, 5 pluviôse an II, reprinted in Caron, *Rapports des agents secrets*, vol. 3, 135.

40. AN F^7 3688^3, Grivel, 22 nivôse an II, reprinted in Caron, *Rapports des agents secrets*, vol. 1, 124.

41. AN F^{11} 201, Grivel, 28 nivôse an II, reprinted in Caron, *Rapports des agents secrets*, vol. 1, 132-133.

42. AN W 191, Grivel, 21 pluviôse an II, reprinted in Caron, *Rapports des agents secrets*, vol. 4.

43. AN W 191, Pourvoyeur, 8 pluviôse an II, reprinted in Caron, *Rapports des agents secrets*, vol. 3, 184.

44. Mathiez, *La vie chère*, 170.

45. AN F^7 3688^3, Bacon, 14 nivôse an II, reprinted in Caron, *Rapports des agents secrets*, vol. 2, 151.

46. AN F^7 3688^3, Monic, 21 nivôse an II, reprinted in Caron, *Rapports des agents secrets*, vol. 2, 291-292.

47. AN W 191, Pourvoyeur, 12 pluviôse an II, reprinted in Caron, *Rapports des agents secrets*, vol. 3, 257.

48. AN W 3688^3, 28 nivôse an II, reprinted in Caron, *Rapports des agents secrets*, vol. 3, 3.

49. AN W 112, Bacon, 24 ventôse an II, reprinted in Caron, *Rapports des agents secrets*, vol. 5.

50. AN F^7 3688^3, Deuxième rapport de Pourvoyer, 7 nivôse an II, reprinted in Caron, *Rapports des agents secrets*, vol. 2, 41.

51. AN F^7 3688^3, Bacon, 22 nivôse an II, reprinted in Caron, *Rapports des agents secrets*, vol. 2, 297.

52. Anne Montenach's study of seventeenth-century markets reveals how marketplace actors participated in "illicit and licit trade" in tandem. This created an "économie parallèle" that diverged from official regulations but remained embedded in the licit economy. Anne Montenach, *Espaces et pratiques du commerce alimentaire à Lyon au XVIIe siècle* (Grenoble: Presses universitaires de Grenoble, 2009), 15, 18.

53. On the domestic and international dimensions of illicit trade in the eighteenth century, see Michael Kwass, *Contraband: Louis Mandarin and the Making of a Global Underground* (Cambridge: Harvard University Press, 2014).

54. AN F^{11} 201, Grivel, 27 frimaire an II, reprinted in Caron, *Rapports des agents secrets*, vol. 1, 272-273.

55. George E. Rudé, "Prices, Wages and Popular Movements in Paris during the French Revolution," *The Economic History Review*, 6, no. 3 (1954): 257-258.

56. I calculated this price based on the Maximum price of 51 livres 12 sous for 1,000 eggs from Mortagne and 41 livres 6 sous 8 deniers for 1,000 eggs from Picardie. BnF YE 14068-71, Citoyen B***, *Almanach républicain chantant; La déclaration; Le Maximum*, 127.

57. AN F⁷ 3688³, Le Breton, 20 nivôse an II, reprinted in Caron, *Rapports des agents secrets*, vol. 2, 271.

58. AN W 191, Dugas, 9 pluviôse an II, reprinted in Caron, *Rapports des agents secrets*, vol. 3, 193.

59. AN F⁷ 3688³, Grivel, 13 et 14 nivôse an II, reprinted in Pierre Caron, ed., *Paris pendant la Terreur: Rapports de Grivel et Siret sur les subsistances et le maximum (sept 1793–mars 1794)* (Collected and reprinted from *Bulletin trimestriel de la Commission de recherche et de publication des documents relatifs à la vie économique de la Révolution*, vol. 2 [1907], 67–231) (1910), vol. 1, 106.

60. Siret, 3 pluviôse an II, reprinted in Leroux, *Commission de Recherche*, 142.

61. AN W 112, Dossier 4: Rapports Polices, 12 ventôse an II.

62. Grivel or Siret, 26 nivôse an II, reprinted in Leroux, *Commission de Recherche*, 129.

63. AN W 191, Pourvoyeur, 5 pluviôse an II, reprinted in Caron, *Rapports des agents secrets*, vol. 3, 134.

64. AN W 191, Prévost, 5 pluviôse an II, reprinted in Caron, *Rapports des agents secrets*, vol. 3, 135.

65. Siret, 3 pluviôse an II, reprinted in Leroux, *Commission de Recherche*, 141–142.

66. AN F¹¹ 201, Grivel, 7 pluviôse an II, reprinted in Caron, *Rapports de Grivel et Siret*, vol. 1, 144–145.

67. George Rudé and Albert Soboul, "Le maximum des salaires parisiens et le 9 thermidor," *Annales historiques de la Révolution française*, 134 (1954): 5; Mathiez, *La vie chère*, 587.

68. As quoted in Mathiez, *La vie chère*, 590.

69. AN W 191, Prévost, 16 pluviôse an II, reprinted in Caron, *Rapports des agents secrets*, vol. 3, 328.

70. AN W 112, Mercier, 1 ventôse an II, reprinted in Caron, *Rapports des agents secrets*, vol. 4, 212; AN W 112, Prévost, 18 ventôse an II, reprinted in Caron, *Rapports des agents secrets*, vol. 5, 166.

71. AN W 191 Pourvoyeur, 30 pluviôse an II, reprinted in Caron, *Rapports des agents secrets*, vol. 4, 194.

72. AN W 112, Dossier 4: Rapports Polices, Rolin, 21 ventôse an II; Merchants did not create black markets alone. Anne Montenach has illustrated how small-scale women smugglers, marginal traders, urban merchants, and consumers alike shaped local illicit practices in response to the state's regulation of salt and Indiennes in Dauphiné. Anne Montenach, *Femmes, pouvoirs, et contrebandes dans les Alpes au XVIIIᵉ siècle* (Grenoble: Presses universitaires de Grenoble, 2017).

73. AN W 191, Prévost, 11 pluviôse an II, reprinted in Caron, *Rapports des agents secrets*, vol. 3, 238; AN W 191, Prévost, 11 pluviôse an II, reprinted in Caron, *Rapports des agents secrets*, vol. 3, 238.

74. AN W 191, Bacon, 14 pluviôse an II, reprinted in Caron, *Rapports des agents secrets*, vol. 3, 279.

75. AN W 112, Pourvoyeur, 4 ventôse an II, reprinted in Caron, *Rapports des agents secrets*, vol. 4, 283.

76. AN W 191, Grivel, 21 pluviôse an II, reprinted in Pierre Caron, ed., *Rapports de Grivel et Siret sur les subsistances et le maximum (sept 1793-mars 1794)*, (Collected and reprinted from *Bulletin d'histoire économique de la Révolution*, vol. 11 [1920–1921], 371–427), vol. 2, 384.

77. AN W 191, Perrière, 29 pluviôse an II, reprinted in Caron, *Rapports des agents secrets*, vol. 4, 173–176.

78. AN W 191, Perrière, 29 pluviôse an II, reprinted in Caron, *Rapports des agents secrets*, vol. 4, 175.

79. AN W 112, Harivel, 1 ventôse an II, reprinted in Caron, *Rapports des agents secrets*, vol. 4, 212.

80. AN W 191, Mercier, 22 pluviôse an II, reprinted in Caron, *Rapports des agents secrets*, vol. 6, 30.

81. AN W 112, Perrière, 6 ventôse an II, reprinted in Caron, *Rapports des agents secrets*, vol. 4, 316–319.

82. *Moniteur*, 4 ventôse an II, reporting on the session of 3 ventôse, n°154, vol. 19, 528.

83. *Moniteur*, 5 ventôse an II, reporting on the session of 3 ventôse, n°155, vol. 19, 533.

84. *Moniteur*, 5 ventôse an II, reporting on the session of 3 ventôse, n°155, vol. 19, 533–534.

85. *Moniteur*, 5 ventôse an II, reporting on the session of 3 ventôse, n°155, vol. 19, 534–535.

86. *Moniteur*, 5 ventôse an II, reporting on the session of 3 ventôse, n°155, vol. 19, 535.

87. *Moniteur*, 5 ventôse an II, reporting on the session of 4 ventôse, n°155, vol. 19, 536.

88. *Moniteur*, 7 ventôse an II, reporting on the session of 6 ventôse, n°157, vol. 19, 555.

89. *Moniteur*, 8 ventôse an II, n°158, vol. 19, 558.

90. As quoted in Mathiez, *La vie chère*, 562–563.

91. *Moniteur*, 8 ventôse an II, n°158, vol. 19, 558.

92. *Moniteur*, 9 ventôse an II, n°159, vol. 19, 569–570.

93. AN W 112, 6 ventôse an II, reprinted in Caron, *Rapports des agents secrets*, vol. 4.

94. AN W 112, Rolin, 7 ventôse an II, as reprinted in Caron, *Rapports des agents secrets*, vol. 4, 338.

95. AN F^{11} 205, Mémoires, lettres, pétitions adressées au Comité de salut public et relatifs aux subsistances et au maximum an II–an IV, report on Paris, 8 ventôse an II.

96. AN F^{11} 205, Extraits des Rapports de la Surveillance de la Police à la Mairie, 7 ventôse an II.

97. Grivel, 15 ventôse an II, reprinted in Caron, *Rapports des agents secrets*, vol. 1, 200–201.

98. *AP*, 8 ventôse an II, 85:509–510.

99. Tackett, *The Coming of the Terror*, 328.

100. Peter McPhee, *Liberty or Death: The French Revolution* (New Haven: Yale University Press, 2016), 250.

101. As quoted in Mathiez, *La vie chère*, 543.

102. Mathiez, *La vie chère*, 544.

103. As quoted in Mathiez, *La vie chère*, 546.

104. Mathiez, *La vie chère*, 549.

105. Mathiez, *La vie chère*, 551.

106. AN W 112, Hanriot, 12 ventôse an II, reprinted in Caron, *Rapports des agents secrets*, vol. 5, 32.

107. AN AD XVIIIe 315, "Instruction sur le tableau général du maximum, rédigée par la Commission des subsistances et approvisionnements, et approuvée par la Convention," 14 ventôse an II, reprinted in Caron, *Le Maximum général*, 65.

108. Grivel, 13 ventôse an II, reprinted in Leroux, *Commission de Recherche*, 192.

109. AN W 78, n°4, "Déclarations des citoyens de la Section des Marchés, reçues par Étienne Masson, l'un des juges du Tribunal révolutionnaire, en présence de Fouquier-Tinville, accusateur public," 23 ventôse an II; AN W 112, Bacon, 14 ventôse an II, reprinted in Caron, *Rapports des agents secrets*, vol. 5, 61; AN W 76, "Lettre anonyme, en date du 9 nivôse, à l'adresse des citoyennes marchandes à la Halle," 12 ventôse an II, as quoted in Alexandre Tuetey, *Répertoire Général des sources Manuscrits de L'Histoire de Paris pendant la Révolution Française*, vol. 11 (Paris: Imprimerie Nouvelle [Association Ouvrière], 1890), 70–71.

110. AN F^{11} 201, Grivel, 14 ventôse an II, reprinted in Caron, *Rapports de Grivel et Siret*, vol. 1, 198–199.

111. AN F^{11} 201, Grivel, 14 ventôse an II, reprinted in Caron, *Rapports de Grivel et Siret*, vol. 1, 199.

112. Carnavalet, AFF341, Affiche, "N° 2216 Décret de la Convention Nationale le 16e jour de Ventôse, an second de la République Française, Relatif à des Pamflets [*sic*] contre-révolutionnaires répandus dans les Halles & Marchés" (Paris: Imprimerie nationale exécutive du Louvre, 1794).

113. Grivel, 15 ventôse an II, reprinted in Caron, *Rapports de Grivel et Siret*, vol. 1, 200–201.

114. Grivel, 15 ventôse an II, reprinted in Caron, *Rapports de Grivel et Siret*, vol. 1, 200–201.

115. AN W 112, Rolin, 18 ventôse an II, reprinted in Caron, *Rapports des agents secrets*, vol. 5, 168.

116. AN W 112, Rolin, 18 ventôse an II.

117. AN W 112, Dossier 4: Rapports Polices, Grivel, 20 ventôse an II.

118. AN W 78, n°3, "Déclarations de membres du Comité révolutionnaire de la section des Marchés, reçues par Gabriel Deliège, juge au tribunal révolutionnaire," le 21 ventôse an II.

119. AN W 78, n°4, "Déclarations de membres du Comité révolutionnaire de la section des Marchés," le 21 ventôse an II.

120. AN W 112, Dossier 4, Rapports Polices, 19 ventôse an II.

121. AN W 112, Dossier 4, Rapports Polices, Bouchiseuche, 17 ventôse an II.

122. AN W 112, Dossier 4, Rapports Polices, 21 ventôse an II.

123. AN W 112, Perrière, 18 ventôse an II.

124. AN W 112, Dugas, 12 ventôse an II, reprinted in Caron, *Rapports des agents secrets*, vol. 5, 28–30.

125. AN W 112, Dossier 4: Rapports Polices, Rolin, 21 ventôse an II.

126. AN W 112, Dossier 4: Rapports Polices, 21 ventôse an II.

127. *Révolutions de Paris*, March 9–16, 1793, n°192. Dominique Godineau astutely observes that the Dames' abrasive complaints "were manifestations of acute feeling against the present situation [especially food crises] rather than real counterrevolutionary sentiment." Godineau, *The Women of Paris and their French Revolution*, trans. Katherine Streip (Berkeley: University of California Press, 1998), 254.

128. AN BB³ 76, "Extrait de l'ordre du jour de la force armée de Paris," 23 ventôse an II.

129. AN W 112, Dossier 4: Rapports Polices, Grivel, 20 ventôse an II.

130. AN W 112, Dossier 4: Rapports Polices, R.J., 19 ventôse an II.

131. Mathiez, *La vie chère*, 557–558.

132. Charles Gomel, *Histoire Financière de la Législative et de la Convention*, vol. 2 (Paris: Guillaumin et Cⁱᵉ, 1905), 241.

133. Mathiez, *La vie chère*, 560, 561.

134. McPhee, *Liberty*, 249.

135. AN F⁷ 3688³, Mercier, 19 nivôse an II, reprinted in Caron, *Rapports des agents secrets*, vol. 2, 255.

136. AN W 174, Perrière, 3 germinal an II, reprinted in Caron, *Rapports des agents secrets*, vol. 6, 64–68.

137. Adolphe Schmidt, *Paris pendant la Révolution d'après les rapports de la police secrète 1789–1800*, vol. 2 (Paris: Champion, 1885), 242.

138. Tackett, *The Coming of the Terror*, 329.

139. McPhee, *Liberty*, 251.

140. William Shepard, *Price Control and the Reign of Terror: France, 1793–1795* (Berkeley: University of California Press, 1953), 24.

141. AdPP DB 396, Commerce de la Marée, Lois, ordonnances, arrêtés, 14 vendémiaire an III, Maximum de la Merluche.

142. AN W 174, J.B.B., "Observations du 5 germinal"; AN W 174, Pourvoyeur, 6 germinal an II, reprinted in Caron, *Rapports des agents secrets*, vol. 6, 134.

143. AN W 174, Perrière, 7 germinal an II, reprinted in Caron, *Rapports des agents secrets*, vol. 6, 151.

144. AN W 174, Grivel, 6 germinal an II.

145. AN W 174, Charmont, 6 germinal an II, reprinted in Caron, *Rapports des agents secrets*, vol. 6, 128; AN W 174, Bacon, 7 germinal an II, reprinted in Caron, *Rapports des agents secrets*, vol. 6, 141.

146. AN W 174, Charmont, 9 germinal an II, reprinted in Caron, *Rapports des agents secrets*, vol. 6, 188.

147. AN W 174, Prévost, 8 germinal an II.

148. AN W 174, Bacon, 9 germinal an II, reprinted in Caron, *Rapports des agents secrets*, vol. 6.

149. AN W 174, Charmont, 5 germinal an II, reprinted in Caron, *Rapports des agents secrets*, vol. 6, 96.

150. AN W 174, Monic, 5 germinal an II, reprinted in Caron, *Rapports des agents secrets*, vol. 6, 110.

151. AN W 174, Charmont, 4 germinal an II, reprinted in Caron, *Rapports des agents secrets*, vol. 6, 76.

152. Across France, the Maximum on goods was most successful in Jacobin strongholds where local officials and clubs committed to enforcing price points. Mathiez, *La vie chère*, 574.

153. AN W 174, Béraud, 6 germinal an II, reprinted in Caron, *Rapports des agents secrets*, vol. 6.

154. Mathiez, *La vie chère*, 574, 576–577, 569.

155. Haïm Burstin, "Problèmes du travail à Paris sous la Révolution," *Revue d'histoire moderne et contemporaine* 4, no. 4 (1997): 669.

156. Schmidt, *Paris pendant la Révolution*, 246.

157. As quoted in Schmidt, *Paris pendant la Révolution*, 251–252.

158. Burstin, "Problèmes," 669, 660.

159. George E. Rudé, "Prices, Wages and Popular Movements," 260.

160. Mathiez, *La vie chère*, 591–592; Rudé and Soboul, "Le maximum des salaires," 9–10.

161. "Arrêté du Comité de salut public interdisant aux administrations, aux sections, aux entrepreneurs, d'accorder aux ouvriers et journaliers employés par eux un salaire supérieur au maximum. Du 13 prairial an II—1er juin 1794," in Caron, *Le Maximum général*, 83.

162. Rudé and Soboul, "Le maximum des salaires," 5.

163. Rudé and Soboul, "Le maximum des salaires," 5.

164. Mathiez, *La vie chère*, 574.

165. BnF NUMM-42404, Conseil-Général de la Commune de Paris, *Tarif du maximum des salaires, façons, gages, main d'oeuvres, journées de travail dans l'étendue de la commune de Paris* (Paris: Nicolas et Desbrières, circa 5 Thermidor an II), 23, 59–60, 28, 61.

166. From figures in Rudé and Soboul, "Le maximum des salaires," 15.

167. Rudé and Soboul, "Le maximum des salaires," 1.

168. Burstin, "Problèmes," 671. On the French deputies' continued purging of their ranks after Robespierre's execution, see Mette Harder, "A Second Terror: The Purges of French Revolutionary Legislators after Thermidor," *French Historical Studies* vol. 38, no. 1 (2015), 33–60.

169. Rudé, "Prices, Wages and Popular Movements," 260.

170. As quoted in Rudé and Soboul, "Le maximum des salaires," 17.

171. Rudé and Soboul, "Le maximum des salaires," 19.

172. Rudé and Soboul, "Le maximum des salaires," 22, 21.

173. François Hincker, "Comment sortir de la terreur économique?" in *Le Tournant de l'an III: Réaction et Terreur blanche dans la France révolutionnaire*, ed. Michel Vovelle (Paris: Éditions du CTHS, 1997), 149–150.

174. As quoted in Shepard, *Price Control and the Reign of Terror*, 55–56.

175. Shepard, *Price Control and the Reign of Terror*, 59, 57.

176. Rudé, "Prices, Wages and Popular Movements," 260.

177. Shepard, *Price Control and the Reign of Terror*, 57, 80.

178. BnF Lb41 1509, Jean-René Loyseau, *Réflexions sur la loi du maximum et sur les réquisitions* (Paris: Chez Vialard, 1795), 10, 59.

179. BnF Le38 1111, Giraud, Marc-Antoine-Alexis, "Rapport et projet de décret sur la nécessité de rapporter la loi sur le maximum, présentés au nom du comité de commerce et d'approvisionnemens" (Paris: Imprimerie nationale, 1795), 6.

180. As quoted in Shepard, *Price Control and the Reign of Terror*, 81.

181. Loyseau, *Réflexions sur la loi*, 22.

182. "Décret contenant proclamation sur l'abolition des lois relatives au maximum. Du 9 nivôse an II—29 décembre 1794," reprinted in Caron, *Le Maximum général*, 126.

183. Caron, *Le Maximum général: Instruction, recueil de textes et notes* (Paris: Imprimerie Nationale, 1930), 126–127.

184. Hincker, "Comment sortir de la terreur économique?," 157.

185. AN AF^{IV} 1472, Commissaire Reports, Frimaire an III and 24 ventôse an III.

186. François-Alphonse Aulard, *Paris pendant la réaction thermidorienne et sous le directoire*, vol. 3 (Paris: Librairie Léopold Cerf, 1899), 381.

187. Kåre Tønnesson, *La Défaite des Sans-Culottes* (Paris: Presses Universitaires d'Oslo, 1978), 127–133, 230–236.

188. Rudé, "Prices, Wages and Popular Movements," 263–265.

189. Schmidt, *Paris pendant la Révolution*, 282.

190. Rudé, "Prices, Wages and Popular Movements," 263–265.

191. François-Alphonse Aulard, *Paris pendant la réaction thermidorienne*, vol. 1 (Paris: Librairie Léopold Cerf, 1898).

192. Laura Mason, "Thermidor and the Myth of Rupture," in *The Oxford Handbook of the French Revolution*, ed. David Andress (Oxford: Oxford University Press, 2015), 524; Laura Mason, "The Thermidorian Reaction" in *A Companion to the French Revolution*, ed. Peter McPhee (Oxford: Wiley-Blackwell, 2013), 317–318.

193. Jean-Luc Chappey, "The New Elites: Questions about Political, Social, and Cultural Reconstruction after the Terror," in Andress, ed., *The Oxford Handbook of the French Revolution*, 557–561.

194. *Moniteur*, August 28, 1795, vol. 25, 578–579, 341.

195. BHVP #962985, in 8°, Camille Saint-Aubin, "Marchand d'oignons devroit se connaître en ciboules, ou Application de cette maxime à plusieurs articles d'un arrêté du comité de Sûreté générale concernant la vente des comestibles à la halle et aux marchés, rendu le fructidor, sur le rapport de la commission administrative de la commune de Paris" (Paris: Imprimerie de Pougin, 1795).

196. Laura Mason, "Never Was a Plot So Holy: Gracchus Babeuf and the End of the French Revolution," in *Conspiracy in the French Revolution*, ed. Peter Campbell, Thomas Kaiser, and Marisa Linton (Manchester: Manchester University Press, 2007), 175.

197. *Le Miroir*, 6 Prairial an IV, 98.

198. Mason, "Never Was a Plot So Holy," 172, 184.

199. Bouton, "Les Mouvements de Subsistance," 72.

200. Margairaz and Minard, "Marché des subsistances et économie morale," 84, 91, 95.

201. After the initial General Maximum, the Dames advocated for more price regulation that would carve out a place for retailers in 1793 and 1794. This sharply diverged from how the Dames used free market principles to justify capitalist competition among parasol renters in 1792.

202. Bruno Blondé and Natacha Coquery note the same definition in the 1730 *Dictionnaire universal de commerce*. "Introduction," in *Retailers and Consumer Changes in Early Modern Europe: England, France, Italy, and the Low Countries*, ed. Bruno Blondé, Eugénie Briot, Natacha Coquery, and Laura Van Aert (Tours: Presses Universitaires François-Rabelais, 2005), 5–19.

Chapter 7

1. BnF Le29 1729 *Adresse des Dames de la Halle, à l'Assemblée nationale, séance du 27 août 1791* (Paris: Imprimerie Nationale, 1791), 2. The confraternity of Saint Louis, which the female merchants of cod had composed, had donated already their holdings of 3,000 livres on November 2, 1789. They now sought to have this original donation acknowledged; AN C 75, n°745, August 27, 1791.

2. *La Chronique de Paris*, August 28, 1791, n° 240, 974; AN C 75, n°745, August 27, 1791.

3. BnF Le29 1729, *Adresse des Dames de la Halle*, 2.

4. *AP*, August 27, 1791, 29:754. There is a typo with "savoir" in place of "servir" in the published version *Adresse des Dames de la Halle, à l'Assemblée nationale, séance du 27 août 1791*.

5. AdPP D^B 389, Dossier Révolution, Droits d'entrée, Contributions, Patentes, "D) le modèle de Patente," in "Loi Portant établissement d'un droit de patente pour l'an V, du 6 fructidor, an IV."

6. John Shovlin, *The Political Economy of Virtue: Luxury, Patriotism, and the Origins of the French Revolution* (Ithaca: Cornell University Press, 2006), 11–12.

7. William Sewell, *Work and Revolution in France: The Language of Labor from the Old Regime to 1848* (Cambridge: Cambridge University Press, 1980), 80, 113. Sewell calls this the "moral collectivism" of the sans-culottes.

8. Yanni Kotsonis, *States of Obligation: Taxes and Citizenship in the Russian Empire and Early Soviet Republic* (Toronto: University of Toronto Press, 2014), 5.

9. Anne Verjus, *Le Cens de la famille: Les femmes et le vote, 1789–1848* (Paris: Éditions Berlin, 2002), 33.

10. As quoted by Auguste-Philippe Herlaut, "Les certificats de civisme," *Annales historiques de la Révolution française*, 90 (November–December 1938), 492.

11. André Neurisse, *Histoire de la Fiscalité en France* (Paris: Economica, 1996), 45.

12. Henry Laufenburger, *Histoire de l'impôt* (Paris: Presses Universitaires de France, 1959), 18; Nicolas Delalande and Alexis Spire, *Histoire sociale de l'impôt* (Paris: La Découverte, 2010), 10.

13. "L'Assemblée Nationale aux François, relativement aux contributions publiques, proclamation décrétée le 24 juin 1791," in *Œuvres du comte P.L. Roederer*, ed. A. M. Roederer, vol. 6 (Paris: Imprimeurs de l'Institut, 1857), 545; Roederer, "Discours sur les motions ajournées relativement à la Liste Civile," September 1791, in Roederer, *Œuvres,*562.
14. Delalande and Spire, *Histoire sociale de l'impôt*, 13.
15. This language comes from Article 13 of the *Declaration of the Rights of Man and Citizen*, which established "fiscal equality"; Michel Bottin, *Histoire des Finances publiques* (Paris: Economica, 1997), 37.
16. Bottin, *Histoire des Finances publiques*, 37. On the fierce resistance to indirect taxes in the early Revolution, see Noelle Plack, "Drinking and Rebelling: Wine, Taxes, and Popular Agency in Revolutionary Paris, 1789–1791," *French Historical Studies* 39, no. 3 (2016): 599–622.
17. "Rapport sur les Patentes, fait au Nom du Comité des Contributions Publiques, le 15 février 1791," in Roederer, *Œuvres*, vol. 6, 523.
18. Kotsonis, *States of Obligation*, 10, 56; Jean Lafourcade, *Détermination et Contrôle de la Patente* (J. Delmas et Cie, 1968), G5.
19. As quoted in Gabriel Ardant, *Histoire de l'Impôt*, vol. 2 (Paris: Fayard, 1972), 168.
20. Bottin, *Histoire des Finances publiques*, 39.
21. "L'Assemblée Nationale aux François," in Roederer, *Œuvres*, vol. 6, 552.
22. Ardant, *Histoire de l'Impôt*, vol. 2, 169. For a discussion of "active" versus "passive" citizenship, see William Sewell, "Le Citoyen, La Citoyenne: Activity, Passivity and the French Revolutionary Concept of Citizenship," in *The French Revolution and the Creation of Modern Political Culture*, ed. Colin Lucas (Oxford: Pergamon Press, 1988), vol. 2, 105–125.
23. *AP*, "Décret et instruction de l'Assemblée nationale du 13 janvier 1791 sur la Contribution mobilière," January 13, 1791, 22:174.
24. Bottin, *Histoire des Finances publiques*, 39.
25. Michael Fitzsimmons, *From Artisan to Worker: Guilds, the French State, and the Organization of Labor, 1776-1821* (New York: Cambridge University Press, 2010), 43–44.
26. Delalande and Spire, *Histoire sociale de l'impôt*, 3.
27. *AP*, February 15, 1791, 23:202.
28. *Réimpression de l'ancien Moniteur*, n°48, February 17, 1791, vol. 7 (Paris: Henri Plon, 1861), 399–400. Reporting on the session of February 16, 1791.
29. Lafourcade, *Détermination et Contrôle*, A1. The Constitution of 1793 and the Constitution of 1795 likewise characterize the "fruit de son travail" as an individual's property.
30. Bottin, *Histoire des Finances publiques*, 39.
31. "Lettres" and "Patente," in *Dictionnaire de l'Académie française*, 1st Edition (1694), Project ARTFL.
32. *Le Grand Vocabulaire François*, vol. 20 (Paris: Panckouche, 1772), 211–212.
33. Rafe Blaufarb, *The Great Demarcation: The French Revolution and the Invention of Modern Property* (Oxford University Press, 2016), 2, 5. On the *lettres patentes* and *métiers jurés*, see Sewell, *Work and Revolution*, 26–28.
34. *AP*, September 23, 1790, 19:181.
35. *AP*, February 15, 1791, 23:202.
36. See the 1791 model patente licences in AdPP D^B 389, Département de Paris, "Loi Relative aux Patentes," Affiche n°1339, 19 octobre 1791.
37. Blaufarb, *The Great Demarcation*, 2.
38. Delalande and Spire, *Histoire sociale de l'impôt*, 14.
39. "Rapport sur les Patentes," in Roederer, *Œuvres*, vol. 6, 523.
40. *Moniteur*, n°48, February 17, 1791, vol. 7, 396. Report on session of February 15, 1791. D'allarde quoted Turgot's Edict of 1776. Thomas Brassey, On *Work and Wages* (Vancouver: Read Books, 2009, original 1872), 2.
41. *AP*, February 15, 1791, 23:203.
42. See William Sewell on Turgot in *Work and Revolution*, 127–133.
43. On the genealogy of "propre," see Sewell, *Work and Revolution*, 115.
44. *Révolutions de Paris*, February 12–19, 1791, Reporting on session of February 16, 1791.
45. *AP*, March 2, 1791, 23:629.

46. *Révolutions de Paris*, February 19–26, 1791, n°85. Reporting on the session of February 17, 1791, and "follow-up on the Patente Decree."

47. "L'Assemblée Nationale aux François," in Roederer, *Œuvres*, vol. 6, 548.

48. *AP*, March 2, 1791, 23:629–630; BnF 8-Lc2-171, *Révolutions de Paris*, September 24, 1791, n°115, 556. Reporting on the session of September 17, 1791.

49. *Moniteur*, February 17, 1791, n°48, 397.

50. "Décret portant suppression de tous les droits d'aides, de toutes les maîtrises et jurandes, et établissement des Patentes," March 2–17, 1791, in *Recueil Général des Lois, Décrets, Ordonnances, etc.*, ed. LePec, vol. 2, n°100, (Paris: L'administration du Journal des Notaires et des Avocats, 1839), 37.

51. Roger Price, *An Economic History of Modern France, 1730–1914* (London: Macmillan Press, 1981), 162.

52. Taxes, like patente, that are calculated from material markers are "index" taxes. Delalande and Spire, *Histoire sociale de l'impôt*, 14.

53. "Patente," in *Répertoire méthodique et alphabétique de Législation de Doctrine et de Jurisprudence en matière de droit civil, commercial, criminel, administratif, de droit des gens et de droit public*, ed. M. D. Dalloz and M. Armand Dalloz, vol. 35 (Paris: Imprimerie par E. Thunot, 1855).

54. Marcel Marion, *Histoire financière de la France depuis 1715*, vol. 2 (New York: Brut Franklin, 1919), 218; see "Décret portant suppression de tous les droits d'aides, de toutes les maîtrises et jurandes, et établissement des Patentes," March 2–17, 1791, in LePec, *Recueil Général des Lois, Décrets*, vol. 2, n°100, 37.

55. "Rapport sur les Patentes," in Roederer, *Œuvres*, vol. 6, 527.

56. LePec, *Recueil Général des Lois, Décrets*, vol. 2, 35.

57. Fitzsimmons, *From Artisan to Worker*, 60.

58. *Moniteur*, February 18, 1791, n°49, 405–406.

59. LePec, *Recueil Général des Lois, Décrets*, vol. 2, 35.

60. *Révolutions de Paris*, February 19–26, 1791, n°85. Reporting on session of February 17, 1791.

61. *AP*, February 17, 1791, 23:230.

62. *Moniteur*, February 17, 1791, n°48.

63. AdPP D^B 389, Dossier Révolution, Droits d'entrée, Contributions, patentes: Département de Paris "Loi Relative aux Assemblées d'Ouvriers & Artisans de même état & profession, donné à Paris le 17 juin 1791."

64. BnF Le29 1729 *Adresse des Dames de la Halle*.

65. Marion, *Histoire financière*, vol. 2, 219.

66. *AP*, March 2, 1791, 23:629–630. *Révolutions de Paris*, September 24, 1791, n°115. Reporting on the session of September 17, 1791. All taxed occupations except for peddlers and wine merchants were assigned licenses from these three categories.

67. "Décret relatif aux patentes," September 20–October 9, 1791, in Dalloz and Dalloz, *Répertoire méthodique*, vol. 35, 45.

68. AdPP D^B 389 Dossier Marché, Pendant la révolution (affaires diverses): Poster: 9 octobre 1791, Loi Relative aux patentes (suite à la loi du 3 mars 1791); Loi du 2 septembre 1791; Loi du 17 septembre 1791.

69. In order to overturn Old Regime privilege, the earliest revolutionary tax agents were elected officials. Thus, patente holders potentially interacted with the very government agents they helped elect. This changed when the Directory began to appoint agents to collect taxes and created departmental "Agences des Contributions directes" to supervise each municipality's tax rolls. Delalande and Spire, *Histoire sociale de l'impôt*, 13–15.

70. "Rapport sur les Patentes" in Roederer, *Œuvres*, vol. 6, 521–530.

71. Ruth Scurr, "Social equality in Pierre-Louis Roederer's interpretation of the modern republic, 1793," *History of European Ideas* 26, no. 2, (2000): 106, 118.

72. Scurr, "Social equality in Pierre-Louis Roederer's interpretation," 112.

73. "Cours d'organisation sociale," 1793, in Roederer, *Œuvres*, vol. 8, 235; Scurr, "Social equality in Pierre-Louis Roederer's interpretation," 118.

74. "Cours d'organisation sociale," 1793, in Roederer, *Œuvres*, vol. 8, 142.

75. Scurr, "Social equality in Pierre-Louis Roederer's interpretation," 112, 118; "Cours d'organisation sociale" 1793, in Roederer, *Œuvres*, vol. 8, 141–142.

76. Scurr, "Social equality in Pierre-Louis Roederer's interpretation," 112, 118.

77. "Cours d'organisation sociale," 1793, in Roederer, Œuvres, vol. 8, 239, 266.

78. "Cours d'organisation sociale," 1793, in Roederer, Œuvres, vol. 8, 267.

79. Of course, the sans-culottes would frown upon Roederer's idea of substantial economic disparity as just. See Patrice Higonnet, Goodness beyond Virtue: Jacobins during the French Revolution (Harvard: Harvard University Press, 1998), 84–85.

80. Herlaut, "Les certificats de civisme," 492.

81. Colin Jones, The Longman Companion to the French Revolution (Longman: New York, 1990), 123.

82. On the trajectory of the Comités de surveillance révolutionnaire, see Réimpression de l'Ancien moniteur, 25 frimaire an III, n°85, vol. 22, 734.

83. AP, March 21, 1793, 60:379, 372

84. Marion, Histoire financière, vol. 2, 222.

85. Jeanne Gaillard, "Les Intentions d'une Politique Fiscale, la Patente en France au XIXᵉ Siècle" Bulletin du Centre d'histoire de la France contemporaine, n°7, 1986, 18.

86. AP, March 21, 1793, 60:379–380.

87. Fitzsimmons, From Artisan to Worker, 61.

88. AP, March 21, 1793, 60:386.

89. AP, April 24, 1793, 63:281.

90. Herlaut, "Les certificats de civisme," 519.

91. AdPP Dᴮ 389, Merlin, Ministre de la Justice, "Loi Portant établissement d'un droit de patente pour l'an V," 6 fructidor an IV, n°679 (Paris: Ballard, an IV).

92. Moniteur, 9 thermidor an III, n°309. Reporting on the session of 4 thermidor an III.

93. Bottin, Histoire des Finances publiques, 47.

94. Déclaration des droits et devoirs de l'homme et du citoyen, art. 16, in Constitution du 5 fructidor an III.

95. AP, March 21, 1793, 60: 371.

96. AdPP Dᴮ 389, Dossier Révolution, Droits d'entrée, Contributions, patentes, "Par le maire et les Officiers Municipaux, Avis Concernant les patentes publiés le 10 avril 1792."

97. "L'Assemblée Nationale aux François," in Roederer, Œuvres, vol. 6, 554; AP, January 13, 1791, 22:174.

98. AdPP Dᴮ 389, "Loi portant établissement d'un droit de patente pour l'an V, Du 6 fructidor, an IV."

99. AdPP Dᴮ 389, Dossier Révolution, Droits d'entrée, Contributions, patentes, "Loi Portant établissement d'un droit de patente pour l'an V, du 6 fructidor, an IV."

100. Moniteur, 27 nivôse an V, n°117.

101. Blaufarb, The Great Demarcation, 10, 120.

102. Verjus, Le Cens de la famille, 33.

103. Jones, The Longman Companion, 71, 73, 75.

104. James Livesey, Making Democracy in the French Revolution (Cambridge: Harvard University Press, 2001), 86.

105. Shovlin, The Political Economy of Virtue, 207.

106. Verjus, Le Cens de la famille, 44, 16.

107. Verjus, Le Cens de la famille, 80.

108. Verjus, Le Cens de la famille, 71. See also Jennifer Heuer, The Family and the Nation: Gender and Citizenship in Revolutionary France, 1789–1830, (Ithaca: Cornell University Press, 2005), 76–78.

109. Ewa Lajer-Burcharth, "David's Sabine Women: Body, Gender, and Republican Culture under the Directory," Art History 14, no. 3 (1991): 397–399.

110. Martyn Lyons, France under the Directory (Cambridge: Cambridge University Press, 1975), 64–66.

111. AdPP Dᴮ 389, Dossier Révolution, Droits d'entrée, Contributions, patentes, "Loi Portant établissement d'un droit de patente pour l'an V, du 6 fructidor, an IV."

112. Rates calculated using the tables conforming to the laws of 6 fructidor an IV, 9 frimaire an V, and 7 brumaire an VI in AdPP Dᴮ 389, Régisseurs de l'Enregistrement et du Domaine

national, "Circulaire n°1417: Patentes de l'an VI, loi du 1er brumaire an VII, et instructions pour son exécution."

113. AdPP D^B 389, Dossier Révolution, Droits d'entrée, Contributions, patentes, "Loi Portant établissement d'un droit de patente pour l'an V, du 6 fructidor, an IV."

114. *Déclaration des droits et devoirs de l'homme et du citoyen*, art. 5 in Constitution du 5 fructidor an III.

115. AdPP D^B 389, Dossier Révolution, Droits d'entrée, Contributions, patentes, "Loi Portant établissement d'un droit de patente pour l'an V, du 6 fructidor, an IV."

116. AdPP D^B 389, Dossier Révolution, Droits d'entrée, Contributions, patentes, "Loi Portant établissement d'un droit de patente pour l'an V, du 6 fructidor, an IV."

117. AdPP D^B 389, "Le Bureau Central du Canton de Paris aux Commissaires de Police et aux Contrôleurs et Inspecteurs sur les Ports et dans les Halles et Marchés," n°721, nivôse an VI.

118. AdPP D^B 389, Dossier Révolution, Droits d'entrée, Contributions, patentes, "Loi Portant établissement d'un droit de patente pour l'an V, du 6 fructidor, an IV."

119. AdPP D^B 389, "B) le modèle de quittance," in "Loi portant établissement d'un droit de patente pour l'an V, Du 6 fructidor, an IV." Wealthier individuals regularly claimed work property such as workshops, factories, stores, fixed boutiques, and so forth, as occupational structures.

120. AdPP D^B 389, "A) le modèle du registre des déclarations et recettes," in "Loi portant établissement d'un droit de patente pour l'an V, Du 6 fructidor, an IV."

121. AdPP D^B 389, Dossier Révolution, Droits d'entrée, Contributions, patentes: "Le Bureau Central du Canton de Paris aux Commissaires de Police, et aux Contrôleurs et Inspecteurs sur les Ports et dans les Halles et Marchés," nivôse an VII.

122. AdPP D^B 389, Merlin, Ministre de la Justice, "Loi Portant établissement d'un droit de patente pour l'an V," 6 fructidor an IV, n°679 (Paris: Ballard, an IV).

123. AdPP D^B 389, Dossier Révolution, Droits d'entrée, Contributions, patentes: "Le Bureau Central du Canton de Paris aux Commissaires de Police, et aux Contrôleurs et Inspecteurs sur les Ports et dans les Halles et Marchés," nivôse an VII.

124. AdPP D^B 389, Dossier Révolution, Droits d'entrée, Contributions, patentes, "Loi Portant établissement d'un droit de patente pour l'an V, du 6 fructidor, an IV."

125. AdP D.4 U^1 29, Justice de Paix du 4ème Arrondissement Ancien, Section Marché des Innocents, le troisième jour complémentaire an V.

126. AdPP D^B 389, Dossier Révolution, Droits d'entrée, Contributions, patentes, "Loi Portant établissement d'un droit de patente pour l'an V, du 6 fructidor an IV."

127. AdPP D^B 389, Dossier Révolution, Droits d'entrée, Contributions, patentes, "Loi Portant établissement d'un droit de patente pour l'an V, du 6 fructidor an IV."

128. AdP D.4 U^1 28, Justice de Paix du 4ème Arrondissement Ancien, Section Marché des Innocents, n°20, 7 thermidor an V. Commercially active widows also paid autonomous patentes including the droit proportionnel by default. The justice of the peace summoned one fashion merchant, Citoyenne Veuve Millot, to pay the fixed taxes for her patente as well as the proportional taxes for the property that she held as a widow. AdP D.4 U^1 28, n°160, 12 fructidor an V.

129. AdPP D^B 389, Dossier Révolution, Droits d'entrée, Contributions, Patentes: "Le Bureau Central du Canton de Paris aux Commissaires de Police, et aux Contrôleurs et Inspecteurs sur les Ports et dans les Halles et Marchés," nivôse an VII.

130. AdP D.4 U^1 29, n°288, 7 vendémiaire an VI.

131. Guillaume Mazeau and Clyde Marlo Plumauzille, "Penser avec le genre: Trouble dans la citoyenneté révolutionnaire," *La Révolution française*, no. 9 (2015), http://lrf.revues.org/1458, 14 (accessed October 24, 2016).

132. AdPP D^B 374 Marché de Paris, couverts; Dossier Marchés interlopes: Commissionnaires aux abords des Halles, "loi du 2 mars 1791."

133. AdP D.4 U^1 29, n°266, 2 vendémiaire an VI. Herbault was also spelled Herbauls.

134. AdP D.4 U^1 28, n°153, 12 fructidor an V.

135. AdP D.4 U^1 28, n° 53, 17 thermidor an V.

136. AdP D.4 U^1 28, n° 168, 12 fructidor an V.

137. AdP D.4 U¹ 28, n°161, 12 fructidor an V.
138. AdP D.4 U¹ 29, n°266, 2 vendémiaire an VI.
139. AdP D.4 U¹ 28, n° 53, 17 thermidor an V.
140. AdP D.4 U¹ 29, n°330, 7 vendémiaire an V.
141. AdP D.4 U¹ 28, n° 59, 17 thermidor an V.
142. AdP D.4 U¹ 28, n°237, fructidor an V. The Directory did not codify judges' ability to "remit fines" until October 1798; AdPP Dᴮ 389 Dossier Révolution, Droits d'entrée, Contributions, patentes: "Code de patentes ou recueil Méthodique, des lois des 6 fructidor an IV, 9 frimaire an V, 11 germinal an V, et 7 brumaire an VI, sur les patentes, 'A l'usage de toutes les Administrations centrales et municipales, des juges de paix, des commissaires du Directoire exécutif et des Contribuables de la République.'"
143. AdPP Dᴮ 389 Dossier Révolution, Droits d'entrée, Contributions, patentes: "Code de patentes ou recueil Méthodique, des lois des 6 fructidor an IV, 9 frimaire an V, 11 germinal an V, et 7 brumaire an VI, sur les patentes."
144. AdPP Dᴮ 389 Dossier Révolution, Droits d'entrée, Contributions, patentes: Les Régisseurs de l'Enregistrement et du Domaine national, 24 Brumaire an VII, circulaire n°1417, "Patentes de l'an 7. Loi de 1ᵉʳ bumaire an 7, et instructions pour son exécution."
145. AdPP Dᴮ 389 *Code des Patentes ou Recueil Méthodique des lois des 6 fructidor an IV, 9 frimaire, 11 germinal an V, et 7 brumaire an VI sur les Patentes*, ed. Département de la Seine (Paris: Ballard, an VI).
146. AdPP Dᴮ 389 Dossier Révolution, Droits d'entrée, Contributions, patentes: Les Régisseurs de l'Enregistrement et du Domaine national, 24 Brumaire an VII, circulaire n°1417, "patentes de l'an 7. Loi de 1ᵉʳ bumaire an 7, et instructions pour son exécution."
147. Husbands and wives would only continue to pay for personal patentes in the infrequent marital arrangement of *séparation des biens* (legal separation of goods). These dual patentes were no way connected to wife's possible *femme marchande* status. AdPP Dᴮ 389 Dossier Révolution, Droits d'entrée, Contributions, patentes: Les Régisseurs de l'Enregistrement et du Domaine national, 24 Brumaire an VII, circulaire n°1417, "Patentes de l'an 7. Loi de 1ᵉʳ bumaire an 7, et instructions pour son exécution."
148. AdPP Dᴮ 389 Dossier Révolution, Droits d'entrée, Contributions, patentes: Le Bureau Central du Canton de Paris aux Commissaires de Police, et aux Contrôleurs et Inspecteurs sur les Ports et dans les Halles et Marchés pour assurer l'exécution des Loix des patentes, nivôse an VII.
149. The national government decreed that the regionally calculated "journée de travail" (the average daily local wages) could not be below 50 centimes or above 1.5 francs. "Loi sur le mode d'assiette, de perception et de dégrèvement, dans l'intérieur des départemens, de la contribution personnelle, mobilière, et somptuaire de l'an 7," 3 nivôse an 7 (23 décembre 1798), in *Collection Complète des Lois, Décrets, Ordonnances, Réglemens*, 12th ed., ed. J. B. Duvergier, vol. 11 (Paris: Chez Guyot et Scribe, 1835), 139.
150. Book 1, Title V, Chapter VI, Articles 214 and 220 of the *French Civil Code* (1803), The Napoleon Series, http://www.napoleon-series.org/research/government/code/ (accessed January 17, 2017).
151. Sewell, *Work and Revolution*, 114. Rafe Blaufarb notes that "'absolute property'—that is, property owned fully and independently by a single person—existed nowhere in France before the Revolution." Blaufarb, *The Great Demarcation*, 3.
152. In his trajectory from 1789 to 1848, Sewell does not recognize this intermediary step in the transition from land, physical possessions, and privileges as Old Regime personal "property" to capital as the bourgeois form of Napoleonic household "property."
153. Delalande and Spire, *Histoire sociale de l'impôt*, 15. Jean Tulard, Jean-François Fayard, and Alfred Fierro, *Histoire et Dictionnaire de la Révolution française* (Paris: Robert Laffont, 1998), 212–213, 821. Without an income tax or a nationally reliable land register, the French state leaned more heavily on indirect taxes in the nineteenth century. In contrast, the United States and Great Britain began to partially rely on income tax. Kimberly J. Morgan and Monica Prasad, "The Origins of Tax Systems: A French-American Comparison," *American Journal of Sociology*, 114, no. 5 (2009): 1350; Robert Schnerb, Jacques Wolff, and Jean

Bouvier, *Deux siècles de fiscalité française: XIXᵉ-XXᵉ siècle, histoire, économie, politique, recueil d'articles* (Paris: Mouton, 1973), 97.

154. Neurisse, *Histoire de la Fiscalité*, 52–53.

155. Dominique-Vincent Ramel de Nogaret, *Des finances de la République française en l'an IX* (Paris: Chez Agasse, 1800), 113.

156. Lafourcade, *Détermination et Contrôle*, A2.

157. Delalande and Spire, *Histoire sociale de l'impôt*, 14, 60. The government did not tax "interest, dividends, [and] salaries" throughout the nineteenth century. Stephen Owen, "The Politics of Tax Reform in France, 1906–1926," (PhD diss., University of California, Berkeley, 1982), 78.

158. Verjus, *Le Cens de la famille*, 200.

159. Jeanne Gaillard, "Les Intentions d'une Politique Fiscale, la Patente en France au XIXᵉ Siècle," 17. Russia experienced similar tensions between taxes and the right to vote in the nineteenth century. Russia started its own patente modeled on the French example in 1824 and made every citizen eligible to buy one in 1863. This had significant consequences since, in 1870, "the payment of any tax, duty, or license fee" enfranchised Russians in town government elections. Kotsonis, *States of Obligation*, 58, 60.

160. Jeanne Gaillard, "Les Intentions d'une Politique Fiscale, la Patente en France au XIXᵉ Siècle," 20, 35–37.

161. Stephen Owen, "The Politics of Tax Reform in France, 1906–1926," 64.

162. All four of the direct taxes that the revolutionaries established lasted until at least 1917.

163. Kotsonis, *States of Obligation*. 151.

164. Jean Lafourcade, *Détermination et Contrôle*, C1, B3, A4; "La Patente," on "Le portail de l'Économie et des Finances," maintained by Centre des Archives Économiques et Financières, http://www.economie.gouv.fr/caef/patente#histoire (accessed February 9, 2017).

165. The *taxe professionnelle* was abolished in 2010 and was replaced by the *contribution économique territoriale* (the territorial economic contribution) based on the rental value of business tangible property and a value added tax. "La Patente," on "Le portail de l'Économie et des Finances," maintained by Centre des Archives Économiques et Financières, http://www.economie.gouv.fr/caef/patente#histoire (accessed February 9, 2017).

Conclusion

1. "France: Preparation for the Great Fete," *New York Daily Times* (New York), August 28, 1852; "France: The National Fete in August," *New York Daily Times*, September 15, 1852.

2. BnF Estampes Réserve FT4 QB 370 (132), "Programme Complet et officiel des Fêtes et Cérémonies qui vont avoir lieu dans Paris le 15 août 1852, à l'occasion de la Fête de Saint-Napoléon" (Paris: Boucquin, 1852).

3. BnF Yth 304, Clairville and Adolphe Choler, *Le Bal de la Halle* (Paris: Beck Libraire, 1852), 1.

4. BnF YE 7180 (508), Louis-Charles Durand, "Les Dames de la Halle: Hommage aux Dames des Halles" (Paris: Impr. de Beaulé, 1852).

5. BnF YE 970 (47), Léon Guilleman, "Les Aventures de la mère Caquet-Bon-Bec au bal des dames de la halle. Chansonnette comique" (Paris: E. de Sote, 1852). The placard reprinted the *Moniteur*'s description of the ball.

6. Sudhir Hazareesingh, "'A Common Sentiment of National Glory': Civic Festivities and French Collective Sentiment under the Second Empire," *Journal of Modern History* 76, no. 2 (June 2004): 280.

7. For an analysis of the Madame Angot plays, see "Playing the Poissarde: Madame Angot, the Dames des Halles, and Political Influence, 1795–1804" in Katie Jarvis, "Politics in the Marketplace: The Popular Activism and Cultural Representation of the Dames des Halles during the French Revolution" (PhD diss., University of Wisconsin-Madison, 2014). For the first Madame Angot blockbuster, see BnF Z Rothschild-4589, Antoine-François Ève Maillot, *Madame Angot, ou la Poissarde parvenue, opéra-comique en 2 actes, joué sur le Théâtre d'Émulation* (Paris: Chez Barba, An V).

8. Quoted in Elizabeth Colwill, "Sex, Savagery and Slavery in the Shaping of the French Body Politic," in *From the Royal to the Republican Body: Incorporating the Political in Seventeenth- and Eighteenth-Century France*, ed. Sarah Melzer and Kathryn Norberg (Berkeley: University of California Press, 1998), 213, 211.

9. Suzanne Desan, *The Family on Trial in Revolutionary France* (Berkeley: University of California Press, 2004), 314.

10. Sophie Wahnich argues that the revolutionaries' different interpretations of "universality" ultimately created "political cleavages." Wahnich, "L'Universel, Le Singulier, le Sujet, à l'Epreuve de la Révolution française," in *Universel, Singulier, Sujet*, ed. Jelica Sumic (Paris: Éditions Kimé, 2000), 159.

11. There is no denying that the Dames had exceptional opportunities for legal, commercial, and fiscal autonomy due to their occupations as female retailers. For the peasant-citizens who composed more than two-thirds of the population, heavy agricultural regulation and forced collections significantly troubled the connection between volition and useful work. However, peasants did promote the idea of the autonomous citizen, according to Jean-Pierre Jessenne, "Une Révolution sans ou contre les paysans?," in *La Révolution française: Une histoire toujours vivante*, ed. Michel Biard (Éditions Tallandier: 2010), 253, 258, 262.

12. James Livesey has contrasted the rewards of property and labor during the Directory: "While property ownership was a fundamental element of civil liberty, labor, the common capacity for work, was the fundamental element that allowed participation in the economy and in society." Livesey, *Making Democracy in the French Revolution* (Cambridge: Harvard University Press, 2001), 70.

13. Philip Dawson, "Introduction," in *The French Revolution and the Meaning of Citizenship*, ed. Renée Waldinger, Philip Dawson, and Isser Woloch (Westport, CT: Greenwood Press, 1993), xxi; See also William Sewell's excellent study on propertyles wage laborers, corporatism, collective action, and labor history as related to the manual laborer. *Work and Revolution in France: The Language of Labor from the Old Regime to 1848* (Cambridge: Cambridge University Press, 1980).

14. For example, Haim Burstin's article on urban work and citizenship focuses on male wage laborers because he limits "travail" to remunerated labor. Burstin perceptively seeks to use this category of "travail" to unhinge the passive/active distinctions among citizens. But since his main question is which actions does the government compensate and why, his definition of work only encompasses services rendered for wages. He argues officials paid men in the National Guard, the army, and the sectional assemblies in order to replace the wages individuals lost during their service. Burstin, "Travail et citoyenneté en milieu urbain sous la Révolution," in *Citoyens et citoyenneté sous la Révolution française*, ed. Raymonde Monnier (Paris: Société des Études Robespierristes, 2006), 263-270.

15. Historians have extensively debated how to delineate the revolutionary bourgeoisie and their economic activities vis-à-vis their Old Regime predecessors. Colin Jones argued venal office holders at the end of the Old Regime bought their positions as entrepreneurial investments rather than socially loaded titles. He argues, "These groups were more genuinely bourgeois than ever before, and exuded a new civic professionalism which had its roots in a developing 'market-consciousness.'" Jones, "Bourgeois Revolution Revivified: 1789 and social change," reprinted in an abridged format from *The French Revolution and Social Change*, ed. Colin Lucas (Oxford: Oxford University Press, 1990), 69-118, in *The French Revolution: Recent Debates and Controversies*, ed. Gary Kates (New York: Routledge, 2006), 100. In his study of the Parisian bourgeoisie over the longue durée, David Garrioch also spotlights venal offices as a means to bypass corporations and to solicit privileges from the government. Garrioch argues that, in the second half of the eighteenth century, "as the local kinship network became less important [for the bourgeoisie], the weight of other components of notability grew: personal reputation, size of business, and particularly wealth." He concludes that the bourgeoisie did not solidify as a class until 1830. Garrioch, *The Formation of the Parisian Bourgeoisie, 1690-1830* (Cambridge: Harvard University Press, 1996), 121, 281. Sarah Maza has argued that no

self-aware bourgeois class existed, while Lynn Hunt reads revolutionary discourse as "bourgeois" in so much as "it expressed the will to break with the past of aristocratic domination." Lauren Clay discerns a politically active "commercial bourgeoisie" during the calling of the Estates General. Maza, *The Myth of the French Bourgeoisie: An Essay on the Social Imaginary, 1750–1850* (Cambridge: Harvard University Press, 2003), 6. Hunt, *Politics, Culture, and Class in the French Revolution* (Berkeley: University of California Press, 2004, orig. ed. 1984), 50. Lauren Clay, "The Bourgeoisie, Capitalism, and the Origins of the French Revolution" in *The Oxford Handbook of the French Revolution*, ed. David Andress (Oxford: Oxford University Press, 2015), 21–35.

16. For a perceptive genealogy of these debates from 1789 to 1848, see Sewell, *Work and Revolution*, 8.

17. As studies on the marginalization of care workers and work-from-home employees illustrate, space continues to partially orient gender and modern labor history. For recent theories on gender, space, and class, see Anaïs Albert, Fanny Gallot, Katie Jarvis, Anne Jusseaume, Eve Meuret-Campfort, Clyde Plumauzille, and Mathilde Rossigneux-Méheust, "Introduction: Le lieu à l'épreuve du genre et des classes populaires," *Genre & Histoire* 17 (Printemps 2016), http://genrehistoire.revues.org/2416.

18. For example, Nimisha Barton has analyzed how, among working-class immigrant women in the early twentieth century, "a particularly female form of mutual aid and neighborhood association functioned as foreign women's primary path to acculturation." Scrimping and saving in neighborhoods offered both economic resources and inroads to community membership. Barton, "Foreign Affairs, Family Matters: Gender and Acculturation in Paris, 1914–1940" (PhD. diss., Princeton University, 2014).

19. In the commercial terms of the nineteenth century, liberal citizenship involved reconciling self-interest and public good within a free market economy. Victoria Thompson, *The Virtuous Marketplace: Women and Men, Money, and Politics in Paris, 1830–1870* (Baltimore: Johns Hopkins University Press, 2000), 4.

20. I do not maintain that this is a universally empowering concept determined by free will alone. Indeed, socioeconomic realities and familial survival more frequently dictate the contours of occupational choices than personal inclination. However, I am arguing that this perspective offers us new ways of conceptualizing society in which work and gender operate on the same discursive sociopolitical plane.

21. Madelyn Gutwirth cites Germaine de Staël and Olympe de Gouges to illustrate that "even the most militant women . . . feel moved to make their pleas as *épouses et mères* or to disclaim their ambition in the very midst of sweeping pronouncements or demands." Gutwirth, "Citoyens, Citoyennes: Cultural Regression and the Subversion of Female Citizenship in the French Revolution," in Waldinger et al., *The French Revolution and the Meaning of Citizenship*, 21. However, the Dames show us that these gendered appeals do not have to be bracketed as posturing or insincere gestures. The Dames did not choose between gendered and militant discourses, because the two did not inherently conflict in their logic of civic work.

22. Thompson, *The Virtuous Marketplace*, 53, 61–62, 65.

23. We can also consider the political ramifications for interpreting types of work through a male example: Male novelists could write novels and male journalists could compose reports from their desks at home. But the domestic location of their work would not emasculate them nor politically stunt them. The novelists' and the journalists' occupational products are aimed directly at others in society at large. Their work extends beyond their own family. Therefore, their work is unmediated with regard to beneficiaries in the community. In her study of women workers in the sewing and garment industry in the nineteenth century, Judith Coffin similarly seeks to get beyond binaries of "home and work, family and market, paid and unpaid labor." She argues that the minimum wage law of 1915 reflected a major change in the relationship among place, gender, and work when it categorized women who performed outsourced labor at home as workers. Judith Coffin,

The Politics of Women's Work: The Paris Garment Trades, 1750–1915, (Princeton: Princeton University Press, 2014), 9, 251.

24. Thompson, *The Virtuous Marketplace,* 76–77, 79, 99, 90.

25. Sewell, *Work and Revolution,* 244, 245, 249. Louis Blanc's February 25, 1848, decree on the "right to labor" declared, "The Government of the French Republic commits itself to guarantee the existence of the worker by labor. It commits itself to guarantee labor to all citizens. It recognizes that workers should associate with one another in order to enjoy the legitimate benefits of their labor."

BIBLIOGRAPHY

Archival Sources

ARCHIVES NATIONALES

Archives imprimées: AD XVIIIe 315

Archives de pouvoir exécutif (1789–1815); AF^{II} 42, AF^{IV} 1329, AF^{IV} 1470, AF^{IV} 1472, AF^{IV} 1478

Ministère de la Justice: BB 87, BB^3 76, BB^3 81^A, BB^3 91

Assemblées nationales: C 33, C 48, C 75, C 128, C 139, C 143, C 147, C 149, C 152, C 163, C 167, C 287

Missions des représentants du peuple et Comités des assemblées: D VI 1, D VI 8

Comité de salut public: D XLII 11

Conseil du roi: E 2653

Esprit public: F^{1c} III Seine 14, F^{1c} III Seine 27

Ministère de l'Intérieur, Police générale: F^7 3688^3, F^7 3702, F^7 3830, F^7 7611, F^7 7745^a

Subsistances: F^{11} 201, F^{11} 205, F^{11} 1185

Commerce et industrie: F^{12} 1239, F^{12} 1266

Bâtiments civils: F^{13} 1162

Instruction publique: F^{17} 1692

Contributions directes: F^{31} 79^{01}, F^{31} 79^{20}

Maison du Roi: O^1 4000, O^1 5000

Domaines: Q^1 1183, Q^1 1186, Q^1 1187

Biens des établissements religieux supprimés: S 4688

Juridictions extraordinaires: W 76, W 78, W 112, W 174, W 191

Parlement de Paris; parlement civil, minutes: X^{1b} 9084

Juridictions spéciales et ordinaires: Z^3 85

Chambre de la Marée: Z^{11} 1

ARCHIVES DE PARIS

Tribunal de commerce de la Seine, Actes de société, 1786–an XI: D.1 U^3 35

Justice de Paix du 4ème Arrondissement Ancien: D.4 U^1 23, D.4 U^1 24, D.4 U^1 25, D.4 U^1 26, D.4 U^1 27, D.4 U^1 28, D.4U^1 29, D.4U^1 30

Biens nationaux: D.Q^{10} 1, D.Q^{10} 39, D.Q^{10} 482, D.Q^{10} 742, D.Q^{10} 743, D.Q^{10} 1392

Affaires Économiques (Administration Communale): V2F^4 9

Administration générale de la Commune de Paris 1789–1800: VD* 3, VD* 8, VD* 40, VD* 47, VD* 46

ARCHIVES DE LA PRÉFECTURE DE POLICE

Procès-verbaux des commissaires de police des sections de Paris, 1789–1820: AA 68, AA 72, AA 88, AA 166

Réglementation et vie quotidienne: commerces et industrie, mendicité, voirie: D^A 23, D^A 24

La préfecture de police: documents administratifs et coupures de presse: D^B 258, D^B 374, D^B 387, D^B 389, D^B 396, D^B 515

BIBLIOTHÈQUE HISTORIQUE DE LA VILLE DE PARIS

7530. *Récit exact de ce qui s'est passé hier à Sainte Geneviève par les Dames du Marché Saint Martin.*

10073 (tome II, n°57) in 8°. Municipalité de Paris par le maire et les officiers municipaux. "Extrait du registre des délibérations du Corps municipal." Du samedi 24 septembre 1791. Paris: Imprimerie Lottin l'aîné et J.R. Lottin, 1791.

10073 (tome II, n°59) in 8°. Municipalité de Paris par le maire et les Officiers-Municipaux. "Extrait du registre des délibérations du Corps municipal, Arrêté sur les échoppes et étalages fixes et mobiles." Du lundi 3 octobre 1791. Paris: Lottin l'aîné & J.R. Lottin, 1791.

10073c (tome II n°68) in 8°. Municipalité de Paris, Par le maire et les officiers municipaux. "Extrait du registre des délibérations du Corps municipal." Du vendredi 4 novembre 1791. Paris: Lottin l'aîné et J.R. Lottin, 1791.

31598 (n°2) in 8°. "Grand détail concernant les dévots et les dévotes qui ont été fouettés par les dames de la Halle à Paris." Paris: Baudouin.

131912 in 4°. Municipalité de Paris, Département de police. "Le M. le Maire, M. le lieutenant de Maire et MM. les Conseillers, Administration règlement provisoire, pour le Marché des SS Innocents." 2 mai 1790. Paris: Lottin l'aîné & Lottin, 1790.

600056. Claude-François de Beaulieu, Assemblée nationale. "Séance et suite des Nouvelles de Versailles du 8 octobre 1789. Découverte d'un complot contre la liberté nationale. Réclamation des dames des halles et marchés contre des faussetés publiées contre elles." Paris: Imprimerie de Seguin-Thiboust, 1789.

959739 in 8°. "Démolition totale des harangues de la halle, faite hier au soir par le peuple." Paris: LL Girard.

962985, in 8°. Camille Saint-Aubin. "Marchand d'oignons devroit se connaître en ciboules, ou Application de cette maxime à plusieurs articles d'un arrêté du comité de Sûreté générale concernant la vente des comestibles à la halle et aux marchés, rendu le fructidor, sur le 1794–1795."

BIBLIOTHÈQUE NATIONALE DE FRANCE, MITTERRAND

F 21216 (31). "Arrêt du Conseil d'État du Roi, qui fixe l'époque à laquelle seront démolies les échoppes du parquet à la Marée, du Carreau du Pilori & du Marché aux Poirées." Paris: L'imprimerie Royale, 1786.

F-21193 (22). *Édit du Roi, Par lequel Sa Majesté en créant, de nouveau, six Corps de Marchands & quarante-quatre Communautés d'Arts & Métiers, conserve libres centaines genres de Métiers ou de Commerce: Réunit les Professions qui ont de l'analogie entr'elles; & établit à l'avenir des règles dans le régime desdits Corps & Communautés.* Paris, 1776.

F 23631 (891). "Lettres Patentes du Roi, sur un Décret de l'Assemblée Nationale, du 26 Juillet 1790, relatif aux droits de Propriété & de Voyerie sur les chemins publics, rues & places de villages, bourgs ou villes, & arbres dépendans." 15 août 1790. Paris: Chez Nyon, 1790.

F 23675 (99). Parlement de Paris, Arrêts de Règlement du Parlement de Paris. "Concernant les Droits de Voierie, des 21 juillet & 27 août 1779." Paris: Imprimerie de Ph. D. Pierres, 1779.

GR FOL LK7 6043. Edme Verniquet. "Atlas du plan général de la ville de Paris, levé géométriquement par le cen Verniquet rapporté sur une échelle d'une demie ligne pour toise, divisée en 72 planches, compris les cartouches et plan des opérations trigonométriques." Dessiné et gravé par les cens Bartholomé et Mathieu. Paris: rue de l'Oratoire, 1795.

HP 750. *Lettre de Marie Bon-bec harangère de la halle à l'auteur des "Rèflexions occasionées par la Conférence d'un franc maçon et d'un profane."* Lb38 682. *Dialogue entre deux poissardes, sur la prise du fort Saint Philippes.* 1756.

Lb39 1229. *Les trois poissardes, buvant à la santé du Tiers-État.*

Lb39 1635. *Compliment des Dames poissardes à leurs frères du Tiers-État.*

Lb39 2085. *Entrée triomphante de M. Necker à l'Hôtel-de-Ville, accompagnée du compliment de M. le marquis de la Fayette & de M. Bailly, maire, suivie de la réponse de M. Necker, & de la présentation du bouquet des poissardes.* Paris: Chez Cressonnier, 1789.

Lb39 2089. *Les Poissardes à la Reine.* Paris: Imprimerie P. de Lormel, 1789.

Lb39 2239. *Bouquet du roi: Pour le 25 août 1789.* Versailles: Imprimerie Royale, 1789.

Lb39 2352. *Réclamation de toutes les poissardes, avec un petit mot à la gloire de notre bonne Duchesse d'Orléans.* Paris: Chez Guillaume, fils, 1789.

Lb39 2411. *Les héroïnes de Paris, ou l'entière liberté de la France par les femmes, police qu'elles doivent exercer de leur propre autorité.* Paris: Knapen.

Lb39 2472. Jean-Gabriel Peltier. *Domine salvum fac regem.* Sur les bords du Gange: October 21, 1781.

Lb39 5296. *V'là c'que s'est dit et passé à la Halle.*

Lb39 5505. *Liste des Culs Aristocrates et Anti-Constitutionnels, qui ont été fouettés hier au soir à tour de bras, par les Dames de la Halle, et du Faubourg Saint-Antoine.* Paris: Imprimerie Patriotique, 1791.

Lb39 6234. *La Joie des halles, conversation entre Madame Giroflée, Marchande Bouquetière, Madame Saumon, Marchande de la marée, & Monsieur Jacquot-la-grosse-patte, Marinier, sur le Joyeux Avénement du Roi à la Couronne.* Imprimerie de D'Houry, 1774.

Lb39 6294. *Harangue des Dames de la Halle aux citoyens du faubourg Saint Antoine prononcée par Ma. Engueule.* 1789.

Lb39 7354. *Compliment des poissardes de Paris à MM. Les électeurs qui ont été à Versailles pour solliciter l'amnistie des Gardes Françaises.* 1789.

Lb39 7705. signé Lebois. *Procession solennelle des dames fripières de la Halle et des marchandes du cimetière des innocents, suivie du Compliment à M. de la Fayette.* Paris: Imprimerie de la Jorry, 1789.

Lb39 7744. signé Lebois. *Récit exact de ce qui s'est passé hier à Sainte Geneviève par les Dames du Marché Saint Martin; & de-là à l'Hôtel-de-Ville; avec Compliment prononcé au Roi par Mlle Bourbau, âgée de 17 ans au nom des dames du Marché Saint Martin; Et la réception agréable de la part de Sa Majesté.* Imprimerie Ballard.

Lb39 7744. *Compliment prononcé au Roi par Mademoiselle Bourbau, âgée de 17 ans, au nom des dames du marché S. Martin et la réception agréable de la part de Sa Majesté.* Paris: Imprimerie de P.R.C.

Lb39 7577. *Premier dialogue entre une poissarde et un fort de la Halle.*

Lb39 7758. Reine d'Hongrie, Mesdames Pluvinet, DeVille, Chevalier, Lefebvre, Lamy, Doute, Genet, Cochois, Baronet. *Lettre d'invitation des dames marchandes du marché d'Aguesseau, à un Te Deum.* 1789.

Lb39 7802. Louise-Félicité Guinement de Kéralio, *Observations sur quelques articles du projet de constitution de M. Mounier.* Paris: Imprimerie de N.H. Nyon, 1789.

Lb39 8267. *Demande de la Reine d'Hongrie à M. le Directeur de la Comédie-Française.*

Lb39 8416. *Le Goûter de la Courtille ou Dialogues sur les affaires présentes, entre quatre dames de la halle: Mme Saumon, La Mère Gogo, La Mère Écorche-Anguille et Manon L'Écailleuse.*

Lb39 9028. *Avis important d'une dame des Halles pour la diminution des vivres.* Paris: De la Cloye.

Lb39 9193. *Départ de M. d'Artois pour se rendre à Paris et détail intéressant de la réception qu'il a faitte [sic] aux dames de la halle pour le ramener à Paris.* Imprimerie de Calais & Dubois.

Lb39 9451. *Adresse aux dames parisiennes. Le voyage à St. Cloud. Paris ou Le Service du Bout de l'An, Pour faire suite au Voyage de Versailles.* Paris: Imprimerie de J. Legueum, 1790.

Lb39 9542. *Le Club des Halles établi à l'instar de celui des Jacobins à la nouvelle Halle ci- devant le charnier des innocents.* Paris: Imprimerie des Halles, 1790.

Lb39 9938. "Grand événement arrivé à un patriote de la Halle, à cause de l'échange d'un assignat. Grande difficulté à ce sujet. Formation d'un club aux Halles."

Lb39 10208. *Grande motion des Halles.* 1791.

Lb39 11705. *Le Roi d'Yvetot à la Reine d'Hongrie tenant sa cour plénière aux Halles de Paris.* Paris: Chez Debray.

Lb40 1245. *Discours adressé au roi par les dames de la Halle, membres de la Société Fraternelle, dont, le 14 Février 1791, elles sont venues donner lecture au Conseil-Général de la Commune, qui en a ordonné l'impression à la distribution.* Paris: Imprimerie de Lottin l'aîné & J.R. Lottin, 1791.

Lb41 1509. Jean-René Loyseau. *Réflexions sur la loi du maximum et sur les réquisitions.* Paris: Chez Vialard, 1795.

Lc2 513. Le Père Duchêne. *Je suis le véritable père Duchêne, foutre,* n°8. Paris: Imprimerie du véritable père Duchêne.

Lc2 2268. "Du brave La Fayette on connaît la valeur. En suivant ses drapeaux, on suit ceux d'un vainqueur." *La Gazette des Halles* n° 1. Paris: Imprimerie de N.H. Nyon, 1789.

Lc2 2382. "Petit mot d'avis en passant. Lettre du général La Pique aux dames de la Halle." In *Journal des Halles.* n° 1 juin 1790.

Ld4 7148. *Liste de toutes les sœurs & dévotes qui ont été fouettées par les Dames des Marchés des différents Quartiers de Paris, avec leur nom, celui de leur Paroisse, & un détail très-véritable de toutes leurs aventures avec les Curés Vicaires à Habitués desdites Paroisses.* Paris: L'imprimerie de Tremblay, 1791.

Le29 1729. *Adresse des Dames de la Halle, à l'Assemblée nationale, séance du 27 août 1791.* Paris: Imprimerie Nationale, 1791.

Le38 344. Jacques Louis David, Convention nationale. "Rapport et décret sur la fête de la Réunion républicaine du 10 août, présentés au nom du Comité d'Instruction publique." 11 juillet 1793. Paris: Imprimerie Nationale, 1793.

Le38 1111. Giraud, Marc-Antoine-Alexis, "Rapport et projet de décret sur la nécessité de rapporter la loi sur le maximum, présentés au nom du comité de commerce et d'approvisionnemens." Paris: Imprimerie nationale, 1795.

LI3-52 (I,2). Louis-Sébastien Mercier. *Tableau de Paris.* Vol. 2 Amsterdam: 1782.

LI3-52 (J,1). Louis-Sébastien Mercier. *Tableau de Paris.* Vol. 1. Amsterdam: 1793.

LI3-52 (1,4). Louis-Sébastien Mercier. *Tableau de Paris.* Vol. 4. Amsterdam, 1782.

LK7 31662. "Adresse à M. le Maire de Paris, ou à son lieutenant, pour les marchands merciers-fripiers-tailleurs, et autres habituellement attachés au marché des SS Innocens." Paris: Imprimerie de Hérault, 1790.

M 12884. Mme Dupray. *Chanson des Dames des Marchés Saint Paul; des Quinze-vingts, la Halle & d'Aguesseau.*

NUMM 42404. Conseil-Général de la Commune of Paris. *Tarif du maximum des salaires, façons, gages, main d'oeuvres, journées de travail dans l'étendue de la commune de Paris.* Paris: Nicolas et Desbrières, circa 5 Thermidor an II.

NUMM 42495. Jacques-René Hébert. *Grande colère du Père Duchesne contre les jean-foutres de calomniateurs des Dames de la halle, & des Bouquetières du palais-royal, au sujet du beau discours qu'elles ont fait au roi.* Paris: Imprimerie de Tremblay, 1791.

Rés YE 3065. *Motion des harangères de la Halle.*

Rés YE 3069. *Le Divorce, Dialogue entre Madame Engueule et Madame Saumon harangères, et M. Mannquin, fort de la halle.* 1790.

Yth 304. Clairville and Adolphe Choler. *Le Bal de la Halle.* Paris: Beck Libraire, 1852.

YE 4787. *Justification des Messieurs et des Dames de la Halle de Paris, sur les crimes de l'exécrable révolution française, notamment de ceux des 5 et 6 octobre 1789, commis à Versailles, auxquels on les accusoit d'avoir pris part.*

YE 7180 (508). Louis-Charles Durand. "Les Dames de la Halle: Hommage aux Dames des Halles." Paris: Impr. de Beaulé, 1852.

YE 14068-71. Citoyen B***. *Almanach républicain chantant pour l'an 2e de la République française: commençant le 22 septembre 1793, et finissant le 21 septembre 1794; La déclaration des droits de l'Homme; Le Maximum.* Paris: Chez Lallemand, 1793.

YE 32173. *Riche-en-Gueule ou Le Nouveau Vadé publié par un enfant de la joie et dédié aux dames des halles et marchés.* Paris: Quai des Augustins n° 9.

YE 35763 (13). *Chanson Poissarde: Leur arrivée à Versailles, & leur retour à Paris avec le Roi & la Famille Royale.*

Z Le Senne 2974. *Dictionnaire de voierie.*

Z Le Senne 4329. Anne Claude Philippe de Pestels de Lévis de Tubières-Grimoard. *Les Citrons de Javotte. Histoire de Carnaval.* Amsterdam, 1756.

Z Le Senne 5128. *Les Bienfaits de l'Assemblée Nationale ou entretiens de la Mère Saumon, doyenne de la Halle: suivis des vaudevilles.* Paris: Au Palais Royal, 1792.

Z Le Senne 6366 (9). Louis-Sébastien Mercier. *Tableau de Paris.* Vol. 9. Amsterdam: 1788.

Z Le Senne 6366 (11). Louis-Sébastien Mercier. *Tableau de Paris.* Vol. 11. Amsterdam: 1788.

Z Le Senne 9438. *Recueil complet de tout ce qui s'est passé à la fête de l'Unité et de l'Indivisibilité de la République Française, suivi des inscriptions tracées sur les pierres de la Bastille et sur les monumens destinés pour cette cérémonie.* Paris: Imprimerie de Chaudrillié.

Z Rothschild-4589. Antoine-François Ève (known as Maillot or Demaillot). *Madame Angot, ou la Poissarde parvenue, opéra-comique en 2 actes, joué sur le Théâtre d'Émulation.* Paris: Chez Barba, An V (1796).

BNF, ARCHIVES DE LA BASTILLE

BL 21306. Fr.-Ch. Huerne de La Mothe. *Histoire nouvelle de Margot des Pelotons; ou la Galanterie naturelle.* 2 parties en 1 vol. Genève, 1775.

BL 19584. *Étrennes aux Messieurs les Ribauteurs les Supplémens aux Écosseuses, ou Margot La Mal-Peignée en Belle Humeur, et ses qualités* (1759). In *Recueil d'œuvres comiques et poissardes.* 1756–1760.

GD 9001. *Dialogue pas mal raisonnable, entre un ancien commis de barrière, un passeur, un couvreur, un charpentier et une Dame de la Halle.*

GD 11044. *La Gazette des Halles.* n° 2 Paris: Imprimerie de N.H. Nyon, 1789.

GD 23459. *La joie de la nation: dialogue sur l'heureuse naissance de monseigneur le Dauphin entre Bruletout, Dragon; Margot, Poissarde: Frisotin, Garçon Perruquier, et Mlle Fontanges, Marchande de Moses au S. Esprit par un clerc de procureur.* Paris: À tous les coins de rues, 1781.

BNF, DÉPARTEMENT DES ARTS DU SPECTACLE

Ra4 659. Augustin de Piis. *Le Bouquet du vaudeville, ou Dialogue d'un charbonnier et d'une poissarde sur la naissance de Mgr le Dauphin.* Imprimerie de Chardon, 1781.

BNF, DÉPARTEMENT CARTES ET PLANS

GESH18PF37DIV3P56. "Paris au XVIIIe siècle. Plan de Paris: en 20 planches, dessiné et gravé sous les ordres de Michel-Étienne Turgot, prévôt des marchands, commencé en 1734, achevé de graver en 1739; levé et dessiné par Louis Bretez." Paris, 1739.

BNF, DÉPARTEMENT DES ESTAMPES

De Vinck 3497. "Fait miraculeux arrivé à Paris l'an de salut de 1791, le six avril." Etching, 25.5 cm × 30 cm, 1791.

De Vinck, 4857. "Les Dames de la Halle de Paris vont complimenter la Reine aux Tuileries." Watercolor, 20.5 cm × 15 cm, 1792.

M 98953. "Médaille aux bonnes citoyennes le 8 octobre 1789, donnée par la commune de Paris."

M 99404. "4e événement du 5 8bre 1789: Les Femmes Parisiennes siégant à l'Assemblée Nationale parmi les deputés."

M 99412. "5, 8bre Départ des Dames de la Halle pour aller chercher le Roi à Versailles."

M 99429. Guyot. "Arrivée des Femmes à Versailles le 5 oct. 1789." Paris: Chez Graveur et Md d'Estampes Rue S. Jacques n°10.

M 99431. "Événement du 5 octobre 1789: Les Dames de la Halle et autres femmes partant de Paris pour Versailles."

M 99433. Ph. Caresme. *Dédiée aux Femmes: Bravoure des Femmes Parisiennes à la Journée du 5 octobre 1789, Paris.* Paris: rue de la Lune, n°38, 1789.

M 99442. "Vue du Château de Versailles à l'époque du 5 8bre 1789: Le Roi la Reine et Msr le Dauphin présentant au Balcon donnant sur la Cour des Miracles."

M 99448. "Le Roi reçoit les Femmes de la Halle."

M 99468. "Vue de la Lanterne de la Place de Grève: Le courage des Héroïnes Françaises passant le 6 octobre devant l'Hôtel de Ville et faisant porter devant elles les têtes de deux Gardes du Corps qui avaient eut l'imprudence de faire feu sur elles à leurs arrivées à Versailles."

M 99487. Medal, "Aux bonnes citoyennes le 8 octobre 1789."

M 99968. "J'sommes du Tiers."

M 100435. "Les femmes de la halle donnant à Mr Barnave un bouquet et le compliment sur son patriotisme."

M 100570. "Le Fanatisme corrigée ou La Discipline Patriotique." Paris: Chez Villeneuve Graveur.

M 100995. "18 septembre Proclamation de la première Constitution."

M 100996. "Proclamation de la Constitution Place du Marché des Innocens le 14 septembre 1791."

M 100997. Detail of "Proclamation de la Constitution Place du Marché des Innocens le 14 septembre 1791."

P 21379. "Eh bien, J ... F ..., dira-tu encore vive la noblesse?" London: 1789.

P 21381. Berthault. "Les Dames de la Halle Partant Pour Aller Chercher le roi à Versailles le 5 octobre 1789."

P 21385. "À Versailles! À Versailles: ou la Journée du 5 Octobre 1789."

P 21390. "Les Dames de Paris Allant à Versailles."

P 21409. "Vive le roi! Vive la Nation! Lang leeve de Koning! Lang leeve de natie!"

P 21428. "La terrible Nuit du 5 au 6 Octobre 1789." Gravure anonyme.

P 22029. "La Discipline patriotique ou le fanatisme corrigée."

P 22731. "Les Parques Nationales Parisiennes."

P 23562. "La Correction Républicaine."

P 23880bis. "Événement de 14 7bre 1792."

QB-1 (1789-10-08). "Les Dames de la halle félicitant leurs Majestés sur le commencement de la Constitution." Etching, 1789 or 1790.

Réserve Fol VE-53 (F). Jacques François Joseph Swebach. "Fontaine des innocents, Élevée sur la place de la halle. Les bas-reliefs des Cens Jean-Gougeon [sic], et de Pujet." Drawing with pen and brown ink, 26.7 cm × 19.6 cm, 1793.

Réserve Fol QB 201 (124). "Le Fanatisme corrigée ou la Dicipline [sic] patriotique." Paris: Chez Villeneuve. Etching, 14.5 cm × 11 cm, 1791.

Réserve FT4 QB-370 (132). "Programme Complet et officiel des Fêtes et Cérémonies qui vont avoir lieu dans Paris le 15 août 1852, à l'occasion de la Fête de Saint-Napoléon." Paris: Boucquin, 1852.

BNF, DÉPARTEMENT DES MANUSCRITS

Mf 34833. Mss fonds français 11697. Letters between Bailly and Gouvion, 23 juillet 1791.

Nouv. Acq. Fr. 2651, fol. 187. "Délibération de la section du Marché-des-Innocents." 5 mai 1792.

MUSÉE CARNAVALET, PARIS, CABINET DES ARTS GRAPHIQUES

AFF341, Affiche. "N° 2216 Décret de la Convention Nationale le 16e jour de Ventôse, an second de la République Française, une & indivisible, Relatif à des Pamflets [sic] contre-révolutionnaires répandus dans les Halles & Marchés." Paris: Imprimerie nationale exécutive du Louvre, 1794.

G.13561, Jacques Aliamet (engraver) and Étienne Jeaurat (painter). "La Place des Halles." Etching, 35 cm × 42 cm, 1757–1761.

Histoire 8 Chemise C couleurs G 23922. "Une femme de condition, fouettée pour avoir craché sur le portrait de Mr Necker."

Histoire PC 007, G 2796. "Les Dames de la Halle félicitant leurs Majestés sur le commencement de la Constitution."

Histoire PC 007, G 2796. "Le Roi reçoit les Femmes de la Halle," 1789.

Histoire PC 007, G 25375. "Vive le Roi! Vive la Nation!"

Histoire PC 007, G 26246. "Pariser Poisarden sonst Fisch Weiber."

Histoire PC 007, G 26247. "La Journée Mémorable de Versailles, Le lundi 5 Octobre 1789."

Histoire PC 007, G 27952. "Les Dames de la Halle partant pour aller chercher le roi à Versailles le 5 octobre 1789."

Histoire PC 007, G 27952. "Le Roi arrivant à Paris escorté de plus de trente mille âmes le 6 octobre 1789."

Histoire PC 007, G 27958. "Départ des Femmes de la Halle Pour Versailles."

Histoire PC 007, Chemise C, G 27973 87CAR 037NB. "Le Roi paroisseant au Balcon donnant sur la Cour de marbre: dit Mes enfans j'irai à Paris mais à condition que ce sera avec ma femme et mes enfans."

Histoire PC 007, G 27974. "Le Roi Reçoit les Dames de la Halle."

Histoire PC 007, G 27978. "Époque du 6 octobre 1789, l'après dîné à Versailles."

Histoire PC 007, G 27982. "Journée Mémorable du 6 octobre 1789."

Histoire PC 007, G 27983. "Retour des Héroïnes Parisiennes après l'expédition de Versailles du 6 octobre 1789."

Histoire PC 007, G 29383. "La Journée à jamais Mémorable aux François où Louis XVI Restaurateur de la liberté Françoise se rendit à l'Hôtel de Ville le 17 du mois de Juillet 1789."

P190, Lafontaine, Pierre. Le marché des Innocents. Oil on canvas, 49.5 cm × 60.5 cm, around 1791.

Printed Primary Sources

Avis important d'une Dame des Halles pour la Diminution des vivres. Paris: Chez LaCloye, Librarie à L'Orme Saint-Gervais, 1789. Reprinted in Réclamations de Femmes, 1789, edited by Milagros Palma. Paris: Côté femmes éditions, 1989.

Biré, Edmond. Journal d'un Bourgeois de Paris pendant la Terreur. "La Fête-Dieu," Jeudi le 30 mai 1793. Vol. 2. Paris: Librairie Académique Didier.

Cahier des plaintes et doléances des Dames de la Halle et Marchés de Paris, Rédigé au grand salon des Porcherons, le premier dimanche de Mai, pour être présenté à Messieux les États-Généraux, Avec des augmentations sur la nouvelle du premier samedi du mois de Juin, au sujet du pain. 1789. Reprinted in Réclamations de Femmes, 1789, edited by Milagros Palma. Paris: Côté femmes éditions, 1989.

Compliment des dames poissardes à leurs frères du Tiers État (1789). In Charles-Louis Chassin, Les Élections et les cahiers de Paris en 1789. Volume II. Paris, 1888–1889, 252–253. Reprinted in Women in Revolutionary Paris, 1789–1795, edited by Darline Gay Levy, Harriet Branson Applewhite, and Mary Durham Johnson. Urbana: University of Illinois Press, 1980.

Déclaration des droits et devoirs de l'homme et du citoyen. In Constitution du 5 fructidor an III.

Diderot and d'Alembert, eds. Encyclopédie, ou dictionnaire raisonné des sciences, des arts et des métiers. Vol. 3. (1751–72). The Project for American and French Research on the Treasury of the French Language (ARTFL). http://portail.atilf.fr/encyclopedie/.

"France: The National Fete in August." New York Daily Times, September 15, 1852.

"France: Preparation for the Great Fete." New York Daily Times, August 28, 1852.

Franz Gabriel Fiesinger, engraver. "Assignat de vingt-cinq livres." Paris: Domaines nationaux, 1791. In Images de la Révolution française: catalogue du vidéodisque. 1990. 35034-2506.

Godard, M. Exposé des Travaux de l'Assemblée-Générale des Représentans de la Commune de Paris, Depuis le 25 Juillet 1789, jusqu'au mois d'Octobre 1790, époque de l'organisation définitive de la Municipalité, fait par ordre de l'Assemblée. Paris: Imprimerie de Lottin l'aîné, 1790.

Granville Levenson-Gower Sutherland, George. "April 15, 1791." In The despatches of Earl Gower, English ambassador at Paris from June 1790 to August 1792: To which are added the despatches of Mr. Lindsay and Mr. Monro, and the diary of Viscount Palmerston in France during July and August 1791, edited by Oscar Browning. London: C. J. Clay and Son, Cambridge University Press Warehouse, 1885.

Les Facteurs et factrices à la Halle aux Farines, à leurs concitoyens. France: 1792.

"Letter IX on the French Revolution," December 1793. In *The Kentish Register and Monthly Miscellany, From August to December 1793.* Vol. 1. Canterbury: Simmons, Kirkgy, and Jones, 1792.

Maleissye, Marquis de. *Mémoires d'un Officier aux Gardes Françaises (1789–1793).* Paris: E. Plon, Nourrit, 1897.

Marivaux, Pierre Carlet de Chamblain de. *Le Jeu d'amour et du hasard.* 1730.

Mémoires secrets de Fournier l'Américain. Edited by F.-A. Aulard. Paris, 1890. Reprinted in *Women in Revolutionary Paris, 1789–1795,* edited by Darline Gay Levy, Harriet Branson Applewhite, and Mary Durham Johnson. Urbana: University of Illinois Press, 1980.

Montaigne, Michel de. *Essais de Michel de Montaigne.* Vol. 1. Paris: Chez Jean Serviere et Chez Jean-François Bastion, 1793.

Prévost, Antoine François. *L'Histoire du chevalier des Grieux et de Manon Lescaut.* 1731.

Procédure criminelle instruite au Châtelet de Paris, sur la dénunciation des faits arrivés à Versailles dans la journée du 6 Octobre 1789. Vol. 1. Paris: Chez Baudouin, 1790.

Prudhomme, ed. *Les Crimes des Reines de France Depuis Le Commencement de la Monarchie jusqu'à la Mort de Marie-Antoinette: Avec les Pièces Justificatives de son Procès.* Paris: Bureau des Révolutions de Paris, an II.

Roux, Jacques. "Le Manifeste des Enragés." In *Scripta et Acta,* edited by Walter Markoc. Berlin: Akademie-verlag, 1969.

Rutledge, James. *Le Creuset, Ouvrage Politique et Critique.* Vol. I, n° XVIII. Du jeudi 3 mars 1791. Paris: 1791.

Sirey, J.-B., ed. *Recueil Général des Lois et des Arrêts, en Matière Civile, Criminelle, Commerciale et de Droit public.* Vol. 21. Paris: Imprimerie de D'Hautel, 1821.

Société des Citoyennes républicaines révolutionnaires de Paris. *Règlement de la Société des citoyennes républicaines révolutionnaires de Paris.* Paris, 1793.

Thiery. *Le Voyageur à Paris: Extrait du Guide des amateurs & des étrangers voyageurs à Paris.* Vol. 2. Paris: Chez Gattey, 1790.

Vireau-Beavoir, Jean Loup de, and Giuseppe de Lama. *La Révolution française racontée par un diplomate étranger. Correspondance du bailli de Virieu, ministre plénipotentiaire de Parme (1788–1793).* Edited by Emmanuel Henri Vicomte de Grouchy and Antoine Guillois. Paris: E. Flammarion, 1903.

Von Kotzebue, August Friedrich Ferdinand. *Sketch of the Life and Literary Career of Augustus Von Kotzebue with the Journal of His Tour to Paris at the Close of the Year 1790.* Translated by Anne Plumptre. December 31, 1790. London: C. Whittingham, 1800.

Weston, Stephen. "Letter XXXIX, August 1791." In *Letters from Paris during the Summer of 1791.* London: J. Debrett, Piccadilly, and W. Clarke, 1792.

Zola, Émile. *Le Ventre de Paris.* Paris: Charpentier et Cie, 1873.

NEWSPAPERS

L'Ami du Peuple ou le Défenseur des Patriotes persécutés
L'Ami du Roi
La Chronique de Paris
La Correspondance Littéraire Secrète
Le Courrier de Lyon
Le Courrier de Paris dans les 83 Départements
Le Créole patriote: bulletin de Milscent-Créole, journal du soir
Le Journal des Débats et des Décrets
Le Journal de Paris
Le Journal général de France
Le Journal officiel de la République française
Le Mercure de France
Le Miroir

Révolutions de Paris

Réimpression de l'ancien Moniteur: depuis la réunion des États-Généraux jusqu'au Consulat

Révolutions de France et de Brabant par Camille Desmoulins

PRIMARY SOURCE COLLECTIONS AND REFERENCE VOLUMES

Aulard, François-Alphonse, ed. *Paris pendant la réaction thermidorienne et sous le directoire*. 5 volumes. Paris: Librairie Léopold Cerf, 1899.

————. ed. *La Société des Jacobins: Receuil de documents*. 6 vols. Paris: Librairie Jouaust, 1899.

Ballard, Richard. *A New Dictionary of the French Revolution*. London: I.B. Yauris, 2012.

Baecque, Antoine de. *La caricature révolutionnaire*. Italy, Presses de CNRS et l'imprimerie Arti Grafiche Vincenzo Bona, 1988.

Bély, Lucien, ed. *Dictionnaire de l'Ancien Régime: Royaume de France, XVIᵉ–XVIIIᵉ siècle*. Paris: Presses universitaires de France, 1996.

Boischevalier, Louis Joseph Hullin de. *Répertoire, ou Almanach historique de la Révolution française*. Paris: Lefort, 1793.

Boursin, Elphège, and Augustin Challamel, eds. *Dictionnaire de la Révolution française: Institutions, Hommes & Faits*. Paris: Librairie Furne, 1893.

Buchez, Philippe-Joseph-Benjamin, and Prosper-Charles Roux, eds. *Histoire parlementaire de la Révolution française, ou, Journal des assemblées nationales, depuis 1789 jusqu'en 1815*. 40 vols. Paris: Paulin, 1834–1838.

Caron, Pierre, ed. *La Commission des Subsistances de l'an II: Procès-verbaux et Actes*. 2 vols. Paris: E. Leroux, 1925.

————. ed. *Le Maximum général: Instruction, recueil de textes et notes*. Paris: Imprimerie Nationale, 1930.

————, ed. *Paris pendant la Terreur: Rapports des agents secrets du ministre de l'intérieur*. 7 vols. Paris: A. Picard, 1910–1978.

————, ed. *Paris pendant la Terreur: Rapports de Grivel et Siret sur les subsistances et le maximum (sept 1793–mars 1794)*. Vol. 1 [Collected and reprinted from *Bulletin trimestriel de la Commission de recherche et de publication des documents relatifs à la vie économique de la Révolution*, vol. 2 (1907), 67–231]. 1910.

————. ed. *Paris pendant la Terreur: Rapports de Grivel et Siret sur les subsistances et le maximum (sept 1793–mars 1794)*. Vol. 2 [Collected and reprinted from *Bulletin d'histoire économique de la Révolution*, vol. 11 (1920–1921), 371–427].

Chassin, Charles-Louis, ed. *Les élections et les cahiers de Paris en 1789: Documents recueillis, mis en ordre, et annotés*. 4 vols. Paris: D. Jouaust, Charles Noblet, and Maison Quantin, 1888–1889.

Clémencet, Suzanne. "Chambre de la Marée." In *Guide des recherches dans les fonds judiciaires de l'Ancien Régime*, edited by Michel Antoine. Paris: Imprimerie nationale, 1958.

Collection Générale des Décrets rendus par l'Assemblée Nationale Législative, avec la mention des sanctions et des mandats d'exécution donnés par le Roi. Vol. 3. Paris, 1792.

Dalloz, M. D., and M. Armand Dalloz, eds. *Répertoire méthodique et alphabétique de Législation de Doctrine et de Jurisprudence en matière de droit civil, commercial, criminel, administratif, de droit des gens et de droit public*. Vol. 35. Paris: Imprimerie par E. Thunot, 1855.

Déclaration des droits et des devoirs de l'homme et du citoyen. Conseil Constitutionnel. http://www.conseil-constitutionnel.fr/conseil-constitutionnel/francais/la-constitution/les-constitutions-de-la-france/constitution-du-5-fructidor-an-iii.5086.html. Accessed December 1, 2016.

Depeyrot, Georges, ed. *Monnaie et Papier-Monnaie Pendant la Révolution (1789–1803)*. Paris: Maison Florange, 1996.

Dictionnaire de l'Académie française, 1st ed. 1694.

Dictionnaire de l'Académie française, 4th ed. 1762.

Dictionnaire de l'Académie française, 5th ed. 1798.

Dictionnaire historique des institutions, mœurs et coutumes de la France. Paris: Librairie de L. Hachette, 1855.

Dictionnaire historique de la Révolution française. Edited by Albert Soboul, Jean-René Suratteau, François Gendron, Jean-Paul Bertaud, et al. Paris: Presses Universitaires de France, 2005.

Duvergier, J. B., ed. *Collection Complète des Lois, Décrets, Ordonnances, Réglemens.* 12th ed., vol. 11. Paris: Chez Guyot et Scribe, 1835.

Elyada, Ouzi, ed. *Lettres bougrement patriotiques de la Mère Duchêne suivi de Journal des Femmes, 1791.* Paris: Les Éditions de Paris/EDHIS, 1989.

Franklin, Alfred. *Dictionnaire Historique des Arts, Métiers et Professions depuis le Treizième siècle.* Paris: Chez H. Welter, 1906.

French Civil Code (1803). The Napoleon Series, http://www.napoleonseries.org/research/government/code/.

French National Assembly. "The Constitution of 1791." In *The Old Regime and the French Revolution,* edited by Keith Baker. University of Chicago Readings in Western Civilization, vol. 7. Chicago: University of Chicago Press, 1987.

Gerbaux, Fernand, and Charles Schmidt, eds. *Procès-Verbaux des Comités d'Agriculture et de Commerce de la Constituante de la Législative et de la Convention.* Vol. 2. Paris, 1906.

Hanson, Paul. *Historical Dictionary of the French Revolution.* Lanham, MD: Scarecrow Press, 2004.

Hould, Claudette, Annie Jourdan, Rolf Reichardt, and Stéphane Roy, eds. *La Révolution par la Gravure: Les Tableaux historiques de la Révolution française.* Vizille: Musée de la Révolution française, 2002.

Jones, Colin. *The Longman Companion to the French Revolution.* New York:Longman, 1990.

Kuscinski, A. *Dictionnaire des Conventionnels.* Paris: Société de l'histoire de la Révolution française, 1916.

Lacroix, Sigismond, ed. *Actes de la Commune de Paris pendant la Révolution.* New York: AMS Press, 1974.

"La mémoire des Lieux." Paris Révolutionnaire. http://www.parisrevolutionnaire.com/.

Lazare, Félix, and Louis Lazare. *Dictionnaire administratif et historique des rues et monuments de Paris.* Paris: Au bureau de la revue municipale, 1855.

Le Grand Vocabulaire François. Vol. 20. Paris: Panckouche, 1772.

Lemay, Edna Hindie, ed. *Dictionnaire des Constituants, 1789–1791.* Vol. 2. Paris: Universitas, 1991.

———. *Dictionnaire des Législateurs, 1791–1792.* Vol. 1. Paris: Ferney-Voltaire, 2007.

"Le portail de l'Économie et des Finances." Centre des Archives Économiques et Financières. http://www.economie.gouv.fr/caef/patente#histoire.

Leroux, Ernest, ed. *Commission de Recherche et de Publication des Documents Relatifs à la Vie Économique de la Révolution.* Bulletin Trimestrial. Paris: Imprimerie Nationale, 1907.

Lottin, Augustin Martin. *Catalogue Chronologique des Libraires et des Libraires-Imprimeurs de Paris, Depuis l'an 1470, époque de l'établissement de l'Imprimerie dans cette Capitale, jusqu'à présent.* Paris: Chez Jean-Roch Lottin de S. Germain, 1789.

Madival, J., and E. Laurent, eds. *Archives parlementaires de 1787 à 1860; recueil complet des débats législatifs & politiques des chambres françaises.* Series I. 102 vols. Paris: P. Dupont, Comité national de la recherche scientifique.

Marion, Marcel, ed. *Dictionnaire des institutions de la France aux XVIIᵉ et XVIIIᵉ siècles.* Paris: À Picard, 1923.

Mémoires de la Société de l'Histoire de Paris. Vol. 11. Paris: Chez Champion, 1885.

Quérard, Joseph-Marie. *La France littéraire ou Dictionnaire bibliographique des savants, historiens et gens de lettres de la France, ainsi que des littérateurs étrangers qui ont écrit en français, plus particulièrement pendant les XVIIIᵉ et XIXᵉ siècles.* Paris: Firmin Didot père et fils, 1827–1839.

Recueil Général des Lois, Décrets, Ordonnances, etc. Edited by LePec. Vol. 2. Paris: L'administration du Journal des Notaires et des Avocats, 1839.

Roederer, A. M. ed. *Oeuvres du comte P.L. Roederer.* Vol. 6. Paris: Imprimeurs de l'Institut, 1857.

Schmidt, Adolphe. *Paris pendant la Révolution d'après les rapports de la police secrète 1789–1800.* Vol. II. Paris: Champion, 1885.

Simonin, Anne, and Pierre Serna, eds. *Décrets et Lois 1789–1795: Collection Baudouin* http://collection-baudouin.univ-paris1.fr/.

Stanford University Libraries and the Bibliothèque nationale de France. *French Revolution Digital Archive.* http://frda.stanford.edu/.

Soboul, Albert, ed. *Dictionnaire historique de la Révolution française.* Paris: Presses Universitaires de France, 2006.

Tuetey, Alexandre. *Répertoire Général des sources Manuscrits de L'Histoire de Paris pendant la Révolution Française.* Paris: Imprimerie Nouvelle (Association Ouvrière), 1890.

Tulard, Jean, ed. *Almanach de Paris: De 1789 à nos jours.* Paris: Encyclopaedia universalis, 1990.

Tulard, Jean, Jean-François Fayard, and Alfred Fierro, eds. *Histoire et Dictionnaire de la Révolution française.* Paris: Robert Laffont, 1998.

Vermorel, A., ed. *Oeuvres de J. P. Marat l'Ami du Peuple.* Paris: Décembre-Alonnier, 1869.

Secondary Sources

Ågren, Maria, ed. *Making a Living, Making a Difference: Gender and Work in Early Modern European Society.* New York: Oxford University Press, 2016.

Albert, Anaïs, Fanny Gallot, Katie Jarvis, Anne Jusseaume, Eve Meuret-Campfort, Clyde Plumauzille, and Mathilde Rossigneux-Méheust. "Introduction: Le lieu à l'épreuve du genre et des classes populaires." *Genre et Histoire* 17 (Printemps 2016). http://genrehistoire. revues.org/2416.

Alpaugh, Micah. *Non-Violence and the French Revolution: Political Demonstrations in Paris, 1787–1795.* Cambridge: Cambridge University Press, 2015.

———. "The Politics of Escalation in French Revolutionary Protest: Political Demonstrations, Nonviolence and Violence in the Grandes journées of 1789." *French History* 23, no. 3 (Fall 2009): 336–359.

Applewhite, Harriet. "Citizenship and Political Alignment in the National Assembly." In *The French Revolution and the Meaning of Citizenship,* edited by Renée Waldinger, Philip Dawson, and Isser Woloch, 43–58. Westport, CT: Greenwood Press, 1993.

Applewhite, Harriet, and Darline Levy, eds. *Women and Politics in the Age of Democratic Revolution.* Ann Arbor: University of Michigan Press, 1990.

Ardant, Gabriel. *Histoire de l'Impôt.* Vol. 2. Paris: Fayard, 1972.

Aubert, Françoise. *Sylvain Maréchal: Passion et Faillite d'une Égalitaire.* Paris: Gliardica, 1975.

Baecque, Antoine de. *La caricature révolutionnaire.* Italy: Presses de CNRS et l'imprimerie Arti Grafiche Vincenzo Bona, 1988.

Baczko, Bronislaw. *Ending the Terror: The French Revolution after Robespierre.* Cambridge: Cambridge University Press, 1994.

Bailey, Merridee Tania Colwell, and Julie Hotchin, eds. *Women and Work in Premodern Europe: Experiences, Relationships, and Cultural Representation, c. 1100–1800.* London: Routledge, 2018.

Baker, Keith. "Public Opinion as Political Invention." In *Inventing the French Revolution.* Cambridge: Cambridge University Press, 1990.

Barton, Nimisha. "Foreign Affairs, Family Matters: Gender and Acculturation in Paris, 1914–1940." PhD diss., Princeton University, 2014.

Brassey, Thomas. On *Work and Wages.* Vancouver: Read Books, 2009, original 1872.

Baurit, M. *Les Halles de Paris des romains à nos jours.* Paris: Chez M. Baurit, 1956.

Blaufarb, Rafe. *The Great Demarcation: The French Revolution and the Invention of Modern Property.* New York: Oxford University Press, 2016.

Biard, Michel ed. *Les Politiques de la Terreur, 1793–1794: Actes du Colloque International de Rouen, 11–13 janvier 2007.* Paris: Société des Études Robespierristes, 2008.

Biollay, Léon. *Les anciennes Halles de Paris.* Mémoires de la Société de l'Histoire de Paris et de l'Ile-de-France, vol. 3, Paris: Société de l'Histoire de Paris, 1877.

Biver, Marie-Louise. *Fêtes révolutionnaires à Paris.* Paris: P.U.F., 1979.

Blackman, Robert. "Did Cicero Swear the Tennis Court Oath?" *French History* 28, no. 4 (2014): 471–497.

Bottin, Michel. *Histoire des Finances publiques*. Paris: Economica, 1997.

Bossenga, Gail. "Financial Origins of the French Revolution." In *From Deficit to Deluge: The Origins of the French Revolution*, edited by Thomas Kaiser and Dale Van Kley. Stanford: Stanford University Press, 2011.

———. *The Politics of Privilege: Old Regime and Revolution in Lille*. Cambridge: Cambridge University Press, 1991.

———. "Protecting Merchants: Guilds and Commercial Capitalism in Eighteenth-Century France." *French Historical Studies* 14 (Autumn 1988): 693–703.

———. "Review Article: Rights and Citizens in the Old Regime." *French Historical Studies* 20 (Spring 1997): 217–243.

Bouchary, Jean. *Les Compagnies financières à Paris à la fin du XVIIIᵉ siècle*. Vol. 2. Paris: Librairie des Sciences Politiques et Sociales Marcel Rivière et Cie, 1941.

———. *Les Faux-Monnayeurs sous la Révolution Française*. Paris: Librairie Marcel Rivière et Cie, 1946.

Bouton, Cynthia. "Les Mouvements de Subsistance et le problème de l'économie morale sous l'Ancien Régime et la Révolution française." *Annales historiques de la Révolution francaise* 319 (Janvier/mars 2000): 71–100.

———. *The Flour War: Gender, Class, and Community in Late Ancien Régime France*. University Park: Pennsylvania State University Press, 1993.

Boudon, Françoise, André Chastel, Hélène Couzy, and Françoise Hamon. *Système de l'Architecture Urbaine: Le Quartier des Halles à Paris*. Volume I. Paris: Éditions du Centre National de la Recherche Scientifique, 1977.

Braesch, Frédéric. *La Commune du dix août 1792: Étude sur l'histoire de Paris du 20 juin au 2 décembre 1792*. Paris: Librairie Hachette et Cⁱᵉ, 1911.

Bruno, Blondé, and Natacha Coquery. "Introduction." In *Retailers and Consumer Changes in Early Modern Europe: England, France, Italy, and the Low Countries*, edited by Bruno Blondé, Eugénie Briot, Natacha Coquery, and Laura Van Aert, 5–19. Tours: Presses Universitaires François-Rabelais, 2005.

Brive, Marie-France Brive, ed. *Les Femmes et la révolution française: Actes du colloque international, 12-13-14 avril 1989*. 3 vols. Toulouse: Presses universitaires du Mirail, 1989–1991.

Burstin, Haim. "Problèmes du travail à Paris sous la révolution." *Revue d'histoire moderne et contemporaine* 44, no. 4. (October/December 1997): 669–670.

———. *Révolutionnnaires: Pour une anthropologie politique de la Révolution française*. Paris: Vendémiaire, 2013.

———. "Travail et citoyenneté en milieu urbain sous la Révolution." In *Citoyens et citoyenneté sous la Révolution française*, edited by Raymonde Monnier. Paris: Société des Études Robespierristes, 2006.

Cage, Claire. "'Celibacy is a Social Crime': The Politics of Clerical Marriage, 1794–1799." *French Historical Studies* 36, no. 4 (Fall 2013): 601–628.

———. *Unnatural Frenchmen: The Politics of Priestly Celibacy and Marriage, 1720–1815*. Charlottesville: University of Virginia Press, 2015.

Caiani, Ambrogio. *Louis XVI and the French Revolution, 1789–1792*. Cambridge: Cambridge University Press, 2012.

Caron, Pierre. "Rapports de Grivel et Siret, Commissaires Observateurs Parisiens du Conseil Exécutif Provisoire sur les subsistances et le maximum." *Bulletin d'histoire économique de la Révolution*. Paris: Imprimerie Nationale, 1907.

Cerati, Marie. *Le Club des Citoyennes Républicaines Révolutionnaires*. Paris: Éditions Sociales, 1966.

Chappey, Jean-Luc. "The New Elites. Questions about Political, Social, and Cultural Reconstruction after the Terror." In *The Oxford Handbook of the French Revolution*, edited by David Andress, 556–572. Oxford: Oxford University Press, 2015.

Chevalier, Clara. "Des émeutières passées sous silence? 'invisibilisation de la violence des femmes au prisme du genre (Paris, 1775).'" In *Penser la violence des femmes*, edited by Coline Cardi and Geneviève Pruvost, 85–94. Paris: La Découverte, 2012.

Choudhury, Mita. *Convents and Nuns in Eighteenth-Century French Politics and Culture.* Ithaca: Cornell University Press, 2004.

Cheney, Paul. *Revolutionary Commerce: Globalization and the French Monarchy.* Cambridge: Harvard University Press, 2010.

Clay, Lauren. "The Bourgeoisie, Capitalism, and the Origins of the French Revolution." In *The Oxford Handbook of the French Revolution.* edited by David Andress, 21–35. Oxford: Oxford University Press, 2015.

Cobb, Richard. *The People's Armies.* New Haven: Yale University Press, 1987.

———. *The Police and the People: French Popular Protest, 1789–1820.* Oxford: Oxford University Press, 1970.

Cobban, Alfred. *The Social Interpretation of the French Revolution.* Cambridge: Cambridge University Press, 1964.

Cochon, Anne. "Paris et les transports sous la Révolution." In *À Paris sous la Révolution: Nouvelles approches de la ville,* edited by Raymonde Monnier, 105–116. Paris: Publications de la Sorbonne, 2008.

Coffin, Judith. *The Politics of Women's Work: The Paris Garment Trades, 1750–1915.* Princeton: Princeton University Press, 2014.

Colwill, Elizabeth. "Sex, Savagery and Slavery in the Shaping of the French Body Politic." In *From the Royal to the Republican Body: Incorporating the Political in Seventeenth and Eighteenth-Century France,* edited by Sarah Melzer and Kathryn Norberg, 198–223. Berkeley: University of California Press, 1998.

Coquery, Natacha. *Tenir boutique à Paris au XVIIIᵉ siècle: Luxe et demi-luxe.* Paris: Comité des travaux historiques et scientifiques, 2011.

Crooks, Malcolm. "The New Regime: Political Institutions and Democratic Practices under the Constitutional Monarchy, 1789–1791." In *The Oxford Handbook of the French Revolution,* edited by David Andress, 218–235. Oxford: Oxford University Press, 2015.

Crow, Thomas. *Emulation: David, Drouais, and Girodet in the Art of Revolutionary France.* New Haven: Yale University Press, 2006.

Crowston, Clare Haru. *Credit, Fashion, Sex: Economies of Regard in Old Regime France.* Durham: Duke University Press, 2013.

———. *Fabricating Women: The Seamstresses of Old Regime France, 1675–1791.* Durham: Duke University Press, 2001.

———. "Moral Credit beyond the Old Regime: Making a Case for Continuities." Paper presented at the annual meeting for Western Society for French Historical Studies, Portland, Oregon, November 10–12, 2011.

Darnton, Robert. *The Literary Underground of the Old Regime.* Cambridge: Harvard University Press, 1982.

Davidson, Denise. *France after Revolution: Urban Life, Gender, and the New Social Order.* Cambridge: Harvard University Press, 2007.

Davis, Natalie Zemon. "Women on Top." In *Society and Culture in Early Modern France,* 131–151. Stanford: Stanford University Press, 1975.

Dawson, Philip. "Introduction." In *The French Revolution and the Meaning of Citizenship,* edited by Renée Waldinger, Philip Dawson, and Isser Woloch. Westport, CT: Greenwood Press, 1993.

Delalande, Nicolas. *Les batailles de l'impôt: Consentement et résistances de 1789 à nos jours.* Paris: Seuil, 2011.

Delalande, Nicolas, and Alexis Spire. *Histoire sociale de l'impôt.* Paris: La Découverte, 2010.

Desan, Christine. *Making Money: Coin, Currency, and Capitalism.* Oxford: Oxford University Press, 2015.

Desan, Suzanne. "'Constitutional Amazons': Jacobin Women's Clubs in the French Revolution." In *Re-creating Authority in Revolutionary France,* edited by Bryant T. Raganjr. and Elizabeth A. Williams, 11–35. New Brunswick: Rutgers University Press, 1992.

———. *The Family on Trial in Revolutionary France.* Berkeley: University of California Press, 2004.

————. "The French Revolution and the Family." In *A Companion to the French Revolution*, edited by Peter McPhee, 470–485. Oxford: Wiley-Blackwell, 2013.

————. "Making and Breaking Marriage: An Overview of Old Regime Marriage as Social Practice." In *Family, Gender, and Law in Early Modern France*, edited by Suzanne Desan and Jeffrey Merrick, 1–25. University Park: The Pennsylvania State University Press, 2009.

————. *Reclaiming the Sacred: Lay Religion and Popular Politics in Revolutionary France*. Ithaca: Cornell University Press, 1990.

————. "Recent Historiography on the French Revolution and Gender." In Special Forum: "The French Revolution is Not Over: An Introduction." *Journal of Social History* 52, no. 4 (Summer 2019).

————. "Transatlantic Spaces of Revolution: The French Revolution, Sciotomanie, and American Lands." *Journal of Early Modern History* 12 (2008): 467–505.

————. "What's after Political Culture? Recent French Revolutionary Historiography." *French Historical Studies* 23, no. 1 (2000): 163–196.

DiCaprio, Lisa. *The Origins of the Welfare State: Women, Work, and the French Revolution*. Urbana: University of Illinois Press, 2007.

Dominique, Pierre. *Paris enlève le roi: Octobre 1789*. Paris Librairie Académique Perrin, 1973.

Doyle, William. *Origins of the French Revolution*. 3rd ed. Oxford: Oxford University Press, 1999.

————. "The Outbreak of the Revolution, 1787–1789." In *The French Revolution: Conflicting Interpretations*, 5th ed., edited by Frank A. Kafker, James M. Laux, and Darline Gay Levy, 33–44. Malabar, FL: Krieger, 2002.

Dudley, Christopher. "Party Politics, Political Economy, and Economic Development in Early Eighteenth-Century Britain." *The Economic History Review* 66 (2013): 1084–1100.

Dulaure, J.-A. *Histoire Civile, Physique et Morale de Paris*. Vol. 9. Paris: Baudoin Frères, 1825.

Durham Johnson, Mary. "Old Wine in New Bottles: Institutional Changes for Women of the People during the French Revolution." In *Women, War, and Revolution*, edited by Carol Berkin and Clara Lovett, 107–144. New York: Holmes & Meier, 1980.

Edelstein, Dan. *The Terror of Natural Right: Republicanism, the Cult of Nature, and the French Revolution*. Chicago: University of Chicago Press, 2009.

Edelstein, Melvin. *The French Revolution and the Birth of Electoral Democracy*. London: Routledge, 2006.

Elyada, Ouzi. "La Mère Duchesne. Masques populaires et guerre pamphlétaire, 1789–1791." *Annales historiques de la Révolution française* 271 (1988).

————. *Presse populaire & feuilles volantes de la Révolution à Paris 1789–1792*. Paris: Société des Études Robespierristes, 1991.

Epstein, Anne R., and Rachel G. Fuchs, eds. *Gender and Citizenship in Historical and Transnational Perspective: Agency, Space, Borders*. London, Palgrave, 2017.

Estrée, Paul d'. *Le Père Duchesne: Hébert et la Commune de Paris (1792–1794)*. Paris: Librairie Ambert, 1908.

Farge, Arlette. *La Vie fragile: violence, pouvoirs, et solidarités à Paris au XVIIIe siècle*. Paris: Hachette, 1986.

Fauré, Christine. "Doléances, déclarations et pétitions, trois formes de la parole publique des femmes sous la Révolution." *Annales historiques de la Révolution française* 344 (2006): 3–4.

Fitzsimmons, Michael P. *From Artisan to Worker: Guilds, the French State, and the Organization of Labor, 1776–1821*. New York: Cambridge University Press, 2010.

————. "The National Assembly and the Abolition of Guilds in France." *The Historical Journal* 39 (1996): 133–154.

————. "The National Assembly and the Invention of Citizenship." In *The French Revolution and the Meaning of Citizenship*, edited by Renée Waldinger, Philip Dawson, and Isser Woloch, 29–41. Westport, CT: Greenwood Press, 1992.

Fontaine, Laurence. *L'économie morale: Pauvreté crédit et confiance dans l'Europe préindustrielle*. Paris: Gallimard, 2008.

Forrest, Alan. *The French Revolution and the Poor*. New York: St. Martin's Press, 1981.

Fraisse, Geneviève. *Muse de la Raison: la démocratie exclusive et la différence des sexes.* Aix-en-Provence: Alinéa, 1989.

Fredona, Robert and Sophus Reinert, eds. *New Perspectives on the History of Political Economy.* 2 volumes. Springer Nature: Palgrave Macmillan, 2018.

Fuchs, Rachel, and Victoria Thompson. *Women in Nineteenth-Century Europe.* New York: Palgrave Macmillan, 2005.

Furet, François. *Penser la Révolution française.* Paris: Éditions Gallimard, 1978.

Gaillard, Jeanne. "Les Intentions d'une Politique Fiscale, la Patente en France au XIXᵉ Siècle." *Bulletin du Centre d'histoire de la France contemporaine,* n°7 (1986): 15–38.

Garrioch, David. *The Formation of the Parisian Bourgeoisie, 1690–1830.* Cambridge: Harvard University Press, 1996.

———. *The Making of Revolutionary Paris.* Berkeley: University of California Press, 2002.

———. *Neighbourhood and Community in Paris, 1740–1790.* Cambridge: Cambridge University Press, 1986.

Gaston-Breton, Tristan. *Banque de France: Deux siècles d'histoire.* Paris, 1999.

Godineau, Dominique. *Citoyennes tricoteuses: Les femmes du peuple à Paris pendant la Révolution française.* Aix-en-Provence: Alinéa, 1988.

———. *Les Femmes dans la France moderne, XVIᵉ–XVIIIᵉ siècle.* Paris, 2015.

———. *The Women of Paris and Their French Revolution.* Translated by Katherine Streip. Berkeley: University of California Press, 1998.

Gomel, Charles. *Histoire Financière de la Législative et de la Convention.* Vol. 2. Paris: Guillaumin et Cie, 1905.

Goodman, Dena. "Public Sphere and Private Life: Toward a Synthesis of Current Historiographical Approaches to the Old Regime." *History and Theory* 3, no. 1 (1992): 1–20.

Gottschalk, Louis, and Margaret Maddox. *Lafayette in the French Revolution: From the October Days through the Federation.* Chicago: University of Chicago Press, 1973.

Guibert-Sledziewski, Elisabeth. *Révolutions du Sujet.* Paris: Méridiens Klincksieck, 1989.

Guilhaumou, Jacques. *Sieyès et l'Ordre de la Langue: L'invention de la politique moderne.* Paris: Editions Kimé, 2002.

Guillon, Claude. *Deux Enragés de la Révolution: Leclerc de Lyon & Pauline Léon.* Quimperlé: Éditions La Digitale, 1993.

———. "Pauline Léon, révolutionnaire." *Annales historiques de la Révolution française* 344 (2006): 147–159.

Gutwirth, Madelyn. "Citoyens, Citoyennes: Cultural Regression and the Subversion of Female Citizenship in the French Revolution." In *The French Revolution and the Meaning of Citizenship,* edited by Renée Waldinger, Philip Dawson, and Isser Woloch, 19–28. Westport, CT: Greenwood Press, 1993.

Hafter, Daryl. "French Industrial Growth in Women's Hands." In *Women and Work in Eighteenth-Century France,* edited by Nina Kushner and Daryl Hafter, 177–201. Baton Rouge: Louisiana State University Press, 2015.

Hafter, Daryl, and Nina Kushner. "Introduction." In *Women and Work in Eighteenth-Century France,* edited by Nina Kushner and Daryl Hafter, 1–15. Baton Rouge: Louisiana State University Press, 2015.

Hanson, Paul R. *Contesting the French Revolution.* Malden, MA: Wiley-Blackwell, 2009.

———. *The Jacobin Republic under Fire: The Federalist Revolt in the French Revolution.* University Park: Pennsylvania State University Press, 2003.

Harder, Mette. "A Second Terror: The Purges of French Revolutionary Legislators after Thermidor." *French Historical Studies* 38, no. 1 (February 2015): 33–60.

Hardwick, Julie. *Family Business: Litigation and the Political Economies of Daily Life in Early Modern France.* Oxford: Oxford University Press, 2009.

Harouel, Jean-Louis. "La question financière et ses rapports avec l'aménagement urbain." In *À Paris sous la Révolution: Nouvelles approches de la ville,* edited by Raymonde Monnier, 29–38. Paris: Publications de la Sorbonne, 2008.

Harris, S. E. *The Assignats*. London: Oxford University Press, 1930.

Hazareesingh, Sudhir. "'A Common Sentiment of National Glory': Civic Festivities and French Collective Sentiment under the Second Empire." *Journal of Modern History* 76 (June 2004): 280–311.

Hénaff, Marcel, and Tracy Strong. "The Conditions of Public Space: Vision, Speech, Theatricality." In *Public Space and Democracy*, edited by Marcel Hénaff and Tracy Strong, 1–32. Minneapolis: University of Minnesota Press, 2001.

Herlaut, Auguste-Philippe. "Les certificats de civisme." *Annales historiques de la Révolution française* 90 (Nov–Dec 1938).

Hesse, Carla. *The Other Enlightenment: How French Women Became Modern*. Princeton: Princeton University Press, 2001.

Heuer, Jennifer. "Citizenship, the French Revolution, and the Limits of Martial Masculinity." In *Gender and Citizenship in Historical and Transnational Perspective: Agency, Space, Borders*, edited by Anne R. Epstein and Rachel G. Fuchs, 19–38. London, Palgrave, 2017.

———. *The Family and the Nation: Gender and Citizenship in Revolutionary France, 1789–1830*. Ithaca: Cornell University Press, 2005.

———. "Hats on for the Nation! Women, Servants, Soldiers and the 'Sign of the French.'" *French History* 16 (2002): 28–52.

———. "The Limits of Martial Masculinity? Revolutionary Veterans as Citizens and Family Men." Paper presented at the Society for French Historical Studies, Cambridge, Massachusetts, April 4–7, 2013.

Higonnet, Patrice. *Goodness Beyond Virtue: Jacobins during the French Revolution*. Cambridge: Harvard University Press, 1998.

———. "The Social and Cultural Antecedents of Revolutionary Discontinuity: Montagnards and Girondins." *The English Historical Review* 396 (1985): 513–544.

Hincker, François. "Comment sortir de la terreur économique?" In *Le Tournant de l'an III: Réaction et Terreur blanche dans la France révolutionnaire*, edited by Michel Vovelle, 149–158. Paris: Éditions du CTHS, 1997.

Hoffman, Philip T., Gilles Postel-Vinay, and Jean-Laurent Rosenthal. *Priceless Markets: The Political Economy of Credit in Paris, 1660–1870*. Chicago: University of Chicago Press, 2000.

Horn, Jeff. *Economic Development in Early Modern France: The Privilege of Liberty, 1650–1820*. Cambridge: Cambridge University Press, 2015.

Huet, Marie-Hélène. *Mourning Glory: The Will of the French Revolution*. Philadelphia: University of Pennsylvania Press, 2015.

Hufton, Olwen. *Women and the Limits of Citizenship in the French Revolution*. Toronto: University of Toronto Press, 1992.

Hugueney, Louis. *Les Clubs Dijonnais sous la Révolution*. Dijon: J. Nourry Libraire-Éditeur, 1905.

Hunt, Lynn. "Afterword." In *The French Revolution and the Meaning of Citizenship*, edited by Renée Waldinger, Philip Dawson, and Isser Woloch, 211–213. Westport, CT: Greenwood Press, 1993.

———. "Engravings." In *The French Revolution: Conflicting Interpretations*, 5th ed., edited by Frank A. Kafker, James M. Laux, and Darline Gay Levy, 270–286. Malabar, FL: Krieger, 2002.

———. *The Family Romance of the French Revolution*. Berkeley: University of California Press, 1992.

———. "The French Revolution in Global Context." In *The Age of Revolutions in Global Context, c. 1760–1840*, edited by David Armitage and Sanjay Subrahmanyam, 20–36. New York: Palgrave Macmillan, 2009.

———. "The Global Financial Origins of 1789." In *The French Revolution in Global Perspective*, edited by Suzanne Desan, Lynn Hunt, and William Max Nelson, 32–43. Ithaca: Cornell University Press, 2013.

———. *Inventing Human Rights: A History*. New York: W.W. Norton, 2007.

———. "La visibilité du monde bourgeois." In *Vers un ordre bourgeois? Révolution française et changement social*, edited by Jean-Pierre Jessenne, 371–381. Rennes: Presses Universitaires de Rennes, 2007.

————. *Politics, Culture, and Class in the French Revolution.* Berkeley: University of California Press, 1984.

————. "Relire l'histoire du politique." In *La Révolution à l'œuvre: Perspectives actuelles dans l'histoire de la Révolution française,* edited by Jean-Clément Martin, 117–124. Rennes: Presses Universitaires de Rennes, 2005.

Jarvis, Katie. "Allez, Marchez Braves Citoyennes: A Study of the Popular Origins of and the Political Reactions to, the October Days of the French Revolution." Bachelor's thesis, Boston College, 2007.

————. "The Cost of Female Citizenship: How Price Controls Gendered Democracy in Revolutionary France," *French Historical Studies* 41, 4 (October 2018): 647–680.

————. "Exacting Change: Money, Market Women, and the Crumbling Corporate World in the French Revolution." *Journal of Social History* 51, 4 (Summer 2018): 837–868.

————. "'Patriotic Discipline': Cloistered Behinds, Public Judgment, and Female Violence in Revolutionary Paris." In *Practiced Citizenship: Women, Gender, and the State in Modern France,* edited by Nimisha Barton and Richard Hopkins, 20–50. Lincoln: University of Nebraska Press, 2019.

————. "Politics in the Marketplace: The Popular Activism and Cultural Representation of the Dames des Halles during the French Revolution." PhD diss., University of Wisconsin-Madison, 2014.

Jessenne, Jean-Pierre. "Une Révolution sans ou contre les paysans?" In *La Révolution française: Une histoire toujours vivante,* edited by Michel Biard, 253–267. Paris: Éditions Tallandier: 2010.

————, ed. *Vers un ordre bourgeois? Révolution française et changement social.* Rennes: Presses Universitaires de Rennes, 2007.

Jones, Colin. "Bourgeois Revolution Revivified: 1789 and Social Change." Abridged from *The French Revolution and Social Change,* edited by Colin Lucas, 69–118. Oxford: Oxford University Press, 1990. Reprinted in *The French Revolution: Recent Debates and Controversies,* edited by Gary Kates, 87–112. New York: Routledge, 2006.

————. *Charity and Bienfaisance: The Treatment of the Poor in the Montpellier Region, 1740–1815.* Cambridge: Cambridge University Press, 1982.

Jouhaud, Christian. *Mazarinades: La Fronde des mots.* Paris: Éditions Aubier Montaigne, 1985.

Kaiser, Thomas. "From Fiscal Crisis to Revolution: The Court and French Foreign Policy, 1787–1789." In *From Deficit to Deluge: The Origins of the French Revolution,* edited by Thomas Kaiser and Dale Van Kley, 139–164. Stanford: Stanford University Press, 2011.

Kafker, Frank, James Laux, and Darline Gay Levy, eds. *The French Revolution: Conflicting Interpretations.* 5th ed. Malabar, FL: Krieger 2002.

Kalifa, Dominique. *Les Bas-Fonds: Histoire d'un imaginaire.* Paris: Éditions du Seuil, 2013.

Kaplan, Steven. *La Fin des corporations.* Translated by Béatrice Vierne. Paris: Fayard, 2001.

————. *Provisioning Paris: Merchants and Millers in the Grain and Flour Trade during the Eighteenth Century.* Ithaca: Cornell University Press, 1984.

————. "Social Classification and Representation in the Corporate World of Eighteenth-Century France: Turgot's 'Carnival.'" In *Work in France,* edited by Steven L. Kaplan and Cynthia Koepp, 176–228. Ithaca: Cornell University Press, 1986.

Kaplan, Steven and Sophus Reinert, eds. *The Economic Turn: Recasting Political Economy in Eighteenth-Century Europe.* 2 volumes. London: Anthem, forthcoming.

Kates, Gary. "Introduction." In *The French Revolution: Recent Debates and Controversies,* edited by Gary Kates, 1–14. New York: Routledge, 2006.

Kennedy, Michael L. *The Jacobin Clubs in the French Revolution, 1793–1795.* New York: Berghahn Books, 2000.

Kessler, Amalia. *A Revolution in Commerce: The Parisian Merchant Court and the Rise of Commercial Society in Eighteenth-Century France.* New Haven: Yale University Press, 2007.

Kotsonis, Yanni. *States of Obligation: Taxes and Citizenship in the Russian Empire and Early Soviet Republic.* Toronto: University of Toronto Press, 2014.

Kushner, Nina, and Daryl Hafter, eds. *Women and Work in Eighteenth-Century France.* Baton Rouge: Louisiana State University Press, 2015.

Kwass, Michael. "Big Hair: A Wig History of Consumption in Eighteenth-Century France." *American Historical Review* 111, no. 3 (June 2006): 631–659.

———. "Capitalism and Inequality in Eighteenth-Century France: Writing History after the Great Recession." (Plenary Lecture at the Society for the Study of French History, Warwick, July 2018.

———. *Contraband: Louis Mandrin and the Making of a Global Underground.* Cambridge: Harvard University Press, 2014.

———. "The Global Underground: Smuggling, Rebellion, and the Origins of the French Revolution." In *The French Revolution in Global Perspective,* edited by Suzanne Desan, Lynn Hunt, and William Max Nelson, 15–31. Cornell: Cornell University Press, 2013.

———. *Privilege and the Politics of Taxation in Eighteenth-Century France: Liberté, Égalité, Fiscalité.* Cambridge: Cambridge University Press, 2000.

Lafurie, Jean. *Les Assignats et les Papiers-Monnaies émis par l'état au XVIIIᵉ siècle.* Paris, 1981.

Landes, Joan. *Women and the Public Sphere in the Age of the French Revolution.* Ithaca: Cornell University Press, 1988.

Lanza, Janine. *From Wives to Widows in Early Modern Paris: Gender, Economy, and Law.* Aldershot: Ashgate, 2007.

Lapied, Martine. "Une absence de Révolution pour les femmes?" In *La Révolution Française: Une histoire toujours vivante,* edited by Michel Biard, 303–316. Paris: Éditions Tallandier: 2010.

———. "Histoire du Genre en Révolution." In *La Révolution à l'œuvre: Perspectives actuelles dans l'histoire de la Révolution française,* edited by Jean-Clement Martin, 77–87. Rennes: Presses Universitaires de Rennes, 2005.

Larrère, Catherine. "Sieyès, lecteur des physiocrates: Droit naturel ou économie?" In *Figures de Sieyès,* edited by Pierre-Yves Quiviger, Vincent Denis, and Jean Salem., 195–211 Paris: Publications de la Sorbonne, 2008.

Laufenburger, Henry. *Histoire de l'impôt.* Paris: Presses Universitaires De France, 1959.

Lajer-Burcharth, Ewa. "David's *Sabine Women*: Body, Gender, and Republican Culture under the Directory." *Art History* 14, no. 3 (1991): 397–430.

Leclercq, Henri. *Les journées d'octobre et de la fin de l'année 1789.* Paris: Librairie Letouzey et Ane, 1924.

Lefebvre, Georges. *The Coming of the French Revolution.* Translated by R. R. Palmer. Princeton: Princeton University Press, 1947.

Levy, Darline Gay, and Harriet Branson Applewhite. "A Political Revolution for Women? The Case of Paris." Originally from *Becoming Visible: Women in European History,* 3rd ed., edited by Renate Bridenthal, Susan Mosher Stuard, and Merry E. Weisner. Boston: Houghton Mifflin Company, 1998. Reprinted in *The French Revolution: Conflicting Interpretations,*5th ed., edited by Frank A. Kafker, James M. Laux, and Darline Gay Levy. Malabar, FL: Krieger, 2002.———

—. "Women and Militant Citizenship in Revolutionary Paris." In *Rebel Daughters: Women and the French Revolution,* edited by Sara Melzer and Leslie Rabine, 79–101. New York: Oxford University Press, 1992.

Linton, Marisa. *Choosing Terror: Virtue, Friendship, and authenticity in the French Revolution.* Oxford: Oxford University Press, 2013.

Livesey, James. "Free Trade and Empire in the Anglo-Irish Commercial Propositions of 1785." *Journal of British Studies* 52 (2013): 103–127.

———. *Making Democracy in the French Revolution.* Cambridge: Harvard University Press, 2001.

———. "The Political Culture of the Directory." In *A Companion to the French Revolution,* edited by Peter McPhee, 328–342. Oxford: Wiley-Blackwell, 2013.

Lombard-Jourdan, Anne. *Les Halles de Paris et leur Quartier (1137–1969).* Paris: École Nationale des Chartes, 2009.

Lucas, Colin. "The Crowd and Politics between the Ancien Régime and Revolution in France," *Journal of Modern History* 60 (1988): 421–457.

————. "Nobles, bourgeoisie and the origins of the French Revolution," *Past & Present* 60 (August 1973): 84–126.

Lyons, Martyn. *France under the Directory*. Cambridge: Cambridge University Press, 1975.

Lytle, Scott. "The Second Sex (September, 1793)" *Journal of Modern History* 27, no. 1 (March 1955): 14–26.

Marion, Marcel. *Histoire financière de la France depuis 1715*. Vol. 2. New York: Brut Franklin, 1919.

Margairaz, Dominique, and Philippe Minard. "Marché des subsistances et économie morale: Ce que 'taxer' veut dire." *Annales historiques de la Révolution française* 352 (2008).

Markoff, John. *Abolition of Feudalism: Peasants, Lords, and Legislators in the French Revolution*. University Park: Pennsylvania State University Press, 1996.

Marion, Rene. "The Dames de la Halle: Community and Authority in Early Modern Paris." PhD diss., Johns Hopkins University, 1994.

Marsden, Kathryn. "Married Nuns in the French Revolution: The Sexual Revolution of the 1790s." PhD. diss, University of California-Irvine, 2014.

Martineau, Jean. *Les Halles de Paris des Origines à 1789: Évolution matérielle, juridique, et économique*. Paris: Éditions Montchrestien, 1960.

Mason, Laura. "Never was a plot so holy: Gracchus Babeuf and the end of the French Revolution." In *Conspiracy in the French Revolution*, edited by Peter Campbell, Thomas Kaiser, and Marisa Linton, 172–188. Manchester: Manchester University Press, 2007.

————. *Singing the French Revolution: Popular Culture and Politics, 1787–1799*. Ithaca: Cornell University Press, 1996.

————. "Thermidor and the Myth of Rupture." In *The Oxford Handbook of the French Revolution*, edited by David Andress, 521–537. Oxford: Oxford University Press, 2015.

————. "The Thermidorian Reaction." In *A Companion to the French Revolution*, edited by Peter McPhee, 317–318. Oxford: Wiley-Blackwell, 2013.

Mathiez, Albert. "All Republicans Benefited." Originally from "La Révolution française." In *Annales historiques de la Révolution française* 10 (1933): 19–24. Reprinted in *The French Revolution: Conflicting Interpretations*, 5th ed., edited by Frank A. Kafker, James M. Laux, and Darline Gay Levy, 395–400. Malabar, FL: Krieger, 2002.

————. "Étude critique sur les journées des 5 & 6 octobre." *Revue Historique* 67 (1898): 241–281.

————. "Le maximum des salaires et le 9 thermidor." *Annales historiques de la Révolution française* 4 (1927): 1–22.

————. *La Révolution française*. 3 vols. Paris: Armand Colin, 1922–1924.

————. *La vie chère et le mouvement social sous La Terreur*. Paris: Payot, 1927.

Mayer, Arno. *The Furies: Violence and Terror in the French and Russian Revolutions*. Princeton: Princeton University Press, 2002.

Maza, Sarah. *The Myth of the French Bourgeoisie: An Essay on the Social Imaginary, 1750–1850*. Cambridge: Harvard University Press, 2003.

Mazeau, Guillaume, and Clyde Marlo Plumauzille. "Penser avec le genre: Trouble dans la citoyenneté révolutionnaire." *La Révolution française*, no. 9 (2015). http://lrf.revues.org/1458.

McPhee, Peter. *Liberty or Death: The French Revolution*. New Haven: Yale University Press, 2016.

————. *Robespierre: A Revolutionary Life*. New Haven: Yale University Press, 2012.

————. *The French Revolution, 1789–1799*. Oxford: Oxford University Press, 2002.

Merrick, Jeffrey. "The Cardinal and the Queen: Sexual and Political Disorders in the Mazarinades." *French Historical Studies* 18, no. 3 (Spring 1994): 667–699.

Michelet, Jules. *Les Femmes de la Révolution*. 2nd ed. Paris: Adolphe Delahays, 1855.

Minard, Philippe. "L'héritage historiographique." In *Vers un ordre bourgeois? Révolution française et changement social*, edited by Jean-Pierre Jessenne, 21–35. Rennes: Presses Universitaires de Rennes, 2007.

Montenach, Anne. *Espaces et pratiques du commerce alimentaire à Lyon au XVIIᵉ siècle*. Grenoble: Presses universitaires de Grenoble, 2009.

———. *Femmes, pouvoirs, et contrebandes dans les Alpes au XVIIIe siècle*. Grenoble: Presses universitaires de Grenoble, 2017.

Moore, A. P. *The Genre Poissard and the French Stage of the Eighteenth Century*. New York: Institute of French Studies, 1935.

Morgan, Kimberly J., and Monica Prasad. "The Origins of Tax Systems: A French–American Comparison." *American Journal of Sociology* 114, no. 5 (2009): 1350.

Morini-Comby, Jean. *Les Assignats: Révolution et Inflation*. Paris: Nouvelle Librairie Nationale, 1925.

Navarro, Joe, with Marvin Karlins. *What Everybody Is Saying*. New York: Harper Collins, 2008.

Neurisse, André. *Histoire de la Fiscalité en France*. Paris: Economica, 1996.

Nicolas, Jean. *La rébellion française: Mouvements populaires et conscience sociale (1661–1789)*. Paris: Éditions du Seuil, 2002.

Nogaret, Dominique-Vincent Ramel de. *Des finances de la République française en l'an IX*. Paris: Chez Agasse, 1800.

Offen, Karen. "The New Sexual Politics of French Revolutionary Historiography." *French Historical Studies*, 16, no. 4 (1990), 909–922.

———. *The Woman Question in France, 1400-1870*. New York: Cambridge University Press, 2017.

Stephen, Owen. "The Politics of Tax Reform in France, 1906–1926." PhD diss., University of California, Berkeley, 1982.

d'Orliac, Jehanne. *Dames de la Halle*. Paris: Éditions Frances, 1946.

Ozouf, Mona. *Festivals and the French Revolution*. Translated by Alan Sheridan. Cambridge: Harvard University Press, 1988.

Palmer, R. R. "Popular Democracy in the French Revolution: Review Article." *French Historical Studies* 1. no 4 (Autumn 1960): 445–469.

———. *The Twelve who Ruled*. Princeton: Princeton University Press, 2005.

Parker, Lindsay. *Writing the Revolution: A French Woman's History in Letters*. Oxford: Oxford University Press, 2013.

Parsons, Jotham. *Making Money in Sixteenth-Century France: Currency, Culture, and the State*. Ithaca, Cornell University Press, 2014.

Pateman, Carole. *The Sexual Contract*. Stanford: Stanford University Press, 1988.

Pincus, Steven. "Empires and Capitalisms: Competing Political Economies and Eighteenth-Century Imperial Crises." Paper presented at the annual meeting for the Social Science History Association, Vancouver, British Columbia, November 1–4, 2012.

———. "Rethinking Mercantilism: Political Economy, the British Empire, and the Atlantic World in the Seventeenth and Eighteenth Centuries." *The William and Mary Quarterly* 69 (January 2012): 3–34.

Plack, Noelle. "Drinking and Rebelling: Wine, Taxes, and Popular Agency in Revolutionary Paris, 1789–1791." *French Historical Studies* 39, no. 3 (2016): 599–622.

Plumauzille, Clyde. "La nouvelle publicité de la prostitution dans le Paris révolutionnaire: information, marchandisation et banalisation d'une transgression sexuelle (1789–1799)." In *Le Genre entre transmission et transgression*, edited by Lydie Bodiou, Marlaine Cacouault-Bitaud, and Ludovic Gaussot, 79–93. Rennes: Presses Universitaires de Rennes, 2014.

———. *Prostitution et Révolution: Les femmes publiques dans la cité républicaine (1789–1804)*. Paris: Ceyzérieu, 2016.

———. "Tolérer et réprimer: Prostitués, prostitution et droit de cité dans le Paris révolutionnaire (1789–1799)." PhD diss., Université Paris I, 2013.

Potofsky, Allan. *Constructing Paris in the Age of Revolution*. London: Palgrave Macmillan, 2009.

Price, Roger. *An Economic History of Modern France, 1730–1914*. London: Macmillan Press, 1981.

Reinhard, Marcel. *Paris pendant la Révolution*. Paris: Centre de documentation universitaire, 1962.

Rétat, Pierre. "The Evolution of the Citizen from the Ancien Régime to the Revolution." In *The French Revolution and the Meaning of Citizenship*, edited by Renée Waldinger, Philip Dawson, and Isser Woloch, 3–16. Westport, CT: Greenwood Press, 1993.

Revel, Jacques. "Présentation" to the issue "Corps et communautés d'Ancien Régime." *Annales. Économies, Sociétés, Civilisations* 43, no. 2 (1988): 295–299.

Roche, Daniel. *The People of Paris: An Essay in Popular Culture in the 18th Century.* Translated by Marie Evans. Berkeley: University of California Press, 1987.

Roessler, Shirley. *Out of the Shadows: Women and Politics in the Age of the French Revolution, 1789–1795.* New York: P. Lang, 1996.

Rudé, George. *The Crowd in the French Revolution.* London: Oxford University Press, 1967.

———. *The French Revolution.* London: Weidenfeld and Nicolson, 1988.

———. "Prices, Wages and Popular Movements in Paris during the French Revolution." *The Economic History Review* 6, no. 3 (1954): 246–267.

Rudé George and Albert Soboul. "Le maximum des salaires parisiens et le 9 thermidor." *Annales historiques de la Révolution française* 134 (1954).

Sargent, Thomas, and François Velde. *The Big Problem of Small Change.* Princeton: Princeton University Press, 2002.

Schnerb, Robert, Jacques Wolff, and Jean Bouvier. *Deux siècles de fiscalité française: XIXᵉ- XXᵉ siècle, histoire, économie, politique, recueil d'articles.* Paris, France: Mouton, 1973.

Scott, Joan. *Only Paradoxes to Offer: French Feminists and the Rights of Man.* Cambridge: Harvard University Press, 1996.

Scott, Samuel F. *The Response of the Royal Army to the French Revolution: The Role and Development of the Line Army, 1787–93.* Oxford: Clarendon Press, 1978.

Scott, William. "The Pursuit of 'Interests' in the French Revolution: A Preliminary Survey." *French Historical Studies* 19, no. 3 (Spring 1996): 811–851.

Scurr, Ruth. "Social Equality in Pierre-Louis Roederer's Interpretation of the Modern Republic, 1793." *History of European Ideas* 26, no. 2 (2000): 105–126.

Sewell, William, Jr. "Le Citoyen, La Citoyenne: Activity, Passivity and the French Revolutionary Concept of Citizenship." In *The French Revolution and the Creation of Modern Political Culture.* Vol. 2: *Political Culture of the French Revolution,* edited by Colin Lucas, 105–125. Oxford: Pergamon Press, 1988.

———. *Logics of History: Social Theory and Social Transformation.* Chicago: University of Chicago Press, 2005.

———. *A Rhetoric of Bourgeois Revolution: The Abbé Sieyes and "What Is the Third Estate?"* Durham: Duke University Press, 1994.

———. *Work and Revolution in France: The Language of Labor from the Old Regime to 1848.* Cambridge: Cambridge University Press, 1980.

Shepard, William. *Price Control and the Reign of Terror: France, 1793–1795.* Berkeley: University of California Press, 1953.

Shovlin, John. *The Political Economy of Virtue: Luxury, Patriotism, and the Origins of the French Revolution.* Ithaca: Cornell University Press, 2006.

Sirich, John Black. *The Revolutionary Committees in the Departments of France, 1793–1794.* Cambridge: Harvard University Press, 1943.

Slavin, Morris. *The Making of an Insurrection: Parisian Sections and the Gironde.* Cambridge: Harvard University Press, 1986.

Sluhovsky, Moshe. *Patroness of Paris: Rituals of Devotion in Early Modern France.* Leiden: Brill, 1998.

Smart, Annie. *Citoyennes: Women and the Ideal of Citizenship in Eighteenth-Century France.* Newark: University of Delaware Press, 2011.

Soboul, Albert. "Classes and Class Struggles during the French Revolution." *Science and Society* 17 (Summer 1953): 238–257.

———. "The French Revolution in the History of the Contemporary World." Reprinted and abridged from Albert Soboul, *Understanding the French Revolution,* translated by April Ane Knutson. New York: International Publishers, 1988, in *The French Revolution: Recent Debates and Controversies,* edited by Gary Kates, 17–32. New York: Routledge, 2006.

———. *The Parisian Sans-culottes and the French Revolution, 1793–1794.* Translated by Gwynne Lewis. Oxford: Clarendon Press, 1964.

———. "The Sans-Culottes." Originally from *The Parisian Sans-culottes and the French Revolution, 1793–1794.* Translated by Gwynne Lewis. Oxford: Clarendon Press, 1964. Reprinted in

The French Revolution: Conflicting Interpretations, 5th ed., edited by Frank A. Kafker, James M. Laux, and Darline Gay Levy. Malabar, FL: Krieger, 2002.

———. *The Sans-Culottes: The Popular Movement and Revolutionary Government, 1793–1794*. Translated by Remy Inglis Hall. Princeton: Princeton University Press, 1980.

———. "The Triumph of a New Bourgeoisie." Originally "Classes and Class Struggles during the French Revolution." *Science & Society* 17 (Summer 1953): 252–257. Reprinted in *The French Revolution: Conflicting Interpretations*, 5th ed., edited by Frank A. Kafker, James M. Laux, and Darline Gay Levy. Malabar, FL: Krieger, 2002.

———. "Un Épisode des luttes populaires en septembre 1793: La guerre des cocardes," *Annales historiques de la Révolution française* 163 (1961): 52–55.

Sonenscher, Michael. "Les sans-culottes de l'an II: Repenser le langage du travail dans la France révolutionnaire." *Annales. Économies, Sociétés, Civilisations* 5 (1985): 1087–1108.

Spagnoli, Paul. "The Unique Decline of Mortality in Revolutionary France." *Journal of Family History* 22, no. 4 (1997): 425–461.

Spang, Rebecca. "The Ghost of Law: Speculating on Money, Memory, and Mississippi in the French Constituent Assembly." *Historical Reflections/Réflexions historiques* 31, no. 1 (Winter 2005): 3–25.

———. "Money, Money, Money." *History Workshop Journal* 69 (Spring 2010): 225–233.

———. *Stuff and Money in the Time of the French Revolution*. Cambridge: Harvard University Press, 2014.

Stanziani, Alessandro. *Rules of Exchange: French Capitalism in Comparative Perspective, Eighteenth to Early Twentieth Centuries*. New York: Cambridge University Press, 2012.

Szulman, Eric. "Les évolutions de la boucherie parisienne sous la Révolution." In *À Paris sous la Révolution: Nouvelles approches de la ville*, edited by Raymonde Monnier, 117–126. Paris: Publications de la Sorbonne, 2008.

Tackett, Timothy. *Becoming a Revolutionary: The Deputies of the French National Assembly and the Emergence of a Revolutionary Culture (1789–1790)*. University Park: Penn State University Press, 1996.

———. *The Coming of the Terror in the French Revolution*. Cambridge: Belknap Press of Harvard University, 2015.

———. *When the King Took Flight*. Cambridge: Harvard University Press, 2003.

Talamante, Laura. "Les Marseillaises: Women and Political Change during the French Revolution, 1789–1794." PhD diss., UCLA, 2003.

Tønnesson, Kåre. *La Défaite des Sans-Culottes*. Paris: Presses Universitaires d'Oslo, 1978.

Tulard, Jean. *Les Thermidoriens*. Paris: Librairie Arthème Fayard, 2005.

Thompson, E. P. "The Moral Economy of the English Crowd in the Eighteenth Century." *Past & Present*, no. 50 (February 1971): 76–136.

Thompson, Victoria. *The Virtuous Marketplace: Women and Men, Money and Politics in Paris, 1830–1870*. Baltimore: Johns Hopkins University Press, 2000.

Vardi, Liana. "The Abolition of the Guilds during the French Revolution." *French Historical Studies* 15 (1988): 704–717.

Vause, Erika. "'The Business of Reputations: Secrecy, Shame, and Social Standing in Nineteenth-Century French Debtors' and Creditors' Newspapers." *Journal of Social History* 28 (2014): 47–71.

———. *In the Red and in the Black: Debt, Dishonor, and the Law in France between Revolutions*. Charlottesville: University of Virginia Press, 2018.

Verjus, Anne. *Le bon mari: Une histoire politique des hommes et des femmes à l'époque révolutionnaire*. Paris: Fayard, 2010.

———. *Le Cens de la famille: Les femmes et le vote, 1789–1848*. Paris: Editions Berlin, 2002.

———. "Gender, Sexuality, and Political Culture." In *A Companion to the French Revolution*, edited by Peter McPhee, 196–211. Oxford: Wiley-Blackwell, 2013.

Verjus, Anne, and Denise Davidson. *Le Roman conjugal. Chroniques de la vie familiale à l'époque de la Révolution et de l'Empire*. Seyssel: Champ Vallon, 2011.

Villiers, Marc de. *Histoire des clubs des femmes et des légions d'amazones*. Paris: Plon-Nourrit, 1910.

———. *Reine Audu: Les Légendes des journées d'octobre*. Paris: Émile-Paul Frères, 1917.

Wahnich, Sophie. *In Defence of Terror: Liberty or Death in the French Revolution*. London: Verso Books, 2012.

———. "L'universel, le singulier, le sujet, à l'epreuve de la Révolution française." In *Universel, singulier, sujet*, edited by Jelica Sumic, 159–186. Paris: Éditions Kimé, 2000.

Walton, Charles. "Capitalism's Alter Ego: The Birth of Reciprocity in Eighteenth-Century France." *Critical Historical Studies* 5, no. 1 (2018): 1–43.

———. "The Fall from Eden: The Free-Trade Origins of the French Revolution." In *The French Revolution in Global Perspective*, edited by Suzanne Desan, Lynn Hunt, and William Max Nelson, 44–56. Cornell: Cornell University Press, 2013.

———. "*Les Graines de la Discorde*: Print, Public Spirit, and Free Market Politics in the French Revolution." In *Into Print: Limits and Legacies of the Enlightenment, Essays in Honor of Robert Darnton*, edited by Charles Walton, 158–174. University Park: Pennsylvania State University Press, 2011.

———. *Policing Public Opinion in the French Revolution: The Culture of Calumny and the Problem of Free Speech*. New York: Oxford University Press, 2009.

———. "Reciprocity and the French Revolution (abstract)." In *e-France: New Perspectives on the French Revolution*, vol. 4, (2013).

White, Andrew Dickson. *Fiat Money Inflation in France*. San Francisco: Cato Institute, 1980, original 1933.

INDEX

Note: Page numbers in *italic* type indicate images or graphics.

Printed in the USA/Agawam, MA
October 15, 2019

740200.011